ANNUAL REVIEW OF
POLITICAL SCIENCE

EDITORIAL COMMITTEE (2002)

CHRISTOPHER ACHEN
ANN CRIGLER
ROBERT L. JERVIS
MARGARET LEVI
GERHARD LOEWENBERG
NELSON W. POLSBY
NANCY ROSENBLUM
ALAN J. WARE

RESPONSIBLE FOR THE ORGANIZATION OF VOLUME 5
(EDITORIAL COMMITTEE, 2000)

DAVID BRADY
JEAN BETHKE ELSHTAIN
BRUCE BUENO DE MESQUITA
DONALD GREEN
ROBERT L. JERVIS
MARGARET LEVI
NELSON W. POLSBY
SIDNEY TARROW
ALAN J. WARE
MARK BLITZ (GUEST)
ARTHUR BURRIS (GUEST)
ANN CRIGLER (GUEST)
JOHN ZALLER (GUEST)

Production Editor: KIM TRANSIER
Bibliographic Quality Control: MARY A. GLASS
Electronic Content Coordinator: SUZANNE K. MOSES
Subject Indexer: BRUCE TRACY

ANNUAL REVIEW OF POLITICAL SCIENCE

VOLUME 5, 2002

NELSON W. POLSBY, *Editor*
University of California, Berkeley

www.annualreviews.org   science@annualreviews.org   650-493-4400

ANNUAL REVIEWS
4139 El Camino Way • P.O. BOX 10139 • Palo Alto, California 94303-0139

ANNUAL REVIEWS
Palo Alto, California, USA

COPYRIGHT © 2002 BY ANNUAL REVIEWS, PALO ALTO, CALIFORNIA, USA. ALL RIGHTS RESERVED. The appearance of the code at the bottom of the first page of an article in this serial indicates the copyright owner's consent that copies of the article may be made for personal or internal use, or for the personal or internal use of specific clients. This consent is given on the condition that the copier pay the stated per-copy fee of $14.00 per article through the Copyright Clearance Center, Inc. (222 Rosewood Drive, Danvers, MA 01923) for copying beyond that permitted by Section 107 or 108 of the US Copyright Law. The per-copy fee of $14.00 per article also applies to the copying, under the stated conditions, of articles published in any *Annual Review* serial before January 1, 1978. Individual readers, and nonprofit libraries acting for them, are permitted to make a single copy of an article without charge for use in research or teaching. This consent does not extend to other kinds of copying, such as copying for general distribution, for advertising or promotional purposes, for creating new collective works, or for resale. For such uses, written permission is required. Write to Permissions Dept., Annual Reviews, 4139 El Camino Way, P.O. Box 10139, Palo Alto, CA 94303-0139 USA.

International Standard Serial Number: 1094-2939
International Standard Book Number: 0-8243-3305-5

All Annual Reviews and publication titles are registered trademarks of Annual Reviews. ⊗ The paper used in this publication meets the minimum requirements of American National Standards for Information Sciences—Permanence of Paper for Printed Library Materials, ANSI Z39.48-1992.

Annual Reviews and the Editors of its publications assume no responsibility for the statements expressed by the contributors to this *Annual Review*.

TYPESET BY TECHBOOKS, FAIRFAX, VA
PRINTED AND BOUND IN THE UNITED STATES OF AMERICA

164,25

(3,11)

11(1o2

PREFACE

Now that the *Annual Review of Political Science* has published five volumes, the process that creates each volume has begun to settle into a pattern that we can describe to our slowly expanding corps of faithful readers. Most of the articles we print are originally proposed as topics by members of the editorial committee. The committee meets annually with a few invited guests in an all-day brainstorming session convened for the purpose of surveying the landscape of the discipline and figuring out what subjects we ought to be covering and who ought to be writing about them.

This makes for a stimulating day. Participants are varied in their perspectives and quite forthcoming. Sometimes even a little noisy. Here is the decision rule that generally prevails. If a committee member can offer a description of a topic that seems coherent to the rest of us, we more frequently than not urge that member to go ahead and recruit an author. We try to be conscientious about covering the main branches of the discipline. Gaps in any given volume are more likely owing to missed deadlines by authors than to neglect by the editors.

More and more we hear ideas proposed to us by prospective authors. If we like these ideas we give a green light and subject the finished product to a peer review, just as we do for articles we solicit.

Each editor takes responsibility for a stable of articles and authors in varying stages of production. Once a manuscript is submitted, it is read by one or more editors. Sometimes they pass suggestions back to authors. Sooner or later, each manuscript gets a thorough going over by Kim Transier, a superb professional editor who upholds the high standards of the publisher with a shrewd eye and a deft touch that is exactly as light as it needs to be. Readers are greatly in her debt, although they will never know how greatly. But we know.

The process relies on the knowledge, the enthusiasm and the dedication of the editors. Each of them has an opportunity to put a thumbprint on the table of contents. In this very important sense, the *Annual Review* is a collegial product.

This is, on the whole, a high-morale operation. The editors think having an annual shot at laying out the current agenda of political science is a worthwhile enterprise. We have managed to do it five times now, in a mutually supportive, collegial way. When we fall short of perfection, as we regularly do, we console ourselves with the thought that next year may be better.

Nelson W. Polsby
Editor

*Annual Review of Political Science*
Volume 5, 2002

CONTENTS

INDEXES

ERRATA

An online log of corrections to *The Annual Review of Political Science*
chapters (if any have yet been occasioned, 1997 to the present) may be
found at http://polisci.annualreviews.org/

RELATED ARTICLES

From the *Annual Review of Anthropology*, Volume 31, 2002

Politics of Archaeology in Africa, Nick Shepherd

Migrant "Illegality" and Deportability in Everyday Life, Nicholas P. De Genova

Critical Perspectives on Contemporary Democracies, Julia Paley

Street Children, Human Rights, and Public Health: A Critique and Future Directions, Catherine Panter-Brick

From the *Annual Review of Psychology*, Volume 53, 2002

Rationality, Eldar Shafir and Robyn A. LeBoeuf

Intergroup Bias, Miles Hewstone, Mark Rubin, and Hazel Willis

From the *Annual Review of Sociology*, Volume 28, 2002

Ethnic Boundaries and Identity in Plural Societies, Jimy M. Sanders

Race, Gender, and Authority in the Workplace: Theory and Research, Ryan Smith

The Study of Boundaries in the Social Sciences, Michele Lamont and Virag Molnar

Variants of Social Violence, Mary Jackman

Ideas, Politics, and Public Policy, John L. Campbell

Welfare Reform: How Do We Measure Success?, Daniel T. Lichter and Rukamalie Jayakody

From Factors to Actors: Computational Sociology and Agent-Based Modeling, Michael W. Macy and Robert Willer

ANNUAL REVIEWS is a nonprofit scientific publisher established to promote the advancement of the sciences. Beginning in 1932 with the *Annual Review of Biochemistry*, the Company has pursued as its principal function the publication of high-quality, reasonably priced *Annual Review* volumes. The volumes are organized by Editors and Editorial Committees who invite qualified authors to contribute critical articles reviewing significant developments within each major discipline. The Editor-in-Chief invites those interested in serving as future Editorial Committee members to communicate directly with him. Annual Reviews is administered by a Board of Directors, whose members serve without compensation.

2002 Board of Directors, Annual Reviews

Richard N. Zare, *Chairman of Annual Reviews*
  Marguerite Blake Wilbur, Professor of Chemistry, Stanford University
John I. Brauman, *J. G. Jackson–C. J. Wood Professor of Chemistry, Stanford University*
Peter F. Carpenter, *Founder, Mission and Values Institute*
W. Maxwell Cowan, *Vice President and Chief Scientific Officer, Howard Hughes Medical Institute, Bethesda*
Sandra M. Faber, *Professor of Astronomy and Astronomer at Lick Observatory, University of California at Santa Cruz*
Eugene Garfield, *Publisher*, The Scientist
Samuel Gubins, *President and Editor-in-Chief, Annual Reviews*
Daniel E. Koshland, Jr., *Professor of Biochemistry, University of California at Berkeley*
Joshua Lederberg, *University Professor, The Rockefeller University*
Gardner Lindzey, *Director Emeritus, Center for Advanced Study in the Behavioral Sciences, Stanford University*
Sharon R. Long, *Professor of Biological Sciences, Stanford University*
J. Boyce Nute, *President and CEO, Mayfield Publishing Co.*
Michael E. Peskin, *Professor of Theoretical Physics, Stanford Linear Accelerator Ctr.*
Harriet A. Zuckerman, *Vice President, The Andrew W. Mellon Foundation*

Management of Annual Reviews

Samuel Gubins, President and Editor-in-Chief
Richard L. Burke, Director for Production
Paul J. Calvi, Jr., Director of Information Technology
Steven J. Castro, Chief Financial Officer
John W. Harpster, Director of Sales and Marketing

Annual Reviews of

Anthropology
Astronomy and Astrophysics
Biochemistry
Biomedical Engineering
Biophysics and Biomolecular
  Structure
Cell and Developmental
  Biology
Earth and Planetary Sciences
Ecology and Systematics
Energy and the Environment
Entomology

Fluid Mechanics
Genetics
Genomics and Human Genetics
Immunology
Materials Research
Medicine
Microbiology
Neuroscience
Nuclear and Particle Science
Nutrition
Pharmacology and Toxicology
Physical Chemistry

Physiology
Phytopathology
Plant Biology
Political Science
Psychology
Public Health
Sociology

SPECIAL PUBLICATIONS
Excitement and Fascination of
  Science, Vols. 1, 2, 3, and 4

Annu. Rev. Polit. Sci. 2002. 5:1–30
DOI: 10.1146/annurev.polisci.5.092601.141138
Copyright © 2002 by Annual Reviews. All rights reserved

BARGAINING THEORY AND INTERNATIONAL CONFLICT

Robert Powell

*Department of Political Science, 220 Barrows Hall, University of California at Berkeley,
Berkeley, California 94720-1950; e-mail: rpowell@socrates.berkeley.edu*

Key Words   causes of war and conflict, inefficiency and breakdown

■ **Abstract**   International relations theory has long seen the origins, conduct, and
termination of war as a bargaining process. Recent formal work on these issues
draws very heavily on Rubinstein's (1982) seminal analysis of the bargaining problem and the research that flowed from it. There is now what might be called a
standard or canonical model of the origins of war that sees this outcome as a bargaining breakdown. This essay reviews this standard model and current efforts to
extend it to the areas of (*a*) multilateral bargaining, which is at the heart of old issues such as balancing and bandwagoning as well as newer ones such as the role of
third-party mediation; (*b*) the effects of domestic politics on international outcomes;
(*c*) efforts to explicitly model intra-war bargaining; and (*d*) dynamic commitment
problems.

INTRODUCTION

Bargaining—be it over the terms of a peace settlement, an alliance, a treaty, a
trade agreement, or the structure of an international institution—is at the center of
many of the most important issues in international politics. Not surprisingly, then,
international relations theory has often looked to bargaining theory.[1] This is especially true of the most recent formal work on the origins, conduct, and termination
of war, which draws very heavily on Rubinstein's (1982) seminal analysis and
the research that flowed from it. Grounded in bargaining theory and building on
earlier formal and nonformal analyses of war, the latest efforts are maturing into
a coherent and cumulating body of research with well-defined questions; clear,
deductive analyses; and empirically testable hypotheses. Most of this work is still
largely theoretical, as might be expected in this relatively early stage in the development of this latest wave of research. Some testing has already been done,

---

[1]Conversely, the study of international politics seems to have stimulated important work in
bargaining theory, most notably Schelling's *The Strategy of Conflict* (1960).

but the challenge for the future—as with so much of the broad thematic work in international relations—is to conduct compelling empirical tests while continuing to develop the theory.

This essay reviews the theoretical work on bargaining and war. The next section surveys results derived from noncooperative bargaining theory. Subsequent sections describe the basic bargaining-problem framework for studying war and its application to four areas: (*a*) multilateral bargaining, which is being used to study old issues such as balancing and bandwagoning as well as newer ones such as the role of third-party mediation; (*b*) the effects of domestic politics on international outcomes; (*c*) efforts to explicitly model intra-war bargaining; and (*d*) dynamic commitment problems.[2]

AN OVERVIEW OF NONCOOPERATIVE BARGAINING THEORY

Bargaining is about deciding how to divide the gains from joint action. That is, coordinated action frequently increases the size of the "pie"—for example, the exchange of goods often creates gains from trade; revising the territorial status quo peacefully rather than through the costly use of force means that the resources that would have been destroyed by fighting can now can be divided. The existence of potential gains from acting jointly creates an incentive to cooperate. But, of course, each actor also wants to maximize its share of those gains and, indeed, may take steps that reduce the chances of agreement when such steps promise a sufficiently large share of the gains if there is an agreement.

In 1982, Rubinstein's striking analysis renewed interest in studying bargaining with noncooperative game theory. The noncooperative approach focuses on the setting in which the negotiations take place and on how that setting shapes the bargaining strategies and ultimate outcomes. In particular, it models the bargaining problem as a noncooperative game and characterizes the equilibria of this game. Once this is done, changes in the bargaining setting are modeled by changing the underlying game and then tracing the effects of these changes on the game's equilibria. This section briefly reviews Rubinstein's (1982) analysis and some of the work that grew out of it [see Fudenberg & Tirole (1991, pp. 397–434), Kennan & Wilson (1993), and Muthoo (1999) for more extensive

---

[2]Space limitations preclude the discussion of important work on war (e.g., Fearon 1994, Kydd 1997, Downs & Rocke 1994) that is not based on bargaining models. Although the distinction is somewhat arbitrary, bargaining models give players a significant range of options when deciding how much of the bargaining surplus to demand. This contrasts with, for example, a war of attrition in which each player must demand everything or give in.

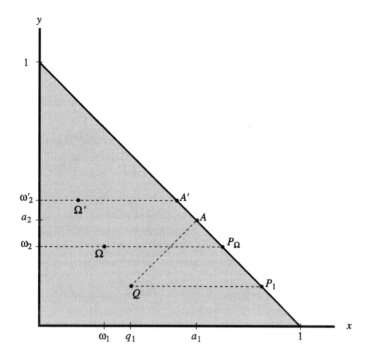

Figure 1 The bargaining problem.

reviews]. Special emphasis is given to the bargaining structures that have been used in applied work, and the outcomes these structures typically induce.[3] Suppose two players, *1* and *2*, are bargaining about how to divide the gains from cooperation. The shaded region in Figure 1 depicts the set of feasible outcomes and payoffs. For expositional simplicity, the bargainers are assumed to be risk-neutral, which means that the players' utilities to agreeing to (x, y) are, respectively, $U_1(x) = x$ and $U_2(y) = y$. Points along the upper-right edge of the set of feasible outcomes are Pareto-optimal or Pareto-efficient outcomes, i.e., making one bargainer better off entails making the other worse off. Point Q represents the status quo, which defines what the players receive if they cannot agree on a new allocation.

---

[3]Unlike noncooperative bargaining theory, which emphasizes the bargaining process, cooperative or axiomatic bargaining theory generally focuses on the properties of a bargaining outcome. In particular, this approach specifies a priori properties or axioms that agreements are assumed to satisfy and then looks for feasible divisions of the surplus that satisfy these conditions. For example, the Nash bargaining solution posits that the outcome will be Pareto-optimal, whereas the noncooperative approach specifies the bargaining setting and then asks whether this setting leads to Pareto-efficient outcomes.

In addition to specifying the stakes, the noncooperative approach also requires specifying a bargaining protocol—how the players bargain about these stakes. Three protocols are widely used in applied work. In the first, player *1* makes a take-it-or-leave-it offer. If *2* accepts, both players receive the agreed payoffs; if *2* rejects, the status quo remains in place. In the second protocol, only one bargainer makes offers, but now that bargainer can make as many offers as she wants. In the third, offers alternate back and forth. If *2* rejects an offer, she can then make a counteroffer. If *1* rejects the counteroffer, he can counter the counter, and so on. There is typically no limit to the number of offers.

In addition to describing who can make offers and in what order, the bargaining protocol also specifies the other actions that the bargainers can take. One possibility is especially relevant to the recent work on war. Sometimes one or both bargainers have an outside option that they can pursue after terminating the bargaining. A seller, for example, might stop bargaining with one potential buyer in order to start bargaining with another. One litigant might give up negotiating a settlement and go to trial. One state might stop bargaining and try to use force to impose a settlement.

In general, what happens if one player terminates the bargaining is not modeled explicitly (see Fudenberg et al. 1987 for an exception) and is simply abbreviated in the payoffs. That is, if one of the bargainers stops the bargaining, the game ends and the players receive the payoffs associated with the outside option. Point Ω denotes these payoffs in Figure 1. Note further that player *2* prefers the outside option Ω to the status quo Q whereas *1* prefers the status quo. As will be seen, these preferences affect the players' ability to make credible threats to exercise the outside option and thereby obtain a more favorable agreement.

The outside-option payoffs Ω are what the bargainers obtain if they fail to reach an agreement because they terminate the bargaining. By contrast, the players receive the payoffs associated with the status quo as long as they have failed to reach an agreement but have not yet ended the bargaining by pursuing an outside option. For this reason, the status quo is sometimes referred to as an inside option (Muthoo 1999, pp. 137–43).

How do different bargaining settings affect the outcome? Rubinstein (1982) studied a situation in which two players were trying to decide how to divide a "pie" and got nothing if they could not agree on the division. [This means $Q = (0, 0)$ in terms of Figure 1.] In his alternating-offer, infinite-horizon model, the players took turns making offers and there was no limit on the number of offers allowed.[4] The bargainers also had complete information about the bargaining setting, and, in particular, each knew the other's payoffs. Rubinstein proved two remarkable facts. First, although the game has infinitely many Nash equilibria, it has a

---

[4]Ståhl (1972) studied the less natural case in which the bargainers could only make a predetermined number of offers.

unique subgame perfect equilibrium.[5] Moreover, as the time between offers becomes arbitrarily small, the payoffs associated with this outcome converge to the Nash bargaining solution, which in this case is $(^1/_2, ^1/_2)$.[6]

The intuition for these results is straightforward. If offers alternate back and forth and can do so without limit, then in effect each player alternates between two roles. A player is either making an offer or receiving one, and the game always looks the same whenever a player assumes one of these roles. Let m and r, respectively, be the equilibrium payoffs to a player who is making an offer and to a player receiving an offer. If a player accepts an offer, he obtains r. If, by contrast, he rejects an offer, he assumes the role of the offerer. The payoff to this role is m, except that it must be discounted because time passes between the the player's rejection of an offer and his subsequent counteroffer. Let δm denote the discounted value of obtaining m after this delay, where δ is the players' common discount factor. Then, a player is choosing between r and δm when deciding whether to accept an offer. Knowing this, the offerer "buys" acceptance at the cheapest possible price by offering the lowest price the receiver would accept. This means that the offerer must give the receiver a payoff r that satisfies $r = \delta m$, which leaves the offerer with what is left, namely, $m = 1 - r$. Solving these two equations for the equilibrium payoffs m and r gives $m = 1/(1 + \delta)$ and $r = \delta/(1 + \delta)$.

Now suppose that the time before a bargainer can make a counteroffer is arbitrarily small. This means the receiver pays almost nothing to reject an offer and thereby become the offerer. Formally, δ becomes arbitrarily close to 1 as the time between offers becomes arbitrarily small, and as δ goes to 1, $(m, r) = (1/(1 + \delta), \delta/(1 + \delta))$ goes to $(^1/_2, ^1/_2)$. More substantively, as the time between offers becomes very small, there is virtually no difference between the roles of making and receiving an offer, for anyone in the latter role can always take on the former by rejecting the offer at little cost if there is a short time between rounds. Thus, the unique equilibrium gives identical players identical payoffs. These stunning results—uniqueness and convergence to the Nash bargaining solution—renewed interest in noncooperative bargaining theory and led to an explosion of work.

When offers alternate back and forth and the time between offers is small, the bargainers are in almost identical situations and therefore have about the same bargaining power. In these circumstances they divide the surplus or pie in half. When only one player makes all the offers, that player has all the bargaining power. Suppose player *1* can make a take-it-or-leave-it offer. If player *2* rejects it,

---

[5]Unlike a Nash equilibrium, a subgame perfect equilibrium requires the threats implicit in the bargainer's strategies to be credible. Because they exclude incredible threats and promises, subgame perfect equilibria offer more plausible predictions about outcomes than do Nash equilibria.

[6]Binmore (1987), Muthoo (1999), and Osborne & Rubinstein (1990) discuss the Nash bargaining solution, and Roth (1979) discusses axiomatic bargaining theory more generally.

he obtains zero. Exploiting this, *1* claims all of the surplus for herself by offering *2* zero.[7] The same result obtains if *1* can make more than one offer.

The existence of outside options can affect a player's bargaining power. Suppose that *1* makes a take-it-or-leave-it offer. In response, *2* can accept or reject the offer or exercise an outside option that ends the game and yields the payoffs associated with Ω in Figure 1. If *2* did not have this option, *1* would maximize her payoff by offering *2* the smallest share that he would be willing to accept and claiming the rest. That is, *1* would propose $P_1 = (1 - q_2, q_2)$. If, by contrast, *2* has the outside option Ω, which he prefers to the status quo (since $\omega_2 > q_2$), then he can credibly threaten to exercise the outside option if he is offered anything less than ω_2. Understanding this, *1* proposes $P_\Omega = (1 - \omega_2, \omega_2)$. In this case, the existence of an outside option and *2*'s ability to credibly threaten to exercise it improves his bargaining position and gets him better terms. The same outcome results if *1* can make more than a single offer.

The situation is different if, as in the Rubinstein model, offers alternate. Suppose that when considering an offer, a bargainer can accept it, reject it in order to make a counteroffer, or exercise the outside option Ω. The outcome of this game would be *A* in Figure 1 if the players did not have this option and if the interval between offers were very short. (Point *A*, the Nash bargaining solution relative to threat point *Q*, divides the bargaining surplus evenly between the bargainers relative to the status quo *Q*.) Note further that the bargainers prefer *A* to Ω. That is, both bargainers prefer the agreement they would reach absent an outside option to the payoffs associated with that option. In these circumstances, neither bargainer can credibly threaten to exercise the outside option, and that option has no effect on the bargaining outcome. *A* is the outcome regardless of the presence of Ω.[8] Matters are different if the outside option is Ω'. Now *2* prefers Ω' to *A* and therefore can credibly threaten to exercise the outside option unless offered ω_2', which is strictly greater than a_2. In this situation, *1* offers *2* just enough to make the exercise of the outside option incredible, namely $A' = (1 - \omega_2', \omega_2')$.

A striking feature of actual bargaining is that it often results in costly delays and inefficient outcomes. Haggling between a buyer and seller delays agreement. Labor negotiations break down in costly strikes. Litigants fail to reach out-of-court settlements and engage in expensive trials. States fall short in their diplomatic efforts to resolve a conflict and go to war. In all these cases, the outcome of the bargaining is not Pareto-optimal. Whatever the final agreement, both sides would have been better off agreeing to it at the very outset and thereby at least avoiding the bargaining costs. The eminent economist Hicks (1932) believed that these

---

[7]Player 2 clearly would accept any offer greater than zero. One can formally show that player 2 in equilibrium is sure to accept an offer of zero although there is no difference between accepting and rejecting it.

[8]Technically, this result also depends on the precise protocol and in particular on exactly when the bargainers can exercise the outside option (see Osborne & Rubinstein 1990, pp. 54–63).

inefficiencies resulted from irrational or misguided behavior. By the early 1980s, economists believed that incomplete or asymmetric information would provide a much better explanation, and this belief motivated a great deal of work.

The basic idea was that if, say, a seller was uncertain about how much a buyer was willing to pay for something, then he might begin by charging a high price and subsequently lowering it. Obviously a low-valuation buyer would not pay a high price and would wait for a lower one. But a high-valuation buyer might pay a higher price rather than wait for a lower one if the benefits of a buying at a lower price were outweighed by the costs of delaying an agreement. Indeed, if the buyer were sufficiently likely to agree to a high price, then it would be optimal for the seller to start the bargaining by demanding a high price and then gradually lower it. In this way, asymmetric information would explain delay.

Unfortunately, efforts to explain delay and other bargaining inefficiencies on the basis of asymmetric information have not been entirely successful. For example, as the time between offers becomes very small, bargainers generally reach agreement without delay even in the presence of uncertainty. Thus, it is not asymmetric information per se that accounts for delay, but the rather unsatisfying assumption that a significant amount of time must elapse before the seller can make a new offer. Asymmetric information is related to bargaining inefficiencies, but its limited ability to explain delay, which is the simplest kind of inefficiency, should serve as a note of caution that the work on war discussed below will have to address.[9]

WAR AS A BARGAINING PROCESS: THE BASIC FRAMEWORK

Much of the recent formal work on international conflict shares a common, unifying theme. The origin, conduct, and termination of war are part of a bargaining process. This perspective is, of course, not new. Schelling, perhaps most famously, observed that most conflicts "are essentially *bargaining* situations" (1960, p. 5). What is new is the set of game-theoretic tools that makes it possible to follow through on this perspective to a greater extent.[10] This section describes the bargaining-problem framework.

---

[9]Kennan & Wilson (1993) review the work on bargaining with private information. For an introduction to the problem of delay and the related issue of the Coase conjecture, see Fudenberg & Tirole (1991, pp. 397–434); Gul & Sonnenschein (1988); and Gul et al. (1986).

[10]To appreciate the importance of the new tools, note that uncertainty plays a crucial role in bargaining. Sellers, for example, are uncertain about buyers' unwillingness to pay; states are uncertain about each other's resolve. Despite its importance, no one knew how to study uncertainty and asymmetric information formally until Harsanyi's (1967–1968) work was combined with ideas about credibility and perfect equilibria in the early 1980s. These developments underpin the latest wave of work on bargaining theory as well as the explosion of work that revolutionized economics in the 1980s and 1990s. See Kreps (1990) for an accessible overview of these developments and some of their limitations.

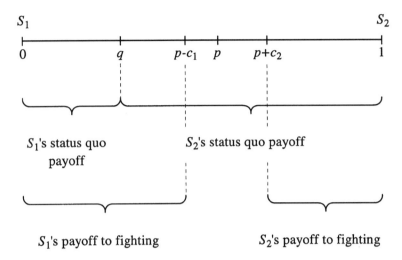

Figure 2   Bargaining over territory.

Figure 2 illustrates the basic setup. Two states, S_1 and S_2, are bargaining about revising the status quo. The bargaining can be about any issue, but it is usually taken to be about territory. In this interpretation, S_1 controls all territory to the left of q, from which it obtains utility q. S_2 controls all territory to the right of q, from which it derives utility $1 - q$. The interval $[0, 1]$ defines the range of possible territorial agreements, and the states receive utilities $U_D(x) = x$ and $U_S(x) = 1 - x$ by agreeing to $x \in [0, 1]$. (Bargaining models typically assume states maximize their absolute gains. See below for a discussion of the implications of "relative-gains" concerns.)

In addition to revising the status quo through mutual agreement, the states may also use force to try to impose a settlement. If they fight, S_1 pays cost c_1 and wins all the territory with probability p. With probability $1 - p$, S_1 loses everything and also pays cost c_1. Thus, S_1's expected payoff to fighting is $p(1 - c_1) + (1 - p)(0 - c_1) = p - c_1$. Similarly, S_2's payoff to fighting is $1 - p - c_2$. In this setting, it is natural to interpret p as the distribution of power between S_1 and S_2.[11]

In Figure 2, S_1 prefers fighting to accepting any point to the right of $p - c_1$ and prefers accepting any point to the left of $p - c_1$ to fighting. Similarly, S_2 prefers the distribution y to fighting if $1 - y > 1 - p - c_2 \Leftrightarrow p + c_2 \leq y$. Consequently, S_1 is dissatisfied with the status quo, i.e., prefers fighting to accepting q, if $q < p - c_1$, whereas S_2 is satisfied since $q \leq p + c_2$. Thus, the set of feasible peaceful

---

[11]The assumption that one state or the other wins everything has no effect on the formal analysis, since the results are the same if p is taken to be the expected territorial outcome. However, if p is defined that way, it may no longer make sense to think of p as the distribution of power. Suppose, for example, the expected territorial outcome remains the same but the variance of the outcome goes up. Is the distribution of power the same or not?

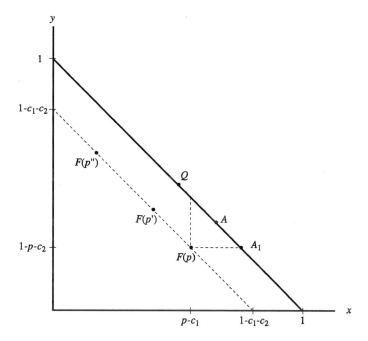

Figure 3 War as an outside option.

agreements, i.e., territorial divisions that both states prefer to fighting, lies between $p - c_1$ and $p + c_2$.

Figure 3 recasts the bargaining problem. S_1's and S_2's utilities are plotted along the horizontal and vertical axes, respectively. The set of peaceful outcomes, including the continuation of the status quo Q, are on the line between $(1, 0)$ and $(0, 1)$ and define the Pareto frontier of the bargaining problem. If the states fight, they obtain the payoffs at $F(p)$. That this outcome lies inside the Pareto frontier reflects the fact that fighting is costly and therefore inefficient. Nevertheless, S_1 prefers $F(p)$ to Q, since the former lies to the right of the latter. The allocations on the Pareto frontier above and to the right of $F(p)$ are the peaceful outcomes that both states prefer to fighting.

Figure 3 shows how shifts in the distribution of power affect the bargaining problem. As the distribution of power shifts in favor of S_2, say from p to p' to p'' (where $p > p' > p''$), S_2's payoff to fighting increases, S_1's decreases, and $F(p)$ slides upward along the line from $(1 - c_1 - c_2, 0)$ to $(0, 1 - c_1 - c_2)$.[12] At p', both states prefer Q to $F(p')$ and neither is dissatisfied. At p'', by contrast, S_2 prefers $F(p'')$ to Q, while S_1 prefers Q and is satisfied.

---

[12]If $p = c_1$, then S_1's and S_2's expected payoffs are 0 and $1 - p - c_2 = 1 - c_1 - c_2$, respectively. Thus, $F(c_1) = (0, 1 - c_1 - c_2)$, and similarly, $F(1 - c_2) = (1 - c_1 - c_2, 0)$.

In an important article, Fearon (1995) uses the basic bargaining setup in Figure 2 and a take-it-or-leave-it protocol to reframe the theories of the origin of war by linking them to a more general problem in bargaining theory, namely that of explaining why bargaining ever breaks down in inefficient outcomes. Because fighting is costly, $F(p)$ lies inside the Pareto frontier and there are agreements that *both* states prefer to fighting (e.g., A in Figure 3). A rationalist theory of war, Fearon argues, must explain why states end up at $F(p)$ and not at a peaceful settlement such as A, which makes them both better off.

Once the question is posed this clearly, it is immediately evident that three of the then most prominent theories of war fail to address this fundamental puzzle. Theories that appeal to anarchy as an important structural cause of war (e.g., Waltz 1959, 1979) assume that there is nothing to stop states from using force to further their ends if doing so appears to be in their best interest. But the puzzle is to explain why states use force when it is not in their interest, i.e., there are outcomes that both prefer to fighting. The idea that a state goes to war when it has a positive expected utility for fighting (e.g., Bueno de Mesquita 1981) also falters. S_1 has a positive expected utility for fighting, i.e., it prefers $F(p)$ to q, but this does not explain why the states would end up at $F(p)$ rather than A, since the expected utility of A is higher for both states than that of $F(p)$. Finally, the theory of preventive war argues that a declining state may attack a rising power in order to avoid having to fight later on worse terms (see Levy 1987 for a survey of nonformal theories of preventive war). This perspective introduces a dynamic component, namely the effects of shifts in the distribution of power on bargaining. But as it stands, this theory also fails to explain why bargaining breaks down in inefficient outcomes. For as long as fighting is costly, the "pie" is larger and there is more to be divided if the states avoid fighting. This means that there should be divisions that leave both sides better off.

In addition to these three theoretical schools, offense-defense theory and relative-gains concerns also suffer from the same weakness. As shown below, neither explains why states use force when there are Pareto-superior alternatives that the states prefer to fighting (see Lynn-Jones 1995 and Van Evera 1998 for reviews of offense-defense theory).

Fearon suggests that coherent rationalist explanations will take one of two general forms.[13] The first appeals to asymmetric information. Suppose S_1 can make a take-it-or-leave-it offer, which S_2 can accept or reject by fighting. If the states have complete information, then S_1 maximizes its payoff by making the largest demand that S_2 will accept. To wit, S_1 demands the border $p + c_2$ in Figure 2, which leaves S_2 with $1 - p - c_2$. S_2 cannot do better by fighting, so it accepts. As is typical in take-it-or-leave-it bargaining, the player making the offer obtains all of the surplus by leaving the other player indifferent between accepting and

---

[13]Fearon (1995) notes a third kind of rationalist explanation that is logically coherent but seems empirically unlikely. If the states are bargaining about an issue that is indivisible or "lumpy," then there may not be any feasible outcome that both states prefer to fighting.

rejecting the offer. If, by contrast, S_1 is unsure of S_2's cost of fighting c_2, S_1 no longer knows what it can demand of S_2 without provoking war. S_1 now faces a risk-return trade-off between possibly obtaining better terms and a higher probability of not obtaining any settlement at all. The more S_1 demands, the better off it will be if S_2 accepts. But the more it demands, the less likely S_2 is to accept. Typically, the optimal solution to this trade-off is not to "buy" zero risk. That is, the demand that maximizes S_1's expected payoff will be rejected with positive probability, in which case there will be war. Thus, war—or, more generally, inefficiency—results from asymmetric information.

The second explanation of why states may fail to agree on an outcome that both prefer to fighting is that they are unable to credibly commit themselves to following through on the agreement. The prisoner's dilemma is the classic example of this problem. Both actors prefer the cooperative outcome (C, C) to mutual defection (D, D), but this agreement is not self-enforcing, since at least one state, and in this case both, has an incentive to renege. Figure 3 makes the same point in a more general context. If none of the agreements above and to the right of $F(p)$ are self-enforcing, then the states may fight. Of course, the interesting part of this kind of explanation lies in explaining what about a particular strategic environment makes it impossible to credibly commit to these agreements. Fearon and others have addressed this in several settings.[14]

This very simple formulation can help cut through seemingly endless debates by posing central issues more clearly. Consider, for example, the idea that concerns about relative gains make cooperation more difficult and war more likely (Grieco 1988, Waltz 1979). Formally, S_1's and S_2's utilities for territorial division x are $U_1(x) = x - k(1 - x - x) = (1 + 2k)x - k$ and $U_2(x) = 1 - x - k[x - (1 - x)] = 1 + k - (1 + 2k)x$, where $k \geq 0$ measures the states' concern about relative gains.[15] Then S_1's payoff to fighting is $pU_D(1) + (1 - p)U_D(0) - c_1 = p(1 + 2k) - k - c_1$ and S_2's payoff is $1 - [(1 + 2k)p - k + c_2]$. Hence, the bargaining range, i.e., the set of territorial divisions that both states prefer to fighting, is given by $p(1 + 2k) - k - c_1 \leq x \leq (1 + 2k)p - k + c_2$. This implies that even if states are concerned about relative gains, there is still a set of agreements they prefer to fighting. Indeed, the length of this range, i.e., the difference between the upper and lower ends of this range, is just $c_1 + c_2$. This length does not depend on k. Nor does the probability

---

[14] It is important to stress that the rational choice approach (whether or not it is formalized mathematically) is based on the "methodological bet" (see Lake & Powell 1999) that trying to understand war as the outcome of instrumentally rational actors in a particular strategic setting will prove fruitful. This emphasis on the strategic setting contrasts with other "bets" that focus on other factors, such as psychological or cognitive factors (e.g., Jervis 1976), as did Hicks's (1932) explanation of strikes.

[15] As I have emphasized elsewhere (Powell 1994, p. 336; 1999, pp. 54–58), modeling relative-gains concerns through the utility function is really a reduced-form approach that begs the prior question of whether the international system actually induces relative-gains concerns. Many theorists claim it does, but this has yet to be shown deductively.

of war. More specifically, if S_2 is uncertain of S_1's cost c_1 and believes that this cost is uniformly distributed over $[\underline{c}_1, \overline{c}_1]$, and S_2 makes a take-it-or-leave-it offer, then the probability of war is $(\overline{c}_1 - c_2)/[2(\overline{c}_1 - \underline{c}_1)]$. Clearly, relative-gains concerns alone cannot explain why states fight rather than agree on peaceful divisions that both prefer to fighting.

Take-it-or-leave-it protocols are widely used because they do capture important aspects of bargaining and are easier to analyze. But they are also somewhat unnatural. The risk-return trade-off described above reflects the fact that the state receiving the offer can respond only by accepting it or going to war. In most circumstances a state could make a counteroffer or, at minimum, neither agree nor attack and simply wait. How would this more natural setting affect the bargaining?

Powell (1996a,b, 1999) addresses this issue in the context of a Rubinstein model with outside options. In that infinite-horizon, alternating-offer game, the state receiving an offer can accept it or reject it, as in the Rubinstein model, or end the game by exercising an outside option. This option is interpreted as trying to use force to impose a settlement and gives the players payoff $F(p)$. If one state rejects the other's offer and does not exercise its outside option of fighting, the round ends and that state makes the offer in the next round.

Powell studies the case in which there is two-sided incomplete information in that neither state knows the other's cost of fighting. Somewhat surprisingly, this game turns out to have a unique equilibrium,[16] in which the status quo remains unchanged and there is no risk of war if both states are satisfied. If one state is dissatisfied, then this state either accepts the satisfied state's initial offer or attacks. Anticipating this reaction, the satisfied state makes its optimal de facto take-it-or-leave-it offer. The probability of war is simply the probability that the dissatisfied state rejects this offer.

As Figure 3 suggests, both states are satisfied if the distribution of benefits mirrors the distribution of power. That is, if $p' = q$, then Q and F will lie on the same ray from the origin as do Q and $F(p')$. Consequently, Q is Pareto-superior to $F(p')$ and both states will be satisfied when the distribution of power is p'. By contrast, S_1 is dissatisfied at p when there is a large disparity between the distributions of power and benefits ($|p - q| \gg 0$), and S_2 is dissatisfied at p'', where there also is a large disparity between the distributions of power and benefits ($|p'' - q| \gg 0$).

This result undercuts many of the claims about the relationship between the distribution of power and the likelihood of war. The balance-of-power school (Claude 1962, Morgenthau 1967, Mearsheimer 1990, Wright 1965, Wolfers 1962) claims that war is least likely when there is an even distribution of power ($p = 1/2$), whereas the preponderance-of-power school (Blainey 1973, Organski 1968, Organski & Kugler 1980) argues that war is least likely when there is a preponderance of power ($p \approx 1$ or $p \approx 0$). (See Levy 1989 for a review of this debate and Wagner 1994 for a discussion of conceptual and modeling issues.)

---

[16]Bargaining games in which offers are made by a player with private information (e.g., one who knows her own cost of fighting while the other player does not) are typically plagued by a plethora of equilibria.

However, substantial empirical efforts to answer this question have yielded conflicting results. Siverson & Tennefoss (1984) find an even distribution of power to be more peaceful, as does Ferris (1973). By contrast, Kim (1991, 1992), Moul (1988), and Weede (1976) determine that a preponderance of power is more peaceful. Singer et al. (1972) find evidence for both claims depending on the historical period—an even distribution of power is more peace prone in the nineteenth century but less so in the twentieth. Mansfield (1992, 1994) uncovers evidence of a nonlinear, quadratic relationship in which the probability of war is smallest when there is both an even distribution of power and a preponderance of power. The greatest instability occurs somewhere between a preponderance and a balance of power. Finally, Maoz (1983) and Bueno de Mesquita & Lalman (1988) find no significant relation between stability and the distribution of power.

The formal results above may account for these conflicting results: The probability of war is likely to be related to the relationship between the distributions of power and benefits, not solely to the distribution of power. Consequently, any effort to assess the relationship between the distribution of power and the probability of war must control for the distribution of benefits.

This model also illuminates the effects of the offense-defense balance on the likelihood of war. Jervis' (1979) important and enormously influential article linked the security dilemma to the offense-defense balance and laid the foundation for what has become the offense-defense theory of war (see Glaser 1997 for a review of work on the security dilemma). The basic idea is that factors that make attacking relatively more attractive than defending make war more likely. Jervis framed his discussion in terms of a repeated prisoner's dilemma and a 2×2 stag hunt. But it is not immediately evident from a bargaining perspective why increasing a state's payoff to attacking should make war more likely. Suppose that the probability that S_1 prevails is $p + f$ if it attacks and $p - f$ if it is attacked. Then the difference between S_1's probability of prevailing if it attacks and its probability of prevailing if it is attacked is $2f$, so f can be thought of as the size of the offensive advantage. In terms of Figure 2, the presence of an offensive advantage narrows the bargaining range to the interval between $p + f - c_1$ and $p - f + c_2$. The length of this interval is $c_1 + c_2 - 2f$, which clearly decreases as the offense becomes more favorable. But as long as the size of the offensive advantage f is not too large, there will still be a set of agreements that both sides prefer to fighting. Why, then, do the states not agree to one of these? Offense-defense theory provides no general explanation. Powell's (1999, pp. 110–13) analysis of the asymmetric-information bargaining model shows that larger offensive advantages as well as decreases in the cost of fighting do make war more likely.

There is a natural link between bargaining and arms races: One can see a state's attempt to build up its military strength as an effort to create a more advantageous bargaining environment (Schelling 1966). Kydd (2000) pursues this line in his analysis of the "deterrence model" of arms racing. In the deterrence model (Jervis 1976), arms races are a symptom of an underlying conflict of interest between states. Consequently, the outbreak of war may be correlated with arms races, but the link is not causal. In the "spiral model" (Jervis 1976), by contrast, there is no fundamental conflict. Rather, misperceptions and arms races interact to fuel a spiral of hostilities that may eventually end in war. In the spiral model, arms races are causal in the sense that if one could stop the cycle of misperception, no state would want to attack the other. (Recent contributions to the empirical literature on arms racing include Diehl & Crescenzi 1998 and Sample 1997.)

In Kydd's (2000) formulation, a state, say S_1, makes a take-it-or-leave-it offer to S_2. If S_2 rejects, the states can choose to increase their military capabilities, after which there is another round of take-it-or-leave-it bargaining. If the states have complete information about each other's ability to sustain an arms race, there will be no arms racing because any mismatch between the distributions of power and benefits will be brought into line in the first round of bargaining. If, however, S_2 is unsure of S_1's ability to run an arms race, S_2 may reject S_1's initial demand because S_2 believes that S_1 is bluffing. In turn, S_1, if it is not bluffing, will build up its military capabilities in order to "signal" to S_2 that it is deadly serious. Kydd's analysis provides a firm, formal footing for the deterrence model. The challenge now is to integrate this work with that on the spiral model in an effort to assess their relative empirical importance.[17]

MULTILATERAL BARGAINING: BALANCING AND BANDWAGONING, EXTENDED DETERRENCE, AND THIRD-PARTY INTERVENTION

Most of noncooperative bargaining theory, as well as the preceding applications, focuses on two-party bargaining. This emphasis probably reflects the fact that although n-player games are not necessarily any more difficult to analyze formally, it is often harder to specify a substantively convincing or "natural" bargaining protocol. For example, it seems natural in a two-player, Rubinstein game for the players to take turns making offers (although, in fact, there is nothing really natural about this). But what is the "natural" bargaining protocol if there are three players? Should the offers be made round-robin, i.e., *1* makes an offer, then *2*, then *3*, then *1* again and so on? This hardly seems natural. Suppose, instead, that the player who makes the next offer is chosen randomly. That is, *1*, *2*, or *3* each make the first offer with probability $1/3$. The player making the next offer is then selected randomly again (see Baron & Ferejohn 1989 for an important analysis of parliamentary bargaining based on this kind of protocol). This protocol has the advantage of symmetry. But it does not feel very natural.

Nevertheless, recent work has begun to study interactions between three or more actors, sometimes finessing the problem by formalizing the situation so that

---

[17]See Kydd (1997) for a formal analysis of the spiral model. Because this analysis is not based on a bargaining model, it is not reviewed here.

bargaining only occurs between two actors. Two areas of research are discussed here. The first is central to balancing, bandwagoning, and states' alignment behavior. The second is a small but growing body of work on third-party intervention in military disputes.

The idea that states balance against power can be traced back to Thucydides and Xenophon and to the politics of ancient Greece—or, at least, David Hume (1898 [1752]) thought so. According to Mattingly (1955), balance-of-power politics framed the diplomacy of Northern Italy in the late fifteenth century.[18] More recently, Waltz observed, "If there is any distinctively political theory of international politics, balance-of-power theory is it. And yet one cannot find a single statement of it that is generally accepted" (1979, p. 117).

Wagner's (1986) path-breaking article renewed interest in trying to understand balancing and bandwagoning as the equilibrium outcome of an underlying noncooperative dynamic game.[19] He sketched a very complicated n-player game, which Niou & Ordeshook (1990) refined and analyzed more extensively. In their game, states bargain by proposing coalitions. A state is chosen randomly to make a proposal, and one coalition prevails over another if the resources of its members exceed the resources of the other's members. The primary finding is that no state is ever eliminated as long as it is an essential part of some winning coalition. This disappointing result suggests that balance-of-power politics has very few observational implications. Unfortunately, these models are so complex, as indeed they must be in order to do what Wagner and Niou & Ordeshook want them to do, that it is difficult to know what is driving the results.

Powell (1999, pp. 149–96) looks at a much simpler game that is more closely tied to the bilateral bargaining models discussed above. In his formulation, a potential attacker, A, can attack S_1 only, S_2 only, both S_1 and S_2, or neither. If A attacks only one of the other states, say S_2, then S_1 has the following options: (a) balance against A by joining S_2, (b) bandwagon with A by joining the attack on S_2, or (c) stand aside while A and S_2 fight. As in the models above, fighting always results in the elimination of one of the opposing sides. Thus, at most two states will remain after the first round of fighting. These two states then bargain about revising the territorial status quo given the distribution of power and benefits that results from the outcome of the first round of fighting.

This formulation highlights the trade-off a state faces when deciding whether to balance or bandwagon. Balancing with a weaker state puts the balancer in a stronger bargaining position relative to its coalition partner and thus makes for a more favorable division of the spoils of victory—if this coalition prevails against the third state. By contrast, aligning with the stronger state puts the bandwagoner in a weaker bargaining position relative to its coalition partner and makes for a less

---

[18]See Haas (1953), Hinsley (1963), and Knutsen (1997) for historical overviews of balance-of-power theories and thinking. Butterfield (1966, p. 139) offers a skeptical view of the existence of a coherent conception of balancing before the middle of the seventeenth century.
[19]See Kaplan et al. (1960) for a very early, partially game theoretic effort to study balancing.

favorable division of the spoils of victory. But bandwagoning, relative to balancing, increases the probability of being on the winning side and having any spoils to divide.[20] Balancing in Powell's formulation turns out to be much less likely than bandwagoning.

Werner's (2000) interesting analysis focuses on the attacker's decision. In her model, an attacker, A, makes "offers" by choosing the size of the stakes of a dispute it is thinking about provoking with another state. The latter is the protégé of a third state, D, and D must decide whether to intervene on its protégé's behalf if A attacks. Since the stakes are endogenous, A faces a risk-return trade-off. The more it demands, the more likely D is to intervene. This trade-off induces selection effects that help to explain some empirical anomalies regarding intervention. For example, if D is relatively powerful, A will moderate its demands and thereby reduce the chances that D intervenes. Consequently, there should be no strong relation between D's strength and the likelihood that it will intervene. This runs counter to the intuitive conjecture that more powerful states are more likely to intervene (Altfeld & Bueno de Mesquita 1979; Walt 1988, 1992; Labs 1992) and helps account for the empirical finding that they are not (Huth & Russett 1984).

The role of third-party mediators in dispute resolution has recently received a good deal of empirical attention (see Bercovitch 1996, Dixon 1996, and Kleibor 1996 for recent efforts and reviews). Kydd[21] and Rauchhaus[22] analyze this problem formally in order to provide a firmer theoretical foundation for the empirics. In Kydd's formulation, a state, say S_1, can make a take-it-or-leave-it demand of S_2. The former is uncertain of the latter's cost of fighting and so faces a risk-return trade-off. Kydd introduces a mediator into this setup by allowing the mediator to report its beliefs about these costs to S_1 before S_1 makes its demand. The mediator is also uncertain of S_2's cost but does have some independent information it can pass on.

Kydd defines a mediator to be biased in favor of one of the states if it prefers territorial distributions that favor that state. The mediator is unbiased if it does not care about the terms of a territorial settlement and only wants to minimize the risk of war. Kydd then shows that, surprisingly, a mediator must be biased in order

---

[20] Awareness of this trade-off is of course not new and not the result of formal analysis. But, strangely, some widely accepted claims that states generally balance appear to disregard the trade-off. Waltz, for example, argues that secondary states balance because they are "both more appreciated and safer, *provided, of course, that the coalition they join achieves enough deterrent or defensive strength to dissuade adversaries from attacking*" (1979, p. 127, emphasis added).

[21] Kydd A. 2001. Which side are you on? Mediation as cheap talk. Unpublished manuscript, Department of Political Science, University of California, Riverside.

[22] Rauchhaus RW. 2000. *Third-party intervention in militarized disputes: primum non nocere*. Unpublished PhD dissertation, Department of Political Science, University of California, Berkeley.

to have any effect on the outcome of the bargaining. The intuition is that if the mediator only cares about preventing war, then the mediator will always tell S_1 that S_2 is resolute (regardless of whether the mediator believes it) and therefore S_1 should moderate its demands. This advice, if followed, minimizes the probability of war. Of course, S_1 understands that the mediator has an incentive to lie and consequently discounts its advice.

Rauchhaus (2000, see footnote 22) generalizes this result. Suppose that a mediator is so strongly biased in favor of a state, or, perhaps more accurately, a particular territorial outcome, that it is willing to act as an *agent provocateur*. During the Cold War, for example, the United States tried to exclude the Soviet Union from a mediating role out of concern that the Soviet Union would "stir up trouble." This type of "mediator," the opposite of the one who prefers a peaceful outcome to any other, would encourage S_1 to make maximal demands. Kydd excludes this case, whereas Rauchhaus allows for it by letting the motivations of the mediator range from caring only about avoiding war to caring only about the distribution of territory.[23] Rauchhaus shows that in order to sustain an equilibrium in which the mediator tells the truth, it must pay a "reputational" cost if it lies (and, presumably, will be caught out at some future time). Moreover, the reputational cost needed to sustain a truth-telling equilibrium is smallest when the mediator is unbiased. This suggests, contra Kydd, that unbiased mediators are preferable. Kydd's and Rauchhaus's formulations are not completely comparable and much work remains to be done. But they have opened up an interesting avenue of work on the increasingly important post–Cold War problem of mediation and intervention.

STRUCTURING APPEALS TO DOMESTIC POLITICS

One of the oldest debates in international relations theory is over the relative importance of domestic and structural explanations (see Fearon 1998b for the distinction between these types of explanation). Definitions of what counts as a domestic or structural explanation vary, but at a minimum, structural theories treat states as unitary actors. However defined, domestic and structural explanations are typically thought to be rivals. But this is misguided. Although some structural theories (e.g., Waltz 1979) seem to suggest that one can explain at least the outline of state behavior without reference to states' goals or preferences (except possibly the very general goal of survival), this assertion runs counter to most of the recent formal work in international relations theory (as well as much of the nonformal work).[24] In order to specify or close a game theoretic model, the actor's preferences and beliefs must be defined. Moreover, most conclusions derived from these models turn out to be at least somewhat sensitive to the actor's preferences and, especially,

---

[23]Kydd (2001, p. 37, see footnote 21) implicitly excludes the latter possibility when he assumes that if S_1 prefers a given settlement to the risk of war, then so does the mediator.
[24]Powell (2002) addresses this notion of structural explanation.

beliefs. This dependence suggests a more fruitful way to think about the relation between domestic and structural explanations. Domestic politics is terribly complicated, and it is not at all clear what aspects of it are likely to have significant international effects. Treating states as unitary actors creates a baseline and helps isolate domestic factors that are most likely to provide significant explanatory leverage.

Schultz's (1998, 2001) work on the democratic peace is an exciting example of the fruitfulness of this perspective. The empirical finding that democratic states do not fight each other is quite robust (see Schultz 2001 for a review and Gowa 1999 for the most powerful challenge to the democratic peace thesis). But we do not yet have an empirically established, theoretical explanation of the democratic peace, i.e., an explanation that predicts other empirical patterns that have been verified. Schultz's effort to provide one grows out of the work surveyed above that identifies asymmetric information as a critical cause of war. If war results from asymmetric information and if there are systematic differences in the likelihood of war between democratic versus nondemocratic states, he conjectures, then perhaps democratic institutions tend to moderate informational asymmetries between states during a time a crisis. With that in mind, Schultz develops a simple model of crisis bargaining in which there is an opposition party in a democratic state. This party's preferences differ from those of the party in power in that, if nothing else, it would prefer to be in power. This difference in preferences (along with a relatively open press) makes it more difficult for the party in power in a democracy to make threats it is unwilling to carry out. Since it is the uncertainty regarding states' willingness to follow through that leads to breakdown and war, democracies should be less likely to be involved in war.

Schultz (1998, 2001) tests his informational explanation against a competing explanation of the democratic peace that is based on the notion that the costs of going to war are systematically higher for democratic states than for nondemocratic states. He shows that these two mechanisms make different predictions about a state's response to a challenge made by a democratic or a nondemocratic state. The informational mechanism predicts that a state is less likely to resist a challenge coming from a democratic state (because there is less uncertainty and the challenge is less likely to be a bluff) than one from a nondemocratic state, whereas the cost-based explanation predicts the opposite. Schultz finds strong empirical support for the informational mechanism.

Bueno de Mesquita et al. (1999a,b)[25] also break down the unitary-actor assumption in a fruitful way. They describe a domestic regime in terms of two dimensions. The first is the size of the "selectorate," which is the group that participates in the selection of a state's leader, and the second is the size of the winning coalition, which is the group whose support a leader must retain in order to remain in power. A democracy, for example, has both a large selectorate and a large winning coalition.

---

[25]See also: Bueno de Mesquita B, Smith A, Siverson RM, Morrow JD. 2001. *Staying Alive: The Logic of Political Survival*. Unpublished manuscript, The Hoover Institution, Stanford University.

In a monarchy or junta, both are small. An autocracy may have a large or small selectorate, but the winning coalition is always small.

Bueno de Mesquita et al. study how these different institutional settings affect the bargaining surrounding a leader's efforts to sustain a winning coalition. Suppose a leader has limited resources that he can allocate to the production of private or public goods. Private goods channel benefits to specific individuals, such as those inside the leader's coalition, whereas public goods benefit everyone. The leader wants to spend the minimal amount needed to remain in office and pocket the rest, and the bargaining proceeds accordingly.

The leader faces a trade-off. On the one hand, offering private goods is the best way of buying loyalty, because it creates a wedge between the benefits of those inside the coalition, who receive the private benefits, and those outside the coalition. This wedge increases the cost to defecting from the winning coalition and supporting someone else's bid for leadership. Buying political support through public goods does not create a wedge because both those inside and outside the winning coalition receive the benefits. On the other hand, providing benefits to a large number of people through private payoffs may be much more expensive than providing them with the same level of benefits through public goods. This suggests that a leader tends to maintain support through the provision of private benefits when the winning coalition is small, as in juntas or authoritarian regimes, and through public goods in democracies.

Bueno de Mesquita et al. (1999a; also see footnote 25) use this framework to explain the democratic peace. When confronted by international conflict, democracies resolve this trade-off by allocating more resources to fighting than autocracies do. This makes democracies unattractive targets and more selective in the states they threaten, thereby reducing the chances that democratic states engage in war.

WAR AS AN INSIDE OPTION

Most of the bargaining theory literature on the causes of war, including the work discussed above, formalizes war as an outside option in a bargaining game. Going to war is typically modeled as a game-ending move, the payoffs of which reflect the distribution of power and the states' costs of fighting. For instance, S_1's expected payoff to fighting in the example above was given by the costly lottery $p \cdot 1 + (1 - p) \cdot 0 - c_1 = p - c_1$. Representing war as a costly lottery raises three issues that recent work is beginning to address by treating war as an inside option.

The first issue is whether modeling war in this way leads to misleading conclusions. All models make simplifying assumptions and are designed to answer some questions and not others. A simplification is neutral with respect to a set of questions if relaxing that assumption would not significantly affect the model's answers to those questions. By contrast, a simplification is distorting if relaxing it would significantly affect those answers. Modeling war as a costly lottery clearly simplifies the analysis in that it assumes away any further strategic interaction after the states go to war. To the extent that the anticipation of that interaction influences the states' pre-war behavior, failing to model intra-war interactions explicitly may lead to misleading conclusions about the causes of the initial decision to fight. In these circumstances, treating war as a costly lottery would be a distorting simplification.

Second, even if the costly-lottery assumption is neutral, this simplification makes it impossible to ask important questions about the strategic dynamics of inter-war behavior and war termination. This alone is a good reason for relaxing the assumption by modeling war as a costly process during which strategic inter-action continues (see Wittman 1979 for a path-breaking effort to model conflict and war as a process).

The third issue raised by the costly-lottery assumption is more general. One of the advantages of casting the problem of the origins of war in terms of a bargaining breakdown is that this conceptualization, as noted above, links it to a number of other substantive and theoretical literatures. Ideally, the work on bargaining and war should help us understand the exercise of coercive power—be it economic, military, or political. But in order for the work on the causes of war to contribute more fully to our understanding of these other forms of coercion, and vice versa, it is important to relax the assumption that the imposition of the costly sanction of going to war is a game-ending move. Even if this assumption is a plausible first approximation for some analyses of the causes of at least major war, it is much less plausible in other contexts, where the issue in dispute (e.g., trade policies) is only one of many issues over which the bargainers continue to interact while applying costly coercive pressure.

Wagner (2000) challenges the game-ending, costly-lottery assumption in two ways. First, following Blainey (1973), Wagner argues that most wars arise because of uncertainty over the distribution of power and continue until the belligerents' perceptions of the distribution of power come into line. However, most existing formal models of bargaining and war (e.g., Fearon 1995; Powell 1996a, 1999) appeal to uncertainty over states' costs or, more generally, their preferences or levels of resolve. It is not clear to what extent conclusions inferred from asymmetric information about preferences carry over to settings in which there is information about the distribution of power.

Wagner's second, broader concern begins with the observation that wars generally end because the states agree to stop fighting and not because the states are incapable of continuing to fight. "Thus to explain why wars occur one must explain why states must fight before reaching an agreement" (2000, p. 469). Wagner maintains that the costly-lottery assumption is distorting even with respect to questions about the origins of war and "can only lead to misleading conclusions" (2000, p. 469).

Smith & Stam,[26] Filson & Werner,[27] and Powell[28] unpack various aspects of the costly-lottery formulation in their efforts to model war as a costly process

---

[26]Smith A, Stam A. 2001. Bargaining through conflict. Unpublished manuscript, Department of Political Science, Yale University.

[27]Filson D, Werner S. 2001. Bargaining and fighting. Unpublished manuscript, Department of Political Science, Emory University.

[28]Powell R. 2001. Bargaining while fighting. Unpublished manuscript, Department of Political Science, University of California, Berkeley.

during which the states can still bargain. Smith & Stam treat the distribution of capabilities in a much more sophisticated way than does the standard costly-lottery formulation. They assume that two states, S_1 and S_2, are competing for a prize and that there are N forts of which S_1 controls n and S_2 controls $N - n$ at the start of the game. At the start of each round, S_1 proposes a division of the prize, say x for itself and $1 - x$ for S_2. S_2 then accepts or rejects. Acceptance ends the game with the agreed division. Rejection ends the round in a battle in which S_1 wins one fort from S_2 with probability p and loses one fort to S_2 with probability $1 - p$, and both states pay a cost of fighting. Given this new division of forts, S_1 starts the next round by making another proposal, and the bargaining continues in this way until the states agree on a division or until one state loses all of its forts. The states also start the game with different beliefs about the value of p, which they update as the fighting continues.

Although still relatively simple, this way of formalizing the distribution of capabilities has a number of appealing properties (see Smith 1998 for an earlier, related formulation). First, the distribution of power, which may be taken to be the probability that S_1 captures all the forts given the number of forts it currently controls, can rise and fall instead of only changing monotonically as in Powell (2001, see footnote 28). One need only think of the initial German successes in World War II to see why the distribution of power should be able to rise and fall in a model. A second appealing property is that gains can accumulate: The more forts a state captures, the higher the probability that it will defeat the other state. The model may therefore shed light on the debate about the importance of accumulated and relative gains.

This formulation has many potential applications. Smith & Stam use it to study the likelihood of future conflict given a previous conflict. In their model, the longer any previous conflict lasted, the less likely future disputes are to end in war. As in the standard costly-lottery formulations, conflicts arise because of different beliefs about the expected payoffs to fighting. These beliefs converge over the course of the conflict, and the longer that conflict lasts, the closer together both states' beliefs will be. If, however, fighting is costly, a conflict may not last very long and beliefs may still be far apart when it ends. This disparity between the states' beliefs is the seed for future conflict.

Unfortunately, this analysis treats beliefs in a nonstandard game theoretic way, as the authors acknowledge (Smith & Stam 2001, p. 9, see footnote 26). To wit, each state knows that the other has different beliefs about p; indeed, it knows precisely what those beliefs are. Yet, each state disregards this knowledge when updating its own beliefs about p.[29] Filson & Werner (2001, see footnote 27) open up the costly-lottery assumption in a different way. For Smith & Stam,

---

[29]More formally, the states do not share a common prior over p. A discussion of the common-prior assumption in game theory is beyond the scope of this review. Suffice it to say that this assumption is extremely strong and, in my view, quite problematic. But disregarding it also raises serious consistency issues.

the distribution of power shifts as the distribution of forts changes, but fighting does not destroy the forts. For Filson & Werner, the states start out with limited military resources that are destroyed by fighting, and a state is eliminated when all of its military resources have been destroyed. S_1 begins by making an offer to S_2, which can either reject the offer or accept it and thereby end the game. If S_2 rejects, S_1 can end the game by quitting or continue by attacking. If the latter, then S_1 wins a battle with probability p and S_2 wins with probability $1 - p$. Winning and losing both destroy resources but differentially so. The bargaining and fighting continue in this way until the states reach agreement or one of them is eliminated. There is also one-sided asymmetric information about the distribution of power. S_1 does not know p.

Filson & Werner (2001, see footnote 27) analyze this model in two kinds of cases. In the first, S_1 cannot sustain any losses and is eliminated as soon as it loses a battle; S_2 is eliminated after losing two battles; and S_1 is uncertain of p (i.e., of S_2's type) but believes that it is either one of two values. These restrictions mean that the states can fight no more than two battles before the game ends. The second kind of case is a set of numerical examples. In particular, the authors posit the number of types, the specific values of p associated with each type, and S_1's distribution over these types.

Beliefs are treated in the standard way with S_1 using all of its information to update its beliefs. As the fighting progresses, victories make S_1 more confident that it is facing weaker (lower p) types, whereas defeats make it more confident that it is facing tougher types. Consequently, the distribution of power—that is, the probability that a state will be eliminated—can rise and fall, and gains can accumulate as in Smith & Stam (2001, see footnote 26). This tends to make S_1 more likely to propose an offer that is sure to be accepted by all types following a defeat.

Powell (2001, see footnote 28) opens up the costly-lottery assumption in yet a third way. He studies an alternating-offer, infinite-horizon model. At the start of each round, state S_1 makes a proposal to which S_2 can respond by accepting the offer, waiting, or fighting. Accepting the offer ends the game in the proposed division of benefits. If S_2 fights, S_1 and S_2 pay costs c_1 and c_2, respectively. Fighting also generates some possibly very small risks (k_1 and k_2) that S_1 and S_2, respectively, collapse militarily. If one state collapses and the other does not, the latter prevails and obtains all the benefits. If both collapse simultaneously, the status quo division of benefits remains unchanged. If neither state collapses, the round ends and the next begins with another offer from S_1. If S_2 waits in response to S_1's offer, S_1 can fight or wait. The consequences of fighting are as before: The states pay costs c_1 and c_2 and generate risks of collapse k_1 and k_2. If S_1 waits, the round ends and the next begins with S_1's making another offer.

Powell analyzes the cases in which S_1 is uncertain about S_2's cost of fighting (c_2) and in which S_1 is unsure about S_2's probability of collapse (k_2). If one defines the distribution of power as the probability that a state prevails in a fight to the finish, then the distribution of power is a function of the probabilities that the states collapse. Hence, S_1's uncertainty about k_2 is equivalent to being uncertain about the distribution of power.

The equilibrium dynamics in these cases turn out to be similar. If the distribution of benefits mirrors the distribution of power, neither state prefers fighting to accepting the status quo, and the status quo remains unchanged. If, however, S_2 is dissatisfied, then in equilibrium S_1 makes a series of strictly increasing concessions. These offers "screen" S_2 according to its type. Weaker types, i.e., those with higher costs or larger probabilities of collapse, accept earlier offers. Tougher types never pass and always fight until they eventually accept a more favorable offer, albeit at the price of having had to fight longer.

There is, however, an interesting difference between these mechanisms. Suppose, in keeping with the economics literature, we examine what happens as the time between offers becomes small. The substantive idea here is that states can make and respond to offers much more quickly than they can prepare for and fight battles. Formally, S_1 can make n offers between battles while the states prepare to fight. Preparation is costly, with S_1 and S_2 paying c_1' and c_2' during each round (where these costs are defined so that the total cost of preparing for and fighting one battle remains c_1 or c_2 regardless of the number of offers between battles). However, the states fight and therefore only generate a risk of collapse in rounds $n, 2n, \ldots$. Paralleling the results obtained in buyer-seller models (e.g., Fudenberg et al. 1985, Gul et al. 1986), as the time between offers becomes small, the states reach agreement almost immediately and without fighting if the states are uncertain about costs. By contrast, if the states are uncertain about the distribution of power and if there is any delay, then there will be some fighting.

In sum, relaxing or unpacking the costly-lottery assumption is a natural next step in the development of the literature on bargaining and war, and much work is under way. This work promises to deepen our understanding of intra-war bargaining, war termination, and, ideally, the dynamics of coercive bargaining more generally. It is too soon to tell, but it also appears that the costly-lottery assumption is generally neutral with respect to questions about the origins of war and serves as a useful analytic simplification in some settings.

WAR WITH COMPLETE INFORMATION

Most of the recent work on bargaining and war has focused on the role of asymmetric information. But some work in comparative as well as international politics has begun to focus on commitment problems (Fearon 1995), especially dynamic commitment problems. As long as fighting destroys valuable resources, there is more to be divided between the bargainers if they can avoid fighting. Because there is more to go around if the states avoid fighting, there are divisions of this larger "pie" that are Pareto-superior to the expected outcome of fighting. Indeed, even in the presence of asymmetric information, there are generally divisions that are known to be Pareto-superior to fighting. Suppose, for example, S_2 makes all the offers to S_1 and is uncertain of S_1's cost of fighting but believes it is at least $\underline{c}_1$. Then S_2 can buy zero risk of war by appeasing the toughest possible type by offering $x = p - \underline{c}_1$. However, this offer is more than would be needed to appease higher-cost types, and asymmetric-information models explain war as the result of a risk-return trade-off in which the bargainers make smaller concessions at the cost of accepting some risk of breakdown.

This simple formulation provides a dubious reading of some important historical cases. If there were no uncertainty, then there would never be any war. Put another way, no matter how expansive an adversary's demands, a state would always prefer satisfying those demands to fighting as long as that state were sure of what the demands were and of precisely what it would take to appease its adversary. In symbols, S_2's payoff to appeasing an adversary with known cost c_1 by offering $x = p - c_1$ is $1 - x = 1 - p + c_1$, which is greater than its cost to fighting $1 - p - c_2$ as long as fighting is costly ($c_1 + c_2 > 0$). Uncertainty is surely an important cause of many wars, but a much more plausible reading of, say, the 1930s in Europe is that over time Britain and France became more confident of Germany's or Hitler's "type" and that this was a type they preferred to fight rather than appease. Many of the existing bargaining models miss this dynamic, because they assume that a state, if sure of its adversary's type, always prefers to appease it.

Dynamic commitment problems do not appeal to asymmetric information in order to explain bargaining breakdowns. Rather, they explain inefficiency and breakdown by the inability of the bargainers to abide by the Pareto-superior divisions because at least one of them will have an incentive to renege on or "renegotiate" any agreement. Shifts in the distribution of power or, more generally, in the cost of fighting are often at the heart of this dynamic-commitment approach or mechanism. When the distribution of power or the costs of fighting shift very quickly, then the larger pie is still not big enough to satisfy their minimal demands.

More formally, suppose that S_1 and S_2 are bargaining about a flow of benefits or series of pies. That is, a new pie has to be divided in each period. The value of this series (to risk-neutral bargainers) is $1 + \delta + \delta^2 + \cdots = 1/(1 - \delta)$, where δ is the states' common discount factor. Suppose further that if the states fight, S_1 wins the entire series with probability p and pays total cost $c_1/(1 - \delta)$, and S_2 wins everything with probability $1 - p$ at cost $c_2/(1 - \delta)$. In effect, S_1 can "lock in" the payoff or share $(p - c_1)/(1 - \delta)$ by attacking. That is, S_1 is indifferent between fighting and having the share $(p - c_1)/(1 - \delta)$ of the series. Hence, S_1 would never agree to a division that gave it a smaller payoff. Similarly, S_2 can "lock in" $(1 - p - c_2)/(1 - \delta)$ by fighting. The difference between these lock-ins, $(c_1 + c_2)/(1 - \delta)$, is what the states save by not fighting and is what they are bargaining about.

If S_2 makes all the offers and the distribution of power is expected to remain constant at p, then S_2 concedes just enough to make S_1 indifferent between fighting and accepting the offer. In symbols, S_2 proposes a division $x = p - c_1$ of each period's pie. But now suppose that the distribution of power will shift in the next period in S_1's favor so that the probability that S_1 would prevail will be $p + \Delta p$. If S_2 fights before this shift, it can still lock in $(1 - p - c_2)/(1 - \delta)$. Similarly, if S_1

waits one period until it is stronger and then attacks, it can lock in $(p - c_1) + \delta (p + \Delta p - c_1)/(1 - \delta)$, where the first term assumes S_2 offers $x = p - c_1$ to S_1 in the first period in order to prevent it from attacking then.

The sum of these lock-ins, $\delta(\Delta p - c_1 - c_2)/(1 - \delta)$, exceeds the total value there is to be divided, $1/(1 - \delta)$, if the distribution of power shifts more than the sum of the per-period costs of fighting, i.e., if $\delta \Delta p > c_1 + c_2$ or, more simply, $\Delta p > c_1 + c_2$. In these circumstances, bargaining breaks down in fighting even though there is complete information, i.e., each state knows the other's cost of fighting, because the larger pie created by not fighting is not large enough to be divided in a way that always gives each state at least as much *from that time forward* as the payoff it can lock in by fighting at that time. Because fighting destroys resources and there is less to be divided if the states fight, there are divisions that both sides would prefer to fighting if the states were sure to abide by those divisions in each and every period. But those divisions would at some point in the series specify an allocation that would give one state less than it could secure by fighting. Since the states cannot credibly commit themselves to not exploiting these situations, the bargainer that loses by waiting fights immediately.

Fearon (1998a) looks at ethnic conflict from the perspective of this mechanism. Imagine that a majority group M and a minority group m are bargaining about the extent of minority rights. Agreements are thought of as points on the interval $[0, 1]$; m prefers agreements closer to one and M prefers agreements closer to zero. If the groups fight, m prevails with probability p at cost c_m and M prevails with probability $1 - p$ at cost c_M. To keep the bargaining simple, assume that M can make a take-it-or-leave-it offer to m. If so, then M offers just enough to keep m indifferent between fighting and accepting, $x = p - c_m$.

Suppose, however, that after any agreement, majority groups generally consolidate their positions in a state. This effectively increases M's power and reduces m's to, say, $p - \Delta p$. This in turn reduces m's payoff to fighting, and this reduction gives M an incentive to renege on or renegotiate the agreement by offering $x' = p - \Delta p - c_m$. If we assume that M has been unable to commit itself to abiding by the original agreement, the choice facing m is a payoff of $p - c_m$, which it secures by fighting at the outset, or the lower payoff of $p - \Delta p - c_m$, which is what it ultimately would obtain through a peaceful and subsequently renegotiated settlement. Fighting is clearly better, so war results despite complete information. More substantively, this analysis very clearly highlights the importance of the majority group's ability to commit itself either through domestic or international institutions or guarantors. It also suggests a trade-off. The more the distribution of power is expected to change, the more credible these guarantees have to be (see Walter 1997 for an empirical assessment of this analysis).

At least since Thucydides, shifts in the distribution of power have been considered a significant source of international stress and potential conflict. Powell (1999) uses this basic dynamic-commitment approach to study this problem. As before, states are bargaining about revising the territorial status quo, but now the distribution of power is shifting in one state's favor throughout the bargaining. If, as in the example above, the distribution of power shifts quickly ($\Delta p > c_1 + c_2$), then the sum of the shares the states can lock in by fighting exceeds the amount there is to be divided. Bargaining breaks down in war in these circumstances despite complete information. If, by contrast, the distribution of power shifts more slowly, then the declining state makes a series of concessions to the rising state, and the bargaining does not break down unless there is also asymmetric information.

The same mechanism is at the heart of Acemoglu & Robinson's (2001) arguments about extending the franchise and about democratic transitions. Why, they ask, would an elite ever transfer political power to the masses in order to "buy off" social unrest? Why not buy them off through direct transfers financed by higher taxes on the elite—a more economically efficient policy that would not reduce the elite's political power? (As before, fighting, whether instigated by the elite or the masses, destroys resources, so there are agreements that all parties prefer to fighting.)

Acemoglu & Robinson (2001) argue that the transfer of political power serves as a means for the elite to commit itself to following through on its promise. That is, economic and social circumstances that create "revolutionary moments," which are formalized as times when the relative cost of challenging the elite is low, come and go. When a revolutionary moment passes and the cost of challenging the elite rises, there is nothing to keep the elite from reneging on its promises by ending the transfers. The promise of greater transfers is therefore incredible and cannot "buy off" pending social unrest and the threat of revolution. One way to make it credible is for the elite to give the beneficiaries of the promise the power to enforce it, which is what extending the franchise does. Of course, the leaders in a democracy may face the same kind of credibility problem in buying off potential coups, and Acemoglu & Robinson (2001) put this problem at the center of their analysis of democratic transitions. When breakdown does occur in these analyses, either through civil unrest or a coup, it is not the result of asymmetric information but of rapidly shifting lock-ins.

Finally, Fearon[30] looks at a different aspect of the way that shifting power distributions affect bargaining. In all the examples above, the reasons for the shift are unrelated to the bargaining settlement. Fearon examines the case in which shifts in the distribution of power arise endogenously because a gain in one period makes a bargainer stronger in the next. This prospect seems likely to create the kind of commitment problem illustrated above. A bargainer would fight today rather than make a concession because the concession makes it weaker tomorrow and more will be demanded of it. Surprisingly, this is not the case. Bargaining does not break down. Fighting today imposes immediate costs, whereas having to make concessions in the distant future is not very costly because of discounting. Thus, a state is willing to make concessions very slowly even if it ultimately

---

[30]Fearon JD. 1996. Bargaining over objects that influence future bargaining power. Unpublished manuscript, Department of Political Science, Stanford University.

has to concede a great deal (over the very long run), and it turns out that the other state also prefers this stream of concessions to bearing the immediate cost of fighting.

CONCLUSION

An apparently remarkable thing has happened in the past decade and a half. Twenty years ago Waltz lamented, "nothing in international politics seems to cumulate, not even criticism" (1979, p. 18). The work on bargaining and war is now a coherent, cumulating literature. Key puzzles have been framed as specific, well-defined problems. Generally, these problems have been studied first in the context of simpler models, which are subsequently refined and generalized and which raise previously unappreciated issues. These new issues are the springboard for new analyses. The literature on war and bargaining has taken on a self-sustaining quality that deals with issues spanning both international and comparative politics. So far, this work has been largely theoretical, as one would expect when new tools are first brought to bear. This theoretical work will continue and, ideally, be more fully complemented by serious empirical testing in an evolving modeling dialogue (Myerson 1992).

ACKNOWLEDGMENTS

Robert Jervis provided many helpful comments and criticisms, and I gratefully acknowledge the financial support of the NSF (SES-9911075).

The *Annual Review of Political Science* is online at http://polisci.annualreviews.org

LITERATURE CITED

Acemoglu D, Robinson JA. 2000. Why did the West extend the franchise? *Q. J. Econ.* 115:1167–99

Acemoglu D, Robinson J. 2001. A theory of political transitions. *Am. Econ. Rev.* 91:938–63

Altfeld MF, Bueno de Mesquita B. 1979. Choosing sides in war. *Int. Stud. Q.* 23:87–112

Baron DP, Ferejohn JA. 1989. Bargaining in legislatures. *Am. Polit. Sci. Rev.* 83(4):1181–1206

Bercovitch J. 1996. *Resolving International Conflicts*. Boulder, CO: Lynne Reinner

Binmore K. 1987. Nash bargaining theory. In *The Economics of Bargaining*, ed. K Binmore, P Dasgupta, pp. 27–46. New York: Blackwell

Blainey G. 1973. *The Causes of War*. New York: Free

Bueno de Mesquita B. 1981. *The War Trap*. New Haven, CT: Yale Univ. Press

Bueno de Mesquita B, Lalman D. 1988. Systemic and dyadic explanations of war. *World Polit.* 41:1–20

Bueno de Mesquita B, Morrow JD, Siverson RM, Smith A. 1999a. An institutional explanation of the democratic peace. *Am. Polit. Sci. Rev.* 93:791–807

Bueno de Mesquita B, Morrow JD, Siverson

RM, Smith A. 1999b. Political competition and economic growth. *J. Confl. Resolut.* 43:147–61

Butterfield H. 1950. The tragic element in modern international conflict. *Rev. Polit.* 12:147–64

Butterfield H. 1966. The balance of power. In *Diplomatic Investigations*, ed. H Butterfield, M Wright. London: Allen & Unwin

Claude I. 1962. *Power and International Relations.* New York: Random House

Crescenzi M, Diehl P. 1998. Reconfiguring the arms-race debate. *J. Peace Res.* 35:111–18

Dixon WJ. 1996. Third-party techniques for preventing conflict escalation and promoting peaceful settlements. *Int. Organ.* 50:653–81

Downs G, Rocke D. 1994. Conflict, agency, and gambling for resurrection. *Am. J. Polit. Sci.* 38:362–80

Fearon JD. 1994. Signaling versus the balance of power and interests. *J. Confl. Resolut.* 38:236–69

Fearon JD. 1995. Rationalist explanations for war. *Int. Organ.* 49:379–415

Fearon JD. 1998a. Commitment problems and the spread of ethnic conflict. In *The International Spread of Ethnic Conflict*, ed. DA Lake, D Rothchild, pp. 107–26. Princeton, NJ: Princeton Univ. Press

Fearon JD. 1998b. Domestic politics, foreign policy, and theories of international relations. *Annu. Rev. Polit. Sci.* 1:289–313

Ferris W. 1973. *The Power Capabilities of Nations.* Lexington, MA: Lexington Books

Fudenberg D, Levine D, Tirole J. 1985. Infinite-horizon models of bargaining with one-sided incomplete information. In *Game Theoretic Models of Bargaining*, ed. A Roth, pp. 73–98. New York: Cambridge Univ. Press

Fudenberg D, Levine D, Tirole J. 1987. Incomplete information bargaining with outside opportunities. *Q. J. Econ.* 102:37–50

Fudenberg D, Tirole J. 1991. *Game Theory.* Cambridge, MA: MIT Press

Glaser CL. 1997. The security dilemma revisited. *World Polit.* 50:171–210

Gowa J. 1999. *Ballots and Bullets.* Princeton, NJ: Princeton Univ. Press

Grieco J. 1988. Anarchy and the limits of cooperation. *Int. Organ.* 42:485–507

Gul F, Sonnenschein H. 1988. On delay in bargaining with one-sided uncertainty. *Econometrica* 56:601–11

Gul F, Sonnenschein H, Wilson R. 1986. The foundations of dynamic monopoly and the Coase conjecture. *J. Econ. Theory* 39:155–90

Haas E. 1953. The balance of power. *World Polit.* 5:442–77

Harsanyi J. 1967–1968. Games with incomplete information played by Bayesian players, parts 1–3. *Manage. Sci.* 14:159–82, 320–34, 486–502

Hicks J. 1932. *The Theory of Wages.* New York: Macmillan. 2nd ed.

Hinsley FH. 1963. *Power and the Pursuit of Peace.* New York: Cambridge Univ. Press

Hume D. 1898 (1752). *Essays: Moral, Political, and Literary.* New York: Longmans, Green

Huth P, Russett B. 1984. What makes deterrence work? *World Polit.* 36:496–526

Jervis R. 1976. *Perception and Misperception in International Politics.* Princeton, NJ: Princeton Univ. Press

Jervis R. 1979. Cooperation under the security dilemma. *World Polit.* 30:167–214

Kaplan M, Burns AL, Quandt R. 1960. Theoretical analysis of the balance of power. *Behav. Sci.* 5:240–52

Kennan J, Wilson R. 1993. Bargaining with private information. *J. Econ. Lit.* 31:45–104

Kim W. 1991. Alliance transitions and great power war. *Am. J. Polit. Sci.* 35:833–50

Kim W. 1992. Power transitions and great power war from Westphalia to Waterloo. *World Polit.* 45:153–72

Kleibor M. 1996. Understanding success and failure of international mediation. *J. Confl. Resolut.* 40:360–89

Knutsen T. 1997. *A History of International Relations Theory.* New York: Manchester Univ. Press. 2nd ed.

Kreps D. 1990. *Game Theory and Economic Modeling.* New York: Oxford Univ. Press

Kydd A. 1997. Game theory and the spiral model. *World Polit.* 49:371–400

Kydd A. 2000. Arms races and arms control. *Am. J. Polit. Sci.* 44:228–44

Labs EJ. 1992. Do weak states balance? *Sec. Stud.* 1:383–416

Lake DA, Powell R. 1999. International relations: a strategic-choice approach. In *Strategic Choice and International Relations*, ed. DA Lake, R Powell, pp. 3–38. Princeton, NJ: Princeton Univ. Press

Levy J. 1987. Declining power and the preventive motivation for war. *World Polit.* 40:87–107

Levy J. 1989. The causes of war. In *Behavior, Society, and Nuclear War*, ed. P Tetlock, J Husbands, R Jervis, P Stern, C Tilly, 1:209–333. New York: Oxford Univ. Press

Lynn-Jones S. 1995. Offense-defense theory and its critics. *Sec. Stud.* 4:660–94

Mansfield E. 1992. The concentration of capabilities and the onset of war. *J. Confl. Resolut.* 36:3–24

Mansfield E. 1994. *Power, Trade, and War.* Princeton, NJ: Princeton Univ. Press

Maoz Z. 1983. Resolve, capabilities, and the outcomes of interstate disputes, 1815–1976. *J. Confl. Resolut.* 27:195–229

Mattingly G. 1955. *Renaissance Diplomacy.* Boston: Houghton Mifflin

Mearsheimer J. 1990. Back to the future. *Int. Sec.* 15:5–56

Morgenthau H. 1967. *Politics Among Nations.* New York: Knopf. 4th ed.

Moul W. 1988. Balances of power and the escalation to war of serious international disputes among the European great powers, 1815–1939. *Am. J. Polit. Sci.* 35:241–75

Muthoo A. 1999. *Bargaining Theory with Applications.* New York: Cambridge Univ. Press

Myerson R. 1992. On the value of game theory in social science. *Ration. Soc.* 4:62–73

Niou E, Ordeshook PC. 1990. Stability in anarchic international systems. *Am. Polit. Sci. Rev.* 84:1207–34

Organski AFK. 1968. *World Politics.* New York: Knopf

Organski AFK, Kugler J. 1980. *The War Ledger.* Chicago: Univ. Chicago Press

Osborne MJ, Rubinstein A. 1990. *Bargaining and Markets.* San Diego: Academic

Powell R. 1994. The neorealist-neoliberal debate. *Int. Organ.* 48:313–44

Powell R. 1996a. Bargaining in the shadow of power. *Games Econ. Behav.* 15:255–89

Powell R. 1996b. Stability and the distribution of power. *World Polit.* 48:239–67

Powell R. 1999. *In the Shadow of Power.* Princeton, NJ: Princeton Univ. Press

Powell R. 2002. Game theory, international relations theory, and the Hobbesian stylization. In *The State of the Discipline*, ed. I Katznelson, H Milner. Washington, DC: APSA. In press

Roth A. 1979. *Axiomatic Models of Bargaining.* Berlin: Springer-Verlag

Rubinstein A. 1982. Perfect equilibrium in a bargaining model. *Econometrica* 50(1):97–110

Sample G. 1997. Arms races and dispute escalation. *J. Peace Res.* 34:7–22

Schelling TC. 1960. *The Strategy of Conflict.* Cambridge, MA: Harvard Univ. Press

Schelling TC. 1966. *Arms and Influence.* New Haven, CT: Yale Univ. Press

Schultz KA. 1998. Do democratic institutions constrain or inform? *Int. Organ.* 53:233–66

Schultz KA. 2001. *Democracy and Coercive Diplomacy.* New York: Cambridge Univ. Press

Singer JD, Bremer S, Stukey J. 1972. Capabilities distribution, uncertainty and major power wars 1820–1965. In *Peace, War, and Numbers*, ed. B Russett, pp. 19–48. Beverly Hills, CA: Sage

Siverson R, Tennefoss M. 1984. Power, alliance, and the escalation of international conflict, 1815–1965. *Am. Polit. Sci. Rev.* 78:1057–69

Smith A. 1998. Fighting battles, winning wars. *J. Confl. Resolut.* 42:310–20

Ståhl I. 1972. *Bargaining Theory.* Stockholm: Stockholm School Econ.

Van Evera S. 1998. Offense, defense, and the causes of war. *Int. Sec.* 22:5–43

Wagner RH. 1986. The theory of games and the balance of power. *World Polit.* 38:546–76

Wagner RH. 1994. Peace, war, and the balance of power. *Am. Polit. Sci. Rev.* 88:593–607

Wagner RH. 2000. Bargaining and war. *Am. Polit. Sci. Rev.* 44:469–85

Walt SM. 1988. Testing theories of alliance formation. *Int. Organ.* 42:275–316

Walt SM. 1992. Alliance, threats, and U.S. grand strategy. *Sec. Stud.* 1:448–82

Walter BF. 1997. The critical barrier to civil war settlement. *Int. Organ.* 51:335–64

Waltz KN. 1959. *Man, the State, and War.* New York: Columbia Univ. Press

Waltz KN. 1979. *Theory of International Politics.* Reading, MA: Addison-Wesley

Weede E. 1976. Overwhelming preponderance as a pacifying condition among contiguous Asian dyads, 1950–1969. *J. Confl. Resolut.* 20:395–411

Werner S. 2000. Deterring intervention. *Am. J. Polit. Sci.* 44:720–32

Wittman D. 1979. How a war ends: a rational model approach. *J. Confl. Resolut.* 23:743–63

Wolfers A. 1962. *Discord and Collaboration.* Baltimore, MD: Johns Hopkins Univ. Press

Wright Q. 1965. *A Study of War.* Chicago: Univ. Chicago Press

Annu. Rev. Polit. Sci. 2002. 5:31–61
DOI: 10.1146/annurev.polisci.5.091001.170657
Copyright © 2002 by Annual Reviews. All rights reserved

EXPERIMENTAL METHODS IN POLITICAL SCIENCE

Rose McDermott

*Department of Government, McGraw Hall, Cornell University, Ithaca, New York 14850;
e-mail: rmm21@cornell.edu*

Key Words   experiments, behavioral economics, political economy, game theory,
individual choice, methodology

■ **Abstract**   This article reviews the use of experiments in political science. The
beginning section offers an overview of experimental design and measures, as well as
threats to internal and external validity, and discusses advantages and disadvantages
to the use of experimentation. The number and placements of experiments in political
science are reviewed. The bulk of the essay is devoted to an examination of what we
have learned from experiments in the behavioral economics, political economy, and
individual choice literatures.

INTRODUCTION

Anyone who takes an antibiotic, confident that illness will remit, is implicitly
trusting in the power and validity of experiments as applied to real-world contexts.
Indeed, the hard sciences, including biology, chemistry, physics, and medicine,
all rely primarily on experimentation to examine and illuminate basic processes.
Psychology embodies a long and distinguished history of experimentation, and
behavioral economics, which involves a great deal of experimentation, has recently gained increasing prominence within the larger field of economics. But
the methodology of experimentation has been slow to garner a following in political science. Experimentation might easily dovetail with methods more established in political science, such as formal modeling, to produce and cumulate
useful knowledge; however, political scientists typically prefer archival work,
case studies, field work, surveys, quantitative analysis, and formal modeling instead. Yet these other methods need not compete with experimentation. Indeed,
the most exciting opportunity for methodological advancement using experimentation lies at the intersection of formal modeling and experimental testing: Formal models present hypotheses that are tested, refined, and explored through
experimentation in a reciprocal manner. This process is widely and successfully employed within behavioral economics. As yet, however, political science
remains slow to embrace the added value offered by the methodology of
experimentation.

1094-2939/02/0615-0031$14.00   **31**

This essay addresses the use of experiments and the experimental method in political science. Following a brief background discussion of the experimental method, including threats to internal and external validity, relative advantages and disadvantages, and ethics, the essay concentrates on what we have learned of substance from experiments in behavioral economics and political science that should be of interest to mainstream political scientists.

My overall goal is to advocate for the utility of experiments for political science. I do not argue that experiments are the only, nor the best, form of methodological inquiry. Rather, I argue that experimentation can be particularly useful under certain circumstances: when existing methods of inquiry have produced inconsistent or contradictory results; when empirical validation of formal models is required; when investigators want to triangulate in on specific processes that have already been examined in a more general way using other methodologies; and when evidence is needed to support strong causal claims. Experiments can combine with other methods to provide what Campbell described as a "fish scale model of omniscience," whereby each methodological layer serves to illuminate and support other component parts.

EXPERIMENTAL METHODS

What do we mean by experiments? I take the term to refer primarily to laboratory studies in which investigators retain control over the recruitment, assignment to random conditions, treatment, and measurement of subjects. This definition assumes that experimenters take pains to assure that the experimental situation does not vary in any way other than the intended independent variables in order to assure the internal validity that allows causal claims.

To be sure, other forms of experimentation exist, including field studies, field experiments, and even simulation studies. Field studies typically look retrospectively at the effect of naturally occurring events. Although such studies seek to achieve maximum realism and representative subject samples, the experimenter has no control whatsoever over the variables of interest. The ideal subject of a field study is a naturally occurring situation with both "before" and "after" data, such as students' test results before and after implementation of an educational reform program (Walker 1976).

Field experiments take place outside the laboratory but allow the experimenter to retain some limited control over the central variables. At their best, field experiments can offer a reasonable trade-off between internal and external validity through increased realism without too much loss of control. Simulations offer a similar compromise between the concerns of internal and external validity. Some experiments use people as subjects; other rely solely on computerized models. But for purposes of the discussion below, laboratory experiments are the gold standard.

Experimental Design

Why do we need experiments? We need experiments because they help to reduce the bias that can exist in less rigorous forms of observation. Experiments reduce the impact of bias by introducing standardized procedures, measures, and analyses.

Important aspects of experimental design include standardization, randomization, between-subjects versus within-subject design, and experimental bias.

1. *Standardization* remains crucial in experimentation because it ensures that the same stimuli, procedures, responses, and variables are coded and analyzed. This reduces the likelihood that extraneous factors, of which the experimenter might not even be aware, could influence the results in decisive ways. Standardization requires that the same set of experimental procedures, or experimental protocol, is administered in the same way to subjects across conditions; only the independent variable (or variables) of interest is manipulated. This process ensures that the data elicited from subjects are comparable and are not the result of some extraneous feature in the environment.

2. *Randomization* refers to the assignment of subjects to experimental conditions. Experimenters assign subjects randomly to ensure that no unrelated or spurious factors vary consistently within a given population and therefore bias the results. The idea is that background differences cancel each other out in the course of random assignment, since each individual is as likely to be placed in one condition as in another. Thus, no systematic differences in subjects can bias the results of the study. Many people unfamiliar with probability might think that random assignment is little more than alternately assigning Condition A or B as subjects walk in the door. However, the most elegant and pure way to ensure random assignment of subjects to conditions is to use a random number table to assign manipulations.

   Experimental design can be between-subjects or within-subject. Typically, one experimental condition is compared to another experimental condition and then to a control condition. The control condition creates a baseline against which investigators compare the results of their manipulations. In between-subjects designs, different groups of subjects are randomly assigned to various experimental or control conditions. In within-subject designs, otherwise known as the A-B-A experimental design strategy, each person serves as his or her own control by participating across time in both control and treatment conditions. Subjects begin with a baseline (A), are then administered a treatment or manipulation condition (B), and are measured again at baseline (A) once the treatment ends (Zimbardo & Gerrig 1996). The comparison of before and after measures on the variable of concern inform the investigator as to the impact, if any, of the treatment on the subject.

3. *Placebo effects*, in medicine, account for patients whose condition improves as a result of a fake treatment, such as a sugar pill. These effects can cause quite powerful changes in outcome based on an individual's belief that the

treatment will work. Control conditions are important in experimental verification precisely because they help determine the extent of placebo effects in an experimental manipulation.

4. *Experimental bias.* Although experiments seek to maximize experimenter control over the independent variables in a study, the experimental process itself can introduce potential sources of bias. Three important forms of experimental bias are expectancy effects, experimenter bias, and demand characteristics.

EXPECTANCY EFFECTS   Expectancy effects occur when an experimenter communicates, usually in a subtle, unconscious way, how he or she wants the subject to behave or respond (Rosenthal 1966). Results then take the form of a self-fulfilling prophecy as experimenters create the reactions they hope to elicit with their subtle signals and not with their controlled manipulation. Ways to overcome this bias include having various experimenters run some subjects in all conditions, making the experimenter blind to the subjects' conditions, designing the experiment to avoid experimenter involvement (as can be done with computer-generated experiments), or treating the experimenter as a factor or variable in the statistical analysis at the end of the experiment to determine if any particular experimenter elicited distinctive responses from the subjects.

EXPERIMENTER BIAS   Experimenter bias can overlap with expectancy effects but is in fact distinct from them theoretically. Many experimental choices originate from the experimenter's beliefs and attitudes, and these choices can influence the design of an experiment in a nonrandom way. Sometimes this may be acceptable, but concerns arise especially when an investigator remains unaware that his beliefs have unduly affected the design of the study (Roth 1988).

DEMAND CHARACTERISTICS   Demand characteristics are similar to expectancy biases as well, although the cues emerge from the subject's interpretation of the experiment rather than from anything the experimenter says or does directly (McConahay 1973). A systematic bias can be introduced if the purpose of the experiment is too obvious. This bias can be exacerbated if subjects, experiencing evaluation apprehension (Rosenberg 1965), try to make the experimenter like them by doing what they believe the experimenter wants. Ways to reduce the impact of this problem on experimental outcomes include using deception to ensure that subjects cannot determine the relevant hypotheses or tests, evaluating the demand characteristics of the experiment in the analysis at the end of the study, and using computer technology to complicate and/or depersonalize the experiment to reduce the likelihood that subjects can discern its true purpose.

Experimental Measures

Experimental measures strive for reliability as well as internal and external validity. Reliability and validity are central concepts in all experimental measurement.

Reliability refers to the extent to which an experimenter tests the same thing time and time again. A reliable result is one that is easily replicable. Reliability improves when measures are standardized, when a larger number of measures have been taken, and when factors that might bias the data are controlled in advance (Zimbardo & Gerrig 1996).

Experimental measures can take several forms: self-reports, behavioral measures, physiological measures, and incentives.

SELF-REPORTS, BEHAVIORAL MEASURES, AND PHYSIOLOGICAL MEASURES   Self-reports are usually verbal or written reports of a subject's responses to a particular set of stimuli. They can take the form of paper-and-pencil questionnaires, surveys, or interviews. Some of these data, which might be originally obtained in qualitative form, can be coded into quantitative categories for later analysis. Behavioral measures require experimenters to observe the behavior of subjects by, for example, videotaping them and later examining the tapes for characteristics such as facial expressions or tendency to dominate in a group. Physiological measures include such data as heart rate, galvanic skin response, blood pressure, or more extensive tests such as magnetic resonance imaging (MRI) or positron-emission tomography (PET) tests. More intrusive tests, such as those that analyze saliva, urine, or blood, might also be conducted to determine hormone levels or other variables of interest.

INCENTIVES   Most experiments in psychology do not offer incentives other than extra credit in a course for participants. Indeed, many introductory psychology classes require students to participate in experiments. However, many behavioral economics experiments do offer material incentives, typically money or a lottery that offers the chance of a cash reward to subjects. There are two kinds of incentives: those offered to subjects merely for showing up to participate in a study, and those intrinsic to the experiment itself.

Threats to Internal and External Validity

Campbell & Stanley (1963) describe the classic distinction between internal and external validity as follows: Internal validity asks, "Did in fact the experimental treatments make a difference in this specific experimental instance?" External validity investigates the generalizability of the results by inquiring, "To what populations, settings, treatment variables, and measurement variables can this effect be generalized?" As McConahay (1973) noted, "Generally, with a large number of specific exceptions, psychologists are more concerned about the internal validity of a research design while political scientists are more concerned with external validity." Walker (1976), bemoaning the fact, went so far as to argue that herein lay one of the main reasons for the lack of productive communication between the two disciplines: "The social psychologist, with his reliance on controlled laboratory experiments, has different interests and concerns than the political scientist, who is more at home in the field."

Once an investigator has determined what to investigate and how to assess and measure the relevant variables, he or she must ensure that the design of the experimental protocol does not fall prey to one of the flaws that can confound the results (see Campbell & Stanley 1963 and Campbell & Ross 1968 for the classic discussion of these confounds).

THREATS TO INTERNAL VALIDITY   There are nine potential threats to internal validity in experimentation:

1. *History* refers to any event that occurs outside the experimenter's control in the time between the measures on the dependent variable. This phenomenon becomes a concern when there is a lot of time between the measurements on the dependent variable.

2. *Intersession history* refers to events that occur inside the study itself, which are beyond the control of the investigator and may affect the outcome of the study. Extreme temperature fluctuation, unexpected fire drills, or unknown preexisting relationships between some subjects might affect one session of an experiment but not another. These confounds all threaten the internal validity of the experiment.

3. *Maturation* refers to the natural needs, growth, and development of individuals over time. For example, an experiment that relies on deprivation for motivation depends on maturation effects for thirst to occur. Maturation processes that work independently of the investigator over the course of an experiment can bias results as well.

4. *Performance effects*. Performance can change as a result of experience. Test performance can be affected by the very act of having taken the test before. Therefore, pre- and post-tests with exactly the same questions do not constitute identical assessments because, independent of the intervening manipulation, taking the first test may influence the answers to the second test through the natural process of learning and experience.

5. *Regression toward the mean*. Since all scores represent some combination of the real score and some random error, subjects who manifest an extreme score are likely to move closer to the mean on the next measurement, as the random error fluctuates. Experimenters who specifically pick subjects because they manifest an extreme score on some dimension, like authoritarianism, are likely to confound their results through their failure to incorporate regression effects into their subject selection procedures.

6. *Subject self-selection*. Subjects who self-select into particular experiments or conditions are likely to differ in some systematic way from those who are randomly assigned to a condition.

7. *Mortality* occurs not only when subjects die but also when they are lost to follow-up by the investigator. In political science, mortality occurs most often in experiments that require the same subject to show up more than once, and

the subject fails to show up for the second part of the experiment. This can also happen in longitudinal and field studies that examine dynamics over time; as people move and change their living situations, they can become hard to trace. Sometimes financial and other incentives can alleviate this problem. From an ethical perspective, the most important cases of experimental mortality occur when subjects leave in the middle of an experiment because some aspect of the experiment has made them uncomfortable. If a study has a high degree of interexperimental drop-out, the investigator should take pains to ascertain that the experiment is being conducted in an appropriate and ethical manner.

8. *Selection-maturation interaction* occurs when subjects are placed into an experimental condition in a nonrandom manner and some aspect of the group differs in maturation from the other groups in an important or systematic way.

9. *Unreliable measures.* If measures are unreliable, if the subject population shifts, or if some other aspect of the experimental condition is affected in a nonrandom manner, results can become biased.

THREATS TO EXTERNAL VALIDITY   Campbell (1968) outlines the six major threats to external validity in experimentation:

1. *Testing interaction effects.* Testing can increase subjects' sensitivity to the variables under investigation, which makes it difficult to generalize the results to a population that has not been pretested.

2. *Unrepresentative subject population.* What can college sophomores tell us about real-world decision makers? Sears (1986) argues that college sophomores differ in systematic and marked ways from other people: They are more self-absorbed; they have less crystallized attitudes, a less clear sense of self, higher rates of compliance, less stable peer relationships, and stronger cognitive skills. Remarkably, many experimental findings using college sophomores have proved remarkably robust (Roth 1988). However, many people remain concerned about subject pools. Obviously, the best way to deal with this problem of external validity would be to sample directly from the populations of interest. Etheredge (1978) did this in his extensive study of 126 career foreign service officers at the State Department to examine "how emotional predispositions might shape elite foreign policy thinking." But often this is not possible because such people are either too busy or not interested in participating in experiments. Another strategy against this limitation involves simulations with real or former decision makers using a hypothetical or past crisis as a stimulus. Such simulations have produced very accurate results. In one of the most powerful examples of a simulation's prescient prediction of a real-world outcome, a Joint War Games Agency of the Joint Chiefs of Staff conducted a major war game simulation of the conflict in Vietnam. The goal was to start with current resources as of July of 1965 and simulate the likely outcome through September of 1966. The results indicated that the United States would not be able to win the conflict in the long

run and was unlikely to do better than stalemate in the short run (as reported in Burke & Greenstein 1989). Simulations that accurately mimic real-life problems and resources can engage the same psychological processes that operate in the real world.

3. *Hawthorne effect.* The third limitation on external validity involves the so-called Hawthorne effect (Roethlisberger & Dickson 1939), whereby people change their behavior merely because they are aware of being observed. People who know they are in an experiment may behave differently than they would if they were not in an experiment or were unaware of the experiment.

4. *Professional subjects.* On large and relatively anonymous college campuses, a student eager to earn money can participate in many experiments across departments without any one experimenter realizing how experienced this subject has become. Overly experienced or jaded subjects may be more likely to guess the underlying hypothesis or manipulation in an experiment if they have participated in similar ones in the past.

5. *Spurious measures.* Some unexpected aspect of the experiment may induce subjects to give systematically irrelevant responses to particular measures, which are then understood to be experimental effects.

6. *Irrelevant measures.* Irrelevant aspects of the experimental condition might produce results that appear to be experimental effects.

ADVANTAGES AND DISADVANTAGES OF EXPERIMENTS

Since most of the threats to internal and external validity can be anticipated, what are the benefits that a skilled experimenter might accrue from using experimentation as opposed to other research strategies, such as case study work or formal models? What problems would still plague the interpretation and utility of his or her results?

Advantages

The comparative advantages of experiments lie in their high degree of internal validity. No other methodology can offer the strong support for the causal inferences that experiments allow. Correlational studies, for example, do not show causation. Since a laboratory setting allows investigators to control all aspects of the environment so that only the independent variables differ, any differences on the dependent variable can be attributed to the manipulation, and thus offer support for causal inferences. Experiments offer at least five such advantages:

1. *Ability to derive causal inferences.* "The major advantage of laboratory experiments is in its [sic] ability to provide us with unambiguous evidence about causation" (Aronson & Carlsmith 1968). Because of the randomization of subjects and the control of the environment, experiments allow

confidence regarding causal inferences about relationships among the variables of interest.

2. *Experimental control.* The experimenter has control over the recruitment, treatment, and measurement of subjects and variables.

3. *Precise measurement.* Experimenters design and implement the desired measures and ensure that they are administered consistently.

4. *Ability to explore the details of process.* Experiments offer the opportunity to explore phenomena of interest in great detail. Complex relationships can be broken down and investigated in smaller units in order to see which part of the process results in the differences of interest. In addition, experiments allow particular relationships to be explored in the presence or absence of other variables, so that the conditions under which certain relationships hold can be examined as well.

5. *Relative economy.* Although experiments may be more costly and time-consuming than some research methodologies, such as formal modeling, they are certainly more economical than conducting large surveys or field experiments. Students are a relatively inexpensive and reliable subject pool, and a large number of them can be run in a semester. Experiments embedded in larger surveys (Sniderman et al. 1991, Kuklinski et al. 1997) may provide a more representative sample but would also require a great deal more time and money to administer.

Disadvantages

Experiments are not always the ideal methodology. Most concerns about their disadvantages within political science revolve around questions of external validity and how widely the findings of the laboratory apply to real-world actors and phenomena. There are four main disadvantages to the use of experiments:

1. *Artificial environment.* Many experimental settings are artificially sterile and unrepresentative of the environments in which subjects might normally perform the behavior under study. There are at least two important aspects of this limitation. First, it might be impossible or unethical to create the desired situation within a laboratory. An experimenter could not study the effects of a life-threatening illness by causing such disease in a subject. Second, it may be very hard to simulate many phenomena of interest—an election, a war, an economic recession, and so on.

2. *Unrepresentative subject pools.* As noted above, subject pools may be unrepresentative of the populations of interest.

3. *External validity.* For political scientists, questions surrounding external validity pose the greatest concern with experimentation. What can experiments tell us about real-world political phenomena? Beyond the nature of the subject pool, this concern is at least twofold. First, in the laboratory it is difficult to replicate key conditions that operate on political actors in the real world.

Subjects typically meet only for a short period and focus on a limited task. Even when money serves as a material incentive, subject engagement may be low. In the real world, actors have histories and shadows of the future with each other, they interact around many complex issues over long periods, and they have genuine strategic and material interests, goals, and incentives at stake. Can the results of a single-session experiment tell us anything about such a complicated world?

Second, and related, many aspects of real-world complexity are difficult to simulate in the laboratory. Cultural norms, relationships of authority, and the multitask nature of the work itself might invalidate any results that emerge from an experiment that does not, or cannot, fully incorporate these features into the environment or manipulation (Walker 1976). In particular, subjects may behave one way in the relative freedom of an experiment, where there are no countervailing pressures acting on them, but quite another when acting within the constrained organizational or bureaucratic environments in which they work at their political jobs. Material and professional incentives can easily override more natural psychological or ethical concerns that might manifest themselves more readily in the unconstrained environment of the laboratory. Failure to mimic or incorporate these constraints into experiments, and difficulty in making these constraints realistic, might restrict the applicability of experimental results to the real political world.

There are two important things to understand about external validity. First, external validity is only fully established through replication. Experiments testing the same model should be conducted on multiple populations using multiple methods in order to determine the external validity of any given experimental paradigm. Second, external validity is more closely related to the realism created within the experiment than to the external trappings of similarity to real-world settings, which is referred to as mundane realism. As long at the experimental situation engages the subject in an authentic way, experimental realism has been constructed; under these circumstances, mundane realism may be nice but is hardly required to establish causality. Moreover, even if the experiment closely approximates real-world conditions, if its subjects fail to engage in an experimentally realistic way, subsequent findings are useless.

4. *Experimenter bias*. Experimenter bias, including expectancy effects and demand characteristics, can limit the relevance, generalizability, or accuracy of certain experimental results.

EXPERIMENTAL ETHICS

As a result of concerns about the ethical treatment of human subjects, the U.S. Department of Health and Human Services imposes strict guidelines on all research involving human subjects. Institutional review boards at major research institutions oversee the administration of these guidelines and require advance approval on all experiments with human subjects to ensure their ethical treatment. These boards have the power to reject proposals that they deem to inadequately protect human subjects from unnecessary pain and suffering. The job of these boards involves weighing the risks and benefits of each study for the appropriate balance between risk to the subject and benefit for science or society. The guidelines include four important components:

1. *Informed consent*. Informed consent requires that the experimenter provide every subject with a disclosure statement prior to the experiment, describing the experimental procedures, along with expected gains and risks for the subject. Subjects are told they can leave the experiment at any time without penalty and are given contact information to report any concerns about their experience in the experiment to the institutional review board.

2. *Risk/gain assessment*. Experimenters are required to take every reasonable precaution to reduce the potential risks to their human subjects.

3. *Deception*. Some critics argue that any deception is not consistent with informed consent (Korn 1987), and others argue that deception is unethical and damages the reputation of experimental scientists in the larger society and is thus unjustified in any circumstance (Baumrind 1985). However, in some instances, deception may be necessary to ensure that subjects cannot guess the hypotheses under investigation. Were subjects to be aware of these hypotheses, their behavior would likely shift as a result of that knowledge, and results would be biased. When deception is used, institutional review boards are particularly careful to ensure that it is necessary. In addition, they may require experimenters to minimize its use, deny the application altogether, or require careful monitoring and reporting on the experiment while it is running.

4. *Debriefing*. At the end of an experiment, experimenters should be careful to tell the subjects as much as possible about the experiment. If deception was involved, experimenters should explain what the deception was and why it was deemed necessary for the unbiased collection of the data. In particular, subjects should be reassured that all their data will be confidential and that the experimenter will obtain subjects' written permission before any of their information is shared publicly.

REVIEW OF EXPERIMENTS RELEVANT
TO POLITICAL SCIENCE

As noted, experiments have not been as widely employed in political science as in either psychology or behavioral economics. Why have we, as a discipline, been so slow to adopt experimental methodology? Why have all other social sciences used experiments to their advantage, and yet political scientists, with few exceptions, resist incorporating experimental methodology into their own work or trusting those who do? Where has our field gone methodologically, and why has this movement been away from experimentation?

There are at least four reasons why political science has not been as receptive to the use of experiments as other social sciences. First, methodology in political science has moved toward large-scale multiple regression work. There is nothing wrong with this; indeed, in behavioral economics, there is a robust subfield devoted to using experiments in concert with formal models and statistical analysis to generate, test, and develop original hypotheses. So although experimental and formal or statistical methods need not be contradictory, the topics studied using these methods tend to be orthogonal to each other. For example, whereas multiple regression tends to concentrate on large groups, experimental work often focuses on small numbers of individuals.

Second, an alternative movement in political science, which tends to eschew the large-scale regression work, focuses on cultural and social aspects of particular phenomena. Although constructivists and postmodern scholars pursue some of the same issues as social psychologists, such as status concerns and the evolution of norms, most cultural analysts remain disinclined to believe that experimental work can get at phenomena as complex and multidimensional as political institutions or cultural and social structures.

The third concern is more practical. Lack of experimental training in political science at the graduate level means that few students add experimental design to their arsenal of research tools as a matter of course. As a result, only especially motivated students will contact an experimenter in a psychology or economics department to learn the basics of experimental design and procedure. The best way to learn how to do experiments is to run experiments. When training and experience are difficult or unavailable, the concentration of experimentalists required to shift disciplinary culture and practice fails to emerge.

Last, many political scientists, unlike other social scientists, seem to believe that experimentalists expect experimental work to stand on its own, the way it does in physics, chemistry, or biology. Unlike in biology, where every aspect of a particular investigation can take place within a petri dish, most phenomena of interest to political scientists are complex and involve many different variables. Experiments can be used very effectively, as they have been in experimental economics, to provide a middle ground between theory and naturally occurring empirical data.

Reciprocation between formal models and experimental testing has advanced both theory and method in behavioral economics, and can serve a similar function in political science as well. In addition, experimentation can be used to triangulate in on various issues for which other methods have produced either inconsistent or contradictory results. Finally, experiments can be effective in breaking down complex processes into isolated pieces, which can then be examined and explored in detail and in interaction. This process might demonstrate, for instance, that small changes in seemingly meaningless variables produce huge shifts in outcome, or that huge shifts in certain ostensibly important factors effect little change in outcome. These insights, gained from the experimental procedure, help with theory development as well as theory testing.

Political science may have significant historical, cultural, or practical reasons for its lack of affinity to the use of experimentation; nonetheless, the past need not predict the future in this arena. Experimentation can achieve the same kind of successful impact in political science that it has had in other fields such as psychology and economics. We can learn from other social sciences that experiments need not stand on their own, as in biology, in order to be effective and useful in refining theory, providing evidence, and testing causal claims. Rather, experiments can dovetail with other methods in order to produce a cumulation of knowledge and an advancement in both theory and method within political science.

How might we respond to the previous lack of experimental work in political science? As noted, one of the mistakes that many political scientists make is to assume that experiments in political science need to mimic those in biology, if not in substance, at least in process. Yet, this stringent standard is not required; we need only note that experiments can dovetail with other methods to produce useful knowledge in order to adequately justify their utility.

In order to illustrate this process in action, the remainder of this essay is devoted to an explication of some of the experimental literature of relevance to mainstream political science. Certain experimental literature in behavioral economics and social psychology is addressed as well, since much of this work is relevant to issues of concern to political science. This article does not have the space to cover accomplishments in all experimental areas of interest to political science. Moreover, it is only through a sequence of experiments exploring related topics in different ways and on different populations that cumulative knowledge and external validity emerge. Therefore, following a brief overview of the presence of experiments in political science, I concentrate on systematic programs of larger research within behavioral economics and political science that have produced results with great relevance to major issues of interest in political science.

Overview

A comprehensive overview of experiments published by established political scientists reveals a total of 105 articles between 1926 and 2000. Only about 57 of them were published in political science journals. Many more strong articles written by political scientists, often in collaboration with economists, on political topics have been published in either psychology or economics journals. I examined 48 articles that appeared in non–political science journals but were written by political scientists; six or seven individuals, either alone or in collaboration, wrote the majority of them. The list of 105 articles does not include those published in the now-defunct *Experimental Study of Politics*. This journal was founded in 1971 because many believed that their experimental work had been unfairly rejected from the established political science journals (McConahay 1973); *Experimental Study* was created expressly to redress this difficulty. However, most of the articles published in this journal were not as experimentally sophisticated as those published in psychology journals (McConahay 1973), and the journal ceased publication in 1975. A casual perusal of contemporary journals reveals that the same double standard exists today, with the experimental sophistication of typical articles in psychology or economics journals outstripping that of many articles published in political science journals. In addition, my review excluded some very good experiments published in edited volumes but not in journals (Iyengar & McGuire 1993, Palfrey 1991, Kagel & Roth 1995).

This overview revealed an increase in the number of published experiments over time. A single article was published in the 1920s, 5 in the 1950s, 7 in the 1970s, 42 in the 1980s, and 45 in the 1990s. (Note that the increase between the 1970s and the 1980s may have been at least partly due to the demise of the aforementioned *Experimental Study of Economics* journal in 1975.) Also interesting is the concentration of experiments in a small number of journals: *Public Opinion Quarterly* (*POQ*) and *American Political Science Review* (*APSR*) account for the most articles, with 21 each. These journals, with very few peripheral exceptions, were the only place that experiments were published in political science until the 1980s. *Political Psychology* has published 18 experimental articles since the 1980s. *American Journal of Political Science* (*AJPS*) has published 13 experiments and *Journal of Politics* has published 7. These five journals together account for 80 of the 105 experimental articles published by established political scientists in this period. Interestingly, the trend appears to be shifting, such that in the 1990s only 2 experimental articles were published in *POQ* and only 5 in *APSR*. *AJPS* captured the majority of the experimental articles published in the 1990s. Moreover, the remaining articles published in the 1990s appeared mostly in one of three additional journals [*Political Behavior* (*PB*); *Journal of Risk and Uncertainty*; and *Games and Economic Behavior*], only one of which (*PB*) is primarily a political science journal.

It is quite striking that so few journals account for the majority of published experimental work in political science. The odds of getting an experimental article published drastically improve if it is submitted to one of these five journals. Although it is possible that political scientists simply do not submit experimental work to other political science journals by chance, the larger number of articles by political scientists on political topics published in either psychology or economic journals (*Econometrica* and *American Economic Review* in particular) suggest otherwise. The relatively low prevalence of experimental work in political science journals suggests that only a few are genuinely receptive to this form of methodological investigation. Indeed, personal communication from the editor of one major journal indicated that he could "never" put any experiment into print because he believed that experiments held no relevance whatsoever for political science. Such entrenched biases are difficult to overcome.

In addition, the bias toward experiments focused primarily on American topics is reflected in the predominance of voting behavior as a primary concern of experimental work. Out of the 105 articles surveyed, 25 were related to voting behavior. The second, third, and fourth most popular topics were bargaining (13), games (10), and international relations topics (10). Other topics that attracted experimental interest included committee work (8), experimental bias (6), race (6), field experiments (5), media (4), leadership (4), and experiments embedded in surveys (3). Given the high percentage of experimental articles focused on voting, the question arises whether more experimenters actually focus on voting, or whether experiments on voting simply find more receptive journals available, and thus are more likely to be published overall.

Several areas of experimental research are relevant to the concerns of mainstream political scientists. Rather than examine each experiment individually, I discuss the major relevant findings in two broad areas of experimental research. In both of these areas, practitioners have developed sequences of experimental work on different populations using different measures in order to clarify and contextualize the generalizability of their results. Such sequences allow investigators to produce more reliable results, as one set of findings spurs another test that might narrow, reinterpret, or extend previous conclusions. Steady and gradual progress can thus attack seemingly impenetrable work. This essay concentrates on behavioral economics, political economy, and psychological studies of individual choice.

Experiments in Behavioral Economics

Within the past 15 years in particular, behavioral economics has grown exponentially and transformed itself through the systematic use of experimentation. These experiments often focus on issues of concern to political scientists. However, behavioral economics, like psychology, embraces some core assumptions about human nature and experimentation that not all political scientists share: skepticism toward notions of perfect rationality; emphasis on experimental validation of modeling assumptions; integration of micro level data; and adoption of lessons about human cognitive processing from experimental social and cognitive psychology (Laibson 2000). Further, experiments deemed successful in economics share certain central characteristics: clear instructions; absolutely no deception; stylized, stripped-down settings; anonymity; cash incentives; experimental tests of formal models, which can include comparisons with rational models; and, ideally, subsequent validation of the findings with supportive field data (Laibson 2000).

Obviously, economic topics have preoccupied political scientists using other methodologies, such as game theory and rational choice forms of analysis. In behavioral economics, theoretical development has profited from the interchange between formal models and experimental tests of such models. Formal models present hypotheses, which are then tested under experimental conditions. The experimental findings are used to refine and develop hypotheses to produce new theoretical models and predictions, which can then be experimentally tested in turn. Political scientists might benefit from this process as well in order to both establish empirical validation of formal models and speed the cumulation of knowledge.

Although the venues and contexts for investigation may differ, a great potential for substantive overlap exists between behavioral economics, psychology, and political science, which might be exploited for greater cross-disciplinary and interdisciplinary work. Current areas of research in psychology and economics offer promising opportunities for collaboration with political scientists who share such interests: social preferences, including investigations of norms, social networks, altruism, status, and trust; bounded rationality, involving decision making in complex environments; learning and expectation formation; attitudes toward risk; and cognitive biases (Laibson 2000).

Behavioral economics has concentrated on six main substantive areas since its experimental work began in the 1930s. These are (Roth 1995) (*a*) Prisoner's Dilemma and public goods issues; (*b*) problems of coordination and cooperation; (*c*) dynamics of bargaining; (*d*) experimental markets; (*e*) auction behavior; and (*f*) individual choice. Some experimental work has also been done in the area of industrial organization, although the majority of work in this area has been conducted by social psychologists.

PRISONER'S DILEMMA AND PUBLIC GOODS   The Prisoner's Dilemma game was developed by Dresher and Flood at the Rand Corporation in 1950 (Flood 1952); the story was added by Tucker (1950) later (Straffin 1980). The central conundrum was that although cooperative play was transparently more profitable in the long run, equilibrium choice favored defection, producing less benefit for each player. Thus, the game produced a challenging test for equilibrium predictions. It was ideal for experimental investigation, which could examine alternative predictions in a controlled setting. In this environment, scholars developed a preference for repeated-play games. Most of these experiments demonstrated that cooperation begins early but breaks down over time, such that in multiround repeated games, players learn to defect earlier and earlier (Selten & Stoecker 1986). In most of these experiments, subjects know that a better outcome of mutual cooperation exists, but fear of exploitation makes mutual defection the only stable strategy over time. Even more interesting are recent findings suggesting that at least some players hold values independent of the payoffs embedded in the game structure, such as fairness, altruism, or concern with reputation building (Andreoni & Miller 1993). These findings will no doubt prompt further experimental work to test the nature and limits of these seemingly noneconomic motivations. Political science readers will also remember the famous Axelrod testing of Prisoner's Dilemma strategies in large-scale computer tournaments (Axelrod 1984). In his simulation, a "tit for tat" strategy, in which the player begins with cooperation and makes the same move as the opponent did the previous round, emerged as the most effective strategy for maximizing payoffs.

Apparently the public goods problem was first presented by Swedish economist Knut Wicksell in the nineteenth century (Roth 1995). Most experimental work on the public goods and free rider problem has focused on the conditions under which it might be most problematic and how its impact can be reduced in those situations.

Early work using single examples of public goods problems indicated little free riding (Johansen 1977). Like the work in Prisoner's Dilemma, experimental work on public goods problems moved toward repeated plays, demonstrating that in successive rounds, voluntary contributions decline (Isaac et al. 1985). Future work will no doubt explore the conditions under which free riding produces the greatest problems and examine ways in which to ameliorate its effects.

COORDINATION   Economists investigating coordination problems experimentally study how subjects playing games with multiple equilibria decide on one in particular. In other words, how do players achieve a "meeting of the minds" (Ochs 1995)? Coordination clearly is influenced by particular aspects of the situation or environment, some of which are not adequately captured by traditional economic models. In many cases, coordination problems prevent optimal decision making from a rational perspective. For example, a factor that should not matter from a traditional economic perspective may exert a tremendous influence, as when the mere presence of a dominated strategy affects the equilibrium chosen (Cooper et al. 1990).

In an experiment involving only problems of coordination, with no inherent conflict of interest, Van Huyck et al. (1990) found that in a repeated game where outcomes are made public after each round, behavior quickly converges around the least profitable equilibrium. Obviously, this outcome does not represent economic rationality in the traditional sense. Crawford (1991) and others have sought to explain these findings using learning models and other game theory models offered by evolutionary biologists. Such models suggest that stable equilibria occur when strategies are not subject to invasion and dominance by new strategies. Crawford does not argue that the coordination problem itself is evolutionary in nature; rather, learning within the game allows stable, albeit economically nonrational, equilibria to emerge and dominate over time.

BARGAINING   Experiments on bargaining behavior also examine how individuals arrive at an agreeable compromise equilibrium, with the added constraint of conflict of interest between players. According to most game theoretic models, player preferences and opportunities should determine outcomes of bargaining behavior. But experimental evidence has shown that bargaining outcomes are affected by variables that are not incorporated into player preference or opportunity, including the player's subjective expectations about the behavior of his opponent, which appears to be learned through experience (Roth & Schoumaker 1983).

The main debate in the bargaining literature has been between those who concentrate on game theoretic predictions and those who are interested in more sociological or cultural considerations. First, important findings in this area include the significance and frequency of disagreements and costly delays during the bargaining games. Second, many experiments demonstrate clear "deadline effects," which support the notion that many agreements are reached very close to the final deadline for agreement (Roth et al. 1988). Both these sets of findings have spurred additional work to determine the impact of these factors on the nature of bargaining

(Roth 1995). This topic is discussed below in the political science section on co-operation.

EXPERIMENTAL MARKETS   Experimental markets typically draw on the basic design established by Chamberlain (1948) to encourage subjects to behave according to the laws of supply and demand, often with the goal of comparing alternative types of markets. Many of the important experiments in this area have been conducted by Plott and colleagues in response to specific policy questions surrounding the potential market effects of instituting particular government regulations (Hong & Plott 1982, Grether & Plott 1984).

Other work on experimental markets examines how traders use and share information. For example, work on asset valuation (Forsythe et al. 1982) demonstrates that prices tend to converge to a perfect equilibrium after replication. In addition, information aggregation (Forsythe & Lundholm 1990) has been examined within the context of experimental markets. Security markets have been examined in this way as well (Plott & Sunder 1988). Forsythe et al. (1992) used an experimental market whose ultimate value was tied to a future election outcome to examine how markets aggregate information. They found that their experimental market prices did a reasonable job of predicting the outcome of the election. On the basis of these results, Forsythe et al. (1992) argue that market transactions reduce the impact of biases such as political opinions on subjects' pricing decisions.

Provocative work on cross-cultural behavior in bargaining and experimental market environments suggested that market outcomes converged to equilibrium and that there were no payoff differences between subjects in Jerusalem, Ljubljana, Pittsburgh, and Tokyo (Roth et al. 1991). However, differences that deviated from equilibrium predictions did occur everywhere in both the agreement and the frequency of disagreement. The experimental procedures employed made the experimenters confident that observed differences in bargaining behavior did not result from differences in language or currency; rather, the investigators tentatively attributed these discrepancies to cultural differences.

AUCTIONS   Auction behavior is familiar to anyone who is a fan of, or knows an addict of, eBay. The most consistent and prominent result of the study of auction behavior is the "winner's curse" (Bazerman & Samuelson 1983, Thaler 1992), wherein the winner of an auction pays much more for the prize than either its real value or the price he intended to pay at the outset. In addition, the average bid is often well below the objective value of the auctioned object. Uncertainty about the true value of the object appears to exacerbate this effect. These findings, suggestive of persistent mistakes on the part of bidders, are clearly contradictory to what established economic theory would predict about equilibrium behavior in auctions (Milgrom & Weber 1982).

INDIVIDUAL CHOICE   Experimental work on individual choice has produced important findings in behavioral economics. This area of work retains the greatest overlap between social psychologists and experimental economists in theory, method, and practice. Research on individual choice encompasses at least three important topics: preference reversals, judgment under uncertainty, and decision making under risk.

The topic of preference reversals has proved particularly problematic for economists attempting to sustain the accuracy of rational models (Tversky et al. 1990). Early experimental work by psychologists Slovic & Litchenstein (1968; Litchenstein & Slovic 1971) noted the anomaly that people will put a higher price on a given lottery when asked to buy or sell it (bids), but when asked to participate in one, most individuals will choose the other lottery (choice). These results remain remarkably robust. Preference reversals seem to result from differences in the way people process information about probabilities and payoffs. Bids appear to be governed by payoffs, whereas choices tend to be driven by probabilities. Although these findings remain inconsistent with expected utility and other rational models of decision making, psychologists readily explain this result as an example of the anchoring and adjustment heuristic (Kahneman et al. 1982), whereby people initially latch onto a value, which can be arbitrary and irrelevant, and fail to adequately adjust that value to present circumstances in making subsequent judgments. The first anchor people fix on is the monetary payoff, and then they insufficiently adjust choices to shifts in probabilities. Preference reversals result from this inadequate adjustment from the initial monetary anchor.

The second main area of research within the individual choice literature is judgment under uncertainty (Kahneman et al. 1982). This experimental work examines how individuals judge the frequency or likelihood of certain outcomes. This work consistently and robustly demonstrates at least three important judgmental heuristics that appear to control people's assessments of frequency: anchoring and adjustment (described above), representativeness, and availability. The representativeness heuristic claims that individuals assess frequency based on the similarity between the judged object or event and the categories to which it might belong. The availability heuristic argues that people judge likelihood based on salience, i.e., the ease of retrieval or imagination of the example from memory. All three judgmental heuristics contradict central assumptions in most expected utility models, which expect dominance, invariance, and intransitivity to hold sway in judgments about probabilities.

Decision making under risk has been most closely examined by the same psychologists who conducted the seminal work on judgmental biases (Kahneman & Tversky 2000). In attempting to develop a descriptively accurate model of choice as an alternative to expected utility models, Kahneman & Tversky (1979; Tversky & Kahneman 1992) delineated prospect theory. Prospect theory incorporates two successive phases: editing and evaluation. In editing, prospects or choices are framed for a decision maker. Robust experimental evidence indicates that trivial aspects of framing options can consistently exert profound impacts on the substance of choice. Specifically, seemingly trivial changes in the method, order, or form in which options are presented to a decision maker systematically affect the content of choice. Evaluation itself encompasses two components as well: the value function and the weighting function. The value function has three central characteristics: (*a*) outcomes are judged in relative, not absolute, terms; (*b*) individuals tend to be risk-seeking in the domain of losses and risk-averse in the domain of gains; and (*c*) people tend to be loss-averse in general. The role of the weighting function is similar to, but distinct from, that of probability assessments in expected utility models. First, people have great difficulty incorporating extremes such as impossibility and certainty into their decision-making strategies. Second, individuals tend to overweight low probabilities while simultaneously underweighting moderate and high probabilities. All these empirical results surrounding the value and weighting functions contradict the predictions of standard expected utility models.

Experiments in Political Science

As in economics, some political scientists are beginning to use experimentation to test formal models in a controlled empirical setting. The three main areas of research in this area are (*a*) voting and elections, (*b*) committee and jury decision making, and (*c*) problems of coordination and cooperation (Palfrey 1991). This third area is similar in some theoretical ways to work on coordination in behavioral economics, but the domains of application differ. Palfrey (1991) argues that these topics have produced at least three important themes in the relationship between formal modeling and experimental research in political science. These include the importance of strategic behavior in studying complex political actions and actors; the critical significance of incomplete or asymmetric information, especially as related to issues of reputation, communication, and signaling; and finally, the importance of explicitly building dynamic models, which are aided by experimental methods and impact problems related to party identification, realignments, incumbency, and political business cycles.

EXPERIMENTAL VOTING AND ELECTIONS   Since Downs's *An Economic Theory of Democracy*, many scholars have tried to examine the foundations of democratic elections with formal models. Increasingly, these models are being tested experimentally (Palfrey 1991). Plott (1991), for one, tested the spatial model to examine certain aspects of elections, including voter turnout.

Voter turnout lends itself nicely to experimental investigation. For example, Palfrey & Rosenthal (1985) argued that according to game theoretic analysis under assumptions of complete information, analysts should expect equilibria of high turnout, even when the costs of voting are high. Instead, they demonstrated experimentally that under conditions of uncertainty about the preferences and costs of others for voting, only voters with very low voting costs will vote in a large election. In other work on voter turnout, Green and colleagues have attempted to rehabilitate the use of field experiments begun by Gosnell (1926). In a study on the effects of canvassing, phone calls, and direct mail on voter turnout, Gerber

& Green (forthcoming[1]) found that personal canvassing increased voter turnout, whereas phone calls appeared to have no impact. Direct mail appeared to have a slight impact on voter turnout. In addition, they found that asking voters whether they could be "counted on" to vote increased the impact of personal canvassing.

Other topics that have been investigated experimentally under the rubric of voting and elections include candidate competition (Plott 1991), retrospective voting (McKelvey et al. 1987), political competition (Boylan et al. 1991), and voter information costs.

Lau and Sears have used experiments to examine related topics. Their study of the evaluation of public figures (Lau et al. 1979) concluded that the so-called positivity bias often found in survey results is not an artifact of the measurement process alone but rests on some real bias in assessment. Related work on political preferences (Sears & Lau 1983) showed that self-interest may result from political and personal cues in surveys that trigger artifactual results. Finally, these authors have experimentally explored the nature of political beliefs (Lau et al. 1991).

Political party identification has also been examined experimentally (Cowden & McDermott 2000). We were intrigued by previous work, using different methodologies, that achieved somewhat contradictory results regarding the long-term stability of party identification. We designed an experiment that assessed student subjects' party identification, among other things, early in the semester. Later, after participating in one experiment that manipulated the extremity of real candidates in experimental elections, or another in which subjects role-played either the prosecutor or defender of Clinton in the impeachment hearing, subjects filled out a second, standard party identification measure. Our results indicated that party identification, even in a young population that should have had less time to develop strong associations, showed remarkable stability.

Media effects on candidate evaluation and voting have been another extremely productive research topic. Some of the best and most imaginative experimentation has been conducted in the area of media studies and political communication by Iyengar and colleagues. Their creative studies have demonstrated that television news influences how viewers weight problems and evaluate candidates (Iyengar et al. 1982); that television news frames individuals' explanation of events (Iyengar 1987); that negative advertising reduces voter turnout (Ansolabehere et al. 1994); and that candidates gain the most by advertising on issues over which they can claim "ownership" (Ansolabehere & Iyengar 1994). Iyengar continues to advance the methodology of experimentation itself as well, with recent studies that use new technology and field strategies to ameliorate some of the traditional criticisms of external validity problems (Iyengar 2000). These strategies include bringing the experiments into natural settings by creating living room environments in shopping malls and asking subjects to watch television in those settings, with experiments embedded in the programming. Further, Iyengar has begun to use the internet

---

[1]Gerber A, Green D. *The Effects of Canvassing*, *Phone Calls and Direct Mail on Voter Turnout: A Field Experiment*. Unpublished manuscript.

to reach more diverse populations, which increases experimenter access to more representative samples.

Experimental studies of candidate evaluation by gender have produced some interesting findings as well. In an evaluation of campaign coverage of senatorial candidates, Kahn (1992) found that the press presented male and female candidates in systematically different ways. Such differences appeared to benefit male candidates, who were seen as more viable; this may disadvantage female candidates at the polls. Nevertheless, sex stereotypes sometimes benefit women because they were judged more frequently than men to be compassionate and honest. Further work by Kahn (1994) examining both gubernatorial and senatorial candidates found that voter perceptions were affected by both news coverage and sex stereotypes. Interestingly, these factors appear to affect incumbents differently from challengers, and gubernatorial candidates differently from senatorial candidates. In particular, gender differences in press coverage were more pronounced in the senate race and for incumbents. This pattern appears to hurt female senatorial candidates. On the other hand, sex stereotypes produce more positive evaluations of women and appear to benefit gubernatorial candidates the most. Note that Kahn's further experimental testing of her earlier findings allowed her to further refine and conditionalize her results. The findings of Huddy & Terkildsen (1993) on gender stereotyping in the perception of candidates are consistent with Kahn's. They too find that female candidates are seen in a positive light on traits such as compassion, whereas men are perceived to be more competent on military issues. Huddy & Terkildsen suggest that a gender trait approach best explains the differences they find.

COMMITTEE AND JURY DECISION MAKING   A second arena of systematic research in political science considers committee and jury decision making. Experiments on committee decision making are typically modeled on legislatures in which results emerge from a combination of bargaining and voting. Much research thus focuses on how the bargaining process and the voting rules affect the outcome of committee decision making, especially under different decision rules. Various scholars have examined committee decision making under majority rule (Fiorina & Plott 1978, McKelvey & Ordeshook 1979), plurality (Neimi & Frank 1985), approval voting (Neimi 1984), noncooperative games (Felsenthal et al. 1988), competitive solutions (McKelvey & Ordeshook 1983), and universalism (Miller & Oppenheimer 1982). In particular, agenda setting (Levine & Plott 1977, Wilson 1986) and time constraints (Wilson 1986) offer perfect topics for experimental investigation based on strategic models. Guarnaschelli et al. (2000), among others, have recently used experimental work in the investigation of jury decision-making analysis as well.

Work on committee decision making often uses the ultimatum game as an experimental tool. Typically, two players must divide a sum of money, such as $10. The procedure requires one player to offer an amount to the second, who can then accept or reject it. If the second player rejects it, no one gets the money, whereas if the player accepts it, both players split the money in the percentage agreed. The theoretical question investigated is whether something about a subject's partner will affect either person's willingness to bargain.

Much work on committee decision making grew out of observations about the problems inherent in conventional game theory's treatment of these issues. The results of many experimental bargaining games seemed askew (Ostrom 1998) and players often exhibited consistent behavioral play (Camerer 1997), neither of which should be true according to traditional models. In particular, self-interest does not always work or dominate in these ultimatum games. This was also found in so-called dictator games, where the first player can solely dictate the division of goods. Specifically, unequal splits tend to be rejected in favor of "fair" splits. This outcome should not happen under subgame perfect backward induction equilibria, which would be predicted by expected utility models.

The promise of behavioral game theory rests on its ability to explore various aspects of this conundrum experimentally. In particular, experimental work can build on previous anomalous findings from ultimatum games to examine altruism, inequality aversion, and so-called mind reading (Wilson 2001). Altruism refers to a consistent desire to help others, even when it might hurt oneself. Numerous models of altruism (Forsythe et al. 1994, Eckel & Grossman 1996) typically assume that altruism is an embedded character trait within a given individual. Altruism succeeds because it gives people a positive feeling about themselves as a result of their actions. From an evolutionary standpoint, altruism may exist within communities because it advances the ability of the society to survive and prosper even when key individuals, such as mothers after childbirth, are too overwhelmed to perform their normal tasks successfully. Altruism in this sense may amount to little more than reciprocal selfishness.

Inequality aversion refers to many individuals' empirical preference for equal over unequal distributions of goods, even when extreme self-interest is possible, as in the dictator game. Examinations of this phenomenon explore how the same individual might act differently in different situations. What constraints control the extent to which an individual might cooperate in one circumstance but not in anther? Early indications suggest that meaningful comparisons are important (Bolton & Ockenfels 2000) and that at least some inequality aversion derives from concerns surrounding relative status (Fehr & Schmidt 1999).

Mind reading refers to discerning the intentions of others (Rabin 1993; Levine 1998; Falk & Fischbacher, unpublished manuscript[2]). Unlike altruism, mind reading allows for the emergence of both positive and negative emotions (Frank 1988, Smith 1998). Once another person's intentions have been determined through an empirical process, people will tend to treat a nice person nicely and a mean person as they deserve.

Wilson (2001) has conducted a series of experiments investigating these phenomena. He demonstrates the ideal experimental procedures by learning from the

---

[2]Falk A, Fischbacher U. 1998. Kindness is the parent of kindness: modeling reciprocity. Unpublished manuscript.

experiences of previous studies and designing future studies to address past anomalies or to ameliorate procedural difficulties. He finds that beliefs about others are important and can change over time. These beliefs appear to be contingent on cues that individuals receive over time about others. In this way, interaction develops lasting reputations and labels. Wilson's work suggests that theoretical models of individual choice might be impaired by their failure to incorporate such seemingly nonrational factors as altruism, inequality aversion, and mind reading.

COORDINATION AND COOPERATION   Work on coordination and cooperation in political science resembles similar work in behavioral economics, discussed above. However, applications differ, and work on cooperation in political science can easily be applied to problems in security as well as political economy. Topics include alliances, arms races, trade wars, and sanctions. For example, Geva and Skorick have used experimentation to test their cognitive calculus model of decision making in foreign policy (Geva & Skorick 1999, Geva et al. 2000, Geva & Skorick 2000). These authors use experimentation to test the predictions of their model against actual behavior in a laboratory setting.

Work on coordination and cooperation remains closely tied to work in social psychology and behavioral economics. Typically, scholars investigate this topic using noncooperative game theory (Palfrey 1991). Experimentalists seek to provide data related to certain models and push those models further by presenting evidence that might either refute or extend the current theoretical claims. Specific results indicate that communication increases group cooperation. Ostrom and colleagues (e.g., Ostrom & Walker 1991) have demonstrated that face-to-face communication, particularly in repeated-play settings involving common pool resources, exerts a powerful impact on propensity for cooperation.

Palfrey and colleagues have undertaken a systematic program of experimental research on topics related to coordination and cooperation. In one experiment, discounted repeated play proved more effective in generating cooperation than a single shot trial in a public goods game with incomplete information; however, results depended on the ability to monitor others and on the specific environmental conditions (Palfrey & Rosenthal 1994). Palfrey and colleagues have concentrated on the centipede game, in which two players alternately have a chance to take a larger portion of a continually escalating amount of money (McKelvey & Palfrey 1992, Fey et al. 1996). Once one person takes the money, the game ends. According to game theory predictions under assumptions of complete information, the first player should take the larger pile in the first round of play. However, this does not happen in reality. Rather, subjects operating under conditions of uncertainty and incomplete information about the payoff appear willing to consider the small possibility that they are playing against an altruistic opponent. Although the probability increases over time that a player will take the pile of money, the game typically continues into subsequent rounds. Palfrey has also investigated choice in other games (McKelvey & Palfrey 1995). This work shows great richness in its ability to combine formal modeling with experimental testing of such models.

The combination of methods allows greater confidence in results that point in the same direction.

Experimental work by Miller and colleagues has explored a variety of topics, including committees (Miller & Oppenheimer 1982). In work on games, Eavey & Miller (1984a) demonstrate that when universalist options, which offer "something for everyone," exist in legislatures, concerns about fairness go beyond what expected value expectations would predict. Further, Miller & Oppenheimer (1982) find that competitive coalitions with a minimum winning coalition occur only when universal options are unavailable. In work on bargaining, Eavey & Miller (1984b) show that a bureaucratic monopoly on agenda setting allows bargaining with a voting body without necessarily imposing the agenda setter's preferences on all. They conclude that bureaucratic agenda control in legislative bodies supports a bargaining model over an imposition one. Although some of this work (Miller & Oppenheimer 1982, Palfrey & Rosenthal 1994) points out the discrepancies between rational choice theory and the behavior of individuals in the real world, experiments are used not only to test and critique existing formal models but also to discover anomalies and challenges that are then incorporated into the next generation of model development.

Bolton (1991) has used experimentation to investigate how actual bargaining behavior differs from game theoretic predictions. Bolton & Zwick (1995) demonstrate that the opportunity to punish an opponent who treats you unfairly presents a more accurate explanation for deviations from perfect equilibrium solutions than the existence of anonymity for the subject. Note that although experimental findings may be at odds with some predictions of formal theory, the overall relationship between game theoretic modeling and experimentation in these exercises is collaborative; experiments empirically test formal models and suggest discrepancies as well as validations, and then formal modelers can attempt to incorporate these empirical demonstrations into later, more sophisticated models.

In our work on topics related to international relations, we investigate the impact of factors such as sex, uncertainty, and framing effects on arms races and aggression. In one experiment involving three rounds of a simulated crisis (McDermott & Cowden, forthcoming), we find that although uncertainty exerts no systematic effect on weapons procurement or likelihood of war, men are significantly more likely to purchase weapons and engage in aggressive action than women. In another experiment involving a simulated crisis game (McDermott et al. 2002), we examine the impact of framing in terms of striving for superiority or parity with the opponent, two kinds of uncertainty, and the tone of messages on weapons procurement. We find that embracing the frame of striving for superiority does indeed increase weapons procurement on the part of subjects. The tone of the message exerts a tremendous impact as well; recipients of hostile messages are much more likely to procure weapons than recipients of friendly messages. As in our other work, uncertainty appears to have no effect on weapons procurement. Finally, in more recent work, as yet unanalyzed, we manipulated the incentive to go to war to further examine the impact of sex differences on levels of aggression. We plan to expand this paradigm to include other populations, including military officers, to further explore the impact of factors such as hormones, including testosterone, and nonverbal gestures on tendencies toward aggression.

CONCLUSIONS

Experimentation is one of many methods that can be used to examine political phenomena. Experiments have a long and distinguished history of effective usage in other disciplines, including hard sciences such as physics and biology, medicine, and social sciences such as psychology and economics. Unfortunately, experiments have been slower to acquire a dedicated following of practitioners in political science, mostly because of concerns about external validity. In many cases, this concern merely reflects a misunderstanding of the replication requirements necessary to establish external validity. But this concern may also indicate a failure to understand the difference between experimental realism, which is essential and requires the subject to be actively engaged in the process under investigation, and mundane realism, which refers to inessential trappings of the experimental situation that increase only the appearance, not the reality, of external validity (McDermott, under review[3]).

The primary advantage of experiments is that they offer unparalleled control over the variables of interest. This is because the experimental method permits the systematic manipulation of variables in a controlled environment with randomly assigned subjects. Experiments thus offer the highest degree of internal validity; experimenters can be pretty confident that outcomes differ on the basis of the variables manipulated systematically within the experimental conditions. This enables experimenters to make causal arguments about which factors cause certain outcomes, or contribute to them, and which do not.

Another advantage of experiments results from the scientific rigor built into the process. Experimenters remain aware of, and retain control over, the independent variables of interest. Experimenters carefully record results as dependent variables. Later statistical analysis allows the detailed testing of the relationships between these variables and any interactions among them. With this process, results that might not have been obvious to less systematic or large-scale analysis become prominent. Experiments allow causal inference, precise measurement and control, and clarity of detail.

Unfortunately, many political scientists assume that experimental results in political science need to be able to stand on their own, as in biology, and that if they cannot, they are useless. Nothing could be further from the truth. Experimentation can readily dovetail with other methodologies to produce systemic bodies of knowledge. As demonstrated by much of the work in behavioral economics and

---

[3]McDermott R. Experimental methodology in political science. Submitted.

some of the work in political science, the intersection of formal modeling and experimental testing is highly productive. Experiments can be, and have been, effectively used to test formal models, demonstrate unpredicted anomalies in outcomes that then provoke more sophisticated models, and suggest extensions and limitations of existing models under particular conditions.

In addition, experiments provide effective methodological help in examining areas in which other methodologies have produced inconsistent or contradictory findings, as was the case in our work on party identification. Experiments also offer clear advantages over other methods in particular areas of investigation, such as the validation of theories developed by formal modeling, or in further theory testing and refinement. Experiments offer useful insights in work that investigates the underlying process of a particular phenomenon as opposed to its outcome. Finally, invoking multiple methods, including experimentation, in investigating a phenomenon allows greater confidence in consensual results. In this way, experiments can help in triangulating in on research questions. Indeed, experimentation can serve a useful purpose, as it has in behavioral economics, to advance knowledge in political science more quickly and systematically and to cumulate such knowledge through the process of building on previous experimental work.

ACKNOWLEDGMENTS

I would like to thank Jonathan Cowden, Margaret Levi, one anonymous reviewer, the participants in the CBRSS Experimental Methods Conference at Harvard, and especially Sidney Tarrow for enormous help in writing this review.

The *Annual Review of Political Science* is online at http://polisci.annualreviews.org

LITERATURE CITED

Andreoni J, Miller J. 1993. Rational cooperation in the finitely repeated Prisoner's Dilemma: experimental evidence. *Econ. J.* 103:570–85

Ansolabehere S, Iyenger S. 1994. Riding the wave and claiming ownership over issues: the joint effects of advertising and news coverage in campaigns. *Public Opin. Q.* 58:335–57

Ansolabehere S, Iyengar S, Simon A, Valentino N. 1994. Does attack advertising demobilize the electorate? *Am. Polit. Sci. Rev.* 88:829–38

Aronson E, Carlsmith M. 1968. Experimentation in social psychology. In *The Handbook of Social Psychology*, ed. G Lindzey, E Aronson, Vol. 2. Reading, MA: Addison-Wesley. Rev. ed.

Axelrod R. 1984. *The Evolution of Cooperation.* New York: Basic Books

Baumrind D. 1985. Research using intentional deception: ethical issues revisited. *Am. Psychol.* 40:165–74

Bazerman M, Samuelson W. 1983. I won the auction but don't want the prize. *J. Confl. Resolut.* 27:618–34

Bolton G. 1991. A comparative model of bargaining: theory and evidence. *Am. Econ. Rev.* 81:1096–36

Bolton G, Ockenfels A. 2000. Measuring motivations for the reciprocal responses observed in a simple dilemma game. *Am. Econ. Rev.* 90:166–93

Bolton G, Zwick R. 1995. Anonymity versus punishment in ultimatum bargaining. *Games Econ. Behav.* 10:95–121

Boylan R, Ledyard J, Lupia A, McKelvey R, Ordeshook P. 1991. Political competition in a model of economic growth: an experimental study. In *Laboratory Research in Political Economy*, ed. T Palfrey, pp. 33–68. Ann Arbor: Univ. Mich. Press

Burke J, Greenstein F. 1989. *How Presidents Test Reality: Decisions on Vietnam, 1954 and 1965.* New York: Russell Sage Fdn.

Camerer C. 1997. Progress in behavioral game theory. *J. Econ. Persp.* 11:167–88

Campbell DT. 1968. Quasi-experimental design. In *International Encyclopedia of the Social Sciences*, ed. DL Sills, Vol. 5. New York: Macmillan

Campbell DT, Ross HL. 1968. The Connecticut crackdown on speeding: time-series data in quasi-experimental analysis. *Law Soc. Rev.* 3:33–53

Campbell DT, Stanley JC. 1963. Experimental and quasi-experimental designs for research on teaching. In *Handbook of Research on Teaching*, ed. NL Gage. Chicago: Rand McNally

Chamberlain R. 1948. An experimental imperfect market. *J. Polit. Econ.* 56(2):95–108

Cooper R, DeJong D, Forsythe R, Ross T. 1990. Selection criteria in coordination games: some experimental results. *Am. Econ. Rev.* 80:218–33

Cowden J, McDermott R. 2000. Short term forces and partisanship. *Polit. Behav.* 22: 197–222

Crawford V. 1991. An "evolutionary" interpretation of Van Huyck, Battalio and Beil's experimental results on coordination. *Games Econ. Behav.* 3:25–59

Eavey C, Miller G. 1984a. Fairness in majority rule games with a core. *Am. J. Polit. Sci.* 28: 570–86

Eavey C, Miller G. 1984b. Bureaucratic agenda control: imposition or bargaining? *Am. Polit. Sci. Rev.* 78:719–33

Eckel C, Grossman P. 1996. Altruism in anonymous dictator games. *Games Econ. Behav.* 16:181–91

Etheredge L. 1978. *A World of Men: The Private Sources of American Foreign Policy.* Cambridge, MA: MIT Press

Fehr E, Schmidt K. 1999. A theory of fairness, competition and cooperation. *Q. J. Econ.* 114:817–68

Felsenthal D, Rapoport A, Maoz A. 1988. Tacit cooperation in three alternative noncooperative voting games: a new model of sophisticated behavior under the plurality procedure. *Elect. Stud.* 7:143–61

Fey M, McKelvey R, Palfrey T. 1996. An experimental study of a constant-sum centipede game. *Int. J. Game Theory* 25:269–87

Fiorina M, Plott C. 1978. Committee decisions under majority rule: an experimental study. *Am. Polit. Sci. Rev.* 72:575–98

Flood M. 1952. *Some experimental games.* Res. Memo. RM-789, RAND Corp., June

Forsythe R, Horowitz J, Savin N, Sefton M. 1994. Fairness in simple bargaining games. *Games Econ. Behav.* 6:347–69

Forsythe R, Lundholm R. 1990. Information aggregation in an experimental market. *Econometrica* 58:309–48

Forsythe R, Nelson F, Neumann G, Wright J. 1992. Anatomy of an experimental political stock market. *Am. Econ. Rev.* 82:1142–61

Forsythe R, Palfrey T, Plott C. 1982. Asset valuation in an experimental market. *Econometrica* 50:537–67

Frank R. 1988. *Passions Within Reason: The Strategic Role of Emotions.* New York: Norton

Geva N, Mayhar J, Skorick JM. 2000. The cognitive calculus of foreign policy decision making: an experimental assessment. *J. Confl. Resolut.* 44:447–71

Geva N, Skorick JM. 1999. Information inconsistency and the cognitive algebra of foreign policy decision making. *Int. Interact.* 25:333–62

Geva N, Skorick JM. 2000. *Process and outcome consequences of simultaneous foreign policy decisions.* Presented at Annu. Meet.

Int. Soc. Polit. Psychol., July 4–8, Seattle, WA

Gosnell H. 1926. An experiment in the stimulation of voting. *Am. Polit. Sci. Rev.* 20:869–74

Grether D, Plott C. 1984. The effects of market practices in oligopolistic markets: an experimental examination of the ethyl case. *Econ. Inq.* 22:479–507

Guarnaschelli S, McKelvey R, Palfrey T. 2000. *An experimental study of jury decision rules.* Presented at Exp. Methods Conf., May 11–12, Cambridge, MA

Hong J, Plott C. 1982. Rate filing policies for inland water transportation: an experimental approach. *Bell J. Econ.* 18:187–97

Huddy L, Terkildsen N. 1993. Gender stereotypes and the perception of male and female candidates. *Am. J. Polit. Sci.* 37:119–47

Isaac R, McCue K, Plott C. 1985. Public goods provisions in an experimental environment. *J. Public Econ.* 26:51–74

Iyengar S. 1987. Television news and citizens' explanations of national affairs. *Am. Polit. Sci. Rev.* 81:815–32

Iyengar S. 2000. *Experimental designs for political communication research: from shopping malls to the internet.* Presented at Exp. Methods Conf., May 11–12, Cambridge, MA

Iyengar S, McGuire W, eds. 1993. *Explorations in Political Psychology.* Durham, NC: Duke Univ. Press

Iyengar S, Peters MD, Kinder D. 1982. Experimental demonstrations of the "not-so-minimal" consequences of television news programs. *Am. Polit. Sci. Rev.* 76:848–58

Johansen L. 1977. The theory of public goods: misplaced emphasis? *J. Public Econ.* 7:147–52

Kagel J, Roth A, eds. 1995. *The Handbook of Experimental Economics.* Princeton, NJ: Princeton Univ. Press

Kahn K. 1992. Does being male help? An investigation of the effects of candidate gender and campaign coverage on evaluations of U.S. senatorial candidates. *J. Polit.* 54:497–517

Kahn K. 1994. Does gender make a difference? An experimental examination of sex stereotypes and press patterns in statewide campaigns. *Am. J. Polit. Sci.* 38:162–95

Kahneman D, Slovic P, Tversky A, eds. 1982. *Judgment Under Uncertainty: Heuristics and Biases.* Cambridge, UK: Cambridge Univ. Press

Kahneman D, Tversky A. 1979. Prospect theory: an analysis of decision under risk. *Econometrica* 47:263–91

Kahneman D, Tversky A. 2000. *Choices, Values and Frames.* New York: Cambridge Univ. Press/Russell Sage Fdn.

Korn J. 1987. Judgments of acceptability of deception in psychological research. *J. Gen. Psychol.* 114:205–16

Kuklinski J, Sniderman P, Knight K, Piazza T, Tetlock P, et al. 1997. Racial prejudice and attitudes toward affirmative action. *Am. J. Polit. Sci.* 41:402–19

Laibson D. 2000. Untitled. Presented at Exp. Methods Conf., May 11–12, Cambridge, MA

Lau R, Sears D, Centers R. 1979. The "positivity bias" in evaluations of public figures: evidence against the instrument artifacts. *Public Opin. Q.* 43:347–58

Lau R, Smith R, Fiske S. 1991. Political beliefs, policy interpretations, and political persuasion. *J. Polit.* 53:644–75

Levine D. 1998. Modeling altruism and spitefulness in experiments. *Rev. Econ. Dyn.* 1:593–622

Levine M, Plott C. 1977. Agenda influence and its implications. *Va. Law Rev.* 63:561–604

Litchenstein S, Slovic P. 1971. Reversal of preferences between bids and choices in gambling decisions. *J. Exp. Psychol.* 89:46–55

McConahay J. 1973. Experimental research. In *Handbook of Political Psychology*, ed. JN Knutson, pp. 356–82. San Francisco: Jossey-Bass. 542 pp.

McDermott R, Cowden J. 2001. The effects of sex and uncertainty in a crisis simulation game. *Int. Interact.* 27:353–80

McDermott R, Cowden J, Koopman C. 2002. The effects of framing, uncertainty and hostile communications in a crisis simulation game. *Polit. Psychol.* In press

McKelvey R, Ordeshook P. 1979. An experimental test of several theories of committee decision making under majority rule. In *Applied Game Theory*, ed. S Brams, A Schotter, G Schwodiauer. Wurzburg, Ger.: Physica Verlag

McKelvey R, Ordeshook P. 1983. Some experimental results that fail to support the competitive solution. *Public Choice* 40:281–91

McKelvey R, Ordeshook P, Collier K, Williams K. 1987. Retrospective voting: an experimental study. *Public Choice* 53:101–30

McKelvey R, Palfrey T. 1992. An experimental study of the centipede game. *Econometrica* 60:803–36

McKelvey R, Palfrey T. 1995. Quantal response equilibria for normal form games. *Games Econ. Behav.* 10:6–38

Milgrom P, Weber R. 1982. Predation, reputation, and entry deterrence. *J. Econ. Theory* 27:280–312

Miller G, Oppenheimer J. 1982. Universalism in experimental committees. *Am. Polit. Sci. Rev.* 76:561–74

Neimi R. 1984. The problem of strategic behavior under approval voting. *Am. Polit. Sci. Rev.* 78:952–58

Neimi R, Frank A. 1985. Sophisticated voting under the plurality procedure: a test of a new definition. *Theory Decision* 19:151–62

Ochs J. 1995. Public goods. In Kagel & Roth 1995, pp. 195–253

Ostrom E. 1998. A behavioral approach to the rational choice theory of collective action. *Am. Polit. Sci. Rev.* 92:1–22

Ostrom E, Walker J. 1991. Communication in a commons: cooperation without external enforcement. In Palfrey 1991, pp. 287–322

Palfrey T, ed. 1991. *Laboratory Research in Political Economy*. Ann Arbor: Univ. Mich. Press. 323 pp.

Palfrey T, Rosenthal H. 1985. Voter participation and strategic uncertainty. *Am. Polit. Sci. Rev.* 79:62–78

Palfrey T, Rosenthal H. 1994. Repeated play, cooperation and coordination: an experimental study. *Rev. Econ. Stud.* 61:545–65

Plott C. 1991. A comparative analysis of direct democracy, two-candidate elections, and three-candidate elections in an experimental environment. In *Laboratory Research in Political Economy*, ed. T Palfrey, pp. 11–32. Ann Arbor: Univ. Mich. Press

Plott C, Sunder S. 1988. Rational expectations and the aggregation of diverse information in laboratory security markets. *Econometrica* 56:1085–118

Rabin M. 1993. Incorporating fairness into game theory and economics. *Am. Econ. Rev.* 83:1281–302

Roethlisberger FJ, Dickson WJ. 1939. *Management and the Worker*. Cambridge, MA: Harvard Univ. Press

Rosenberg MJ. 1965. When dissonance fails: on eliminating evaluation apprehension from attitude measurement. *J. Pers. Soc. Psychol.* 1:28–42

Rosenthal R. 1966. *Experimental Effects in Behavioral Research*. New York: Appleton-Century-Crofts

Roth A. 1988. Laboratory experimentation in economics: a methodological overview. *Econ. J.* 393:974–1031

Roth A. 1995. Introduction. In Kagel & Roth 1995, pp. 3–109

Roth A, Murnighan K, Schoumaker F. 1988. The deadline effect in bargaining. *Am. Econ. Rev.* 78:806–23

Roth A, Prasnikar V, Okuno-Fujiwara M, Zamir S. 1991. Bargaining and market behavior in Jerusalem, Pittsburgh, and Tokyo: an experimental study. *Am. Econ. Rev.* 81:1068–95

Roth A, Schoumaker F. 1983. Expectations and reputations in bargaining: an experimental study. *Am. Econ. Rev.* 73:362–72

Sears D. 1986. College sophomores in the laboratory: influences of a narrow data base on social psychology's view of human nature. *J. Pers. Soc. Psychol.* 86:515–30

Sears D, Lau R. 1983. Inducing apparently self-interested political preferences. *Am. J. Polit. Sci.* 27:223–52

Selten R, Stoecker R. 1986. End behavior in sequences of finite Prisoner's Dilemma supergames: a learning theory approach. *J. Econ. Behav. Org.* 7:47–70

Slovic P, Litchenstein S. 1968. Relative importance of probabilities and payoffs in risk taking. *J. Exp. Psychol. Monogr. Suppl.* 78:1–18

Smith V. 1998. The two faces of Adam Smith. *South. Econ. J.* 65:1–19

Sniderman P, Piazza T, Tetlock P, Kendrick A. 1991. The new racism. *Am J. Polit. Sci.* 35:423–47

Straffin P. 1980. The Prisoner's Dilemma. *UMAP J.* 1:102–3

Thaler R. 1992. *The Winner's Curse: Paradoxes and Anomalies of Economic Life*. Princeton, NJ: Princeton Univ. Press

Tucker A. 1950. A two-person dilemma. Mimeo, Stanford Univ.; republished 1980. On jargon: the Prisoner's Dilemma. *UMAP J.* 1:1

Tversky A, Kahneman D. 1992. Advances in prospect theory: cumulative representation of uncertainty. *J. Risk Uncertain.* 5:297–323

Tverksy A, Slovic P, Kahneman D. 1990. The causes of preference reversal. *Am. Econ. Rev.* 80:204–17

Van Huyck J, Battalio R, Beil R. 1990. Tacit coordination games, strategic uncertainty, and coordination failure. *Am. Econ. Rev.* 80:234–48

Walker T. 1976. Microanalytic approaches to political decision-making. *Am. Behav. Sci.* 20:93–110

Wilson R. 1986. Forward and backward agenda procedures: committee experiments on structurally induced equilibrium. *J. Politics* 48:390–409

Wilson R. 2001. Untitled. Presented at Exp. Methods Conf., May 11–12, Cambridge, MA

Zimbardo P, Gerrig R. 1996. *Psychology and Life*. New York: HarperCollins. 14th ed.

Annu. Rev. Polit. Sci. 2002. 5:63–85
DOI: 10.1146/annurev.polisci.5.092801.093759
Copyright © 2002 by Annual Reviews. All rights reserved

POLITICS, POLITICAL SCIENCE, AND URBAN GOVERNANCE: A Literature and a Legacy

Russell D. Murphy
Department of Government, Wesleyan University, Middletown, Connecticut 06459;
e-mail: rmurphy@mail.wesleyan.edu

Key Words   administrative state, local self-rule, municipal reform,
politics-administration

■ **Abstract**   Politics has not always fared well in the political science literature
on the cities, at least not in the United States. Since the mid-nineteenth century, a
substantial literature has either decried or discounted the role of politics in urban
governance. Much of the early literature, written before and just after the creation
of the American Political Science Association in 1903, urged politics be banished
and administration privileged as a way to remedy "one conspicuous failure of the
United States . . . the government of cities." Subsequent literature reinstated politics—
though some claimed elected officials were simply agents of special interests or upper-
class elites. The prevailing view today is that political leadership is an important,
independent factor in the governing equation, although it is arguable that of late national
and state administrators have been empowered at the expense of local self-rule—thus
approximating, albeit by different means, the system envisioned by early municipal
reformers.

INTRODUCTION

It is hard to wrap your arms around a city; harder still your mind. Cities, by
definition, are large and complex, which helps explain why there is no unified and
universally accepted theory of urban life. To be sure, there are utopian visions
of what the ideal city should be and, less grandly, tidy-town awards promoting
some partial view of gracious urban living. But as yet there is no single theory
that transcends time and place and fully describes, let alone explains, how cities
work. There are instead numerous theories and studies that examine broad areas
of city life, each seeking to leave the reader a little less bewildered than before.
This includes the literature on urban politics and government in the United States,
the focus of what follows.

The focus, less generally, is on academic writing about cities, principally, though
not exclusively, writings by American political scientists. The survey is not exhaustive but selective and personal—such is the editorial warrant—and centers on
writings that contribute to understanding key questions about city politics. The

1094-2939/02/0615-0063$14.00
63

selections derive from more than 100 years of articles, essays, books, and reports, beginning with mid–nineteenth century efforts to adapt intellectually and institutionally to the big city.

Cities in the United States share much with cities across the globe. The nation's big cities are a nineteenth-century phenomenon and their growth here coincided with urbanization elsewhere, especially in Western Europe. According to Weber, this concentration of population in cities was the most remarkable social phenomenon of a century not lacking for remarkable phenomena. As he noted, urbanization, along with other "agencies of modern civilization . . . worked together to abolish rural isolation" and subject it increasingly to urban influences (Weber 1899, pp. 1, 7, 448).

If the timing was similar, so too were the challenges. Large, densely settled communities create problems that intensify the needs associated with any human settlement. These include an adequate and healthy supply of food and water, effective methods for disposing of human and animal waste, shelter against the elements and against predators, and measures to deal with the extremes of material well-being and material deprivation. Failure to address these problems is a deadly constraint on all human places, especially on cities, which, because of their sheer size, are more vulnerable for example to epidemics or threats to the civil order.

URBANIZATION AND URBAN GOVERNANCE

Although similar in these respects, American cities are politically distinctive. This distinctiveness lies in the tradition and expectation of local self-government combined with a broad-based suffrage. It also lies in the character of urban populations, especially the impact of immigration on the politics and governance of the nation's big cities. These factors have helped frame the dialogue about cities and how we go about governing them.

Bryce's oft-repeated claim that "the government of cities is the one conspicuous failure of the United States" was a commonplace among political observers by the time he published *The American Commonwealth* in 1888 (Bryce 1891 [1888], I:608). By 1888 there was already a substantial literature reflecting widespread alarm about the sudden and sharp growth of cities—some relative newcomers, such as Chicago, but older, larger cities as well.

There was alarm, further, about the broadening of municipal functions—about increased spending and taxes, increased regulation of private property, and increased initiatives in social welfare. And there was alarm, most of all, about the management of municipal affairs—concerns not simply that city governments were reaching beyond the proper limits of state action but that essential functions were poorly tended and poorly administered by corrupt and unqualified officials.

This was one dimension of the "conspicuous failure," much of it detailed, early on, in accounts of individual cities. "It is not that the city government, so far as controlled by politicians, sometimes steals. We do not make that charge. We say it does nothing *but* steal," Parton wrote in a lengthy review essay, "The Government of the City of New York" (Parton 1866, pp. 448–49). Parton's assessment derived partly from direct observation of the City Council (pp. 417–28) and its machinations, but chiefly from a review of various reports on New York City, most conducted by the Citizens Association of the City of New York, some few by the City or County of New York. The latter included the *Manual of the Corporation of the City of New York*—"a most superb and lavishly illustrated duodecimo volume of 879 pages [containing] one hundred and forty-one pictures, of all degrees of expensiveness—steel-plate, wood cut, plain lithograph and colored lithograph—" for which the City paid $57,172.30 compared with production costs of $15,000 (1866, pp. 431–33). "Such is the book," Parton concluded, "which the taxpayers of the city are called upon every year to pay for, in order to swell the income of sundry printers, lithographers, politicians and the compilers" (Parton 1866, p. 432).

For Parton, the *Manual* showed just how far the spoils system had penetrated City government. "In the precious Manual ... the reader, amazed at the interminable lists of persons employed by the city, is every now and then puzzled by such items as these." The items ranged from such low-level positions as "manure inspectors" and "distributors of corporation ordinances" to more prestigious-sounding positions, "inspectors of encumbrances," for example, and "health wardens and their assistants." Whatever the title, he added, the officials were little more than

> bar-keepers, low ward politicians, nameless hangers-on of saloons, who absolutely performed no official duty whatever except to draw the salary attached to their places. They were the merest creatures of the worthless man who appointed them—the man who sold or gave away blanket internment permits, signed to favored undertakers. (Parton 1866, p. 439)

Parton's extended essay is an early and noteworthy example of a genre that would become more commonplace in the literature on city governance. In a sense, it presaged the more celebrated exposés associated with the muckrakers of the late nineteenth and early twentieth centuries—politically engaged and faithful to the facts, but selective, not systematic, in their reporting. Aware that "we are all disposed to exaggerate evils [and that] good people are not quite as good nor bad people as bad as popular rumor gives them out," (Parton 1866, p. 416), Parton nonetheless emphasized the "bad." To do otherwise would be to complicate the story and undermine its purpose, which was to rally honest citizens by dramatizing just how much the system was costing them.

Though city-specific, Parton's account was addressed to a broader national audience. "Let no one suppose this is a subject which concerns the people of New York only," he counseled. "The insidious beginnings of that misgovernment which has made New York the by-word and despair of the nation can already be [found] in Brooklyn, Philadelphia, Boston, New Orleans, San Francisco, Chicago, Albany, Rochester, Buffalo, St. Louis," and, he added, "many other cities" (Parton 1866, p. 464).

RETHINKING POPULAR RULE

By the end of the nineteenth century, accounts of municipal mismanagement across the country were commonplace in an expanding literature on the cities. Many such accounts, like Parton's, were city-specific, based on the work of local civic organizations and circulated through an emerging national network of local reform organizations. But there were more systematic accounts as well, including comparative financial data on individual cities first published by the U.S. Census in 1890 (U.S. Bureau of the Census 1946, p. 286).

More important, reports of widespread municipal mismanagement prompted speculation that the problem was inherent in the very nature of city politics, not simply the result of occasional "defalcations" by a few venal public officials. The speculation centered principally on whether received notions of popular rule and the institutions embodying them were still suitable for governing the modern city—whether the ideas and the institutions could simply be adjusted or, instead, required radical rethinking and restructuring.

The issues were crucial to the fate of the democratic experiment. It was not simply that municipal responsibilities had broadened or were being mismanaged. The issues were crucial, as well, because city life was becoming the dominant culture in the United States and because city populations challenged the assumption that suffrage and self-government were suited to all peoples. In his Presidential Address at the Fourth Annual Meeting of the American Political Science Association, Judson noted:

> It is in the government of our cities that representative government has had its most conspicuous failure, and it is therefore clear that the future of representative government is closely connected with and indeed dependent upon reform in municipal administration.... The civilized world is now watching with interest the struggle for representative government, where heretofore from the dawn of history autocracy has held an undisputed sway. It is for this country to show that the hopes and anticipations of the founders of our government will be realized through the only means whereby self-government can be preserved over an extended territory, and that is by true representative government. (Judson 1908, pp. 199–202)

These broad concerns figured prominently on the early agenda of the American Political Science Association. By the time the Association was founded in 1903, there was already a substantial "political science" literature on city government. Much of this had been published in such established journals as the *Political Science Quarterly* (founded in 1886), the *Annals of the American Academy of Political and Social Science* (1890), the *Proceedings of the American Statistical Association* (1888), or in the publications of the American Economic and American Historical Associations.

Much of it, moreover, was written by early leaders in the profession, among them Frank Goodnow, James Bryce, Woodrow Wilson, Albert Bushnell Hart,

A. Lawrence Lowell, and Charles Merriam. According to its founders, the Association provided an additional and more focused venue for the "scientific study of the great and increasingly important question of practical and theoretical politics," including municipal government and politics (American Political Science Association 1904, p. 11).

The central question, as Judson asked, was whether popular rule and universal male suffrage were suited to managing the modern city. Democratic theory presumed voters would make informed, intelligent, and independent choices and that in doing so they would choose men of caliber and competence, the "fittest men" (Judson 1908, p. 186), and the "most highly gifted and highly activated" (Parkman 1878, p. 15). This was the republican tradition, or its presumption, one sanctified by Madison in *The Federalist 10* (p. 62). A republican form of government, Madison assured his readers, would "refine and enlarge the public views by passing them through the medium of a chosen body of citizens, whose wisdom may best discern the true interest of their country and whose patriotism and love of justice will be least likely to sacrifice it to temporary or partial considerations." The record in the cities was otherwise.

The record was otherwise, according to a generation of political scientists, public intellectuals, and reformers, principally because of the party system, which, Bryce speculated (1891 [1888], I:608), "[had] not perhaps created, but certainly enormously aggravated [the evils] and impressed on them their specific type." Nominations and ballot access were two sources of its power. Another was its control of jobs, public revenues, and municipal regulatory authority, all of which, Bryce noted, the party used to "consolidate, extend and fortify its power." Once in power, moreover, a party tended to remain in power—unregulated electoral competition, it seems, created public monopolies (Bryce 1891 [1888], II:130 ff).

A third source of the party's staying power was its constituency base. The party was extraordinarily attentive to its constituents. It had developed elaborate grassroots organization "among the people" where party leaders would "see them and be seen" (Riordan 1963, p. 25). "Everybody in the district knew him," Riordan (1963, p. 90) said of Tammany Hall's legendary George Washington Plunkitt, "and everybody knew where to find him and nearly everybody went to him for assistance of one sort or another, especially the poor of the tenements" (1963, p. 90). Or, as Ostrogorski (1902, II:471) reported in his detailed, two-volume study *Democracy and the Organization of Political Parties*, "The politicians of the Machine looked after the electors day after day, they attended to this business morning and evening, for years together, and not only during election time."

The character and competence of urban voters, without whose support party systems could not have endured, was an added matter of concern. The suffrage had been broadened earlier in the nineteenth century with the elimination of property and tax-paying qualifications. These changes, Martin Van Buren complained at the time, admitted to the polls "tens of thousands of ignorant and vicious men" who threatened to overwhelm responsible citizens and corrupt the ideals of local popular control (Parton 1866, p. 446). The threat had since intensified. Not only had city populations grown but so too, it was said, had the relative numbers of ignorant and ill-informed voters.

Much of this growth was due to dramatic changes in the size and nature of foreign-born populations. Immigration, Mayo Smith allowed (1888, p. 48), had been one of the prime factors in the nation's development, but he questioned whether immigrants were "any longer a desirable element for the community to acquire." One concern was the source of immigration. The heaviest immigration, he reported, was now coming from those areas where poverty was the most striking— from the west of Ireland, for example, from the eastern provinces of Prussia, from the southern regions of Italy, and from those sections of Hungary "where the condition of the people is so strikingly inferior that it attracts universal attention." Smith concluded that emigration was "no longer culling and bringing . . . the cream of the working classes, the men of energy, thrift and enterprise . . . but as likely the indolent, vagrant and vicious" (1888, pp. 69–76).

It was also bringing individuals from "a class of society which [did] not concern itself about the form of government . . . and who [knew] little of our institutions and of our history, and [cared] less." Smith continued, "The franchise means to them simply an opportunity to sell their votes, and liberty is license to do as they please." As a result of "the infusion of so much alien blood into our social body," he added, there was a danger the nation would "lose [its] capacity and power of self-government, or that the elements of our national life shall become so heterogeneous that we shall cease to have the same political aspirations and ideals and thus be incapable of consistent political progress" (Smith 1888, pp. 415–22).

The immigrant's capacity for self-government was a common concern among a generation of scholars and intellectuals. "In those days," Steffens remarked (1931, p. 400), "educated citizens of the cities said, and I think they believed—they certainly acted upon the theory—that it was the ignorant foreign riff-raff of the big congested towns that made municipal politics so bad." Lacking a sense of civic duty, immigrants were nonetheless, according to Bryce (1891, II:358), "admitted to full civic rights before they [had] come to shake off European notions and habits. These strangers," he continued,

> enjoy political power before they either share or are amenable to American opinion. Such immigrants are at first not merely a dead weight in the ship, but a weight which the party managers can, in city politics, so shift as to go near upsetting her. They follow blindly leaders of their own race, are not moved by discussion, exercise no judgment of their own. (Bryce 1891, II:358)

Still, Bryce was optimistic. "The younger sort [of] foreigners," he suggested, "when . . . they have learnt English, when, working among Americans, they have imbibed the sentiments and assimilated the ideas of the country, are thenceforth scarcely to be distinguished from the native population" (Bryce 1891, II:358). Even Mayo Smith conceded that the children of immigrants "do often, in one generation, become good citizens," although he was less sanguine than Bryce in this regard (Smith 1888, p. 54). There was thus some hope the system could socialize and assimilate the "other" and "make citizens intellectually and morally fit to conduct their government," which, Bryce told the profession in his 1909 Presidential Address (p. 12), was "the chief problem of democracy."

REDEFINING URBAN DEMOCRACY

Whatever the prospects, there were hesitations, widely shared among intellectuals, about the wisdom and practicality of urban democracy. There were concerns about big-city voters and whether they would choose the right kind of leadership, namely competent, honest, public-spirited individuals. And there were concerns about urban political systems and whether an excess of democracy made proper city government unlikely.

These were some of the questions "agitating the public mind," as Goodnow put it in his 1904 Presidential Address to the first annual meeting of American Political Science Association (1904, p. 36). Such questions prompted an extensive reexamination of democratic theory and practice as it had evolved in the nation's cities, along with an extensive literature on municipal government and politics.

Much of the literature was prescriptive and "busied itself," in Goodnow's phrase, "with agitation for some particular reform" (1904, p. 36). By the time Goodnow spoke, the catalogue of "particular reforms" was already as lengthy as it was familiar—voter registration laws, for example, including literacy tests and residency requirements; civic education; the direct primary, the short-ballot, and the nonpartisan election; proportional representation and at-large elections. Often advocated as discrete and even disjointed initiatives, most shared a common dimension, namely an ambivalence toward popular rule.

In principle, such prescriptions were fully consonant with the mission of the new Association. The "ultimate object of political science is moral . . . the improvement of government among men," Lowell told his colleagues in his 1910 Presidential Address (p. 14), and he chided "students of politics [for] not lead[ing] public thought as much as they ought to" in this regard (Lowell 1910, p. 4). At the same time, he insisted such leadership required that government be studied "as a science, as a series of phenomena of which [the investigator] is seeking to discover the causes and effects" (Lowell 1910, p. 14).

Lowell urged more scientific study of democracy, a novel experiment that had "lasted long enough to produce many of its normal results, and a vast deal of information may be obtained by observing them with scientific thoroughness and accuracy" (Lowell 1910, p. 14). And he challenged the profession to "observ[e] . . . with scientific thoroughness and accuracy" such phenomena as voting and nonvoting, political recruitment and turnover in office, and political parties and party bosses. With respect to the last, little was actually known—why, for example, bosses had thrived only intermittently and had been permanent in so few places; or why they ruled autocratically on some but not all issues. "If we knew these things accurately," he concluded, "we should be a much better position to contrive a remedy" (Lowell 1910, pp. 11–12).

According to Lowell, such studies were rare. "To advocate in this twentieth century the importance of studying the actual working of government may seem like watering a garden in the rain. But that this is not the case everyone must be aware who is familiar with the current political literature on such living topics as . . . the reform of municipal government" (Lowell 1910, pp. 2–3). There were exceptions: Merriam (1908) and Munro (1909), both of whom Lowell singled out for praise, and others whom he did not, including Ostrogorski (1902), who had already published an encyclopedic comparative study of political parties, and Steffens (1904), whose powerful exposé of city bosses and nouveau arrivé entrepreneurs had been presaged some years earlier, though not as colorfully, by Parkman (1878). But most writing on city politics, Lowell complained, was "theoretical," "conducted in the air," and "treat[ed] what ought to happen rather than what actually occurs." Many of these writers, he allowed, were "earnest men, overflowing with public spirit." But they were "prone to imagine a new device [would] work as they intended and [were] disappointed that it [did] not." The resulting "waste of precious efforts at reform, from a failure to grasp the actual forces at work" was, he concluded, "one of the melancholy chapters of our history" (Lowell 1910, p. 3)—a judgment reminiscent of George Washington Plunkitt's playful jibe that reformers "were mornin' glories—looked lovely in the mornin' and withered up in a short time, while the regular machines went on flourishing forever, like fine old oaks" (Riordan 1963, p. 17).

In an important sense, the record belies the rhetoric. Whatever the fate of individual reform initiatives, key reform ideals endured. Some were variants on traditional values and beliefs, for example, the faith in the efficacy of institutional engineering. Others combined old ideals with powerful new ones, notably professionalism.

A key objective was achieving the right kind of municipal leadership. "Democracy," Judson explained in his Presidential Address at the Fourth Annual Meeting of the Association (1908, p. 186), was not "merely a means of securing an expression of the average intelligence in legislation . . . [T]he ideally perfect government was that in which the intelligence of the community, the fittest men, should be selected." Whatever the quality of municipal leadership in the past—and some, such as Parton, insisted there was a "time . . . when the city was governed by its natural chiefs—the men who had the divine right to govern it" (Parton 1866, p. 446)—"the very best of citizens" were no longer engaged in the enterprise. The reason, according to Bryce, was that they had either withdrawn from the struggle or were engaged in other more profitable activities. "Able citizens," Bryce reported (1891, I:613), "[are] absorbed in their private business, cultivated citizens unusually sensitive to the vulgarities of practical politics, and both sets therefore specially unwilling to sacrifice their time and tastes and comfort in the struggle with sordid wire-pullers and noisy demagogues." Or they were simply outnumbered, or outmaneuvered and outvoted by the political bosses and their allies.

One way to correct this was to reform city charters, state statutes, and state constitutions. Though frequently dismissed as overly mechanical—as Steffens once quipped, "paper government did not count" (1931, p. 409)—this type of reform had notable precedents. One was the nation's long-standing reliance on written constitutions and the faith that well-designed laws could produce desired political and policy outcomes. This included Madison's claim, noted above, that a "republican form of government" would result in the election to office of public-spirited men.

Others, moreover, had shown "boss rule" was not inevitable even in large industrial cities and that municipalities could be governed effectively, efficiently, and with a high degree of integrity. Prussian municipalities were oft-cited examples. "Among the local elective organs of the various countries of Europe and America none have been more successful than the Prussian city councils in securing as members men of ability, integrity and general prestige," Munro reported in his exhaustive study of *"Government in European Cities"* (1909, pp. 150–51). Equally successful in this regard was the Magistrat, a local Prussian administrative board with broad municipal powers. Some of its appointed members were paid, professional administrators chosen for their special skill; the rest were men of financial means who could forego paid employment to serve the community. There was, as well, a professional bureaucracy, appointed and promoted "with due regard for merit and experience, security of tenure and protection against arbitrary dismissal." In Munro's mind, these features were key to the success of the system and to "much of the integrity and efficiency which characterize civic bureaucracy, particularly in Prussia" (Munro 1909, p. 205).

Although much admired, there were features of the Prussian system that, prima facie, made it an unrealistic proposition in the United States. One was the Magistrat, which was appointed, not elected—to choose its members "by universal suffrage would be to alter greatly its conservative character," which was, according to Bishop (1908, p. 410), "its greatest merit." Nor was the elected Council any less conservative, largely because of the electoral system employed. The city electorate was organized into three distinct classes, with each group paying one third of the total taxes and each electing one third of the councilors. As Munro observed, this arrangement put "the preponderance of influence in the hands of the wealthier citizens." It also brought "social and economic distinctions into the polling-room, where, according to the fiction that American cities have vigorously attempted to maintain, all citizens are equal" (Munro 1909, pp. 132–33).

Although the nation's egalitarian impulse made the Prussian system unlikely in the United States, its ideals remained at the core of municipal reform. It was unlikely, for example, that votes could be weighted as radically as in Prussia, but access to the vote could be limited through registration laws, residency requirements, and literacy tests. Nor was it likely city councilors in the United States would ever be "a well selected elite drawn from the professional, mercantile, and academic circles" or that there would come a day when their decisions would consistently represent not "the hasty transitory judgments of the masses but the best business sense of the community" (Munro 1909, p. 151). On the other hand, the unwholesome influence of elections could be minimized by constraining those most to blame, namely the political parties. This could be done by limiting the parties' role in the electoral process—through, for example, the direct primary, the short ballot, and nonpartisan and at-large elections—as well as by denying them important resources, such as patronage and regular and special party financial assessments.

The "hasty, transitory judgments of the masses" could be minimized further by limiting the range of choices entrusted to voters and their elected representatives. Issues could instead be handled by professional administrators, appointed, not elected, on the basis of merit and free from partisan influence. Important municipal matters would thus be entrusted to those most qualified to deal with them, achieving indirectly what could not be achieved through elections. Of all the reform initiatives, these were arguably the most far-reaching and influential.

The justification for this vision of popular rule can be found in the early literature on the administrative state. Two such works stand out: Wilson's "The Study of Administration," published in the *Political Science Quarterly* in 1887, and Goodnow's *Politics and Administration*, published three years later. Both advocated a greater role for administration as distinct from politics in the governmental process. Politics, Goodnow explained (1890, p. 18), had to do with "policies or expressions of the state will"; administration with the "execution of these policies." Administration, moreover, was "removed from the hurry and strife of politics" (Wilson 1887, p. 209). The distinction was by no means straightforward, as Wilson himself confessed. "No lines of demarcation, setting apart administrative from non-administrative functions," he cautioned, "can be run between this and that department of government without being run up hill and down dale, over dizzy heights of distinction and through dense jungles of statutory enactment, hither and thither around 'ifs' and 'buts,' 'whens' and 'howevers' until they become altogether lost to the common eye not accustomed to this sort of surveying and consequently not acquainted with the use of the theodolite of logical discernment" (Wilson 1887, p. 211). Still, like Goodnow, Wilson was confident the distinction had meaning as well as merit. The "discrimination between administration and politics," Wilson insisted (1887, p. 211), "is now, happily, too obvious to need further discussion."

Though perhaps "too obvious," it plainly was not compelling, and Wilson complained the United States had been slow to act on the importance of the distinction. This was due largely to the country's long-standing suspicion of government power and the instruments of this power, namely "administrative organization and administrative skill." The nation, he complained, had stressed "curbing executive power to the constant neglect of the art of perfecting executive methods" and had invested "much more in controlling than in energizing government" (Wilson 1887, p. 206).

Changing this would be a major challenge. "The very fact we have realized popular rule in its fullness," he mused (Wilson 1887, pp. 207–9), "has made organizing that rule just so much more difficult" and made "practical reform slow and ... full of compromises." Reform would be difficult because "in order to make any advance at all [reformers would need to] instruct and persuade a multitudinous monarch called public opinion ... the bulk of which is rigidly unphilosophical ... [but] votes." Even so, it was imperative the nation adopt "a science of administration," Wilson believed, "to straighten the paths of government, to make its business less unbusinesslike, to strengthen and purify its organization, to crown its duties with dutifullness ... and [to counter] the poisonous atmosphere of city government" (1887, p. 201).

The significance of all this for municipal government was in the specification of what constituted the administrative sphere and what constituted the political. The answer, in brief, was that "municipal government [was] ... almost exclusively a matter of administration" (Goodnow 1900, p. 84). Politics thus would play a limited part in municipal affairs. There would be little need for those schooled in the art of politics, and there would be little need for burdening the electorate with matters beyond their competence. Such matters were more appropriately left to administrators specially educated and trained to handle them. In this way, previously vague urgings that the best people should be running municipal government became somewhat less indeterminate, since ideally municipal administrators would be recruited from the ranks of established professions and occupations with their seemingly scientific criteria for judging excellence. In this way, additionally, urban politics would be transformed. "Any reasonable man would willingly renounce his privilege of dropping a piece of paper into a box," Parkman had predicted in 1878 (p. 10), "provided good government were assured to him and his descendants." Or, as some had urged, the "right to good government" would finally take precedence over the "asserted right to self-government" (*North American Review* 1866, p. 250).

Though radical, this broad vision of urban politics found important institutional expression in the civil service and in the council-manager plan. To some, such as Tammany's George Washington Plunkitt, civil service was "the biggest fraud of the age and the curse of the nation" (Riordan 1963, p. 11). But the proposition that government personnel be hired, fired, and promoted solely on the basis of ability and performance is in principle quite unexceptional and proved attractive even to elected officials.

The devil, however, was in the details, namely specifying who would judge ability and performance and according to whose standards. In the case of the civil service, these determinations were to be made by boards or commissions that would be free of partisan and political pressures. Guided by the spirit of professionalism and with assistance from experts in each field, a civil service commission would classify jobs and write and administer exams that would produce personnel who satisfied the commission's a priori definition of a "good public servant." The electoral process is far less presumptuous in this respect, since it does not presume to tell citizens what kinds of people they must choose to govern them.

The council-manager plan was a second reform that sought to institutionalize the role of professionals and experts in the governance of cities. As set forth in the National Municipal League's revised *Model City Charter of 1915*, this innovative form of government called for an uncluttered hierarchical arrangement of municipal agencies. Ideally, the city council would be the sole elected body and as such responsible for establishing the broad outlines of municipal policies. These would be carried out by administrators chosen under the merit system, and the administrators, in turn, would be under the general direction of a professional manager chosen by the council solely on the basis of managerial skills. The chief executive was thus appointed, not elected; accountable to the council, not the voters; and, in theory at least, indifferent to political and policy matters.

The manager plan thus embodied that vision of democratic politics in which elections and elected officials were to play a minimal role. True, there was an elected council, but the council consisted of part-time citizen legislators, volunteers who agreed to serve intermittently as the community principal policy makers. Councilors were to be paid token salaries—"lest the salary attract candidates whose real ambition is to get the money," as the plan's chief architect Richard Childs put it (Childs 1965, p. 69)—and would be thus forced to divide their time between the city's business and their own. They would have no staff and would be prohibited from dealing with "city officers and employees who [were] subject to the direction and supervision of the manager." Managers, on the other hand, would be full-time, as would the civil servants under them. And while the council attended to policy matters, the manager would attend to the day-to-day running of the city's business, most of which, according to orthodox reform thinking, was administrative, not political, in nature.

The council-manager plan represented a radically different vision of democratic politics from that which had prevailed earlier in the city. What had prevailed earlier, according to many, was too much democracy—too many elected officials and too frequent elections. These were perhaps entirely appropriate to earlier times, when municipal responsibilities were fewer and less complex, but no longer. Government's responsibilities were now greater, the suffrage had expanded, the electorate was radically different; voters and elected officials were generally more suspect and increasingly underqualified, technically and morally, to run city governments. There was virtual consensus in the literature on these points, as there was on the proposition that less democracy and more administration were what municipal government needed.

REINSTATING POLITICS

The broad vision of municipal government embodied in turn-of-the-century reforms proved remarkably durable. The proposition that cities are principally administrative, not political, entities is still widely though by no means universally accepted, and institutions such as the council-manager plan, nonpartisan elections, and at-large elections are now commonplace in city and town charters, albeit less so in the largest cities than elsewhere. For much of the century, moreover, this broad perspective on city government was accepted uncritically.

By mid-century, however, key assumptions were being challenged, especially the administrative principles on which so much of the reform initiative was based. The distinction between administration and politics, for example, no longer seemed as clear-cut as it had, even to reasonable, well-informed and public-spirited men and women. Nor were the principles of administrative science as scientifically certain as before. These principles, or "proverbs of administration," to use Simon's phrase (1946, pp. 53–67), were often contradictory and inconsistent as well as unproved. Nor were they entirely value-free. Professional administrators, according to reform orthodoxy, would promote government efficiency, and efficiency was a value that was simply assumed, or asserted, to be the core value for city governments.

Though increasingly influential within the profession, these challenges had relatively little impact on the municipal government literature. In 1957, for example, Herson complained that "administrative dogma, based upon the premise of a value-free administrative process sank—in the literature of administration—beneath the waters of empirical investigation. But in the literature of city government, the dogma exists, an ice-age inhabitant of a lost Atlantis" (Herson 1957, p. 334). This was especially true of city government textbooks, where, he noted, "the administrative theory that entered the city government texts in 1920 did not adapt itself to subsequent changes in this theory, but persists unchanged" (Herson 1957, p. 334). Indeed, by 1920 the theory was well established in the innumerable textbooks published during the late nineteenth and early twentieth centuries. With notable exceptions, such as Beard's *American City Government* (1912), these texts promoted city government as chiefly an administrative and not a political concern.

It was not simply that the assumptions had gone unchallenged but, as well, that the claims and consequences of reform had not been systematically scrutinized. There was little evidence, for example, on the record of the council-manager plan—for many, the centerpiece of municipal reform. By 1957, the plan had been widely adopted, and, as Herson notes, this record was often cited as evidence that the plan delivered on its promise of honest and efficient city government (Herson 1957, p. 340). But despite a great deal of celebratory literature, much of it published in and by the *National Municipal* (now *Civic*) *Review* and in various publications of the International City Managers (now Management) Association, little was known about the structure and functioning of council-manager–plan cities: whether, for example, all council-manager plans were created equal with respect to the scope of municipal responsibilities, charter authority, and professional credentials of managers; whether these features varied over time with changes in the size and demographics of the city; whether manager-plan cities were more likely than others to be run by "able, public spirited, non-political councils" (Childs 1952, p. 189); or whether, finally, manager-plan cities were more efficient than non–manager-plan cities, assuming efficiency was a universal value for which there were agreed-upon standards and adequate data to make systematic comparisons.

There was little attention, additionally, to the consequences of reform and especially to the implications of the administrative state for the workings of popular rule. This was a major theoretical and practical challenge. "Whether popular government will endure," Lowell wrote in the concluding paragraph of *Public Opinion and Popular Government* (1926 [1913], p. 303), "depends on its success in solving its problems, and among these none is more insistent than the question of its capacity both to use and to control experts." Others had since addressed the issue but largely outside the context of municipal government. The literature, Herson reported (1957, p. 341, note 22), "offer[ed] little evidence [of having] thought through the problem of the expert and his proper role in democratic government." There was scant information on the policy process and on the extent to which, as a result of the reforms, municipal policy making had shifted to the administrative arena; and on whether such shifts, along with other institutional changes affecting elections, parties, and city councils, had reshaped political participation to the detriment of mass publics and to the benefit of the media and of intense policy minorities (interest groups) with special access to the bureaucracy.

This neglect coincided with shifts in professional interests during these years. These in turn reflected major shifts in the public agenda, in particular a more active national government. The change had been foreshadowed during the late nineteenth century. But it was not until World War I and especially until the New Deal and its aftermath that the political science agenda shifted dramatically to the national arena, with a consequent decline in research interest in the city.

By the time Herson's article appeared in 1957, there were already signs of renewed scholarly interest in urban governance. As had been the case in the late nineteenth century, the interest was prompted partly by dramatic changes in the demographics and economics of the nation's cities. Cities were in decline following World War II as population, housing construction, retail trade, service industries, and employment generally shifted from the core to the ring. Although the process had begun decades before, the earlier suburbanization had not outpaced the city (Warner 1978 [1962]). Now deconcentration appeared to be the dominant trend, raising alarms about the future of a society without a dynamic and defining urban culture (Jacobs 1961, Mumford 1961). It raised concerns as well about a still sizable urban population, those left behind and those newly arrived, living in communities with declining physical infrastructures and declining public and private resources, where the old "tenement trail" (Lubell 1952) seemed overgrown and no longer visible, let alone passable.

Reports of a widespread urban crisis prompted a remarkably ambitious set of policy initiatives and policy proposals. Though varied and at times conflicting, these proposals shared the assumption that the private sector alone could not be counted on to preserve and revitalize the city and consequently that the public sector needed to intervene. This meant not only city governments themselves but state and federal governments with their greater taxing and borrowing powers. And it meant more extensive use of government power generally, including government's power to regulate and to coerce.

Most of the early initiatives stressed economic development—for example, the revitalization of central business districts or the construction of industrial parks—using the city's power of eminent domain to assemble the land, public subsidies for new construction or rehabilitation, and tax incentives to encourage retail trade and industry to remain or relocate. Although they stressed economic development, these early initiatives assumed success would be broadly beneficial—that a rising tide would, as it were, improve the lot of citizens generally. Some observers, however, were skeptical, or at least insisted more direct investment in human capital was also needed. The latter was the main thrust of such federal legislation as the Economic Opportunity Act of 1964 (P.L. 88-452); the Manpower Development and Training Act of 1962 (P.L. 87-145); and the Elementary and Secondary Education Act of 1965 (P.L. 89-10). It was also, along with economic development, the thrust of the Housing and Community Development Act of 1972, in this instance with the stated congressional objective of "deconcentrating" the city's poor by resettling them in suburban communities (P.L. 93-383, Sec. 101(c)(6); National Commission on Urban Problems 1968; Downs 1973).

Proposals calling for deconcentrating the city's poor had profound implications for urban governance and especially for the way local government was organized in metropolitan areas. As matters stood, the system was highly decentralized, with authority distributed among an at times bewildering array of governments—counties, municipalities, independent school districts, public authorities, and numerous and varied other special districts. This "system" had long been a source of consternation to critics, who insisted there were more rational ways to organize local governments and adapt them to the realities of suburbanization.

As in earlier times, the stress was on institutional engineering and the adjustment of governmental forms to deal with whatever problems cities faced. In this case it was the long-standing recommendation the many units of local government in metropolitan areas be reorganized into a single larger one. Doing so, it was said, would eliminate duplication, allow for greater economies of scale, and reduce competition for population and taxes. It would also broaden perspectives of lawmakers and make it easier for the ordinary citizen to find out who was responsible for what. And, according to one of its champions (Gulick 1957, p. 59), once there was "a single center for coordinated analysis, planning and action," a "rational attack" on the city's "underlying problems" would finally be possible.

Whatever the promise, the metropolitan government movement, as it is sometimes called, has had limited success in the United States. There are exceptions— Unigov in Indianapolis-Marion County and the Miami-Dade County Metropolitan Federation. But even these are at best only approximations of the ideal, since each lacks jurisdiction over important locally administered programs such as education, police, and public housing. For the most part, the nation's system of local government remains highly decentralized, reflecting a political rationality quite different from that underpinning blueprints of how metropolitan government ought to be organized.

Understanding this rationality is at the core of political science—not simply to treat what "ought to happen" but, as Lowell had counseled in his 1910 Presidential Address (p. 3), to determine "what actually occurs," and "to grasp the actual forces at work." Such questions, long a concern in mainstream political science, were now posed increasingly in the literature on urban politics as well—who stood to gain or lose, for example, from metropolitan government; and whether, if adopted, metropolitan governments would operate according to plan, such that the effective distribution of political power actually corresponded to the formal provisions of reform charters. In brief, the study of urban government and politics was now no longer the stagnant professional backwater described by Herson. Within a decade of Herson's article, there was a substantial and richly empirical literature describing government and politics in the city. It was a literature that was also lively and often quite roiled.

Topics varied. Some scholars addressed institutional matters, including such reform initiatives as the council-manager plan, at-large elections, and administrative reorganization plans, or such reform nemeses as political parties, city councils, and the electoral systems. Others examined major policy initiatives, most notably those in housing, urban renewal, and welfare broadly defined. Methods varied as well. Some investigators produced case studies, rich contextual analyses of individual cities or of discrete policies or political controversies. Others approached the city from more comparative and quantitative perspectives, testing general hypotheses about the causes and consequences of institutions or the relative importance of political, social, and economic variables on policy outcomes.

Although there were widely shared epistemologies and methodologies, the literature was also quite varied and as such difficult to summarize. In this respect, it lacked the unifying vision that pervaded so much of the early literature on municipal government. Still, important themes can be noted and important studies cited, albeit selectively, illustrating the new directions in the study of urban governance.

One was the emphasis on process and the proposition that governing is more than simply acts in the law—a commonplace proposition, except in the earlier literature on the city. It is more than simply acts in the law inasmuch as (a) few laws cover all contingencies and none are self-executing, and (b) laws are not spontaneous acts. People value different things differently, except perhaps in a utopia or dystopia. Elsewhere, lawmaking involves choices among competing values, interests, and peoples. It typically imposes differential costs and bestows differential benefits on citizens and, in normal course, provokes conflict.

Although politics was thus restored to the literature on urban governance, there was disagreement about what kinds of politics counted and just how much. The disagreements were evident, for example, in the political economy literature and especially in the large-scale comparative studies. These studies typically examined differences in public policy using statistical models to test the relative influence of various factors on outcomes. Few studies, it is true, focused specifically on local as opposed to state or national governments (Fabricant 1952, Dawson & Robinson 1963, Dye 1966). But the methods and the models, as well as the findings, had broader significance for understanding how city governments functioned.

They had significance among other reasons because they gave pause to easy generalizations about the importance of government and politics. Many studies suggested that socioeconomic variables such as income and education were, statistically, far more significant in the policy equation than were governmental and political ones. (See, however, Lineberry & Fowler 1967, Fry & Winters 1970.) This did not mean, as even investigators admitted, that politics was irrelevant or that only fools contested forms of government, as Alexander Pope suggested long ago. These were statistical models designed to test relationships among variables, and the results depended heavily on the kinds of data and measures employed—whether, for example, they adequately captured, in all their complexities, such important political and governmental variables as party competition, the budget process, or administrative rule making. Even so, the findings were a powerful reminder that one could not assume politics and government somehow vaguely counted, and that it would be very difficult to demonstrate empirically they did.

These questions also figured prominently in the debates over interest groups and the structure of power in city government. For some, interest groups were key, not only as the principal unit of analysis, as in sociological research, but as the principal explanatory variable in political and governmental life as well. According to Bentley's influential *The Process of Government*, politics was essentially conflict between groups, each pursuing its own interests, and governments, whatever their form or composition, were nothing more than the "adjustments or balance" of these interests. There was no "interest of society as a whole" and little by way of an independent, autonomous role for public officials, whether appointed or elected. Even in their roles as "umpires," government officials would at best be reactive, without a life force of their own, responding to problems and proposals defined by others, and enacting policies that simply registered the strength of competing pressure groups (Bentley 1908, pp. 258–71). Although Bentley was neglected at the time by political scientists (Barnes 1921, pp. 493–94), interest group theory emerged as a dominant perspective on politics in the post World War II period (Latham 1952, Truman 1958).

For many group theorists, especially those who wrote in the late nineteenth and early twentieth centuries, "the adjustment of the conflicting interests always emerge[d] in one specific manner, namely the domination of the economically inferior majority by the economically powerful minority" (Barnes 1921, p. 494). The claim, or an important variant thereof, soon emerged as commonplace in the literature on local government and politics. In 1929, for example, Robert and Helen Lynd's pioneering study *Middletown* reported that business dominated civic affairs in Muncie, Indiana. Their findings were subsequently affirmed in numerous other community studies—in Atlanta as well as in Newburyport (MA), in Morris (IL) as well as in Philadelphia and Seattle, and in the Lynds' own follow-up study of Muncie, *Middletown in Transition*, published in 1937.

Stratification theory, as it came to be known, pictured communities as divided along socioeconomic lines (Polsby 1963). A single, upper-class group ruled in its own interests and against the competing interests of the lower class. The upper class ruled, moreover, by controlling public officials, who, though endowed with legal authority, were in practice subordinate to the ruling class. In Muncie, for example, "the business class [had] . . . little respect for local politics and politicians," viewing the "typical city official as a man of meager caliber" whom the "inner business ignore[d] economically and socially and used politically" (Lynd & Lynd 1937, cited in Polsby 1963, p. 16). Like interest group theory, stratification theory restored politics to the governing process, but it did so, ironically, by assigning little or no independent role to public officials.

These findings were questioned on several grounds, not least the assumption, common in the stratification literature, that political power and social economic status were one and the same, with the former inherent in the latter. This, critics noted, could not be taken for granted, any more than it could it be assumed the unequal distribution of resources such as money, social status, or prestige necessarily produced an unequal distribution of power. All resources were inert. Even if used to influence political outcomes, there were no guarantees they would be used effectively, or if so in one case, thus used in all. All these were questions to be studied empirically and, as Sayre & Polsby urged, by examining the "changes in behavior brought about by the actions of one person upon another." And they were to be studied by observing and analyzing "concrete decisions," not by simply reporting who informants believed had power (Sayre & Polsby 1965, p. 129).

Investigators who studied actual policy making reported a far less structured and determinative process than those reported by stratification or interest group theorists. "No single ruling elite dominates the political and governmental system of New York City," Sayre & Kaufman concluded from their classic study, *Governing New York City: Politics in the Metropolis* (1960, pp. 709–38). It was, rather, a highly decentralized system with policies emanating from "a multiplicity of decision centers" (p. 710). It was intensely political as well. The "system is . . . vigorously and incessantly competitive. The stakes of the city's politics are large, the contestants are numerous and determined, the rules of competition are known to and enforced against each other by the competitors themselves, and the city's electorate is so uncommitted to any particular contestant as to heighten competition for the electorate's support or consent" (p. 709–10). Interest groups were an important part of this. But "even they [were] compelled by the nature of the rules to accept roles as satellites," competing with other interest groups and with government and political officials to influence those "invested by the rules with the formal authority to legitimize decisions" (p. 712).

Though in many respects sui generis, New York City's government and politics were similar in many ways to those reported in other communities (Polsby 1971, Banfield & Wilson 1966). In New Haven, for example, Dahl and his colleagues found a fragmented system with numerous small groups active within, but seldom across, specific policy areas (Dahl 1961). It was a highly fluid system, one that had changed radically over the long term and in the short term was characterized by shifting political coalitions that often formed and re-formed from one set of issues to the next.

It was a system, further, in which public officials often acted autonomously and not simply as agents of a ruling elite or of interest groups; one in which public officials often used and even manipulated the private sector to advance their own policy goals. Although it was hard to define, Dahl and his associates pointed up the importance of political leadership, and how different city officials used the same resources with varying degrees of skill and success. These included not only the mayor, who was the central actor in the account, but city bureaucrats, in staff and line agencies alike, some of whom were quintessentially bureaucratic, others of whom were independent, imaginative, and innovative.

It was a system, finally, that was generally accessible to citizens, even though in normal course "the great body of citizens use[d] their political resources at a low level," leaving the active political stratum to a relatively small group of professionals (Dahl 1961, p. 305). There were a number of reasons for this, among them demographic changes in the city. Population changes often gave rise to new groups demanding access to the system. In some instances they might act largely on their own, relying principally on the mobilization of large numbers of similarly situated citizens or on the dedication, determination, and intensity of a small, newly engaged policy minority. Or they might be stirred into action by political mavericks, who are typically unconstrained by the prevailing rules of the game (Coleman 1957). In other instances, they might be courted by members of the political stratum hoping to transform a losing coalition into a winning one (Schattschneider 1942, Riker 1962). Most disagreements, it is true, were probably settled within the activist stratum—there are powerful incentives to do so (Vidich & Bensman 1958). But it is difficult to contain conflict entirely, especially when the stakes are high, as they are in large cities, and when there are what Dahl termed "slack resources" (1961, p. 305), including individuals and groups to be mobilized on behalf of one's political goals.

Conflict was difficult to contain additionally because of elections. Many citizens, of course, do not participate in elections or any other form of politics. But many do, and elections, like the hangman's noose, wonderfully focus the minds of public officials, serving as both a constraint and as a stimulus for those who hold or seek office. Elections are an occasion for heightened information on policies and performance across a wide range of issues, and although the information may be imperfect and citizens less than fully attentive, elections are unrivaled in this respect. They also provide a periodic opportunity for citizens to pause and reflect on their corporate responsibilities and to voice and to vote their support of candidates and issues. Moreover, as regularly scheduled occasions for public debate, elections can also be used by mavericks and outsiders to reach a broader audience as well as to distract regular candidates, cost them votes, and perhaps even be part of a coalition that throws the rascals out.

On the other hand, political leaders can also use elections to test and legitimate their policy agendas. Admittedly electoral mandates are notoriously ambiguous and it is difficult to establish precise causal links between the vote and specific policy outcomes. Elections, other than referenda and initiatives, are not structured for such analysis. Still, elections generally are an important occasion for proposing and debating broad policy initiatives, especially those affecting large numbers of citizens, widely shared values, or the future character of the community. And campaigns and elections, including but not limited to the actual vote, are important feedback mechanisms that may prompt leaders to continue on their current course or abandon it altogether. Or they may cause leaders to pause and redirect their efforts, as happened in New Haven when political costs of the city's urban renewal projects prompted its political leaders to embark on an ambitious anti-poverty project (Murphy 1971).

THE LEGACY

Much has been rediscovered in the "Lost World of Municipal Government" since the publication some 40 years ago of Herson's article, not least the re-affirmation of the proposition that there is more to governing cities than finely drawn municipal charters, carefully drafted ordinances, or the prescriptions of scientific management. Whether this constitutes a lost innocence is doubtful, though the view that governing was largely a matter of well-structured institutions and formal acts in the law is simpler and less cluttered and than what has been reported since. Indeed, its very simplicity may be key to its widespread appeal.

Although the literature is now richer and more nuanced—especially with respect to such core political science questions as who, if anyone, rules—the agenda is far from exhausted. The number and range of unresolved research questions remain as substantial today as when Sayre & Polsby (1965) proposed a scholarly agenda for "urban political science" some 35 years ago. Sayre & Polsby outlined several broad areas for investigation—a partial list includes "comparative analysis of community power," "emerging metropolitan systems," "political parties in urban America," "external political forces," and "urbanization and democracy in emergent nations"—and within each area, they suggested discrete research questions political scientists might profitably explore.

The agenda is comprehensive, so there is little warrant to expand it. The task, rather, is to revisit some of the questions posed by Sayre & Polsby in the context of broad issues raised earlier in this essay. I have in mind particularly whether the administrative state and federalism now constrain local self-government in ways akin to, yet radically different from, the constraints urged by municipal reformers at the close of the nineteenth century. Municipal reformers, it will be recalled, urged the separation of politics and administration, declared municipal affairs to be principally an administrative concern, and thereby hoped to limit the role of political parties, voters, and elected public officials. At the same time, they urged greater reliance on municipal administrators chosen for their special knowledge and protected by the classified service from the vagaries and uncertainties of politics.

Conditions have changed substantially since then. The public sector has grown and the role of state governments in local matters has expanded—even allowing for the earlier state legislative "meddling" that spurred the so-called Home Rule Movement. So too has the role of the national government, partly a heritage of the New Deal but more especially of the Great Society and its aftermath. Always supreme constitutionally, these governments are now major actors in such areas as public education, land use regulation, environmental policy, local law enforcement, and public health and welfare. All this, in turn, has arguably resulted in a narrowing of local discretion, especially as a result of the rules, regulations, and policies adopted by national and state administrators. Acting under broad mandates and delegations from their respective legislatures, these administrators do more than simply fill in the details, as judges sometimes claim, and even when simply filling in the details they constrain local officials in substantial ways.

Or so it seems from an admittedly casual review of administrative regulations, case law, and the public and private complaints of local public officials. But the case remains speculative, since there are no systematic data on these or competing perspectives. It may be, for example, that a rising tide lifts all boats, which is to say that an increase in the size of the public sector generally may increase authority and power at all levels of government. Or it may be, as Grodzins (1966) once suggested, that professionalism binds bureaucrats across governments, thus increasing the chances of some local input in the process, albeit not from local elected officials. Still, the broad issues warrant an occasional nod, to see not only whether local discretion has been narrowed but also the conditions under which this has occurred or is likely to occur. Interest groups with a national or statewide constituency might be one factor, since they might find it more economical to deal with one or a few governments rather than thousands. So too would external diseconomies, i.e., problems that spill over local governmental boundaries and require intervention by a more comprehensive jurisdiction. Still others might be "leveling" effects of democratic politics, or the trade-offs made by local elected officials wishing to shift their community's financial burdens elsewhere, albeit at the expense of local autonomy.

To pose these questions is not to imply American local government is in imminent danger of being reduced to parish pump politics. But the trends warrant investigation, as does the prior question, namely what if anything is at stake? Would it really matter whether local voters and local elected officials were limited still further in what they could do on their own? And what would it mean if cities and local governments generally were reduced to the status of administrative units that simply enforced the policy mandates of state and national governments? To what extent would such a shift benefit organized as opposed to unorganized interests, or at least those who can afford to mobilize statewide or nationally? And is it the case, finally, that shifting so much policy making to national and state agencies has produced the kind of governmental system advocated by earlier reformers, namely one in which policy making is insulated from local electoral politics—whether or not, as before, such an outcome is based on hesitations about the character and competence of today's urban voters and their ability to govern themselves?

The *Annual Review of Political Science* is online at http://polisci.annualreviews.org

LITERATURE CITED

American Political Science Association. 1904. Organization. *Proc. Am. Polit. Sci. Assoc.* 1:5–15

Banfield EC, Wilson JQ. 1966. *City Politics.* New York: Vintage Books

Barnes HE. 1921. Some contributions of soci-

ology to modern political theory. *Am. Polit. Sci. Rev.* XV:487–533

Beard CA. 1912. *American City Government: A Survey of Newer Tendencies.* New York: Century

Bentley AF. 1967 (1908). *The Process of*

Government, ed. PH Odegard. Cambridge, MA: Belknap Press of Harvard Univ. Press

Bishop JT. 1908. The burgermeister: Germany's chief municipal magistrate. *Am. Polit. Sci. Rev.* 2:396–410

Bryce J. 1891 (1888). *The American Commonwealth*. Vols. I, II. London/New York: Macmillan. 2nd ed.

Bryce J. 1909. The relations of political science to history and to practice. *Am. Polit. Sci. Rev.* III:1–19

Childs RS. 1952. *Civic Victories: The Story of an Unfinished Revolution*. New York: Harper & Brothers

Childs RS. 1965. *The First Fifty Years of the Council Manager Plan of Municipal Government*. New York: Natl. Municipal League

Coleman JS. 1957. *Community Conflict*. Glencoe, IL: Free

Dahl RA. 1961. *Who Governs? Democracy and Power in an American City*. New Haven, CT: Yale Univ. Press

Dawson RE, Robinson JA. 1963. Inter-party competition, economic variables and welfare policies. *J. Polit.* XXV:265–89

Downs A. 1973. *Opening Up the Suburbs*. New Haven, CT: Yale Univ. Press

Dye TR. 1966. *Politics, Economics and the Public: Policy Outcomes in the States*. Chicago: Rand McNally

Fabricant S. 1952. *The Trend of Government Activity in the United States Since 1900*. New York: Natl. Bur. Econ. Res.

Fry B, Winters R. 1970. The politics of redistribution. *Am. Polit. Sci. Rev.* LXIV:508–22

Goodnow FJ. 1900. *Politics and Administration*. New York: Macmillan

Goodnow FJ. 1904. The work of the American Political Science Association. *Proc. Am. Polit. Sci. Assoc.* 1:35–46

Grodzins M. 1966. *The American System: A New View of Government in the United States*, ed. DJ Elazar. Chicago: Rand McNally

Gulick L. 1957. Metropolitan organization. *Ann. Am. Acad. Soc. Polit. Sci.* 314:57–65

Herson JJR. 1957. The Lost World of Municipal Government. *Am. Polit. Sci. Rev.* LI:330–45

Jacobs J. 1961. *The Death and Life of Great American Cities*. New York: Random House

Judson FN. 1908. The future of representative government. *Am. Polit. Sci. Rev.* II:185–203

Latham E. 1952. *The Group Basis of Politics*. Ithaca, NY: Cornell Univ. Press

Lineberry RL, Fowler EP. 1967. Reformism and public policies in American cities. *Am. Polit. Sci. Rev.* LXI:701–16

Lowell AL. 1910. The physiology of politics. *Am. Polit. Sci. Rev.* IV:1–15

Lowell AL. 1926 (1913). *Public Opinion and Popular Government*. New York: Longmans Green

Lubell S. 1952. *The Future of American Politics*. New York: Harper

Lynd RS, Lynd HM. 1929. *Middletown*. New York: Harcourt Brace

Lynd RS, Lynd HM. 1937. *Middletown in Transition*. New York: Harcourt Brace

Merriam EC. 1908. *Primary Elections*. Chicago: Univ. Chicago Press

Mumford L. 1961. *The City in History: Its Origins, Its Transformation, and Its Prospects*. New York: Harcourt, Brace & World

Munro WB. 1923 (1909). *The Government of European Cities*. New York: Macmillan

Murphy RD. 1971. *Political Entrepreneurs and Urban Poverty*. Lexington, MA: DC Heath, Lexington Books

National Commission on Urban Problems. 1968. *Building the American City: A Report to Congress and to the President*. Washington, DC: US Gov. Print. Off.

North American Review. 1866. The right of suffrage. *North Am. Rev.* CIII:250

Olson M. 1965. *The Logic of Collective Action: Public Goods and the Theory of Groups*. Cambridge, MA: Harvard Univ. Press

Ostrogorski M. 1902. *Democracy and the Organization of Political Parties*. Vols. 1, 2. New York: Macmillan

Parkman F. 1878. The failure of universal suffrage. *North Am. Rev.* CCLXIII:1–20

Parton J. 1866. The government of New York City. *North Am. Rev.* CIII:413–65

Polsby N. 1963. *Community Power and Political Theory*. New Haven, CT: Yale Univ. Press

Riker WH. 1962. *The Theory of Political Coalitions*. New Haven, CT: Yale Univ. Press

Riordan WL. 1963. *Plunkitt of Tammany Hall*. New York: Dutton

Sayre WS, Kaufman H. *Governing New York City: Politics in the Metropolis*. New York: Russell Sage Fdn.

Sayre WS, Polsby NW. 1965. American political science and the study of urbanization. In *The Study of Urbanization*, ed. PM Hauser, LF Schnore, pp. 115–56. New York: Wiley

Schattschneider EE. 1942. *Party Government*. New York: Farrar & Rinehart

Smith RM. 1888. Control of immigration. *Polit. Sci. Q.* 3(1,2,3):46–77, 197–225, 409–24

Steffens L. 1904. *The Shame of the Cities*. New York: McClure Phillips

Steffens L. 1931. *The Autobiography of Lincoln Steffens*. New York: Harcourt Brace

Truman D. 1952. *The Governmental Process*. New York: Knopf

United States Bureau of the Census. 1949. *Historical Statistics of the United States: 1789–1945*. Washington, DC: US Gov. Print. Off.

Vidich AJ, Bensman J. 1958. *Small Town in Mass Society*. Princeton, NJ: Princeton Univ. Press

Warner SB. 1978 (1962). *Streetcar Suburbs: The Process of Growth in Boston, 1870–1900*. Cambridge, MA: Harvard Univ. Press. 2nd ed.

Weber A. 1899. *The Growth of Cities in the Nineteenth Century: A Study in Statistics*. New York: Publ. for Columbia Univ. by Macmillan

Wilson W. 1887. The study of administration. *Polit. Sci. Q.* 2:197–222

Annu. Rev. Polit. Sci. 2002. 5:87–110
DOI: 10.1146/annurev.polisci.5.100201.101909
Copyright © 2002 by Annual Reviews. All rights reserved

DEMOCRACY AND TAXATION

Andrew C. Gould and Peter J. Baker

*Department of Political Science, University of Notre Dame, Notre Dame, Indiana 46556;
e-mail: agould@nd.edu, pbaker@nd.edu*

Key Words   democratic institutions, spatial voting, veto players, agenda setter, fiscal policy

■ **Abstract**   Does democracy affect taxation? Do varieties of democratic institutions affect levels of revenue, methods of collection, and distributions of tax burdens? Many political scientists believe so despite the currently mixed evidence. Moreover, prominent models of fiscal politics yield differing predictions about whether and how elections, parties, constitutions, and legislative and executive decision rules influence policy choices. This essay reviews recent works on taxation under democracy with a focus on how scholars derive hypotheses about institutional effects. It evaluates the leading theories' main assumptions and implications, including the results of empirical tests so far. Many explanations focus mainly on electoral competition or on post-electoral governing, but not both, and draw their evidence from a small set of countries. Promising works develop more complete models of decision making, test hypotheses against a broader range of countries' experiences, and point toward more persuasive answers to current research questions.

INTRODUCTION

This essay provides an analytic summary of works in political science and political economics on the politics of taxation in democracies. Citizens and politicians alike care about tax revenue, collection techniques, and the distribution of tax burdens, all of which vary widely over time and across cases. For scholars, the recently widespread presence of democratic institutions reinforces the desire to understand the democratic politics of taxation, both in positive theory and in new empirical instances. Our survey focuses on hard-won insights about the workings of political institutions, clearly formulated models of economics and politics, and innovative research strategies. Nevertheless, more work remains to be done on how citizens and legislators work within and modify the core institutions of democracy and taxation.

The literature on the politics of taxation addresses three main types of dependent variables: revenue, methods of collection, and incidence. Revenue is important to scholars concerned with the overall size of government and to scholars interested in fiscal performance (Roubini & Sachs 1989, Alesina et al. 1997, Lieberman 2002). Methods of collection, such as tax rates and types, capture the attention

1094-2939/02/0615-0087$14.00

of researchers focused on tax law itself. Such a focus permits questions about the complexity versus simplicity of tax legislation (Steinmo 1993), reform episodes (Brownlee 1996, Zelizer 1998), and the use of special incentives (King 1993, Howard 1997). Finally, a bottom-line question for many scholars is: Who pays? This question inspires scholars to measure progressivity versus regressivity (Slemrod 1994, Bradford 1995); the contributions of various tax instruments (taxes on wages, income, sales, etc.) as shares of their respective bases, gross domestic product, or total government revenue (Campbell & Allen 1994, Williams & Collins 1997); and comparisons of rates on capital and labor incomes (Tanzi 1995). Choices among these dependent variables contribute to diversity within the literature.

In the first section of this essay, we examine a stylized view of policy making as a sequence of setting key objectives, making laws, and implementing policies. For each stage, we identify the main actors and institutions involved; we also find that the current scholarship concentrates on one stage at the expense of the others, missing opportunities for additional insights. The second section reviews the leading political and political-economic theories of fiscal policy with the aid of a heuristic typology. We argue that recent advances have been made by researchers using theories that hypothesize representational and governance effects of political institutions. In the third section, we examine in greater detail some of the leading models from which researchers derive hypotheses about how institutions influence policy. Our comparison of these models focuses on their main assumptions, their testable implications (including empirical confirmations so far), and the issues that remain unsettled. Space constraints force us to be selective. We limit ourselves to studies that include both theory and empirical testing. For broader surveys of political economics, see Drazen (2000) and Persson & Tabellini (2000). For a general introduction to the politics of taxation, see Peters (1991).

STAGES OF TAX POLICY

Political institutions shape fiscal policies at different stages in the policy-making process. By policy making, we mean an episode of political authorities acting within a formal or informal process to make a binding decision for a polity. To facilitate a review of the roles played by institutions, we employ what is labeled a stages heuristic model that organizes decision-making processes into three general phases: design, law making, and implementation. What follows is a brief discussion of how the literature treats institutions at each stage.

The design stage refers to specifying policy goals, establishing priorities among them, and comparing the means of achieving them. Economists and political economists studying fiscal policy in developing countries have made fiscal policy design a primary focus, whereas its processes are generally understudied in other fields of political science and policy studies.

Scholars of this stage focus on trade-offs. Tax reform requires governments to address several issues simultaneously, including the breadth and scope of reform, revenue goals, equity goals, resource allocation goals, and timing (Gillis 1989a).

Fiscal policies involve inherent trade-offs among administration, efficiency, equity, political acceptability, and revenue (Burgess & Stern 1993). Policy design in the context of development, in particular, allows us to observe more clearly the evidence of the clash of values or objectives in the drafting process (Goode 1990). Given this context, observers debate the strengths and weaknesses of comprehensive (Gillis 1989a) versus incremental (Jenkins 1989) reform in achieving desired results.

The literature also suggests that the people facing the dilemma of trade-offs vary. In developed countries, accountants, economists, lawyers, policy analysts, professional lobbyists, and even regular citizens can provide input during the design phase of tax law. Developing-country cases involve far fewer actors (Gordon & Thuronyi 1996). However, in these cases, international actors are more likely to be involved [e.g., technical assistants from international financial institutions (Tanzi 1994)].

Designers can anticipate the law-making and implementation stages. Legally articulated principles such as equality, fair play, proportionality, ability to pay, nonretroactivity, and other possible legal limitations (e.g., a tax payer bill of rights or international agreements) may constrain legislative options (Vanistendael 1996). There may also be constraints on the extent to which the legislature is allowed to delegate tax law-making authority. In addition to these institutional constraints, language and local techniques in drafting contribute to variation in law design (Thuronyi 1996a).

However, many studies of design omit important issues. The highly descriptive nature of these works gives little indication as to why certain principles and objectives are chosen over others in the trade-off scenario. Elections are often inappropriately disregarded as a determinant of which trade-offs occur. Finally, there is still much to learn about how actors involved in policy design anticipate the challenges that arise in subsequent stages.

The second stage, law making, includes the official drafting and proposal of fiscal legislation, the resulting debate, the attachment of amendments, voting, and signing into law. What differentiates this stage from the design stage, where multiple debates can take place, is who controls access. Law making begins when an item becomes part of the institutional agenda in the legislature or executive, after which that branch directly controls access to legislation under consideration. Two broad types of institutions frame the law-making stage: exogenous and endogenous institutions. Exogenous institutions are those rules and procedures that cannot legally be changed by a legislature (Cox 2000) or executive acting alone, such as the division of power and often the electoral and party systems. These institutions have been explored for their ability to explain variation in decision making and policies (Alesina et al. 1999, Hallerberg & von Hagen 1999). Endogenous institutions can be changed by a unilateral act of one branch; examples include choices regarding proposal and amendment rights and committee systems within a legislature and choices regarding fiscal contracts versus delegation to a strong finance minister within executives (Hallerberg 1999). We view work on the interaction of exogenous and endogenous institutions and on the choices among endogenous institutions as especially promising.

The third and final stage of policy making is implementation. Perhaps the boldest declaration regarding implementation asserts, "tax administration is tax policy" (Casanegra 1987, p. 25). Analysts develop two themes. First, some suggest that reform-minded legislators should assume problems of implementation and write legislation accordingly. The World Bank insists that reformers ensure that "changes in tax policy are compatible with administrative capacity" (1991, p. 51); on the same subject, Bird cautions that "policy change without administrative change is nothing" (1991, p. 39). Policy analysts often call for straightforward reforms to address administrative constraints. They claim that rationalizing state bureaucracies through computerization, better taxpayer registration, and auditing techniques, and constructing appropriate penalty structures can accomplish this (Bird & Casanegra 1992, Casanegra et al. 1992). Others disagree with the notion that weak administrations can so easily be fixed. Limited administrative capacity is more likely the function of more profound conditions than the simple lack of proper incentives and techniques (Bird 1989). In sum, anticipated administrative (in)capacities are conceptualized as yet another institutional constraint on the policy-making process (Bird & Oldman 1990).

A second research theme within the implementation phase addresses the principal-agent relationship between legislators and bureaucrats. Investigation into the bureaucratic drift that separates lawmakers' intentions from actual administrative behavior demonstrates how interests on each side affect policy choices (McCubbins et al. 1987, 1989; Calvert et al. 1989; Bawn 1995). Scholars are now developing a comparative theory of delegation, in which legislators wrestle with the trade-offs between giving bureaucrats a great deal of discretion in implementation, allowing bureaucrats to collect valuable information while exercising their expertise, or writing detailed statutes that allow for little discretion, resulting in administrative delays and less information for elected policy makers (Huber et al. 2001). However, we know even less about what this give and take looks like in new, institutionally weaker democracies. Compared with their colleagues in developed countries, legislators in developing countries or countries in transition often lack the ability to make effective decisions. State agents are in a position of greater bargaining power. Problems with implementation are expected, then, when newly passed laws conflict with the financial interests or authoritative control currently enjoyed by bureaucrats (Way 2001).

Like the design phase, the implementation phase merits much more work to understand its political dynamics. Research agendas exploring general administrative constraints are highly descriptive of implementation procedures and too often focus on prescribing policy in response. There is little analysis of how the politics of implementation explains observed policy choices. Applications of principal-agent theories can be tested with developing-country experiences and can be oriented to explaining why a particular reform policy was chosen over alternative choices.

This initial overview suggests ways to improve our understanding of how political institutions affect policy. Scholars can develop research strategies that better incorporate the stages of design and implementation theoretically and empirically, employ evidence that is balanced between new and old democracies, and devote more attention to actors' use of and modifications to decision-making procedures.

POLITICAL EXPLANATIONS FOR TAXATION

Virtually every scholar agrees that taxes involve politics. Yet the leading explanations of taxation employ different analytic perspectives and generate different hypotheses about the roles of political institutions. One dimension on which explanations differ is whether the researcher adopts a predominantly top-down perspective, in which elites and their interactions are the major determinants of tax policies, or a predominantly bottom-up perspective, in which the main determinants emerge from the underlying society. A second dimension on which explanations differ is whether the researcher employs a micro-analytic perspective, which specifies individual motivations and how they aggregate in particular settings to generate behavioral predictions, or a macro-analytic perspective, which begins with regularities about collectivities and shows how they combine to produce broad generalizations. The combination of these two dimensions yields four basic types of explanations and associated hypotheses (see Table 1).

Explanations in the first group focus on the fiscal goals of elites in a macro-analytic perspective. The basic logic is that an organized group of people that collects taxes can be seen as a unitary actor that pursues a basic goal such as maximizing revenue, security, or efficiency; the label for this actor is the overall organization (e.g., the state) or its head (the ruler). Schumpeter coined the label "tax state" to summarize the centrality of the modern state's fiscal needs and to

TABLE 1   Analytic perspectives and hypothesized roles for political institutions in theories of fiscal policy

	Micro-analytic	Macro-analytic
Top-down	**Constraints on Policy Makers**	**Leviathan or Benevolent Dictator**
	Strategic interactions among policy makers limit possible policies	Ruler maximizes revenue or efficiency
	Laver & Schofield 1990	Schumpeter 1991 [1918]
	Roubini & Sachs 1989	Brennan & Buchanan 1980
	models of post-electoral governance	Barro 1979
Bottom-up	**Preference Filters**	**Structurally Determined**
	Preference aggregation determines whose voice enters policy making	Underlying society (culture, economy, geopolitics) drives policy
	Hansen 1998	Peters 1980
	Powell 2000	Tarschys 1988
	models of voting in elections	Tilly 1990

express his concern that the revenue demands of the tax state could go so far as to undermine capitalism itself (1991 [1918], p. 100). More recently, Brennan & Buchanan (1980) develop what they term the Leviathan model, in which the ruler seeks simply to maximize revenue. Also in this category are benevolent-dictator models, in which the rulers maximize a variable that is more positively evaluated by analysts. For example, in optimal taxation models, a benevolent social planner sets tax rates to maximize the welfare over time of a representative consumer in the society (Barro 1979, Lucas & Stokey 1983).

The generality of the top-down, Leviathan, and benevolent-dictator models diminishes their usefulness in developing explanations for cross-national or temporal differences. Rulers may want to maximize revenue or efficiency, but they do so under constraints that remain to be specified. A more productive research agenda investigates the conditions of maximization with a different set of hypotheses (a move toward the upper-left cell of Table 1). This is the path taken by Levi (1988). Although she starts with the assumption that rulers maximize revenue under constraints, the explanatory work is done by the constraints (the ruler's bargaining power vis-à-vis society, transaction costs, and the ruler's discount rate). For example, Levi contends that representative institutions have reduced transaction costs by publicizing the fairness of the system and by assuring taxpayers that funds will be used as intended.

Other explanations take a bottom-up, macro-analytic perspective (lower-right cell of Table 1). In these explanations, policies emerge out of underlying societal conditions, and political institutions are hypothesized to be mainly structurally determined. Peters argues that political culture explains the "stable clusterings of taxation patterns among groups of industrialized democracies that persisted even with economic and political change" (1980, p. 6; 1991). Haycraft (1985) argues that the anti-statist values of many French and Italian citizens explains in part why their states' respective tax systems are highly dependent on indirect taxation. In the development literature, scholars investigate cultural barriers to tax reform (Newbery & Stern 1987, Bird & Oldman 1990, Burgess & Stern 1993). Political culture is often only the starting point of an investigation that turns to a more detailed study of how regime institutions mediate social norms. Other research agendas explore how economic structures and the geopolitical context affect taxation. For example, Tarschys (1988) describes how each of the basic means of revenue extraction (tributes, tariffs, taxes, and trade) emerged at a different phase of economic development. Tilly (1990) similarly points to the monetarization of economies as an important factor for explaining fundamental changes in taxation, but he also emphasizes that geopolitical settings and war exerted varying pressures on rulers to extract the resources necessary to compete successfully.

Theoretical lacunae characterize the demand-driven models, especially when applied to democratic politics, for they leave out the crucial steps between the demands generated in the society and the outputs produced in the political process. Do all political systems equally and fully translate demands into output? If not, which institutions select the expression of various demands and with what effects? Are there variations in the supply of public goods across political systems? Why do some political systems produce decisive action, whereas others seem to be stuck with an undesirable status quo? These are the questions that pure demand models cannot address on their own. To answer them, analysts develop explanations that incorporate the means by which demands are expressed, aggregated, and balanced against each other.

A third group of explanations takes a bottom-up, micro-analytic perspective (lower-left cell of Table 1). In several versions of this view, regime institutions filter out some demands so that they cannot affect the formation of fiscal policy and amplify other demands so that they have more say in decision making. The primary institutions that are thought to have these filtering and amplifying effects are associated with elections, the central way that mass preferences work their way into the decision-making of governments and ultimately into policy outputs. Thus, scholars emphasize characteristics of elections, variations in the right to vote and turnout, majoritarian versus proportional rules for converting votes into legislative seats, rules for election scheduling, and two-party versus multiparty systems.

The filtering and amplifying effects of institutions are observed in empirical works from diverse theoretical traditions. For the United States, Hansen (1998) takes advantage of the single distribution of underlying public preferences that is projected into government through three different rules for aggregating preferences via the House, Senate, and Presidency. With a natural experiment created by different institutions in the same country, Hansen explores how the different rules of aggregation explain the different positions of these three governing institutions in fiscal policy debates of the 1980s. Cross-national research on governments and opinion in the advanced industrial democracies finds that majoritarian systems produce governments distant from the preferences of the median voter, whereas proportional systems produce governments more consistently close to the preferences of the median voter (Huber & Powell 1994, Powell 2000). Scholars of comparative political economy contend that proportional systems (along with other institutions such as organized labor) grant voice to diffuse societal interests, rather than to privileged and narrow special interests as in majoritarian systems, and that this broader interest representation yields more redistributive public policy (Birchfield & Crepaz 1998, Steinmo & Tolbert 1998, Wilensky 2002). Spatial models of voting fit within this third group of explanations and are widely employed as a foundation for explanations of fiscal policies (several spatial models are discussed more fully in the next section).

Finally, the fourth group of explanations employs top-down micro-analytic perspectives (upper-left cell of Table 1). According to these accounts, decision makers have policy preferences and strategic reasoning abilities. Their interactions within a particular institutional setting produce policies. The main research hypotheses examine whether varied institutions alter the calculations of actors and thereby ultimately influence the final policy. Institutions that figure prominently in these models include constitutions and party systems that affect the number of actors involved and their possible actions. For example, Laver & Schofield (1990, p. 248) contend that single-party governance entails partisan cycles, rapid policy making, and quick fiscal adjustments. Coalition governments, they argue, avoid partisan cycles and produce a long-lived status quo, even in the face of new external conditions. Many scholars find that multiparty and divided governments ran larger deficits than single-party and unified governments (Roubini & Sachs 1989, Alesina & Rosenthal 1995, Alesina et al. 1997; but see Borelli & Royed 1995). Constitutions and other institutions specify what happens if no new policy is adopted and which political actors have the rights to draw up, propose, and amend new revenue legislation. Research hypotheses building on Romer & Rosenthal's (1978) agenda-setter model therefore investigate whether varied assignments of these rights lead to different policy choices.

In our judgment, exciting work on the politics of fiscal policies pursues hypotheses about the influence of regime institutions on policies. By contrast, and despite their important contributions, pure Leviathan, benevolent-dictator, and demand models are too broadly drawn to help answer the questions that currently motivate research in political science and political economics. In seeking explanations for variation across countries and over time, researchers can turn to theories that permit them to model constraints on maximization and the deviations from optimal performance. Similarly, rather than assuming that demands are satisfied, researchers can explain how individual preferences enter the political process and consider whether they are differentially influential. In addition, some research questions effectively presuppose the possibility that institutions matter: Does democracy affect taxation? Do the varieties of democratic decision-making institutions have fiscal implications? These are hard but tractable questions. The next section examines leading research strategies for answering them.

ASSESSING MODELS OF POLICY DETERMINATION

This section considers how researchers derive and test hypotheses about the role of institutions. As we have seen, many scholars view elections as the core institution that determines policies. In the first subsection below, we discuss several spatial voting models centered on elections. Other scholars are more impressed by the problems of governing after elections, so, in the second subsection, we turn to post-electoral governing and models of decision-maker interactions. In the third subsection, we review models that integrate electoral and post-electoral politics. Wherever possible, we compare empirical findings associated with the various models. We cannot always make direct contrasts, however, because the models frequently do not try to explain the same dependent variables, and not all of the models have so far been used to guide systematic empirical research.

Spatial Voting

In spatial models, elections translate public preferences into government policies. Several assumptions are common to most spatial models applied to fiscal politics: Each voter cares about her own post-tax, post–government spending income and considers the candidates' announced policies from this point of view; each voter chooses the candidate who puts forward the policy that is best for her own situation. A candidate has some knowledge of the electorate and announces a policy platform to maximize some goal, such as gaining office or ensuring the best policy. Each candidate knows that any other candidate is also announcing a platform. The strategic policy selections of the candidates thus introduce elements of top-down analysis focused on elites. Nevertheless, the main empirical emphasis is from the bottom up, for the electorate's characteristics determine which candidate (and platform) wins. With an emphasis on electorate characteristics in mind, researchers can use a spatial model to generate policy predictions from observable features of societies and their electoral behavior, such as overall income, inequality, and turnout.

MEDIAN VOTER   The median voter theorem is the spatial model most widely applied to fiscal politics (see Table 2). This approach assumes the existence of (only)

TABLE 2   Two policy-convergent spatial-voting models of policy determination

	Median voter	**Probabilistic voting**
Actors	Policy-oriented voters, office-seeking candidates[a]	Policy-oriented voters, office-seeking candidates[b]
What determines policy?	Candidates converge on median voter's preference	Candidates converge on weighted preferences of all voters
Impact on policy of:		
–elections?	Via turnout, a large effect on which voter occupies median	Via political costs, a large effect on marginal benefits of policy
–parties?	Not modeled	Not modeled
–constitutions?	Via turnout, a small effect on which voter occupies median	Not modeled
–decision rules?	Not modeled	Not modeled
Testable implications	Tax revenue varies with: turnout inequality and development interaction of democracy and development Meltzer & Richard 1981, 1983; Boix 2001; Franzese 2002	Elections and diverse voters jointly cause multiple rates, bases, and special provisions No flat tax in democracy Tax complexity varies with franchise, competitiveness Hettich & Winer 1999
Unsettled issues	Multidimensional policies Multiple and fractile fallacies Policy-seeking candidates Divergence in platforms Post-election policy making	Unobserved voter preferences Few testable predictions Institutions not modeled Policy-seeking candidates Divergence in platforms Post-election policy making

[a]One-dimensional policy choice; candidates know electoral impact of choice with certainty.

[b]Multidimensional policy choice; candidates uncertain about electoral impact of choice.

one manipulable element of tax policy (the first such applications are Romer 1975 and Roberts 1977). In the influential formulation of Meltzer & Richard (1981), society has the one-dimensional policy choice of setting a linear income tax rate. Candidates know with certainty the electoral implications of selecting a particular tax rate and care only about holding office. It can be shown that candidates converge on the same policy platform in equilibrium. (Additional assumptions include that all tax revenue goes to transfer payments in equal lump sums to individuals, that the budget is balanced, and that voters know the costs and benefits of the redistribution they demand, including incentive effects on work and consumption.)

The regime institutions that are hypothesized to matter are those that increase (decrease) turnout and therefore typically select a voter relatively low (high) on the income distribution to occupy the median position; such a voter wants more (less) taxing and spending. Meltzer & Richard (1981, 1983) test a model with time-series data on the United States (1937–1940, 1946–1976) and the United Kingdom (1953–1979). Elaborations of the model and pooled time-series analyses cover OECD (Organisation for Economic Co-operation and Development) countries (Franzese 2002) and 65 countries (Boix 2001). Among OECD democracies, Franzese finds that higher rates of voter participation were associated with higher demands for taxing and spending; this turnout effect is magnified by greater income inequality. Boix (2001) finds that public sectors grew in parallel to the structural changes associated with economic development under democratic regimes, but in authoritarian regimes, the size of the public sector remained smaller (but see Cheibub 1998 for contrasting results). Boix also finds a turnout effect and relatively small effects on the size of the state from varied constitutional arrangements (presidentialism exerts a negative indirect effect by suppressing turnout; proportional representation exerts an indirectly positive effect by enhancing turnout; federalism has a small indirect and direct effect).

Notwithstanding the simplicity of its premises and its explanatory power for certain questions, the median voter model has limitations. One problem is the restrictive condition that the fiscal decision concerns only one dimension. In practice, policy makers consider multiple tax instruments and multiple tax bases. Tax incidence involves multiple dimensions as well, especially the balance between regressivity and progressivity of the tax system, in addition to the overall burden of taxation. Unfortunately, the unidimensional policy assumption does not provide a starting point for explaining the different ways that states collect revenue or the different patterns of incidence. Purely self-serving candidates do not square with partisans who care about policies. The equilibrium prediction of policy convergence is difficult to match with competing candidates who offer dissimilar campaign platforms. An observational limit to the model is that characteristics of the median voter are highly correlated with characteristics of other voters, and thus most tests of the model cannot distinguish between median voter–driven results and results that are driven by voters in other areas of the distribution. Finally, the model abstracts away intraparty and intragovernmental bargaining and provides few insights into how campaign platforms become laws.

PROBABILISTIC VOTING   Probabilistic voting models permit analysts to incorporate many-sided political issues into the analysis and derive hypotheses about complex policy choices (see Table 2). A key assumption is that candidates do not know for certain the electoral implications of their platforms (see Austen-Smith 1991 for a critique). Each voter, not just the median voter, has at least some positive probability of voting for a given candidate. With this in mind, a candidate seeking to maximize vote plurality (or likelihood of winning) needs to direct programmatic adjustments to the vote choices of all voters. According to the representation theorem (analogous to the median voter theorem), probabilistic voting in a multidimensional policy space yields an equilibrium prediction in which competing candidates converge on the same (multidimensional) policy.

With candidates converging on the same platform in probabilistic models, the research problem similarly becomes a bottom-up question of ascertaining the electorate's demands for taxation. For example, in a comparative analysis of state and local taxation in the 50 US states, Chernick & Reschovsky (1996) seek to explain differences in the progressivity and regressivity of tax structures. Volkerink & de Haan (1999) seek to explain variation in the mix of tax instruments (personal income taxation, public pension contributions, and consumption taxes) across OECD countries from 1965 to 1995. Nevertheless, the difficulty of imputing interests to fiscal interest groups, partly due to individual mobility across income groups over time, and other obstacles (discussed in greater detail below), have so far limited the successful empirical applications of probabilistic voting to explaining tax structures.

A probabilistic spatial voting approach to fiscal politics is most fully elaborated by Winer and Hettich (Winer & Hettich 1998, Hettich & Winer 1999). They model the minimal conditions under which the optimal political platform of a governing party has the important features of actual tax systems observed in advanced democracies, namely multiple rates, bases, and special exemptions. Such realistically complex tax platforms emerge from the electoral struggle between parties that must propose fiscal policies that cost-effectively distinguish among economically and politically heterogeneous taxpayers. A simple and provocative statement is that no party hoping to win a general election in a democracy would ever propose a real flat tax, because more revenue can be raised with less political opposition if the party proposes varied rates across individuals.

The limitations of the probabilistic voting model of fiscal policy require further attention. First, the model's current formulation does not yet offer predictions about how institutions other than elections produce varied fiscal calculations, nor does it include any room for policy making apart from campaign positioning. Hettich & Winer themselves informally examine how the constitutional separation of powers in the United States, compared with the parliamentary system in Canada, contributes to observed differences in tax policies and tax policy–making processes. Fully in the spirit of this essay, they call for researchers to model the effects of such institutions on measured economic variables. Second, it is difficult to reconcile the central assertion that every feature of tax policy is an equilibrium choice of the incumbent party with the potential for political market failure. In other words, a researcher using the probabilistic model alone cannot determine if a particular policy rule indeed emerged from a fiscal-political calibration. Only a detailed historical reconstruction of a given policy decision can rule out other possibilities, such as that a policy developed as a trade-off for some other nonfiscal policy (such as a regulation) or even from a failed drive for efficiency. Third, in many cases the competing models of policy determination produce observationally equivalent predictions; even more problematically, the probabilistic model employs hard-to-measure independent variables (such as the weights assigned to each voter and the detailed calculations of costs and benefits that each type of voter receives under various policies). Although some general predictions can be sustained, researchers using the model have not yet produced a full range of empirically testable implications (Poterba 1999, p. 431). Fourth, the reliance on policy convergence may not satisfy scholars impressed by persistent divergence among political parties.

PARTISAN COMPETITION   A formal treatment of economic and political equilibria in which competing parties offer different policies can be found in the partisan competition model (see Table 3). This model avoids purely venal candidates and takes a different view of party formation. Roemer (2001) conceives of parties as composed of three factions of activists. The first two factions are the familiar opportunists who seek office (Downs 1957) and reformers who seek the best

TABLE 3   A policy-divergent spatial-voting model of policy determination

	Partisan competition

Actors	Policy-seeking voters;
	  parties composed of three factions:
	  office-, policy-, and publicity-seeking activists[a]

What determines policy?	Platforms in party unanimity Nash equilibria
Effect on policy of:	
–elections?	Competition between parties leads to partial convergence
–parties?	Factional bargaining within each party prevents complete convergence
–constitutions?	Not modeled
–decision rules?	Not modeled

Testable implications	Both left and right parties support progressive taxes;
	  competing parties offer different tax policies;
	  taxes vary inversely with salience of non-fiscal issues.
	Roemer 2001

Unsettled issues	Empirical confirmation Post-election policy making

[a]Multidimensional policy choice; activists uncertain about electoral impact of choice.

attainable policy outcomes under present circumstances (Wittman 1973). The third faction is new to formal modeling, although well-known to most political observers. This third group contains militants who place no value on winning the current election, nor on influencing the next government's policy. Instead, militants seek publicity for their ideal policy so that voters eventually will adopt that policy as their own ideal as well. Another way to conceive of reformers and militants is that they both care about policy but at different time discount rates. The model assumes multidimensional policy choices as inputs as well as uncertainty among parties about the electoral implications of policy platforms. Bargaining among the factions within each party crucially reduces the acceptable policy space for each party and thus goes a long way toward generating stable pairs of policies offered by competing parties. Each party offers a platform from which its three factions do not unanimously wish to deviate, given the platform of the other party, which defines a party unanimity Nash equilibrium.

Several stylized facts about democratic politics fit the model. In particular, candidates generally make importantly divergent policy proposals in the course of political campaigns. The campaigns, moreover, typically generate debates that simultaneously involve many dimensions, such as taxes, deficits, social spending, defense spending, and additional nonfiscal issues, such as religion, nationalism, and citizenship. Moreover, parties are indeed uncertain about the outcome of elections and even with modern polling techniques cannot predict unfailingly the electoral implications of their policy pronouncements.

The partisan model also offers novel explanations for some important puzzles. Why do political parties on both the left and right of the political spectrum support progressive taxation? Why do the poor not expropriate the rich? Each has been answered before, and Roemer's answers involve complex computations. It is nevertheless laudable that a single theory resolves them (and others) without resort to ad hoc amendments.

An important limitation invites further attention. Empirical tests of the partisan competition model do not yet employ time-series and cross-national research designs. Such tests would help the model compete with other formal models as a foundation for explaining different features of politics and economics. For example, Roemer formally derives the hypothesis that tax levels should vary inversely with the political salience of nonfiscal issues (such as ethnicity or religion) and provides rough anecdotal confirmation; a systematic test would be worthwhile.

SUMMARY   Despite their limitations, spatial voting models of how elections determine tax policies help researchers make key findings about institutions. Median voter models contend that electoral turnout and democracy boost tax revenues because both institutions select for a relatively income-poor median decision maker who demands taxation to fund redistribution and public goods. Yet many analysts question the applicability of median voter models to multidimensional policy choices under electoral uncertainty; in addition, scholars disagree about the empirical relationships between income inequality and tax revenues and between democracy and revenues (both of which are implied by the theorem). Probabilistic models powerfully explain the complexity of taxation under democracy as the product of competitive elections in a heterogeneous electorate. Such models effectively set out a research agenda for understanding varied structures of taxation across cases, but so far the empirical testing has been slowed by difficulties in modeling and measuring complex voter preferences. A partisan competition model explains the ubiquity of divergent but still progressive taxation platforms from both left and right parties as the joint product of electoral competition and intraparty bargaining, but this positive theory requires additional cross-national and time-series testing to become a robust explanation for policy choices. A final limitation applies to all of the models that focus on elections: None devotes sustained attention to the post-electoral process of making decisions. The key steps of proposing, enacting, and implementing legislation all appear under the rubric of fulfilling campaign promises and/or choosing platforms as part of the run-up to the next election. In the spatial models of voting, politicians campaign and citizens vote, but no one governs.

Post-Electoral Governance

For sustained attention to policy-making processes, scholars can turn to several models of post-electoral governance. The basic insight is that decision making in democracies frequently involves several elected officials. Policy can be seen to emerge from their strategic interactions. Like other micro-analytic, actor-centered approaches, such models require making certain assumptions about who is involved, their preferences, their available options, and the sequence in which they make choices. The rest of this subsection spells out how analysts define these elements.

VETO PLAYERS   A veto players model is one of the two predominant post-electoral governance models (see Table 4). Tsebelis (1995a,b) builds on collective choice theory to construct the basics of this type of model. A veto player is a person or group whose agreement is required for a new policy to be adopted. Each player is assumed to have preferences over possible policies. When a player is a group, the decision rule for that group (e.g., unanimity, super-majority, majority) must be specified. The status quo is the location of the current policy within the policy space (of one or more dimensions). The winset of the status quo is defined as the set of policies that can defeat the status quo according to the institutional voting rule in place for these veto players. (For example, in a three-party coalition government deciding by unanimity, the winset of the status quo is the set of all policies that all three parties prefer to the status quo.) In the veto players model, policy stability does not decrease as the number of players increases, as their policy preferences diverge, and as the internal coherence of group players (such as parties) increases.

Who or what counts as a veto player in an empirical analysis? The coding procedures depend on constitutional structures and parties. In a parliamentary-ministerial system, each party in the government coalition counts as one (partisan) veto player; in a congressional-presidential system, each branch controlled by a different party counts as one (institutional) veto player; in a multicameral system,

TABLE 4 Two post-electoral models of policy determination

	Veto players	Agenda setter
Actors	Policy-seeking partisan and institutional players	Policy-seeking committee and chamber
What determines policy?	Players approve law that all prefer to status quo	Committee proposes law nearest ideal that chamber prefers to status quo
Effect on policy of:		
–elections?	PR increases number of partisan veto players	Not modeled
–parties?	Internal divisions increase status quo bias[a]	Not modeled
–constitutions?	Presidential-congressionalism and multicameralism increase number of institutional veto players	Not modeled
–decision rules?	Not modeled	Majoritarian proposal and amendment rules enhance agenda control
Testable implications	Status quo bias increases with players' number	Status quo bias increases with agenda control
	Policy reform *iff* some policy jointly preferred to status quo	Policy nearest to committee's ideal that chamber prefers to status quo
	No-action policy anticipates reform/stability	Stewart 1991, Huber 1996
	Hallerberg & Basinger 1998, Bawn 1999, Steinmo 1993	
Unsettled issues	Counting players in new democracies	Origins of decision rules
	Broader empirical confirmation	Agenda control in new democracies
	Citizen responses	Broader empirical confirmation
	Origins of player preferences	Citizen responses
		Origins of player preferences

[a]Assumes that parties are collective actors deciding by majority rule. We have yet to find an empirical test of the proposition that internal party coherence/incoherence affects status quo bias in fiscal policy.

each chamber controlled by a different party counts as one (institutional) veto player. Given the relatively frequent changes in governing coalitions and partisan control of varied institutions, measures of veto players exhibit greater variability over time than do measures of constitutional and party systems alone.

Comparative research tests the proposition that multiple veto players lead to more stable tax policy. For example, the number of veto players in advanced industrial democracies was associated with sticky statutory tax rates in the late

1980s (Hallerberg & Basinger 1998, 1999; Wagschal 1998; but see Ganghof 1999). The consequences of multiple veto players can accumulate over time, as well: Boix (2001) finds that presidentialism (compared with parliamentarism) has a strongly negative direct effect on government revenue through a status quo bias in an otherwise upward-trending series.

With the aid of additional information beyond the number of veto players, this type of model can also generate more finely grained hypotheses about the nature of change and its timing. In particular, the analyst needs information about the precise preferences of the players and about the nature of the status quo policy outcome (Bawn 1999, p. 708). For example, Bawn's analysis of German fiscal policies from 1961 to 1989 (on the spending side) shows that policies changed in response to shifts in the partisan composition of government, but only when a winset analysis predicts policy change.

A veto player model of fiscal policy in a large-N analysis remains to be tested. The country studies of Haggard & McCubbins (2001) assemble characterizations of key variables that are required to develop the more detailed, one-case-at-a-time empirical implications of a veto player analysis. In particular, the case studies focus on agenda control (who can propose new legislation), the identification of veto players and their preferences, and reversionary outcomes (the outcome that obtains if no new legislation is passed). The empirical chapters cover single countries, except for one chapter that compares two countries. At the outset, Haggard & McCubbins seek to uncover how and when institutions affect policy outcomes; at the end of the book, they claim to have presented a theory of institutional effects on policy (2001, pp. 1, 324), yet the book never gets beyond general assertions about institutional effects. Given the foundation provided by case studies and synthetic statements, some scholars may pursue a more clearly specified, comparative treatment of veto players in a medium- to large-N analysis.

AGENDA SETTER   Agenda setter models allow scholars to explore the impact of different distributions of proposal and amendment rights among decision makers (see Table 4). In these models, an institution, such as a committee, has the right to propose new legislation; where this right is exclusive, the committee exercises monopoly agenda control or perfect gate-keeping ability. Another institution, such as the whole chamber, then has the right to vote the (amended) proposal up or down against the status quo. The actors in both institutions have preferences over policies. The strategic interaction of the actors can be examined by working backward from the last move: The chamber will approve any policy it prefers to the status quo and will vote down any policy that it does not prefer to the status quo. On the first move, the agenda setter anticipates what will unfold later by proposing the policy nearest to its own ideal that the chamber will approve. Baron & Ferejohn (1989) developed an influential Rubenstein-Ståhl bargaining model of this type for the US Congress. Diermeier & Feddersen (1998) elaborate a model in which agenda setting is valuable to explain why legislators in parliamentary-ministerial systems vote more cohesively with other legislators (even across party lines) than legislators do in congressional-presidential systems.

Applications of agenda setter models to national fiscal policy have little to say about different types of elections, parties, or constitutions, but instead concentrate on the legislative decision rules that most other types of models ignore. The main hypothesis of agenda setter models of fiscal policy is that restrictive proposal and amendment rules enhance agenda control by the majority. A testable implication is that agenda control should lead to a status quo bias, especially when the preferences of the chamber have changed more than the preferences of the committee. Stewart (1991) develops such an explanation for the absence of major tax reform in the United States in the post–World War II period up through the early 1980s.

Huber's (1996) analysis of the package vote procedure in the French National Assembly develops an agenda setter model in a comparative context supported by evidence regarding debates over fiscal legislation. Under the package vote procedure, the government requires the assembly to consider a bill and government-sponsored amendments as a single package in an up-or-down vote without further amendments. This procedure thus reflects a very strong monopoly agenda and amendment control by the government. The hypothesis is that the governing coalition uses the package vote to protect bargains among governing parties from subsequent log-rolls. Huber finds empirical support for two tests implied by the main hypothesis. First, distributive bargains, such as those involved in tax legislation, received package protections more frequently than did the nondistributive bargains of other types of legislation. Second, complex bargains received more frequent protection than simple bargains (1996, pp. 92–96).

The origins of decision rules are not settled by generic agenda setter models, and in this area scholars can expect new findings in the future. Scholars of the US Congress debate the relative merits of partisan (Binder 2001), informational (Krehbiel 1998), and median voter (Schickler 2000) explanations. For France, Huber (1996) provides historical and analytic accounts of how restrictive voting procedures emerged. Powell (2000) contends that the majoritarian versus proportional balance in decision rules tends to match the majoritarian versus proportional balance in electoral laws, although there are important exceptions and the theory on this question is not yet fully developed. Hallerberg & von Hagen (1998, 1999) explain the choice of varied executive decision rules as alternative resolutions of the common-pool resource problem that governments confront in allocating spending authority over tax revenue. Hallerberg & von Hagen contend that multi-party coalition governments employ fiscal contracts, whereas single-party governments delegate to strong finance ministers. Such explanations view decision rules not as fixed constraints on policy makers but rather as solutions to problems (moral hazard, time inconsistency, informational asymmetry, and so on) that emerge in the course of governing.

SUMMARY   Research on post-electoral bargaining confirms that tax policies are slower to change in the short run when there is more than one veto player involved in decision making. This status quo bias is in turn associated with slower growth in tax revenue. Some agenda setter research finds that strong agenda control is associated with stability in tax policies, but broader empirical testing of agenda setter models is necessary to bolster this finding. Agenda setter and veto player models share the characteristic that they have been most successfully applied to the United States and to comparative studies of other advanced democracies. A limiting condition is that veto players can be identified only when parties can be seen as unitary actors. Scholars of new democracies may have to base their models more rigorously on the choices of individual legislators rather than party groupings; with a focus on legislators, analysts can treat party and majority formation endogenously. In addition, for many post-electoral models to be useful, the institutions that are asserted to be influential in policy making must actually exercise that influence in practice. As in the case of parties, if in a given democracy a given policy is settled outside of the formal institutions, then a veto player account framed by the constitutional arrangements may not aid the analysis of that policy. Agenda control in many new democracies and especially in comparative research designs likewise remains to be investigated.

Most post-electoral governance models omit citizen responses to policy making and the formation of elite actors' policy preferences. One author's statement about his own analysis applies to many: "Electoral competition is not modeled . . . . In order to focus on the process of governing, the time until the next required election is initially assumed to be infinite" (Baron 1998, p. 595). Exogenous citizen preferences, campaigns, and voting results simplify the models. But leaving out elections limits these models' abilities to explain the influence of democratic institutions on policy choices.

Elections and Governance

A few recent models integrate electoral competition and governing. In these models, candidates select platforms, citizens vote in elections, winning candidates become elected officials and negotiate policies, and then the sequence repeats. Huber (1996) develops a model of post-electoral policy making in which the decision makers seek higher office and reelection. This model usefully builds on the desire of French National Assembly deputies in the majority to support their governing coalition's policy compromise while also signaling their ideal policy positions to voters; deputies achieve these twin aims when they force the Prime Minister to invoke confidence votes on such legislative compromise. Persson et al. (1997, 2000) and Persson & Tabellini (2000, pp. 251–73; 2001) present several abstract models that integrate elections and governing. Austen-Smith (2000) formally explores tax rates and post-tax income under two typical institutional combinations of elections and governance (proportional elections with legislative bargaining versus majoritarian elections with winner-take-all legislative decision making), although systematic empirical testing remains to be done.

Integrated models such as these should help us to make sense of both top-down governance effects and bottom-up representation effects that are implicit in the core findings of empirical studies. Gould (2001) observes a difference in revenue levels across OECD democracies that use proportional representation (PR), even controlling for other political and economic factors: PR countries with at least one large party collected more tax revenue than did PR countries with only small parties (confirming Steinmo & Tolbert 1998). Theoretical and empirical work is needed to test the top-down explanation that large parties count on stable governments and make long-term, high-yield fiscal bargains, whereas small parties alone foresee frequent coalition changes and strike short-term, low-yield fiscal policies. A second finding is that majoritarian democracies collect lower revenue than PR democracies (Steinmo & Tolbert 1998, Gould 2001, Persson & Tabellini 2001). Constituents of majoritarian parties that expect to govern alone may support beggar-thy-neighbor competitive taxation that in the long run produces lower revenue, whereas constituents of parties that expect to govern in coalition favor broader revenue bases. In this case, we need to test a bottom-up account. Whatever the ultimate status of these particular explanations, stronger theory should help scholars sort through complex empirical patterns of association.

In our view, integrated models usefully recognize that voters and politicians alike respond to institutional incentives. One argument for integrated models is that a model's assumptions about actors should be consistent across actors. Accordingly, a rational-actor-based explanation for institutional effects should be consistent with rational voters. A second argument focuses on completing the modeling shift from candidate to policy maker. Candidates in most election models seek office and their platforms become policy, whereas the elected officials in most governance models seek policies according to given preferences. Neither the election-based models nor the governance-based models sufficiently explain how office holders running for reelection balance the demands of policy and office. In sum, consistent elaborations of complete electoral and governing models suitable for applications to fiscal politics have the potential to produce even more compelling results than we currently have.

CONCLUSION

Democratic institutions affect taxation at every stage of the policy-making process. The outlines of policy reform are frequently established in the design stage, and analyses of this stage emphasize varied institutions and actors. For democracies, the design stage of tax policy includes elections. Campaign platforms have tax implications, even if essential details remain to be elaborated. Most importantly, elections determine the success or failure of candidates and their tax platforms, thereby selecting who will exercise the rights of proposal, amendment, and veto in the legislative phase. Legislation is at the core of this review, and many political scientists and political economists consider their analytic work to be finished once a policy proposal becomes law. Yet the implementation stage is not solely the province of applied policy research. Rather, political scientists who employ principal-agent models of the legislature and the tax administration can study the efforts of legislators to structure incentives for bureaucrats in the writing of statutes and in the establishment of bureaucratic procedures. Joint models of elections and governance can help researchers incorporate key elements from all three stages of policy making and specify their effects on policy choices.

Another reason we advocate joint models of elections and governing is simply to provide stronger tests for ideas about the impact of democratic institutions. Hypotheses about the institutional effects will be more analytically persuasive and more amenable to empirical testing if they can be derived from models that make a consistent assumption about citizens, candidates, legislators, and members of executives: All of them can respond to political and economic incentives. Such integrated models can be evaluated with information from a broader range of democracies, a research strategy that we recommend. Several databases permit cross-national, time-series studies that go beyond the OECD democracies (Alvarez et al. 2000, Beck et al. 2000, Gould 2001, Persson & Tabellini 2001). The incorporation of evidence from new democracies can also proceed via theoretically guided case studies (following a few examples in the literature) and in small-N comparative analyses (a research design we have yet to observe in published work in this field). Using such broader evidence is not only feasible but also desirable because researchers who wish to investigate and develop positive theories of democracy can more fully evaluate their hypotheses with evidence from all democracies.

Our last recommendation is for expanded research on the decision rules employed by the world's democratic legislatures and executives. Many of these rules are not fully constitutionalized but are instead endogenous to legislation and government formation. Moreover, a particular decision to employ a previously established decision rule, even a constitutionally mandated decision rule, is virtually always endogenous to a particular policy-making episode. As we have seen, a promising way to understand decision rules is as the product of politicians' attempts to resolve problems in collective decision making. In short, our understanding of how citizens and politicians adjust to varied democratic institutions in the process of designing, legislating, and implementing fiscal policies can be improved if we also consider how certain actors modify and select aspects of those institutions.

ACKNOWLEDGMENTS

We gratefully acknowledge comments from Daniel Brinks, Howard Chernick, Georges Enderle, Matt Gabel, Thomas Gresik, Mark Hallerberg, Walter Hettich, Karrie Koesel, Margaret Levi, A. James McAdams, Luis Pásara, Jaime Ros, Paul Vasquez, Daniel Verdier, Bjørn Volkerink, and Stanley Winer. Previous versions were presented at the 2001 Annual Meeting of the American Political Science Association, San Francisco, CA, August 30–September 2, and to the Political Economy Working Group of the Kellogg Institute for International Studies, University of Notre Dame. Any errors that remain are ours.

The *Annual Review of Political Science* is online at http://polisci.annualreviews.org

LITERATURE CITED

Alesina A, Hausmann R, Hommes R, Stein E. 1999. Budget institutions and fiscal performance in Latin America. *J. Dev. Econ.* 59:253–73

Alesina A, Rosenthal H. 1995. *Partisan Politics, Divided Government, and the Economy.* Cambridge, UK: Cambridge Univ. Press

Alesina A, Roubini N, Cohen GD. 1997. *Political Cycles and the Macroeconomy.* Cambridge, MA: MIT Press

Alvarez M, Cheibub JA, Limongi F, Przeworski A. 2000. Regime and development database. http://pantheon.yale.edu/~jac236

Austen-Smith D. 1991. Rational consumers and irrational voters: a review essay on *Black Hole Tariffs and Endogenous Policy Theory*, by Stephen Magee, William Brock and Leslie Young, Cambridge University Press 1989. *Econ. Polit.* 3(1):73–92

Austen-Smith D. 2000. Redistributing income under proportional representation. *J. Polit. Econ.* 108(6):1235–69

Baron DP. 1998. Comparative dynamics of parliamentary governments. *Am. Polit. Sci. Rev.* 92(3):593–609

Baron DP, Ferejohn J. 1989. Bargaining in legislatures. *Am. Polit. Sci. Rev.* 83(4):1181–206

Barro RJ. 1979. On the determination of public debt. *J. Polit. Econ.* 87:940–47

Bawn K. 1995. Political control versus expertise: congressional choices about administrative procedures. *Am. Polit. Sci. Rev.* 89(1):62–73

Bawn K. 1999. Money and majorities in the Federal Republic of Germany: evidence for a veto players model of government spending. *Am. J. Polit. Sci.* 43(3):707–36

Beck T, Clarke G, Groff A, Keefer P, Walsh P. 2000. *New tools and new tests in comparative political economy: the database of political institutions.* Policy Res. Work. Pap. No. 2283. Washington, DC: World Bank, Dev. Res. Group

Binder S. 2001. *Parties and institutional choice revisited.* Presented at Annu. Meet. Midwest Polit. Sci. Assoc., Chicago, April 19–22

Birchfield V, Crepaz MML. 1998. The impact of constitutional structures and collective and competitive veto points on income inequality in industrialized democracies. *Eur. J. Polit. Res.* 34:175–200

Bird RM. 1989. The administrative dimension of tax reform in developing countries. See Gillis 1989b, pp. 315–46

Bird RM. 1991. Tax administration and tax reform: reflections on experience. In *Tax Policy in Developing Countries*, ed. J Khalilzadeh-Shirazi, A Shah, pp. 38–56. Washington, DC: World Bank

Bird RM, Casanegra M. 1992. The reform of tax administration. In *Improving Tax Administration in Developing Countries*, ed. RM Bird, M Casanegra, pp. 1–15. Washington, DC: Int. Monet. Fund

Bird RM, Oldman O. 1990. *Taxation in Developing Countries.* Baltimore, MD: Johns Hopkins Univ. Press. 4th ed.

Boix C. 2001. Democracy, development, and the public sector. *Am. J. Polit. Sci.* 45:1–17

Borelli SA, Royed TJ. 1995. Government "strength" and budget deficits in advanced democracies. *Eur. J. Polit. Res.* 28(2):225–60

Bradford DF, ed. 1995. *Distributional Analysis of Tax Policy.* Washington, DC: AEI Press, Am. Enterp. Inst.

Brennan G, Buchanan JM. 1980. *The Power to Tax: Analytical Foundations of a Fiscal Constitution.* Cambridge, UK: Cambridge Univ. Press

Brownlee WE. 1996. *Federal Taxation in America.* Cambridge, UK: Woodrow Wilson Cent. Press and Cambridge Univ. Press

Burgess R, Stern N. 1993. Taxation and development. *J. Econ. Lit.* 31(2):762–830

Calvert RL, McCubbins MD, Weingast BR. 1989. A theory of political control and agency discretion. *Am. J. Polit. Sci.* 33(3): 588–611

Campbell JL, Allen MP. 1994. The political economy of revenue extraction in the modern state: a time-series analysis of U.S. income taxes, 1916–1986. *Soc. Forces* 72(3):643–69

Casanegra M. 1987. *Problems in administering a value-added tax in developing countries: an overview.* Rep. No. DRD246. Dev. Res. Dep., World Bank

Casanegra M, Silvani C, Vehorn CL. 1992. Modernizing tax administration. In *Fiscal Policies in Economies in Transition,* ed. V Tanzi. Washington, DC: Int. Monet. Fund

Cheibub JA. 1998. Political regimes and the extractive capacity of governments: taxation in democracies and dictatorships. *World Polit.* 50:349–76

Chernick H, Reschovsky A. 1996. The political economy of state and local tax structure. In *Developments in Local Government Finance,* ed. G Pola, G France, R Levaggi, pp. 253–72. Cheltenham, UK/Brookfield, MA: Elgar

Cox GW. 2000. On the effects of legislative rules. *Legis. Stud. Q.* 25(2):169–92

Diermeier D, Feddersen TJ. 1998. Cohesion in legislatures and the vote of confidence procedure. *Am. Polit. Sci. Rev.* 92(3):611–21

Downs A. 1957. *An Economic Theory of Democracy.* New York: HarperCollins

Drazen A. 2000. *Political Economy in Macroeconomics.* Princeton, NJ: Princeton Univ. Press

Franzese R. 2002. *Macroeconomic Policies in Developed Democracies.* New York: Cambridge Univ. Press

Ganghof S. 1999. Steuerwettbewerb und Vetospieler: stimmt die These der blockierten Anpassung? *Polit. Vierteljahresschr.* 40(3):458–72

Gillis M. 1989a. Toward a taxonomy for tax reform. See Gillis 1989b, pp. 7–26

Gillis M, ed. 1989b. *Tax Reform in Developing Countries.* Durham, NC: Duke Univ. Press

Goode R. 1990. Obstacles to tax reform in developing countries. See Bird & Oldman 1990, pp. 121–28

Gordon RK, Thuronyi V. 1996. Tax legislative process. See Thuronyi 1996b, pp. 1–14

Gould AC. 2001. Party size and policy outcomes: an empirical analysis of taxation in democracies. *Stud. Comp. Int. Dev.* 36(2):3–26

Haggard S, McCubbins MD, eds. 2001. *Presidents, Parliaments, and Policy.* New York: Cambridge Univ. Press

Hallerberg M. 1999. The importance of domestic political institutions: why and how Belgium and Italy qualified for EMU. www.pitt.edu/~hallerb/homeframes.html

Hallerberg M, Basinger S. 1998. Internationalization and changes in tax policy in OECD countries: the importance of domestic veto players. *Comp. Polit. Stud.* 31:321–52

Hallerberg M, Basinger S. 1999. Globalization and tax reform: an updated case for the importance of veto players. *Polit. Vierteljahresschr.* 40:618–27

Hallerberg M, von Hagen J. 1998. Electoral institutions, cabinet negotiations and budget deficits in the European Union. In *Fiscal Institutions and Fiscal Performance,* ed. J Poterba, J von Hagen. Chicago: Univ. Chicago Press

Hallerberg M, von Hagen J. 1999. Electoral institutions and the budget process. In *Democracy, Decentralisation and Deficits in Latin America,* ed. K Fukasaku, R Hausmann, pp. 65–94. Washington, DC/Paris: Inter-Am. Dev. Bank and Dev. Cent. of Organ. Econ. Co-op. Dev.

Hansen JM. 1998. Individuals, institutions, and public preferences over public finance. *Am. Polit. Sci. Rev.* 92:513–31

Haycraft J. 1985. *Italian Labyrinth.* Harmondsworth: Penguin

Hettich W, Winer SL. 1999. *Democratic Choice and Taxation: A Theoretical and Empirical Analysis.* Cambridge, UK: Cambridge Univ. Press

Howard C. 1997. *The Hidden Welfare State: Tax Expenditures and Social Policy in the United States.* Princeton, NJ: Princeton Univ. Press

Huber JD. 1996. *Rationalizing Parliament: Legislative Institutions and Party Politics in France*. New York: Cambridge Univ. Press

Huber JD, Powell GB. 1994. Congruence between citizens and policymakers in two visions of liberal democracy. *World Polit.* 46(April):291–326

Huber JD, Shipan CR, Pfahler M. 2001. Legislatures and statutory control of bureaucracy. *Am. J. Polit. Sci.* 45(2):330–45

Jenkins GP. 1989. Tax changes before tax policies: Sri Lanka, 1977–88. See Gillis 1989b, pp. 233–51

King RF. 1993. *Money, Time, and Politics: Investment Tax Subsidies and American Democracy*. New Haven, CT: Yale Univ. Press

Krehbiel K. 1998. *Pivotal Politics*. Chicago: Univ. Chicago Press

Laver M, Schofield N. 1990. *Multiparty Government: The Politics of Coalition in Europe*. New York: Oxford Univ. Press

Levi M. 1988. *Of Rule and Revenue*. Berkeley: Univ. Calif. Press

Lieberman ES. 2002. Taxation data as indicators of state-society relations: possibilities and pitfalls in cross-national research. *Stud. Comp. Int. Dev.* 36(4). In press

Lukas R, Stokey N. 1983. Optimal fiscal and monetary policy in an economy without capital. *J. Monet. Econ.* 12:53–93

McCubbins MD, Noll RG, Weingast BR. 1987. Administrative procedures as instruments of political control. *J. Law Econ. Organ.* 3(2): 243–77

McCubbins MD, Noll RG, Weingast BR. 1989. Structure and process, politics and policy: administrative arrangements and the political control of agencies. *Va. Law Rev.* 75:431–82

Meltzer AH, Richard SF. 1981. A rational theory of the size of government. *J. Polit. Econ.* 89:914–27

Meltzer AH, Richard SF. 1983. Tests of a rational theory of the size of government. *Public Choice* 41:403–18

Newbury D, Stern N, eds. 1987. *The Theory of Taxation for Developing Countries*. New York: Oxford Univ. Press

Persson T, Roland G, Tabellini G. 1997. Sepa-

ration of powers and political accountability. *Q. J. Econ.* 112(4):1163–202

Persson T, Roland G, Tabellini G. 2000. Comparative politics and public finance. *J. Polit. Econ.* 108:1121–61

Persson T, Tabellini G. 2000. *Political Economics: Explaining Economic Policy*. Cambridge, MA: MIT Press

Persson T, Tabellini G. 2001. Political institutions and policy outcomes: What are the stylized facts? http://www.iies.su.se/data/home/perssont/papers/gtfeb 19.pdf

Peters BG. 1980. Determinants of choice in tax policy. In *The Determinants of Public Policy*, ed. TR Dye, V Gray, pp. 203–11. Lexington, MA: Lexington Books

Peters BG. 1991. *The Politics of Taxation: A Comparative Perspective*. Cambridge, MA: Blackwell

Poterba JM. 1999. Public finance and public choice. See Slemrod 1999, pp. 429–34

Powell GB. 2000. *Elections as Instruments of Democracy: Majoritarian and Proportional Visions*. New Haven, CT: Yale Univ. Press

Roberts K. 1977. Voting over income tax schedules. *J. Public Econ.* 8:329–40

Roemer JE. 2001. *Political Competition: Theory and Applications*. Cambridge, MA: Harvard Univ. Press

Romer T. 1975. Individual welfare, majority voting and the properties of a linear income tax. *J. Public Econ.* 7:163–68

Romer T, Rosenthal H. 1978. Political resource allocation, controlled agendas, and the status quo. *Public Choice* 33:27–44

Roubini N, Sachs J. 1989. Political and economic determinants of budget deficits in the industrial democracies. *Eur. Econ. Rev.* 33:903–33

Schickler E. 2000. Institutional change in the House of Representatives, 1867–1998: a test of partisan and ideological power balance models. *Am. Polit. Sci. Rev.* 94:269–88

Schumpeter JA. 1991 (1918). The crisis of the tax state. Reprinted in *The Economics and Sociology of Capitalism*, ed. R Swedberg, pp. 99–140. Princeton, NJ: Princeton Univ. Press

Slemrod J, ed. 1994. *Tax Progressivity and*

Income Inequality. Cambridge, UK: Cambridge Univ. Press

Slemrod J, ed. 1999. *Tax Policy in the Real World.* Cambridge, UK: Cambridge Univ. Press

Steinmo S. 1993. *Taxation and Democracy: Swedish, British, and American Approaches to Financing the Modern State.* New Haven, CT: Yale Univ. Press.

Steinmo S, Tolbert CJ. 1998. Do institutions really matter? Taxation in industrialized democracies. *Comp. Polit. Stud.* 31(2):165–87

Stewart CH. 1991. The politics of tax reform in the 1980s. In *Politics and Economics in the Eighties,* ed. A Alesina, G Carliner, pp. 143–73. Chicago: Univ. Chicago Press

Tanzi V. 1994. The IMF and tax reform. In *Tax Policy and Planning in Developing Countries,* ed. A Bagchi, N Stern, pp. 445–73. Delhi: Oxford Univ. Press

Tanzi V. 1995. *Taxation in an Integrating World.* Washington, DC: Brookings Inst.

Tarschys D. 1988. Tributes, tariffs, taxes and trade: the changing sources of government revenue. *Br. J. Polit. Sci.* 18(1):1–20

Thuronyi V. 1996a. Drafting tax legislation. See Thuronyi 1996b, pp. 71–94

Thuronyi V. 1996b. *Tax Law Design and Drafting,* Vol. 1. Washington, DC: Int. Monet. Fund

Tilly C. 1990. *Coercion, Capital, and European States: AD 990–1992.* Cambridge, MA: Blackwell

Tsebelis G. 1995a. Decision-making in political systems: veto players in presidentialism, parliamentarism, multicameralism, and multipartyism. *Br. J. Polit. Sci.* 25:289–326

Tsebelis G. 1995b. Veto players and law production in parliamentary democracies. In *Parliaments and Majority Rule in Western Europe,* ed. H Doering, pp. 83–111. New York: St. Martin's

Vanistendael F. 1996. Legal framework for taxation. See Thuronyi 1996b, 1:15–70

Volkerink B, de Haan J. 1999. Political and institutional determinants of the tax mix: an empirical investigation for OECD countries. http://www.eco.rug.nl/medewerk/bjorn/

Wagschal U. 1998. Blockieren Vetospieler Steuerreformen? *Polit. Vierteljahresschr.* 40(4):628–40

Way LA. 2001. *Informal policymaking and reform in weak states: the case of post-Soviet intergovernmental fiscal policy.* Presented at conf. on State-Building in Post-Communist States: Toward Comparative Analysis, Yale Univ., New Haven, CT, Apr. 27–28

Wilensky HL. 2002. *Rich Democracies: Political Economy, Public Policy, and Performance.* Berkeley: Univ. Calif. Press

Williams JT, Collins BK. 1997. The political economy of corporate taxation. *Am. J. Polit. Sci.* 41:208–44

Winer SL, Hettich W. 1998. What is missed if we leave out collective choice in the analysis of taxation? *Natl. Tax J.* 51(2):373–89. Reprinted in Slemrod 1999, pp. 411–27

Wittman D. 1973. Parties as utility maximizers. *Am. Polit. Sci. Rev.* 67:490–98

World Bank. 1991. *Lessons of Tax Reform.* Washington, DC: World Bank

Zelizer JE. 1998. *Taxing America: Wilbur D. Mills, Congress, and the State, 1945–1975.* Cambridge, UK: Cambridge Univ. Press

Annu. Rev. Polit. Sci. 2002. 5:111–25
DOI: 10.1146/annurev.polisci.5.102601.115116
Copyright © 2002 by Annual Reviews. All rights reserved

FORECASTING FOR POLICY MAKING
IN THE POST–COLD WAR PERIOD

Stanley A. Feder
PolicyFutures, LLC, Washington, DC 20015; e-mail: sfeder@policyfutures.com

Key Words   prediction, uncertainty, complexity, scenario analysis, political
expected utility models

■ **Abstract**   Political science has given policy makers many useful methods and
models for understanding continuities in the world. The utility of many models that
were specified with statistical analysis is likely to be undermined as relations among
variables change. Today, globalization, the rapid diffusion of technology, the internet, nongovernment organizations, environmental stresses, and population growth and
migration present policy makers with unfamiliar challenges. To keep from being surprised, policy makers need methods that indicate possible outcomes but do not specify
probabilities, which can be misleading. Instead, policy makers should have analytic
methods that warn of discontinuities and illuminate the forces and processes shaping events. Methods based on or compatible with complexity theory seem promising.
I describe two methods that can meet the needs of policy makers: Bueno de Mesquita's
political expected utility models and multiple scenario analysis. But methods or theories alone will not keep policy makers from being surprised by future developments.
It will also be crucial to ask the right questions.

A POLICY PERSPECTIVE

Policy makers responsible for the national security and foreign policy of the United
States face many challenges. They establish and maintain diplomatic relationships, international regimes, and memberships in intergovernmental organizations,
treaties, and alliances. They plan and make huge investments in defensive and
offensive weapons systems that often take decades to procure and presumably will
have useful lives of 25 to 50 or more years. Those who craft foreign and national
security policy ideally should have the foresight to design and build diplomatic
and military capabilities that will be useful in managing conflict and promoting
cooperation to preserve US interests, whatever they may be over the next 20 years.
Ideally, too, policy makers should be able to deal with crises that they could not
foresee or could not prevent.

This is a tall order at a time when the international system and many countries are
going through transitions. The processes of globalization, diffusion of technology,

population growth and migration; the increasing role of nongovernment organizations; environmental stress; and the restructuring of the international system are presenting policy planners with a range of uncertainties seemingly unimaginable during the Cold War.

Policy makers now have a great need to divine the possible directions in which global relations may evolve. Political and other social scientists can play a useful role in developing concepts for understanding new and emerging patterns of global relations. They can also develop models and methods that reliably warn of changes and forecast potential outcomes in the international system, or in subsystems, during this period of uncertainty.

In this essay I examine "political science forecasting" in light of my nearly 20 years' experience with organizations responsible for making and carrying out the foreign and national security policies of the United States. From 1981 to 1998 I was a research political scientist and political analyst in the Office of Research and Development and the Directorate of Intelligence at the CIA and at the National Intelligence Council. In this capacity, I had an opportunity to evaluate a number of analytic and forecasting methods for their utility in supporting policy makers and for helping intelligence analysts make sense of the reports they were getting from around the world. Testing many of these methods involved using them with interagency teams of experts. Policy makers, academics, and business people were often part of those teams. This experience taught me to look at forecasting methods pragmatically and skeptically. The basic question in evaluating a forecasting method is not "Can it tell us what will happen?" The question of primary value in policy making is "Can it keep us from being surprised?"

My arguments are as follows:

- These uncertain times require forecasting methods not based on tacit assumptions of continuity. Correlations among variables that obtained in the past may continue into the future, but there are huge risks in assuming that they will.

- Although the ability to forecast accurately is supposed to be a touchstone of a good theory, the world, especially the political and social world, is not that deterministic. Therefore, political scientists should not neglect theories that allow for more than one possible outcome. Indeed, they should make such theories more rigorous.

- Prediction and forecasting entail risks for policy makers. Prediction provides only one possible outcome; forecasting provides several, usually with probabilities for each. Probabilities make it too easy for decision makers to focus on the "most likely" outcome. A better practice would be what I call surveying the future. This entails understanding the dynamics of a situation, taking account of uncertainties, and identifying what can and cannot happen within a given time frame. Surveying also requires an awareness of the questions to which the policy maker needs answers.

- Policy makers and political scientists have much to learn from each other. I suspect that between the academic's desire to develop theories and the policy maker's need to avoid surprises the seeds of new paradigms can be found.

I hope that this essay will spur the academic community to develop new ways of thinking about political forecasting—especially regarding global relations—and about the needs of policy makers and those who support them. Similarly, I hope that policy makers and those who support them will develop a greater appreciation for methodological developments in the academic community.

DISCONTINUITY AND UNCERTAINTY ARE THE CHALLENGE

Wilson (2000) wrote his essay, "How Social Science Can Help Policymakers: The Relevance of Theory," to help academic political scientists understand what officials responsible for foreign policy do and how a dialogue between academics and policy makers can be more fruitfully conducted. It is well worth reading. During Wilson's tenure in the first Clinton Administration, he found that as much as 90% of the time, "foreign policy like domestic policy consists mainly of modest adjustments to current standard operating procedures to meet slightly new conditions." He describes ways in which political scientists can be helpful to policy makers during these periods of continuity (Wilson 2000, p. 112).

Intelligence organizations and policy makers' staffs spend a lot of time monitoring conditions around the world. Largely they report the news. But they also monitor reactions to and the effectiveness of US policies or those of international organizations, and they look for signs of emerging problems. When such signs appear, policy makers and intelligence analysts must figure out what is going on— whether a problem really is emerging and, if so, what its nature is and how the situation might develop. Policy makers must also consider policy responses and forecast the potential impacts of various policy options.

The effectiveness of monitoring depends as much on what is being looked for as it does on what is being looked at. Organizations tend to develop their own cultures. Moreover, they are susceptible to mindsets. A mindset is "'a fixed attitude or state of mind' that provides a context for the interpretation of data or events or for making decisions" (Feder 2000; definition from *Webster's Collegiate Dictionary*, 1991). They develop standard operating procedures for monitoring areas of their responsibility. Mindsets have been a major cause of intelligence and policy failures for decades, even though managers of intelligence organizations are well aware of their danger (Feder 2000, pp. 28–30). Organizations—governmental as well as academic—often go to great lengths to defend their mindsets.

During my government career, my colleagues and I were particularly concerned about anticipating discontinuities and avoiding policy and intelligence failures. In 1978, the policy, intelligence, and academic communities were surprised by the overthrow of the Shah of Iran. In all three communities, the conventional wisdom was that the Shah's regime was strong and its opponents were weak and fragmented. Evidence to the contrary was dismissed for months. Nearly two decades later, those three communities were again surprised by the collapse of the Soviet Union. Gaddis (1992a,b) saw this as evidence of the failure of international relations theory. Perhaps if theory had been more effective, it would have suggested the possibility that the Cold War could end.

Theories help us answer questions; they do not ask them. People ask questions. During the 1980s, how many people considered that the end of the Cold War or the collapse of the USSR was a possibility? Within the government, so many people believed that the USSR would last forever that few dared to ask if collapse was possible. I know of only one organization, Royal Dutch/Shell Oil, that by the early 1980s had considered the possibility of radical changes in the USSR and had monitored events in the USSR for leading indicators of significant change. In the early 1980s, the planning team at Shell had asked what factors, however unlikely, would cause world oil prices to fall and result in a lifting of Europe's restriction of importing no more than 35% of its natural gas from the Soviet Union. They speculated that one of those factors was "massive political and economic restructuring" in the USSR. They sought evidence that such an event was possible and found it. Shell's insight came "from asking the right question. From having to consider more than one scenario" (Schwartz 1991, pp. 56–58).

There have been other policy and intelligence failures over the years, but there have also been many successes. The critical differences between them were the openness of analysts and policy makers to discontinuities, a curiosity about anomalous data, and a willingness to engage in speculative thinking. Analytic and forecasting methods can reinforce or undermine these patterns of thinking, as can organizational cultures.

Dealing with Uncertainty from an Enlightenment Perspective: Single Outcomes and Probabilities

There is a relatively small but rich political science literature on forecasting, especially in international relations. Choucri & Robinson's compendium, *Forecasting in International Relations* (1978), stands out for the scope and quality of its coverage from several political science perspectives: theory, criteria for evaluation forecasts, and range of forecasting methods, to name a few. In rereading it, I was struck both by the quality of the work and by what, in retrospect, looks like a mindset about the nature of forecasting.

Choucri (1978, p. 4), like most other political scientists who have written about prediction and forecasting, defined prediction as the foretelling of a single future development. Single-outcome forecasts have long been recognized as dangerous. For example, a 1984 evaluation of intelligence estimates, analytic reports produced within the intelligence community on a particular issue or country, found that "the major factor in failed estimates was overly cautious, overly conservative, single-outcome forecasting . . . . This addiction to single-outcome forecasting defied both estimative odds and much recorded history. It reinforced some of the worst analytical hazards—status quo bias and a prejudice toward continuity of previous trends." Single-outcome forecasts "do not reduce uncertainty. They only increase the margins of surprise" (Armstrong et al. 1995, pp. 241–42).

The solution to this problem is forecasting, which Choucri (1978, p. 5) and many others defined as being "concerned with the ranges of possibilities and contingencies and probabilities associated with each." The authors of the critique of single-outcome forecasting quoted above recommended that analysts provide several possibilities for future developments and attach probabilities to each. In the intelligence-policy and academic communities, this has been the conventional wisdom for decades.

When helping policy makers think about the future, it is important to forecast several possible outcomes. But the use of probabilities is a two-edged sword. On the positive side, probability is a concept for which most people have an intuitive feel. They use it to discuss the weather and sports. They think they understand it. On the negative side, what does the probability of a forecasted outcome mean? Many of the political events being forecast do not occur often enough for frequency-based probabilities to be meaningful, especially during periods of flux. Even subjective probabilities are subject to misinterpretation. Moreover, reactions to forecasted probabilities depend on policy makers' willingness to take risks. If told that the odds of a war breaking out in the Middle East over the next six months are 1 in 20, some policy makers would consider the risk small enough to ignore. Others would start implementing diplomatic and military plans to deal with a potential crisis. Their response depends on their interpretation of the odds and their willingness to accept risks.

The use of probabilities also feeds the desire of many policy makers for a "bottom line." They want an expert judgment about what is going to happen. When offered several outcomes, each with a probability attached, they are too willing to bet on the most probable outcome and ignore the others. This too, increases "the margins of surprise." In other words, forecasters' customers drive them toward prediction.

Policy makers need to consider, if not plan for, contingencies. Therefore, an approach is needed that does not bias the analyst or the decision maker to focus on only one outcome. An alternative is "surveying the future"—considering plausible outcomes and presenting them to policy makers in ways that enable them to manage uncertainty. At least two forms of surveying have been known for decades. The first is to provide several possible outcomes, without probabilities, but with a unique set of leading indicators for each. Leading indicators are sets of discrete, observable events or conditions portending a particular outcome. This surveying approach encourages policy makers and analysts to plan for contingencies; monitoring indicators gives them a way to manage uncertainty. A slightly different alternative is to identify several outcomes and provide a "mechanistic" description of how events could lead to each of them from conditions today. Ascher & Overholt (1983, p. 132) advocated this approach and recommended adding information about how others might disagree with the forecast outcomes and the developments leading to them. In a policy-making environment, these approaches reduce the likelihood of being surprised.

Facing Uncertainty

Forecasting and prediction are antidotes to uncertainty or to the anxiety it can engender. But surprisingly, the political science literature deals less with the malady than with the cure. For example, some game theorists have studied the effects of one form of uncertainty, imperfect information, on escalation of international conflicts. Incomplete or inaccurate information can be a serious problem for policy makers. But policy makers face other forms of uncertainty as well. These include inadequate conceptual frameworks and weak theoretical foundations for understanding unfamiliar situations. Here, political scientists can play an important role by helping policy makers understand new situations and providing what Wilson calls contextualization (Wilson 2000, pp. 115–16).

We have, not surprisingly, a good foundation for understanding and forecasting familiar situations. Much of this foundation consists of quantitative work done in political science during the past 50 years. Two cornerstones of this foundation are probability theory and statistical analysis. Both provided an array of forecasting methods from simple extrapolation of trends to more sophisticated techniques of causal modeling, econometric modeling, dynamic models, and computer simulations.

All of these approaches are founded on the notion that correlations noted in the past will continue into the future. "Goodness of fit" in postdiction has been a criterion for evaluating forecasting models. But in forecasting, goodness of fit carries certain risks. As Leavitt (1978, p. 249) said of forecasting with computer simulations in the mid 1970s,

> For many planning purposes, knowing what is likely to happen is of some interest, but of greater import is knowing what low-probability (but high-cost or high-benefit) situations might be possible. Models that are developed to fit the former criteria will be hard pressed to perform the latter. If an international relations model is developed that has forecast real-world events at some point in the past (postdicted them), its precision will necessarily exclude most events that did not occur. But in international relations, with relatively few actors and poor descriptive theory, can the experimenter be confident enough to make the deterministic assumption that the other events could not have happened?... The point is that forecasting in international relations should perhaps take the form of "systematic speculation" rather than strict range-prediction.

Implicit here is the notion that models estimated with statistical techniques imply that political events are manifestations of a certain kind of order—that the fit between statistically based models and political events is good enough to describe certain political phenomena and to forecast future developments. And many of these models worked well enough for the 45 relatively stable years following World War II. But today, Enlightenment paradigms such as probability theory and Newtonian, mechanistic concepts may no longer be sufficient for understanding the world and managing political uncertainty. Instead, increasing evidence seems to indicate that political systems are better described by what mathematicians call complexity theory.

Complexity theory describes systems of autonomous actors that can exhibit nonlinear behavior. Very small changes in one variable can have enormous consequences. These systems can go through alternating periods of dynamic equilibrium and instability after which they organize themselves into a new pattern of dynamic equilibrium. During periods of instability, they can develop in any of several possible ways. This process of "bifurcation" and emergent reorganization is characterized by great uncertainty. Complexity theory should be a useful heuristic for political research. It might, for example, explain the huge impact of certain leaders, the impact of programs such as the Marshall Plan, and why some regimes collapsed so easily. Several political scientists, including Jervis (1997–1998), Axelrod (1997), and Bueno de Mesquita (1998), have begun to explore the usefulness of approaches consistent with complexity theory. Allen (1998, p. 37), another explorer of the new frontier of modeling complex systems, has written: "Instead of the classical view of science eliminating uncertainty, the new scientific paradigm accepts uncertainty as inevitable." There is a lot of fertile ground to plow here.

MANAGING UNCERTAINTY

In the meantime, several methods can support policy making in the face of uncertainty. Below, I highlight two dissimilar approaches: political expected utility models and evidence-based multiple scenario analysis. One is quantitative, the other qualitative. One is deterministic; the other is deliberately open to a number of possibilities. One is narrowly focused on policy decisions; the other is focused broadly enough to take into account economic, social, technical, and environmental factors if appropriate. Both have roots in political science. In describing them, I emphasize the features that make them useful for dealing with uncertainty and avoiding surprises.

Political Expected Utility Models

Bueno de Mesquita's policy forecasting models, first described in *The War Trap* (1981) and later elaborated on in *Forecasting Political Events: The Future of Hong Kong* (Bueno de Mesquita et al. 1985) and *European Community Decision Making* (1994), brought new power to political forecasting. Although Bueno de Mesquita's models are deterministic, they can effectively be used to manage uncertainty.

A decision maker who uses them will have a good sense of what is politically feasible—and what is not—and what strategies are likely to produce desired policy outcomes.

Bueno de Mesquita developed two forecasting models that he uses in a series of iterations or sequential games. Together these models provide a policy forecast and the political dynamics leading to that outcome. As the inputs are varied in plausible ways, the models indicate what outcomes are possible and which are impossible.

The first model uses a variation of the median voter theorem to forecast a policy decision. The median voter theorem states that if a group of people employs simple majority voting to choose among a number of options, and those options can be ordered on a single dimension, and each person has single-peaked preferences, then the outcome selected will be the one preferred by the median voter (see Black 1968 [1958], pp. 15–25). Bueno de Mesquita assumed that policy selection processes in nearly any political system are analogous to voting in committees. But instead of individuals voting, groups and leaders—each having their own political resources and political priorities—compete to have their preferred policy selected. Bueno de Mesquita also uses a voting procedure suggested by Condorcet: pitting each option against every other option in a series of pairwise contests. "The policy forecast is the alternative that defeats all other alternatives in pairwise head-to-head voting . . .. This forecast is the Condorcet winner and occupies the weighted median voter position" (Bueno de Mesquita et al. 1985, p. 40; see also Bueno de Mesquita 1994, pp. 75–80).

Bueno de Mesquita's second model, based on political expected utility theory, is used in conjunction with the voting model. "In practice, perceptions or beliefs often lead decision makers to grant concessions or give in to a rival's point of view, sometimes even needlessly. Such concessions or capitulations can change the location of the median voter" (Bueno de Mesquita 1994, p. 80). The expected utility model forecasts how players will interact on the issue and who will concede to whom, thus permitting an adjustment of players' policy preferences in the voting model. By iterating back and forth between the voting model and the expected utility model until a stable policy forecast is reached, Bueno de Mesquita has achieved impressive results in real-time forecasting. Organski & Eldersveld, evaluating real-time forecasts made with the expected utility model of 21 policy decisions in the European Community, concluded that "the probability that the predicted outcome was what indeed occurred was an astounding 97 percent" (1994, pp. 232–33). (See Bueno de Mesquita & Stokman 1994, pp.7–104, for a description of both models and an application.)

During my government career, I used Bueno de Mesquita's voting model on more than 1200 issues in more than 75 countries. Between 1982 and 1986, issues forecasted included the following (Feder 1995, p. 283):

- What policy is Egypt likely to adopt toward Israel?
- How fully will France participate in the Strategic Defense Initiative?
- What is the Philippines likely to do about US bases?

■ What policy will Beijing adopt toward Taiwan's role in the Asian Development Bank?

My colleagues and I found that compared with conventional intelligence analyses, those based on Bueno de Mesquita's voting model had more precise forecasts without sacrificing accuracy. In 1983, for example, using traditional methods to forecast how large a budget deficit the Italian government would approve, an analyst typically would have used vague language such as, "We believe this year's budget deficit will be moderately larger than last year's." Using Bueno de Mesquita's model, we forecasted a budget deficit of 70 trillion lira, an error of <1% (Feder 1995, p. 277).

Because Bueno de Mesquita's models are deterministic, the outputs are conditional forecasts. That is, the policy forecast is contingent on conditions as the experts described them. If some players lose interest in an issue or if others alter their policy goals, the policy forecasted can change. At the CIA, we tested the voting model by making real-time, conditional forecasts for about 80 issues in more than a score of countries. We found that the voting model alone was accurate almost 90% of the time (Feder 1995, p. 275).

For policy and intelligence agencies, one advantage of these models is that their data inputs are the observations of country or issue experts. Use of the models, particularly the way in which analysts provided the data, also made it easy to avoid analytic traps such as expecting the future to look like the past and failing to consider alternative outcomes (Feder 1995, p. 276). (Despite the advantages of Bueno de Mesquita's models, which became known as "factions" models within the CIA, the vast majority of analysts do not use them. My hypothesis is that this kind of systematic analysis does not fit into an organizational culture that sees an "analyst" as someone who writes reports, often evaluating and summarizing available information. In contrast, people who use models and quantitative techniques are considered "methodologists.")

In addition to providing policy forecasts, the models also make possible reliable inferences about the stability of a government and the emergence of new leaders. Within a parliamentary system, if a policy supported by the head of government or ruling party is defeated, the government collapses. When using Bueno de Mesquita's models, if the forecasted outcome is politically far from the position of the head of government, that leader is vulnerable to defeat. Several times in the past 20 years, we foresaw the collapse of a number of governments based on this kind of analysis. (The Italian deficit issue mentioned above is one instance.) This pattern also obtains in authoritarian governments. If the head of government is far from the forecasted outcome on an issue that is important to players that have military or police powers at their disposal, there is a high likelihood of a forced resignation or coup.

Conversely, a leader who is not head of the government, and who consistently takes positions on key policies that are at the forecasted outcomes or very close to them, is in a strong political position. It is highly likely he or she will be a contender for very high government position.

Bueno de Mesquita's models facilitate surveying the future by making it easy to explore the implications of possible changes in a political environment. This can be done systematically or on an ad hoc basis. When I forecast policy decisions, I always perform systematic sensitivity analyses to see what plausible errors or changes in the data could produce significantly different forecasts. One can also explore the policy consequences of specific plausible changes in a policy environment. For example, what will be the policy impacts of a change of leadership in China? Or what will be the effect on US health policies if labor unions make education in general, and worker retraining in particular, their primary issues during the next two years?

By using the voting model to examine "what if" scenarios, one can develop a sense of which changes in the political environment will have a significant effect on a particular issue. Because the forecasts are conditional and conditions can change, the sensitivity analysis provides a list of political factors to monitor. Testing "what if" scenarios also provides an indication of how much change is possible and how quickly it can occur. If a particular policy outcome required the members of a relatively weak lobbying group to greatly increase their political clout, could they do it? How long would that take? How would other conditions have to change for them to increase their organizational and fund-raising capabilities? This is an ad hoc, but effective, way to manage uncertainty and reduce the likelihood of being surprised over a six- to 24-month period.

Bueno de Mesquita (1998) has described a systematic way to explore the long-term implications of random, plausible changes in some of the input data in a simulation of the evolution of the post–World War II international system. This intriguing study involved using data for 36 states in 1948 from the Correlates of War project as the only inputs for his voting and expected utility models. By randomly varying the salience of security as an issue to each of 36 states within the international system through 25 iterations of the models, Bueno de Mesquita simulated their interactions and alignments over what he estimated to be a 50-year period. By repeating these simulations 100 times, he found that a "US wins" pattern occurred in 67% to 78% of the simulations, depending on how victory was defined (Bueno de Mesquita 1998, p. 153). Soviet victory, war, and a continuation of the Cold War made up the rest of the outcomes. The study thus identifies several possible forms of "emergent behavior" in the international system, based only on conditions in 1948. It also identifies changes in international alignments that could have been used as a leading indicator of which path the international system was following. I can imagine how such an approach might be used (or misused) to explore ways in which the current international system might evolve over the next 10 or 20 years. This kind of modeling deserves real-time testing.

Evidence-Based Multiple Scenario Analysis

Scenario analysis has not been used much in academic political science. This is a shame, since it is a qualitative form of simulation well suited for studying potential developments in a wide range of areas. Moreover, scenario exercises, or a course based on scenario analysis directed by a good teacher or facilitator, can sharpen the critical-thinking skills of participants and motivate them to acquire knowledge.

The scenario technique was promoted by Herman Kahn and his colleagues at RAND in the 1950s. They used scenarios to think about the unthinkable consequences of thermonuclear war and to examine the implications of global and regional trends on international relations. Soon thereafter, other think tanks, consulting firms, military organizations, and some businesses also used scenarios for long-term thinking and planning over the past 50 years. In the late 1960s, Pierre Wack at Royal Dutch/Shell Oil led a planning team that advanced the methodology and made it a valuable tool for long-term planning. Wack's two articles in the *Harvard Business Review* in 1985 describe how his team's use of scenarios enabled Shell to foresee the 1973 oil crisis (Wack 1985a,b).

An even more readable description of the scenario approach and a guide to its application is Schwartz's *The Art of the Long View: Planning for the Future in an Uncertain World* (1991). An excellent example of scenario analysis is Yergin & Gustafson's *Russia 2010* (1993), which examined what forces were shaping Russia's transition to a democracy and market economy and how these might play out.

Scenario analysis is best used for strategic planning over periods of more than three years. It relies mostly on qualitative methods, although quantitative analysis is often critical to the construction of particular scenarios.

There are many forms of multiple scenario analysis. Most of the scenario analyses I have seen in agencies responsible for national security and foreign policy differed in terms of a single, driving factor such as rate of economic growth. Such scenarios are not useful, for they neglect the impact of other variables, thereby increasing the likelihood of surprise. There are, however, analytic groups in the intelligence community that are successfully using more complex methods of scenario analysis.

Scenario analysis is best done to answer a particular question. This focuses the effort and makes it more useful to those on whose behalf it is being done. For example, a university might use scenario analysis to decide how much to invest in a new library or online teaching capabilities. A corporation might use scenario analysis to decide whether to build a chain of retail outlets in Mexico. A nongovernment organization might use it to project the humanitarian relief capabilities it might need over the next 10 years.

The next step, after identifying a focal question and specifying the time horizon for the analysis, is to identify and describe the forces or factors that can influence the outcome. These are then sorted into those that can be forecast with a good deal of confidence (e.g., demographics over a 10–15-year period) and those that cannot (e.g., the health of the economy or the state of communications technology). These groups are also referred to as the "certainties" or "predetermined elements" and the "uncertainties." The forces or factors are also sorted by the size of their likely impact on the focal question. Uncertainties that are judged likely to have the greatest impact and that are independent of each other provide the basic framework for the scenarios. Creating this framework is easiest if two key uncertainties are chosen, but it is possible to work with three or four. The scenarios are created by combining sets of extreme outcomes for each uncertainty and creating a plausible story of how the world can develop from the present condition to one in which those extremes are reached. The scenarios must also take account of the key certainties. Once the scenarios are outlined, they should be fleshed out in ways that make them plausible. For example, a skilled work force cannot magically appear in a country that does not have one. A plausible process of how a skilled work force develops must be described. Various quantitative and qualitative methods can be used.

After the scenarios are fleshed out, their implications must be considered. What does each mean for the focal question or for decisions that have to be made? Is there a strategy that would work in all scenarios? Which strategies will work in some scenarios but not in others?

Finally, it is important to identify leading indicators for each scenario. These indicators must be monitored so that the decision makers and the people who support them can take advance action or change strategies as appropriate.

Creating scenarios has several advantages. First, it requires a critical examination of the forces likely to shape future developments. This promotes a deeper understanding of situational dynamics. Second, it makes explicit the key uncertainties, reducing the likelihood of surprise. Third, it highlights developments that are inevitable. Many of these inevitabilities are rarely obvious. Fourth, it indicates ways in which a system can change and ways in which it cannot. Fifth, it requires analysts and, we hope, decision makers to consider ways to deal with contingencies.

Scenario analysis requires a lot of work. In many ways, it is far less elegant than expected utility modeling. But like expected utility analysis, it is an effective way to manage uncertainty. Both approaches should find increasing currency as the world gets more complex.

SURVEYING THE FUTURE

Political science has given policy makers many useful methods and models for understanding the continuities in the world. The utility of many of those models that were specified with statistical analysis is likely to be undermined as relations among variables change. During the relatively stable Cold War period, political forecasters overcame the fallibility of their models by providing sets of alternative outcomes and assigning probabilities to each. Despite its questionable validity, the practice is followed to this day. Many policy makers like to "know" the odds they face. Today, assigning probabilities can be dangerously misleading. Instead, policy makers should have analytic methods that warn of discontinuities and illuminate the forces and processes shaping events.

Both Bueno de Mesquita's political expected utility models and multiple scenario analysis do this adequately. Both can be used to anticipate discontinuities and, to some extent, the characteristics of systems that might emerge. Bueno de

Mesquita posits that patterns of political interactions depend on the groups and leaders vying to influence policy decisions, their political agendas, and the amount and kinds of political resources they control. He provides mathematical models that indicate the policy consequences of various political configurations. Knowledgeable country experts and experienced forecasters can use the models to identify situations that would destabilize a regime or its leadership; these models can also indicate what its likely replacements may be. The models even seem to provide insights into the dynamics of international systems. In short, the models can show what is politically feasible and what is infeasible. In the face of disorder, they provide a way to palpate the structure of systems that can emerge.

Evidence-based scenario analysis is a systematic way to speculate about plausible changes in complex situations. Although it lacks the mathematical precision of Bueno de Mesquita's models, scenario analysis has a much broader scope. Once the basic drivers of the future are specified, their interactions can be explored, and the range of possible outcomes becomes limited and manageable.

But analytic methods alone will not guarantee that policy makers and academics will not be surprised by political events. Preventing surprise depends on asking the right questions—often those that meet someone's need to make a decision, whether that someone is a government official, on the board of a nongovernment organization, the head of a corporation, the leader of an international organization, or a researcher curious about the possibility of a development that would surprise most people.

From a US national security perspective, the "right" questions now include the following:

- How might relations between the United States and China develop over the next 20 years?
- In what ways can fundamentalist religions affect global relations and the internal politics of countries in the Middle East and Asia?
- What attitudes and beliefs about the United States are prevelant abroad and how are those attitudes and beliefs likely to change over the next 20 years?
- What are likely to be key threats to US national security over the next 20 years?
- Economically and in global politics, how successful will the European Union be?
- What are the prospects for peace in the Middle East?
- Over the next 20 years, how adequate will energy supplies be in the United States? In China? India? Europe? How will politics affect those supplies?
- In what ways will global warming and other environmental issues affect the interactions and interests of the United States and other countries?

These questions come from a primarily US-oriented perspective. Similar questions can usefully be asked from European, Russian, Arab, Indian, Chinese, Latin American, or other perspectives.

We as political scientists or policy makers do not want to be surprised by the next discontinuity in global relations or in the internal politics of a major state. We have theories and methods at our disposal to help us answer questions about possible future developments. As we better understand the sources of uncertainty in politics, we will develop theories and methods that help us survey the future with more precision and reliability.

The *Annual Review of Political Science* is online at http://polisci.annualreviews.org

LITERATURE CITED

Allen PM. 1998. Evolving complexity in social science. In *Systems: New Paradigms for the Human Sciences*, ed. G Altman, WA Koch pp. 3–38. Berlin: Walter de Gruyter

Armstrong WC, Leonhart W, McCaffrey WJ, Rothenberg HC. 1995. The hazards of single-outcome forecasting. See Westerfield 1995, pp. 238–54

Ascher W, Overholt WH. 1983. *Strategic Planning and Forecasting: Political Risk and Economic Opportunity*. New York: Wiley. 311 pp.

Axelrod R. 1997. The dissemination of culture: a model with local convergence and global polarization. *J. Confl. Resolut.* 41(2):203–26

Black D. 1968 (1958). *The Theory of Committees and Elections*. Cambridge, UK: Cambridge Univ. Press. 241 pp.

Bueno de Mesquita B. 1981. *The War Trap*. New Haven, CT: Yale Univ. Press. 223 pp.

Bueno de Mesquita B. 1994. Political forecasting: an expected utility method. See Bueno de Mesquita & Stokman 1994, pp. 71–104

Bueno de Mesquita B. 1998. The end of the Cold War: predicting an emergent property. *J. Confl. Resolut.* 42(2):131–55

Bueno de Mesquita B, Newman D, Rabushka A. 1985. *Forecasting Political Events: The Future of Hong Kong*. New Haven, CT: Yale Univ. Press. 198 pp.

Bueno de Mesquita B, Stokman FN, eds. 1994. *European Community Decision Making*. New Haven, CT: Yale Univ. Press. 259 pp.

Choucri N. 1978. Key issues in international re-

lations forecasting. See Choucri & Robinson 1978, pp. 3–22

Choucri N, Robinson TW, eds. 1978. *Forecasting in International Relations: Theory, Methods, Problems, Prospects*. San Francisco: Freeman. 468 pp.

Feder SA. 1995. Factions and Policon: new ways to analyze politics. See Westerfield 1995, pp. 274–92

Feder SA. 2000. Overcoming "mindsets": what corporations can learn from government intelligence failures. *Compet. Intell. Rev.* 11:28–36

Feder SA, Schwartz AR. 1999. *Policy forces analysis—forecasting the policy impact of the Russian elections*. Lunch Sem., Brookings Inst., Jan. 14

Gaddis JL. 1992a. Point of view. *Chron. Higher Educ.*, July 22, p. A44

Gaddis JL. 1992b. International relations theory and the end of the Cold War. *Int. Sec.* 17(3):5–58

Jervis R. 1997–1998. Complexity and the analysis of political and social life. *Polit. Sci. Q.* 112(4):569–93

Leavitt MR. 1978. Computer simulation in international relations forecasting. See Choucri & Robinson 1978, pp. 239–51

Organski AFK, Eldersveld S. 1994. Modeling the EC. See Bueno de Mesquita & Stokman, pp. 229–42

Schwartz P. 1991. *The Art of the Long View: Planning for the Future in an Uncertain World*. New York: Doubleday. 258 pp.

Wack P. 1985a. Scenarios: uncharted waters ahead. *Harv. Bus. Rev.* 5:72–89

Wack P. 1985b. Scenarios: shooting the rapids. *Harv. Bus. Rev.* 6:139–50

Westerfield HB, ed. 1995. *Inside the CIA's Private World: Declassified Articles from the Agency's Internal Journal, 1955–1992.* New Haven, CT: Yale Univ. Press. 489 pp.

Wilson EJ III. 2000. How social science can help policymakers: the relevance of theory. In *Being Useful: Policy Relevance and International Relations Theory*, ed. M Nincic, J Lepgold, pp. 109–28. Ann Arbor: Univ. Mich. Press. 392 pp.

Yergin D, Gustafson T. 1993. *Russia 2010 and What It Means for the World.* New York: Random House. 302 pp.

Annu. Rev. Polit. Sci. 2002. 5:127–49
DOI: 10.1146/annurev.polisci.5.101501.145837
Copyright © 2002 by Annual Reviews. All rights reserved

THE ORIGINS, DEVELOPMENT, AND POSSIBLE DECLINE OF THE MODERN STATE

Hendrik Spruyt
Department of Political Science, Arizona State University, Tempe, Arizona 85287-2001;
e-mail: hspruyt@asu.edu

Key Words sovereignty, capstone government, institutionalism, quasi-states, Westphalia

■ **Abstract** Some contemporary states seem subject to aggregational dynamics that bring them together in larger regional associations, whereas others fall prey to centrifugal forces that pull them apart. The autonomy of all states has been drawn into question by the globalization of trade and finance. For these reasons, scholars have returned to examining the historical origins and development of the modern state in the hope that this may shed light on its future, and on the process through which new logics of organization may be emerging that might displace the state. This essay discusses various accounts of the emergence and development of the modern state, comparing security, economic, and institutionalist approaches. It then links these approaches to insights regarding contemporary statehood. Arguments regarding the autonomy of the state must be distinguished from discussions of territorial sovereignty as a constitutive principle of international relations. The latter, juridical notion of sovereignty as a regulative device in international relations has retained its influence, even if the autonomy of the state has declined.

INTRODUCTION

Recent scholarship in political science has returned with vigor to examining the origins and development of the modern state. On the one hand, this revival of interest has been due to expectations that the state might have reached its high water mark. Such supranational entities as the European Union, and the increasing powers of such multinational entities as the World Trade Organization, seem to foreshadow an end to the ultimate authority of national governments. From that perspective, state sovereignty appears to be shifting, albeit imperfectly, to multilateral and supranational levels of authority (Rosenau 1989, Rosenau & Czempiel 1992).

On the other hand, we are daily confronted with states fractionating into multiple entities. Some polities, which once appeared to be coherent territorial units, have broken apart, sometimes with remarkable speed. And these centrifugal tendencies have not been limited to developing states, where one might presuppose that ethnic tensions would have a rich feeding ground in artificial borders imposed by former colonial powers, and in feeble economies. Advanced capitalist and socialist states have not been immune. Few foresaw the demise of the Soviet Union as a federal entity. The Quebecois only narrowly lost a referendum that would have brought Canadian territorial integrity into doubt.

Aggregational dynamics and centrifugal forces seem to uneasily coexist in the post–Cold War world. Some scholars have thus turned to tracing the historical origins and subsequent evolution of the state in the hope that this may shed light on the future of the state and the process through which new logics of organization may be emerging. Examining the modes of previous transitions might lead to insights concerning current transitions.

Other paradoxes come to mind as well. Some modern states excel in their ability to regulate many spheres of social activity and in their capacity to affect economic outcomes. Many such states are located in regions that have been blessed by a period of "Long Peace." Other states have lacked such abilities, and they have been unable to provide welfare and security to their citizens in regions fraught with peril. Nominally juridically equivalent with other states in the system, they in fact differ markedly from developed countries in their capacity and functions. Jackson (1987) has aptly described these entities as "quasi-states." Here, a study of different historical trajectories might clarify why such states exist as international legal entities but lack the positive trappings of modern states.

For many years, the study of the state and its origins has been relegated to secondary status. Neo-Marxist arguments, world systems theory, and structural functionalist perspectives accounted for the rise of the state as a response to macro structural changes. Linear and teleological in nature, such theories pictured the modern state as the logical endpoint in the evolutionary development of polities. International relations scholarship too found little reason to examine how states evolved, since structural realism argued that structure fully determined state behavior. Different types of states engaged in similar patterns of behavior. Macro-level patterns and deductive arguments obfuscated a far more complex and diverse pattern of state formation and made closer inspection of state development superfluous.

Such macro-structural accounts have been found wanting. Empirically, they fail to recognize the multiplicity of institutional types that often coexist in any period. Theoretically, they neglect agency, the variant choices that individuals make to pursue their interests given existing constraints and opportunities. Recent scholarship has addressed these deficiencies. It has at once opened up the empirical universe by examining often neglected and alternative institutional arrangements, and it has interjected a micro-level perspective to complement macro-level analyses.

Before entering these discussions, however, modern states must be differentiated from their predecessors. I highlight two features in particular: the capacity of modern states to intervene in their societies, and the principle of international legal sovereignty based on the recognition of domestic sovereignty and the juridical equivalence of states. Both features, though first appearing in the Late Middle

Ages, took many centuries to come to fruition. Indeed, the full extension of international legal sovereignty across the globe only came in the wake of World War II.

This essay then turns to a discussion of various accounts for the emergence of the modern state and links them to insights about contemporary statehood. Admittedly, this essay concentrates on materialist accounts, leaving culturalist explanations aside despite their relevance (Ruggie 1993). I do, however, examine the constructivist insights on the origins of the state and the implications of the constructivist challenge for state theory and the study of international relations.

Accounts of the origins of the state can be divided into three categories: scholarship that stresses changes in the military environment; economic perspectives that highlight the growth of trade and production; and institutionalist views that accentuate the particular features of territorial sovereignty. The key argument of this essay is that although the first two perspectives contain many insights, a micro-level institutionalist perspective forms a necessary complement to macro-level accounts that focus on military and economic functions. Macro-level explanations must take human agency into account. The institutional framework, however, mediates individual choices. I argue for a three-tiered perspective incorporating macro-level variations, institutional constraints and opportunities, and individual preferences and choices given the conditions at the first two levels.

I then examine why contemporary debates in political science have returned to the study of the origins and development of the state. Scholars of comparative politics have turned to such analysis in order to elucidate the various patterns of state formation in developing areas. Students of transition economies have also found value in examining how early modern states constructed market economies, created institutional frameworks that tied rulers' hands, and formalized bureaucratic administration. In international relations, with the waning of structural realist primacy, scholars have started to realize that the nature of the polities in the system, and, hence, the nature of the state, fundamentally affects the structural properties of the system.

DIFFERENTIATING EARLY AND MODERN STATES

Premodern States

Discussing the origins of the state has widely divergent meanings across the various social sciences. For anthropologists, sociologists, and historians, the origins of the state lie in the earliest transitions from tribal or kin-based societies to stratified forms of organization. Indeed, accounts of state formation become virtually synonymous with accounts of agricultural settlement, civilization, and recorded history (Mair 1962). The ability to govern corresponded closely to the ability to keep records, to issue orders, to organize large-scale forces, and to exercise legal authority. Thus, such accounts of state formation might—by examining the Egyptian dynasties, the Mesopotamian region, China, or early Greece

(Runciman 1982)—stress the ability to issue laws and administrative decrees and to create a bureaucracy and army.

At a second level of generalization, accounts of early state formation tend to emphasize how formal authority structures replaced personalistic rule. The ability to command individuals who were not blood relatives enabled rulers to expand their domains over much larger population bases and territories. This required, however, alternative modes of legitimation. Blood ties of the clan, tribe, or kin group were relatively obvious. But how could one bind others to one's rule? Rulers needed to expand conceptions of tribal affinity and grant others the means to join. The ascriptive markers used to delineate membership and authority had to be replaced with associational criteria if the polity wished to transcend its temporal boundaries (legitimate rule would then attach to roles rather than individuals) and to expand its geographical frontiers (the polity could then incorporate more potential members). As Doyle (1986) suggests, the Roman willingness to expand its basis of rule from tribal affinity to associational citizenship, and to extend that citizenship to all parts of the empire, greatly aided the long-term viability of Roman imperial rule. One might similarly explore the earliest formations of polities in the Middle East and East Asia (Mann 1986).

This separation of personal connections between ruler and ruled, however, requires a second transformation before rule becomes fully formalized and abstract. In early states, even when rulers and ruled were not personally related, rulers still governed people. Clovis the Merovingian, who ruled the Frankish empire in the late fifth century, ruled as "King of the Franks." Less than a millenium later, however, the Capetians were considered "Kings of France," that is, rulers of a fixed and defined territory (Claesen 1985). In the Early Middle Ages, one spoke of Rex Anglorum (King of the English), but by the Late Middle Ages, he had become Rex Anglie (King of England). Similarly, the systems of law that emerged in the wake of the Roman Empire specified the group for whom that law was meant. The "Lex Burgundium" applied to Burgundians, wherever they might be. Authority attached to people, not to a defined geographical area. But by the Late Middle Ages, systems of law started to emerge that were demarcated by territorial parameters.

Thus, a variety of key features distinguish early states from the variants that we know today (Claesen 1985, p. 212). Most forms of early statehood revolved around some form of kingship and the relationship between the king and his retinue. Kings and aristocracy acted within a reciprocal set of obligations: The king's retinue remained loyal as long as he succeeded in war and could distribute booty. The exercise of authority flowed from loyalty to the king as a person, rather than to the kingship as a public function. Such early states had only weakly defined market economies and property rights. Formal administration through salaried officials, legislative frameworks, and taxation hardly existed.

The interactions between such polities also looked markedly different from the state system of today. Given the personalistic nature of rule and the lack of any conception that rule affixed to territory (the analog of property rights), such polities were neither territorially defined nor exclusive in character (Kratochwil 1986). Universal empires recognized only material frontiers, not mutually acknowledged borders. Such borders entail juridical equivalence, which such universal empires as the Roman or the Chinese did not recognize. Multiple authority structures also coexisted side by side. Such contemporary distinctions as secular and religious authority blurred in early state practice. For example, medieval European emperors claimed sacral status and the right to appoint members of the clergy, while the papacy claimed the authority to levy taxes, raise armies, and depose secular rulers, including the emperor himself (Tierney 1964).

The personalistic aspects of rule permeated Europe until the Late Middle Ages and arguably even later. The feudal state revolved around personal ties of obedience and loyalty. Kings and dukes commanded those lords who had sworn fealty to them. Those lords in turn commanded lesser vassals. Only through this command of men did one control territory. Thus, the control of a lord over his vassals resembled social networks and bundles of rights rather than the exclusive control over a fixed territory. Individuals might be subject to multiple patterns of rule from various lords, from the ecclesiastical authorities, and occasionally from urban authorities that had their own distinct modes of governance (Strayer 1965, 1970; Cheyette 1975).

Finally, early states only tangentially affected their societies. Premodern states constituted capstone governments (Gellner 1983, Mann 1986, Crone 1989, Hobsbawn 1990). Ruling elites were often integrated and dispersed throughout the area of control, but society remained relatively untouched. Society consisted of multiple divided communities, differentiated along ethnic, religious, and linguistic lines. Horizontal elites (the capstone government) overlaid vertically segregated societies.

In short, the capacity of early states remained relatively limited. Their abilities to tax, to raise troops, and to forge any sense of national identity remained weak. Early states ran wide but not deep.

The Transition to Modern Statehood

Modern statehood first took form in late medieval Europe. Although early states in many regions of the world showed similar traits, the modern European state evolved in a unique manner (for general accounts, see Strayer 1970, Poggi 1978). Here governments developed institutional capacities far beyond the capstone polities of the premodern age, and here states became synonymous with sovereign territorial rule. That model was subsequently transplanted from Europe to other areas. On such empirical grounds, and following the methodological maxim that the explication of a specific case or several cases can demonstrate more generalizable logics of organization (Evans 1995), this account focuses on developments in Europe during the past millenium, beginning at the end of the feudal era, to shed light on the contemporary world-wide system of states.

In the course of the fourth century and culminating in the fifth century, the Roman Empire came under increasing pressure of internal power struggles and external enemies. By the middle of the fifth century, only the East Roman Empire (the Byzantine empire) survived while a variety of tribes from beyond the imperial border overran the western empire. Church leaders took on some of the imperial administration (indeed the dioceses overlaid the previous provincial borders), while local chieftains provided a measure of security. Economic transactions and public security thus became highly localized with a large degree of barter exchange, and the use of coin declined greatly. The Carolingian empire momentarily brought greater unity, particularly under Charlemagne (crowned emperor in 800), but without primogeniture, the empire soon fell apart in smaller kingdoms. Once again, foreign invasions (the Maygar, Viking, and Muslim intrusions) advantaged localized defense, thus empowering local barons over any centralized rule. Feudal rule dominated with serfs who were tied to the land and local lords, and local lords who in turn were enfeoffed to higher aristocrats through personalistic, reciprocal ties (Duby 1968, 1978). Kingship and centralized authority remained contested and weak. Such was the fate of Western Europe until the middle of the eleventh century.

By the late eleventh century, however, the situation in Western Europe started to change, and here we find the beginnings of the modern state. Shifts in climate, advances in military and agricultural technology, declining levels of external threat, and expanding trade placed ever-increasing pressure on the feudal order (Pirenne 1952 [1925], 1956; Duby 1974). Aspiring monarchs started to assert themselves against local rulers.

Capstone governments gave way to far more intrusive authority. Taxation, administration, and the subsequent policing of society increased the ability of the state to intervene in all aspects of social life. The increasing economic productivity allowed rulers to raise more revenues. By giving lesser lords a stake in central rule through pensions and tax sharing, royal authority gradually extended the royal domain (Fawtier 1960, Strayer 1980, Dunbabin 1985). Higher revenues in turn allowed kings to eventually raise standing armies to replace the ad-hoc feudal service, which often amounted to no more than 40 days a year. Thus, by the mid fifteenth century, the French monarchy could finally raise a standing army of almost 15,000 troops.

Homogeneous governance and formalized legal codes, evinced by the reappearance of Roman law from the thirteenth century on, replaced the previous juridical segmentation of society based largely on informal customs and traditions. This enhanced the formal legitimation of royal authority as the rule over subjects rather than the personalistic ties of the feudal period. Monarchy became a public office rather than a private possession. Roman law also aided the rise of a market economy: Private property replaced possession (*seisin*); written contract supplanted oral agreement; formal courts took the place of trial by ordeal and combat (Berman 1983).

These trends would continue in subsequent centuries. Advances in military technology, production techniques, and transportation enabled mercantilist states to consolidate their rule. Externally, they began to project force at ever-greater distances and to incorporate even non-European territories into the European economy (Wallerstein 1974, Braudel 1984).

The process came to full fruition in the wake of the French Revolution of 1789. Napoleonic rule extended formal legal codes over much of continental Europe, extinguished the last vestiges of aristocratic particularism and clerical privilege, and standardized weights, measures, and administration. Democratic ideals gave rise to increasing levels of integration and identification of subjects and rulers. Indeed, subjects became citizens. In the course of the nineteenth century, public education and conscript service led to linguistic homogeneity and uniformity (Weber 1976).

Territorial states thus became nation-states. Whereas the term nation originally referred only to the linguistic background of university students, it later came to denote the aggregation of individuals that had come to consider itself a coherent political entity. State building (the attempt to enhance the capacity to rule) and nation building (the attempt to construct a shared political identity among the subjects of that particular territorial state) thus went hand in hand. States became increasingly homogeneous entities, with governments that had the loyalty of their citizens and thus the commensurate ability to deploy those citizens in service of the state on an unprecedented scale.

But the European state evolved not only in terms of capacity. The institutional logic of state organization changed. First, the state became coterminous with territorial sovereignty. Sovereignty, as a claim to final jurisdiction, had originated in Roman law. The emperor was deemed sovereign in the sense of being the ultimate source of law. Hence, he himself could not be bound by any other authority (Hinsley 1969, 1986).

Following the defeat of the Roman Empire in the West, the Roman legal tradition continued in the East Roman, Byzantine empire. Here again the emperor remained superior to any other authority including the church. In the West, however, imperial authority had faded, and the church had usurped many previously imperial functions. Thus, when the German emperors tried to revive the empire in the West, designating it the Holy Roman Empire, clashes between imperial and papal authority became unavoidable.

In the twelfth century, therefore, the German emperor Frederick Barbarossa returned to Roman sources of law to claim superiority vis-à-vis the rival claims of the papacy (Gerbenzon & Algra 1975). This conflict should not be interpreted in the contemporary context of secular and ecclesiastical contests. Both sides advanced secular and transcendental claims. The issue revolved around ultimate hierarchy. Who had the authority to appoint bishops? Could a pope depose an emperor and vice versa? Importantly, because authority claims were both secular and sacerdotal, these claims to rule were not territorially restricted. Both emperor and pope invoked their rights to rule over all the faithful (Pizzorno 1987). Both, at least nominally, could judge kings (even though the emperor seldom pressed the issue).

Emperor and pope both sought allies in their contest. Nominally lesser rulers, kings and powerful dukes, were solicited for support. But aspiring monarchs, who wished to free themselves from either imperial or theocratic oversight, soon advanced their own claims to sovereignty. Less than a century after the emperor had claimed sovereignty, the kings of France and England argued that they were emperors in their own kingdoms (*rex imperator est in regno suo*). Hence, they could not be held subject to any higher authority within their domain. The papacy, desperate for allies, supported such monarchical ideas to gain royal aid against German imperial pretensions. Besides, the kings initially did not seem to advance claims against ecclesiastical authority. In contrast to the universalistic claims of empire and papacy, the kings laid no claim to rule outside their realms. They merely claimed sovereignty within their territorial domains.

For centuries thereafter, sovereignty remained contested. Dynastic linkages and remnants of feudal rule continued to litter the European political landscape arguably until the Napoleonic era. Empire and papacy retained considerable authority for centuries after the beginning of the conflict, thus constraining the latitude for territorial states, but neither emperor nor pope escaped unscathed from the imperial battles. German imperial pretensions met opposition from lords and towns, thus limiting any hierarchy within German borders (Rörig 1969, Fleckenstein 1978, Leuschner 1980, Fuhrmann 1986). The failure of the imperial project gave rise to city-leagues in the North (Dollinger 1964) and powerful city-states in the South (Martines 1979, Becker 1981, Burke 1986, Tabacco 1989). In the West, assertive kings soon curtailed papal universalist pretensions (Reynolds 1984). Territorial sovereignty remained imperfect but started to make inroads into the political landscape of Europe.

Many scholars have argued that the Treaty of Augsburg (1555), which delimited religious claims by territorial borders, and particularly the Peace of Westphalia (1648), firmly established the principle of sovereign, territorial rule. Mutually recognized borders circumscribed the extension of political authority. Within such borders, authority would be exclusive (Gross 1968). So strongly has Westphalia been identified with these principles that scholars sometimes denote the contemporary system as the Westphalian system. As said, however, the early articulation of such principles started well before Westphalia and took many years thereafter to complete. Indeed, according to Krasner (1993, 1999), sovereignty was not even uniformly extended by the nineteenth century. Indeed, sovereign equality was not fully extended to other parts of the globe until decolonization in the post–World War II period.

Whatever the exact periodization, it remains clear that the principle of territorial sovereignty is now a constitutive feature of the modern state. Rule is territorially demarcated. Rulers have no legal claims to ultimate authority beyond their own borders. Conversely, within their borders, their authority is absolute. Sovereignty is mutually constitutive. Only if leaders have voluntarily signed away some of their states' prerogatives may another state claim authority over those states. The sovereignty principle has become a keystone of international law, at once regulating juridical autonomy and the means through which societal interests can be pursued at the international level. The logic of state organization thus changed internal government and external relations (for the dual nature of the state, see Nettl 1968).

THEORETICAL EXPLANATIONS OF THE EMERGENCE OF THE MODERN STATE

Recent scholarship on the origins of the state and its subsequent development differs in three respects from its predecessors. The older literature tended to focus on the macro historical transformations that swept through Europe from the Late Middle Ages through the Renaissance to the present. By starting from the modern state, and by retracing the process through which the state had evolved, such accounts provided a linear, teleological explanation for the observed outcome. More recent scholarship, however, has criticized such unilinear evolutionary accounts (Unger 1987) and drawn attention to the myriad forms of polities that emerged in response to the macro historical contextual variations (Tilly 1990, Spruyt 1994).

In contrast to such macro-level, unilinear accounts, modern scholarship tends to analyze the variation in institutional types and looks for explanations of such variations at the micro level. While recognizing the impact of broad environmental shifts, the attention has shifted to the particularities of individual calculations, coalitional bargaining, and contractual relations. Methodological individualism has augmented macro accounts.

Traditional explanations for the rise of the modern state also focused on the capacity of the state rather than on the particular institutional logic of state sovereignty. Such accounts thus highlighted two features in particular: the ability of the modern state to wage war at an unprecedented scale and the ability of governments to directly intervene in and mobilize their economies. Without denying these functions of the state, the more recent institutionalist scholarship has drawn attention to states' ability to facilitate collective action at the domestic level and to stabilize relations at the international level.

War as the Catalyst for State Formation

One prominent explanation for the emergence of the modern state emphasizes the effects of war making on state capacity. Starting roughly around the end of the fourteenth century, the nature of military technology changed dramatically. Massed infantry of archers and pikemen started to displace the mounted heavy cavalry that had typified feudal warfare for several centuries (Parker 1979, 1988; Delbrück 1982 [1923]; Contamine 1984).

This had several repercussions. Most obviously, the privileged position of the mounted knight declined. Under feudal obligations, vassals were responsible for their own equipment of horse, armor, and retinue. This private possession of armed force in turn gave vassals and lower lords the opportunity to resist hierarchical obligations without reciprocal privileges. Service (usually no more than 40 days) corresponded with considerable autonomy and jurisdiction in one's own feudal domain. Lords thus retained considerable political and economic rights.

The changes in the mode of warfare now led to changes in the composition of the armed forces. Kings and dukes desired larger armies of individually cheap, although collectively more expensive, manpower. The leverage of lower lords on their superiors thus declined. Since armored cavalry declined in importance, monarchs and dukes were not obliged to make concessions to counts, barons, and lesser lords. Indeed, the army might be used against such lesser lords themselves. Mercenary armies could be turned with equal ease on foreign enemies or internal foes.

The increasing scope of warfare gradually led to the emergence of standing armies and the advent of large mercenary contingents. These changes required rulers to raise ever larger sums of capital to fund such forces. Money is the sinews of power, argued Machiavelli succinctly, observing the winds of military change in his day. This transformation in warfare led to a greatly expanded royal administration and a rise in the levels of taxation (Bean 1973, Tilly 1975, Ames & Rapp 1977, Webber & Wildavsky 1986).

Changes in the fifteenth and sixteenth centuries exacerbated these trends. The advent of artillery and eventually hand-held firearms reduced the role of the mounted knight even further. Simple fortifications no longer sufficed. Elaborate, and thus far more expensive, fortifications such as the *trace italienne* required ever larger sums of money. Efficiencies of scale, both in terms of manpower resources and tax base, gave bigger units an advantage. Whereas the army of France at the end of the Hundred Years War amounted to no more than 15,000 troops, by the late 1600s France had more than 300,000 men under arms (Parker 1979). These developments continued unabated because of the high frequency of warfare. Some of the great powers of the sixteenth and seventeenth centuries, such as Spain and France (and, to a slightly lesser extent, England and the Netherlands), were constantly at war for those two centuries.

The French Revolution and the *levee en masse* raised warfare yet one step higher. Rather than rely on vast mercenary contingents, governments now managed to mobilize their own populations on a heretofore unknown scale. The Napoleonic armies could bring hundreds of thousands of troops to bear, as they did in the Russian campaign. In reaction to these challenges, France's rivals, Prussia, Austria, Russia, and Britain, altered their army structures and manpower levels. Ratchet effects permeated all of Europe.

Such earlier accounts that stress the changes in warfare as the primary causal mechanism behind the emergence of the modern state tend to emphasize macro pressures at the systemic level. The long revolution in military affairs and the incessant struggle for hegemony and counterhegemony forged the high-capacity states of Europe.

More recently, scholars have turned to micro-level analyses of how the military context provided new opportunities for individuals to reshape existing political organizations. Macro-level accounts focus primarily on the selective aspects of warfare. Given that defeated powers would fall by the wayside, the remaining polities would all have roughly similar abilities to wage war and would all have the administrative and economic capacity to support such a war effort. Micro-level accounts, by contrast, concentrate on the changing balances of power within the state that favored individual monarchs over lesser lords and created new incentives for such rulers to forge alliances with heretofore excluded groups.

Sophisticated scholarship in this vein blends both macro- and micro-level perspectives. For instance, Tilly uses systemic selective explanations. States that could not wage modern warfare were simply weeded out (Tilly 1990). Simultaneously, he also wields a micro-level account. Comparing states to organized crime syndicates, he suggests that rulers operate similarly to protection rackets (Tilly 1985; also see Levi 1988). They contract with their subjects to exchange protection for taxes. The ability of rulers to offer subjects a more reliable protection racket favored centralized rule over feudal lordship. The strengthening of central authority over decentralized rule, in turn, increased the state's capacity to wage external war. International conflicts then fed back on the rulers' demands on society.

Economic Explanations for the Rise of the State

Like military accounts, economic explanations for the emergence of the modern state may operate at a variety of levels. At the macro level, neo-Marxists tend to emphasize the inherent weakness of economic arrangements that required subsequent adjustment. Other economic accounts might emphasize selective mechanisms. Those rulers who failed to create states that facilitated trade and production lost out to rival modes of organization that succeeded. And here, too, some offer micro-level accounts that concentrate on the changing incentive structures for individuals to alter the older arrangements.

At the macro level, the neo-Marxist variant of this school emphasizes the connections between the rise of capitalism and the emergence of modern states, particularly of absolutist states. Anderson (1974a,b) submits that the inherent flaws of feudal production necessitated state intervention, as occurred in France and Eastern Europe. Wallerstein (1974) too suggests that capitalism emerged simultaneously with the rise of strong states in Europe, which then incorporated peripheral states into the world economy.

Macro-level accounts that focus on the selection of fit and unfit states sometimes note the close ties between military state development and the emergence of early capitalism. If money did indeed constitute the sinews of power, then military competition between states meant that political rulers had vested interests in stimulating their respective economies. It is no surprise, therefore, that the earliest state ventures in capitalism took place in military enterprises. The production of Venetian galleys, for example, in the eleventh century, arguably constituted one of the first capitalist firms (McNeill 1974). Similarly, governments matched mercantilist economic ambition with intervention in such key military sectors as gunpowder production (Nef 1940). States that lacked the means to modernize their economies beyond elementary feudal agricultural modes of production were at a disadvantage. Hence, maritime powers such as Britain and the Netherlands, with more advanced economies (because of trading skills, financial techniques, and the protection of private property), displaced less advanced powers such as Spain and Portugal.

Like new perspectives on the effects of military changes that blend macro- and micro-level narratives, new perspectives on the economic changes permeating late medieval Europe blend macro-level with micro-level accounts that emphasize changes in economic incentive structures. These incentive structures changed in a variety of ways. First, the dispersion of political authority over multiple states (Europe around 1500 included about 500 of them) prevented the blatant exploitation of trade by capricious rulers. Unlike imperial rulers in the Middle East and the Orient, rulers in Europe needed to take mercantile interests into account. Should the level of public protection decline or should the tax burden on traders become too heavy, such merchants could take their business elsewhere. Random predation by rulers was thus checked by the ever-present exit option open to the merchants (North & Thomas 1973, Unger 1987).

Second, with changing demographic patterns and with dispersed political authority, labor could seek less repressive means of production. The worst cases of lordly repression would lead to labor flight; thus, the possessor of labor, land, and capital made compromises, which prevented the autocratic forms of rule seen in non-European imperial polities. These contractual relations at once gave a measure of protection to trade and early industrial interests, and in so doing brought private profit incentives in line with public welfare maximization.

Third, because rulers had a vested interest in enhancing their economies, they also had a stake in defending private wealth. The more rulers recognized this link between public and private welfare, the greater the likelihood of economic success. Rulers and the possessors of capital (merchants and early industry) came to be mutually dependent.

The Institutionalist View of the Modern State

New institutionalism sees institutions as means to resolve cooperation and coordination problems (Moe 1984). Squarely based in rational choice theory and its attention to individual preferences, new institutionalism examines transaction costs, information asymmetries, and principal-agent problems to explain the choice of particular institutional arrangements. In this sense, institutions are the dependent variables. The choice of territorial sovereignty thus has micro-level origins, and we should explain the rise of the state as an institutional solution to cooperation and coordination problems and as a provider of information and reducer of transaction costs.

At the same time, however, other versions of institutionalist analysis, particularly the historical institutionalist school, convincingly demonstrate that choices are constrained by prior institutional arrangements. Institutions are only moderately amenable to dramatic change. More often than not, they follow in the footsteps of long-gone historical predecessors. Institutions form the independent variables to explain agent behavior. Thus, between the macro-structural context and agency, institutions act as conduits of choice and constraint.

The institutionalist explanation makes little effort to place primacy on either the military or economic aspects of state formation. And indeed, empirically, for early modern rulers the pursuit of power was synonymous with the pursuit of plenty. Mercantilist doctrine formalized the sentiments. Even England and the Netherlands, often considered proponents of laissez-faire relative to France and Spain, practiced mercantilism to a considerable degree. The aims of English navigation acts and Dutch attempts to protect key economic sectors differed little from those of absolutist rulers elsewhere. Also, as seen, the earliest large-scale enterprises often blended economic and military functions. Although it is true that the larger part of public revenues (until the late-nineteenth- and early-twentieth-century nascence of a welfare state) went to warfare (Brewer 1989), this is not evidence that the state had no economic effects. The state's protection of private property, its enforcement of legal codes, and its creation of institutions (such as the Bank of England) that remained untouched by the whims of the government might have taken up little of the overall revenue, but they clearly had profound effects on the subsequent development of the economy and the state.

Thus, institutionalists do not try to disentangle whether military or economic explanations are the more powerful. They do not focus on the growing capacity of the state but on the particular institutional logic of state organization. Here institutionalist accounts provide insights into why the particular mode of territorial sovereign state organization has become predominant.

Seen from a new institutionalist perspective, the modern state provided more efficient solutions to cooperation and coordination problems than its predecessors did. Internally, sovereign state institutions formalized relations between subjects and rulers, and between subjects themselves. By justifying rule as the public and exclusive provision of collective goods (defense, legal frameworks), sovereignty also created homogeneity in governance and greater stability in social interactions. Contrary to the multiple and overlapping feudal jurisdictions, sovereignty created hierarchical authority structures. Roman law not only facilitated the extension of royal authority, it also created a legal system that would form the basis of legal codes to this very day. Rather than be subject to multiple and competing taxation, central authority standardized the type and level of exactions. Monarchs also worked to regulate their economies through standardization of coinage, weights, and measures (Zupko 1977, Kula 1986).

In short, internally, sovereignty proved a more efficient form of organization than feudal arrangements. It reduced cooperation and coordination problems between rulers and ruled, as well as between subjects themselves. Social and economic life became regularized, and transaction and information costs were reduced. Sovereign territorial states even proved better than the fragmented city-states or the loose confederal town-leagues at organizing their own subjects (Spruyt 1994).

But the sovereign territorial state also operates as a gatekeeper to the external environment (Nettl 1968). Internationally, the organization of the state represents domestic society to the outside. Here as well, states resolved cooperation and coordination problems more successfully than rival forms of organization. Externally, territorial sovereignty delimited claims to rule by fixed borders, in contrast to universal claims to empire or theocratic organization. In this sense, sovereignty geographically delimited a domestic sphere of jurisdiction (subject to the ruler of that area) and an international sphere of jurisdiction with all actors nominally (but not de facto) equal. Indeed, it created the distinction of domestic and international politics (Holzgrefe 1989). Within the international arena, agreements between the sovereigns would regulate the interactions of private actors of their respective realms that went beyond the geographic extension of the territorial state.

Consequently, rulers who could credibly commit their realms and their subjects were more attractive to other rulers in such international negotiations. Polities with less formal geographic boundaries and less hierarchical authority, such as the city-leagues of the late medieval and Renaissance eras, proved less reliable and thus less attractive as partners (Lloyd 1991). This demand for convergence further aided the spread of territorial sovereignty as the dominant form of state organization through Europe and ultimately across the globe.

Institutionalists have also shed new light on the consequences of variations among modern states. North suggests that states with limited coercive abilities, such as Britain and the Netherlands, fared better in relative terms than more absolutist governments. State institutions that curtailed the ability of rulers to intervene in society created incentives at the micro level for individuals to pursue innovation and profit. Conversely, this incentive at the individual level enhanced the capacity of the state to compete at the international level. Britain and the Netherlands were able to raise larger funds than their absolutist competitors (North & Thomas 1973; North 1981, 1990). Not only were sovereign states superior to nonsovereign entities, but within the group of sovereign states, less coercive institutions had a decisive advantage.

THE CONTEMPORARY RELEVANCE OF DISCUSSIONS ON THE ORIGINS OF THE STATE

Recent scholarship has emphasized the need to blend both comparative perspectives and views from international relations in order to elucidate the various trajectories of state formation (Zolberg 1980). External, macro-historical processes propel individuals to seek new political arrangements, but internal conditions provide the constraints and opportunities through which such choices are mediated. Studying the historical nuances of state formation in the past clarifies the current predicament and future of the modern state.

Whereas European states concurrently developed state capacity and international legal sovereignty, the non-European states often had the latter imposed on them. Juridically sovereign entities, their governments lack the institutional and economic features of advanced capitalist polities. Herbst's (1989, 2000) analyses of African states compares the European historical trajectory to African experiences. Taking the militarist view of the origins of the state, he notes that Africa lacked Europe's long periods of high-intensity warfare. If war made the European states, the lack of technologically advanced large-scale warfare in Africa implies that African states will remain weak. Incentives may thus exist for political entrepreneurs in that continent to engage in risky external relations in order to build their own state capacity.

Those emphasizing economic or institutionalist functions of the state, however, might suggest that the African experience need not mimic the European. Instead, one might argue that judiciously interventionist states, governments that create incentives for private wealth maximization that translate into overall welfare gains as well, might be an alternative outcome. As with early European states, the question would not be whether states have the capacity to compete in external war but whether they have the institutional arrangements to bring private welfare maximization in line with public welfare gains. Some late-developing countries, such as Korea (Amsden 1989), have apparently managed to build state capacity and provide public rather than private goods. Others, such as some African countries, have seen the state cater to narrower clienteles (Bates 1981).

Students of recent transitions in formerly communist countries have similarly returned to examining the origins of states in the West. The questions faced by reformers in Eastern Europe resemble those of early state development. How does one create an efficient market? How does one create a formal institutional network that ties the ruler's hands? (See, for example, North & Weingast 1989.)

In international relations, the predominance of the structural realist perspective precluded any careful examination of the emergence of the state. International relations showed a strong continuity across historical periods. Anarchy constituted the key structural feature of the international system, which explained the behavior of units, be they states or other forms of organization (Waltz 1979, 1986).

But, as critics pointed out, this presumes that domestic politics (organized hierarchically) and international politics (where anarchy reigned) could clearly be distinguished. That presupposition has been criticized across a range of epistemological vantage points. One set of critiques has focused on the particular logic of organization invoked by the principle of territorial sovereignty (Ruggie 1986; Wendt 1987, 1999; Spruyt 1994). The feudal order, for example, revealed heteronomous and cross-cutting jurisdictions, as argued above. In the same spirit, one can criticize structural realism for neglecting the variety of modalities between anarchy and hierarchy (Deudney 1995a). The emergence of territorial sovereignty, with the separation of jurisdictional power into discrete territorial units—what has been described as the Westphalian system—creates anarchy. Anarchy is not a transhistorical given.

Neoliberal institutionalists as well criticize the strict demarcation of domestic hierarchy and international anarchy (Milner 1991). Neoliberal institutionalists also suggest that the Hobbesian anarchy of structural realism fails to recognize how states may create institutions to mitigate the consequences of anarchy. Indeed, some institutional arrangements, such as the European Union, might even create a measure of supranational organization, thus bringing international legal sovereign units under higher multilateral bodies (Sbragia 1992).

Even some realists themselves suggest that different types of polities conducted different international interactions (Gilpin 1981, p. 42). They have also started to pay attention to the various modalities between anarchy and hierarchy (Krasner 1999, Lake 1999). While still acknowledging material interests and relative distributions of power as the primary factors driving international relations, they suggest that territorial sovereignty with juridically equivalent units has often been denied to less powerful states. Studying why certain types of units predominate an international system (states, informal empires, formal empires) and examining how the set of predominant units may change over time sheds light on the patterns of international relations one should expect.

The same conclusion emerges from a radically different epistemological perspective. Constructivists have argued that international relations needs an account of the state (Wendt 1987), because the particular nature of the state, its moral purpose and identity, profoundly affect the type of international system that states create. Stressing cultural and ideational factors rather than materialist variables, constructivists suggest that the state's perspective regarding its internal function and its external role will determine how it acts toward other states. This identity is partially self-constructed and partially determined by the role configurations developed by previous exchanges with others. Social networks and mutual expectations inform and are in turn determined by state identity. Thus, even if the separation of states may be described as a condition of anarchy (the absence of hierarchical authority), polities may create a variety of institutional arrangements that transform the condition from potential conflict to a more benign environment (Reus-Smit 1999). States may interact as predators, as in Hobbesian anarchy, or they may create Lockean societies or Kantian cosmopolitanism (Wendt 1999).

WITHER THE STATE?

The discussion of the origins of the state has gained further relevance because of questions regarding the future of the state. However, some debates regarding the origins, role, and future of the state in contemporary political science confuse changes in the autonomy of the state with changes in the institutional logic of territorial sovereignty. Whereas the autonomy of the state has undergone a transformation in some respects, the principle of territorial sovereignty remains robust.

Recent changes in the international environment have led some to suggest that the state and the state system have been undergoing fundamental changes in the past decades. Accounts that stress the state's military, economic, or institutionalist dimensions generate divergent expectations regarding the future of the Westphalian system. Within each of these approaches there remains considerable variation as well.

An examination of the security environment does not lead to uniform conclusions regarding the future of the state. On the one hand, some argue that nuclear-weapons technology has made the state obsolete (e.g., Herz 1976). If the state's primary function is to protect its populace from foreign attack, the state today can no longer serve that function, as it cannot guarantee the safety of its citizens. Similarly, other scholars (e.g., Deudney 1995b) argue that nuclear weapons have turned the analogy between states in the international system and colliding billiard balls into fiction. The hard shells of the nation-states have been breached, and catastrophic conflict might be avoided in the long run only by mutual binding mechanisms, for which Deudney deploys the term macro-republicanism.

One might also infer from other developments in weapons technology that the scale of the political unit matters less than it once did. Previous centuries rewarded efficiencies of scale. The transition from feudal warfare to large-scale infantry combat had advantaged larger units, or units that had other means of raising the revenue necessary for the new mode of war. Thus, scale (either of geographical size or economic wealth) was vital to the survival of the state. Twentieth-century warfare, however, has diminished territorial size as a key measure of military standing. Territory has not become altogether irrelevant, but the ability to project force rapidly over great distance has diminished the use value of large numbers of troops and buffer zones. Even if one were to disregard the independent effects of nuclear-weapons technology, the third revolution in military technology (in precision-guided munitions, stealth technology, and advanced communications) has expanded the zone of immediate military action.

On the other hand, one might argue that the state still reigns supreme. If the key feature of the modern state is its monopoly on the use of force, as Max Weber argued, then states are still the primary possessors of military might (Gilpin 2001, pp. 15–17). Despite some attempts to forge supranational or multilateral forces, most force structures still resemble traditional alliances, with individual states reluctant to yield their sovereign control. Realist views of international relations remain valid.

Such debates between state-centric realists and state declinists deservedly receive much attention, particularly when one examines the implications of weapons of mass destruction, such as missiles and nuclear weapons, for conventional interstate relations. But such debates neglect the transnational actors who deploy means of violence below the level of the state. The dispersal of such means to terrorist groups, drug cartels, and rogue military units of imploded states has created a new "security problematique" necessitating unexplored types of responses (for one discussion, see Falkenrath 2001). This has led to greater transnational cooperation in some areas, such as international policing, as states attempt to reassert their authority over such actions. But it has also led to the emergence of shadow states within legitimate states. The latter problem poses unique questions of accountability, which the juridical notion of territorial sovereignty had sought to resolve. As Thomson shows (1990, 1994), the introduction of sovereign authority over transnational possessors of violence (mercenaries, pirates) by means of international agreements enhanced the violence monopoly of states, but it also made sovereigns accountable. Whether the same mechanism might apply to contemporary problems is open to debate.

Economic factors as well have led some to question whether the state in its current form will survive. The most prevalent argument has focused on the effects of globalization. Increasing trade and financial flows are said to put pressure on national economies. This has led to a loss of governments' autonomy to set their own economic policy. Given the spread of international trade and commensurate organizations, and given the disciplining effect of financial markets, governments must heed external demands. An inward-looking mercantilist strategy runs the risk of international confrontation (through dispute panels or state retaliation) and capital flight. For example, some have argued that international pressures on the French interventionist economy in the late 1980s led to a retreat from *dirigisme* and to a greater willingness to accept liberal perspectives and further regionalization of the European economy (Moravcsik 1991, Garrett 1992).

The economic theory of clubs further elucidates why states must conform to international dictates. As the group of liberal trading states increases, the opportunity costs of not joining the club increase. Since liberal trade leads to net efficiency gains, and restrictions lead to deadweight losses, the gains for the group of free traders increase not only by the addition of new members but also by the growth in overall welfare efficiency. Conversely, the losses of mercantilists include both the loss of members and the increasing deadweight losses due to trade distortions. This logic holds true even for nonmarket economies. In the absence of real price mechanisms, the difference between world market prices and the assigned prices will increase (Frieden & Rogowski 1996). In short, the movement of some states to regional organizations and greater liberalization precipitates domino effects (Baldwin et al. 1995, ch. 2). Pressures to join regional and multilateral organizations will thus mount. Even prior to formal accession, governments will adopt institutions and standards that should make them viable partners. States seeking to join the European Union will start to amend their institutions to make them compatible with current members. Similarly, states seeking International Monetary Fund or World Bank support will conform to their institutional expectations (such as their demands for an independent central bank). In this sense, state autonomy has decreased.

On the one hand, then, states have incentives to pursue welfare gains by joining regional and multilateral institutions. Some regional organizations, particularly in the case of the European Union, will in fact take on tasks that were previously handled by sovereign governments. Indeed, although the European Union does not yet fulfill all conditions of Mundel's optimal currency area, the liberalization of trade in goods and services and the advent of the Euro currency have greatly integrated the European economies.

On the other hand, liberalism reduces the costs of secessionism. In a mercantilist world with barriers to the free exchange of goods and services, scale becomes a decisive asset. Small states simply lack the domestic markets required for the efficient production of goods (hence, small states tend to rely far more on trade as a percentage of gross national product than large states). But if few barriers exist, size becomes a less important prerequisite. Some scholars have argued that progress on the North American Free Trade Agreement (NAFTA) in fact assisted secessionist sentiments in Quebec.

Although institutionalists recognize that dramatic changes have taken place in the security and economic environment, they see greater durability in the existing state system. Institutions are often the end result of long historical processes and of individual choices mixed with serendipitous and unintended outcomes. Agents no doubt seek to design institutions to best serve their interests (to increase their chances at reelection, to achieve cherished policy goals, or to enhance welfare gains), but their choices are constrained by the available options (Thelen & Steinmo 1992). Thus, although external changes provide an impetus for change, the modalities of response are determined by previous choices. The timing of industrialization and the security position of the state have often determined the degree of state intervention and the degree of liberal democracy. In this sense, institutions are often path-dependent. Once chosen, they subsequently structure a range of other choices around themselves. Lock-in will result (David 1985).

Institutionalists further argue that external economic and military challenges can be met in a variety of ways. The particular response is determined by strategic choices on the part of politicians and economic actors and by previous historical legacies. Thus, at certain points, some models might seem to have an advantage over others, but these findings remain inconclusive. The East Asian development model had great currency during the 1980s and early 1990s. However, with the crisis of the late 1990s, the model has lost favor, and less interventionist strategies gained credence. In light of the downturn in some of the less interventionist states, the latter model too seems to have its flaws. The drive toward convergence might thus be overstated (see Weiss 1998). Empirically, at the level of the firm, evidence of convergence seems ambiguous (Pauly & Reich 1997). In short, institutionalists see less convergence and less pressure on the state.

Most arguments regarding the future of the state pertain to the capacity of states to act autonomously, or they pertain to state dissolution and secession. They do not have a direct bearing on whether territorial sovereignty as a constitutive principle of international relations is diminishing. Contrary to Krasner (1999), I would argue that international legal sovereignty remains robust, although I agree that domestic sovereignty in the past has often been infringed. Even by his own account, international legal sovereignty has been violated less often. Moreover, voluntary association in international or even supranational organizations, which he takes as evidence that sovereignty has not been respected, hardly constitutes a violation of the principle. On the contrary, the very notion that governments are the primary contracting parties validates their supremacy as the key actors in international relations (over, say, nongovernmental organizations or intersocietal networks). Giddens (1987) argues that international organizations in fact reaffirm territorial states as the key actors. Finally, as Zacher shows (2001), the forceful imposition of rule over other polities has declined, particularly in the post-1945 period. The most egregious breaches of sovereignty have vanished with the end of colonialism.

The juridical notion of territorial sovereignty as a regulative device in international relations retains its influence. This is true even for regions where trans-state claims to affinity, such as Pan-Arabism, have vied with national statehood for individual loyalties (Piscatori 1986, Gause 1992). Thus, although interdependence and globalization have diminished the capacity of governments to act autonomously, the principle that states have governments that are supreme within their borders, and that international relations are conducted between juridical equals, remains the key feature of the state and international relations today.

The *Annual Review of Political Science* is online at http://polisci.annualreviews.org

LITERATURE CITED

Ames E, Rapp R. 1977. The birth and death of taxes: a hypothesis. *J. Econ. Hist.* 37:161–78

Amsden A. 1989. *Asia's Next Giant: South Korea and Late Industrialization.* Cambridge, UK: Cambridge Univ. Press

Anderson P. 1974a. *Passages from Antiquity to Feudalism.* London: Verso

Anderson P. 1974b. *Lineages of the Absolutist State.* London: Verso

Baldwin R, Haaparanta P, Kiander J, eds. 1995. *Expanding Membership of the European Union.* New York: Cambridge Univ. Press

Bates R. 1981. *Markets and States in Tropical Africa.* Berkeley: Univ. Calif. Press

Bean R. 1973. War and the birth of the nation state. *J. Econ. Hist.* 33,1:203–21

Becker M. 1981. *Medieval Italy.* Bloomington: Indiana Univ. Press

Berman H. 1983. *Law and Revolution: The Formation of the Western Legal Tradition.* Cambridge, MA: Harvard Univ. Press

Braudel F. 1984. *The Perspective of the World.* New York: Harper & Row

Brewer J. 1989. *The Sinews of Power.* New York: Knopf

Burke P. 1986. City-states. In *States in History,* ed. J Hall, pp. 137–53. New York: Blackwell

Cheyette F, ed. 1975. *Lordship and Community in Medieval Europe.* New York: Krieger

Claesen H. 1985. From the Franks to France— the evolution of a political organization. In

Development and Decline, ed. H Claesen, P van de Velde, M Smith, pp. 196–218. South Hadley, MA: Bergin & Garvey

Contamine P. 1984. *War in the Middle Ages.* New York: Blackwell

Crone P. 1989. *Pre-Industrial Societies.* Oxford, UK: Blackwell

David P. 1985. Clio and the economics of QWERTY. *Am. Econ. Rev.* 75:332–37

Delbrück H. 1982 (1923). *Medieval Warfare.* Lincoln: Univ. Nebraska Press

Deudney D. 1995a. The Philadelphian system: sovereignty, arms control, and balance of power in the American states—union, circa 1787–1861. *Int. Organ.* 49:191–228

Deudney D. 1995b. Nuclear weapons and the waning of the real-state. *Daedalus* 124(2):209–31

Dollinger P. 1964. *The German Hansa.* Stanford, CA: Stanford Univ. Press

Doyle M. 1986. *Empires.* Ithaca, NY: Cornell Univ. Press

Duby G. 1968. *Rural Economy and Country Life in the Medieval West.* Columbia (SC): Univ. South Carolina Press

Duby G. 1974. *The Early Growth of the European Economy.* Ithaca, NY: Cornell Univ. Press

Duby G. 1978. *The Three Orders.* Chicago: Univ. Chicago Press

Dunbabin J. 1985. *France in the Making 843–1180.* Oxford, UK: Oxford Univ. Press

Evans P. 1995. The role of theory in comparative politics: a symposium. *World Polit.* 48(1): 2–10

Falkenrath RA. 2001. Problems of preparedness: U.S. readiness for a domestic terrorist attack. *Int. Secur.* 25(4):147–86

Fawtier R. 1960. *The Capetian Kings of France.* New York: St. Martin's

Fleckenstein J. 1978. *Early Medieval Germany.* Amsterdam: North-Holland

Frieden J, Rogowski R. 1996. The impact of the international economy on national policies: an analytical overview. In *Internationalization and Domestic Politics*, ed. R Keohane, H Milner, pp. 25–47. New York: Cambridge Univ. Press

Fuhrmann H. 1986. *Germany in the High Middle Ages c. 1050–1200.* Cambridge, UK: Cambridge Univ. Press

Garrett G. 1992. International cooperation and institutional choice: the European community's internal market. *Int. Organ.* 46:533–60

Gause G. 1992. Sovereignty, statecraft and stability in the Middle East. *J. Int. Aff.* 45:441–69

Gellner E. 1983. *Nations and Nationalism.* Ithaca, NY: Cornell Univ. Press

Gerbenzon P, Algra N. 1975. *Voortgangh des Rechtes.* Groningen, Netherlands: Tjeenk Willink

Giddens A. 1987. *The Nation-State and Violence.* Berkeley: Univ. Calif. Press

Gilpin R. 1981. *War and Change in World Politics.* Cambridge, UK: Cambridge Univ. Press

Gilpin R. 2001. *Global Political Economy.* Princeton, NJ: Princeton Univ. Press

Gross L. 1968. The peace of Westphalia, 1648–1948. In *International Law and Organization*, ed. R Falk, W Hanrieder, pp. 45–67. Philadelphia: Lippincott

Herbst J. 1989. The creation and maintenance of national boundaries in Africa. *Int. Organ.* 43:673–92

Herbst J. 2000. *States and Power in Africa: Comparative Lessons in Authority and Control.* Princeton, NJ: Princeton Univ. Press

Herz J. 1976. *The Nation-State and the Crisis of World Politics.* New York: McKay

Hinsley FH. 1969. The concept of sovereignty and the relations between states. In *In Defense of Sovereignty*, ed. W Stankiewicz, pp. 275–88. New York: Oxford Univ. Press

Hinsley FH. 1986. *Sovereignty.* Cambridge, UK: Cambridge Univ. Press

Hobsbawn EJ. 1990. *Nations and Nationalism Since 1780.* New York: Cambridge Univ. Press

Holzgrefe JL. 1989. The origins of modern international relations theory. *Rev. Int. Stud.* 15:11–26

Jackson R. 1987. Quasi states, dual regimes, and neo-classical theory: international jurisprudence and the Third World. *Int. Organ.* 41:519–49

Krasner S. 1993. Westphalia and all that. In *Ideas and Foreign Policy*, ed. J Goldstein, R Keohane, pp. 235–64. Ithaca, NY: Cornell Univ. Press

Krasner S. 1999. *Sovereignty: Organized Hypocrisy.* Princeton, NJ: Princeton Univ. Press

Kratochwil F. 1986. Of systems, boundaries and territoriality: an inquiry into the formation of the state system. *World Polit.* 39:27–52

Kula W. 1986. *Measures and Men.* Princeton, NJ: Princeton Univ. Press

Lake D. 1999. *Entangling Relations.* Princeton, NJ: Princeton Univ. Press

Leuschner J. 1980. *Germany in the Late Middle Ages.* Amsterdam: North-Holland

Levi M. 1988. *Of Rule and Revenue.* Berkeley: Univ. Calif. Press

Lloyd TH. 1991. *England and the German Hanse 1157–1611.* New York: Cambridge Univ. Press

Mair L. 1962. *Primitive Government.* Harmondsworth, UK: Penguin

Mann M. 1986. *The Sources of Social Power.* Cambridge, UK: Cambridge Univ. Press

Martines L. 1979. *Power and Imagination.* New York: Vintage

McNeill W. 1974. *Venice: The Hinge of Europe 1081–1797.* Chicago: Univ. Chicago Press

Milner H. 1991. The assumption of anarchy in international relations theory: a critique. *Rev. Int. Stud.* 17:67–85

Moe T. 1984. The new economics of organization. *Am. J. Polit. Sci.* 28:739–77

Moravcsik A. 1991. Negotiating the single European act: national interests and conventional statecraft in the European community. *Int. Organ.* 45:19–56

Nef J. 1940. *Industry and Government in France and England, 1540–1640.* Ithaca, NY: Cornell Univ. Press

Nettl JP. 1968. The state as a conceptual variable. *World Polit.* 20:559–92

North D. 1981. *Structure and Change in Economic History.* New York: Norton

North D. 1990. *Institutions, Institutional Change and Economic Performance.* Cambridge, UK: Cambridge Univ. Press

North D, Thomas R. 1973. *The Rise of the Western World.* Cambridge, UK: Cambridge Univ. Press

North D, Weingast B. 1989. Constitutions and commitment: the evolution of institutions governing public choice in 17th century England. *J. Econ. Hist.* 49:803–32

Parker G. 1979. Warfare. In *New Cambridge Modern History*, ed. P Burke, 13:201–19 Cambridge, UK: Cambridge Univ. Press

Parker G. 1988. *The Military Revolution.* New York: Cambridge Univ. Press

Pauly L, Reich S. 1997. National structures and multinational corporate behavior: enduring differences in the age of globalization. *Int. Organ.* 51:1–30

Pirenne H. 1952 (1925). *Medieval Cities.* Princeton, NJ: Princeton Univ. Press

Pirenne H. 1956. *Economic and Social History of Medieval Europe.* New York: Harcourt Brace Jovanovich

Piscatori J. 1986. *Islam in a World of Nation-States.* New York: Cambridge Univ. Press

Pizzorno A. 1987. Politics unbound. In *Changing Boundaries of the Political*, ed. C Maier, pp. 27–62. Cambridge, UK: Cambridge Univ. Press

Poggi G. 1978. *The Development of the Modern State.* Stanford, CA: Stanford Univ. Press

Reus-Smit C. 1999. *The Moral Purpose of the State.* Princeton, NJ: Princeton Univ. Press

Reynolds S. 1984. *Kingdoms and Communities in Western Europe 900–1300.* Oxford, UK: Clarendon

Rörig F. 1969. *The Medieval Town.* Berkeley: Univ. Calif. Press

Rosenau J. 1989. Global changes and theoretical challenges: toward a post-international politics for the 1990s. In *Global Changes and Theoretical Challenges*, ed. EO Czempiel, J Rosenau, pp. 1–20. Lexington, MA: Heath

Rosenau J, Czempiel EO, eds. 1992. *Governance Without Government: Order and Change in World Politics.* New York: Cambridge Univ. Press

Ruggie J. 1986. Continuity and transformation in the world polity. In *Neorealism and Its Critics*, ed. R Keohane, pp. 131–57. New York: Columbia Univ. Press

Ruggie J. 1993. Territoriality and beyond: problematizing modernity in international relations. *Int. Organ.* 47:139–74

Runciman WG. 1982. Origins of states: the case of archaic Greece. *Comp. Stud. Soc. Hist.* 24:351–77

Sbragia A. 1992. Thinking about the future: the uses of comparison. In *Europolitics*, ed. A Sbragia, pp. 257–91. Washington, DC: Brookings Inst.

Spruyt H. 1994. *The Sovereign State and Its Competitors.* Princeton, NJ: Princeton Univ. Press

Strayer J. 1965. *Feudalism.* New York: Van Nostrand Reinhold

Strayer J. 1970. *On the Medieval Origins of the Modern State.* Princeton, NJ: Princeton Univ. Press

Strayer J. 1980. *The Reign of Philip the Fair.* Princeton, NJ: Princeton Univ. Press

Tabacco G. 1989. *The Struggle for Power in Medieval Italy.* Cambridge, UK: Cambridge Univ. Press

Thelen K, Steinmo S. 1992. Historical institutionalism in comparative politics. In *Structuring Politics*, ed. S Steinmo, K Thelen, F Longstreth, pp. 2–32. New York: Cambridge Univ. Press

Thomson J. 1990. State practices, international norms, and the decline of mercenarism. *Int. Stud. Q.* 34:23–48

Thomson J. 1994. *Mercenaries, Pirates, and Sovereigns*. Princeton, NJ: Princeton Univ. Press

Tierney B. 1964. *The Crisis of Church and State 1050–1300*. Englewood Cliffs, NJ: Prentice Hall

Tilly C, ed. 1975. *The Formation of National States in Western Europe*. Princeton, NJ: Princeton Univ. Press

Tilly C. 1985. War making and state making as organized crime. In *Bringing the State Back In*, ed. P Evans, D Rueschemeyer, T Skocpol, pp. 169–91. Cambridge, UK: Cambridge Univ. Press

Tilly C. 1990. *Coercion, Capital and European States, AD 990–1990*. Cambridge, UK: Blackwell

Unger R. 1987. *Plasticity into Power*. New York: Cambridge Univ. Press

Wallerstein I. 1974. *The Modern World System*, Vol 1. Orlando, FL: Academic

Waltz K. 1979. *Theory of International Politics*. New York: Random House

Waltz K. 1986. Reflections on *Theory of International Politics*: a response to my critics. In *Neorealism and Its Critics*, ed. R Keohane, pp. 322–46. New York: Columbia Univ. Press

Webber C, Wildavsky A. 1986. *A History of Taxation and Expenditure in the Western World*. New York: Simon & Schuster

Weber E. 1976. *Peasants into Frenchmen: The Modernization of Rural France 1870–1914*. Stanford, CA: Stanford Univ. Press

Weiss L. 1998. *The Myth of the Powerless State*. Ithaca, NY: Cornell Univ. Press

Wendt A. 1987. The agent-structure problem in international relations theory. *Int. Organ.* 41:335–70

Wendt A. 1999. *Social Theory of International Politics*. New York: Cambridge Univ. Press

Zacher M. 2001. The territorial integrity norm: international boundaries and the use of force. *Int. Organ.* 55:215–50

Zolberg A. 1980. Strategic interactions and the formation of modern states: France and England. *Int. Soc. Sci. J.* 32:687–716

Zupko R. 1977. *British Weights and Measures*. Madison: Univ. Wisc. Press

Annu. Rev. Polit. Sci. 2002. 5:151–79
DOI: 10.1146/annurev.polisci.5.102301.084508
Copyright © 2002 by Annual Reviews. All rights reserved

DEMOCRATIC INSTITUTIONS AND REGIME SURVIVAL: Parliamentary and Presidential Democracies Reconsidered

José Antonio Cheibub[1] and Fernando Limongi[2]

[1]*Department of Political Science, Yale University, New Haven, Connecticut 06511;*
e-mail: jose.cheibub@yale.edu
[2]*Departmento de Ciência Política, Universidade de São Paulo, São Paulo, SP 05508-900,*
Brazil; e-mail: fdmplimo@pop.usp.br

Key Words   democratic stability, minority governments, coalitions, legislative
institutions

■ **Abstract**   We review arguments and empirical evidence in the comparative literature that bear on the differences in the survival rates of parliamentary and presidential democracies. Most of these arguments focus on the fact that presidential democracies are based on the separation of executive and legislative powers, whereas parliamentary democracies are based on the fusion of these powers. The implications of this basic distinction lead to radically different behavior and outcomes under each regime. We argue that this perspective is misguided and that one cannot deduce the functioning of the political system from the way governments are formed. Other provisions, constitutional and otherwise, also affect the way parliamentary and presidential democracies operate, and these provisions may counteract some of the tendencies that we would expect to observe if we derived the regime's performance from its basic constitutional principle.

INTRODUCTION

The idea that the form of government influences the survival of democracies was a major point of contention among students of comparative politics in the late 1980s and 1990s. The argument, first developed by Linz (1978), about the superiority of parliamentary over presidential institutions guided much of the discussion about the prospects of democracies born in the wake of the so-called third wave of democratization. The new conventional wisdom among comparative politics scholars was that, if these democracies were to succeed, they should adopt parliamentary institutions.

Indeed, parliamentary democracies seem to outperform presidential democracies in many key aspects, notably in their capacity to survive under a wide set of conditions. Between 1946 and 1999, one in every 23 presidential regimes died (that is, became a dictatorship), whereas only one in every 58 parliamentary regimes

1094-2939/02/0615-0151$14.00   **151**

died. At very low levels of economic development, say at the level observed in sub-Saharan Africa, neither parliamentary nor presidential democracies are likely to survive; under these circumstances, one in every eight democracies, of either type, dies. At higher levels of development, however, things are different. Not only are parliamentary democracies consistently more likely to survive than presidential democracies, their chances of survival under economic crisis are at least as good as presidential democracies' chances of survival under economic expansion.[1] Moreover, although presidential democracies are more likely to emerge from military dictatorships than from civilian dictatorships, and thus are more likely to become dictatorships themselves, when origin is held constant we still find that presidential democracies die sooner than parliamentary democracies (Przeworski et al. 2000).

This fact has commonly been interpreted as evidence that the instability of presidential democracies stems from the principle of separation between executive and legislative authorities, which distinguishes presidentialism from parliamentarism. Several implications are derived from this basic difference that would explain why survival rates differ between these democratic regimes. The fusion of powers characteristic of parliamentarism is supposed to generate governments capable of governing because they are supported by a majority in parliament, composed of highly disciplined parties prone to cooperate with one another, which, together, would produce a highly centralized decision-making process. Presidential regimes, however, frequently generate presidents who cannot count on a majority of seats in congress. Congress is composed of individual legislators who have little incentive to cooperate with one another, with their parties, or with the executive. As a consequence, decision making under presidentialism is highly decentralized. Presidential regimes, therefore, are characterized by weak political parties and frequent stalemates between the president and congress in a context of loose decision making. Because presidential regimes lack a mechanism to resolve conflicts between executives and legislatures (such as the votes of confidence or censure of parliamentary regimes), minority presidents, divided government, and deadlock would drive actors toward extraconstitutional means of resolving their differences, thus making presidential regimes prone to instability and eventual death. This view, now widespread, was originally formulated by Linz (1978, elaborated in 1994). Other proponents include Stepan & Skach (1993), González & Gillespie (1994, p. 172), Hartlyn (1994, p. 221), Valenzuela (1994, p. 136), Jones (1995a, pp. 34, 38), Mainwaring & Scully (1995), Linz & Stepan (1996, p. 181), Niño (1996, pp. 168–69), Huang (1997, pp. 138–39), and Ackerman (2000, p. 645).

This view, however, is problematic. Parliamentary and presidential regimes are indeed founded on different constitutional principles, and this is a central choice in any democratic constitution. However, the operation of the political system cannot be entirely derived from the mode of government formation. Other provisions, constitutional and otherwise, also affect the way parliamentary and presidential

---

[1]These figures are based on the Regime and Development Database, available at http://pantheon.yale.edu/~jac236/.

democracies operate, and these provisions may counteract some of the tendencies that we would expect to observe if we derived the regime's entire performance from its basic constitutional principles. Moreover, even if these principles were the main factor in shaping incentives under parliamentary and presidential systems, it would not be sufficient to simply assert that they are different and that hence outcomes should also be different. One would need to specify which institutional features are affected by which incentives and with what consequences.

We review arguments and empirical evidence in the comparative literature that bear on the differences in the performance of parliamentary and presidential regimes that emerge from the alleged differences in incentives that these constitutional frameworks generate. We focus on three areas that, according to the traditional view, give an advantage to parliamentary regimes: legislative majorities, incentives for cooperation, and the centralization of the decision-making process. Although we believe that parliamentarism does outperform presidentialism in survival, we have good reasons to doubt that we understand what causes this difference. This is why we advocate a return to a theme about which some believe political science already knows everything there is to know.

THE "MAJORITARIAN IMPERATIVE"

There is a majoritarian imperative in parliamentarism, or so the conventional view implies. This imperative seems to follow from the very definition of parliamentary democracies.

Parliamentarism, according to this view, is a regime in which the government, in order to attain and retain power, must enjoy the confidence of the legislature. Because decisions are made by majority rule, no parliamentary government can exist without the support of a majority. Minority governments could occasionally emerge, but these would be relatively infrequent and necessarily ephemeral, since they would simply reflect the temporary inability of the current majority to crystalize. This inability is temporary because the system contains automatic correctives for these situations: Either a new government supported by a majority will be formed, or, if this is not possible, new elections will be held so that such a majority may emerge.

Presidential regimes, in contrast, lack the majoritarian imperative. But majorities also matter under presidentialism. Voters have two agents who, by design, do not necessarily represent the same majority. These agents have fixed terms in office and do not depend on each other to exist. If elections result in a situation in which the presidential party does not control a majority of legislative seats, there is no mechanism to solve the conflicts between the two legitimate majorities. The most likely outcome, it is believed, is stalemate and impasse between the executive and the legislative branch, which can ultimately result in the collapse of the democratic regime.

However, several theoretical and empirical arguments suggest that the majoritarian imperative that supposedly distinguishes parliamentarism and presidentialism is neither an imperative nor sufficient to distinguish them.

In the first place, as conclusively demonstrated by Strom (1990), parliamentary governments do not necessarily produce majority governments. We consider this issue in more detail below when we discuss coalition formation. Here it is sufficient to say that minority governments existed 22% of the time in parliamentary regimes from 1946 to 1999 (Cheibub et al. 2001). Other counts (see, e.g., Strom 1990, Cheibub 1998), based exclusively on industrialized democracies, find that about one third of governments formed under parliamentarism have a minority status.

More important, Strom's (1990) analysis shows that minority governments are not necessarily a sign of political instability. Rather, the emergence of minority governments can be explained in terms of the calculus made by party leaders about the costs and benefits of participating in government, given that they are concerned not only with achieving office but also with the policies to be implemented by the government. This calculus, Strom argues, is affected by the degree of policy influence parties can exert when outside the government, as well as the competitiveness and decisiveness of the electoral process. Out-of-government policy influence, in turn, depends essentially on the organization of parliament (existence of standing committees, degree of specialization, scope of action, allocation rules). Electoral decisiveness and competitiveness depend on the clarity of the electoral alternatives presented to voters (identifiability), the degree to which the distribution of seats fluctuates from party to party between elections (competitiveness), the direct relationship between electoral success and government participation (responsiveness), and the proximity of elections to government formation.

Thus, it is simply not true that majority governments are the expected outcome of government formation under parliamentarism. Whether they are depends on institutional traits that are not part of what defines a democracy as parliamentary.

Furthermore, there is evidence that minority governments under presidentialism, although frequent, are not as widespread as we would expect them to be. Cheibub (2002), from whose work Table 1 was adapted, shows that about 40% of the years of presidentialism between 1946 and 1996 were under minority governments, a number not far from the estimates for parliamentary regimes. These cases, as he shows, do not occur randomly. The frequency of minority presidential governments is associated with the number of political parties (although not in the expected way), with the type of electoral system, and with the electoral cycle (Mainwaring 1993, Jones 1995, Shugart 1995). However, the occurrence of minority governments has no impact whatsoever on the survival of presidential democracies (Cheibub 2002).

As for deadlock, the specter that supposedly haunts presidentialism, it is neither pervasive nor is it associated with regime breakdown (Cheibub 2002). Deadlock occurs only when the preferences of a majority cannot prevail. These situations depend both on the share of seats controlled by the party of the president in congress and on specific institutional features regarding the presidential veto and legislative override of the presidential veto: whether the president has veto power; the type of congressional majority necessary to override the presidential veto; whether the system is unicameral or bicameral; and whether, in bicameral systems,

TABLE 1 Minority presidents, deadlock situations, and transition probabilities in presidential regimes by type of legislature, effective number of political parties, electoral system, and timing of elections (source: Cheibub 2002)

	% Minority presidents[a] (N)	Deadlock situations[b] (N)	Transition probabilities[c]
All	40.22 (726)	33.52 (710)	0.0395
Type of legislature:			
Unicameral	36.46 (277)	29.67 (273)	0.0464
Bicameral	42.54 (449)	35.96 (437)	0.0353
Electoral system:			
Majority-plurality	39.04 (146)	36.99 (146)	0.0482
Pure proportional	39.42 (553)	32.96 (540)	0.0378
Pure prop. + mixed	40.52 (580)	32.62 (564)	0.0372
Effective number of parties (ENP):			
ENP ≤ 2	35.33 (150)	27.33 (150)	0.0458
$2 < ENP \leq 3$	33.45 (281)	31.49 (280)	0.0209
$3 < ENP \leq 4$	59.69 (129)	49.22 (128)	0.0714
$4 < ENP \leq 5$	28.17 (71)	28.17 (71)	0.0417
ENP > 5	50.60 (83)	32.10 (81)	0.0111
Timing of legislative and presidential elections:			
Non-concurrent	45.16 (124)	40.32 (124)	0.0318
Alternate	66.92 (133)	47.11 (121)	0.0548
Non-conc. + alternate	56.42 (257)	43.67 (245)	0.0429
Concurrent	31.34 (469)	28.17 (465)	0.0374
Political conditions			
Minority presidents			0.0462
Majority presidents			0.0293
Minority governments[d]			0.0392
Majority governments[d]			0.0377
Deadlock situations			0.0378
No deadlock situations			0.0318

[a]"Minority presidents" include the cases in which the party of the president does not control >50% of the seats in the legislature in a unicameral system; or where it does not control >50% of the seats in at least one of the chambers in a bicameral system.

[b]"Deadlock situations" are defined by the number of seats held by the government, by whether presidents can veto legislation, by the requirements for legislative override of the presidential veto, by the legislative structure, and by whether, in bicameral systems, veto override is by a vote in each house or by a joint session of both houses.

[c]"Transition probabilities" indicate the probability that a presidential regime will become a dictatorship (the number of transitions away from presidentialism divided by the number of cases of presidentialism).

[d]"Minority" and "majority" governments are defined by the share of legislative seats held by all the parties that hold cabinet positions.

veto override is by a vote in each chamber separately or in a joint session of both chambers. In combination with the share of seats held by the government, these factors allow one to distinguish three situations: presidential dominance, opposition dominance, and legislative deadlock. The latter occurs only when the president is likely to veto a bill approved by a majority in the legislature but that majority is not sufficient to override the presidential veto.

If arguments about the perils of presidentialism are correct, presidential democracies should face higher risks of dying when conditions for deadlock between the president and congress are met. Yet, as we see at the bottom of Table 1, this is not the case. The difference in the transition probabilities for deadlock and no-deadlock situations, although in favor of the former, is rather small: One in every 26 presidential democracies dies when there is deadlock, one in every 31 when there is no deadlock. This difference does not seem to warrant the level of concern with deadlock that is often expressed in the comparative literature on presidentialism. The belief that the survival prospects of presidential democracies are compromised when presidential parties lack a majority of seats in congress, or when deadlock situations exist, has no empirical basis.

The conventional view is that deadlock will never occur in parliamentary regimes. Indeed, parliamentary regimes are designed so that whenever there is a deadlock between the government and the legislature, either the government changes or the legislature changes. Thus, although divided government may also exist under parliamentarism (for example with minority governments), the fact that the government in these systems exists only as long as there is no alternative majority that can replace it distinguishes them from presidential regimes. Ultimately, divided government in parliamentarism cannot produce deadlock, at least not deadlock in the same sense as in presidentialism.

Yet, the fact that parliamentarism includes a mechanism that can be invoked in case of policy conflict between the government and the legislative majority does not mean that this mechanism will always be invoked, or that, once invoked, it will necessarily put an end to the disagreement that led to its use. For this reason, deadlock under parliamentary regimes may occur over time, as when governments succeed governments and no stable majority is formed even after new elections are held.

The discussion so far has been guided by the supposition that the existence of a majority, either in parliamentarism or in presidentialism, automatically means the ability of the government to govern. However, the scope of action available to the government can also be reduced as it seeks to obtain majority status. What matters is both the number of parties that must come together in order to establish a majority and the cohesion of the party (or parties) that belong to the majority. In spatial terms, government action is necessarily limited to the area that contains policy proposals preferred by its supporters over the status quo. That area, however, may be small, and it may become smaller as the government attempts to broaden its base of support; that is, as it attempts to secure the support of a majority in the legislature. As Tsebelis (1995) has demonstrated, policy change in democratic regimes is associated with the number of actors who can veto a proposal. The number of veto players, in turn, is a function of both institutional and ideological variables: Policy stability increases with the number and the cohesion of, and the distance among, the parties that belong to the government.

The reduction in the scope of governmental action as a by-product of majority building will certainly affect the policies pursued in a given system. Whether it will affect the survival of the regime and whether its impact will be larger under presidentialism than under parliamentarism cannot be specified a priori. The point is that governments may have to pay the price of policy immobility in order to form a majority, and this price may have a negative effect on the survival of the democratic regime.

INCENTIVES FOR COOPERATION

Parliamentary regimes are supposed to foster cooperation. Political parties have an incentive to cooperate with one another; parties in the government will support the executive, and parties out of the government will refrain from escalating conflicts because they may, at any time, become part of the government; individual members of parliament will align themselves with their parties. Consequently, the government is supported by a majority composed of highly disciplined parties, prone to cooperate with one another. Presidentialism, on the other hand, is characterized by the absence of such incentives and hence is likely to generate governments that, even if supported by a majority, are based on undisciplined parties that tend to compete fiercely with each other.

There are, in fact, two distinct issues here: the discipline of political parties and their propensity to enter and stay in governing coalitions. Although related, these issues must be discussed separately.

Party Discipline

There are formal and nonformal arguments relating regime type to party discipline or cohesion in legislative vote.[2] In the nonformal arguments, which originated with Linz and are reproduced by most critics of presidentialism, what matters is

---

[2]Conceptually, party discipline and cohesion are distinct (Ozbudun 1970, Tsebelis 1995). Empirically, however, we can only observe a group of legislators voting together, either as an expression of their true preferences or as the result of disciplinary measures. As Bowler et al. (1999b) note, this distinction matters only when cohesion is moderate. If it is very high, then disciplinary measures are not necessary. If cohesion is very low, it is unlikely that such a heterogeneous group of legislators will agree to any measure that will make them vote together. Only when cohesion is high enough that a group of like-minded representatives will accept a common set of constraining rules, but low enough that they will occasionally find it in their interests to vote against the party's position, do disciplinary mechanisms become relevant. In what follows, unless explicitly noted, we treat discipline and cohesion as synonymous.

the legislators' desire to come to and remain in office. The postulate is that the threat of government dissolution and early elections is necessary and sufficient to induce party discipline. Here is how the argument works.

Under parliamentarism, undisciplined parties may mean a failure to obtain majority support in parliament, the defeat of government bills, and consequently the fall of the government. In order to remain in government, political parties enforce discipline so that their members in parliament can be counted on to support the bills proposed by the government. Individual legislators, in turn, have an incentive to support the government in order to prevent the occurrence of early elections in which they would risk losing their positions. Under presidentialism, since the government and the legislature are independently constituted, office-seeking political parties have no reason to impose discipline on their members; their survival in office does not depend on the result of any particular vote in the legislature. Individual members of congress also lack any incentive to accept the discipline of political parties (if they were to try to impose it); voting against the party or the government would not make them any more likely to lose their mandates in early elections.

Thus, given office-seeking politicians, the fusion of power that characterizes parliamentary regimes generates incentives for individual legislators and political parties to cooperate with the government, resulting in a high level of party discipline. The separation of powers that characterizes presidentialism implies very low levels of party discipline. Even if a president were lucky enough to belong to a party that controlled a majority of seats in congress, he or she could not necessarily count on the support of that majority in order to govern. On the contrary, the president should expect, at least under some circumstances, that no support would be forthcoming from that majority.[3]

There are several problems with this argument. At the highest level of generality, the assumption on which it is based—that politicians care only about office—is not tenable. If it were true, we should never observe minority governments, since the party in charge of forming a government would always be able to lure some party into the government in order to attain a majority. Yet minority governments, as we have seen, are not infrequent in either parliamentary or presidential regimes.

At a lower level of generality, the standard argument that connects the threat of government dissolution with party discipline is inconsistent. If the argument

---

[3]One of the most-noted circumstances appears near the end of the presidential term. As presidential elections near, the argument goes, members of the president's party try to distance themselves from him or her in order to avoid paying the costs associated with the government's policies. This argument neglects the possibility of circumstances in which members of the president's party do want to identify with the president in order to share in the benefits of the government's policies. Implicitly, this argument assumes that control over the government brings no electoral benefit and that presidents are not able to transfer votes for the politicians who support them. This, however, does not seem to be the case. Data on the rates of presidential reelection in the absence of term limits show that incumbency is indeed a big advantage (see, for instance, Cheibub & Przeworski 1999). Note, in addition, that the effect of forthcoming elections on support for the government, if any, should also be expected under parliamentarism (Baron 1998).

assumes at one stage that individual legislators may gain electorally by providing specific benefits to their constituency, it denies the existence of these benefits at the next stage. Let us consider this point in detail.

Suppose a key presidential initiative implies losses for a specific group and gains for the whole society. In the standard view, presidents have no means to induce legislators to support a proposal that removes some special privileges of a given constituency. Because legislators are office seekers, they have a clear preference for distributive policies, that is, policies that concentrate benefits on their constituencies and disperse the costs. Hence, legislators will do better if they vote against the presidential initiative and protect their constituency's narrow interests so that they will obtain its vote again in the future. They bear no costs of acting this way, and they will collect the benefits when elections are due.

The same would not occur under a parliamentary regime. An identical situation would lead to a different result. Because dissolution and early election are possible, legislators will prefer to follow the party line and support the government so that they can guarantee their seats. There are costs to bear, since one may lose his or her seat. By calling (or threatening to call) an early election, the prime minister invites the electorate to judge the behavior of the legislator.

But why would a legislator who voted against the party to protect the interests of his or her constituency be punished by that same constituency? If the legislator loses the seat in early elections because his vote helped bring the government down, it must be because the number of voters who benefited from that action is not large enough to prevail electorally. If this is the case, then the legislator should know that it does not pay electorally to go against the party line and in favor of those voters. In turn, if the number of voters who benefited from the government defeat is large enough to elect a representative, then the legislator can safely defy the party line to protect them, since the legislator can expect to survive an early election.[4] Therefore, with purely office-seeking politicians, early elections are not a credible threat that would induce party discipline.

Hence, one needs something else to argue that the threat of dissolution leads to party discipline. The standard argument includes an unstated presumption that voters in parliamentary regimes base their votes on party labels and not on individual politicians. In other words, it is presumed that under parliamentarism the electoral connection is necessarily different from the one that prevails in the US congress, as analyzed by Mayhew (1974). But whether voters vote on the basis of party labels or of legislators' personal attributes is not necessarily related to the form of government.

As a matter of fact, electoral laws, and not the form of government, are usually seen as the main factor determining whether voters will vote according to personal or party attributes in a given system. In Carey & Shugart's (1994) attempt to rank electoral systems according to the kind of incentives they provide, the key factor is

---

[4]Government dissolution, in fact, is not always an undesired outcome. As Smith (1996) shows in a model of majority governments, early elections are more likely to be called when the times are good (see also Baron 1998).

the control parties exercise over a politician's chances to get elected or reelected. This control, in turn, depends on the access to the ballot, the rules for transferring votes within party lists, the choices offered to vote below the party level, and the district magnitude. Parties are said to be strong and capable of enforcing discipline if these factors allow them to affect the probability that a politician will get elected.

Important as the electoral variables may be in affecting the degree of party discipline in a system, they cannot be the whole story. Electoral laws may provide the incentives for legislators to cultivate the personal vote (by seeking policies that have concentrated benefits and diffuse costs), but the decision-making process may deny them the means to do so (by centralizing decision making so that the preferences of the individual legislator are virtually irrelevant).[5] Indeed, the personal vote in the US congress is closely related to the decentralized decision-making process that characterizes its committee system (Mayhew 1974). On the other hand, as Cox (1987) demonstrated in his analysis of nineteenth-century England, a centralized decision-making process may neutralize the electoral incentives for the cultivation of the personal vote.

What matters is whether we have reasons to expect that parliamentary governments necessarily foster a higher degree of centralization in policy making. Is the process described by Cox inherent to parliamentarism? Are all presidential regimes like the one described by Mayhew? In other words, can we take the United States and England to be the paradigmatic cases of presidential and parliamentary regimes when it comes to policy making? We argue in the next section that they are not, and that we have no reason to expect a systematic variation in the centralization of policy making between the two regimes.

Finally, some of the implications of the standard view concerning the relationship between mode of government formation and party discipline are not supported by the facts. The calculus of the individual legislator under parliamentarism cannot be solely connected with the risk of election because early election is not the necessary consequence, or even the most frequent consequence, of a government dissolution. Cheibub (1998) shows that 56% of all prime ministers in 21 industrialized democracies between 1946 and 1995 changed without elections. In the same data set, 38% of changes in the party of the prime minister, 46% of changes in the partisan composition of the government, and 24% of changes in the major party in the government occurred without elections. Elections are far from being the necessary outcome of government dissolution in parliamentary democracies; hence, the costs they represent are not necessarily high and uniformly distributed across these systems. This point is forcefully made by Mershon (1996 and 1999) in her studies of coalition formation in Italy and other countries.

---

[5]Here the case of post-1988 Brazil, arguably the presidential system with the most permissive party legislation in the world, becomes relevant (Limongi & Figueiredo 1995). In any roll-call vote taken in the lower house of the Brazilian National Congress since 1988, 9 out of 10 representatives voted according to the recommendation of their party leaders. As Limongi & Figueiredo argue, some of this unexpected level of legislative vote cohesion must be attributed to the organizational structure of congress.

On the other hand, as far as presidentialism is concerned, the standard argument assumes that voters use their two votes independently and that representatives are judged exclusively by what they do to defend the narrow and immediate interests of their constituency. Voters do not care about their representative's role in the success or failure of the executive. If this were true, the electoral performance of the presidential party in legislative elections would be entirely dissociated from the performance of the president. Yet, considerable evidence suggests that voters do tend to associate their vote in presidential and legislative elections. This is why concurrent presidential and legislative elections would work to reduce the number of political parties competing in a given political system (Shugart & Carey 1992, Jones 1995, Shugart 1995). Hence, if voters connect their votes in presidential-legislative elections, legislators will have incentives to support the executive in some key votes. Their seats may depend on the good performance of the president.

Formal arguments linking parliamentary regimes with legislative vote cohesion have been recently developed by several authors. Huber's (1996b) spatial model of the interaction between the prime minister, the cabinet, and the prime minister's majority highlights the role of vote-of-confidence procedures in legislative outcomes. Baron (1998) and Diermeier & Feddersen (1998) use a model of legislative bargaining to show how confidence procedures that characterize parliamentary democracies affect legislative cohesion. These papers represent important advances in the understanding of the functioning of parliamentary democracies, but they do not necessarily provide a compelling argument to the effect that levels of legislative cohesion are higher in parliamentary than in presidential democracies.

To begin with, the models proposed by Huber, on the one hand, and Baron and Diermeier & Feddersen, on the other, differ in at least one very important aspect. Whereas the latter models explicitly set up a situation entailing conflict of interests among political parties so that legislative cohesion is not a function of similarity of preferences, Huber's analysis does not. In his case, there is an area of the policy space in which the preferences of all the actors overlap, and what the model shows is that the agenda power of the prime minister will allow her to pick, in that area, the policy that she prefers. Legislators who go against the government do so in order to signal to their constituents that they are defending their interests. They do so, however, knowing that the prime minister will choose a policy that they prefer over the status quo. The contribution of Huber's model, in our view, is not to show that vote-of-confidence procedures induce high levels of party discipline in a context of conflicting preferences, but to show, as he himself notes (Huber 1996b, p. 279), that prime ministers are strategically well-positioned to obtain policies that are to their liking and that, hence, political parties are constrained in their ability to shape policies after the government is formed.[6]

---

[6]This suggests a curious, and unexpected, parallel with complaints about the limited role of political parties and the legislature in some new, presidential, democratic regimes (O'Donnell 1994). What is seen as a positive trait in parliamentary regimes takes on a negative tone when observed in presidential regimes.

Baron (1998) and Diermeier & Feddersen (1998), in contrast, explicitly model a situation in which the preferences of the party or coalition members are in conflict. The mechanism that drives their model is the control over the legislative agenda enjoyed by the parties in the government. Because agenda power guarantees future gains, and because the vote-of-confidence procedure allows the government to link the vote on a policy with the survival of the government, and, hence, to control the legislative agenda, parties and legislators may find it in their interests to vote against their preferences.

Underlying both models, as well as Huber's (1996b, p. 280), is the view of a presidential system such as the one in the United States, in which agenda-setting power lies with the legislature. However, if presidents can control the legislative agenda much in the same way as prime ministers can, then the mechanism that drives party cohesion in parliamentary regimes can also operate under presidentialism. We argue in the next section that if one considers the full range of existing presidential regimes, the United States is exceptional in granting little or no legislative and agenda power to the executive; hence, the United States is by no means representative of what presidents can do. Here it is sufficient to say that presidential regimes are compatible with executives that hold a high level of agenda and legislative powers (see Mainwaring & Shugart 1997b). The specific institutional procedure whereby this is achieved is obviously different from parliamentarism, but the end result may very well be the same.

Finally, as Diermeier & Feddersen (1998) state, confidence procedures may be a sufficient institutional feature to induce legislative vote cohesion, but they are not a necessary feature. Other mechanisms may exist, some of which are institutional (e.g., centralized legislative organization and executive agenda and legislative powers) and some of which are not. In this context, Medina's[7] analysis is particularly relevant because it shows how legislative voting cohesion can emerge from pure congruence of preferences. His analysis demonstrates that cohesion does not necessarily depend on disciplinary measures (such as the vote of confidence) and can be obtained under any institutional set-up.

Thus, it is not at all clear that the existence of cohesive legislative blocs is endogenous to the regime type. We should not presume that presidential regimes invariably generate low levels of party discipline in the legislature.

Coalition Government

The basic argument about coalitions is that presidentialism, unlike parliamentarism, does not offer incentives for political parties to cooperate with the government. This fact is supposed to give rise to legislative paralysis or some other kind of "ungovernability," with all its attendant tragedies. Stepan & Skach (1993, pp. 17–18) summarize the argument well:

[7]Medina LF. 2001. Legislatures vs. political parties: endogenous policy with strategic voters. Unpublished manuscript, Dep. Polit. Sci., Univ. Chicago.

> The essence of pure presidentialism is mutual independence. From this defining (and confining) condition a series of incentives and decision rules for encouraging the emergence of minority governments, discouraging the formation of durable coalitions, maximizing legislative impasses, motivating executives to flout the constitution, and stimulating political society to call periodically for military coups predictably flows. Presidents and legislatures are directly elected and have their own fixed mandates. This mutual independence creates the possibility of a political impasse between the chief executive and the legislative body for which there is no constitutionally available impasse-breaking device.

Coalition governments, thus, are considered rare and unstable in presidential regimes and frequent and stable in parliamentary regimes. Mainwaring (1993) added the complicating factor of party system fractionalization. Whereas parliamentary regimes are equipped to deal with such situations—cooperation, remember, is inherent to the regime—the problems of presidentialism are only compounded by a multitude of political parties in the legislature.

This argument is problematic in many respects. Most fundamentally, it assumes that the institutional differences between the two regimes are sufficient to create divergent incentives for coalition formation. This, however, is not the case. Cheibub et al. (2001) show that the circumstances under which portfolio coalitions are likely to be formed are identical under the two systems.

The crucial difference between parliamentarism and presidentialism, they argue, is the "reversion point," that is, the situation that emerges if no coalition is formed. In parliamentary regimes, the reversion point is an early election; in presidential regimes, since mandates are fixed, it is a situation in which the president keeps all the portfolios. The implication is that whereas in parliamentary regimes every portfolio government enjoys the support of a legislative majority, under presidentialism it is possible for a legislative majority to hold no portfolio. This difference, however, is not sufficient to generate different *incentives* for the formation of portfolio coalitions. Cheibub et al. (2001) show that if there is a large distance in policy space between the party of the formateur and the party closest to it, portfolio coalitions are formed in both parliamentary and presidential systems. In these cases, the formateur uses portfolios to bring the policy closer to its own preferences. Alternatively, when the distance in the policy space between the party of the formateur and the party closest to it is small, and together these two parties would form a majority, no coalition is formed, again in both parliamentary and presidential systems. Because policy preferences are close, the formateur can allow policy to be chosen by a party other than itself. Given that, by definition, mandates are fixed in presidential regimes, what needs to be explained is not so much why coalitions are not formed under presidentialism (which, as we show below, is not true anyway), but why presidents do not always form majority coalitions.

According to Cheibub et al. (2001), the reason majority coalitions are not always formed under presidential regimes has to do with the opposition's beliefs about how much it would gain electorally from opposing the president. If the opposition believes that its vote share will increase in the next election, it may be willing to stay out of the government, in which case a majority of legislators unite against the president and the president remains in office for the duration of the term. This outcome is structurally unavailable under parliamentarism. What is fundamental, though, is not that this outcome may occur but that, if it occurs, it does not invariably imply impasse or deadlock between the executive and the legislature. Legislative paralysis is likely to occur only under very specific institutional configurations, namely, if the legislature cannot initiate legislation or if the president can veto legislation without being overridden. These are relatively infrequent scenarios: Of 20 democratic constitutions that existed in Latin America, 11 contained no provision regarding exclusive introduction of legislation by the executive, and the rest included partial restrictions—usually involving budget laws and/or the armed forces—on the legislature's ability to initiate legislation (Carey et al. 1997). As for veto, in only 4% of the years of presidentialism between 1946 and 1999 could the president veto legislation with no legislative override (Cheibub 2002). Thus, although possible under some specific circumstances, a generalized lack of cooperation between executive and the legislature or chronic legislative paralysis are not the outcomes that would naturally result from the structure of incentives in presidential regimes.

Empirical patterns largely support these considerations. Table 2, based on the work of Cheibub et al. (2001), contains the frequency of majority and coalition governments for parliamentary and presidential regimes according to the share of seats held by the largest party in the legislature. Majority governments are those in which the share of seats held by all parties holding portfolios is >0.50; coalition governments are those in which there are at least two parties that hold portfolios. We can see that, except for the cases in which one party holds more than 50% of the seats in the legislature, the frequency of coalition governments is higher under

TABLE 2 Majority and coalition governments in parliamentary and presidential regimes by the share of seats held by the largest party in the legislature

	Both	Parliamentarism	Presidentialism
Majority government:			
All	0.7474	0.7871	0.6128
>50%	0.9598	1.0000	0.8736
<50%	0.5531	0.5908	0.2892
33.3%–50%	0.5293	0.5688	0.2778
<33.3%	0.6316	0.6857	0.3239
Coalition government:			
All	0.4326	0.4314	0.3034
>50%	0.1250	0.0920	0.1348
<50%	0.7141	0.7443	0.5122
33.3%–50%	0.6581	0.6949	0.4306
<33.3%	0.8982	0.9571	0.7606

parliamentarism than under presidentialism. The difference, however, is not as large as we would expect if it were true that presidential regimes do not provide any incentives for coalition formation. When no party holds a majority of seats in the legislature, coalition governments emerge slightly over half the time. Furthermore, we find that the frequency of coalition and majority governments actually increases significantly when no party holds more than a third of the seats in the legislature. This pattern is identical to that in parliamentary regimes, suggesting, as discussed above, that the incentives for coalition formation are the same under the two regimes. Thus, contrary to the widespread fear expressed in the existing literature, the fragmentation of the party system does not make coalition formation more difficult in presidential systems.

Even if we grant that incentives for coalition formation are the same under parliamentary and presidential regimes, one basic difference between them is that the number of possible coalitions under presidentialism is necessarily smaller than under parliamentarism. When the president is an "outsider" with very little support in congress, the power of his or her party is magnified by the fact that that party must be a member of the government. If this is a frequent occurrence in presidential regimes, then this limitation could become a serious problem.

However, it is simply not the case that presidents tend to belong to small parties or be outsiders (Cheibub et al. 2001). The probability that the chief executive will belong to one of the two largest parties is 0.9492 in parliamentary regimes and 0.9279 in presidential regimes. As Figure 1 shows, the distribution of seats

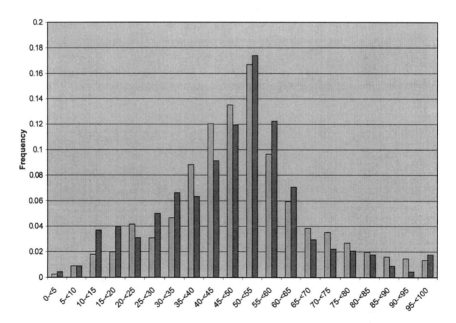

Figure 1 Parliamentary (light grey) and presidential (dark grey) governments by share of seats of party of chief executive.

held by the party of the president and the prime minster is similar under the two regimes. There is nothing in this distribution suggesting that presidential regimes are more likely than parliamentary regimes to produce governments headed by outsiders. Furthermore, presidential regimes are not considerably more constrained than parliamentary regimes in the process of coalition formation. In both regimes, the government tends to be headed by the largest party, and this political factor, rather than any formal rule, seems to be sufficient to constrain the process of government formation in ways that make the two systems look alike.

What are the consequences of coalition governments under the two regimes? If the cycle described by Stepan & Skach (1993) were true, presidential regimes would be less likely to survive when the party of the president does not hold a majority of seats in congress and no coalition is formed. The same should be true of parliamentary regimes. The empirical patterns, however, are complex. As Table 3 indicates, parliamentary regimes do, in fact, have better chances to survive when no party obtains a majority of seats in the legislature and coalitions are formed. Presidential regimes experience the opposite situation: Although the difference is not large (life expectancies of 24.5 versus 22.6 years), the formation of coalition governments reduces survival chances when no party has $>50\%$ of the seats in congress. This, however, is not the whole story. This effect is stronger in presidentialism when the largest party holds between one third and one half of the seats. (The result is the same if instead of the seats of the largest party we use the seats of the party of the chief executive to condition the probabilities reported in the upper panel of Table 3.) In these cases, the expected lifetime of the regime when coalitions are formed is 13.2 years, compared with an expected lifetime of 24.5 years when no coalitions are formed. When the largest party holds less than one third of the seats, that is, when the legislature is highly fractionalized, coalition formation sharply improves the survival chances of the regime: Expected lifetime with coalition is 54.9 years versus 23.9 when no coalitions are formed.

Thus, it seems to be the level of party fractionalization that determines the effect of coalition formation on the survival of presidential democracies. When fractionalization is moderate (for instance, when the effective number of parties is between 3.5 and 4.5, as indicated in the second panel of Table 3), coalition governments are highly fragile: Their expected lifetime is <9 years, compared with 26 years when no coalitions are formed. When fractionalization increases, we find, as expected, that coalition governments increase the survival chances of presidential democracies. We saw above that in situations of high party fractionalization, coalitions are more likely to emerge in both parliamentary and presidential regimes. Now we see that, under these conditions, not only are they more frequent but they also significantly improve the chances that democracy will survive.

The reason why coalitions tend to be less frequent and detrimental to the survival of democracy when the party system is moderately fractionalized is puzzling and deserves further investigation. The third panel in Table 3 presents some of the conditions that transpire under moderate and high party fractionalization and may suggest some clues. When fractionalization is moderate, the party of the president

TABLE 3   Transition probabilities by the share of seats held by the largest party and the effective number of political parties (source: Cheibub et al. 2001)

	All	**Parliamentary**	**Presidential**
Seats held by the largest party:			
>50%	0.0251	0.0139	0.0475
No coalition	0.0266	0.0137	0.0516
Coalition	0.0143	0.0159	0.0000
≤50%	0.0254	0.0191	0.0429
No coalition	0.0301	0.0253	0.0408
Coalition	0.0172	0.0114	0.0443
33.3%–50%	0.0222	0.0131	0.0555
No coalition	0.0307	0.0265	0.0407
Coalition	0.0178	0.0071	0.0753
<33.3%	0.0170	0.0197	0.0224
No coalition	0.0256	0.0000	0.0417
Coalition	0.0161	0.0206	0.0182
Effective number of parties (ENP):			
ENP ≤ 2.5	0.0267	0.0167	0.0480
No coalition	0.0308	0.0192	0.0532
Coalition	0.0000	0.0000	0.0000
2.5 < ENP ≤ 3.5	0.0170	0.0121	0.0325
No coalition	0.0230	0.0165	0.0291
Coalition	0.0117	0.0087	0.0392
3.5 < ENP ≤ 4.5	0.0292	0.0094	0.0886
No coalition	0.0127	0.0000	0.0385
Coalition	0.0342	0.0121	0.1132
ENP > 4.5	0.0163	0.0140	0.0390
No coalition	0.0278	0.0000	0.0555
Coalition	0.0148	0.0148	0.0339

Conditions under moderate and high party fragmentation (effective parties):		
	3.5 < ENP ≤ 4.5	ENP > 4.5
Majority government	0.5760	0.5719
Coalition government	0.7690	0.8824
Party of head of government is the largest party	0.6569	0.5085
Share of seats of party of the head of government	0.3361	0.2319
Share of seats of largest party	0.3809	0.2845
Share of seats of second largest party	0.2512	0.2049
Share of seats of third largest party	0.1600	0.1523
Sum of seat share of first, second, and third parties	0.7921	0.6417
Sum of seat share of second and third parties	0.4112	0.3573

is more often the largest party, holds on average about one third of the seats, and is confronted with other legislative parties that are, themselves, relatively large. The relative strengths of legislative parties may be what makes coalition so detrimental to presidential democracies under these conditions. For the moment, however, we simply emphasize that it is *not* high party fractionalization, and the difficulties of forming majority coalitions that allegedly follow from it, that kills presidential democracies.

Thus, it is not true that incentives for coalition formation are different in presidential and parliamentary democracies. It is not true either that presidential regimes with highly fractionalized party systems make the task of coalition formation even more daunting; to the contrary, the frequency of coalition governments increases with the fractionalization of the party system in both presidential and parliamentary regimes.

CENTRALIZATION OF THE DECISION-MAKING PROCESS

From the constitutional point of view, all legislators, whether in presidential or parliamentary regimes, have the same rights and duties. Their mandates are the same, regardless of the number of votes they received in the electorate, their party affiliation, their degree of seniority in the legislature, and so on. Each legislator has the same right to propose legislation, to amend proposals made by others, and to participate in the process of deliberation. In addition, each legislator's vote has the same weight. In principle, therefore, legislatures are egalitarian institutions.

The reality, of course, is different. In order to manage their workload, legislatures organize themselves in a variety of ways and adopt internal rules that regulate individual legislative rights and access to resources (Kriebhel 1992, p. 2). Legislative rights and resources are not uniformly distributed. Individual legislators' chances to influence the order of business and to have a say in decision making depend on the legislative rights granted to them by the internal rules of their assembly. Hence, legislative organization affects the structure of the decision-making process and the weight of legislators in policy decisions.

Discussions of legislative organization usually make reference to the paradigmatic cases of England and the United States: a centralized and a decentralized legislature, respectively, and, as we know, a parliamentary and a presidential democracy. Most arguments that we find about decision making in democracies contrast these two systems and assume, often implicitly, that all legislatures, and, for that matter, the decision-making process, are centralized under parliamentarism and decentralized under presidentialism.

The English parliament is indeed characterized by the complete control of the cabinet over the legislative agenda. Government bills are appreciated under a special calendar that gives them priority over bills introduced by individual members of parliament and, as a consequence, parliamentary minorities have no way to "close the gates" to governmental proposals. In addition, individual members of parliament are often restricted in their capacity to amend government bills. For instance, since the beginning of the eighteenth century the government has had the sole prerogative to initiate measures that increase expenditures (Lowemberg & Patterson 1979, p. 249). Nowadays, it is rare for the budget presented by the cabinet to be modified by the parliament. In fact, given the high expectations that it will be approved as submitted, "a provisional resolution places it into effect on the day it is delivered, though months may pass before its final enactment" (Lowemberg & Patterson 1979, p. 250).

Because of the government's control over the agenda, legislative output is marked by a high rate of success for the executive's initiatives. Proposals made by the cabinet had a 0.97 chance of being approved during the 1945–1978 period, whereas bills introduced by back-benchers, irrespective of their party affiliation, had a close-to-zero chance of being approved (Rose 1986, p. 11). This means that the cabinet introduces almost all laws that are approved in parliament. The government legislative success rests on disciplined party support. Cabinet defeats are rare events. The cabinet entirely monopolizes the law-making process and, for that matter, all the decisions about policy.

The US congress, in contrast, is supposed to be a decentralized body, organized as it is around a strong committee system. In this view, the committee system allows legislators to have a say in decisions related to policy areas that are important to their electoral survival. The story goes like this. Each committee has a monopoly on initiating legislation in its own policy jurisdiction. The committee reports a bill to the floor, and for reasons that are not entirely clear, the floor accepts the bill as reported [see the debate between Kriebhel (1987) and Shepsle & Weingast (1987)]. Political parties do not control the assignment of legislators to specific committees; this is described as a process of self-selection in which legislators pick the committee that has jurisdiction over the policy area that will bring them the highest electoral payoff. At the same time, electoral considerations dictate that politicians prefer distributive, pork-barrel policies. The committee system in the US congress provides the organizational means to make these distributive policies possible. This textbook (Shepsle 1989) view of the US congress has been challenged by Kriebhel (1992) and Cox & McCubbins (1993), to cite only the most important works. Yet, it is true that even in the informational and the party-as-a-cartel views, the committee system is a key and distinctive feature of the US congress.

Hence, with England as the prototype of executive-legislative relations in parliamentary regimes and the United States as the prototypical presidential system, it follows that "[i]n parliamentary systems the executive (government) controls the agenda, and the legislature (parliament) accepts or rejects proposals, while in presidential systems the legislature makes the proposal and the executive (the president) signs or vetoes them" (Tsebelis 1995, p. 325). The prototypical parliamentary regime is one in which the government has complete control over the legislative agenda; the rights of the individual members of parliament are "expropriated" and monopolized by the cabinet. Hence, all individual legislators can do is to support the party line. Voters know that this is all they can do, and thus have no incentive to cast their ballot on the basis of the candidate's personal characteristics. Through the control of the legislative agenda, therefore, parliamentarism would lead to party vote in the electorate and to party discipline in the parliament.[8]

The prototype of a presidential regime, in turn, is one in which the organization of congress preserves the right of individual representatives to have a say on policy decisions. Separation of powers leads to independent legislators who act on the basis of their individual electoral needs, and in response to these needs, they build personal ties with their constituencies. One is thus led to expect that legislatures in presidential regimes will have strong committee systems and representatives will be elected on the basis of the personal ties they build with their constituencies.

But, as we have known at least since Shugart & Carey published *Presidents and Assemblies* (1992), presidential systems vary considerably in the degree of legislative powers they grant the president. The US president, as a matter of fact, is one of the few presidents in existing systems who cannot initiate legislation. Moreover, the US president only has the package veto, which weakens his capacity to oppose distributive bargains produced in congress. Hence, the US presidency is unique in that the president has only "reactive legislative powers" (Mainwaring & Shugart 1997b). Not only are presidents often endowed with the capacity to initiate legislation; often they also have the exclusive right to initiate legislation in some areas (such as appropriation and budgetary matters), whereas legislators are restricted in their capacity to amend bills in these areas. Hence, contrary to Tsebelis (1995), presidents can do much more than simply sign or veto bills proposed by the legislature.

In addition, some presidents also have decree power; they are constitutionally able to unilaterally alter the status quo. Although there is considerable variation in the specifics (Carey & Shugart 1998), often presidential decrees enter into effect first and the legislature acts second. The legislature acts a posteriori, rejecting, amending, or accepting the new status quo brought about by the executive decree.[9] A president with decree power can dictate the legislative agenda by forcing the legislature to make a decision on some matter it could not have appreciated

---

[8]High rates of executive success and low participation of individual members in law making are, indeed, characteristic of most parliamentary regimes. The data assembled by the Inter Parliamentary Union (Herman & Mendel 1976), covering 14 countries with parliamentary regimes during the 1971–1976 period, register only 3 in which government legislative success is below 80%. There is no case in which individual initiatives represent more than 20% of the laws passed. For three countries (Australia, Ireland, and Malta), there is no case of a bill introduced by an individual legislator that became a law. For the period 1978–1982, Herman & Mendel (1986) register 3 out of 16 countries with government success below 80% and only 3 with individual members' initiatives above 20% (Austria, Italy, and Portugal).

[9]Often, rejection of a presidential decree does not mean a return to the status quo ante. Even if there is a majority in favor of the status quo, once the decree has been in effect, rejecting it may have become an unattractive or unavailable alternative.

otherwise. Thus, no group in the legislature, not even the majority, can "close the gates" against a presidential initiative made by decree.

Note that the power to impose an agenda does not imply that presidents always prevail against the will of the majority. In fact, since a legislative majority can always reject a presidential decree, a model of executive-legislative conflict cannot explain why the executive would ever make use of decrees (Huber 1996a). There are, of course, strategic advantages that the agenda setter may explore. But as Kriebhel (1988, p. 270) has argued, these are not properly antimajoritarian devices.[10]

In addition, the government's legislative and agenda powers, including decree power, need not be interpreted solely as means for solving "vertical" conflicts, that is, conflicts between the government and the opposition. The government's legislative powers are also means for solving "horizontal" conflicts, that is, conflicts between the government and its supporters (Huber 1996a). These powers enable the government to protect the cohesion of its coalition against the opportunistic behavior of its members.[11]

It follows from this that, because of presidents' legislative powers, separation of powers in presidential regimes is not as complete as it is usually considered to be. Presidential legislative powers are commonly interpreted in the context of the US constitution, that is, as means to create checks and balances. But, as we have just seen, the legislative powers of the executive are not only a mechanism for checking the power of the majority or imposing the will of the president. They are also weapons of the majority. Therefore, the fusion of executive and legislative powers is not absent from presidential systems.

This interpretation is at odds with Shugart & Carey's (1992) view, according to which presidential systems that endow presidents with considerable legislative powers—creating what Shugart & Carey call strong presidents—have a greater probability of breaking down. They argue that strong presidents have smaller incentives to negotiate with congress, making paralysis and crisis more likely. This is so because strong presidents have the institutional means to impose their will on congress, whereas weak presidents know that they have no alternative but to negotiate. This argument, however, is based on the "vertical conflict" model and disregards the possibility that the president will try to organize a majority in congress. Once the possibility that the president and the majority have overlapping

---

[10]It is true that, since a decree immediately alters the status quo, decree power increases the power of the agenda setter. When legislatures vote on ordinary propositions, legislators compare the status quo (SQ) with the situation to be created by the proposition. In the case of an executive decree, the legislator compares the situation created by the decree (D) with the new situation created by rejecting a decree that has been in effect for some time (SQD). If the preferences of the majority are SQ > D > SQD, then the majority will approve the decree. If the preferences of the majority are SQD > D (assuming that SQ is no longer a viable alternative), then the majority will reject the decree.

[11]There seems to be no association between minority status and the use of decree power (Figueiredo & Limongi 1998).

preferences is considered, then legislative agenda powers need not imply paralysis, crisis, and eventual breakdown.

The organization of congress and the degree of control the executive has over the legislative agenda does influence the behavior of individual legislators. They act in a constrained environment. If they want to influence policy, they have to do so according to the procedural rules of their legislative body and the terms set by the president. For example, the incentives to cultivate the personal vote that stem from the electoral arena may be entirely neutralized in the legislature through a distribution of legislative rights that favors the executive. For this reason, we cannot deduce, as is commonly done, the behavior of legislators from electoral and party legislation alone.

In this context, the case of Brazil is of central theoretical interest, for it demonstrates the far-reaching effects of the centralization of the decision-making process. The system produced by the 1988 constitution is frequently cited as a prime example of bad institutional design (Ames 2001). All of the institutional choices that should not be made, it seems, were made in 1988: a strong presidential regime [ranked among the strongest in the world by Shugart & Carey (1992, p. 155)]; a proportional representation formula for legislative elections with high district magnitude; very permissive party and electoral legislation (e.g., open-list and low party control over access to the ballot). Under such conditions, the party system is bound to be fragmented and presidents can be virtually certain that their party will not control a majority of seats in both legislative houses. Even if it did, parties would be highly undisciplined, making the majority status of the president a mere formality (Sartori 1994, p. 113; Mainwaring 1991). Hence, to have their agenda approved, presidents would use their strong legislative powers, which would lead to conflict and paralysis. To paraphrase Sartori (1997), the system created in 1988 was nothing but hopeless.

Yet, the performance of the post-1988 Brazilian regime is completely at odds with what we would expect. Brazilian presidents of this period have had great success enacting their legislative agenda. Presidents introduced 86% of the bills enacted since 1988, and the rate of approval of the bills introduced by the executive was 78%. Presidents have formed coalitions to govern and have reliably obtained the support of the parties that belong to the government coalition in approving its legislation; the average discipline of the presidential coalition, defined as the act of voting in accordance with the public recommendation of the government leader in the floor, was 85.6%. This support is sufficient to make a presidential defeat in a roll call a rare event. Thus, despite the "centrifugal" characteristics of Brazilian presidentialism, as indicated by the party and electoral legislation, presidents have governed relying on the support of a disciplined coalition (Figueiredo & Limongi 2000).

This outcome results from both the organization of the Brazilian congress and the president's control of the legislative agenda. The Brazilian congress is highly centralized. Legislative rights heavily favor party leaders, who are taken to be perfect agents of their caucuses (*bancadas*) regarding most procedural decisions, such as the request for roll-call votes, the closing of debates, and, most important, the designation of a bill as urgent for purposes of appreciation. The urgency request is a kind of discharge petition: it removes the bill from the committee and forces its immediate (within 24 hours) deliberation by the floor. Bills that are appreciated as urgent cannot be freely amended; only amendments signed by 20% of the lower house are accepted, which implies that only amendments supported by party leaders will be considered. As Figueiredo & Limongi (2000, p. 157) have shown, the approval of the urgency petition is highly associated with the success of a bill. Centralization, thus, deprives members of congress of the legislative rights they need in order to influence legislation.

The Brazilian presidents, thanks to their constitutional legislative powers, have a direct influence on the definition of the legislative agenda. Using its decree power, the executive places on the agenda the issues it deems most relevant and pressing. The president can also influence the pace of ordinary legislation by requesting urgency for the appreciation of specific bills (which will give each house 45 days to deliberate on them). The president also has the exclusive right to initiate legislation related to the definition of the budget, taxation, and public administration. Therefore, the executive monopolizes the legislative initiative on the most crucial areas of policy making.

Hence, it is through participation in the government that individual legislators obtain access to resources they need for political survival: policy influence and patronage. Leaders bargain with the executive, exchanging political support (votes) for access to policy influence and patronage. The executive thus provides party leaders with the means to punish back-benchers who do not follow the party line: Their share of patronage may be denied. The executive, in turn, given the resources it controls, is in a very advantageous position. Party leaders become, in fact, the main brokers in the bargaining between the executive and the legislators. Contrary to what is currently assumed about Brazil, presidents do not need to bargain on a case-by-case basis. They are in a position to demand support for their entire legislative agenda. Once the government is formed and benefits are distributed among the members of the coalition, the president, with the help of party leaders, may threaten representatives and actually punish those who do not follow the party line. To say it once more, the actual pattern of legislative-executive relations in Brazil's presidential regime is rather different from what one would expect if one deduced it from electoral and partisan legislation.

It should be clear by now that separation of powers does not necessarily imply decentralized decision making. Institutional analyses that stress the negative effects of separation of powers, and that point to specific, often restrictive, electoral laws as a corrective for these effects, miss the point. Presidentialism does not necessarily imply, or require, decentralized decision making and conflict between the executive and the legislature. Once one grants the possibility that coalition governments exist in presidential regimes, the degree of overlap between the executive and legislative majorities has to be adjusted.

Presidential control over the agenda becomes a weapon to be used by the majority rather than against the majority. Thus, presidents are not necessarily as distinct from prime ministers as is normally assumed. As we showed above, outcomes that are usually associated exclusively with parliamentarism, such as executive success and dominance over the legislative output obtained through disciplined parties, can be found even in "hopeless" presidential regimes such as Brazil's.

Now, just as presidential regimes are not all alike, neither are parliamentary systems. Government control over the legislative agenda does not follow from the definition of parliamentarism. Neither is it necessary that the legislative rights of private members be curtailed in parliamentary regimes. Committees may have considerable powers in parliamentary assemblies and may erect barriers to the executive agenda.[12] The weakness of individual members of parliament that characterizes England is not inherent to parliamentary governments, as illustrated by the cases of Italy after 1945 and France in the Third and Fourth Republics. In both cases, the government had no control over the definition of the legislative agenda, committees had considerable power, and the rights of individual legislators were not "expropriated."

In France, until 1911, it was the Chamber presidents who defined the legislative agenda. As Andrews (1978) reports, after this date, a Conference of Presidents assumed control over the definition of the agenda. The government was represented in the Conference, but it was only in 1955 that internal rules were revised so that voting in the Conference of Presidents was weighted by the proportion of seats held by each party. The proposed agendas had to be approved by the Chamber, and this "often became an occasion for a vote of non-confidence through a device called "interpellation'" (Andrews 1978, p. 471). Hence, the government did not have firm control over the definition of the legislative agenda. On several occasions, interpellation led to judgment on the government agenda that caused the fall of the government.

Besides, committees could act as "veto players," since a report from the committee was necessary for consideration of a bill by the floor. The government could expedite the committee report but could not avoid it. Therefore, committees could respond to government pressure with an unsatisfactory report. According to Andrews (1978), the Third and Fourth Republics placed few restrictions on the ability of private members to propose initiatives that would increase expenditures and reduce revenues. In his words, given the absence of serious restrictions, the government's financial projects were often "butchered in parliament" (Andrews 1978, p. 485).

In Italy one finds the same pattern: the parliament's independence to set the legislative agenda, strong committees, and legislative rights that favor individual members' influence over decisions. In the Italian parliament, the presidents of each house, and not the government, define the legislative agenda. Bills introduced by the government have no special calendar or precedence over private members' bills. Article 72 of the Italian constitution grants standing committees the authority to

---

[12]One of the variables used by Strom (1990) to explain the formation of minority governments in parliamentary regimes was the committee structure of parliaments. Obviously there must exist some variation in this structure.

pass laws. This capacity has been widely used. According to Di Palma (1976), the presidents of both houses decide unilaterally whether a bill will have to be considered by the floor. Di Palma labels these alternatives the centralized and the decentralized procedures. Bills scheduled for the decentralized procedure have a much greater chance of becoming laws. Hence, all a president must do in order to "kill" a governmental proposition is to schedule it for the centralized procedure.

Besides being endowed with the power to pass legislation, Italian committees cannot be discharged when a bill follows the decentralized procedure. Although possible, discharges under the centralized procedure are rarely enforced. The committee chairmen are autonomous in defining their agendas and even in convening their committees. Therefore, committees not only are important decision-making bodies but also can act as veto players. As for individual members of parliament, until the 1988 reform, roll calls were secret and could be easily requested at any stage of the law-making process (Cotta 1990, p. 77). Hence, the government fell prey to the action of the *franco attiratori*. In other words, members of the majority could not be sanctioned, either by the government or their parties.

These are obviously not examples of parliamentary regimes performing at their best. In fact, both systems are often cited as examples of pathological development of parliamentarism, and both have been considerably reformed. But this only emphasizes our point: The instability of these systems resulted not from the form of government but from the way decision making was organized. Although policy performance is important for the survival of a democratic regime, we cannot deduce it from the basic constitutional principle that defines the regime. Policy making under parliamentarism is not necessarily centralized, and consequently the government is not always successful in having its policy proposals approved. Similarly, policy making under presidentialism is not necessarily decentralized, and the government is not invariably immobilized in terms of the policies it can implement.

CONCLUSION

The difference between parliamentary and presidential democracies does not seem to attract the same attention today as it did 10 or 15 years ago. Then, as several new democracies were choosing their constitutional frameworks, there was a clear sense of urgency in discussions about which system was more likely to survive. Today, the scholarly imagination has been captured by more immediate concerns (it seems to have rested on federalism and corruption, at least momentarily), and an implicit consensus has emerged to the effect that political scientists know everything that needs to be known about "broad" constitutional choices.

We disagree with this position. We hope this paper has shown that the difference in the survival of parliamentary and presidential regimes cannot be explained by the structure of incentives that supposedly follows from the regime's basic principles. Parliamentary systems do not operate under a "majoritarian imperative"; deadlock is not as frequent as supposed under presidentialism and is not absent from parliamentarism; coalition governments are not foreign to presidential systems and emerge for the same reasons as they do in parliamentary systems; decision making is not always centralized under parliamentarism and is not always decentralized under presidentialism. The reality of both parliamentary and presidential regimes is more complex than it would be if we derived these systems' entire behavior from their first principles.

So what explains the difference? We suspect that the main difference between the two regimes lies in the way the decision-making process is organized. Lack of coordination on policy making and the probability of deadlock increase with the decentralization of the decision-making process. More often than not, we find parliamentary regimes that have a centralized decision-making process, one in which the executive has a monopoly on the policy agenda. However, as the Italian and French cases demonstrate, this is not a necessary feature of parliamentarism. And as the case of Brazil demonstrates, executive-legislative powers, in the presence of political parties, allow for a fusion of powers not predicted by the usual conception of presidential regimes. Presidents with active legislative powers need not impose their will on the congress; they can bargain from a very advantageous position with legislative majorities that can encompass more than one political party. Agenda powers that centralize the decision-making process may be the basis for the "efficient secret" (Cox 1987) of presidential regimes. Thus, if parliamentary regimes have a better record of survival than presidential regimes, it is not because they are parliamentary.

ACKNOWLEDGMENTS

We thank Adam Przeworski, Tasos Kalandrakis, and especially Argelina Cheibub Figueiredo, who has participated in many of the conversations that led to this paper. We also thank the Leitner Program in International Political Economy at Yale University for support for this research and the Fundação de Pesquisa e Amparo à Pesquisa do Estado de São Paulo (FAPESP) for providing the conditions for us to work on this paper together.

The *Annual Review of Political Science* is online at http://polisci.annualreviews.org

LITERATURE CITED

Ackerman B. 2000. The New Separation of Powers. *Harvard Law Rev.* 113(3):642–727

Ames B. 2001. *The Deadlock of Democracy in Brazil*. Ann Arbor: Mich. Univ. Press

Andrews WG. 1978. Parliamentary procedures in France. *Legis. Stud. Q.* 3:465–506

Baron DP. 1998. Comparative dynamics of parliamentary government. *Am. Polit. Sci. Rev.* 92:593–610

Bowler S, Farrell DM, Katz RS, eds. 1999a.

Party Discipline and Parliamentary Government. Columbus: Ohio State Univ.

Bowler S, Farrell DM, Katz RS. 1999b. Party cohesion, party discipline, and parliaments. See Bowler et al. 1999, pp. 3–22

Carey JM, Amorin Neto O, Shugart MS. 1997. Appendix: outlines of constitutional powers in Latin America. See Mainwaring & Shugart 1997b, pp. 440–60

Carey JM, Shugart MS. 1994. Incentives to cultivate a personal vote: a rank ordering of electoral formulas. *Elec. Stud.* 14:417–39

Carey JM, Shugart MS, eds. 1998. *Executive Decree Authority.* Cambridge, UK: Cambridge Univ. Press

Cheibub JA. 1998. *Elections and alternation in power in democratic regimes.* Presented at Annu. Meet. Am. Polit. Sci. Assoc., Boston, Sept. 3–6

Cheibub JA. 2002. Minority governments, deadlock situations, and the survival of presidential democracies. *Comp. Polit. Stud.* In press

Cheibub JA, Przeworski A. 1999. Democracy, elections, and accountability for economic outcomes. In *Democracy and Accountability,* ed. A Przeworski, SC Stokes, B Manin, pp. 222–50. New York: Cambridge Univ. Press

Cheibub JA, Przeworski A, Saiegh S. 2001. *Government coalitions under presidentialism and parliamentarism.* Presented at Conf. Brazilian Political Institutions in Comparative Perspective: The Role of Congress in Presidential Systems, Cent. Brazilian Stud., Oxford Univ., May 28–29

Cotta M. 1990. The 'centrality' of parliament in a protracted democratic consolidation. In *Parliament and Democratic Consolidation in Southern Europe,* ed. U Liebert, M Cotta, pp. 55–91. London: Pinter

Cox GW. 1987. *The Efficient Secret.* Cambridge, UK: Cambridge Univ. Press

Cox GW, McCubbins MD. 1993. *Legislative Leviathan: Party Government in the House.* Berkeley: Univ. Calif. Press

Di Palma G. 1976. Institutional rules and legislative outcomes in the Italian parliament. *Legis. Stud. Q.* 1:147–79

Diermeier D, Feddersen TJ. 1998. Cohesion in legislatures and the vote of confidence procedure. *Am. Polit. Sci. Rev.* 92:611–22

Figueiredo AC, Limongi F. 1998. *Institutional legacies and accountability: executive decrees in Brazil and Italy.* Presented at Conf. Confronting Non-Democratic Legacies During Democratic Deepening: Latin America

and Southern Europe. Buenos Aires, Arg., Aug. 17–19

Figueiredo AC, Limongi F. 2000. Presidential power, legislative organization and party behavior in the legislature. *Comp. Polit.* 32: 151–70

González LE, Gillespie CG. 1994. Presidentialism and democratic stability in Uruguay. In *The Failure of Presidential Democracy: The Case of Latin America,* ed. JJ Linz, A Valenzuela, 2:151–78. Baltimore, MD: Johns Hopkins Univ. Press

Hartlyn J. 1994. Presidentialism and Colombian politics. In *The Failure of Presidential Democracy: The Case of Latin America,* ed. JJ Linz, A Valenzuela, 2:220–53. Baltimore, MD: Johns Hopkins Univ. Press

Herman V, Mendel F. 1976. *Parliaments of the World. A Reference Compendium.* London: Inter-Parliamentary Union/Macmillan

Herman V, Mendel F. 1986. *Parliaments of the World. A Reference Compendium.* Berlin/New York: Inter-Parliamentary Union/De Gruyter

Huang T. 1997. Party systems in Taiwan and South Korea. In *Consolidating the Third Wave Democracies: Themes and Perspectives,* ed. L Diamond, MF Plattner, Y Chu, H Tien, pp. 135–59. Baltimore, MD: Johns Hopkins Univ. Press

Huber JD. 1996a. *Rationalizing Parliament.* Cambridge, UK: Cambridge Univ. Press

Huber JD. 1996b. The vote of confidence in parliamentary democracies. *Am. Polit. Sci. Rev.* 90:269–82

Jones MP. 1995. *Electoral Laws and the Survival of Presidential Democracies.* Notre Dame, IN: Notre Dame Univ. Press

Kriebhel K. 1987. Why are congressional committees powerful? *Am. Polit. Sci. Rev.* 81: 929–35

Kriebhel K. 1988. Spatial models of legislative choice. *Legis. Stud. Q.* 8:259–319

Kriebhel K. 1992. Constituency characteristics and legislative preferences. *Public Choice* 76:21–37

Limongi F, Figueiredo AC. 1995. Partidos

políticos na câmara dos deputados: 1989–1994. *Dados* 38:497–543

Linz JJ. 1978. *The Breakdown of Democratic Regimes: Crisis, Breakdown, and Reequilibration.* Baltimore, MD: Johns Hopkins Univ. Press

Linz JJ. 1994. Presidential or parliamentary democracy: Does it make a difference? See Linz & Valenzuela 1994, pp. 3–87

Linz JJ, Stepan A. 1996. *Problems of Democratic Transition and Consolidation: Southern Europe, South America, and Post-Communist Europe.* Baltimore, MD: Johns Hopkins Univ. Press

Lowemberg G, Patterson SC. 1979. *Comparing Legislatures.* Boston: Little, Brown

Mainwaring S. 1991. Politicians, parties, and electoral systems: Brazil in comparative perspective. *Comp. Polit.* 24:21–43

Mainwaring S. 1993. Presidentialism, multipartism, and democracy: the difficult combination. *Comp. Polit. Stud.* 26:198–228

Mainwaring S, Scully TR. 1995. Introduction: party systems in Latin America. In *Building Democratic Institutions: Party Systems in Latin America*, ed. S Mainwaring, TR Scully, pp. 1–32. Stanford, CA: Stanford Univ. Press

Mainwaring S, Shugart MS. 1997a. Conclusion: presidentialism and the party system. See Mainwaring & Shugart 1997b, pp. 394–439

Mainwaring S, Shugart MS, eds. 1997b. *Presidentialism and Democracy in Latin America.* Cambridge, UK: Cambridge Univ. Press

Mayhew D. 1974. *Congress: The Electoral Connection.* New Haven, CT: Yale Univ. Press

Mershon C. 1996. The costs of coalition: coalition theories and Italian governments. *Am. Polit. Sci. Rev.* 90(3):534–54

Mershon C. 1999. The costs of coalition: a five-nation comparison. See Bowler et al. 1999, pp. 227–68

Nino CS. 1996. Hyperpresidentialism and constitutional reform in Argentina. In *Institutional Design in New Democracies: Eastern Europe and Latin America*, ed. A Lijphart, CH Waisman, pp. 161–74. Boulder, CO: Westview

O'Donnell G. 1994. Delegative democracy. *J. Democr.* 5:55–69

Ozbudun E. 1970. *Party Cohesion in Western Democracies: A Causal Analysis.* Beverly Hills, CA: Sage

Przeworski A, Alvarez M, Cheibub JA, Limongi F. 2000. *Democracy and Development: Political Institutions and Economic Performance, 1950–1990.* Cambridge, UK: Cambridge Univ. Press

Przeworski A, Alvarez M, Cheibub JA, Limongi F. 2001. Regime and development database. http://pantheon.yale.edu/~jac236/

Rose R. 1986. British MPs: more bark than bite? In *Parliaments and Parliamentarians in Democratic Politics*, ed. EN Suleiman. New York: Holmes & Meier

Sartori G. 1994. Neither presidentialism nor parliamentarism. See Linz & Valenzuela 1994, pp. 106–18

Sartori G. 1997. *Comparative Constitutional Engineering. An Inquiry Into Structures, Incentives and Outcomes.* New York: New York Univ. Press

Shepsle K. 1989. The changing textbook congress. In *Can the Government Govern?*, ed. JE Chubb, PE Patterson, pp. 238–66. Washington, DC: Brookings

Shepsle K, Weingast B. 1987. Rejoinder—Why are congressional committees powerful? *Am. Polit. Sci. Rev.* 81:935–45

Shugart MS. 1995. The electoral cycle and institutional sources of divided presidential government. *Am. Polit. Sci. Rev.* 89:327–43

Shugart MS, Carey JM. 1992. *Presidents and Assemblies: Constitutional Design and Electoral Dynamics.* Cambridge, UK: Cambridge Univ. Press

Smith A. 1996. Endogenous election timing in majoritarian parliamentary systems. *Econ. Polit.* 8:85–110

Stepan A, Skach C. 1993. Constitutional frameworks and democratic consolidation: parliamentarism versus presidentialism. *World Polit.* 46:1–22

Strom K. 1990. *Minority Government and Majority Rule*. Cambridge, UK: Cambridge Univ. Press

Tsebelis G. 1995. Decision making in political systems: veto players in presidentialism, parliamentarism, multicameralism and multipartyism. *Br. J. Polit. Sci.* 25:289–325

Valenzuela A. 1994. Party politics and the crisis of presidentialism in Chile: a proposal for a parliamentary form of government. In *The Failure of Presidential Democracy: The Case of Latin America*, ed. JJ Linz, A Valenzuela, 2:91–150. Baltimore, MD: Johns Hopkins Univ. Press

Annu. Rev. Polit. Sci. 2002. 5:181–200
DOI: 10.1146/annurev.polisci.5.112601.144242
Copyright © 2002 by Annual Reviews. All rights reserved

POLITICAL CLEAVAGES AND POST-COMMUNIST POLITICS

Stephen Whitefield

*Department of Politics and Pembroke College, University of Oxford, Oxford, England
OX1 1DW; e-mail: stephen.whitefield@pmb.ox.ac.uk*

Key Words   social divisions, ideological divisions, party support, electoral bases

■ **Abstract**   Considerable attention has been paid over the past decade to political cleavages in post-communist Eastern Europe. Investigators have attempted to establish whether such cleavages exist, to map their character, and to explain their formation theoretically. Research initially focused on whether communist rule had created distinctive forms of cleavage in the region as a whole, or indeed obliterated social capacity to form any structured social or ideological divisions. The results of this work, however, have tended to support a more differentiated and less sui generis understanding in which the character of cleavages varies considerably across the region. Debate has turned to accounting for the formation and variation in cleavages by reference to factors such as long-standing cultural legacies, forms of communist rule and modes of transition from it, the effects of social structure and individual social experience in the post-communist period, and the impact of institutions and party strategies.

1. INTRODUCTION

The concept of a political cleavage is contested in important ways (Daalder 1966, Eckstein 1966, Dogan 1967, Zuckerman 1982, Bartolini & Mair 1990, Neto & Cox 1997), and whether cleavages exist in post-communist Eastern Europe might depend substantially on how the term is defined. Some authors who find that cleavages are weak or absent in the region use a rigorous definition of the term (Lawson 1999). It is argued here, however, that even when the definitional barrier is raised to a high level, political cleavages are in all likelihood present in the region.

Political cleavages are conceived of here as strongly structured and persistent lines of salient social and ideological division among politically important actors. This definition requires social division but is not limited to it, involves social difference to connect not only to varied views of the world but also to political competition, and says that people who are thus divided matter to political outcomes.

Political cleavages are important for political scientists because of their role in providing bases of support for parties (Dalton 1988) and thus in structuring the content of party competition and political conflict more generally. The presence of cleavages, therefore, can contribute to democratic stability by solidifying party-public ties and increasing the predictability of political outcomes (Lijphart et al. 1993). On the other hand, because they can reflect deep and intractable social and ideological divisions, political cleavages may also create potentials for intense political conflict such that, at least in some institutional contexts, democratic politics become less stable (Gunther & Mughan 1993).

Cleavages, in the sense given above, certainly divided politically relevant actors in communist party states. Class and ethnic differences were often highly politicized alongside cognate ideological claims about economic and national policy (Sabel & Stark 1982, Bremmer & Taras 1993, Davies 1996). But with the collapse of communist systems in Eastern Europe in the late 1980s and early 1990s, the comparative study of cleavages in democratic politics could be extended to Eastern Europe.

The concept of a political cleavage, however, is not universally regarded as useful by political observers of the post-communist world (White et al. 1997, Elster et al. 1998). Indeed, in a highly influential and controversial account published soon after the collapse of communist power, Fukuyama (1992) interpreted the event as an indicator of the end of ideological division across all modern societies, East European ones included. Fukuyama emphasized convergence and consensus on and among liberal values. The collapse of communism could be seen as demonstrating either broad support for liberalism or (to put the argument negatively) the absence of any alternative method of organizing modern society. From this perspective, although transition in the region would certainly have its winners and losers, the end of ideological competition meant that the political cleavages that had divided populations across industrial societies, most famously characterized by Lipset & Rokkan (1967), were anachronistic. Differences among politicians and choices among voters would in this context be based on who could best do the job of delivering on liberal, market, and democratic policies.

Most scholars of politics of the region (and elsewhere), however, dissented in various ways from Fukuyama's perspective. Some shared his expectation of an absence of cleavages but also saw the weakness of liberalism; many expected to find cleavages, though they disagreed about their character. But whether cleavages were envisaged or not, scholarly interest in the cleavage structures (or lack thereof) in post-communist states was often strongly grounded in pessimistic assessments of their putative effects on party competition and on the stability of these new democracies (Cirtautas 1994, Comisso 1997, Elster et al. 1998).

Interest in post-communist cleavages, however, resulted not only from their imputed effects on democratic stability but also (in my view and experience) from social scientists' sheer curiosity and desire to uncover the character and structure of public attitudes in Eastern Europe. As an alternative historical model of modernization, communist power had operated intentionally and methodically to transform society. At the same time, it had also prevented systematic empirical investigation of its effects on society. The nature of the social and ideological divisions that might structure post-communist politics once the mass of the population became politically relevant via participation in party competition was therefore largely unknown when the communist order collapsed. Therefore, when the "curtain came up" [in Szelenyi & Selenyi's phrase (1991)] on democratic politics after 1989, Eastern Europe was, if not *terra incognita*, then at least *terra obscura*. Had societies hibernated under communism to emerge divided as before? Had communism reshaped and redivided society so that political cleavages would be new and distinctive, or possibly leveled social relations so that cleavages would be absent? Or might the challenges of the post-communist order quickly provide new sources of politically salient social and ideological division within East European populations?

What has emerged from ten years of empirical study of post-communist societies is a picture of considerable diversity in the structure of social and ideological divisions across the region rather than evidence that communist power had leveled social and ideological divisions. Nor does there appear to be evidence that the collapse of communist power has resulted in a "liberal consensus," with its implication that cleavages are an outmoded concept in the study of the region. Instead, political cleavages have emerged in each state across the region that reflect the country's historical inheritances as well as its post-communist economic and social experiences.

At least two important theoretical and empirical questions remain in the field. First, although the general shape of the cleavage structures of post-communism is better understood, the mechanisms for their formation are unclear or disputed. Most explanations of cleavages in more established democracies emphasize the importance of prior social organization in providing sources of interest and political allegiance among the public that allow coordination of voters and parties in structured and relatively stable ways (Sartori 1969, Przeworski 1985). Such prior social organization, however, was largely absent across Eastern Europe. Various other mechanisms, therefore, have been invoked to account for the evidence of cleavage structure—such as cultural legacies, modes of communist rule, forms of elite and mass mobilization during the democratic transition itself, and the institutionally shaped incentives for parties and politicians to forge links with the electorate—but it is not yet agreed which of these factors, if any, is most important, or indeed exactly how these factors have shaped choices at the individual level so that they result in cleavages at the societal level.

Second, in order to speak with full confidence about the existence of cleavages, it is necessary to see stability and persistence in social and ideological divisions, but naturally these conditions are only weakly established empirically. There are also differing theoretical expectations about the stability of the social and ideological divisions in politics. Considerable volatility is evident in support for particular parties, and political parties themselves have often been short-lived, offering voters little opportunity to reward or punish them. But is this volatility of supply and demand for parties a sign of instability in the cleavage structure? For many countries, there is limited evidence available to test these possibilities because follow-up studies that might allow over-time comparisons have not yet taken place; however, it should be noted that where such evidence is available, it points to more stability than change in the structure of underlying social and ideological divisions, which strengthens claims about the existence of cleavages in the region. This begs a further question, however: If stability of political divisions is the norm, why should this be the case given the extent of broad social transformation in the region over the past decade?

The rest of this chapter is structured to engage these issues and the evidence. Section 2 considers expectations that communism and its collapse would have a profoundly inhibiting effect on cleavage formation or that it would lead to the emergence of common but sui generis post-communist cleavages. Section 3 looks at the evidence that has been built up, which, though sometimes incomplete and contradictory, does point toward a more structured and variegated set of cleavages than initial expectations suggested. Section 4 discusses competing theoretical explanations for these cleavage structures. Section 5 considers the case for cleavage stability and change. The concluding section considers how this evidence sheds light on the two big issues mentioned above: How great are the social and ideological legacies of the communist era? And how great is the effect of cleavages on the stability of democracy in the region?

2. LENINIST LEGACIES

Communist power was expected by many scholars to have long-standing effects. However, the nature and consequences of the Leninist legacy were disputed. Some argued that it would inhibit the formation of any stable social and ideological divisions in mass democratic politics; others expected cleavages to emerge but of a distinctive post-Leninist type.

Many scholars theorizing and investigating post-communist politics shared with Fukuyama the expectation that political cleavages would be absent in post-communist states, but they held this view for quite different reasons. Communist power and the struggle against it were believed to have profoundly affected the character of societal involvement in politics. This position, which continues to attract support from some scholars (Ost 1993, Elster et al. 1998, White et al. 1997, Ahl 1999, Lawson et al. 1999), was initially put in fairly stark terms. Communism was considered to have flattened the social and ideological landscape such that no political cleavages would or could appear, at least without significant long-term social reconstruction. The flattening of the social and ideological landscape was anticipated as an effect of policies of the communist party state that had supposedly atomized social relationships, disaggregated social classes, destroyed or inhibited the formation of civil society, and caused citizens to retreat from the public to the private domain. Ideologically, it was argued that communist rule had removed the capacity of East Europeans to locate themselves on a left-right spectrum and had caused them to so distrust politics and politicians as to be unable to form attachments to political programs. These difficulties were expected to be exacerbated by the immense cognitive deficits of people facing monumental social, economic, and ideological transformation with the collapse of communism.

Post-communist society was expected by some to resemble a *tabula rasa*. Unorganized in intermediate civic groups, society lacked social differentiation, ideological commitments that might structure attitudes to change, and trust or ties to politicians or politics; as some scholars saw it, there was little likelihood of the early emergence of stable sources of mass-level social and ideological differentiation that might constitute cleavages underlying involvement in democratic politics (see Evans & Whitefield 1993 for a critical discussion of this perspective). In this context, and by contrast with Fukuyama, political competition for votes in post-communist states would be based on personalistic, demagogic, and populist appeals, with great volatility and potential instability for democracy in the region.

However, a number of scholars were committed to an alternative perspective on the importance of the Leninist legacy. Along with Fukuyama, they expected to find a consensus among liberals, though not, as he did, a liberal consensus. Rather, post-communist societies were expected to be strongly divided along a single dimension of support for and opposition to liberalism. In this, they were distinct from established democracies that had developed out of prior existing market economies, civil societies, and stable state boundaries and citizenries; in established democracies, the character of liberalism was more fragmented and its connection to democracy attenuated (Fleishman 1988, Heath et al. 1991, Shafer & Claggett 1995). Economic liberals could be socially conservative, and the economic left could be libertarian. At least parts of the anti-market left, moreover, could be more committed to democratic processes than the right. In post-communist states, by contrast, a number of authors (Jowitt 1992, Gray 1993) argued that liberalism was "consolidated"; market liberals were also socially and politically liberal. Against the liberals stood opponents of the market who were also consolidated authoritarians.

Explanations for the emergence of a peculiarly consolidated liberalism in post-communist states—as opposed to the Fukuyama view that this had become a common condition across modern societies—tended to focus on the historical circumstances of ideological opposition to communist rule. However, in a seminal article for the field, Kitschelt (1992) presented the most developed case for the existence of a Leninist ideological legacy, arguing that post-communist societies were divided in a distinctive manner, at least for the period of their transition to established market democracies, along a single liberal-authoritarian axis of political competition. Most importantly, Kitschelt located the position of individuals on this dimension by reference to their personal resource endowments. Those best suited to market conditions—the young, the educated, men, those with transferable skills, or even those who had privileges within the old communist system that they could privatize to themselves in the new order—were likely to be found in the pro-market/libertarian quadrant, whereas those likely to be most adversely affected by change, or cognitively least able to deal flexibly with social flux—the old, the uneducated, industrial workers, etc.—would support anti-market/authoritarian ideologies. Differences between countries in the distribution of individuals on this axis, moreover, were explained in terms of the country's economic development; the more developed the country, the more market liberals it would contain. In some states, such as Czechoslovakia, this group was expected to comprise a majority; in others, like Romania, a minority.

For various reasons, however, these arguments for the importance of the Leninist legacy did not convince all within the field. Scholars could not agree on what the Leninist legacy actually was, given the considerable variation in the character of governance across communist systems (Sabel & Stark 1982, Bunce 1999, Kitschelt et al. 1999). Perhaps most important, the evidence about the content of political competition during the transition (Linz & Stepan 1996) and from elections in their immediate aftermath (Whitefield 1993) was suggestive of highly differentiated sources of social and ideological division. Neither the *tabula rasa* nor uniformity resulting from common communist inheritances appeared to account for the signs of diversity that post-communist societies quickly exhibited.

3. "RETURN TO DIVERSITY": POST-COMMUNIST POLITICAL DIVISIONS

It has become obvious that democratic, liberal, and market transformations have proceeded at widely different paces, and in different ways, across Eastern Europe since 1989 (Karatnycky et al. 1999). Diversity has also appeared on many indicators that are directly relevant to the question of the cleavage structures of the region. The character of the issues expressed in political competition, the ideological fields appropriated by parties, the social bases of support for parties and candidates, the organizational stability of parties, and levels of partisanship themselves all vary considerably. The simple models outlined in the previous section do not adequately characterize these differences.

The existence of diversity across post-communist states in the content of political competition is not evidence for diversity in cleavage structures. Support for political parties may vary as a result of many factors, discussed below, that are not connected to cleavages. And even if partisanship appears to be rooted in ideological and social differentiation, this may not result from social and ideological divisions in the population but rather from party strategies. To defend a cleavage-based approach to post-communist politics, therefore, that takes into account the diversity of issues and social factors mentioned above, it is necessary to show that social differentiation exists, that it has intelligible consequences for citizens' ideological perspectives, and that these consequences are important in shaping vote choice.

Whereas authors discussed in the previous section expected considerable uniformity in the cleavage structure of post-communist states, those who emphasize diversity often claim that each state has a unique set of divisions—a view that tends to be particularly pronounced, not surprisingly, among those whose studies are not comparative in design. It would be difficult to obtain consensus even among scholars working with comparative data. For one thing, few empirical studies of cleavages—as opposed to studies of constitutional arrangements or economic reform programs—have been based on more than two or three states. Moreover, evidence for cleavage structures is drawn from distinctive sources, including aggregate and individual data—regional voting patterns and surveys—as well as studies of party platforms and elite framing of issues. No doubt an investigation that combines these kinds of evidence would be useful and significant, but as yet very little has been done along these lines of a broad comparative nature. What has been done, however, suggests that diversity in the region exists only insofar as the causes of cleavages vary. Put the other way, common causes in many countries also produce strong commonalities in the cleavage structures of some countries.

The broadest empirical investigation of political divisions in Eastern Europe, involving 12 countries, has been undertaken by Evans and myself, using data mainly from 1993 and 1994 (although some over-time studies, discussed in Section 5, have also been undertaken in a narrower range of cases). The results of our joint work are summarized below. Analytically, our research strategy sought to show (*a*) the connection between social locations, identities, and differentiated experiences, (*b*) the connection of ideological and attitudinal perspectives of these socially located individuals, and then (*c*) the connection of these social and ideological elements to vote choice. Methodologically, the analysis used similar or identical measures of social indicators—class, religion, ethnicity, etc.—and attitudes toward issues such as the market, political freedom, social liberalism, and minority rights, which allow for direct comparison of their character across the region, and then for a comparative assessment of their relative impact on vote. The research, therefore, addresses most of the key elements of cleavages in democratic societies outlined in the second paragraph of this chapter: that cleavages should be strongly structured lines of salient social and ideological division at the mass level, that they should involve social difference connected to ideological difference, and that these in turn relate to political competition and party choice.

The results of our analysis showed precisely the relationship among social and ideological differences and partisanship that would be expected if political cleavages were present. Social differentiation was evident, arising from a variety of identities and resource endowments. These were good predictors of attitudes on cognate ideological dimensions; for example, class, age, and education provided bases for varied views about the role of the market; ethnic background and perceptions of ethnic distance were strongly predictive of views of minority rights; and religiosity was in many contexts predictive of attitudes toward social liberalism and conservatism.

Naturally, although economic differentiation was common to all countries (if not always to the same degree), not all social identities and differentiated social experiences were equally present in all states; in particular, the religious and ethnic composition of countries in the region varies markedly. As a consequence, we found that the connection of social division to ideological division also varies; religiosity appears to matter much more to social liberalism in Catholic than in Orthodox states; and issues of ethnic rights are more firmly socially rooted where minorities exist and where the sense of social difference between ethnic groups is more strongly felt. This variation in the nature of social and ideological division is important because it appears to relate to the nature of divisions that emerge in support for political parties.

Table 1 (Evans & Whitefield 2000) shows the social and ideological bases for partisanship in post-communist states. The analysis indicates a complex and variegated social and ideological structure underlying electoral choice across the

TABLE 1   Political cleavages in post-Communist Eastern Europe: social and ideological divisions to partisanship

	Social bases	Ideological bases
Bulgaria	1. Ethnicity (Turkish) 2. Age, Class (professionals vs workers) 3. Religiosity	1. Economic liberalism, pro/anti-West 2. Ethnic liberalism 3. Nationalism, Gypsies
Czech Republic	1. Religiosity 2. Education/class, region (Moravia), settlement size 3. Age, class (urban-rural), sector	1. Economic liberalism, pro/anti-West 2. Social & political liberalism, ethnic liberalism, Gypsies
Estonia	1. Ethnicity (Russians and others) 2. Age 3. Class (urban-rural)	1. Ethnic liberalism 2. Economic, social & political liberalism
Hungary	1. Age 2. Religiosity 3. Class (urban-rural), education/class, settlement size, denomination (Protestant)	1. Economic liberalism, pro/anti-West 2. Social & political liberalism, Jews 3. Social & political liberalism, nationalism
Latvia	1. Ethnicity (non-Latvians), religious denomination 2. Education, class (professionals vs agriculture and workers)	1. Ethnic liberalism, nationalism 2. Economic liberalism, West, social and political liberalism
Lithuania	1. Ethnicity (Russians and Poles), Religiosity, settlement size 2. Religiosity, class (professionals vs workers)	1. Ethnic liberalism, nationalism 2. Economic, social & political liberalism
Moldova	1. Ethnicity (Russians vs Moldovans) 2. Ethnicity (Gagauz and others vs Moldovans) 3. Settlement size, education, private sector, church attendance, gender	1. Ethnic liberalism 2. Social and political liberalism, economic liberalism, West
Poland	1. Settlement size, class (urban-rural) 2. Religiosity 3. Gender, class (professionals vs others) 4. Age, pensioners	1. Economic liberalism, pro/anti-West, nationalism 2. Social & political liberalism, Jews

TABLE 1   (*Continued*)

Romania	1. Age, region (Bucharest), education 2. Ethnicity (Hungarians) 3. Region (Transylvania)	1. Social & political liberalism, economic liberalism, pro/anti-West 2. Ethnic liberalism 3. Pro-West, Jews

Russia	1. Region (Nizhnii-Novogorod),
	   settlement size
	2. Income, class (urban-rural), region
	   (Urals)
		1. Economic liberalism
		2. Social & political liberalism and
		   ethnic rights

Slovakia	1. Ethnicity (Hungarian) 2. Religiosity 3. Ethnicity (other ethnics), class (professionals vs. others) 4. Age, sector	1. Ethnic liberalism 2. Economic liberalism, pro/anti-West 3. Social & political liberalism, Gypsies
Ukraine	1. Region (Western), language 2. Age, gender 3. Ethnicity (Russians and others), region (Crimea)	

region, which reflects the lines of social and ideological differentiation mentioned above, with consequent considerable diversity between countries.[1]

At the same time, there is some commonality across countries in the sources of division, and the extent of diversity is relatively limited, with similar forms of division appearing in countries that on reflection share common characteristics. Almost all states show some element of ideological division over distributional issues, and social class (especially urban-rural), age, and education are frequently social predictors on this dimension. Religiosity and ethnicity and their ideological correlates, social and ethnic liberalism, by contrast, do not matter everywhere, but, as expected, are important sources of division in all Catholic and ethnically divided states. Other factors, such as anti-Semitism, attitudes towards Gypsies, and views of Western involvement also, albeit to a lesser degree, structure partisanship in some cases. Although the issue of stability is still to be addressed below, this evidence does suggest that the term cleavage is appropriate on the basis of the definition provided at the beginning of the chapter: There are strongly structured lines of social and ideological division among the electorate that are relevant to their political choices.

---

[1]The analysis that produced these summary results was undertaken by relating vote, or in some cases (depending on the electoral cycle) intended vote, of respondents drawn from national probability samples in each of the states mentioned, to a range of social characteristics and attitudes that had been scaled into ideological dimensions. The analysis, therefore, was intended to uncover the main forms of social and ideological division, if these exist, revealed by the complex choices and motivations of voters often choosing from 8–10 parties or presidential candidates.

Not all authors agree empirically with the precise characterization of divisions shown in Table 1, and there are certainly additional important factors not shown in the table. Powerful regional divisions, for example, are also present in some countries (Arel 1995, Clem & Craumer 2000, Gehlbach 2000), as shown by both survey and aggregate voting data, and although such divisions require further explanation, they do not disappear when other socioeconomic factors are controlled for. Ideologically, local issues such as the question of Hungarian and Russian "coethnics" living in neighboring states (Slovakia and Romania, or parts of the former Soviet Union) also tap into voters' decision making (Evans & Whitefield 1995, Whitefield & Evans 1998); the same point can be made about the issue of EU and NATO expansion in states targeted for accession. Corruption and crime are other issues that have framed debates during elections. However, where voters stand on apparently country-specific issues such as EU expansion and state borders appears to be strongly related empirically to issue divisions such as support for the market, the West, ethnic rights, and nationalism (Evans & Whitefield 2000), and individual attitudes on these questions are also explicable in terms of the same kinds of social interests. In this sense, many local issues connect to the cleavage structure outlined above.

Party choice is, of course, never solely determined by ideological or social interests; factors such as personalities, competence, and perceptions of party stances on valence questions also shape political competition in each state. But there is no reason to conclude that the divisions just outlined are irrelevant or even weak guides to voters' party choices. Rather, such specificities in the forms of political competition are additional to and not incompatible with the cleavage structures described above. Although it might be argued that there was little reason to expect a strong relationship between elite presentations of issues and mass divisions in the early stages of democracy, and even less reason to suppose that elite conflict should only be about divisions within the electorate, this line does not fit well with (admittedly patchy) evidence that the gap between party elites and supporters is much less pronounced than some commentators have suggested (Lawson et al. 1999). Parties that do not relate themselves to the issues and social experiences that divide the electorate may be electorally weakened (Reisinger et al. 1996, Miller et al. 2000). Evidence about the position of party supporters on each of the social and ideological divisions in Table 1, moreover, suggests a sensible link to the known positions of the parties they support. In the main, therefore, the evidence indicates that divisions within the post-communist electorate pass another test of cleavages from the definition given at the start of the chapter: They help define the behavior of politically relevant mass actors. The flux of politics, parties, and politicians, focused on by many authors (Elster et al. 1998, Lawson et al. 1999, Rose 2000), though of course important at the level of party organization, nonetheless disguises a great deal of structure and commonality across countries in the underlying cleavages. Party choice does appear to result, to a significant degree, from the socially and ideologically differentiated perspectives of voters, even if many parties themselves have had a short and unstable life.

4. EXPLAINING VARIATION: SOCIAL AND POLITICAL FACTORS THAT SHAPE CLEAVAGES

There is considerable evidence that post-communist societies contain structured social and ideological divisions, that social factors—especially age, education, religion, ethnicity, and occupational class—significantly shape ideological perspectives, and that voters choose parties that in large measure programmatically reflect their interests. There is less agreement, however, on the reasons for the emergence of structured divisions and on commonalities in the pattern of divisions. Some of these explanations, moreover, have further implications for the forms and extent of divisions, and these in turn can be considered against the empirical evidence available.

Although most accounts show an awareness of the causal complexities of cleavage formation, within the literature there are two broad categories of explanations of differences and patterns across countries in the nature and extent of post-communist political divisions. One approach is to locate the explanatory factor at some point in a causal chain: in pre-communist historical and cultural traditions, in the form of communist rule or transition from it; in institutional choices and party strategies; or in the character of economic and social post-communist experience itself. The second category of explanation refers to the agent—elite or mass—that had the main effect in shaping the choices of voters that resulted in the cleavages discussed in the previous section. (For a fuller discussion of these issues, see Kitschelt 2002 and Evans & Whitefield 2000.)

4.1. Pre-Communist Cultural Legacies

If historical and cultural traditions are important, then they involve the passing on of identities and interests, formally via institutions or informally through families, and they provide foci for the appeals of parties and cues to be picked up by voters. Demonstrating that historical or cultural factors are at work is frequently difficult. Comparable data from the pre-communist period are generally not available, so that it is difficult to be sure what the old culture was; multiple possible historical foci are available, and an account of why one rather than another is contemporarily relevant is not normally provided in cultural terms; and even if historical similarities of current cleavages can be shown, individual interests and choices that produce them can generally be accounted for by existing rather than historical circumstances and interests.

To demand that a cultural account deal with all of these points, however, may be overly stringent, particularly since the evidence about cleavages shown above is difficult to account for in many cases without reference to a country's historical traditions. To say that current institutions and recent individual experiences and involvements shape identities and values is not to say that distinctive historical traditions did not play a role in their production. Catholicism is clearly a factor in current political socialization, but it makes no sense to deny that it is also a historical and cultural fact about a country. Whereas Catholicism affects social and ideological divisions in historically Catholic countries, Orthodoxy has very little effect on attitudes or cleavages where it is the dominant religion, and the best explanation of this has to do with the relative effects of Orthodoxy on the political culture of these states (Whitefield 2001). By the same token, the most obvious explanation for the greater role of religion in dividing the public in Slovakia relative to the Czech Republic is the historical difference, no doubt socially and institutionally maintained since, between the Reformation experiences of the two states (Evans & Whitefield 1998).

The same points may be made about ethnicity as a divisive force in post-communist politics. The communist system, and the transition from it, affected and politicized ethnic differences in many ways. For example, the very large number of working-class Russians in the Baltic states is a consequence of post-1945 Soviet industrial and migration policy. Similarly, the Polish Communist Party pursued an aggressively anti-Jewish policy in 1968 under the guise of anti-Zionism. Mobilization against communist power, moreover, regularly made overt appeals to ethnic factors, most obviously in the Soviet Union (including within Russia), but also to dire effect in the Balkans. In some cases, therefore, it is very difficult to say whether it was these more recent historical experiences that shaped attitudes and made them currently salient, or whether the status quo is an effect of experience of ethnic mobilization in the communist period. The likelihood is that each temporal point affects the emergence of an ethnic cleavage. But, notably, in every country in the region in which there were historical ethnic divisions of consequence, and, *pace* Germans in Poland and the Czech Republic, where the ethnic minority remains in situ, these appear to be a significant source of contemporary differentiation in the electoral choices of post-communist voters. The intensity of the cleavage does vary in ways that might be accounted for by communist and post-communist social experiences and institutional designs (Pettai & Kreuzer 1999), but their presence appears at least plausibly related to long-standing cultural legacies. This is far from saying, however, that all cleavages in post-communist societies require a deep historical explanation.

4.2. Varieties of Communist Rule and Democratic Transition

Forms of communist power, and the modes of transition from them, have been used to explain observed differences in a number of aspects of post-communist politics (Linz & Stepan 1996, Bunce 1999), such as democratic consolidation, market reform, and the cleavage structure. Effects are produced via three mechanisms: by the politicization of issues in the communist period, by the nature of elite competition and extent of mobilization in the transition and in the institutional choices that are made at this point, and by the party strategies of the communist-successor parties. Cleavages themselves are affected in two ways: in the relative extent of structuring of cleavages and in the content of the cleavages themselves.

These arguments about the intensity of cleavages in post-communist societies differ from those discussed in Section 2 in that weakness of cleavages is not attributed to communist power per se but rather to forms of its exercise and demise. Kitschelt et al. (1999) have expressed this position most clearly and influentially by making the extent of "programmatism" the central focus of research. They define this term as the extent to which political divisions result from choices made by voters about differences in the ideological appeals of parties. Where programmatism is high, Kitschelt et al. expect the strongest political cleavages. Other forms of party competition are possible, however, including patronage or charismatic bases for partisanship. In these cases, partisanship will be much more weakly defined by social and ideological factors, and hence political cleavages will be less pronounced. Which of these three kinds of party competition exists in Eastern Europe is a result of various factors operating at different temporal points in the causal chain, but one of the most important is the form of communist power. (Kitschelt et al. do not deny, however, that this factor was itself shaped by some characteristics of the pre-communist phase.) Where communism was "patrimonial," as in most parts of Eastern Europe, patronage is believed to predominate as the basis on which parties connect with voters. Where communist regimes pursued "national accommodative" strategies, which tended both to be more economically liberal and to allow greater accommodation to a country's historical institutions (e.g., church) and traditions, both counterelite and mass mobilization against communism tended to be weaker, and the issue bases of both the transition and post-transition period were less polarized. Market issues, in particular, were much less contested politically. Because the communist-successor party supported economic liberalism, the main dimension of ideological division, and hence of social mobilization, was expected to involve value-based issues such a religion or ethnicity rather than distributional questions. In "bureaucratic authoritarian" communist regimes, such as East Germany and Czechoslovakia, class and economic issues were heavily mobilized, the Communist Party remained hardline to the end, mass mobilization on class grounds was greater, and post-communist cleavages were expected to be relatively highly programmatic and polarized.

4.3. Institutional and Elite Factors

Institutional and elite factors are also believed to bear on the cleavage structure. Some claim that elite factors account especially strongly for the pattern of cleavages when civil society is weakly developed and when, therefore, political leaders can shape the issue agenda under fewer constraints (Chhibber & Torcal 1997). Moreover, although structural conditions play a role in determining party strategy, elite ideological commitments also count and influence the ways in which parties present issues to the public (Ishiyama 1995). By the same token, although institutional design is the result of the balance of actors at the moment of transition, which was in turn significantly shaped by the form of communist power (Elster et al. 1998, Frye 1997), once they are established institutions may have their own effects on the extent of programmatism. For example, presidential and single-member-district electoral systems, especially in combination, are anticipated to be much less stimulating to cohesive party systems, more likely to produce patronage and personalized charismatic competition for votes, and therefore more likely to weaken cleavage formation (Kitschelt 1995).

Much of the evidence for such claims comes from studies of party elites or party behavior in legislatures rather than from support for parties within the electorate. Interestingly, in Bulgaria, where programmatic structuring was expected to be weak, Kitschelt et al. (1999) found the extent of social and ideological structuring at the mass level much greater than anticipated. Other evidence comparing the United Kingdom with East European societies also shows that programmatic and social structuring of vote in most of Eastern Europe is at high levels and that differences in the extent of cleavage formation at the mass level does not match the expectations of Kitschelt and others. The picture that emerges from the table above also points against these hypotheses. Countries that share the same characteristics of type of communist system or mode of transition from it do not appear to cluster together in the predicted ways; nor do countries in which elites have made similar choices in the post-communist period. To take two obvious examples, the Czech Republic, Hungary, and Poland appear to have strongly similar cleavage structures, although they differed in the type of communist power ascribed to them; and the cleavage structures of the Czech Republic and Slovakia differ despite having had the same mode of communist rule and transition from it.

4.4. Social Experiences and Identities

The final approach to accounting for the differences in cleavage structures—one that Evans and I have argued for—focuses less on institutional forms and elite behavior in communist and post-communist states (Evans & Whitefield 2000). Although these factors may be more important in explaining changes in the cleavage structure (see discussion below), they may be less important in the phase of cleavage formation. At this point, many parties chase voters, and voters make choices without the involvement in civil society discussed in Section 2 and with very limited information or experience about electoral outcomes. In such circumstances, the information most readily available to voters derives precisely from the individual's experiences and identities. Which experiences and identities count most will depend on their historical and cultural salience, as well as their current relevance, and on the extent to which individuals' attitudes are cognitively organized. Ethnic and religious differences, in such contexts, are likely to present to many people an organizing concept that relates closely to elements of salient personal and cultural experience, although these will operate only in states where ethnic and religious identities are historically well-entrenched. In all countries in the region, moreover, economic experiences are likely to be sharply differentiated, and the communist system itself, to a far greater extent than many commentators have suggested, structured attitudes into economic ideologies.

Seeing the problem in terms of historically and culturally located individual experience of contemporary social and economic difference both answers the second of the main issues raised at the beginning of this section, about whether mass or elite and institutional factors are central to shaping cleavages, and addresses the empirical evidence about patterns in the cleavage structures. This view suggests that the locus for formation of cleavages immediately after the collapse of communist power was the mass of the population rather than the political elites; that the electorate were much more cognitively sophisticated and (informally) socially organized than many accounts allow, particularly in regard to issues and identities that had historical and cultural resonance within a state. Individuals in conditions of great uncertainty during transformation overcame potentially severe collective action problems in producing the structured ideological and social divisions that form cleavages by using their experiences and cultural commitments as focal points to allow coordination. Types of communist rule and modes of transition matter only insofar as they influence the interest formation of individuals, and they appear to matter much less than historical legacies and contemporary economic experience.

5. VOLATILITY AND STABILITY IN POST-COMMUNIST POLITICS

The next issue to be addressed concerns theory and evidence for the stability of the social and ideological divisions discussed above. Indeed, given that the term cleavage is meaningful only if divisions are persistent, stability needs to be established if the term is to be properly applied to the post-communist context. Despite clear signs that partisan choices have structure—that social experience and identities connect to ideological perspectives and that these in turn connect to parties in sensible ways—the argument could still be made that this structure is likely to be ephemeral because the parties themselves are so unstable, because elite interests are dominant and fleeting, and because social experience and identities are in such flux in the region. Evidence for structure at one point should not lead to expectations of structure later and certainly not to the same sorts of divisions. Moreover, the very success of transformation should itself cause instability in the cleavage structure. As the memory of communist power fades, and experience of market systems grows, old issues fade and new ones take their place. Although political liberalization and democracy were powerful concerns in the early stages of transition, as democracy consolidates it may fade as a source of division, while greater economic differentiation may lead to an increase in class politics. Over time and with experience, the association between market support, liberalism, and democracy ought to fade, especially if losers from the transition can be brought to pursue their interests via democratic politics.

As mentioned at the beginning of the chapter, there have been few over-time studies across the region as a whole that replicate previous work, so conclusions are necessarily tentative. Some change along the lines just mentioned, however, does seem to have occurred. Political liberalism appears less salient and economic issues have become more powerful, at least in some contexts (Gibson 1996, Whitefield 2001). However, in general, the evidence suggests that political divisions are sticky. In Russia, about which perhaps most is known over time, the character of divisions has remained stable, even though the power of elites and the degree of social uncertainty might lead us to expect the greatest cleavage instability. Social bases of politics in Russia have developed in the sense that class and economic interests now appear more sharply connected with partisanship, but the fundamental nature of the main cleavage has remained the same: Economic winners from change still support economic liberalism, Western involvement, and the breakup of the former Soviet Union, whereas the losers take the opposite positions (Whitefield & Evans 1998). A similar story can be told about Ukraine and Lithuania, where stability in the cleavage structure can be observed between 1993 and 1998; class divisions are related to the same type of economic divide, but more powerful divisions remain between regions and between ethnic, religious, and linguistic groups (Evans & Whitefield 2001).

This picture of relative stability requires explanation, given the extent of social change and party instability in the region. However, from the perspective of the social experience and identity-based explanation of the formation of political divisions, stability is less surprising. Social identities such as ethnicity and religion tend to shift only very slowly over decades and longer. Economic transformation to the market certainly did create winners and losers, mainly among the old, the less educated, and blue-collar and agricultural workers, but there is no reason to think that the relative economic prospects of these groups has changed significantly over time to bring about a realignment in their relative economic attitudes. If anything, greater experience with the market may have clarified the economic attitudes of classes and social groups, sharpening the economic cleavage rather than transforming it. Although parties and politicians have come and gone, in conditions of significant stability in the dispersal of attitudes and their relative salience, successful new politicians may be likely to address the issues that are known to divide the electorate, and voters may decide among new parties in the same way they decided among the old ones—by finding those closest to their position on the experiences that matter most to them. The term cleavage, therefore, is likely to be meaningful for post-communist societies, and the cleavages are likely to continue to resemble those shown in Table 1 for some time.

6. CONCLUSIONS: COMMUNIST LEGACIES, CLEAVAGES, AND DEMOCRACY IN EASTERN EUROPE

Two broad questions remain. What was the impact of communism on the structure of political divisions in Eastern Europe? And, from a broad comparative perspective, what light can the experience of post-communism cast on the connection between the cleavage structures and the stability and quality of democracies?

The first question remains difficult for the reasons given in Section 1; we don't know much about mass political divisions in the pre-communist period. It is relatively easy, however, to note some important things that communist power did not do, despite expectations to the contrary. Communist rule did not destroy social identities of class, religion, region, and ethnicity, which were to prove immediate sources of division; indeed, it probably maintained them and in some cases stimulated them. Nor did it so disorient or cognitively disable its citizens as to make them incapable of having complex and structured attitudes about issues, or making difficult and sophisticated choices about how to sensibly relate these attitudes to parties in conditions of great uncertainty about how other citizens would behave or which parties would win. Indeed, the modernizing effect of communism, by urbanizing and educating the public, probably radically increased the cognitive capacity of many of its citizens to cope with the transformations of the past decade.

There is, therefore, no clear Leninist legacy in the region. The apparent cleavage structures of many countries in Eastern Europe can be compared to those of countries without communist pasts; the countries of Central Europe resemble France, Austria, or Germany in the character of their political divisions much more than they resemble Russia or Ukraine. The most notable area of difference between East and West results from the strength of ethnic divisions in many states—Bulgaria, Estonia, Latvia, Lithuania, Romania, Slovakia—but this results from the ethnic make-up of these countries. Such distinctions as there are in character of divisions in Eastern Europe, in other words, stem from the composition of each country's identities and not from the specific impact of communism.

This claim relates to the second question about democracy. It is clear that there is considerable divergence across post-communist Eastern Europe in the extent of democratic reform. Some countries (Russia, Ukraine) can be considered borderline democracies, and some, such as Belarus, not democracies at all. How are these differences to be accounted for? To go back to Kitschelt's seminal 1992 paper, democracy would appear to be most threatened if there were a majority in the authoritarian/anti-market part of the distribution. For other scholars in a comparative context, ethnic divisions are particularly difficult to manage in a democratic framework. To what extent, then, do differences in democratic reform result from the cleavage structure?

The evidence from the region appears to be mixed. In countries such as Estonia and Latvia, citizenship entitlements were written to exclude many Russians in ways that severely limited their democratic rights, and this is most plausibly linked to the degree to which ethnic divisions constituted a basis for political competition in these countries (Pettai & Kreuzer 1999). However, the mere existence of ethnic cleavages did not lead to such policy conclusions, as the cases of Bulgaria, Lithuania, Moldova, Romania, Slovakia, and Ukraine amply demonstrate. It is important to account for the variation between these states, but cleavages do not, on their own, appear to provide the explanation.

In fact, the most likely explanation for variation in democratic reform shows the limits of value to the discussion above. Political cleavages were defined to refer to lines of division among politically important actors. Democratic deficits and instabilities are most evident in states where the mass public are the least politically important, whether because of overt restrictions on information, participation, and representation or because of institutionalized difficulties in translating public preferences into government control. These are also the circumstances in which elite corruption is most prevalent and where, therefore, elites have interests in inhibiting public political involvement (Hellman 1998). Not surprisingly, these states also tend to have the lowest levels of public support for "democracy" as it has been practiced. Given the weakness of popular political involvement in these cases, however, an explanation of democratic weakness is not likely to come from an examination of the mass cleavage structures of these states. In this case, elite-level communist legacies are much more plausible contenders.

The *Annual Review of Political Science* is online at http://polisci.annualreviews.org

LITERATURE CITED

Ahl R. 1999. Society and transition in post-Soviet Russia. *Communist Post-Communist Stud.* 32(2):175–93

Arel D. 1995. Ukraine: the temptation of the nationalizing state. In *Political Culture and Civic Society in the Former Soviet Union*, ed. V. Tismaneanu, pp. 157–88 Armonk, NY: Sharpe

Bartolini S, Mair P. 1990. *Identity, Competition and Electoral Availability: The Stabilization of European Electorates, 1885–1985*. Cambridge, UK: Cambridge Univ. Press. 363 pp.

Bremmer I, Taras R, eds. 1993. *Nation and Politics in the Soviet Successor States*. Cambridge, UK: Cambridge Univ. Press. 577 pp.

Bunce V. 1999. *Subversive Institutions: The Design and the Destruction of Socialism and the State*. Cambridge, UK: Cambridge Univ. Press. 206 pp.

Chhibber P, Torcal M. 1997. Elite strategy, social cleavages, and party systems in a new democracy: Spain. *Comp. Polit. Stud.* 30(1): 27–54

Cirtautas AM. 1994. In pursuit of the democratic interest: the institutionalization of parties and interests in Eastern Europe. In *The New Great Transformation*, ed. C Bryant, E Mokrzycki, pp. 36–57. London: Routledge

Clem RS, Craumer P. 2000. Regional patterns of political preference in Russia: the December 1999 Duma elections. *Post-Sov. Geogr. Econ.* 41(1):1–29

Comisso E. 1997. Is the glass half full or half empty? Reflections on five years of competitive politics in Eastern Europe. *Communist Post-Communist Polit.* 30(1):1–21

Daalder H. 1966. Parties, elites and political developments in Western Europe. In *Political Parties and Political Development*, ed. J LaPalombara, M Weiner, pp. 43–77. Princeton, NJ: Princeton Univ. Press

Dalton RJ. 1988. *Citizen Politics in Western Democracies: Public Opinion and Political Parties in the United States, Great Britain, West Germany and France*. Chatham, NJ: Chatham House. 270 pp.

Davies N. 1996. *Europe: A History*. Oxford, UK: Oxford Univ. Press. 1365 pp.

Dogan M. 1967. Political cleavage and social stratification in France and Italy. In *Party Systems and Voter Alignments: Cross-National Perspectives*, ed. SM Lipset, S Rokkan, pp. 129–95. New York: Free

Eckstein H. 1966. *Division and Cohesion in Democracy*. Princeton, NJ: Princeton Univ. Press. 293 pp.

Elster J, Offe C, Preusse UK. 1998. *Institutional Design in Post-Communist Societies*:

Rebuilding the Ship at Sea. Cambridge, UK: Cambridge Univ. Press. 350 pp.

Evans GA, Whitefield S. 1993. Identifying the bases of party competition in Eastern Europe. *Br. J. Polit. Sci.* 23(4):521–48

Evans GA, Whitefield S. 1995. Social and ideological cleavage formation in post-communist Hungary. *Eur.-Asia Stud.* 47(7): 1177–1204

Evans GA, Whitefield S. 1998. The structuring of cleavages in post-communist societies: the case of the Czech Republic and Slovakia. *Polit. Stud.* 46(1):115–39

Evans GA, Whitefield S. 2000. Explaining the formation of electoral cleavages in post-communist democracies. In *Elections in Central and Eastern Europe: The First Wave*, ed. H-D Klingemann, E Mochmann, K Newton, pp. 36–70. Berlin: Ed. Sigma

Evans GA, Whitefield S. 2001. *The dynamics of cleavage formation in conditions of economic transformation: comparing cleavages in Russia, Ukraine and Lithuania*. Presented at Annu. Meet. Am. Polit. Sci. Assoc., San Francisco, September

Fleishman JA. 1988. Attitude organization in the general public: evidence for a bidimensional structure. *Soc. Forces* 67(1):159–84

Frye T. 1997. A politics of institutional choice: post-communist presidencies. *Comp. Polit. Stud.* 30(5):523–52

Fukuyama F. 1992. *The End of History and the Last Man*. New York: Free. 418 pp.

Gehlbach S. 2000. Shifting electoral geography in Russia's 1991 and 1996 presidential elections. *Post-Sov. Geogr. Econ.* 41(5):379–87

Gibson JL. 1996. Political and economic markets: changes in the connections between attitudes towards political democracy and a market economy within the mass culture of Russia and Ukraine. *J. Polit.* 58(4):954–84

Gray J. 1993. From post-communism to civil society: the re-emergence of history and the decline of the Western model. *Soc. Philos. Policy* 10(1):26–50

Gunther R, Mughan A. 1993. Political institutions and cleavage management. In *Do Institutions Matter? Government Capabilities in the United States and Abroad*, ed. RK Weaver, BA Rockman, pp. 272–301. Washington, DC: Brookings Inst.

Heath AF, Jowell R, Curtice J, Evans GA, Field J, Witherspoon S. 1991. *Understanding Political Change: The British Voter 1964–1987*. Oxford, UK: Pergamon. 334 pp.

Hellman J. 1998. Winners take all: the politics of partial reform in postcommunist transitions. *World Polit.* 50(2):203–34

Ishiyama J. 1995. Communist parties in transition: structures, leaders, and processes of democratization in Eastern Europe. *Comp. Polit.* 27(2):147–66

Jowitt K. 1992. *New World Disorder: The Leninist Extinction*. London: Univ. Calif. Press. 342 pp.

Karatnycky A, Motyl A, Grabow C. 1999. *Nations in Transit, 1998: Civil Society, Democracy, and Markets in East Central Europe and the Newly Independent States*. New Brunswick, NJ: Transaction. 680 pp.

Kitschelt H. 1992. The formation of party systems in East Central Europe. *Polit. Soc.* 20(1):7–50

Kitschelt H. 1995. Formation of party cleavages in post-communist democracies. *Party Polit.* 1(4):447–72

Kitschelt H. 2002. Accounting for post-communist regime diversity. In *Capitalism and Democracy in Central and Eastern Europe: Assessing the Legacy of Communist Rule*, ed. G Ekiert, S Hanson. Cambridge, UK: Cambridge Univ. Press. In press

Kitschelt H, Mansfeldova Z, Toka G, Markowski M. 1999. *Post-Communist Party Systems: Competition, Representation, and Inter-Party Cooperation*. Cambridge, UK: Cambridge Univ. Press. 457 pp.

Lawson K. 1999. Cleavages, parties and voters. See Lawson et al. 1999, pp. 19–36

Lawson K, Rommele A, Karasimeonov G, eds. *Cleavages, Parties and Voters: Studies from Bulgaria, the Czech Republic, Poland and Romania*. London: Praeger

Lijphart A, Rogowski R, Weaver RK. 1993.

Separation of powers and cleavage management. In *Do Institutions Matter? Government Capabilities in the United States and Abroad*, ed. RK Weaver, BA Rockman, pp. 302–44. Washington, DC: Brookings Inst.

Linz JJ, Stepan A. 1996. *Problems of Democratic Transition and Consolidation: Southern Europe, South America and Post-Communist Europe*. Baltimore/London: Johns Hopkins Univ. Press. 479 pp.

Lipset SM, Rokkan S. 1967. Cleavage structures, party systems and voter alignments. In *Party Systems and Voter Alignments: Cross-National Perspectives*, ed. SM Lipset, S Rokkan, pp. 1–64 New York: Free

Miller AH, Erb G, Hesli V. 2000. Emerging party systems in post-Soviet societies: fact or fiction. *J. Polit.* 62(2):455–90

Neto OA, Cox GW. 1997. Electoral institutions, cleavage structures, and the number of parties. *Am. J. Polit. Sci.* 41(1):149–74

Ost D. 1993. The politics of interest in post-communist East Europe. *Theory Soc.* 22(4): 453–86

Pettai V, Kreuzer M. 1999. Party politics in the Baltic states: social bases and institutional context. *East Eur. Polit. Soc.* 13(1):148–89

Przeworski A. 1985. *Capitalism and Social Democracy*. Cambridge, UK: Cambridge Univ. Press. 269 pp.

Reisinger W, Melville A, Hesli V. 1996. Mass and elite political outlooks in post-Soviet Russia: How congruent? *Polit. Res. Q.* 49(1): 77–102

Rose R. 2000. A supply-side view of Russia's elections. *East Eur. Const. Rev.* 9(1/2):53–59

Sabel C, Stark D. 1982. Planning, politics, and shop-floor power: hidden forms of bargaining in Soviet-imposed state-socialist societies. *Polit. Soc.* 11(4):439–75

Sartori G. 1969. From the sociology of politics to political sociology. In *Politics and the Social Sciences*, ed. SM Lipset, pp. 65–100. Oxford, UK: Oxford Univ. Press

Shafer BE, Claggett W. 1995. *The Two Majorities: The Issue Context of Modern American Politics*. Baltimore, MD: Johns Hopkins Univ. Press. 227 pp.

Szelenyi I, Szelenyi S. 1991. The vacuum in Hungarian politics: classes and parties. *New Left Rev.* 187:121–37

White S, Rose R, McAllister I. 1997. *How Russia Votes*. Chatham, NJ: Chatham House. 331 pp.

Whitefield S, ed. 1993. *The New Institutional Architecture of Eastern Europe*. London: Macmillan. 204 pp.

Whitefield S. 2001. *Liberalism, conservatism and religion in Russia*. Presented at Annu. Meet. Am. Polit. Sci. Assoc., San Francisco, September

Whitefield S, Evans GA. 1998. The emerging structure of partisan divisions in Russian politics. In *Elections and Voters in Post-Communist Russia*, ed. M Wyman, S White, S Oates, pp. 68–99. London: Elgar

Zuckerman A. 1982. New approaches to political cleavage. A theoretical introduction. *Comp. Polit. Stud.* 15:131–44

Annu. Rev. Polit. Sci. 2002. 5:201–21
DOI: 10.1146/annurev.polisci.5.111401.151327
Copyright © 2002 by Annual Reviews. All rights reserved

OF WAVES AND RIPPLES: Democracy and Political Change in Africa in the 1990s

Clark C. Gibson

Department of Political Science, 9500 Gilman Drive, University of California, San Diego, La Jolla, California 92093-0521; e-mail: ccgibson@ucsd.edu

Key Words   democratization, transitions, political liberalization, elections

■ **Abstract**   This chapter reviews the literature concerned with explaining recent political change in Africa. After recounting some of the political transformations on the continent, it explores the economic and political factors most often invoked by scholars to account for these changes. The chapter concludes with a call for more comparative work, as well as more precise measures, models, and tests.

INTRODUCTION

Africa's encounter with the "third wave" of democracy has reinvigorated the study of the continent's politics at the national, regional, and international levels. Political scientists who had been busy exploring the contours of authoritarianism suddenly confronted dozens of African states experiencing political transformations. Such momentous events challenged scholars to explain the origin, process, and possible implications of these political changes. In response, Africanist political scientists have produced a richly varied body of work that continues their tradition of contributing key theoretical and empirical insights to the broader debates of their discipline (Bates et al. 1993).

The goal of this chapter is to explore how political scientists have studied Africa's recent political changes. After a short history regarding the recent political upheaval in Africa, the chapter discusses several major works in the field and examines some of the central arguments provided by political scientists to account for Africa's political reconfiguration. The chapter ends with a more general evaluation of African transitions research.

A caveat is in order regarding language. There is debate about how to label the political change occurring in Africa. Some think the events warrant the moniker of democratization; others scoff at the idea that any democratic transition has taken place. Although I believe we should think of these phenomena more as aspects of political change than as democratization (see, e.g., Joseph 1999d, Sklar 1999), I use the latter term at times to refer to this transitions literature.

1094-2939/02/0615-0201$14.00   **201**

POLITICAL CHANGE IN AFRICA

Authoritarian governments still dominated Africa's political landscape at the end of the 1980s. By the end of 1994, however, 29 countries had held a total of 54 elections, with observers hailing more than half as "free." Further, these elections boasted high turnouts and clear victories: Voters removed 11 sitting presidents, and three more had declined to run in these "founding" elections. During 1995–1997, 16 countries held second-round elections, so that by 1998 only four countries in all of sub-Saharan Africa had not staged some sort of competitive contest during the 1990s (Bratton & van de Walle 1997, pp. 21–22). Given the continent's poor record of competitive elections that followed its first wave of democracy in the 1960s, the rash of elections in the 1990s clearly signaled that some form of political change had come to Africa.

A potent admixture of economic, social, and political crises surrounded these changes. Two decades of authoritarian government policies had driven most African economies into the ground. Observers also blamed structural adjustment programs for exacerbating the economic downturns—or at least faulted them for not doing enough to avert the collapses (Callaghy & Ravenhill 1993c, Mkandawire & Olukoshi 1995, Gibbon et al. 1992). During this period, donors increased their restrictions on foreign aid. When the Berlin Wall collapsed, so did the idea of state socialism in Africa. International financial institutions and bilateral donors became less interested in acting as banker to African autocrats and instead began espousing the concept of accountable government. With domestic and international funds shrinking, many African governments further cut their already skeletal public services [adding fuel to the ongoing debate about the legitimacy of the African state (Jackson & Rosberg 1982, Sandbrook 1985, Boone 1998)]. The number of popular protests in Africa increased. Workers decried their inflation-eaten wages, students clamored for better support, and civil servants increasingly sought unofficial sources of income. All the while, elites gauged the widening cracks in the authoritarian edifice (Bratton & van de Walle 1997, Bates 1994). For most African countries, some combination of these factors triggered political liberalization and, eventually, multiparty elections.

The timing, content, and consequences of recent political change in Africa clearly vary by country (as do countries' previous experience with democratic institutions). Benin could be placed at one end of the transition scale; popular protest led to a national conference in 1990 that effectively ended Mathieu Kérékou's 17-year rule. At the other end of the scale could sit the authoritarian regimes of Mauritania, Burundi, Equatorial Guinea, and Swaziland. Between the two poles lie the harder-to-categorize cases of pseudo-, semi-, and ambiguous democracies such as that of Kenya, where Daniel arap Moi continues to thwart domestic and international pressure with an effective mix of electoral legerdemain and outright corruption (Joseph 1999a, Diamond 1999b, Barkan & Ng'ethe 1999, Kanyinga 1998).

Indeed, whereas nearly all political scientists agree that the political topography of Africa began to change in the 1990s, far fewer assert that a wave of democracy has crashed into—or even lapped at—the continent's shores. Even early optimists became less effusive about democracy's prospects (at least in the short run) as they witnessed what seemed to be politics as usual after historic founding elections (Chege 1996, Villalón 1998, Lemarchand 1992). In 1991, Joseph wrote of the democratic "miracle" that appeared to be taking place in Africa; eight years later he claims that African politicians have constructed "virtual democracies" that do just enough to keep financial aid flowing (Joseph 1991, 1999d). In the eyes of many, the democratic impulse of the early 1990s quickly lost its sheen. Bratton & Posner (1999) point out that although elections in "surviving multiparty systems" are held with "acceptable punctuality," their quality is declining as incumbents devise strategies of questionable legality to retain their positions. Clapham & Wiseman (1995) believe that the continent will at best house "minimalist democracies." Young (1999a) asserts that the democratizing reforms that have occurred in Africa have fallen far short of any reasonable criteria for consolidation. Ake (1996) sees continuity rather than change as elites are merely recycled by so-called transitions (see also Chabal & Daloz 1999, Ottaway 1999a). Mbembe (1995) views Africa's new political transitions merely as new "formulas of domination." And Ihonvbere foretells "intolerance, violence, instability, uncertainty, and stalemate" for Africa in the near future (2000, p. 213). Disturbing trends notwithstanding, political scientists generally remain hopeful, noting that even small political change may help to move African countries away from their previous authoritarianism (Woodward 1998, Wiseman 1999, Young 1999a, Diamond 1999b, van de Walle 2001, Ndegwa 2001).

EXPLAINING POLITICAL CHANGE

Political scientists have applied a variety of theoretical lenses, featured scores of variables, addressed different levels of analysis, and identified various time periods to account for Africa's political changes in the late twentieth century. Despite the diversity of their studies, however, scholars have coalesced around certain kinds of explanations and clusters of variables. This section reviews some of the more important debates that have emerged from the literature by examining several well-known works and the more popular explanatory variables. (For heuristic reasons, it divides the latter into economic and political categories, although their overlap and interaction are acknowledged by all analysts.)

Some Central Work

I single out six books, presented in order of publication, that focus on Africa's recent political transformations. Reading these works would not comprise a complete course on African political transformation over the past decade, and many excellent articles and books are absent from this too-short list. Nevertheless, it provides a good overview of works that represent a range of methods and styles and include most of the salient issues and approaches found in the African transitions literature.

Widner's edited volume *Economic Change and Political Liberalization in Sub-Saharan Africa* (1994b) was one the first collections of studies to address Africa's contemporary political changes. Despite its age, its contributors' analyses remain generally robust after eight years. The book's longevity is due in part to its relatively limited goal, namely "to offer hypotheses about the relationship, if any, between the economic crises of the 1980s and patterns of regime change in sub-Saharan Africa" (Widner 1994a, p. 4). Consequently, and importantly, the contributors stay focused on the impact of economic factors. The volume's structure is somewhat typical for the genre: It contains two theoretical chapters, five single-country case studies, a rare regional-level comparison (between Francophone and Anglophone countries), and three chapters that review political trends in Africa. Much of the work contained in these chapters regarding the economics of political transformation laid the foundation for later, similar studies. Many of the hypotheses in the volume still cry out for rigorous testing.

Mamdani's *Citizen and Subject* (1996) is a broad and impressive examination of the contemporary effects generated by Africa's colonial institutions. Mamdani offers an intriguingly different account of current African politics and the possibility of the continent's democratization. He argues that colonial regimes created—and postcolonial regimes maintained—institutions (the Native Authority system) that deracialized but did not democratize the state. These institutions produced a bifurcated political landscape in which urban dwellers are citizens (allowed some level of political participation), whereas residents of the countryside remain the subjects of traditional authority. Regimes use this duality to maintain their power at the center. From this perspective, Mamdani sees little movement toward democratization despite recent political change in Africa. He argues that only when the rural dwellers are organized as true citizens will democracy be possible in Africa. For the African transitions literature, Mamdani's contribution is both substantive and methodological. He forces readers to evaluate the political importance of historical institutions through a clear theoretical argument and a careful comparison of Uganda and South Africa.

The touchstone for cross-national empirical studies of African political transformation remains Bratton & van de Walle's *Democratic Experiments in Africa* (1997). Using national-level data from 47 sub-Saharan countries, Bratton & van de Walle test some of the better-known theories of democratization, most of them from the non-African transitions literature. The authors seek to account for the causes and consequences of transitions by first separating them into a three-part sequence: political protest, political liberalization, and elections and their aftermath. They argue for an account of African political change based on domestic rather than international phenomena, including civil society and a country's particular political and electoral institutions. Bratton & van de Walle also evaluate (and ultimately discard) much of the conventional wisdom about transitions (e.g., higher levels of economic development lead to democracies, international intervention caused the transitions). Although questions about method and data bedevil any cross-national work, and although the data do not always provide strong support for the authors't arguments, Bratton & van de Walle have constructed clear concepts, useful variables, and important tests.

Reynolds (1999) builds on Bratton & van de Walle's foundational work by constructing a careful comparison of the types and effects of electoral systems and executives in five southern African countries. In *Electoral Systems and Democratization in Southern Africa*, Reynolds provides evidence that the structure of electoral systems matters to the kind of parties, party system, and legislative-executive relations within a country. More important, he argues that these institutions also critically affect the representativeness of government as well as government performance. At base, Reynolds argues that the inclusiveness of electoral and government systems is a good predictor of African countries' political stability and economic performance. It is somewhat unfortunate that the two cases that emerge as "the best" according to Reynolds's well-specified criteria are South Africa and Namibia, given the numerous characteristics that they share in addition to their "inclusive" political structures. This five-country study of democratization stands out because of its commitment to clear research design and its use of data to test hypotheses regarding the effects of political institutions.

Whereas *Democratic Experiments in Africa* works largely at the level of formal institutions, Chabal & Daloz's *Africa Works*: *Disorder as a Political Instrument* accounts for African politics through the "informal, uncodified and unpoliced" (Chabal & Daloz 1999, p. xix). The authors argue that political actors in Africa seek to maximize their own resources by creating and maintaining social disorder. Such a disordered world places a premium on vertical and personalized relationships as exemplified in Africa's neopatrimonial regimes. Through this analytical lens, the informalization of politics is explored with respect to civil society, the state, and political elites. Conventional wisdoms suffer under Chabal & Daloz's examination. Civil society and the state cannot be differentiated, political protest in Africa is about the distribution of spoils and not a rejection of the neopatrimonial system itself, and so-called democratic transitions in Africa are reinterpreted as phenomena that may be unrecognizable to citizens of the West. In this book no concepts are tested, no data systematically marshaled. Instead, this is a book of strong ideas that challenge nearly all the assumptions of modernization and democratic theory.

The final two books described here provide a sampling of more recent work regarding Africa's political changes. Articles culled from the *Journal of Democracy* comprise Diamond & Plattner's edited volume *Democratization in Africa* (1999). This collection of 16 essays is far too broad to summarize quickly, but it includes five chapters that feature the South African case. Intended as a primer on the subject, its contributions are directed at a general reader, and thus few go beyond the level of description and general concepts. Joseph's *State, Conflict, and Democracy in Africa* (1999e) is a wide-ranging edited collection of 23 chapters, with contributions from noted scholars on dozens of aspects of Africa's contemporary politics. Methods and arguments vary, but the volume's overarching topic is the constitution (and reconstitution) of political order in African societies.

These six books outline the contours of most of the essential debates in the African transitions literature. The next sections explore some of these debates by looking at the most commonly invoked causes for Africa's political changes.

Economic Factors

There is almost no debate about the importance of economic phenomena to Africa's recent politics. In fact, many observers claim that both underlying and proximate demands for political reform have come primarily from economic rather than political sources (Hyden 1992; Bratton 1994b, p. 123; Bates 1994). Debate about the importance of economic factors centers on specific variables and their conjectured effects on political transformation. For the purposes of this essay, I split the most-discussed economic factors into two groups: underlying economic structure and current economic trends.

Accounts that use economic structure to account for political change come from the modernization, neo-Marxist, and new institutionalism schools. In modernization theory, increasing industrialization, wealth, education, and urbanization all create conditions conducive to stable elected government (Moore 1966, Lipset 1960). The standard account argues that industrialization begets urbanization, which in turn increases literacy and then a demand for participation in government. Neo-Marxists argue that the formation of classes—especially a bourgeoisie—is necessary before the advent of democracy. New institutionalists have given an account of political change based on both class and political institutions that characterizes African regimes as unaccountable to their citizenry because—thanks to donors—they can opt out of bargaining with domestic capital (Bates 1994, 1999).

Africanists generally agree that standard measures of national-level economic aggregate indicators explain little of Africa's political change. This undermines certain tenets of modernization theory. Although Huntington (1991) argues that democracies tend to "break out" in countries with per capita incomes that range from $1000 to $3000, only a handful of African countries can boast such numbers. Testing different aggregated economic factors, Widner (1994a, pp. 49–51) finds no association linking political liberalization in Africa with growth of gross domestic product (GDP), per capita GDP, defense expenditure, development assistance, inflation, or the rural workforce. Neither is there a relationship between reform and states experiencing windfalls in natural resources or foreign aid. Bratton & van de Walle (1992) find little or no correlation between intensity of political unrest and severity of economic crisis. These analyses resonate with the latest work of Przeworski et al. (2000, pp. 97–100), who see little association between per capita income and a transition to democracy but find a strong relationship between income and the staying power of democracy.

The effectiveness of structural arguments for African political transformation depends, of course, on what is being explained. If the dependent variable is entrenched, legitimate, consolidated democracies in Africa (assuming that we could all agree on a definition and means of measurement for "consolidated"), then arguments that emphasize economic structure are probably more right than wrong, in doubting that democracy has been consolidated. For example, based on 1990 levels of industrialization, income, and education, Huntington (1991) predicted little democracy in Africa for the near to middle term. Most neo-Marxists see little strength in the bourgeoisie when analyzing the average neopatrimonial and nonindustrial African country, and so they expect little progress toward democracy in most, if not all, African cases (see Mamdani 1987, Anyang' Nyong'o 1987, Beckman 1989, Fatton 1992, Sklar 1994, Taylor 1999). Bates's new institutionalism model predicts that although recent political reform may lead to a change of political leaders, consolidated democracies are unlikely so long as overseas development assistance continues to flow. Such structural arguments help us to understand the lack of "deep" democracies across Africa in general, but they are not particularly helpful in explaining other, more specific and contingent political phenomena (Bratton & van de Walle 1997, pp. 22–24; Wilson 1994). Thus, if the dependent variable of an analysis is the timing of Africa's political changes or the precise make-up of opposition groups, structural variables dealing with economic phenomena have little explanatory power (Olukoshi 1998b, p. 15–17).

Arguments that refer to Africa's more recent economic experience figure prominently in most accounts of the continent's political changes during the 1990s. Rare is the article or book that does not argue the economic crisis of the 1980s was a crucial cause—if not *the* crucial cause—of political transformations in the 1990s. Several paths have been described that link economics to politics. Many observers hold that economic decline led to a decline in state legitimacy and an increase in popular protest, eventually catalyzing political opposition (e.g., Ake 1993, Westebbe 1994, Bratton & van de Walle 1997). Others believe African governments' austerity policies in response to economic decline were the principal instigator of social unrest (Olukoshi 1998a). Still others highlight the role of international financial institutions (IFIs) in these economic crises and subsequent political changes. Given the disastrous economic shape of most African countries in the 1980s, the World Bank and International Monetary Funds adjustment and stabilization programs were ubiquitous across the continent, and there is a very large and growing literature regarding the economic and political outcomes of these programs (e.g., Callaghy 1993; Callaghy & Ravenhill 1993a,b; Gibbon & Olukoshi 1996). In several incidences—especially the removal of food subsidies—reform packages clearly led to popular protests (Gibbon et al. 1992, Bangura 1992). One inference is that the high social costs of these externally demanded reform programs, in addition to the state's already austere budgets, led to popular and elite dissatisfaction, prompting growing opposition to incumbent regimes (Nelson 1990, Sandbrook 1990, Lancaster 1991, Lubeck & Watts 1994). Other work views the causation as running from economic crisis through political elites—rather than just popular protest—to political change. Elites working within the regime begin to see its likely demise and so withdraw their support. Elites who were not part of the regime also observe its growing weakness and so plan their own political (or armed) assault (Ake 1996, Ihonvbere 1996b, Chabal & Daloz 1999).

Although some link between economics and politics seems obvious from a casual glance at recent history, careful arguments about the precise relationship between the two are still scarce in the literature. Bratton & van de Walle's (1997) argument that economically based protest formed the foundation for political change leaves out the one third of new African democracies that had no such protest, and their general argument linking protest to political change has been criticized (Barkan 1999). Further, since most African countries had endured economic hardships through most of the late 1970s and 1980s, and yet proceeded with different kinds of political liberalization at different rates, the connection between economics and political liberalization remains murky (Lewis 1996). And few cross-national tests of these arguments exist.

Neither has the role of IFIs in Africa's political transformation been fully explored, especially comparatively. There are several competing and clashing positions. Whereas many see adjustment programs as facilitating political change [either by directly requiring political changes or by exacerbating domestic economic downturns, weakening the state, undermining rent-seeking opportunities, and providing windows of opportunity to opposition (Bates 1994, van de Walle 1994, Westebbe 1994, Clapham 1996, Ould-Mey 1998, Joseph 1999d, Ihonvbere 2000)], others argue African regimes did not follow through on many of their promised economic and political reforms (Gordon 1993, Grosh 1994), or used the reforms to finance their stay in power (Olukoshi & Laakso 1996, Boone 1998, Reno 1998, Bates 1999, Joseph 1999c, van de Walle 2001). Bratton & van de Walle (1997) find the number of structural adjustment programs to be associated with the frequency of political protest in Africa but unrelated to the extent of political liberalization or democratization. The significance of these findings is weakened by the authors' choice of variable—number of programs rather than their value, implementation, etc.—and the lack of an explicit time-series analysis. Grosh's early warnings should be reconsidered by those using IFI-related phenomena as explanatory variables for transitions in Africa. Economic adjustment programs varied in their timing, content, and implementation (Grosh 1994; see also Herbst 1990 and Joseph 1999c).

Political scientists have also pondered the consequences of simultaneous economic and political liberalizations in Africa. Given the economic disasters created by nondemocratic regimes, many argue that economic reforms cannot be meaningfully undertaken without democratic changes (e.g., Sklar 1996, Nzongola-Ntalaja & Lee 1998). Other scholars identify possible hazards in the concurrent pursuit of both liberalizations; because economic reform may impose costs on certain sectors of society, some analysts believe that such reforms would have to be insulated from popular protest to be successful (Nelson 1990, Haggard 1990, Collier 1991, Przeworski 1991, Callaghy 1994, Bienen & Herbst 1996, Lewis 1996, Jeffries 1993, Hellman 1998). Alternatively, new political coalitions will need to be constructed to support the changes (e.g., Lofchie 1993), and economic and democratic liberalization may not be irreconcilable goals (Lewis 1996). Callaghy (1993) contends that even if simultaneous political and economic reform is possible, the combination of factors necessary for both to be successful is rare. Cynics point out that if the two liberalizations are influenced by donors, then democracy will take a back seat to economic reform (Dunn 1999, Monga 1999, Somide 1999). [van de Walle (2001, pp. 268–69) finds evidence for this view, as aid flows increased more for countries that pursued economic rather than political liberalization.] Many of the foregoing positions assume, however, that incumbent governments want either or both kinds of reforms, and that there is some political support for such efforts. van de Walle undermines such a position; he asserts that governments manipulate demands for economic and political reform so that little tension actually exists between the two. He finds that neither the substance nor outcomes of economic policy changed much in most African countries.

Political Factors

Given the complexity of recent political changes in Africa, it is hardly surprising that dozens of political factors have been mustered as partial explanations for transitions or for their failure. The list includes the role of the military (Jeffries & Thomas 1993, Hansen & Twaddle 1995, Diamond 1995, Ihonvbere 1996a, Joseph 1999b), ethnic groups (Mamdani 1996, Ottaway 1999b, Rothchild 1999; but for another view see Young 1994a, 1999b), elections (Bratton & van de Walle 1997, Bratton & Posner 1999), democracy assistance and election observing (Bjornlund et al. 1992, Bebbington & Riddell 1995, Robinson 1995, Carothers 1997, *Journal of Democracy* 1998, Abbink & Hesseling 2000), and the press (Adewale 1996).

Two clusters of political factors stand out in discussions about African transitions. First are those variables that deal with political institutions, especially regime type. The second cluster includes variables regarding civil society. I explore each in turn.

POLITICAL INSTITUTIONS   Nearly every scholarly work in this literature draws on some aspect of neopatrimonialism to explain the pattern and outcomes of political change in Africa. Neopatrimonial regimes are those that have a modern bureaucracy but vest political power in a person and not an institution. Maintaining political authority in such a system requires the giving and granting of favors, "in an endless series of dyadic exchanges that go from the village level to the highest reaches of the central state" (van de Walle 2001, p. 51). Scholars working with this clientelistic view of African politics focus on such phenomena as corruption, rent seeking, and patronage.

Although neopatrimonialism greatly flavors the study of African political change, its importance varies by study. At one end of the scale sit those scholars who believe that neopatrimonial regimes are far too well entrenched to be greatly affected by current political trends (e.g., Chabal & Daloz 1999). There is evidence to support this view: As of 1998, 26 of 39 African countries retained their "big man" in multiparty elections held in the 1990s and only two of these are "free" according to Freedom House rankings (van de Walle 2001, p. 245). Other scholars argue that, even if that individual is removed, the system of neopatrimonialism still decisively shapes political change in Africa. Neopatrimonial systems create a fiercely entrenched political elite within government and a winner-take-all mentality in politics (since control of the government is the source of the most important spoils). If the opposition does succeed in ousting incumbents, it too faces strong incentives to maintain the structure of neopatrimonial politics. This phenomenon provides the foundation for those observers who see political change in Africa as *plus ça change, plus c'est la même chose* (the more things change, the more they stay the same) (Mbembe 1995, Chabal & Daloz 1999, Ottaway 1999a, Ihonvbere 2000). There is evidence for this position as well, since 35 of the 44 countries that were not multiparty regimes in 1989 stayed in the "partly free" or "not free" Freedom House categories as of 1998 (van de Walle 2001, p. 245).

The endurance of patronage politics is an important reason for the emergence of literature that criticizes "electioneering" in Africa. Multiparty elections were considered extremely important in the early democratization literature. No doubt such enthusiasm sprang from the previous pessimism about any chance for democratic change in Africa. With the continued operation of neopatrimonial politics in the post-election era, elections are now generally regarded as—at best—only one of many necessary conditions for democratic transitions on the continent.

But there is also evidence that neopatrimonialism, broadly defined, does not determine the direction of political change in Africa. Among the 13 countries that did throw out their "big man" and did not have extensive experience with multiparty elections before 1989, seven are categorized as "free" on Freedom House scales. The variation in transition outcomes means that the broad category "neopatrimonial" is not a very good predictor for political change in Africa.

Unfortunately, only a few studies attempt to unpack neopatrimonial regimes in systematic and comparative ways. Bratton & van de Walle (1997, pp. 77–82), for example, consider five modal regimes when categorizing neopatrimonialism into the dimensions of political competition and political participation: plebiscitary one-party systems, competitive one-party systems, military oligarchies, settler oligarchies, and multiparty systems. In a coarse test of the effects of their regime types on political change in Africa, Table 1 combines Bratton & van de Walle's (1997) neopatrimonial categories with van de Walle's (2001) reported 1998 Freedom House scores for the same cases.

There are few obvious patterns. Being a military oligarchy in 1989 seems to dim considerably the hope for political freedom in 1998, and residents of settler oligarchies enjoyed great freedom by 1998 (although only two cases fit within this category), but other patterns are not as readily apparent. Using other ways to operationalize political institutions (e.g., number of elections held in the post-independence period), Bratton & van de Walle's (1997) own findings remain highly sensitive to statistical technique and flicker in and out as important explanations for political changes. This indicates that their five types are not capturing well the

TABLE 1   A coarse test of the effects of regime type on political change in Africa

	Freedom House score (1998)		
	Free	Partly free	Not free
Type of neopatrimonial regime (1989)			
Plebiscitary one party	2	4	7
Competitive one party	3	6	4
Military oligarchies	0	5	5
Settler oligarchies	2	0	0
Multiparty systems	2	2	1

institutional determinants for democratic outcomes, and calls for further refinements of institutional types and appropriate tests.

Other authors have investigated different institutions from a smaller set of neopatrimonial regimes. Clark (1995), for example, examines the impact of the national conferences held in nine West African countries, arguing that the conferences are tied importantly to the trajectories of political change in each case. Bratton & van de Walle (1997) similarly argue that the logic of plebiscitary one-party systems led incumbents and challengers to favor the conferences as a negotiating tool. Ten of the 11 countries that held national conferences had some experience with plebiscitary systems. It should be noted, however, that 8 countries the authors list as plebiscitary did not have national conferences (Bratton & van de Walle 1997, pp. 173–74). In the context of explaining economic liberalization, Widner (1994a) suggests that other institutions could be important bases for comparison, including electoral institutions (á la Reynolds 1999), patterns of distributional politics, and interest group organization. Such institutions could be of similar importance in explaining the origin, content, and process of political change in Africa. Good work along these lines can be found for individual countries (e.g., Rothchild & Zartman 1991), and there are scattered two-country comparisons, but the literature is missing systematic comparative work with larger sets of countries.

CIVIL SOCIETY   Some of the most animated debates to emerge from the recent study of African politics have centered on the relationship between civil society and the state. Africanists who had argued in the 1980s for a retreat from state-centered analyses and a stronger focus on nongovernment sources of politics—the state-society approach—set the stage for those who envisioned a pivotal role for civil society in democratic transitions. Although many scholars believed civil society played a role in consolidating democracy, others questioned the normative bias, empirical relevance, and analytical utility that conventional views of civil society have for Africa. The difficulties of Africanists in their attempt to define the concept have had a clear impact on attempts to measure civil society systematically.

The intellectual turn to civil society as an explanation for cause and/or consolidation of African transitions can be traced to earlier work that questioned whether the state was always the paramount political actor. Migdal's (1988) work on strong and weak states echoed Huntington's argument about the relative degrees to which governments actually governed. Precisely when other comparativists were urged to "bring the state back in" (Evans et al. 1985), some Africanists questioned such a statist approach for a region where states were weak, reflexive, and still forming (Jackson & Rosberg 1982, Callaghy 1987, Bratton 1989). The state-society approach emerged from this view of African politics as more personalistic and less formally institutionalized; consequently, "taking the state back out" became the order of the day for many students of African politics (Hyden 1980, Chazan 1983, Bayart 1986, Rothchild & Chazan 1988, Zartman 1995). Political scientists were urged to "devote more research attention to the associational life that occurs in the political space beyond the state's purview" (Bratton 1989, p. 411; see also Diamond 1999a). As African countries experienced the so-called third wave of democratization, it was a short intellectual step from a focus on associational life under authoritarian regimes to a focus on civil society's role in democracy (Harbeson 1994, p. 10).

Although few disputed that nonstate actors and their relationship with the state help to fashion political order, different views of civil society emerged, each with its own combination of ideas culled from Locke, Hegel, Tocqueville, Rousseau, Marx, and Gramsci (Bratton 1994a, Young 1994b). The broadest view conceived of civil society as encompassing all public political nonstate activity occurring between the government and the family (Bratton 1994a, p. 56). For some, individuals, groups, and associations were part of civil society to the extent that they "seek to define, generate support for, or promote changes in the basic working rules of the game by which social values are authoritatively allocated" (Harbeson 1994). Others viewed civil society as more oppositional, i.e., they believed civil society is distinct from society "in so far as it is confrontation with the state" and through "the process by which [it] seeks to 'breach' and counteract the simultaneous 'totalisation' unleashed by the state." (Bayart 1986, p. 11). Kasfir (1998) argues that the conventional view—which he associates with Chazan, Diamond, Hadenius & Uggla, and Schmitter—is even narrower and includes only nonstate organizations in public life that are formally organized with specific and limited purposes, have participatory internal government, and enjoy the autonomy to act beyond the immediate interests of their members (Chazan 1992; Diamond 1996, 1999a; Diamond et al. 1997, pp. xxx–xxxii; Hadenius & Uggla 1996; Schmitter 1997).

The conventional view bestows on civil society a central, if not the central, part in the concinnity of democracy (Bratton 1994a, Diamond et al. 1997). Because it both generates the norms by which its members play the political game and holds governments accountable, civil society is fundamental to sustained political reform, legitimate states and governments, improved governance, viable state-society and state-economy relationships, and the prevention of political decay (Harbeson 1994, pp. 1–4). Diamond (1996) lists 10 functions of civil society, all of which strengthen democracy.

Unlike many discussions within the academy, this one did influence the policy world. For a variety of reasons—not the least being the positive role allotted to civil society by political scientists' thinking—donor countries and IFIs quickly employed the concept in their decision over aid allocation. For the fiscal years 1991–1993, for example, the U. S. Agency for International Development (USAID) spent over a fifth of its democracy budget on civil society projects (Kasfir 1994, p. 134). Nearly all the governance-supporting nongovernmental organizations in Africa were funded by donors (Gyimah-Boadi 1999). Donors saw the concept of civil society as a convenient hat stand for ideas related to human rights, good government, participation, privatization, and public service reform (White 1993, Riddell & Bebbington 1997).

A growing number of scholars critique the conventional view of civil society. No doubt this is partly because of the general pessimism with which observers view the prospects for democratic transition in Africa. But more important is scholars' dissatisfaction with the fit between conventional definitions of civil society and African political reality, the normative rather than analytic underpinnings of the concept, and the lack of convincing data.

Some scholars point out that whatever is left after applying the various requirements of civil society to the African political landscape is certainly not the crucial part of African politics. Civil society, among other things, requires a distinct sphere of autonomous, voluntary, democratic organizations that constrain the state while simultaneously legitimating it. Many Africanists argue that such a concept captures little of extant African politics, which instead boasts ethnic and religious organizations, organizations dominated by a narrow base of elites, unorganized protest, and neopatrimonial relationships between the state and nearly all organizations (Azarya 1994, p. 95; Callaghy 1994, p. 127; Young 1994b; Fine & Rai 1997; Kasfir 1998; Orvis 2001). It may be true that civil society is needed for democratic consolidation, as its advocates argue, but such a civil society is at best a nascent phenomenon in Africa.

To many, the conventional view of civil society, when applied to the African political landscape, seems more like wishful thinking than rigorous analysis. Civil society becomes an "all-good-things-go-together" concept, in which the negative aspects of civil society are eliminated by definition, and important arguments about causality are left unanswered. For instance, if civil society is strong enough to combat tyrannical regimes, what prevents it from undermining democratic governments (Foley & Edwards 1996)? And how can weakly institutionalized states regulate their own civil societies?

Given the yeasty discussion of the concept, it is striking how little effort has been made to measure civil society or employ it in systematic tests of theory. Because of the general lack of data in this area, Bratton & van de Walle (1997) use the admittedly limited variable of the number of trade unions in their models. But they remain among the few who have tried to measure and test how civil society affects democracy in the African context.

OF CONCEPTS, THEORIES, HYPOTHESES, AND DATA

Political scientists have produced a prodigious amount of work regarding recent political change in Africa. This work needs clearer theoretical premises, as well as crisper conceptualizations of causes and effects, more precise hypotheses about the relationship between them, and greater efforts toward their rigorous measurement (see also Wilson 1994, Mahmud 1996, Chabal 1998). I argue that these weaknesses undergird Chabal's description of the literature on African democratization as a "dialogue of the deaf." He claims analysts speak past each other, and focus "attention on different aspects of the recent political transitions. Each can rely on the evidence of what has happened in some African countries, while conveniently neglecting what has happened elsewhere" (Chabal 1998, p. 300). This is not to say that there is no work with conceptual, theoretical, and empirical bona fides; I have identified several such studies in this chapter. Nor do I claim such analyses are easily created; a recent review of the literature regarding democratization in Eastern Europe and Latin America comes to similar conclusions, even though countries in those regions generally boast better-quality data and more research (Munck 2002). What I do say is that plenty of sharp analytical work remains to be done on political change in Africa and, to be more persuasive, I would argue that it needs to address more generalizable theory.

There are several reasons why studies of recent political change in Africa are not as strong as they might be. First, it is difficult for social scientists to analyze an ongoing process of political change, since cause and effect are not very clear in the historic moment. In fact, in the early stages, it is sometimes "not even clear what should be explained" (Herbst 1994, p. 182). Such scholars as Villalón (1998), reminiscent of Zolberg's view of post-independence analyses, question a rush to embrace the apparent positive changes, when measuring democracy in Africa does not really address the most significant political changes occurring there. Second, a strong incentive may exist only to describe what is occurring—and to omit deeper analysis—in order to get information out quickly to the public. Given the historic changes that have certainly occurred in Africa, specialists want others to know the details of "their" country's transformation. Third, the possibility of positive political change in Africa might have encouraged "boosterism" on the part of observers. Such a normative, prodemocracy thread can be seen running through some early (and even some more recent) work on African transitions (see for example Hyden 1992, p. 23; Harbeson 1994, p. 3). Unfortunately, advocacy can hobble good analysis. Fourth, data about African countries are not very good; time series for even the most important and obvious political and economic variables are spotty and often of poor quality. Even well-conceptualized arguments cannot proceed far without reliable data with which to test them. Finally, good social science takes time. Refining concepts, collecting and analyzing data, and generating clear, strong, and well-supported arguments do not occur overnight. Now that some time has passed, we should expect improvement from the second generation of studies about Africa's recent political transformations. Indeed, we can already see such advances, e.g., the movement away from the dichotomous democracy/nondemocracy categories and the critical discussions of terms such as civil society recounted above.

One of the first challenges when confronting the shifting, complex arena of African politics over the past decade is defining a tractable and meaningful dependent variable. The process of political transformation offers no end of possible choices; founding elections alone provide many such variables related to their timing, processes, and outcomes. Post-election phenomena offer another large set of potential explananda (e.g., accounting for the type and extent of changes in post-election government policy, institutional reform, opposition groups, politicians' behavior, electorate behavior and beliefs, and relationships with international organizations). Despite—or perhaps because of—the number of possibilities, it is surprising how few studies in the African transitions literature choose to focus clearly on one (or even a few) dependent variable(s). Instead, most observers avoid such flensing and provide monographic studies of the many political changes occurring within one or more countries. The merit of such studies is their fascinating story; their limitation is a lack of explanatory power. It is important to note that this is not a criticism of the case study approach, as all methods depend on clear conceptualizations of cause and effect.

Theory guides research toward independent variables that can help explain the phenomenon in question. Monographic accounts of an entire transition process tend not to employ sharp theories nor to operationalize them with clear variables and hypotheses. Further, these hypotheses are rarely tested with a specific set of well-defined and measured independent variables (Mahmud 1996). All too often, theoretical statements are made without clear conceptualizations of the causal relationships involved. The global political "climate" may have been propitious for political change in Africa, but exactly how did it influence particular actions and events? Civil society may have been important to an opposition candidate's success in the founding election, but what is civil society, how is it measured, and precisely how did it contribute to the resources or strategies of opposition candidates during an election? IFIs may have affected the timing of transitions, but what instruments, actions, strategies, and power did the IFIs employ? There exist several well-known theories about the various aspects of transition that have emerged from studies of East European and Latin American experiences (e.g., Rueschmeyer et al. 1992, Collier 1999); some of these will apply to the African context, others will not. But it is difficult to know whether these or any other theories offer an explanatory edge without their rigorous formulation and testing. Not only would such rigor offer more explanatory power, but it could also allow something that we rarely see in accounts of African transition: the possibility of being wrong.

In this review, I have clearly pushed for an agenda that includes more comparative work on African political change in the late twentieth century. I believe this is essential. Although it is easy to see the variation at all levels in the experiences of African countries, there are many commonalities, and they cry out for comparative analysis: the timing of political liberalization, the kinds of domestic political institutions, the economic trajectories, and the constraints on political choices emanating from globalization, to name a few. Further commonalities exist at the subcontinent level, such as region, colonial history, currency zone, Cold War alliances, and structure of agricultural and industrial sectors. This comparative work must also construct better concepts, theories, and tests. Data are improving so that theory building and testing are increasingly possible (for example, the Afrobarometer data and new World Bank data series). The mix of comparative research designs, better data, and new ideas will help the next generation of theory building about the crucial political changes occurring in Africa—and help us discern ripples from waves.

ACKNOWLEDGMENTS

This essay has been greatly improved thanks to the insights of Emily Beaulieu, Michael Bratton, David Cunningham, Karen Ferree, Barak Hoffman, Daniel Posner, Stephanie Rickard, and Peter York. Its weaknesses are of my own making.

The *Annual Review of Political Science* is online at http://polisci.annualreviews.org

LITERATURE CITED

Abbink J, Hesseling G, eds. 2000. *Election Observation and Democratization in Africa.* New York: St Martin's

Adewale MP, ed. 1996. *Directory of African Media.* Brussels: Media for Democr., Int. Fed. Journalists

Ake C. 1993. The unique case of African democracy. *Int. Aff.* 69:239–44

Ake C. 1996. *Democracy and Development in Africa.* Washington, DC: Brookings Inst.

Anyang' Nyong'o P, ed. 1987. *Popular Struggles for Democracy in Africa.* Atlantic Highlands, NJ: United Nations Univ. Zed Books

Azarya V. 1994. Civil society and disengagement in Africa. See Harbeson et al. 1994, pp. 83–102

Bangura Y. 1992. Authoritarian rule and democracy in Africa: a theoretical discourse. See Gibbon et al. 1992, pp. 39–82

Barkan J. 1999. Regime change in Africa. *J. Democr.* 10:165–70

Barkan J, Ng'ethe N. 1999. Kenya tries again. See Diamond & Plattner 1999, pp. 184–200

Bates RH. 1994. The impulse to reform in Africa. See Widner 1994b, pp. 13–28

Bates RH. 1999. The economic bases of democratization. See Joseph 1999e, pp. 83–94

Bates RH, Mudimbe VY, O'Barr J, eds. 1993. *Africa and the Disciplines: The Contributions of Research in Africa to the Social Sciences and Humanities.* Chicago: Univ. Chicago Press

Bayart JF. 1986. Civil society in Africa. In *Political Domination in Africa,* ed. P Chabal, pp. 109–25. Cambridge, UK: Cambridge Univ. Press

Bebbington A, Riddell R. 1995. The direct funding of southern NGOs by donors: NEW agendas and old problems. *J. Int. Dev.* 7:879–93

Beckman B. 1989. Whose democracy? Bourgeois versus popular democracy. *Rev. Afr. Polit. Econ.* 45(46):84–97

Bienen HS, Herbst J. 1996. The relationship between political and economic reform in Africa. *Comp. Polit.* 29:23–42

Bjornlund E, Bratton M, Gibson C. 1992. Observing multiparty elections in Africa: lessons from Zambia. *Afr. Aff.* 91:405–31

Boone C. 1998. "Empirical statehood" and reconfigurations of political order. See Villalón & Huxtable 1998, pp. 129–42

Bratton M. 1989. Beyond the state: civil society and associational life in Africa. *World Polit.* 41:407–30

Bratton M. 1994a. Civil society and political transitions in Africa. See Harbeson et al. 1994, pp. 51–82

Bratton M. 1994b. Crisis and political realignment in Zambia. See Widner 1994b, pp. 101–28

Bratton M, Posner DN. 1999. A first look at second elections in Africa. See Joseph 1999e, pp. 377–408

Bratton M, van de Walle N. 1992. Toward governance in Africa: popular demands and state responses. See Hyden & Bratton 1992, pp. 27–56

Bratton M, van de Walle N. 1997. *Democratic Experiments in Africa: Regime Transitions in Comparative Perspective*. New York: Cambridge Univ. Press

Callaghy TM. 1987. The state as lame Leviathan: the patrimonial administrative state in Africa. In *The African State in Transition*, ed. Z Ergas. London: Macmillan.

Callaghy TM. 1993. Political passions and economic interests: economic reform and political structure in Africa. See Callaghy & Ravenhill 1993c, pp. 453–519

Callaghy TM. 1994. Civil society, democracy, and economic change in Africa: a dissenting opinion about resurgent societies. See Harbeson et al. 1994, pp. 231–54

Callaghy TM, Ravenhill J. 1993a. How hemmed in? Lessons and prospects of Africa's responses to decline. See Callaghy & Ravenhill 1993c, pp. 520–64

Callaghy TM, Ravenhill J. 1993b. Vision, politics, and structure: Afro-optimism, Afro-pessimism or realism? See Callaghy & Ravenhill 1993c, pp. 1–17

Callaghy TM, Ravenhill J, eds. 1993c. *Hemmed In: Responses to Africa's Economic Decline*. New York: Columbia Univ. Press

Carothers T. 1997. Democracy assistance: the question of strategy. *Democratization* 4:109–32

Chabal P. 1998. A few considerations on democracy in Africa. *Int. Aff.* 74(2):289–303

Chabal P, Daloz JP. 1999. *Africa Works: Disorder as Political Instrument*. Indianapolis: Indiana Univ. Press

Chazan N. 1983. *An Anatomy of Ghanaian Politics: Managing Political Recession 1969–82*. Boulder, CO: Westview

Chazan N. 1992. Africa's democratic challenge. *World Policy J.* 9(2):279–308

Chege M. 1996. Between Africa's extremes. See Diamond & Plattner 1996, pp. 350–57

Clapham CS. 1996. *Africa and the International System: the Politics of State Survival*. Cambridge, UK: Cambridge Univ. Press

Clapham C, Wiseman JA. 1995. Assessing the prospects for the consolidation of democracy in Africa. See Wiseman 1995, pp. 220–32

Clark JF. 1995. National conferences and democratization in Francophone Africa. See Mbaku & Ihonvbere 1995, pp. 97–122

Collier P. 1991. Africa's external economic relations: 1960–90. *Afr. Aff.* 90:339

Collier RB. 1999. *Paths Toward Democracy: The Working Class and Elites in Western Europe and South America*. New York: Cambridge Univ. Press

Diamond L. 1995. Nigeria: the uncivic society and the descent into praetorianism. In *Politics in Developing Countries: Comparing Experiences with Democracy*, ed. L Diamond, JJ Linz, SM Lipset, pp. 417–91. Boulder, CO: Lynne Rienner

Diamond L. 1996. Toward democratic consolidation. See Diamond & Plattner 1996, pp. 226–40

Diamond L. 1999a. *Developing Democracy:*

Towards Consolidation. Baltimore, MD: John Hopkins Univ. Press

Diamond L. 1999b. Introduction. See Diamond & Plattner 1999, pp. ix–xxvii

Diamond L, Plattner MF, eds. 1996. *The Global Resurgence of Democracy.* Baltimore, MD: John Hopkins Univ. Press. 2nd ed.

Diamond L, Plattner MF, eds. 1999. *Democratization in Africa.* Baltimore, MD: John Hopkins Univ. Press

Diamond L, Plattner MF, Chu Y, Tien H, eds. 1997. *Consolidating the Third Wave Democracies: Themes and Perspectives.* Baltimore, MD: John Hopkins Univ. Press

Dunn K. 1999. The democracy discourse in international relations: identity, development and Africa. See Ojo 1999, pp. 1–23

Evans PB, Rueschemeyer D, Skocpol T, eds. 1985. *Bringing the State Back In.* Cambridge, UK: Cambridge Univ. Press

Fatton R. 1992. *Predatory Rule: State and Civil Society in Africa.* Boulder, CO: Lynne Rienner

Fine R, Rai S, eds. 1997. *Civil Society: Democratic Perspectives.* Portland, OR: Frank Cass

Foley MW Edwards B. 1996. The paradox of civil society. *J. Democr.* 7(3):38–52

Gibbon P, Ofstad A, Bangura Y, eds. 1992. *Authoritarianism, Democracy and Adjustment: The Politics of Economic Reform in Africa.* Coronet Books

Gibbon P, Olukoshi AO, eds. 1996. *Structural Adjustment and Socio-Economic Change in Sub-Saharan Africa: Some Conceptual, Methodological and Research Issues.*

Gordon DF. 1993. Debt, conditionality and reform: the international relations of economic policy restructuring in sub-Saharan Africa. See Callaghy & Ravenhill 1993c, pp. 90–129

Grosh B. 1994. Through the structural adjustment minefield: politics in an era of economic liberalization. See Widner 1994b, pp. 29–46

Gyimah-Boadi E. 1999. The rebirth of African liberalism. See Diamond & Plattner 1999, pp. 34–47

Hadenius A, Uggla F. 1996. Making civil society work, promoting democratic develop-

ment: What can states and donors do? *World Dev.* 24:10

Haggard S. 1990. *Pathways from the Periphery.* Princeton, NJ: Princeton Univ. Press

Hansen HB, Twaddle M. 1995. The advent of no-party democracy. See Wiseman 1995, pp. 137–51

Harbeson JW. 1994. Civil society and political renaissance in Africa. See Harbeson et al. 1994, pp. 1–32

Harbeson JW, Rothchild D, Chazan N, eds. 1994. *Civil Society and the State in Africa.* Boulder, CO: Lynne Rienner

Hellman JS. 1998. Winners take all: the politics of partial reform in postcommunist transitions. *World Polit.* 50:203–34

Herbst J. 1990. The structural adjustment of politics in Africa. *World Dev.* 18:949–58

Herbst J. 1994. The dilemmas of explaining political upheaval: Ghana in comparative perspective. See Widner 1994b, pp. 182–98

Huntington SP. 1991. *The Third Wave: Democratization in the Late Twentieth Century.* Norman: Univ. Oklahoma Press

Hyden G. 1980. *Beyond Ujamaa in Tanzania: Underdevelopment and an Uncaptured Peasantry.* Berkeley: Univ. Calif. Press

Hyden G. 1992. Governance and the study of politics. See Hyden & Bratton 1992, pp. 1–26

Hyden G, Bratton M, eds. 1992. *Governance and Politics in Africa.* Boulder, CO: Lynne Rienner

Ihonvbere JO. 1996a. Are things falling apart? The military and the crisis of democratization in Nigeria. *J. Mod. Afr. Stud.* 34:193–225

Ihonvbere JO. 1996b. Where is the third wave? A critical evaluation of Africa's non-transition to democracy. *Afr. Today* 43:343–68

Ihonvbere JO. 2000. *Africa and the New World Order.* New York: Peter Lang

Jackson RH, Rosberg CG. 1982. *Personal Rule in Black Africa.* Berkeley: Univ. Calif. Press

Jeffries R. 1993. The state, good governance, and structural adjustment in Africa. *J. Commonw. Comp. Polit.* 31:20–35

Jeffries R, Thomas C. 1993. The Ghanaian elections of 1992. *Afr. Aff.* 92:331–66

Joseph R. 1991. Africa: the rebirth of political freedom. *J. Democr.* 2:11–24

Joseph R. 1999a. Africa, 1990–1997: from *Abertura* to closure. See Diamond & Plattner 1999, pp. 3–17

Joseph R. 1999b. Autocracy, violence and ethnomilitary rule in Nigeria. See Joseph 1999e, pp. 359–76

Joseph R. 1999c. The reconfiguration of power in late twentieth-century Africa. See Joseph 1999e, pp. 57–82

Joseph R. 1999d. State, conflict and democracy in Africa. See Joseph 1999e, pp. 3–14

Joseph R, ed. 1999e. *State, Conflict, and Democracy in Africa.* Boulder, CO: Lynne Rienner. *Journal of Democracy.* 1998. 9(2)

Kanyinga K. 1998. Contestation over political space: the state and the demobilisation of opposition politics in Kenya. See Olukoshi 1998b, pp. 39–90

Kasfir N. 1994. Strategies of accumulation and civil society in Bushenyi, Uganda: how dairy farmers responded to a weakened state. See Harbeson et al. 1994, pp. 103–24

Kasfir N, ed. 1998. *Civil Society and Democracy in Africa: Critical Perspectives.* Portland, OR: Frank Cass

Lancaster C. 1991. Democracy in Africa. *For. Policy* 85:148–65

Lemarchand R. 1992. African transitions to democracy: an interim (and mostly pessimistic) assessment. *Afr. Insight* 22:178–85

Lewis P. 1996. Economic reform and political transition in Africa. *World Polit.* 49:92–129

Lipset SM. 1960. *Political Man: the Social Bases of Politics.* Garden City, NY: Doubleday

Lofchie MF. 1993. Trading places: economic policy in Kenya and Tanzania. In Callaghy & Ravenhill 1993, pp. 398–462

Lubeck PM, Watts M. 1994. An alliance of oil and maize? The response of indigenous and state capital to structural adjustment in Nigeria. In *African Capitalists in African Development*, ed. B Berman, C Leys, pp. 214–35. Boulder: Lynne Rienner

Mahmud SS. 1996. Africa's democratic transi-

tions, change, and development. *Afr. Today* 43:405–16

Mamdani M. 1987. Contradictory class perspectives on the question of democracy: the case of Uganda. See Anyang' Nyong'o 1987, pp. 78–95

Mamdani M. 1996. *Citizen and Subject: Contemporary Africa and The Legacy of Late Colonialism.* Princeton, NJ: Princeton Univ. Press

Mbaku JM, Ihonvbere JO, eds. 1995. *Multiparty Democracy and Political Change: Constraints to Democratization in Africa.* Aldershot, UK: Brookfield USA

Mbembe A. 1995. Complex transformations in late twentieth century Africa. *Afr. Demos* 3:28–30

Migdal JS. 1988. Strong societies and weak states: state-society relations and state capabilities in the Third World. Princeton, NJ: Princeton Univ. Press

Mkandawire T, Olukoshi A, eds. 1995. *Between Liberalisation and Oppression: the Politics of Structural Adjustment in Africa.* Dakar, Senegal: Codesria

Monga C. 1999. Eight problems with African politics. See Diamond & Plattner 1999, pp. 48–62

Moore B Jr. 1966. *Social Origins of Dictatorship and Democracy, Lord and Peasant in the Making of the Modern World.* Boston: Beacon

Munck G. 2002. The regime question: theory building in democracy studies. *World Polit.* In press

Ndegwa S, ed. 2001. *A Decade of Democracy in Africa.* Leiden, Netherlands: Brill

Nelson J, ed. 1990. *Economic Crises and Policy Choice: The Politics of Economic Adjustments in the Third World.* Princeton, NJ: Princeton Univ. Press

Nzongola-Ntalaja G, Lee MC, eds. 1998. *The State and Democracy in Africa.* Lawrenceville, NJ: Afr. World

Ojo BA, ed. 1999. *Contemporary African Politics: A Comparative Study of Political Transition to Democratic Legitimacy.* New York: Univ. Press Am.

Olukoshi AO. 1998a. Economic crisis, multipartyism, and opposition politics in contemporary Africa. See Olukoshi 1998b, pp. 8–38

Olukoshi AO, ed. 1998b. *The Politics of Opposition in Contemporary Africa*. Stockholm: Elanders Gotab

Olukoshi A, Laakso L, eds. 1996. *Challenges to the Nation-State in Africa*. Uppsala, Sweden: Nordiska Afrikainst., in cooperation with Inst. Dev. Stud., Univ. Helskinki

Orvis S. 2001. Civil society in Africa or African civil society? In *A Decade of Democracy in Africa*, ed. S Ndegwa, pp. 17–38. Leiden, Netherlands: Brill

Ottaway M. 1999a. *Africa's New Leaders: Democracy or State Reconstruction?* Washington, DC: Carnegie Endow. Int. Peace

Ottaway M. 1999b. Ethnic politics in Africa: change and continuity. See Joseph 1999e, pp. 299–318

Ould-May M. 1995. Structural adjustment programs and democratization in Africa: the case of Mauritania. See Mbaku & Ihonvbere 1995, pp. 33–64

Przeworski A. 1991. *Democracy and the Market: Political and Economic Reforms in Eastern Europe and Latin America*. New York: Cambridge Univ. Press

Przeworski A, Alvarez ME, Cheibub JA, Limongi F. 2000. *Democracy and Development: Political Institutions and Well-Being in the World, 1950–1990*. New York: Cambridge Univ. Press

Reno W. 1998. Sierra Leone: weak states and the new sovereignty game. See Villalón & Huxtable, pp. 93–108

Reynolds A. 1999. *Electoral Systems and Democratization in Southern Africa*. New York: Oxford Univ. Press

Riddell R, Bebbington A. 1997. The direct funding of southern NGOs by northern donors: new agendas and old problems. *J. Int. Dev.* (7)6:879–93

Robinson M. 1995. Towards democratic governance. *Inst. Dev. Stud. Bull.* 26(2):70–80

Rothchild D. 1999. Ethnic insecurity, peach agreements and state building. See Joseph 1999e, pp. 319–38

Rothchild D, Chazan N, eds. 1988. *The precarious balance: state and society in Africa*. Boulder, CO: Westview

Rothchild D, Zartman JW, eds. 1991. *Ghana: The Political Economy of Recovery*. Boulder, CO: Lynne Rienner

Rueschemeyer D, Huber E, Stephens JD. 1992. *Capitalist Development and Democracy*. Chicago: Univ. Chicago Press

Sandbrook R (with J Barker). 1985. *The Politics of Africa's Economic Stagnation*. New York: Cambridge Univ. Press

Sandbrook R. 1990. Taming the African Leviathan. *World Policy J.* 7:673–701

Schmitter P. 1997. Civil society east and west. See Diamond et al. 1997, pp. 239–62

Sklar RL. 1994. Social class and political action in Africa: the bourgeoisie and the proletariat. See Apter & Rosberg 1994, pp. 117–44

Sklar RL. 1996. Toward a theory of developmental democracy. In *Democracy and Development*, ed. A Leftwich, pp. 25–45. Cambridge, MA: Polity

Sklar RL. 1999. African politics: the next generation. See Joseph 1999e, pp. 165–78

Somide AA. 1999. International efforts at democracy and sub-Saharan African development. See Ojo 1999, pp. 24–50

Taylor SD. 1999. Race, class and neopatrimonialism in Zimbabwe. See Joseph 1999e, pp. 239–66

van de Walle N. 1994. Neopatrimonialism and democracy in Africa, with an illustration from Cameroon. See Widner 1994b, pp. 129–57

van de Walle N. 2001. *African Economies and the Politics of Permanent Crisis, 1979–1999*. Cambridge, UK: Cambridge Univ. Press

Villalón LA. 1998. The African state at the end of the twentieth century. See Villalón & Huxtable 1998, pp. 3–26

Villalón LA, Huxtable PA, eds. 1998. *The African State at a Critical Juncture*. Boulder, CO: Lynne Rienner

Westebbe R. 1994. Structural adjustment, rent seeking and liberalization in Benin. See Widner 1994b, pp. 80–100

White GW. 1993. Prospects for civil society in

China: a case study of Xiaoshan City. *Aust. J. Chin. Aff.* 29:63–87

Wilson EJ. 1994. Creating a research agenda for the study of political change in Africa. See Widner 1994b, pp. 253–72

Widner JA. 1994a. Political reform in Anglophone and Francophone African countries. See Widner 1994b, pp. 49–79

Widner JA, ed. 1994b. *Economic Change and Political Liberalization in Sub-Saharan Africa*. Baltimore, MD: John Hopkins Univ. Press

Wiseman JA, ed. 1995. *Democracy and Political Change in Sub-Saharan Africa*. New York: Routledge

Wiseman JA. 1999. The continuing case for demo-optimism in Africa. *Democratization* 6(2):128–55

Woodward P. 1998. Democracy and economy in Africa: the optimists and the pessimists. *Democratization* 1(1):116–32

Young C. 1994a. Evolving modes of consciousness and ideology: nationalism and ethnicity. See Apter & Rosberg 1994, pp. 61–86

Young C. 1994b. In search of civil society. See Harbeson et al. 1994, pp. 33–50

Young C. 1999a. Africa: an interim balance sheet. See Diamond & Plattner 1999, pp. 63–82

Young C. 1999b. The third wave of democratization in Africa: ambiguities and contradictions. See Joseph 1999e, pp. 15–38

Zartman W, ed. 1995. *Collapsed States: The Disintegration and Restoration of Legitimate Authority*. Boulder, CO: Lynne Rienner

Annu. Rev. Polit. Sci. 2002. 5:223–48
DOI: 10.1146/annurev.polisci.5.112801.080933
Copyright © 2002 by Annual Reviews. All rights reserved

HOW CONCEPTUAL PROBLEMS MIGRATE:
Rational Choice, Interpretation, and the Hazards of Pluralism

James Johnson
*Department of Political Science, University of Rochester, Rochester, New York 14627;
e-mail: jjsn@troi.cc.rochester.edu*

Key Words   methodological pluralism, culture, mechanisms, explanation

■ **Abstract**   When they assess competing theories, political scientists typically rely
almost exclusively and rather naively on criteria of empirical performance. They have
correspondingly little to say about conceptual problems and seem generally unaware
of the extent to which their assessments of empirical performance are parasitic on conceptual commitments. This blind spot, in turn, hinders their ability both to persuasively
conduct and critically assess substantive research. I call attention to the importance and
complexity of conceptual problems for ongoing social and political research. As a vehicle for this argument, I examine and criticize recent attempts to integrate interpretive
and rational choice theories in hopes of improving our understanding of how culture
and politics intersect. I argue that these efforts are plagued by important, mostly unrecognized conceptual problems that, in turn, subvert their explicitly stated explanatory
objectives. I also show, in light of this same example, how conceptual problems unintentionally can frustrate laudable pluralist aspirations. This essay illustrates why, if we
take conceptual problems seriously, calls for methodological and theoretical pluralism
are significantly more demanding than they often appear.

INTRODUCTION

Culture and politics are related in intimate, inadequately understood ways. Despite
persistent effort, political scientists grasp those relations so poorly as to invite
skepticism shading into ridicule (e.g., *The Economist* 1996). Indeed, it remains
fair to say that, in the discipline as a whole, the "systematic study of culture and
politics is moribund" (Laitin 1986, p. 171; Kertzer 1988, pp. 7,186 n22). If ever an
area of research demanded a creative, pluralist approach, this is it. Yet it is crucial
not to underestimate the theoretical difficulties that beset seemingly attractive calls
to theoretical and methodological pluralism (e.g., Munck 2001).

I have two related aims in this paper. First, I want to call attention to the importance and complexity of conceptual problems for substantive social and political
research. As a vehicle for this argument, I examine and criticize recent attempts

1094-2939/02/0615-0223$14.00   **223**

to improve our understanding of how culture and politics intersect by integrating interpretive and rational choice theories. I argue that these efforts are plagued by important, mostly unrecognized, and so unresolved, conceptual problems that, in turn, subvert their explicitly stated explanatory objectives. In this respect they resemble other, quite different approaches to the relations between politics and culture (Johnson 2001, 2002). My aim is not wholly critical, however. I also indicate how interpretive and rational choice theories might, when properly combined, productively contribute to our understanding of the relations of culture and politics.

Second, I show how the efforts of rational choice theorists to borrow from interpretive research unintentionally frustrate their laudable pluralist aspirations. In this way I illustrate why, if we take conceptual problems seriously, calls for methodological and theoretical pluralism are significantly more demanding than they often appear. This is an important caution at a time when the discipline is beset by calls for *perestroika*, with which I have considerable, if qualified, sympathy.

Before proceeding, I want to preempt two varieties of skepticism. First, there are good reasons—analytical, normative and empirical—to welcome efforts to integrate interpretive and rational choice theories (e.g., Johnson 1997, 2000; Chwe 2001). Thus, the criticisms I advance here are not nearly as sweeping as the more pervasive skepticism regarding rational choice models that interpretive anthropologists, for example, regularly express. The question is not whether we ought to try to integrate diverse and seemingly incompatible approaches but how we might do so most soundly and fruitfully.

My concern here is not to defend rational choice theory or interpretation per se. My primary concern is substantive: How might we best analyze the ubiquitous relations of culture and politics? That said, we must avoid excessive skepticism regarding the role of social and political theory in this endeavor (e.g., Shapiro 1998). The difficulties here are not primarily empirical. Consider a plausible alternative point of departure. Geertz (1973, p. 312) first defines culture as "the structures of meaning through which men give shape to their experience" and then identifies politics as "one of the principle arenas in which such structures publicly unfold." He observes that analysis of the relations between culture and politics so understood is an "immodest" enterprise because "there is almost no theoretical apparatus with which to conduct it." As a result, instead of systematic analysis of culture and politics, "one is left with a series of anecdotes connected by insinuation, and with a feeling that though much has been touched little has been grasped."

This diagnosis still holds. What we require if we hope to analyze the relations of culture and politics are theoretical resources. And, in ways that might surprise Geertz, rational choice theories provide some of the resources we need. Indeed, rational choice theories sharpen our appreciation for what is at stake, and hence in need of explanation, at the intersection of culture and politics. They also prompt us to speculate about what mechanism we might invoke as the basis for such explanation. That is the sort of matter that political scientists, in their rush to evaluate theories solely in terms of empirical performance, typically neglect. In this area, as as in others, such haste is a standing hindrance to progress in social and political inquiry.

CONCEPTUAL PROBLEMS, THEORETICAL PROGRESS, AND HOW THEY ARE RELATED

When political scientists assess competing theories, they typically fixate immediately and more or less naively on empirical performance (e.g., King et al. 1994, Green & Shapiro 1994). They have correspondingly little to say about conceptual problems and seem generally unaware of the extent to which their assessments of empirical performance are parasitic on conceptual commitments (Johnson 1996, 2002). This weakness, in turn, hinders their ability to both persuasively conduct and critically assess substantive research.

Several questions arise at this point. What is a conceptual problem? How do conceptual problems relate to empirical problems? What constitutes progress in a discipline? And how is it related to the recognition and resolution of conceptual and empirical problems? If we can answer these questions persuasively, what consequences for social and political inquiry follow from explicit awareness that conceptual problems play an important, recurrent role in scientific practice and progress?

My response to these questions draws on the work of Laudan, who advances a pragmatist account of science as a "problem solving" enterprise and a view of scientific progress that, accordingly, assesses competing research traditions in terms of their relative problem-solving capacities (Laudan 1977; 1990, pp. 24–31; 1996, pp. 77–87). I rely on Laudan's work without thoroughly explicating his views, discussing how he has elaborated them over time, or defending them against competing views of science. Ball (1987) provides initial warrant for relying on Laudan's approach in assessing political science.

In Laudan's account, research traditions play a crucial role in the practice and progress of science. Research traditions consist of general assumptions that loosely unite various component theories. At any given time, a research tradition encompasses competing, sometimes outright inconsistent theories. A research tradition nevertheless places consequential conceptual constraints on those theories. It defines the object domain of component theories and specifies the sorts of entity that populate that domain. It identifies the sorts of problems that component theories can be expected to solve. And it designates the methods appropriate for solving them (Laudan 1977, pp. 81–82, 97; 1996, pp. 83–84). Whereas its component theories aim to explain and predict events in the world, a research tradition primarily performs conceptual or theoretical tasks and so is not directly testable. We assess the value of a research tradition by how successfully its component theories solve a range of problems relative to the theories of its competitors (Laudan 1977, pp. 106–14, 119–20; 1996, p. 86). We assess any theory, Laudan claims, in terms of its relative success at solving both conceptual and empirical problems.

Empirical performance is crucial to our assessment of theories. No one—not Laudan, not I—denies that. Indeed, Laudan discusses the role of empirical problems in scientific practice at considerable length (Laudan 1977, pp. 11–45). He simply insists that "a broad range of empirical and conceptual checks are of equal importance in theory testing" (Laudan 1996, p. 80). On this basis, Laudan claims that there may well be circumstances in which we justifiably abandon a theory that appears empirically well-supported in favor of one that has less empirical support but resolves conceptual problems more readily than its competitors (Laudan 1996, p. 80; 1990, pp. 14–20).

In Laudan's account, empirical problems are "first order problems . . . substantive questions about the objects which constitute the domain of a given science." Put otherwise, an empirical problem is anything that "strikes us as odd, or otherwise in need of explanation" about some relevant portion of the world (Laudan 1977, p. 15). Laudan distinguishes between potential, anomalous, and solved problems and suggests that empirical progress consists solely in the resolution of potential and anomalous problems (1996, p. 79; 1977, pp. 17–31). I set aside matters of empirical performance for the remainder of this paper.

Conceptual problems, by contrast, are "higher order questions about the well-foundedness of the conceptual structures (e.g., theories) which have been devised to answer first order questions" (Laudan 1977, p. 48). Laudan distinguishes here between internal and external problems. A theory encounters an internal conceptual problem if it is self-contradictory or invokes implausible, unclear, or vague mechanisms. It encounters an external conceptual problem if, for instance, it makes assumptions about the world and the entities it contains that run counter to current well-founded metaphysical or epistemic doctrines, disregards basic precepts of the more encompassing research tradition in which it is situated, or neglects conceptual resources offered by other theories or research traditions (Laudan 1996, p. 79; 1977, pp. 49–64). Particular conceptual problems, whether internal or external, "have no existence independent of the theories which exhibit them." In other words, they are "exhibited by some theory or other" and so are unlike potential empirical problems—some "odd" feature of the world—which are more or less independent of any given theory (Laudan 1977, p. 48). In this sense, "a conceptual problem will, in general, be a *more* serious one than an empirical anomaly . . . because it is usually easier to explain away" anomalous empirical data "than to dismiss out of hand a conceptual problem" (Laudan 1977, p. 64).

The importance of conceptual problems and their relation to scientific progress should now be fairly clear. We make progress insofar as we resolve conceptual as well as empirical problems. We make theoretical progress, for example, to the extent that we specify more clearly the mechanisms at work in our theories or that we more successfully incorporate conceptual resources available from sources outside our own research tradition.

Scientific practice, of course, is more complicated than that. For example, my efforts to avoid external and internal conceptual problems may operate at cross purposes. The competing theoretical approaches on which would-be pluralists seek to draw could be "inconsistent in their fundamentals" (Laudan 1977, p. 103) if, for instance, they relied on incompatible mechanisms. Thus, my attempt to appropriate theoretical resources from some external source is constrained insofar as those investigators from whom I hope to borrow clearly specify the mechanisms that animate their research. We therefore might be wise to place positive value on small amounts of conceptual ambiguity (Laudan 1977, p. 49; 1988, p. 534).

Of course, ambiguity may just as surely be unhelpful. In order to know whether resources derived from competing research traditions are compatible with the animating assumptions of our own, a minimal requirement is that the mechanisms animating their component theories be specified. In the case of recent efforts by rational choice theorists to borrow conceptual resources from interpretive approaches, poorly specified mechanisms have generated—however unintentionally—conceptual confusion and misspecified substantive research. They thus potentially provide fodder for renewed, unproductive rounds of recrimination between partisans of the competing research traditions.

The impetus to integrate interpretive and rational choice theories comes largely from advocates of rational choice. It stems from the apprehension that since rational choice theories are typically designed for and most plausibly applied to strategic interactions within relatively settled institutional structures, they "may face significant limitations when applied to the less-settled politics of other regions, where ethnic and religious identities play a greater role in politics" (Bates et al. 1998, p. 605). I set aside the obvious objection that politics in more familiar Western polities is as thoroughly influenced by symbolically constituted identities as is politics in "other regions" (e.g., Kertzer 1996). The more pressing objection is that this predicament is not a contingent empirical problem. If, plausibly, we interpret the unsettled circumstances to which Bates et al. refer as one species of "unforeseen contingency" (Kreps 1990a; Dekel et al. 1998), and if such contingencies are an unavoidable feature of all social and political interaction, then rational choice theories confront an especially pressing conceptual problem (Calvert & Johnson 1999). The domain of their theory is, potentially, quite severely restricted. In response, rational choice theorists seek to establish that their own work and interpretive theories are "complementary" and to appropriate from the latter theoretical resources that will enable them "to handle the politics of transition and culture" (Bates et al. 1998, p. 606). The difficulty is that although interpretive theories offer important conceptual resources, they also are plagued by serious, longstanding conceptual problems. In particular, they typically lack a plausible mechanism to account for how symbols, traditions, rituals, and myths influence social and political interaction. This conceptual problem migrates, largely unnoticed, along with the conceptual resources that rational choice theorists seek to appropriate. The upshot is what in later sections I call the reductionist predicament.

THE INTERPRETIVE DILEMMA: CONCEPTUAL
INNOVATION GENERATES CONCEPTUAL PROBLEMS

Geertz (1973) rightly insists that culture and politics are intimately related, and he plausibly ascribes our impoverished grasp of that relationship to inadequate theoretical resources. Geertz also provides crucial elements of the sort of "theoretical apparatus" that we need to systematically analyze the relations of culture and politics. He advances a revisionist conception of culture as consisting in publicly shared symbols and cultural practices that social and political actors deploy in contested efforts to impose conceptual order on otherwise indeterminate experience (Geertz 1973, pp. 250, 325). This conceptual revision has had profound influence on anthropologists and other social scientists because it "gave the hitherto elusive concept of culture a relatively fixed focus, and a degree of objectivity, that it did not have before" (Ortner 1984, p. 129; see also Swidler 1996, p. 299; Kuper 1999, p. 76; Ortner 1999).

Geertz hoped his conceptual revision would enable anthropologists to jettison then extant conceptions of culture that either reified it as a mysterious, larger-than-life, independent source of purpose and activity or reduced it to an essentially psychological, and therefore unobservable and nearly inaccessible, subjective category (Geertz 1973, pp. 10–13). Yet, in this respect, his conceptual innovation highlighted a stark new dilemma. Unlike other interpretive theorists (e.g., Taylor 1985, pp. 52–53), Geertz insists that the credibility of any interpretation rests largely on its firm grounding in an account of social action (Geertz 1973, pp. 17–18). At a more general level, therefore, he sees it as "the central theoretical problem" for those who endorse an interpretive conception of culture to specify how symbols and other cultural practices influence social and political interaction (Geertz 1973, p. 250).

Neither Geertz himself nor his intellectual progeny persuasively address this problem. For reasons I do not examine here, they offer no plausible account of what, even early on, Geertz termed "symbolic action" (1973, pp. 10, 24). This remains an outstanding issue for anthropological theory more generally (Ortner 1984, p. 130; 1990, p. 87; Kuper 1999, p. 100). Interpretive theorists consequently face a twofold task. First, they need to specify "a comprehensible mechanism" to account for the influence of symbols on social and political action. Second, they must avoid determinism, and so any mechanism they propose must allow "a kind of elastic distance" between symbols and relevant actors so that observers can construe the actors as intentional agents rather than as passive vehicles of cultural patterns (Ortner 1990, pp. 84–90).

The difficulties here become apparent if we turn to recent anthropological accounts of how culture and politics have intersected in post-communist Europe, West and East. Kertzer (1996), for instance, depicts the travails of the Italian Communist Party following the demise of the Soviet Union. Much of the internal turmoil that Kertzer details is highly symbolic, and he aims to explain how strategic conflicts over various rituals, over interpretations and reinterpretations of party tradition, and over the redesign of party insignia affected communist party politics. In his account, symbols are politically important because by "promoting a certain view of the world and stirring up emotions, symbols impel people to action" (Kertzer 1996, pp. 6, 127). Kertzer places considerable stress on the role of emotions as an explanatory mechanism in hopes of differentiating his account from analyses that ground politics primarily in rational action (1996, pp. 156–57). Yet he is ambivalent on this score and so also repeatedly attributes a broadly cognitive force to the symbols political actors use in hopes of imposing conceptual order on recalcitrant and unruly events both past and present (Kertzer 1996, pp. 7, 41, 69, 77, 131, 134). His work parallels in this respect Verdery's (1999) analysis of the symbolic politics of burial and reburial of dead bodies, both famous and anonymous, in post-communist Eastern Europe. Verdery too rejects an overly "rationalist and dry sense of politics," one that induces a "narrow and flat," hence inadequate, appreciation of post-communist transformations (1999, pp. 26, 126). To this end, she too stresses the "emotional force" of political symbols (Verdery 1999, p. 114). Yet she places heaviest emphasis on the broadly cognitive force of the symbols that political actors deploy in the contested process of "reordering meaningful worlds" that might sustain regularized expectations in the wake of highly disorienting social, economic, and political dislocations (Verdery 1999, p. 35).

Kertzer and Verdery exemplify the dilemma that besets interpretive approaches. On the one hand, they both invoke emotions as an explanatory mechanism in order to differentiate their accounts from explanations that ground politics in rational action. Although I think that this move is ill-advised, I do not pursue here its specific theoretical difficulties,[1] for both Kertzer and Verdery also more plausibly emphasize the notion that political actors use symbols to impose conceptual order on the world as part of ongoing strategic contests. Kertzer (1996, pp. 41, 134) repeatedly claims that the political actors he studies rely on ritual and other cultural practices in an ongoing struggle to impose a particular "symbolic definition of reality" and, thereby, to "create a world in which current events could be properly interpreted." He also argues that these struggles had important practical consequences. How should we understand such claims? And how should we understand Verdery's (1999, p. 52) more encompassing plea that we interpret post-communist East European politics in "suitably 'cosmic' terms, showing it as rich, complex, and disputatious processes of political meaning-creation?" In short, how might we comply with Ortner's demand for a comprehensible mechanism to explain how symbols influence social and political action? Progress in understanding the relations of culture and politics requires that we squarely address such conceptual problems.

---

[1]For instance, it suggests that rationality and the emotions typically are opposed. More fundamentally, it implies that the things we categorize as emotions form a more or less homogenous category and therefore influence action in roughly the same ways. Each of these presumptions requires substantial argument (see, e.g., Rorty 1985, Elster 1999).

THE DEMAND FOR A COMPREHENSIBLE MECHANISM

The General Problem

The demand that explanations specify comprehensible mechanisms is not peculiar to interpretive inquiry. Efforts to comply with that demand may be considered "the central task for social scientists" more generally (Little 1993, p. 185). This is a contested claim and I do not adequately defend it here. King et al. (1994), for instance, explicitly reject it and have been criticized for not properly attending to such conceptual matters (e.g., Brady 1995, Laitin 1995). That said, there is considerable support for the broad position I assert here (Boudon 1986; Elster 1989a, 1993; Hoover 1990; Little 1991; Stinchcombe 1991; Knight 1995; Hedström & Swedberg 1998; Petersen 1999; Tilly 2001).

What, then, is a mechanism? For present purposes, a mechanism m is a usually unobservable ingredient of some more encompassing theory T. Typically, m operates at an analytical level below that which T seeks to explain and makes T more credible in the sense that m renders more fine-grained the explanations that T generates. Perhaps the most obvious example of such a mechanism in contemporary political science is the way that rational choice theories account for aggregate patterns as the (often unintended) outcome of interdependent decisions made by individual agents. In this instance, m consists of actions taken by strategically rational agents whereas T offers explanations of such aggregate phenomena as collective action, electoral outcomes, or social institutions.

The mechanisms that animate any theoretical account identify those "places where kinds of causal forces . . . are connected to their effects" (Stinchcombe 1991, pp. 371–72). Because social and political research largely is concerned with aggregate patterns, the mechanisms that it invokes typically operate at the individual level (Stinchcombe 1991, pp. 367, 372). Hence, rational choice theorists, for example, typically attribute the behavior of strategic actors to their beliefs or expectations and their desires or preferences (see Elster 1986; but see also Satz & Ferejohn 1994, Hausman 1995). This implies neither that social entities do not exist nor that they have no influence. Rather, it implies that "the only form of causal influence that social entities have is through their effects on individual action" by, for example, altering the incentives that agents face, the options or information available to them, or the powers at their command (Little 1993, pp. 186, 193). In this view, if a theory contains clearly specified mechanisms, it can generate more fine-grained explanations and thereby achieve greater "precision or suppleness or fruitfulness" (Stinchcombe 1991, p. 374).

Laudan (1977, pp. 46–47) details how, in natural science, contests over explanatory mechanisms provide a source of continuing, often heated, conceptual controversy. It also is easy to identify such disputes among social scientists. One important recent example revolves around whether and under what conditions efficiency (variously defined) or distributional conflict is the appropriate mechanism in rational choice accounts of the creation and maintenance of social and political institutions (e.g., North 1990; Knight 1992, 1995; Calvert 1995a,b; Allio et al. 1997; Knight & North 1997; Binder & Smith 1998). A second example of conceptual debate is whether and how "values" might provide a plausible explanatory mechanism for social and political research (e.g., Swidler 1986, Hechter 1992, Hechter & Kanazawa 1993, Chong 1996). Political scientists typically treat such conceptual disputes as subsidiary concerns. Indeed, if we examine actual social scientific practice, my earlier statement that the search for mechanisms is a "central task" of social science is more normative than descriptive.

A Response to the Interpretive Dilemma

In the remainder of this section, I sketch an account of "how culture works" that goes considerable distance toward remedying the interpretive dilemma that rational choice theorists unknowingly inherit.

Symbolic forms and the cultural practices (e.g., ritual, myth, tradition) in which they are embodied afford social and political actors the resources from which they might elaborate a "symbolic strategy" for imposing conceptual order on otherwise indeterminate processes of interaction (Geertz 1973, pp. 89, 230, 250; Ortner 1984, p. 129). This formulation captures what Laitin (1986) labels the "two faces of culture." It is important for theoretical purposes to ascribe proper weight to both symbol and strategy. Ortner, for instance, rightly is skeptical of approaches that reduce symbolic to strategic action. If we depict symbols instrumentally, as useful social and political resources, they must have some identifiable, independent force (Ortner 1990, p. 59). What she neglects to add is that, insofar as symbolic forms have such force, they constitute a potent and thus nearly irresistible resource for strategic actors. I address these two issues in turn.

It is important, first, to see how symbols and cultural practices concretely influence social and political interaction. This requires an analytical distinction between the force and the scope of symbolic forms. The force of a symbol or a cultural practice is its degree of centrality in the lives of relevant actors, the "psychological grip" it exercises over them. The scope of a symbol or practice is the range of social contexts in which those actors find it relevant (Geertz 1968, pp. 111–13). Claims about the scope of particular symbols or practices presuppose that they have force, for if symbols lack force they cannot be relevant to any social context.

As we have seen, even anthropologists who are tempted to ascribe the power of symbolic forms to their emotional impact on relevant actors ultimately identify the force of symbolic forms primarily in the ways that they help constitute a world view. The force of symbolic forms is at bottom conceptual in a broadly cognitive sense (Lukes 1977, pp. 68ff; Gellner 1988, pp. 56–57, 205–10; 1995, pp. 49–56). Thus, "the whole point" of interpretation in social inquiry is "to aid us in gaining access to the conceptual world in which our subjects live" (Geertz 1973, p. 24). Symbolic forms, deployed in cultural practices of various sorts, "structure the way people *think* about social life" (Moore & Myerhoff 1977, p. 4). They provide actors with "extrinsic sources of information" (Geertz 1973, p. 92), less in the sense that they convey detailed messages than in the broader sense that they impart a conception of how the world is constituted—the sorts of entities it contains, how those entities can be expected to behave, and so on. Because symbolic forms establish the focal categories in terms of which social and political interaction is conducted (Laitin 1986), they play a crucial role in coordinating it (Chwe 2001).

Symbolic forms do not represent or express preexisting values and beliefs so much as they provide the medium within which individuals formulate beliefs (Kertzer 1988, p. 68; Cohen 1985, pp. 10–21). Indeed, it is a commonplace among anthropologists that symbols are inherently and irreducibly ambiguous and that they mean diverse things to different people. Consequently, "the mark of a good political symbol" is that it works "not because everyone agrees on its meaning but because it compels interest *despite* (because of?) divergent views of what it means" (Verdery 1999, pp. 31, 125; see also Kertzer 1988; 1996, p. 129).

Symbolic forms, then, do not directly instill beliefs or values. Rather, they provide parameters on belief formation. They help delineate the realm of social and political possibility for relevant actors and thereby establish the range of things to which those actors might attach value or about which they might hold beliefs. They do this in at least two analytically separable, if empirically related, ways.

In the first place, symbolic forms operate indicatively to enable social actors to direct their own attention and, more important, that of others toward certain ranges of alternatives and away from others. Symbolic forms allow relevant actors to assert order, relation, and predictability in the face of indeterminacy (Moore & Myerhoff 1977, p. 18). In this way, social and political actors use symbols to foreclose possibilities. This process is not naive; symbolic force discriminates. By calling attention to certain identities and options, thereby defining them as viable or feasible, it forecloses others. It necessarily constitutes social and political interactions on particular, partial terms (Lukes 1977, pp. 68–69; Kertzer 1988, p. 87).

If symbolic forms operated only indicatively, their impact would be invariably conservative. But symbols also operate subjunctively and so enable social and political actors to *disclose* possibilities often not immediately discernable in mundane existence. They thus enable those actors to reveal options and identities that might otherwise remain unconsidered. Orchestrated in complex cultural practices such as ritual, for example, symbolic forms give palpable existence to as-yet-unrealized possibility (Geertz 1973, p. 112). They nourish the imagination of social and political actors. This process is not naive either. By imaginatively disclosing and exploring possibilities, actors can, within limits, redefine the options and identities available to themselves and those with whom they interact.

Symbolic forms, then, exert force over social and political actors by commanding their attention and capturing their imagination. They govern the mental capacities with which actors delimit the possibilities embodied in their extant situation and envision those that lie beyond it. Symbolic force, as I sketch it here, provides precisely the sort of comprehensible mechanism that we need if we hope to understand how symbols and cultural practices influence ongoing human interaction.

Moreover, it allows us to specify how culture exerts its influence while allowing the requisite distance between symbols and the actors for whom they have force. In short, it enables us to see how symbolic forms affect social and political interaction without programming it. We can see more clearly how symbol and strategy intersect in politics.

Here we arrive at the implication of Ortner's position that she and other interpretive theorists typically neglect. Geertz warns us not to treat culture as "a self-contained 'super-organic' entity with forces and purposes of its own" (1973, p. 11). In the present context, this injunction raises at least two practical tasks. First, we should avoid attributing too much structure to culture. Any culture consists of an array of symbols and practices. It is not a neatly ordered, seamless, self-contained entity. The extent of internal interconnection and coherence among the constituent elements of any given culture is an empirical question (Geertz 1973, p. 407). It is inadvisable to prejudge this question precisely because we risk underestimating the potential "disorder, multiplicity and underdeterminedness" that a given culture encapsulates (Barth 1993, pp. 4–5; see also Geertz 1973, pp. 11, 18). This, in turn, will prompt us to overlook not only the ubiquitous opportunities for strategic action at the unavoidable interstices of culture but also the fact that such coherence as does obtain in a culture emerges from the efforts of strategic actors to resolve disorder and indeterminacy in ways that advantage themselves.

Second, the converse, more constructive task is to ground the force of symbols and cultural practices in a systematic understanding of human action. Symbols and cultural practices are not self-animating. Social and political actors engage in "symbolic action" when they deploy symbolic forms in the effort to impose some conceptual order on otherwise indeterminate processes of social and political interaction. Symbolic action is not a naive process. Because symbolic force discriminates, it has distributional consequences—it forecloses or discloses possibilities and so defines the terms in which social and political coordination can take place. Any culture (understood as a complex of symbols and practices) not only provides agents with repeated occasions on which to engage in strategic action but also offers them strong reasons to do so.

Symbolic action thus has an inescapable strategic dimension. It is the medium for what Geertz calls "the struggle for the real" (Geertz 1968, p. 105; 1973, p. 316). Actors engaged in this struggle often seek not to invent new symbols but to creatively contest and recast the meanings invested in existing symbolic forms. They endeavor, with differential facility and success, to exploit symbolic force in order to define or redefine the context of their ongoing interactions. Their objective is to establish an authoritative, though particular and partial, conception of the world and the social and political possibilities it contains. In the struggle for the real, actors strive to command the attention and capture the imagination of others by controlling the symbolic media with which they think. In this sense, the struggle for the real is a competition for power over others, a strategic contest to control the symbols and cultural practices in terms of which social and political actors envision possibilities and fashion them into viable alternatives (Rorty 1983, Johnson 1997). That is what is at stake at the intersection of culture and politics.

RATIONAL CHOICE AND *CULTURE*?

Those who endorse interpretive inquiry might find the prospect of incorporating rational choice theory into cultural analysis thoroughly misguided (e.g., Kertzer 1996, pp. 3–4, 156–57; Verdery 1999, pp. 26, 126). In part, such incredulity is well-founded because rational choice theorists, as I show below, actively invite it. Yet both sides in this ill-defined encounter overlook the ways that rational choice models actually help us "to ask what role symbolism plays in modern politics, how important it is and why, how it works, and how it fails" (Kertzer 1996, p. 4). In other words, given that symbolic forms have force, the models help us to conceptualize more precisely why strategic actors seek to deploy them for political advantage. Such models thereby help us to see why and how interpretive and rational choice theories can, when soundly integrated, provide a fruitful basis for exploring the ways culture and politics are related.

Rational choice theorists adopt a variety of attitudes toward the role of cultural factors in political analysis. Many, perhaps most, are dismissive. For instance, Tsebelis (1990, p. 44) candidly insists that cultural factors "do not enter directly into any rational choice explanation." A quick glance at recent surveys suggests that this view is widely shared (e.g., McLean 1991, Lalman et al. 1993, Austen-Smith & Banks 1998). None comes close to considering whether or how cultural factors inform rational choice explanations.

Other rational choice theorists, by contrast, are accommodationist. For example, although he suggests that rational choice theory and cultural analysis are "complementary," Ferejohn (1991, pp. 280–82) argues they are dissimilar endeavors that can be pursued along parallel, largely independent tacks. In his view, the two sorts of analysis may, but need not, inform one another. Thus, to use language from Laudan (1977, pp. 53–54), Ferejohn acknowledges that interpretative approaches and rational choice theories are "compatible." But he also suggests that neither approach implies anything about the other and therefore that we need not seek to establish any stronger "positive relevance" between them. Here Ferejohn differs from Chwe (2001), for example, who argues that rational choice theories and interpretive approaches in fact reinforce one another in the sense that each "provides a rationale for (part of)" the other. Yet, unless he can demonstrate something like this stronger claim, Ferejohn's position is not obviously distinct from the dismissive stance of Tsebelis.

Finally, some rational choice theorists endorse some brand of reductionism. On the one hand, some recent analyses insert an element of "symbolic utility" directly into the utility functions of relevant actors (Nozick 1993, Akerlof & Kranton 2000, Schuessler 2001). This approach is misguided. First, it is easy to posit that actors get utility from all sorts of things, but this simply diminishes the analytical purchase of rational choice theories. Second, although such an approach might account for either cultural persistence or change, it is hard to see how it might account for both. On the other hand, there is the seemingly more plausible reductionist posture demonstrated by Bates' statement that contemporary game theory affords the apparatus necessary "to provide formal structure for kinds of symbolic displays" that occupy the intersection of politics and culture. In this view, cultural factors can be modeled as signals in games of incomplete information (Bates 1990, p. 54).

None of these three broad positions is defensible for the simple reason that cultural considerations enter unavoidably and directly, if tacitly, into rational choice accounts of politics. Moreover, they do so in ways that are neither contingent on nor reducible to the formal game-theoretic apparatus that rational choice theorists deploy. Rational choice theorists thus must attend to symbolic as well as strategic action. Unfortunately, not only are they now poorly equipped to address that problem but the formal game-theoretic apparatus they deploy may by itself be incapable of addressing it.

Popkin's *The Rational Peasant* (1979) supplies a convenient, if unlikely, example here. This book was an early exemplar of the sort of empirical study that rational choice theorists might conduct; furthermore, it addresses just the sort of unsettled circumstance that prompts rational choice theorists to seek rapprochement with interpretive approaches in the first place. At the outset, Popkin proclaims that he will treat cultural considerations as givens in order to advance an exclusively rational choice analysis of peasant politics. Toward the end of the book, however, he reflects briefly on the decisive role leaders played in facilitating collective action among Vietnamese peasants. He suggests that the success or failure of these leaders depended crucially on their competence and credibility. But, somewhat surprisingly, Popkin insists that those leaders established credibility on "cultural bases." He attributes the variable success of religious and political leaders over time to their differential ability "to utilize cultural themes," to orchestrate "terms and symbols," that resonated with their potential constituents (Popkin 1979, pp. 260–61). In short, in Popkin's account, political leaders create and sustain credibility through what we might call symbolic action. They seek to coordinate and mobilize relevant constituencies by deploying symbolic forms that have force over them. Here, dismissive rational choice theorists such as Tsebelis notwithstanding, cultural factors emerge centrally, if uncomfortably, in a purportedly austere rational choice explanation.

Rational choice theorists might concede that symbolism is central to Popkin's account of peasant politics. They nevertheless might complain that his informal empirical study is fairly distant from the game-theoretic models central to their research. This is unfair to Popkin. Insofar as we understand political leadership as emerging from coordination problems (e.g., Calvert 1992), Popkin's work is hardly idiosyncratic. More important, such claims radically underestimate the implicit presence of symbolic considerations at the core of the rational choice research tradition. Indeed, the agents who populate more austere game-theoretic models confront precisely the indeterminacy that bedevils Popkin's peasants and leaders. Symbolic action thus enters the game-theoretic framework just as surely as it enters Popkin's account.

The players who populate noncooperative game-theoretic models tacitly rely on symbolic resources at at least two junctures. First, and most obvious, there are the pervasive coordination problems that emerge in those very common, theoretically unsettling instances where games generate multiple equilibria (Harsanyi 1986 [1977], p. 102; Kreps 1990b, pp. 95–99). Schelling (1960) long ago suggested that this indeterminacy requires rational choice theorists to attend to two seemingly irrelevant issues. The first is how strategic actors rely on factors that game theorists eliminate as "incidental detail"—specifically symbols and traditions—to fashion solutions to the coordination problems that are a ubiquitous feature of social and political life. The second is how such factors provide actors with a potent resource as they undertake "strategic moves" in hopes of defining or redefining the context of their interactions. Game theorists tend to find Schelling's recommendations elusive. However, they have yet to improve on his suggestion that actual social and political actors exploit the "symbolic contents of the game" (Schelling 1960, pp. 106, 160) in their efforts to resolve the pervasive coordination problems that game-theoretic models reveal (Kreps 1990b, p. 101; Chwe 2001). Moreover, they almost completely overlook the distributive consequences of actors' efforts. Because coordination problems typically are asymmetrical, and because the symbols and practices that constitute culture discriminate (as described above), any effort to make a particular option salient will necessarily have distributive consequences; in fact, such efforts are typically motivated by those consequences. It thus is a mistake to presume, as Kreps (1990a, p. 91, 106, 125, 127) for instance does, that culture promotes efficiency in any but an indirect sense.

The second and less obvious area where game theorists tacitly incorporate cultural or symbolic factors is in their standard technique for transforming games of incomplete information into equivalent, technically more tractable, games of complete but imperfect information. Myerson (1991, pp. 74–83) provides a succinct discussion of this procedure. For analytical purposes, it reduces all forms of incomplete information regarding the parameters of the game to mutual uncertainty about the payoff functions characteristic of players in the game. Each player then calculates her best strategy in light of conditional probabilities that she constructs over the range of possible types of player that she might encounter. These probabilities, in turn, are premised on common knowledge of an initial objective distribution over possible types.

Game theorists regularly attribute this initial distribution to "nature" (e.g., Kreps 1990b, pp. 19–20; Fudenberg & Tirole 1991, pp. 209, 210; Gibbons 1992, p. 148). This unfortunate rhetorical practice not only brackets the subject of symbolic action but forecloses inquiry into it, implying that the definition of player types is unproblematic. Game theorists, however, offer scant insight into either the source or nature of the common knowledge that obtains among players about the initial distribution of possible types who might populate their models (Binmore 1990, pp. 88–89, 176–77). Since each player's type consists not only of physical attributes but also of such characteristics as language or gender (Myerson 1991, p. 67), it is plausible to attribute common knowledge about the range of possible types in a population to "such factors as a shared cultural heritage" (Binmore 1990, p. 158). Hence,

> The everyday world in which members of any community move, their taken for granted field of social action, is populated not by anybodies, faceless men without qualities, but by somebodies, concrete classes of determinant persons positively characterized and appropriately labeled. And the symbol systems which define these classes are not given in the nature of things—they are historically constructed, socially maintained and individually applied. (Geertz 1973, pp. 363–64)

In this view it is not "nature" but social and political agents operating at the contested intersection of symbol and strategy who construct the range of possible types in any population.

Even within stark game-theoretic models, then, both the range of strategic options that actors confront and the range of identities available to them are constituted and constrained symbolically. Absent some such symbolic constraint, the strategic interactions that game theorists seek to capture in their models remain highly indeterminate. This observation has two implications.

First, symbolic considerations inform rational choice analyses in ways that not only undermine the typical dismissive view but are simply not contingent (as accommodationists such as Ferejohn would have us believe). Moreover, symbolic considerations are analytically prior to, and indeed are a precondition for, the signaling processes that Bates and other reductionists analyze. Reductionist approaches misfire to the extent that they fail to grasp this point.

A second and much more important implication is that symbolic force is strategically important and political actors must try to turn it to their advantage. Simply put, culture works to define the ways that ongoing social and political interactions are coordinated. Game theory, however inadvertently and indirectly, helps us grasp the ways social and political actors use symbolic forms to delineate options and identities and thereby establish the range of social and political possibility.

THE REDUCTIONIST PREDICAMENT

In the previous three sections, I have identified a remarkable convergence between rational choice and interpretive theories. Among rational choice theorists, those who adopt dismissive or accommodationist postures are either unwilling or unable productively to explore this convergence. This leaves reductionists, who, following Bates, seek to represent symbolic action within the signaling framework of game theory. In this section and the next, I use this reductionist approach to illustrate how, when we fail to address conceptual problems and especially the ways they migrate and proliferate, we risk both subverting our explicitly announced explanatory aims and derailing our pluralist ambitions.

In an underappreciated sense, reductionist and interpretive approaches converge still further precisely because they exhibit different versions of the same conceptual problem. The interpretive dilemma results from a failure to identify the mechanisms that account for how symbols and symbolic practices such as ritual, myth, or tradition influence social and political interaction. Reductionists inherit this unresolved conceptual problem yet remain largely unaware of it. They are intent on integrating rational choice and interpretive theories, but, since the latter lack a persuasive theory of action, reductionists simply reduce symbolic considerations to strategic interaction. As a result, their analyses ultimately accord culture little or no independent explanatory force and, however inadvertently, support the skepticism of interpretive theorists such as Ortner, Kertzer, and Verdery.

Bates et al. (1998) exemplify this reductionist predicament. Their paper is commendable for several reasons. It addresses a set of issues—namely rapid, momentous political change and especially the symbolic dimensions of such phenomena—that, by their own admission, is inauspicious terrain for rational choice analysis. In taking up these subjects, Bates et al. acknowledge that culture and politics intersect in just the ways identified above. Indeed, this particular paper is part of an ambitious, creative effort to construct an account of the relations of culture and politics that is pluralist in the sense that it is systematically informed by both interpretive approaches and rational choice theory. (See also Weingast 1998, de Figueiredo & Weingast 1999). Finally, the paper is interesting because the authors explicitly deny they are reductionist. They instead set out to establish "that rational choice and cultural analysis ... are complementary rather than mutually exclusive and antagonistic" and so hope to defend something like the accommodationist stance that Ferejohn advocates (Bates et al. 1998, p. 603).

Bates et al. rely on two case studies of transitional politics—Zambia and the former Yugoslavia, both in the early 1990s—as a vehicle for their analysis of the "less-settled politics" common to developing and transitional states (1998, p. 605). They model both cases as relatively simple signaling games in which one or more of the players has private information that is unavailable to others. The problem for relevant players is how to interpret signals that convey information about matters of uncertainty that are essential to their strategy choice.

For ease of explication, I concentrate on the Yugoslav case, where Bates et al. hope to explain "how ethnic issues moved from the periphery of politics to become its dominating force" (1998, p. 611). This is the proper question, but Bates et al. propose to answer it by specifying a game-theoretic model that reduces cultural or symbolic matters to straightforward strategic considerations.

The players are remnants of the incumbent communist regime and the pivotal member of the Serbian population whose support the regime must enlist if it is to derail political and economic reforms it deems disadvantageous. Incomplete information exists in the form of the Serbian population's uncertainty regarding the actual character (aggressive or peaceful) of other ethnic groups (Croats and

Muslims), given that the regime has an incentive to misrepresent that information (Bates et al. 1998, pp. 621–29).

Bates et al. claim that, by 1989–1990, the average Serb supported dramatic political and economic reforms that, if enacted, would have systematically threatened the power and prerogatives enjoyed by incumbent officials. Faced with this problem, the officials coordinated on ethnicity as an "alternative dimension of politics" that they might use to divert the population's attention from reform proposals. This strategic move, according to Bates et al. (1998, pp. 621–22), accounts for the marked "transformation of Serbian politics" during the period. They show that because ordinary Serbs were uncertain about both the actual propensities of Croats and the veracity of their own regime's signals about those propensities, it was equilibrium behavior for them to support the regime as it pursued the increasingly aggressive "ethnification of politics." In this model, the expected benefits of pursuing this strategy "swamp the expected costs" of foregoing other available equilibrium strategies premised on the probability that the Croats were, in fact, peaceful rather than aggressive (Bates et al. 1998, pp. 623–28). In short, Serbs were driven by fear of aggressive, possibly genocidal, Croats to support the bellicose policies of the incumbent regime.

How do cultural factors enter this account? According to Bates et al., they enter because individual Serbs were compelled to assign probabilities to actions and events that would never transpire because they were "off of the equilibrium path." Rational players rely on Bayesian reasoning to reach decisions concerning observable actions and events. However, in order to reason counterfactually, as it were, they must proceed on the basis of "interpretations advanced by others" (Bates 1998, pp. 627–28). In the case at hand, individual Serbs were at the mercy of potentially misleading information supplied by the incumbent regime.

Two things are important about this account. First, although Bates et al. set out to establish that rational choice and interpretation are compatible, they ultimately accede to an established, untenable pattern of intellectual gerrymandering. They clearly relegate the cultural or symbolic matters that preoccupy interpretive theorists to the realm of irrationality and emotion (Bates et al. 1998, p. 628). They implement a strategy of disciplinary partition that anthropologists such as Kertzer and Verdery, who also sometimes consign symbolic matters to the domain of irrationality and emotion, might well embrace.

Second, and more important, Bates et al. accord no independent causal force to cultural factors. Although they claim that their models afford "insight into the mechanisms that underlie the politics of symbols, identities, and other subjective states," they actually reduce such factors to individual calculations of "the balance . . . between probabilities and payoffs" (Bates et al. 1998, p. 630). In this respect, they do not depart in any significant way from standard rational choice mechanisms. Culture enters, at best, in a subsidiary way.

An uncharitable interpretation might suggest that Bates et al. do not advance a pluralist project at all. Indeed, one might complain that they leave the debate substantially where it began except that various parties might embrace their original views with renewed confidence. On the one hand, dismissive rational choice theorists might claim that Bates et al. demonstrate that cultural factors really do not enter their models in any meaningful way. On the other hand, interpretive theorists skeptical of rational choice might feel vindicated in their suspicion that rational choice accounts cannot adequately illuminate the symbolic dimensions of politics. And even sympathetic critics might conclude that, as they suspected, rational choice theory lends itself too easily to ad hoc and ultimately unpersuasive extensions (Munck 2001).

OPENING THE BLACK BOX OF "NATURE"

The conclusion I just sketched is uncharitable because it is too quick. If we examine how the reductionist account of Bates et al. misfires, we see more precisely what it is about the relations of culture and politics that calls for explanation.

Ironically, it is the narrow limits Bates et al. impose on processes of political interpretation that are most illuminating at this juncture. Like other rational choice theorists, Bates et al. take rational calculations of payoffs and probabilities as primary. Culture, as I have suggested, consists in publicly shared symbols and the cultural practices that social and political actors deploy in the effort to impose conceptual order on otherwise indeterminate experience. Bates et al. insist that our understanding of this interpretative process, and the partial and therefore contested world views on which it necessarily draws, must be disciplined by rational decision making. They therefore insist that the impact of "culture and identity" on political action "must be consistent with Bayes's rule" (Bates et al. 1998, p. 631). [Morrow (1994, pp. 163–66) sketches the technical issues.] One need not be a radical skeptic regarding Bayesian conceptions of rationality (Elster 1989b, p. 85n; Binmore 1990) to see that this view is one-sided. The so-called constraint necessarily operates in both directions because our "view of the world and of ourselves, and our notion of what counts as rational, are in continual interplay" (Nozick 1993, pp. 134–35). It remains to be seen how we might characterize this process of reciprocal constraint between rationality and world view in a nonreductionist way.

Bates et al. are perplexed about how ethnic attachments, having long been largely irrelevant to Yugoslav politics, quickly became perhaps the most salient feature of social and political life in the former Yugoslavia. They portray this as an instance of "discontinuous change" and insist that such transformations involve "not just persuasion but also conversion" (Bates et al. 1998, p. 631). They are right to do so. Yet their analytical models do little to illuminate the properly symbolic or cultural dimensions of such processes. Indeed, although their models specify what it is rational for individual players to do once the political world is constituted symbolically in ethnic terms (e.g., after the players are recognized and labeled as Serbs, Croats, etc.), they tell us nothing about how the world comes to be constituted in those terms in the first place. [Bates et al. are not alone. For example, Fearon & Laitin (1996) are preoccupied with the converse perplexity—why we regularly observe so *little* ethnic violence—and the model they deploy assumes that players are labeled in ethnic terms from the outset. Similarly, the existence of the competing "cultural beliefs" whose implications Greif (1994) examines depends on some prior range of symbolically constituted identities. Thus, although Greif relies on a complete-information framework to model the differential impact of local cultural beliefs on larger patterns of economic development, his analysis too presupposes that social and political actors are already appropriately labeled.]

A culture consists of congeries of symbols and practices that impart to social and political actors a world view—a partial, typically contested conception of the sorts of entities that inhabit the natural, social, and political universe, and of the ways those entities typically behave (Geertz 1973, Verdery 1999). Such world views set the terms within which those social and political actors adopt, abandon, defend, and contest options and identities. Bates et al. not only readily concede this point, they suggest that "world views play a major role in shaping the ways that . . . beliefs are revised" in politics and consequently that "the struggle over world views should itself be treated as a strategic process" (Bates et al. 1998, pp. 633–35). Here again they are correct but offer no account of why this is the case. This is because they largely fail to appreciate how world views emerge from the struggle for the real and, by defining identities and options, establish the bounds of possibility. Symbolically constituted world views delineate the sorts of things about which social and political actors can establish beliefs or expectations, the sorts of things that are appropriate objects of emotions, the sorts of things among which they might have preferences, the sorts of things to which they might attach value or apply moral categories, and so on.

Verdery provides an especially germane example of this process. In the wake of communism, political actors in Eastern Europe sought to endow dead bodies, ranging from the famous to the anonymous, with symbolic force in their effort to redefine the social and political world. In the former Yugoslavia, political leaders encouraged disinterring from mass graves the corpses of people killed in civil conflict during and immediately following World War II. Depending on their own particular strategic aims, these political actors initially identified the anonymous dead as victims of Ustaša, of communists, or of Chetniks. They then quickly redefined the dead as victims of atrocities perpetrated by Croats and Serbs, thereby shifting blame from predecessors to contemporaries. But Verdery is quite clear on a crucial point. These political leaders were not simply seeking to assign blame. Rather, they were deploying the past to redescribe their contemporaries, thereby "creating certain kinds of social actors" defined in ethnic terms to whom they and their prospective constituents might apply the moral and political concept of blame (Verdery 1999, pp. 111–12).

Bates et al. hope but fail to capture this sort of symbolic politics in their model. Their failure is not idiosyncratic. Standard game-theoretic models are ill-suited to represent the ways strategic actors contest or struggle to transform world views. The difficulty is that such models presume a closed universe, a world in which all possible actions and events can be specified and labeled in advance. In a closed universe there are no surprises. Any uncertainty is merely strategic in the sense that although players may not know what relevant others actually will do, they do know, in advance, both the identity of those relevant others (they see them under some description) and all of the actions those others might take (Binmore 1990, pp. 119–20, 144, 178). The cultural or symbolic considerations that game theorists tacitly introduce into their analyses ensure that the players confront a closed universe. This indeed is how we might conceive the way a relatively settled culture works. Thus, Geertz (1983) identifies "common sense" and Kreps (1990a) identifies "principles" as the sorts of cultural resources on which social and political actors fall back when facing true surprises. And it is in this way that culture enters the models that Bates et al. deploy.

Because they model ethnic politics in the former Yugoslavia as a game of incomplete information, Bates et al. postulate "a non-strategic player," identified as "nature," who takes an initial move that "determines the Croatians' type" as either aggressive or not (Bates et al. 1998, pp. 614, 623). The remainder of the game is animated by the fact that ordinary Serbs must assign some conditional probability to the likelihood that the Croats are aggressive and therefore dangerous. The difficulty is that ordinary Serbs are uncertain about this, and their assessment of the matter depends on signals sent by officials within the incumbent regime. All of this presupposes that players conceptualize the social and political world in ethnic terms—that it is common knowledge among them that the relevant dimension for sociopolitical interaction is ethnicity, as opposed to, say, religion or ideology (compare Laitin 1986). In short, the players in this model already are converts. They attach probabilities to the types of other players conditional on the description of those others as Serbs and Croats and on the premise that these specifically ethnic identities are politically relevant. The categories within which they see the world are settled. The problem is that Bates et al. do not set out to explain such "settled" politics.

There is, of course, an obvious fallback position. Bates et al. readily acknowledge that processes of rational belief formation are shaped by some more encompassing world view. So they might claim that they are warranted in assuming that the players who inhabit their model see the world in ethnic terms rather than explaining how and why this came to pass. The crucial question here is how world views emerge and influence current beliefs. Here again Bates et al. formally represent possibilities in terms of probabilities and so reduce the impact of symbols on politics. They propose that the influence of any world view "can be re-conceptualized as a posterior probability of an antecedent process," so long as we recognize that this updating process is based not only on "objective experience" but also on "interpreted experience" (Bates et al. 1998, p. 634). In other words, players update their beliefs at least partially on the basis of interpretations advanced by others, who in turn are strategically motivated.

I set aside the question of whether, in speaking of social and political interaction, we can meaningfully distinguish objective from interpreted experience. I instead wish to make two related observations. First, it is important to appreciate that symbolic and cultural factors actually operate to configure or reconfigure the "priors" from which strategic actors, in light of their experience, update their beliefs. Both of the ways that game-theoretic models tacitly incorporate such factors illuminate how strategic actors aim to define a particular version of the past as relevant to current choice. Thus, when strategic actors seek to make one equilibrium salient among a set of available equilibria, thereby establishing a focal point, they participate in "the creation of traditions" (Schelling 1960, p. 106) in hopes of inducing others to interpret their current interaction as analogous to some purported precedent (Schelling 1960, p. 106; Johnson 2001; Calvert & Johnson 1999). Likewise, when political actors describe or seek to redescribe the range of possible types in a population, they are establishing the basis on which others condition their subsequent beliefs.

Second, the sort of conversion involved when world views—whether one's own or others'—are radically transformed is one variety of "unforeseen contingency" in that it represents "a set of circumstances that *ex ante* the parties to the transaction had not considered" (Kreps 1990a, pp. 116–17). Although the meaning of "unforeseen contingency" is subject to some dispute, it commonly is accepted that it is not merely some event or circumstance that an actor considers but to which she assigns a low or zero probability (Dekel et al. 1998, p. 524). There is "a fundamental difference between a situation in which a decision-maker is uncertain about the state of X and a situation in which the decision-maker has not given any thought to whether X matters or not, between a situation in which a prethought event judged of low probability occurs and a situation in which something occurs that has never been thought about, between judging an action unlikely to succeed and never thinking about an action" (Nelson & Winter 1982, p. 66). In each case, the latter situation would constitute a genuine surprise, an unforeseen contingency. And in those circumstances, "an 'uninformative statement'—such as 'event x might or might not happen'—can change the agent's decision" (Dekel et al. 1998, p. 524). Even such a vacuous statement would prompt social and political actors to consider an outcome they had not thought about at all. It would draw their attention to such an eventuality or invite them to imagine it and, in either case, prompt them to reassess what they heretofore deemed politically possible. In the case at hand, for instance, an uninformative statement could prompt Yugoslavs to entertain the possibility that for political purposes they should describe themselves and others in ethnic terms.

Bates et al. miss both of these points. They stumble over conceptual problems bequeathed to them by the interpretive theories from which they borrow. Because they never adequately resolve the interpretive dilemma, they ultimately reduce symbolic action, and hence culture, to strategic considerations. But their mistake is instructive. Once we understand that world view and rationality are reciprocally constraining, we can appreciate not only that "priors" are malleable but that they are altered for strategic purposes and in truly surprising ways. If game theory presupposes a closed universe, we might here confront a real limit on its scope because we may have identified "a factor that is intrinsically impossible to represent in a game theoretic model" (Myerson 1992, p. 66). But, at the same time, we have identified more precisely what is at stake at the intersection of culture and politics. It is at the many points where symbol and strategy intersect that political possibility is contested and defined. This, we now know, is what we need to explain.

CONCLUSION: THE PERILS OF PLURALISM

Pluralism in matters of theory and method is an extremely attractive position philosophically (Bohman 1991, Little 1991). One also might advocate it on more practical grounds (e.g., Munck 2001). And in this era of disciplinary *perestroika*, one might endorse it for political reasons too. Yet pluralism is a hazardous endeavor. As Laudan remarks (1977, p. 103),

> [I]t would be a serious error to assume that a scientist cannot consistently work in more than one research tradition. If these research traditions are inconsistent in their fundamentals, then the scientist who accepts them both raises serious doubts about his capacity for clear thinking. But there are times when two or more research traditions, far from mutually undermining one another, can be amalgamated, producing a synthesis which is progressive with respect to both the former research traditions.

This paper has aimed to show how important it is to attend to fundamentals in any pluralist undertaking. I think that efforts to integrate rational choice and interpretation can be progressive with respect to both traditions. Such integration might help rational choice theorists address matters of social and political indeterminacy, and it might help interpretative theorists address questions of agency and power. To date, however, these possibilities remain largely unredeemed because political scientists in both traditions have overlooked basic conceptual problems. As a result, our explanatory ambitions are hindered as well. But the demand that we carefully attend to conceptual problems has broader implications than those we can draw from the particular difficulties involved in efforts to integrate rational choice and interpretive theories. Indeed, those efforts illustrate the perils of theoretical pluralism more generally.

In the first place, once we place a premium on clearly specifying the mechanisms that inform our theories, the attraction of pluralism may in particular cases be diminished. For there often is tremendous value in pushing a fairly narrow theoretical or methodological perspective to what may seem extreme lengths. One need only think of Becker's (1986 [1976], p. 110) efforts to press his particular economic approach "relentlessly and unflinchingly" into all realms of human behavior. Likewise, one might think of Skocpol's (1979) macrohistorical structural account of social revolutions. At a minimum, such endeavors serve to illuminate the bounds of the domain where we might expect particular explanatory mechanisms to have purchase (e.g., Taylor 1988). Advocates of what Munck (2001, p. 203) calls "a pluralistic agenda" in political inquiry therefore must use care to avoid rhetorical excess. In particular, it is crucial not to presume that the converse of pluralism in methodological and theoretical matters is dogmatism—or at least to recognize that dogmatism can be a virtue.

Second, enhanced appreciation of the importance of conceptual problems compels us to be clear about which brand of pluralism we mean to defend. If we take conceptual problems seriously, not all interpretations of pluralism are defensible. [I borrow Bernstein's typology of pluralisms (1997, pp. 396–97).] We must avoid versions of pluralism that license extreme fragmentation in the discipline, for such a pluralism subverts both our ability and our willingness to engage with scholars whose approaches and concerns differ from our own. This in turn lays us open to external conceptual problems. We also must avoid "flabby" pluralisms that underwrite calls to eclecticism in the discipline. [Sil (2000) endorses eclecticism unabashedly and Munck (2001, p. 204) does so somewhat more circumspectly. Geertz (1973, p. 5) offers a sharp contrast.] For, in Bernstein's words, this temptation amounts to "little more than glib superficial poaching" without due attention to whether the approaches we seek to amalgamate are conceptually compatible, and if so, how. Likewise, we must avoid polemical pluralism, which willingly recognizes factors others deem important only to demonstrate that those factors are easily reduced to the approach that we ourselves already endorse. Finally, we must avoid the bland, patronizing pluralism that would have us tolerate alternative approaches only insofar as we presume that we have nothing to learn from them. Again we open ourselves to external conceptual problems. This stance in the end is equivalent to the dogmatism that pluralists claim to stand against.

None of these brands of pluralism takes alternative approaches seriously. None demands that we engage with their complex conceptual strengths and shortcomings. Such an engaged pluralism is hazardous. It may, as Bates et al. demonstrate, mean that efforts at theoretical integration, however well-intentioned and thoughtful, fall short. It may also compel us to recognize the deficiencies and limits not only of other theories but of our own as well. It occasionally may convince us that we are wrong, or even that our preferred theory is so misguided or poorly formulated that we should abandon it. An observable increase in any of these consequences would constitute theoretical progress in a discipline where it is sorely lacking.

ACKNOWLEDGMENTS

I presented an earlier, quite different version of this paper to the Third Annual St. Louis Philosophy of Social Science Roundtable, Washington University. I subsequently presented a considerably revised version to the Department of Political Science, Washington University. I thank members of both audiences for their reactions. I also thank Robert Bates, Jack Knight, and David Laitin for more detailed comments. I am especially grateful to Margaret Levi for her very helpful comments and forbearance.

The *Annual Review of Political Science* is online at http://polisci.annualreviews.org

LITERATURE CITED

Akerlof G, Kranton R. 2000. Economics and identity. *Q. J. Econ.* CXV:715–53

Allio A, Dobek M, Mikhailov N, Weimer D. 1997. Post-communist privatization as a test of theories of institutional change. In *The Political Economy of Property Rights*, ed. D Weimer, pp. 319–48. Cambridge, UK: Cambridge Univ. Press

Austen-Smith D, Banks J. 1998. Social choice theory, game theory, and positive political theory. *Annu. Rev. Polit. Sci.* 1:259–87

Ball T. 1987. Is there progress in political science? In *Idioms of Inquiry*, ed. T Ball, pp. 13–44. Albany: State Univ. NY Press

Barth F. 1993. *Balinese Worlds*. Chicago: Univ. Chicago Press

Bates R. 1990. Macropolitical economy in the field of development. In *Perspectives in Positive Political Economy*, ed. J Alt, K Shepsle, pp. 31–54. Cambridge, UK: Cambridge Univ. Press

Bates R, de Figueiredo R, Weingast B. 1998. The politics of interpretation (corrected version). *Polit. Soc.* 26:603–42

Becker G. 1986 (1976). The economic approach to human behavior. In *Rational Choice*, ed. J Elster, pp. 108–22. New York: NY Univ. Press

Bernstein R. 1997. Pragmatism, pluralism and the healing of wounds. In *Pragmatism*, ed. L Menand, pp. 382–401. New York: Vintage

Binder S, Smith S. 1998. Political goals and procedural choice in the senate. *J. Polit.* 60:396–416

Binmore K. 1990. *Essays on the Foundations of Game Theory*. Oxford, UK: Blackwell

Bohman J. 1991. *New Philosophy of Social Science*. Cambridge, MA: MIT Press

Boudon R. 1986. *Theories of Social Change*. Berkeley: Univ. Calif. Press

Brady H. 1995. Doing good and doing better. *Polit. Methodol.* 6:11–19

Calvert R. 1992. Leadership and its basis in problems of social coordination. *Int. Polit. Sci. Rev.* 13:7–24

Calvert R. 1995a. The rational choice theory of social institutions: cooperation, coordination, and communication. In *Modern Political Economy*, ed. J Banks, E Hanushek, pp. 216–67. Cambridge, UK: Cambridge Univ. Press

Calvert R. 1995b. Rational actors, equilibrium, and social institutions. In *Explaining Social Institutions*, ed. J Knight, I Sened, pp. 57–93. Ann Arbor: Univ. Mich. Press

Calvert R, Johnson J. 1999. Interpretation and coordination in constitutional politics. In *Lessons in Democracy*, ed. E Hauser, J Wasilewski, pp. 99–138. Krakow: Jagiellonian Univ. Press

Chwe M. 2001. *Rational Ritual*. Princeton, NJ: Princeton Univ. Press

Cohen A. 1985. *The Symbolic Construction of Community*. London: Havistock

de Figueiredo R, Weingast B. 1999. The rationality of fear. In *Civil Wars, Insecurity and Intervention*, ed. B Walter, J Snyder, pp. 261–302. New York: Columbia Univ. Press

Dekel E, Lipman B, Rustichini A. 1998. Recent developments in modeling unforeseen contingencies. *Eur. Econ. Rev.* 42:523–42

The Economist. 1996. The man in the Bagdad Café. Nov. 9:23–26

Elster J. 1986. The nature and scope of rational choice explanation. In *Actions and Events*, ed. E LePore, B McLaughlin, pp. 60–72. Oxford, UK: Blackwell

Elster J. 1989a. *Nuts and Bolts for the Social Sciences*. Cambridge, UK: Cambridge Univ. Press

Elster J. 1989b. *The Cement of Society*. Cambridge, UK: Cambridge Univ. Press

Elster J. 1993. *Political Psychology*. Cambridge, UK: Cambridge Univ. Press

Elster J. 1999. *Alchemies of the Mind: Rationality and the Emotions*. Cambridge, UK: Cambridge Univ. Press

Fearon J, Laitin D. 1996. Explaining interethnic cooperation. *Am. Polit. Sci. Rev.* 90:715–35

Ferejohn J. 1991. Rationality and interpretation. In *The Economic Approach to Politics*, ed. K Monroe, pp. 279–305. New York: Harper Collins

Fudenberg D, Tirole J. 1991. *Game Theory.* Cambridge, MA: MIT Press

Geertz G. 1968. *Islam Observed.* Chicago: Univ. Chicago Press

Geertz G. 1973. *The Interpretation of Cultures.* New York: Basic Books

Geertz G. 1983. *Local Knowledge.* New York: Basic Books

Gellner E. 1988. *Plough, Sword and Book.* Chicago: Univ. Chicago Press

Gellner E. 1995. *Anthropology and Politics.* Oxford, UK: Blackwell

Gibbons R. 1992. *Game Theory for Applied Economists.* Princeton, NJ: Princeton Univ. Press

Green D, Shapiro I. 1994. *Pathologies of Rational Choice Theory.* New Haven, CT: Yale Univ. Press

Greif A. 1994. Cultural beliefs and the organization of society. *J. Polit. Econ.* 102:912–50

Harsanyi J. 1986 (1977). Advances in understanding rational behavior. In *Rational Choice*, ed. J Elster, pp. 82–107. New York: NY Univ. Press

Hausman D. 1995. Rational choice and social theory: a comment. *J. Philos.* 92:96–102

Hedström P, Swedberg R, eds. 1998. *Social Mechanisms.* Cambridge, UK: Cambridge Univ. Press

Hoover K. 1990. The logic of causal inference. *Econ. Philos.* 6:207–34

Johnson J. 1996. How not to criticize rational choice theory: the pathologies of 'commonsense'. *Philos. Soc. Sci.* 26:77–91

Johnson J. 1997. Symbol *and* strategy in comparative political analysis. *APSA-CP: Newsl. APSA Org. Sec. Comp. Polit.* Summer:6–9

Johnson J. 2000. Why respect culture? *Am. J. Polit. Sci.* 44:405–18

Johnson J. 2001. Inventing constitutional traditions: the poverty of fatalism. In *Constitutional Culture and Democratic Rule*, ed. J Ferejohn, J Rakove, J Riley, pp. 71–109. Cambridge, UK: Cambridge Univ. Press

Johnson J. 2002. Conceptual problems as obstacles to theoretical progress in political science: political culture among the 'sociologists'. *Philos. Soc. Sci.* In press

Kertzer D. 1988. *Ritual, Politics and Power.* New Haven, CT: Yale Univ. Press

Kertzer D. 1996. *Politics and Symbols.* New Haven, CT: Yale Univ. Press

King G, Keohane R, Verba S. 1994. *Designing Social Inquiry.* Princeton, NJ: Princeton Univ. Press

Knight J. 1992. *Institutions and Social Conflict.* Cambridge, UK: Cambridge Univ. Press

Knight J. 1995. Models, interpretations and theories: constructing explanations of institutional emergence and change. In *Explaining Social Institutions*, ed. J Knight, I Sened, pp. 95–119. Ann Arbor: Univ. Mich. Press

Knight J, North D. 1997. Explaining the complexity of institutional change. In *The Political Economy of Property Rights*, ed. D. Weimer, pp. 349–54. Cambridge, UK: Cambridge Univ. Press

Kreps D. 1990a. Corporate culture and economic theory. In *Perspectives on Positive Political Economy*, ed. J Alt, K Shepsle, pp. 90–143. Cambridge, UK: Cambridge Univ. Press

Kreps D. 1990b. *Game Theory and Economic Modeling.* Oxford, UK: Oxford Univ. Press

Kuper A. 1999. *Culture: The Anthropologists' Account.* Cambridge, MA: Harvard Univ. Press

Laitin D. 1986. *Hegemony and Culture.* Chicago: Univ. Chicago Press

Laitin D. 1995. Disciplining political science. *Am. Polit. Sci. Rev.* 89:454–56

Lalman D, Oppenheimer J, Swistak P. 1993. Formal rational choice theory: a cumulative science of politics. In *Political Science: The State of the Discipline, II*, ed. A Finifter, pp. 77–104. Washington, DC: Am. Polit. Sci. Assoc.

Laudan L. 1977. *Progress and Its Problems.* Berkeley: Univ. Calif. Press

Laudan L. 1988. Conceptual problems revisited. *Stud. Hist. Philos. Sci.* 19:531–34

Laudan L. 1990. *Science and Relativism.* Chicago: Univ. Chicago Press

Laudan L. 1996. *Beyond Positivism and Relativism.* Boulder, CO: Westview

Little D. 1991. *Varieties of Social Explanation.* Boulder, CO: Westview

Little D. 1993. On the scope and limits of generalizations in the social sciences. *Synthese* 97:183–207

Lukes S. 1977. *Essays in Social Theory.* New York: Columbia Univ. Press

McLean I. 1991. Rational choice and politics. *Polit. Stud.* 39:486–512

Moore S, Myerhoff B. 1977. Introduction. In *Secular Ritual,* ed. S Moore, B Myerhoff. Amsterdam: Van Gorcum

Morrow J. 1994. *Game Theory for Political Scientists.* Princeton, NJ: Princeton Univ. Press

Munck G. 2001. Game theory and comparative politics. *World Polit.* 53:173–204

Myerson R. 1991. *Game Theory.* Cambridge, MA: Harvard Univ. Press

Myerson R. 1992. On the value of game theory in social science. *Rationality Soc.* 4:62–73

Nelson R, Winter S. 1982. *An Evolutionary Theory of Economic Change.* Cambridge, MA: Harvard Univ. Press

North D. 1990. *Institutions, Institutional Change and Economic Performance.* Cambridge, UK: Cambridge Univ. Press

Nozick R. 1993. *The Nature of Rationality.* Princeton, NJ: Princeton Univ. Press

Ortner S. 1984. Theory in anthropology since the sixties. *Comp. Stud. Soc. Hist.* 26:126–66

Ortner S. 1990. Patterns of history. In *Culture Through Time,* ed. E Ohnuki-Tierney, pp. 57–93. Stanford, CA: Stanford Univ. Press

Ortner S, ed. 1999. *The Fate of Culture.* Berkeley: Univ. Calif. Press

Petersen R. 1999. Mechanisms and structures in comparison. In *Critical Comparisons in Politics and Culture,* ed. J Bowen, R Petersen, pp.

61–77. Cambridge, UK: Cambridge Univ. Press

Popkin S. 1979. *The Rational Peasant.* Berkeley: Univ. Calif. Press

Rorty A. 1983. Imagination and power. *Soc. Sci. Info.* 22:801–16

Rorty A. 1985. Varieties of rationality, varieties of emotion. *Soc. Sci. Info.* 24:343–53

Satz D, Ferejohn J. 1994. Rational choice and social theory. *J. Philos.* 91:71–87

Schelling T. 1960. *The Strategy of Conflict.* Cambridge, MA: Harvard Univ. Press

Schuessler A. 2001. *A Logic of Expressive Choice.* Princeton, NJ: Princeton Univ. Press

Shapiro I. 1998. Can the rational choice framework cope with culture? *PS: Polit. Sci. Polit.* 31:40–42

Sil R. 2000. The foundations of eclecticism. *J. Theor. Polit.* 12:353–87

Skocpol T. 1979. *States and Social Revolutions.* Cambridge, UK: Cambridge Univ. Press

Stinchcombe A. 1991. The conditions of fruitfulness of theorizing about mechanisms in social science. *Philos. Soc. Sci.* 21:367–88

Swidler A. 1986. Culture in action: symbols and strategies. *Am. Soc. Rev.* 51:273–86

Swidler A. 1996. Geertz's ambiguous legacy. *Cont. Soc.* 25:299–302

Taylor C. 1985. *Philosophy and the Human Sciences.* Cambridge, UK: Cambridge Univ. Press

Taylor M. 1988. Rationality and revolutionary collective action. In *Rationality and Revolution,* ed. M Taylor, pp. 63–97. Cambridge, UK: Cambridge Univ. Press

Tilly C. 2001. Mechanisms in political processes. *Annu. Rev. Polit. Sci.* 4:21–41

Tsebelis G. 1990. *Nested Games.* Berkeley: Univ. Calif. Press

Verdery K. 1999. *The Political Lives of Dead Bodies.* New York: Columbia Univ. Press

Weingast B. 1998. Constructing trust: the politics and economics of ethnic and regional conflict. In *Institutions and Social Order,* ed. K Soltan, E Uslaner, V Haufler, pp. 163–200. Ann Arbor: Univ. Mich. Press

Annu. Rev. Polit. Sci. 2002. 5:249–69
DOI: 10.1146/annurev.polisci.5.111201.115816
Copyright © 2002 by Annual Reviews. All rights reserved

THE NEWS MEDIA AS POLITICAL INSTITUTIONS

Michael Schudson

*Department of Communication, University of California, San Diego, La Jolla,
California 92093-0503; e-mail: mschudson@ucsd.edu*

Key Words   political economy, culture, social organization, government sources,
bias

■ **Abstract**   Political science has tended to neglect the study of the news media
as political institutions, despite a long history of party-subsidized newspapers and
despite a growing chorus of scholars who point to an increasing "mediatization" of
politics. Still, investigators in sociology, communication, and political science have
taken up the close study of news institutions. Three general approaches predominate.
Political economy perspectives focus on patterns of media ownership and the behavior
of news institutions in relatively liberal versus relatively repressive states; a second set
of approaches looks at the social organization of newswork and relates news content to
the daily patterns of interaction of reporters and their sources; a third style of research
examines news as a form of culture that often unconsciously incorporates general belief
systems, assumptions, and values into news writing.

INTRODUCTION[1]

Political science has never extended to the news media the lovingly detailed attention it has lavished on legislatures, parties, presidents, and prime ministers.
Journalism is a constituent of political life that political science for the most part
has neglected. This is not to overlook a number of attempts to nominate the media
as an institution worthy of study. The classic effort is Lippmann's *Public Opinion* (1922). For all its brilliance, however, this work focuses more on the social
and psychological implications of mediated experience for public apprehension of
reality than on specifically political implications of news organizations for governing. Decades later, Cater labeled the news media a political institution in the title
of his book, *The Fourth Branch of Government* (1959). Even so, the provocative
title was a loose metaphor to call attention to the media's influence rather than a
blueprint for examining news as a component of the governmental process. Cook's
Governing With The News (1998) meant to correct this; Cook aims to provide a
framework for thinking about the ways in which news organizations operate as
political actors. His insistence that journalism is a political actor is persuasive,

---

[1]This article is original to this volume but draws substantially on Schudson (2000).

but his work has not provided clear direction for a research program or a set of questions to follow up his general claim.

In recent years, more students of politics have turned to the study of news, convinced that the media are an increasingly important and autonomous force in politics, independent of political parties. Such scholars are impressed, as well, that parties, politicians, and pressure groups develop sophisticated strategies regarding the media and devote increasing resources to them. There has been, as Blumler & Kavanagh write (1999, p. 214), a "professionalization of political publicity." This is what turned Cook to the topic of political communication, since he found in his first book that congressional law making, once an "inside game," became by the 1970s and 1980s a process in which publicity was a strategic weapon and making news "a crucial component of making laws" (1989, p. 168). Mazzoleni (1995, p. 308) has called this development in Italy a "Copernican revolution" in political communication—"yesterday everything circled around the parties, today everything circles around, and in the space of, the media." At its best, this "mediatization" of politics is one in which journalism is "capable of standing as spokesperson for civil society, of challenging political arrogance and political roguery," but media institutions—unlike parties, whose weakening hold on popular loyalties has afforded new space for media aggrandizement—are not accountable to the public (Mazzoleni 1995, pp. 309, 315; Mazzoleni & Schulz 1999). Popular thinkers have been especially concerned that mediatization has corrupted political life, civic commitment, or political discourse.

News institutions have long been closely connected with politics. In nineteenth-century states with representative political systems, parties typically controlled the press. A newspaper either directly served as the voice of a party or relied for economic survival on the legal advertising and government printing contracts of local, state, and federal governments when the right party took power. This was the "subsidized press," in Cook's words (1998). Today, the media in some nations are state-controlled or state-directed, self-conscious organs of propaganda, but in Europe, the United States, Japan, and elsewhere, media organizations are formally (and in most respects actually) independent of the state. What kind of organizations are they, and how do they work as a political institution?

Academic consideration of the production of news goes back at least to Weber (1946 [1921]), who wrote of the social standing of the journalist as a political person; Park (1922, 1923), an ex-journalist himself, who wrote about the U.S. immigrant press and news itself as a form of knowledge; Lippmann's extended discussion of journalism in *Public Opinion* (1922); and Hughes' (1940) early study of human interest stories. Formal study of how news organizations produce news products dates to "gatekeeper" studies in the 1950s. Several studies demonstrated that editors who select wire service stories for their newspapers do so in ways that do not mirror the whole array of stories before them but select according to individual prejudice (White 1950) or bureaucratic newsroom routines (Gieber 1964). This kind of work was preface to much more systematic empirical work in the 1960s and 1970s in both political science and sociology.

Generally speaking, social scientists who examine the news-making process have employed three different, if sometimes overlapping, perspectives. The first is the view of political economy or macro-sociology, which relates the outcome of the news process to the structure of the state and the economy and to the economic foundation of the news organization.

The second approach comes primarily out of sociology, especially the study of social organization, occupations, and professions, even though several of the landmark works in this area (Cohen 1963, Epstein 1973, Sigal 1973) have been by political scientists. This perspective typically tries to understand how journalists' efforts are constrained by organizational and occupational demands.

Third, a cultural approach emphasizes the constraining force of broad cultural traditions and symbolic systems, regardless of the structure of economic organization or the character of occupational routines.

All three of these approaches recognize (or, at any rate, should recognize) that news is a form of culture. It is a structured genre or set of genres of public meaning-making. But this is not to suggest that it floats in a symbolic ether. It is a material product and there are political, economic, social, and cultural dimensions to understanding its production, distribution, and appropriation by audiences (Garnham 1990, p. 10). Perhaps most important with respect to government, news gathering is generally an interinstitutional collaboration between political reporters and the public figures they cover. Officials or their media advisers and spokespeople are themselves parajournalists, seeking to prompt journalists to provide favorable coverage.

Each approach to studying news organizations seeks to understand and explain media content. The assumption is that media content matters and is to some degree an independent influence on the world, either through affecting public opinion (this is the most common assumption) or through playing a role in the internal rough and tumble of political insiders. The position of Cook and Mazzoleni, cited above, as well as Kernell (1986) and others, is that the game of politics is increasingly played in the public eye, not behind closed doors. Factors that contribute to mediatization include changes in political institutions that have given the public a greater role in decision making (such as primary elections rather than party caucuses, or public hearings rather than closed sessions to confirm presidential appointments); the weakening of political parties; and the availability and aggressiveness of media organizations themselves. Whatever the causes, the result is that effective politicians must learn to master the arts of media publicity.

THE POLITICAL ECONOMY OF NEWS

The link between ownership of news organizations and the character of news coverage is not easy to determine—and it grows more difficult by the day as public and commercial systems of ownership mix and blend and intersect in a growing variety of ways (Noam 1991). In Europe, it is not clear that public and private broadcasters differ systematically in the ways they present political news and current affairs (Brants 1998, p. 328). Research on the impact on news content of chain ownership compared with independent ownership of American newspapers has been either inconclusive (Demers 1996) or, as Baker puts it (1994, p. 19), "tepid, hardly motivating any strong critique of chain ownership or prompting any significant policy interventions."

Some scholars write as if corporate ownership and commercial organizations necessarily compromise the democratic promise of public communication (McChesney 1997), but the evidence is closer to suggesting that the absence of commercial organizations, or their total domination by the state, is the worst-case scenario. In Latin America, for instance, government officials benefited more from state-controlled media than did the public; for Latin American policy makers in the recent wave of democratization, "strong control, censorship, and manipulation of the mass media during authoritarian and democratic regimes have deeply discredited statist models" (Waisbord 1995, p. 219).

Not that market-dominated systems and state-dominated systems are easy to distinguish these days. Zhao (1998) offers a detailed and persuasive account of the blending of commercial and propagandistic objectives in state-controlled media in post–Tiananmen Square China. After Tiananmen Square, the government tightened controls on the media, closed down three leading publications whose coverage it judged too sympathetic to the protesters, replaced editors at other newspapers, and required all news organizations to engage in self-criticism. The state continues to monitor political news but pays less attention to coverage of economic, social, and environmental issues. In all cases, self-censorship rather than heavy-handed party control is the operating system (Polumbaum 1997).

Despite the tightening of party control, rapid commercialization of the popular press has continued, and there has been a proliferation of sensational, entertainment-oriented tabloids that compete with the established press for advertising revenue. Media outlets in the commercial sector remain political organs, catering to the Communist Party's propaganda needs, but they try to "establish a common ground between the Party and the people" by covering popular topics (Zhao 1998, p. 161). The audience for commercial media has grown rapidly at the expense of traditional Party organs. In response, even Central China Television, the most influential station in the country, has tried new news formats that test the limits of orthodoxy to please the public. "Focus," an innovative program begun in 1994, has raised critical issues, has spoken on behalf of the poor, and has investigated corruption in both business and government. Still, the department that produces it aims to make all the journalists share the same perspective and refrain from airing any segment that could induce political instability. The journalists are "dancing with chains on" (Zhao 1998, p. 121).

In the United States, fewer and fewer corporations control more and more of the news media (Bagdikian 1989). Major media conglomerates control more and more of the world's media. Where media are not controlled by corporations, they are generally voices of the state. Dominant media, whether commercial or state-sponsored, typically reinforce political understandings that reinforce the views of political elites. What matters is how unified are the views of these political insiders (Hallin 1986), how open to dissent is the political culture and the legal and constitutional order, and how great a range of opinion is represented by leading political parties.

With too rigid a view of the control of news by powerful elites, much of the media's output, and for that matter much of recent world history, cannot be understood. Herman & Chomsky's *Manufacturing Consent* (1988, p. xi) holds that the media "serve to mobilize support for the special interests that dominate the state and private activity" and that the propagandistic role of the American press is not in any essential way different from the role *Pravda* played in the Soviet Union. This flat-footed functionalism makes many of the most dramatic changes in the media in the past half century inexplicable. A view that sees large corporations and the media working hand-in-glove to stifle dissent or promote a lethargic public acceptance of the existing distribution of power cannot explain why corporations in the early 1970s were so incensed by the U.S. media coverage of politics, the environment, and business (Dreier 1982).

Functionalism can explain, of course, how the culture industry keeps progressive social change from happening and so why Eastern Europe is ruled today by the Communist Party, why women in western democracies do not hold office, why African-Americans in the United States failed to win civil rights, why no coverage of gays and lesbians can be found in the news media, and why Thatcher rules in Britain, Franco in Spain, and Nixon in the United States. In short, functionalist explanations explain far too much.

The question is what role the media play in social change. The behavior of the American press in questioning the Vietnam War may have emerged precisely because the political elites did not know their own mind. They were deeply divided. Even then, the press seems largely to have gone about its normal business of citing official leaders—but at a time when officials were at odds with one another (Hallin 1986). The result was that the media did not reinforce existing power but amplified elite disagreements in unsettling and unpredictable ways.

Both state and market limit free expression, but this does not make the comprehensiveness and severity of means employed, the coherence of motives involved, or the consequences of controls enacted just the same. Public criticism of state policy is invariably easier in liberal societies with privately owned news outlets than in authoritarian societies with either state or private ownership. In China, published criticism of the state has been tightly constrained; reporters have some freedom to write articles critical of high officials, but they must circulate these as internal documents not available in the public press (Grant 1988).

Within market societies, there are various institutional forms and constitutional regimes for the press. De Mateo's (1989) sketch of the newspaper industry in Spain during the Franco regime, the transition to democracy, and the full restoration of democracy makes it clear that private, profit-making newspapers made ideological purity their first priority under Franco. After Franco, however, the same private, profit-making press has emphasized profits first while providing more opportunity for freedom of expression. This suggests that forms of ownership do not predict as much about news content as the forms of government within which the media operate. The political economy of news neglects the political in favor of the economic at its peril. Whereas state-operated media in authoritarian political systems serve directly as agents of state social control, both public and privately owned media in liberal societies carry out a wider variety of roles, cheerleading the established order, alarming the citizenry about flaws in that order, providing a civic forum for political debate, and serving as a battleground among contesting elites.

The distinction between "market" and "state" organization of media, or between commercial and public forms of broadcasting, masks important differences within each category. For instance, because of the First Amendment tradition, government intervention in the news media is more inhibited in the United States than in European democracies. In Norway, Sweden, France, and Austria, government for several decades has subsidized newspapers directly, especially to strengthen newspapers that offer substantial political information but receive low advertising revenues. These policies have sought to stop the decline in the number of newspapers and so to increase public access to a diversity of political viewpoints. There is no indication that the subsidized newspapers are more likely to withhold criticism of the government than other newspapers; in fact, one Norwegian study indicates just the opposite (Skogerbo 1997, Murschetz 1998).

Consider another domain of variation that has become increasingly salient: How should the news media cover the private behavior of public officials? There is great concern, particularly in Britain and the United States, that commercial motives have led to media preoccupation with pudenda rather than politics. Yet this depends greatly on legal and cultural conditions. Coverage of the sexual behavior of politicians and other celebrities barely exists in Germany; German civil law gives much greater protection to privacy than Anglo-American law (Esser 1999).

Both scholars and critics, including critics in or close to the news business itself, view recent technological and market changes with alarm. When a "new news" responds to corporate concerns and technological imperatives, the ethics of professional journalism seems under ever-growing assault (Kalb 1998). The anecdotal evidence here is sobering, but the baseline of comparison is feebly depicted. The worst incidences of contemporary journalism are compared to the remembered best of another era; there is a need for more careful comparison and more broadly conceived research frameworks. It is very likely that some of the worst instances of contemporary journalism are made possible by some of the same forces—particularly the force of semi-independent professionalism and a declining deference to authority in public culture—that create the best (Schudson 1999). There is now a growing countercurrent to the most common complaints, a sense that a more aggressive, feisty, irreverent, and quasipopulist media has as many virtues as vices (McNair 2000).

THE SOCIAL ORGANIZATION OF NEWSWORK

Journalists operate within constraints—among them the constraint of having to write "accurately" about objectively real occurrences in the world, whoever planned them and however they came to the media's notice. The reality-constructing practices of the powerful will fail (in the long run) if they ride roughshod over the world "out there."

Still, the basic orientation of social scientists is that political news making is a reality-constructing activity that follows the lead of government officials. Sociologist Mark Fishman's study of a mid-sized California newspaper concluded that journalists are highly attuned to bureaucratic organizations of government and that "the world is bureaucratically organized for journalists" (1980, p. 51). That is, the organization of "beats" is such that reporters get the largest share of their news from official government agencies. For the journalist, one great advantage of dealing with bureaucracies is that they provide a reliable and steady supply of the raw materials for news production.

One study after another, whether at the national or local level, comes up with essentially the same observation: Journalism, on a day-to-day basis, is the story of the interaction of reporters and government officials, both politicians and bureaucrats. Most analysts agree that officials have the upper hand (Cohen 1963, p. 267; Gans 1979, p. 116; Schlesinger & Tumber 1994). Government officials themselves do not necessarily see it this way, but there is little doubt that the center of news generation is the link between reporter and official, the interaction of the representatives of news bureaucracies and government bureaucracies.

"News," as Sigal put it (1986, p. 25), "is not what happens, but what someone says has happened or will happen." To understand news, we must understand who the "someones" are who act as sources, and how journalists deal with them.

Most often, the someones are government officials, whether police officers or politicians. They are informed. Their information is judged to be authoritative and their opinions legitimate. And they are eager to satisfy the cravings of the news organizations. They make information available on a regular basis in a form that the media can easily digest. As a Brazilian editor remarked (in Waisbord 2000, p. 95), "All of us have been educated professionally according to the idea that the government is the main source of information, that everything that happens with it is important. . . . That's the journalistic law of the least effort. It's faster and easier to practice journalism based in the world of government than putting emphasis on what's happening in society." Studies of media that see the process of news production beginning in the newsroom—rather than in the halls of power—have rightly been criticized as "too media-centric" (Schlesinger 1990). It is the rare study that has examined news production from the viewpoint of the news source rather than the news organization (Cook 1989, Ericson et al. 1989). When scholars look at the media from the viewpoint of politicians, they are likely to see news coverage as one among several tools in the politician's knapsack for advancing policies, legislation, and career. Regarding election and reelection, national politicians in the United States court local media assiduously but can remain invisible in the national media at little or no cost (Loomis 1988).

Among government sources, routine government sources matter most. That is, most news comes to the news media through scheduled, government-initiated events such as press releases, public speeches, public legislative hearings or deliberations, press conferences, and background briefings for the press. In the 1950s and 1960s, nearly 60% of news channels in foreign and national news in the *New York Times* and the *Washington Post* were routine, only 26% percent "enterprise"—that is, depending on the initiative of the reporters to conduct an interview or otherwise seek out information that did not come to them on a silver platter. However, during subsequent decades and especially during the Vietnam War years, as disagreement and dissent within the government grew more intense and more articulate and as journalists grew more distrustful of government veracity, there was a measurable shift toward enterprise reporting (Sigal 1973).

In some countries, reporter-official relations are far more routinized than in the United States. The most famous case is that of the Japanese Kisha clubs. These clubs of reporters, which date to early in the twentieth century, are maintained by the news organizations that provide their membership. They are formal associations of reporters from different media outlets assigned to a particular ministry and granted privileged—but highly controlled—access to the minister and other high officials. Because most clubs are connected to government agencies, news takes on an official cast. The daily association of reporters at the clubs contributes to a uniformity in the news pages; reporters are constrained by what is described as a "phobia" about not writing what all the other reporters write (Feldman 1993, Freeman 2000, Krauss 2000).

At the other extreme, consider foreign affairs journalists in the Netherlands.

> They do not pound the halls and knock on doors in the Foreign Ministry, as American journalists do. Rather, they work for the most part at home, reading, thinking, perhaps phoning an official whom they know, writing if the muse visits, and not writing if she does not. Since their output is personal and thus explicitly subjective, there is little basis among them for the competitive spirit that animates American coverage of foreign-affairs news and that results in a convergence of judgment of what that "news" is (Cohen 1995, p. 109).

In fact, the independence of these correspondents is so striking that those Cohen interviewed did not have much interaction with one another, did not generally know one another, and seemed generally ignorant of or indifferent to the work styles of their nominal peers (Cohen 1995).

In the United States, conditions that tend toward Kisha-like group journalism are derisively labeled "pack journalism," a term invented by Crouse (1973) in his study of news coverage of the 1972 presidential campaign. Pack journalism happens most when journalists literally travel in packs, as they do in covering the White House or in covering a presidential campaign. In these cases, a single significant source brings the press together and commands their constant attention. This very fact creates a new relationship—not only of journalist to source but of journalist to the corps of reporters. The traveling corps of reporters becomes a set of companions, even comrades, sharing a long, intense, emotional experience (White 1961, pp. 365–66).

Reliance on government officials does not guarantee pro-government news. As sociologist Silvio Waisbord writes (2000, p. 94), "Official wrongdoing is another form of official news and, as such, is more likely than other forms of wrongdoing to become the subject of journalistic investigations." It is difficult to muckrake the government without the government's cooperation. Journalists may have rumors, leads, leaks, near-certain knowledge of a government misdeed, but normally they cannot go to print within the conventions of the craft without getting confirmation from a well-placed figure. Government officials who serve as sources, whether they are promoting the government's position or are lobbying for alternative positions and seeking to discredit their superiors, use the press to their own advantage. In Latin American journalism, the practice of one insider using the press to spread scandal about another insider even has a name—*denuncismo*. From the reporters' perspective, this is simply quick and dirty journalism; from the sources' perspective, it is a form of ventriloquism by which they try to dictate the news and advance their own interests through a reporter (Waisbord 2000, p. 108).

The capacity of journalists to write critically about government even when government is their primary source of information has grown in recent decades as the news media adopt a more professional and critical style and as commercial incentives for the shocking weigh against interpersonal pressures for collegial and congenial reporting. In the United States, campaign coverage of both Democratic and Republican contenders in newspapers, news magazines, and television was significantly more negative in the 1980s and 1990s than it had been in 1960 (Patterson 1993).

A corollary to the power of the government source or other well-legitimated sources is that "resource-poor organizations" have great difficulty in getting the media's attention (Goldenberg 1975). If they are to be covered, as Gitlin's (1980) study of American antiwar activities in the 1960s indicated, they must adjust to modes of organizational interaction more like those of established organizations.

The significance of studies of reporter/source interaction lies not only in detailing the dynamics of news production but in evaluating the power of media institutions as such. Media power looms large if the portrait of the world the media present to audiences stems from the preferences and perceptions of publishers, editors, and reporters unconstrained by democratic controls. However, if the media typically mirror the views and voices of established (and democratically selected) government officials, then the media are more nearly the neutral servants of a democratic order. Policy experts widely attacked American television news for forcing U.S. military intervention in Somalia in 1992 by showing graphic scenes of starving people. But later research showed that the networks picked up the

Somalia story only after seven senators, a House committee, the full House, the full Senate, a presidential candidate, and the White House all publicly raised the issue. When the networks got to it, they framed it very much as Washington's political elites had framed it for them (Mermin 1997, p. 397). This does not mean the television stories made no difference; clearly they rallied public interest and public support for intervention. But where did the television story come from? From established, official sources.

The finding that official sources dominate the news is often presented as a criticism of the media. If the media were to fulfill their democratic role, they would offer citizens a wide variety of opinions and perspectives, not just the narrow spectrum represented by those who have attained political power. But there is an alternate view also consistent with democratic theory. Perhaps the best to hope for in a mass democracy is that people will evaluate leaders, not policies. Perhaps asking the press to offer enough information, history, and context for attentive citizens to make wise decisions on policies before politicians act is asking the impossible. It may be a more plausible task for the media, consistent with representative democracy, that citizens assess leaders after they have acted (Zaller 1994).

There has been more attention to reporter-official relations than to reporter-editor relations, despite some suggestive early work on the ways in which reporters engage in self-censorship when they have an eye fixed on pleasing an editor (Breed 1955). Case studies of newswork regularly note the effects—usually baleful—of editorial intervention (Crouse 1973, p. 186; Gitlin 1980, p. 64–65; Mortensen & Svendsen 1980; Hallin 1986, p. 22). Generally, however, studies do not look at the social relations of newswork from the editor's desk.

Most research, then, has focused on the gathering of news rather than on its writing, rewriting, and "play" in the press. Some research suggests that the play of a story may matter a lot. Hallin (1986), Herman & Chomsky (1988), and Lipstadt (1986) all argue that in the press of a liberal society such as the United States, a great deal of news, including dissenting or adversarial information and opinion, gets into the newspaper. The question is where that information appears and how it is inflected. Hallin (1986, p. 78) suggests there was a "reverse inverted pyramid" of news in much reporting of the Vietnam War. The nearer the information was to the truth, the farther down in the story it appeared.

If more work develops on the relations of reporters and editors inside the newsroom, it will profit from the comparative studies initiated by Donsbach and Patterson (Donsbach 1995) or the careful British-German comparison conducted by Esser (1998). Esser shows that whereas there are many job designations in a British newsroom, all personnel in a German newsroom are *Redakteurs*, editors or desk workers, who combine the tasks of reporting, copyediting, editorial or leader writing, and commentary. Whereas in a British or American newspaper editors read and edit the work of reporters, what a *Redakteur* writes goes into print without any supervision. Different historical traditions have led to different divisions of labor and different understandings of the possibility and desirability of separating facts from commentary, with British and American journalism representing the most vigorously fact-centered form of journalism (Chalaby 1996).

If, on the one hand, the creation of news is seen as the social production of "reality," on the other hand it is taken to be the social manufacture of an organizational product, one that can be studied like other manufactured goods. This latter point of view is evident, for instance, in Epstein's pioneering study (1973) that grew out of James Q. Wilson's political science seminar at Harvard on organizational theory. The working assumption of that seminar was that members of an organization "modified their own personal values in accordance with the requisites of the organization" (Epstein 1973, p. xiv). One should therefore study organizations, not individuals, to analyze their output—in this case, news. Epstein's study, based on fieldwork at national network news programs in 1968 and 1969, emphasized organizational, economic, and technical requirements of television news production in explaining the news product.

Some American scholars have insisted that professional values are no bulwark against a bias in news that emerges from the social backgrounds and personal values of media personnel. Lichter et al. (1986) made the case that news in the United States has a liberal bias because journalists at elite news organizations are themselves liberal. Their survey of these journalists finds that many describe themselves as liberals and tend to vote Democratic. [A 1992 national sample of journalists also finds them more liberal and more Democratic than the adult population as a whole, but not as liberal or Democratic as elite journalists in the Lichter survey (see Weaver & Wilhoit 1996).] This is a moderate liberalism, at most, and only within the peculiar American political spectrum. The group is more socially liberal (53% say adultery is not wrong) than economically liberal (only 13% think government should own big corporations). American elite journalists fully accept the framework of capitalism, although they wish for it a human face.

The approach of Lichter et al. (1986) has been criticized for failing to show that the news product reflects the personal views of journalists rather than the views of the officials whose positions they are reporting (Gans 1985). American journalists, more than their counterparts in Germany, are committed to their ideology of dispassion, their sense of professionalism, and their value of fairness or objectivity (Donsbach 1995). They have a professional commitment to shielding their work from their personal political leanings. Moreover, their political leanings tend to be weak. Several close observers find leading American journalists not so much liberal or conservative as apolitical (Gans 1979, p. 184; Hess 1981, p. 115).

Critics and activists who advocate the hiring of more women and minorities in the newsroom share the intuition of Lichter et al. (1986) that the personal values journalists bring to their jobs color the news they produce. Hiring practices adopted in the United States in the 1970s and 1980s, designed to develop a newsroom more representative of the population by gender and ethnicity, should have transformed the news product itself. News should have become more oriented to groups often subordinated or victimized in society. Some anecdotal evidence (Mills 1989) suggests that a changing gender composition of the newsroom does influence news content, but other reports suggest that definitions of news have not dramatically changed (Beasley 1993, pp. 129–30). In the United States, concerns about a widening gap in economic class have probably overshadowed hopes about the effects of a reduced gap in gender and ethnicity. It is feared that the growing affluence of national journalists, who report by fax and phone and by accessing databases from their computers, will separate them from direct contact with the poor or others who live in places unpleasant to visit.

What is fundamental in organizational approaches such as Epstein's (1973), as opposed to the personal-values approach of Lichter et al. (1986), is the emphasis on (*a*) constraints imposed by organizations despite the private intentions of the individual journalists and (*b*) the inevitability of "social construction" of reality in any social system. A social-organizational perspective holds that news is less a report on a factual world than "a depletable consumer product that must be made fresh daily" (Tuchman 1978, p. 179). It is not a gathering of facts that already exist; indeed, as Tuchman (1978, pp. 82–83) has argued, facts are defined organizationally—facts are "pertinent information gathered by professionally validated methods specifying the relationship between what is known and how it is known . . . . In news, verification of facts is both a political and a professional accomplishment."

Little has been said here about the differences between print and television news. There is much to say, of course. For instance, there is controversy over the existence of a "CNN effect" in the shaping of American foreign policy, in which policy makers respond to the speed, ubiquity, global reach, and vividness of 24-hour global television news (Livingston 1997). Still, in terms of the basic news-gathering tasks, print and broadcast journalism share a great deal. Most television news stories come from print sources, especially the wire services (Krauss 2000). American evidence suggests that, at least for national news, most print and television journalists share common professional values. Separate studies of how print and television journalists use experts, for instance, reveal that in foreign policy coverage, both prefer former government officials to other kinds of experts (Steele 1995, Hallin et al. 1993). What Steele calls the "operational bias" in television news also applies to print journalism—both kinds of journalists seek experts who personally know the key players, who have strong views on a limited range of policy alternatives, and who will make short-term predictions. Even the television preference for experts who can turn a good phrase is one that print journalists share.

CULTURAL APPROACHES

Most understandings of the generation of news merge a cultural view with a social-organizational view. These approaches are, however, analytically distinct. Whereas the organizational view finds interactional determinants of news in the relations between people, the cultural view finds symbolic determinants of news in the relations between "facts" and symbols. A cultural account of news helps explain generalized images and stereotypes in the news media—of predatory stockbrokers just as much as hard-drinking factory workers—that transcend structures of ownership or patterns of work relations. An analysis of British mass media coverage of racial conflict, for instance, finds that "The British cultural tradition contains elements derogatory to foreigners, particularly blacks. The media operate within the culture and are obliged to use cultural symbols" (Hartmann & Husband 1973, p. 274). Another British study, examining media coverage of homosexuals, takes as a theoretical starting point a standard anthropological view that societies like to keep their cultural categories clean and neat and are troubled by anomalies that do not fit them. Homosexuality is an anomaly in societies that take as fundamental the opposition and relationship of male and female; thus, homosexuals provide a culturally charged topic for story telling that seeks to preserve or reinforce the conventional moral order of society—and its conceptual or symbolic foundation. News stories about homosexuals may be moral tales designed to reinforce conventional moral values (Pearce 1973).

A cultural account of this sort can explain too much; after all, news coverage of homosexuality has changed enormously, a universal cultural anxiety about anomalous categories notwithstanding. Gays and lesbians appear much more in the news today than 50 years ago and are covered much more routinely, as ordinary news subjects rather than characters in moral tales (Alwood 1996).

Similarly, broad cultural explanations of the prevalence and character of crime news (Katz 1987) must also be evaluated with some caution. Although it makes sense to assume that broad and long-lasting phenomena—such as heavy news coverage of crime over two centuries across many societies—have deep cultural roots, it is also important to recognize fashions, trends, and changes in crime coverage. Best (1999) provides a useful account of why some newly defined crimes receive only occasional or episodic press coverage whereas others, with better institutionalized support in a "victim industry," receive more systematic and ongoing treatment. What is at stake here is the interaction of general cultural and specific social-organizational dimensions of news.

A cultural account of news is also relevant to understanding journalists' vague descriptions of how they know news when they see it. Tuchman (1972, p. 672) writes that "news judgment is the sacred knowledge, the secret ability of the newsman which differentiates him from other people." This suggests the large cultural dimensions of the subject. The cultural knowledge that constitutes news judgment is too complex and too implicit to label simply "ideology." News judgment is not so unified, intentional, and functional a system as "ideology" suggests. Its presuppositions about what counts as novel, touching, interesting, or shocking are in some respects rooted much more deeply in human consciousness and are much more widely distributed in human societies than capitalism, socialism, industrialism, or any other particular system of social organization and domination can encompass.

One need not adopt assumptions about universal properties of human nature and human interest (although it would be foolish to dismiss them out of hand) to acknowledge that some aspects of news generation go beyond what sociological analysis of news organizations is normally prepared to handle. Why are violent crimes so greatly overreported in relation to their actual incidence (Katz 1987)? The overreporting has been documented in both the United States and Britain, not only in the popular press but (to a lesser degree) in the mid-market and quality press (Schlesinger & Tumber 1994, p. 185). This probably has something to do with a fact-centered pattern of reporting more characteristic of British and American journalism than the more literary, ideological, and intellectual journalism of France (Chalaby 1996), but it may touch on a deep fascination with violence and transgression that crosses national political cultures.

The cultural dimension of news concerns its form as well as its content. By "form," I refer to patterns of narrative, story telling, and the conventions of photographic and linguistic presentation in news production. Weaver (1975) shows systematic differences between the "inverted-pyramid" structure of print news (the convention of reporting the most important facts in a news story first and presenting the rest in declining order of significance) and the "thematic" structure of television news. Schudson (1982, 1995) argues that the inverted-pyramid form is a peculiar development of late nineteenth-century American journalism that implicitly authorized the journalist as a political expert and helped redefine politics itself as a subject appropriately discussed by experts rather than partisans. Hallin & Mancini (1984) demonstrate in a comparison of television news in Italy and the United States that formal conventions of news reporting, which analysts often attribute to the technology of television and which journalists often attribute to "the nature of things," actually stem from features of a country's political culture. All of this work recognizes that news is a form of literature and that among the resources journalists work with are the traditions of story telling, picture making, and sentence construction they inherit from their own cultures, with vital assumptions about the world built in.

Journalists operate not only to maintain and repair their social relations with sources and colleagues but also their cultural image as journalists in the eyes of a wider world. Television news reporters deploy experts in stories not so much to provide viewers with information but to certify the journalist's "effort, access, and superior knowledge" (Manoff 1989, p. 69). Reporters in American broadcast news visually and verbally establish their own authority by suggesting their personal proximity to the events they cover (Zelizer 1990). Regardless of how the news was in fact gathered, it is presented in a style that promotes an illusion of the journalists' adherence to the journalistic norm of proximity. The reality that journalists manufacture provides not only a particular version of the world but also a particular vision of journalism itself.

Most research on news production takes it for granted that, at least within a given national tradition, there is one common news standard among journalists. This convenient simplification merits critical attention. Reporters who may adhere to norms of objectivity in reporting on a political campaign (what Hallin calls the "sphere of legitimate controversy") will report gushingly about a topic on which there is broad national consensus (the "sphere of consensus") or will write derisively on a subject that lies beyond the bounds of popular consensus (the "sphere of deviance") (Hallin 1986, p. 117). It is as if journalists were unconsciously multilingual, code-switching from neutral interpreters to guardians of social consensus and back again without missing a beat. After September 11, 2001, television reporters and anchors spoke more quietly and somberly than usual, and moved from a normal to a "sacerdotal" journalism, a journalism of consensus and reassurance rather than of argument and information. Katz & Dayan note that, in moments of high ceremony or high tragedy, television journalists in Britain, the United States, Israel, and elsewhere abandon a matter-of-fact style for "cosmic lyricism" (1992, p. 108). Peri shows that the same code-switching took place in Israeli print journalism that covered the martyred Prime Minister Yitzhak Rabin. In life, Rabin walked in the sphere of legitimate controversy, but in death, he was absorbed into the sphere of consensus (Peri 1997).

CONCLUSIONS

Many studies of media coverage of politics smuggle in the assumption that the news media should serve society by informing the general population in ways that arm them for vigilant citizenship. I am sympathetic to this as one goal of the news media in a democracy, but it is not a very good approximation of the role that the news media have historically played—anywhere. The news media have always been a more important forum for communication among elites (and some elites more than others) than with the general population. In 1991, when the *Times* of London stopped publishing extracts of parliamentary speeches on a page set aside for this purpose, the editor remarked that he could not find anyone except members of Parliament themselves who read the page (Negrine 1998).

In the best of circumstances, the existence of a general audience for the news media provides a regular opportunity for elites to be effectively embarrassed, even disgraced, as Fisse & Braithwaite (1983) show in their cross-national study of the impact of publicity on corporate offenders. The combination of electoral democracy with a free press, economist Amartya Sen argues, has prevented famines even when crops have failed. Famines have more to do with problems of distribution than with problems of production, and politicians responsible to an electorate and to the press typically respond to the political implications of a potential famine (Sen & Dreze 1989).

Thinking about the media as political institutions has typically been ahistorical, ignoring possibilities for change in the nature of news. It has rarely been comparative, although I emphasize comparative work in this review. Comparative research is cumbersome, even in the age of word processors and computer networking. And it is conceptually bedeviling. How can news be compared across countries when, the press is primarily national in one country and regional and local in the next? How can comparison be made between the news media in a country where intellectual life is concentrated in a few media outlets and another where is it highly dispersed? Media studies are genuinely linked to national political issues—they are an academic metadiscourse on the daily defining of political reality. The motive for research, then, is normally conceived in isolation from comparative concerns. If this strengthens the immediate political relevance of media studies, it weakens their longer-term value as social science.

None of the three perspectives identified here can solely account for what we might want to know. Take just one important example. Several studies from around the world suggest a shift toward reporting styles that are more informal, more intimate, more critical, and more cynically detached or distanced than earlier reporting. British television interviewing style, once formal and deferential toward politicians, changed to a more aggressive and critical style that makes politicians "answerable to the public through the television news interview" (Scannell 1989, p. 146). Japanese broadcasting changed in a similar direction under the influence of news anchor Kume Hiroshi, whose "alienated cynicism and critical stance toward society and government" appear to have charmed a younger, more urban, and more alienated generation (Krauss 1998, p. 686). Kume's style moved toward a type of politics "more cynical and populist" than the old bureaucratic conservatism, a politics that "offers little in the way of the framing of real political alternatives" (Krauss 1998, p. 686). In fact, Krauss argues, the Japanese political establishment now "relies as much on a form of cynical inertia as on strong belief and allegiance to any positive values" (1998, p. 690).

Meanwhile, is the new investigative aggressiveness in Latin American journalism a related force? In Brazil, Argentina, and Peru, revelation of government scandals emerges not from old-fashioned partisan journalism but from a new, more entertainment-oriented journalism that adopts stock narratives and a telenovela-like, personality-focused moralizing style. In Waisbord's view, the results do not contribute to a public accounting of the moral order but come from and reinforce cultural pessimism. Scandal becomes a form of entertainment, at best, and contributes to political cynicism (Waisbord 1997, p. 201).

Evidence of a more aggressive, less deferential style in American television news (Hallin 1994) seems related. Similarly, Norway's most popular newspaper, *Verdens Gang*, has adopted the melodramatic framework of tabloid journalism in covering politics. "Politicians in a way become human beings, while the voters become customers" (Eide 1997, p. 179). There is something at work here consistent with the developments in the Netherlands that Liesbet van Zoonen refers to as "intimization" in the news (1991).

Are these changes explained by shifts in political economy? Or social organization? Or culture? Clearly, all are involved.

The media influence political outcomes—especially election outcomes in democracies—but they also affect the fate of legislative decisions, bureaucratic infighting, and individual political advancement or failure. Enormous effort has been lavished on clarifying the nature and extent of the media's political impact. This is beyond my purview here, but it is still worth two quick cautionary notes. First, whatever influence the media exercise, they may exercise it in ways that reflect very different conclusions about independent media power. The media may have influence by conveying information provided by government officials—in which case any effect is initiated by the officials, not the media. Alternatively, the media may have influence by legitimating or providing a kind of aura to information simply because the information appears in a place that carries prestige and public legitimacy. In this case, the media are exercising a kind of power of their own, but it is independent of any particular framing, shaping, or bias they contribute. Third, the media may exercise influence by framing information in a particular way. This third form of media influence is almost always what students and critics of the media think they are examining, hoping to discover and discount a media bias of some kind—but this is only one dimension of media influence, and in many or most cases it may not be the most important.

A second cautionary note is that sometimes the media exercise little or no measurable influence. Public opinion appears to have been entirely unaffected by the news from the White House that became the Monica Lewinsky scandal— public approval of Clinton's job performance did not decline at all during the congressional and media frenzy over the topic. In fact, it increased (Zaller 1998). This is just one more vivid reminder that, at the heart of media studies, there remains the embarrassing question of whether, or under what circumstances, the media are worth studying at all.

My own response is simply to urge that studies of the media not confine themselves to over-simple models of how the media affect society. For many scholars and most lay people, the model of media influence is a model of propaganda. This view of media power is often referred to as a "hypodermic" model—one in which the media inject ideas into a passive and defenseless public. The problem with this model is not that it posits media power but that it takes the mechanism of power to be indoctrination. Models of indoctrination in mainstream communication research have grown more subtle through the years but have not basically shifted. Notions that have been popular among different scholars through the years, such as agenda setting, hegemony, and priming, all refine but do not fundamentally discard the notion of indoctrination.

The primary, day-to-day contribution the news media make to the wider society is one that they make as cultural actors, that is, as producers—and messengers— of meanings, symbols, messages. Candidates, politicians, and other government officials live in a special world where media messages are central, rather than incidental, to their workaday activity. For political scientists or plumbers, sociologists or sales clerks, it is difficult to imagine what life is like for people whose work is routinely a subject of the news—people for whom good press is the best available proxy for public support and serves as the currency of political reputation. For politicians, news coverage can be direct reward or punishment for their behavior. For the rest of humanity, however, the news offers neither paychecks nor cudgels, neither praise nor criticism, neither license nor confinement. It offers the language in which action is constituted rather than the cause that generates action. To move from an indoctrinational model of media influence to a cultural model, we would not picture the mass media implanting a belief or behavior in individuals but instead establishing a web of meanings and therefore a web of presuppositions, in relation to which, to some degree, people live their lives.

The *Annual Review of Political Science* is online at http://polisci.annualreviews.org

LITERATURE CITED

Alwood E. 1996. *Straight News: Gays, Lesbians, and the News Media.* New York: Columbia Univ. Press

Bagdikian B. 1989. *The Media Monopoly.* Boston: Beacon

Baker CE. 1994. *Ownership of newspapers: the view from positivist social science.* Res. Pap. R-12. Cambridge, MA: Shorenstein Cent. Press, Politics, and Public Policy

Beasley M. 1993. Newspapers: Is there a new majority defining the news? In *Women in Mass Communication*, ed. PJ Creedon. Newbury Park, CA: SAGE

Best J. 1999. *Random Violence: How We Talk About New Crimes and New Victims.* Berkeley: Univ. Calif. Press

Blumler J, Kavanagh D. 1999. The third age of political communication: influences and features. *Polit. Commun.* 16:209–30

Brants K. 1998. Who's afraid of infotainment? *Eur. J. Commun.* 13:305–35

Breed W. 1955. Social control in the newsroom: a functional analysis. *Soc. Forces* 33:326–55

Cater D. 1959. *The Fourth Branch of Government.* Boston: Houghton Mifflin

Chalaby J. 1996. Journalism as an Anglo-American invention. *Eur. J. Commun.* 11:303–26

Cohen BC. 1963. *The Press and Foreign Policy.* Princeton, NJ: Princeton Univ. Press

Cohen BC. 1995. *Democracies and Foreign Policy: Public Participation in the United States and the Netherlands.* Madison: Univ. Wisc. Press

Cook TE. 1989. *Making Laws and Making News: Media Strategies in the U.S. House of Representatives.* Washington, DC: Brookings Inst.

Cook TE. 1998. *Governing with the News.* Chicago: Univ. Chicago Press

Crouse T. 1973. *The Boys on the Bus.* New York: Ballantine

De Mateo R. 1989. The evolution of the newspaper industry in Spain, 1939–87. *Eur. J. Commun.* 4:211–26

Demers D. 1996. Corporate newspaper structure, editorial page vigor, and social change. *Journal. Mass Commun. Q.* 73:857–77

Donsbach W. 1995. Lapdogs, watchdogs and junkyard dogs. *Media Stud. J.* Fall:17–30

Dreier P. 1982. Capitalists vs. the media: an analysis of an ideological mobilization among business leaders. *Media Culture Soc.* 4:111–32

Eide M. 1997. A new kind of newspaper? Understanding a popularization process. *Media Culture Soc.* 19:173–82

Epstein EJ. 1973. *News from Nowhere.* New York: Random House

Ericson RV, Baranek PM, Chan JBC. 1989. *Negotiating Control: A Study of News Sources.* Toronto: Univ. Toronto Press

Esser F. 1998. Editorial structures and work principles in British and German newsrooms. *Eur. J. Commun.* 13:375–405

Esser F. 1999. "Tabloidization" of news: a comparative analysis of Anglo-American and German press journalism. *Eur. J. Commun.* 14:291–324

Feldman O. 1993. *Politics and the News Media in Japan.* Ann Arbor: Univ. Mich. Press

Fishman M. 1980. *Manufacturing the News.* Austin: Univ. Texas Press

Fisse B, Braithwaite J. 1983. *The Impact of Publicity on Corporate Offenders.* Albany: State Univ. NY Press

Freeman LA. 2000. *Closing the Shop: Information Cartels and Japan's Mass Media.* Princeton, NJ: Princeton Univ. Press

Gans HJ. 1979. *Deciding What's News: A Study of* CBS Evening News, NBC Nightly News, Newsweek *and* Time. New York: Pantheon

Gans HJ. 1985. Are U.S. journalists dangerously liberal? *Columbia Journal. Rev.* (Nov./Dec.):29–33

Garnham N. 1990. *Capitalism and Communication.* London: SAGE

Gieber W. 1964. News is what newspapermen make it. In *People, Society and Mass Communications*, ed. LA Dexter, D Manning, D White, pp. 173–80. New York: Free

Gitlin T. 1980. *The Whole World Is Watching.* Berkeley: Univ. Calif. Press

Goldenberg E. 1975. *Making the Papers.* Lexington, MA: DC Heath

Grant J. 1988. Internal reporting by investigative journalists in China and its influence on government policy. *Gazette* 41:53–65

Hallin DC. 1986. *"The Uncensored War": The Media and Vietnam.* New York: Oxford Univ. Press

Hallin DC. 1994. *We Keep America on Top of the World.* London: Routledge

Hallin DC, Mancini P. 1984. Speaking of the President: political structure and representational form in U.S. and Italian television news. *Theory Soc.* 13:829–50

Hallin DC, Manoff RK, Weddle JK. 1993. Sourcing patterns of national security reporters. *Journal. Q.* 70:753–66

Hartmann P, Husband C. 1973. The mass media and racial conflict. In *The Manufacture of News: A Reader*, ed. S Cohen, J Young, pp. 270–83. Beverly Hills, CA: SAGE

Herman ES, Chomsky N. 1988. *Manufacturing Consent.* New York: Pantheon

Hess S. 1981. *The Washington Reporters.* Washington: Brookings Inst.

Hughes HM. 1940. *News and the Human Interest Story.* Chicago: Univ. Chicago Press

Kalb M. 1998. *The rise of the "new news": a case study of two root causes of the modern scandal coverage.* Disc. Pap. D-34. Cambridge, MA: Joan Shorenstein Cent. Press, Politics, and Public Policy

Katz E, Dayan D. 1992. *Media Events: The Live Broadcasting of History.* Cambridge, MA: Harvard Univ. Press

Katz J. 1987. What makes crime "news"? *Media Culture Soc.* 9:47–76

Kernell S. 1986. *Going Public.* Washington, DC: CQ Press

Krauss E. 1998. Changing television news in Japan. *J. Asian Stud.* 57:663–92

Krauss E. 2000. *Broadcasting Politics in Japan: NHK TV News.* Ithaca, NY: Cornell Univ. Press

Lichter SR, Rothman S, Lichter LS. 1986. *The Media Elite: America's New Powerbrokers.* Bethesda, MD: Adler & Adler

Lippmann W. 1922. *Public Opinion.* New York: Macmillan

Lipstadt D. 1986. *Beyond Belief: The American Press and the Coming of the Holocaust 1933–1945.* New York: Free

Livingston S. 1997. Beyond the "CNN effect": the media–foreign policy dynamic. In *Politics and the Press*, ed. P Norris, pp. 291–318. Boulder, CO: Lynne Rienner

Loomis B. 1988. *The New American Politician.* New York: Basic Books

Manoff RK. 1989. Modes of war and modes of social address: the text of SDI. *J. Commun.* 39:59–84

Mazzoleni G. 1995. Towards a "videocracy"? Italian political communication at a turning point. *Eur. J. Commun.* 10:291–319

Mazzoleni G, Schulz W. 1999. "Mediatization" of politics: a challenge for democracy? *Polit. Commun.* 16:247–61

McChesney RW. 1997. *Corporate Media and the Threat to Democracy.* New York: Seven Stories

McNair B. 2000. *Journalism and Democracy.* London: Routledge

Mermin J. 1997. Television news and American intervention in Somalia: the myth of a media-driven foreign policy. *Polit. Sci. Q.* 112:385–403

Mills K. 1989. *A Place in the News.* New York: Dodd, Mead

Mortensen F, Svendsen EN. 1980. Creativity and control: the journalist betwixt his readers and editors. *Media Culture Soc.* 2:169–77

Murschetz P. 1998. State support for the daily press in Europe: a critical appraisal. *Eur. J. Commun.* 13:291–313

Negrine R. 1998. *Parliament and Media: A Study of Britain, Germany and France.* London: R. Inst. Int. Aff.

Noam E. 1991. *Television in Europe.* New York: Oxford Univ. Press

Park RE. 1922. *The Immigrant Press and Its Control.* New York: Harper

Park RE. 1923. The natural history of the newspaper. *Am. J. Sociol.* 29:273–89

Patterson TE. 1993. *Out of Order.* New York: Knopf

Pearce F. 1973. How to be immoral and ill, pathetic and dangerous, all at the same time: mass media and the homosexual. In *The Manufacture of News: A Reader*, ed. S Cohen, J Young, pp. 284–301. Beverly Hills, CA: SAGE

Peri Y. 1997. The Rabin myth and the press: reconstruction of the Israeli collective identity. *Eur. J. Commun.* 12:435–58

Polumbaum J. 1997. Political fetters, commercial freedoms: restraint and excess in Chinese mass communications. In *Regional Handbook of Economic and Political Development*, ed. C Hudson, 1:211–26. Chicago: Fitzroy Dearborn

Scannell P. 1989. Public service broadcasting and modern public life. *Media Culture Soc.* 11:135–66

Schlesinger P. 1990. Rethinking the sociology of journalism: source strategies and the limits of media-centrism. In *Public Communication*, ed. M Ferguson, pp. 61–83. London: SAGE

Schlesinger P, Tumber H. 1994. *Reporting Crime: The Media Politics of Criminal Justice.* Oxford, UK: Clarendon

Schudson M. 1982. The politics of narrative form: the emergence of news conventions in print and television. *Daedalus* 111:97–113

Schudson M. 1995. *The Power of News.* Cambridge, MA: Harvard Univ. Press

Schudson M. 1999. Social origins of press cynicism in portraying politics. *Am. Behav. Sci.* 42:998–1008

Schudson M. 2000. The sociology of news production revisited (again). In *Mass Media and Society*, ed. J Curran, M Gurevitch, pp. 175–200. London: Arnold. 3rd ed.

Sen A, Dreze J. 1989. *Hunger and Public Action.* Oxford, UK: Clarendon

Sigal LV. 1973. *Reporters and Officials.* Lexington, MA: Lexington Books

Sigal LV. 1986. Sources make the news. In *Reading the News*, ed. RK Manoff, M Schudson, pp. 9–37. New York: Pantheon

Skogerbo E. 1997. The press subsidy system in Norway. *Eur. J. Commun.* 12:99–118

Steele JE. 1995. Experts and the operational bias of television news: the case of the Persian Gulf War. *Journal. Mass Commun. Q.* 72:799–812

Tuchman G. 1972. Objectivity as strategic ritual: an examination of newsmen's notions of objectivity. *Am. J. Sociol.* 77:660–79

Tuchman G. 1978. *Making News: A Study in the Construction of Reality.* New York: Free

van Zoonen L. 1991. A tyranny of intimacy? Women, femininity and television news. In *Communication and Citizenship*, ed. P Dahlgren, C Sparks, pp. 217–35. London: Routledge

Waisbord S. 1995. Leviathan dreams: state and broadcasting in South America. *Commun. Rev.* 1:201–26

Waisbord S. 1997. The narrative of exposés in South American journalism. *Gazette* 59:189–203

Waisbord S. 2000. *Watchdog Journalism in Latin America.* New York: Columbia Univ. Press

Weaver P. 1975. Newspaper news and television news. In *Television as a Social Force*, ed. D Cater, R Adler, pp. 81–94. New York: Praeger

Weaver D, Wilhoit GC. 1996. *The American Journalist in the 1990s.* Mahwah, NJ: Lawrence Erlbaum

Weber M. 1946 (1921). Politics as a vocation.

In *Max Weber: Essays in Sociology*, ed. H Gerth, CW Mills, pp. 77–128. New York: Oxford Univ. Press

White DM. 1950. The gatekeeper: a case study in the selection of news. *Journal. Q.* 27:383–90. Reprinted 1964 *in People, Society, and Mass Communications*, ed. LA Dexter, DM White, pp. 160–71. New York: Free

White T. 1961. *The Making of the President 1960.* New York: Atheneum

Zaller J. 1994. Elite leadership of mass opinion: new evidence from the Gulf War. In *Taken by Storm: The Media, Public Opinion, and U.S.*

Foreign Policy in the Gulf War, ed. WL Bennett, DL Paletz, pp. 186–209. Chicago: Univ. Chicago Press

Zaller J. 1998. Monica Lewinsky's contribution to political science. *PS: Polit. Sci. Politics* 31:182–89

Zelizer B. 1990. Where is the author in American TV news? On the construction and presentation of proximity, authorship, and journalistic authority. *Semiotica* 80:37–48

Zhao Y. 1998. *Media, Market, and Democracy in China: Between the Party Line and the Bottom Line.* Urbana: Univ. Ill. Press

Annu. Rev. Polit. Sci. 2002. 5:271–304
DOI: 10.1146/annurev.polisci.5.100201.102917
Copyright © 2002 by Annual Reviews. All rights reserved

THE FIRST DECADE OF POST-COMMUNIST ELECTIONS AND VOTING: What Have We Studied, and How Have We Studied It?

Joshua A. Tucker
Department of Politics and Woodrow Wilson School, Princeton University, 322 Bendheim Hall, Princeton, New Jersey 08544; e-mail: jtucker@princeton.edu

Key Words   electoral, vote, election, methodology, data, Russia, Poland

■ **Abstract**   This review assesses the state of the newly emerging field of the study of post-communist elections and voting by building and analyzing a database of 101 articles on the topic that have appeared in 16 leading academic journals (8 general political science journals and 8 post-communist area studies journals) between 1990 and 2000. The database is then used to make inferences concerning both what is being studied by scholars and how it is being studied. The review systematically assesses which countries have been analyzed, the types of elections examined, the prevalence of comparative analysis, the division between quantitative and qualitative research, and the types of data used in quantitative studies. It then turns to substantive questions, examining both how scholars have explained post-communist election results and voting decisions, and what they have used these elections to explain.

INTRODUCTION

Political science is filled with examples of ideas, approaches, and paradigms that have ebbed and flowed over the years. Indeed, we have had almost as many "revolutions" as the countries we study. But alongside the many debates in political science lie real political phenomena that we hope to understand. Although we often have the opportunity to observe a mode of study develop, the chance to observe a new political phenomenon is more rare. Yet with the collapse of communism in Eastern Europe and the former Soviet Union, such an opportunity has arisen. Prior to 1989, the world had little or no practical experience observing democratic behavior in post-communist societies. And although there are undoubtedly some continuities between the communist and post-communist eras in these countries, there are just as many, if not more, sharp discontinuities. Perhaps nowhere is this more clearly evident than in the realm of elections and voting.

As Colton vividly notes (2000b, p. 34), "The sight of Russians streaming into their local precincts to pronounce on who is fit to rule them is as startling a transposition of conventional imagery as a takeover by Maoist guerillas would be in the

1094-2939/02/0615-0271$14.00

United States." Whereas previously voting had been no more than an act of mass mobilization demanded by a totalitarian (or post-totalitarian) regime to mollify the ruling party, citizens were now faced with choices.[1] Suddenly, votes represented choices between different people, parties, and movements. Moreover, these elections had consequences. How might Russian history have evolved differently had Boris Yeltsin not been elected president of the Russian Federation in 1991 and then been reelected in 1996? And would Slovakia still be on the outside of NATO looking in had the voters rejected the nationalist Vladimir Meciar in the 1994 parliamentary elections after his fellow politicians had twice ousted him from power?

Over a decade after the crucial 1989 Polish parliamentary elections, it is now an appropriate time to pause and survey the literature. What exactly have we been studying for the past decade? What questions have we sought to answer? A crucial task of this article, as a first review of the subject, is to provide a road map to the work in this new field. A retrospective evaluation (no pun intended) of the literature on voting and elections in post-communist countries also holds the tantalizing possibility of telling us something interesting about political science as a discipline. For not only can we assess what have we studied in the first decade of this new field, we can also observe how we have studied it. Unlike earlier waves of democratization, this one has occurred in an age of powerful computers, cheap airfares, leftover funding from the Cold War, and (relatively) easily attainable visas. How have scholars taken advantage of these resources? Have we used quantitative or qualitative research? Employed aggregate or micro-level analysis? Explored one election or multiple ones? Analyzed a single country or many?

In an effort to take advantage of this unique opportunity, this review therefore addresses both the "how" and "what" of the first decade of study of post-communist elections and voting. I examine in detail how the field has studied elections and voting by addressing in turn the countries analyzed, the prevalence of comparative analysis, the types of elections explored, the division between quantitative and qualitative research, and the nature of the data used in quantitative studies. I then turn to the substantive nature of the field's development, exploring both how scholars have explained post-communist election results and voting and what they have used these elections to explain.

A Database of Journal Articles

In order to address these topics, I constructed a database of 101 articles on elections and voting from 16 leading journals—8 general or comparative political

---

[1]Of course, this was not the case in all of the post-Soviet countries, with Turkmenistan being the most glaring exception. But given the fact that, prior to the late 1980s, arguably none of the communist countries were anything close to democratic, the fact that so many of these countries have had meaningful elections—and in most cases multiple meaningful elections—is quite stunning. Indeed, according to one source, only two of the 27 post-communist countries have failed to have multiple competitive elections (Bunce 2001, p. 43).

science journals and 8 post-communist area studies journals—between 1990 and 2000.[2] The criteria for inclusion of an article were as follows.

First, the article had to be primarily written about an election or a series of elections. In most cases, the election functioned as the dependent variable of the analysis: The goal of the article was to explain why the election(s) turned out the way it did and/or why voters voted the way they did. I included in this classification studies that asked voters which parties they preferred (and thus were likely to vote for in an election) even if the survey did not occur at the time of an actual election, but only if the article was primarily concerned with voting, as opposed to the development of party systems more generally.[3]

In some cases, articles were included where an election functioned as an independent variable. I was, however, careful to limit this category to articles in which elections were the primary explanatory variable. I excluded those in which elections were just one of many variables employed to explain some other phenomenon out of fear that such articles would quickly overwhelm the pure elections articles. Had I included any article that mentioned an election as a causal variable, this very quickly would have become a review about democratization as opposed to elections and voting. As it turned out, less than 15% of the articles (13 out of 101) included in the database are there exclusively because an election(s) functioned as an independent variable in the article. Articles were also excluded if elections were a component of a debate on another topic where the focus of the research was not on explaining an election or voting.[4]

The second, perhaps more obvious, criterion was that the article had to be focused on analyzing an election or elections that took place in one or more of

---

[2]The political science journals are *American Journal of Political Science*, *American Political Science Review*, *British Journal of Political Science*, *Comparative Political Studies*, *Comparative Politics*, *Electoral Studies*, *Journal of Politics*, and *World Politics*. A number of area studies journals, not surprisingly, changed their names during this period, so the following list shows the current name of the journal with the previous name in parentheses if necessary. The journals are *Communist and Post Communist Studies* (*Studies in Comparative Communism*), *Demokratizatsiya*, *East European Politics and Society*, *Europe-Asia Studies*, *Post-Soviet Affairs* (*Soviet Economy*), *Post-Soviet Geography and Economics* (*Post-Soviet Geography*), *Problems of Post-Communism* (*Problems of Communism*), and *Slavic Review*. Of these, all published for the entire period with the exception of *Demokratizatsiya*, which appeared in 1993.

[3]Without this rule, the line would quickly fade between scholarship focused on elections and voting and scholarship devoted to the development of party systems. Although both of these interrelated topics are interesting, the focus of the current article is elections and voting.

[4]A good example is the scholarship concerning the development of partisanship in Russia (Rose 1998, Whitefield & Evans 1999, Colton 2000a, Miller & Klobucar 2000, Brader & Tucker 2001). Clearly, the discussion of voting factors into any consideration of partisan identification, but it is really a separate topic with its own literature and theoretical concerns.

the 27 post-communist countries of the former Soviet Union and Eastern Europe.[5] This also excluded any large-N studies that included post-communist countries within a much larger universe of cases. Finally, the article had to represent some attempt at an *analysis* of election results or voting. Articles that merely reported results without attempting to add any independent analysis were not included in the database.[6]

The task of compiling the database involved checking literally thousands of articles to determine whether they ought to be included. In order to avoid the vagaries of search engines, each issue of each journal was examined by hand.[7] Most of the decisions concerning the inclusion of articles were fairly straightforward. Although I doubt that anyone else would have made exactly the same decision I did on every article, I am confident that most other scholars would have made most of the same decisions.

Why Journal Articles?

The composition of the database begs the question of why journal articles. The answer is fourfold. First and foremost, clearly delimiting the universe of cases of writing on the topic is crucial for eliminating selection bias. Selection bias occurs

---

[5]More specifically, the countries included were: Russia, Belarus, Ukraine, Latvia, Lithuania, Estonia, Armenia, Azerbaijan, Georgia, Moldova, Kyrgyzstan, Uzbekistan, Turkmenistan, Kazakhstan, Tajikistan, Poland, Hungary, Slovakia, the Czech Republic, Bulgaria, Romania, Albania, Slovenia, Croatia, Yugoslavia (Serbia or Montenegro), Bosnia-Herzegovina, and Macedonia. In addition, articles focusing on competitive elections in the former East Germany, Czechoslovakia, and the Soviet Union were included.

[6]The primary effect of this rule was to exclude notes that appeared in *Electoral Studies'* "Notes on Recent Elections" section. Although some of these notes were longer and did attempt to provide commentary in addition to details (see for example Krupavicius 1997, Wyman 1997, Chan 1998), many were little more than descriptions of parties and results. Lacking any clear way to differentiate between various notes, I deferred to the editors of *Electoral Studies* and assumed that articles more focused on analysis would be found in the article section of the journal; consequently, I excluded all of the notes. The alternative, to include all of the notes, would have resulted in a substantial portion of the database being based largely on nonanalytical articles.

[7]The initial pass was made by my research assistants, Todd Spiegelman and Sarah Keffer, without whose assistance this project would not have been possible. Final decisions concerning which articles to include were made after two sets of screenings and were mine alone. Undoubtedly, we missed some articles that should have been included in the database. Because such omissions were the result of measurement error, they should not bias any of the inferences made on the basis of the data. Nevertheless, I apologize to anyone whose work was inadvertently omitted. And indeed, after this article had been submitted for publication, I found two additional articles that appeared late in 2000 and should have been included in the database (Bohrer et al. 2000, Colton & McFaul 2000); because these articles are not included in the database, they are not reflected in the summary statistics, but they are referred to in the text.

when the results of a study are influenced by our choice of which cases to include in it. (For example, a study of the effects of repression on some form of political behavior suffers from selection bias if it omits countries that the researcher could not visit because of their severely repressive regimes.) But although selection bias has received the most attention in empirical studies, it also lurks below the surface of any review article. As King et al. (1994, p. 128) note, one of the most obvious manifestations of selection bias occurs when "we, knowing what we want to see as the outcome of the research (the confirmation of a favorite hypothesis), subtly or not so subtly select observations . . . that support the desired conclusion." Like any empirical study, review articles make conclusions on the basis of available evidence, but in this case the literature itself represents the evidence or data. Because it is up to the individual reviewer to decide which "evidence" (i.e., articles, books, papers, etc.) to include in the survey, the possibility always exists that these decisions will introduce selection bias.

Of course, this risk is normally mitigated by the fact that the reviewer has been selected to write the review precisely because someone thinks he or she will introduce a particular kind of selection bias: quality and importance. After all, a review article is not necessarily intended to survey everything ever written on a topic but instead to report on the most important works.

In this particular review article, though, the issue of selection bias is much more serious. A primary goal of my endeavor is to make inferences about how political scientists have approached the study of elections and voting in post-communist countries. In attempting to comment about how research has been conducted, it is crucial that I not limit my survey to research of any particular type. By including all articles that meet the above criteria from a universe of cases defined a priori, the sample should be relatively free of bias. I have thus taken the decision out of my own hands and turned it over to everyone who has ever written a review for an article on the topic for any of the 16 journals mentioned above.[8]

This brings me to my second point, which is that the analysis of journal articles gives us a first-hand observation of what the discipline values as important research in the field of post-communist elections and voting. In order for an article to appear in any of these journals, an editor or reviewers, and in most cases both, must have thought that the article was worth publishing. Because the purpose of this exercise is to examine how political science has gone about studying a new field, a focus on journal articles allows me to comment on not only what individual authors have chosen to write but also what the field has chosen to regard as quality. In a sense, therefore, I have included the "quality" selection bias, but it is what the discipline (as opposed to just the author of this review article) values as quality.

---

[8]Even through the selection of journals, bias can creep into the study. Most of these journals are American or British. Although it would of course have been better to include more journals, considerations of time and effort forced me to draw a line at some point. I apologize to those whose work has been published elsewhere; the omission should not be read as a comment on the quality of the work.

The third reason for relying on journal articles is that they represent a comparable unit of analysis. This is a prerequisite for any quantitative assessments regarding the development of the field (e.g., a third of all articles have been written about country X). If the database included books and edited volumes, it would raise sticky questions about how to count cases. By restricting my analysis to journal articles, I avoid this concern.

Finally, because the field is young, not many books purely devoted to elections and voting in post-communist countries have been published, particularly by university presses.[9] As a result, much of the action, so to speak, in the development of the field has been taking place in journals. For example, in an approximately page-long endnote, Colton (2000b, p. 262) surveys the literature on Russian elections in the 1990s; almost the entire note refers to journal articles.

Figure 1 displays the distribution of the articles across the 16 journals. Not surprisingly, there are more articles on post-communist elections in the area studies journals than there are in the general interest journals. Although there is some variation in the journals' frequency of publication, the relative paucity of articles on post-communist elections and voting in the leading journals of political science is undeniable. The *APSR*, *AJPS*, *BJPS*, *JOP*, *World Politics*, and *Comparative Politics*, combined, averaged one article per year that met the criteria enumerated above. Whether this scarcity is due to a lack of research being submitted to these journals or a low acceptance rate for such work is beyond the scope of this article. Nevertheless, it is clear that there is still a long way to go in moving studies of post-communist elections and voting into the mainstream of political science analysis.[10]

---

[9]However, see Krejcí (1995), Tworzecki (1996), Belin & Orttung (1997), McFaul (1997b), White et al. (1997a), Birch (2000), Colton (2000b), and Moser (2001). In addition, a number of edited volumes have been published, although most appear either to be a part of the *Founding Elections in Eastern Europe* series sponsored by the Fritz Thyssen Foundation in Berlin (Tóka 1995, Gabal 1996, Karasimeonov 1997, Gelman & Golosov 1999, Klingemann et al. 2000), or to be focused exclusively on Russian elections (Lentini 1995, Colton & Hough 1998, Wyman et al. 1998). Moreover, none of the books or edited volumes feature analyses that compare elections from more than one country. Indeed, only one edited volume even addresses elections in more than one country, and this is mainly through a series of chapters on individual countries (Klingemann et al. 2000). Perhaps even more surprising is the lack of doctoral dissertations on elections and voting in post-communist countries. A search of the UMI dissertation abstracts database during the summer of 2001 revealed that of the hundreds of dissertations written on elections and voting generally since 1993, only seven have focused on post-communist countries (Tworzecki 1994, Treisman 1995, Birch 1998, Oates 1998, Perepechko 1999, Stegmaier 2000, Tucker 2000a); two others addressed the development of electoral systems in post-communist countries (Benoit 1998, Jones-Luong 1998). Another source of publications that lie somewhere between articles and books are the University of Strathclyde's Studies in Public Policy (which can be found on the web at http://www.cspp.strath.ac.uk/).

[10]The point is further emphasized by the fact that of the books and edited volumes listed above, only two (Colton 2000b, Moser 2001) were published by an American or British university press, and both appeared in print only recently.

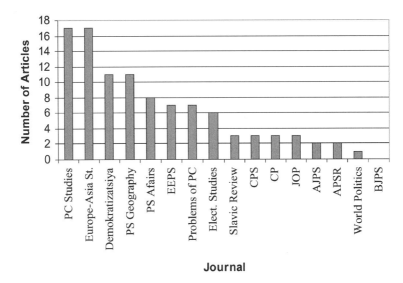

Figure 1   Distribution of articles by journal. Journal listings are based on most recent title and include publications from that journal under previous title. Abbreviations are as follows: PC, post-communist; PS, post-Soviet; EEPS, *East European Politics and Society*; CPS, *Comparative Political Studies*; CP, *Comparative Politics*; JOP, *Journal of Politics*; AJPS, *American Journal of Political Science*; APSR, *American Political Science Review*; BJPS, *British Journal of Political Science*.

HOW ARE WE STUDYING ELECTIONS AND VOTING?

In this section, I focus on how scholars have studied elections and voting in post-communist countries. I explore which countries are being studied, whether they are being studied individually or comparatively, what types of elections have been analyzed, and what methods scholars have chosen to employ in their analyses.

Countries

As Figure 2 demonstrates, the analysis of elections and voting in the post-communist context has been anything but uniformly distributed across countries. Thirteen of the 101 articles in the database analyzed more than one country, ranging generally from two to six countries. Therefore, the bar in Figure 2 for each country is subdivided to show the number of times the country appeared in a single-country article (dark shading) and the number of times it appeared in a multi-country comparative article (no shading). Although there are numerous points of interest in Figure 2, I confine my remarks to four observations.

First, it is clear that the study of elections and voting in post-communist countries is dominated by analyses of Russia. Over half of the articles in the database examine Russian elections, and single-country studies of Russia almost make up a

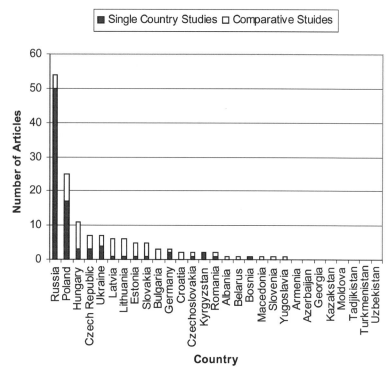

Figure 2   Distribution of articles by country.

majority of the research. (A similar pattern is present in book publication.) This is not entirely surprising, given the legacy of academic attention to the Soviet Union and the importance of Russia in the international sphere relative to most other post-communist countries. Nevertheless, it should raise some red flags. If the field continues to develop in this direction, then there is a realistic danger that much of what we learn about elections and voting in the post-communist context will be based on our understanding of only one country, and one that is hardly representative of the lot. On the other hand, perhaps we should be pleased that even in the immediate post–Cold War era, scholars have devoted considerable attention to countries besides Russia.

This leads to my second observation, which I must confess took me completely by surprise and for which I have no obvious explanation. After Russia, Poland has been by far the most studied of the post-communist countries. It has been the subject of more than twice as many articles as any other country, and four times as many single-country articles have been written about Poland than about any other country. Perhaps most stunningly, there are almost six times as many single country articles about Poland (17) as there are about Hungary (3) or the Czech Republic (3). Because these are the three countries that have joined NATO and are often considered together (along with Slovakia) as the Visegrad four, I was not surprised that all three would be among the most studied in Eastern Europe. However, there was no reason to expect any one of the three to receive more attention than the others. Although difficulty in learning the language might disadvantage Hungary, this cannot explain the distinction between Poland and the Czech Republic. My best guess was that perhaps particularly good survey data existed in the Polish case, but only three of the articles written exclusively on Poland relied on survey data (Powers & Cox 1997, Szelenyi et al. 1997, Shabad & Slomczynski 1999). And although more studies of Poland use regional-level data than either of the other two, I can confirm from personal experience that it is no more difficult to get similar data in Hungary or the Czech Republic. Another guess was that more articles had been written on Poland because it has had direct elections for president and parliament—the Czech Republic and Hungary both have a president elected by the parliament—and therefore there were more articles written simply because there were more elections to study. However, it turns out that of the 17 single-country articles written on Poland, none focused exclusively on presidential elections and only two (Bell 1997, Shabad & Slomczynski 1999) considered both presidential and parliamentary elections. I remain baffled by this trend and am intrigued to see whether it is limited to elections and voting or extends to other fields.[11]

More generally, there is a definite link between the relative importance of a country to the West and the number of scholarly articles on elections and voting in that country. Although "importance to the West" is a nebulous concept, there are some clear patterns in the data. As previously noted, the most popular country for study by far is Russia, with the three countries that have been admitted to NATO occupying the next three slots. The next most popular country is Ukraine, followed by the three Baltic States and Slovakia, all four of which have been considered for NATO and European Union membership; no other country has been the subject of more than three articles.

I can only speculate as to what is driving this pattern. It may be that we are more apt to reward work on more familiar countries through mechanisms such as grants, journal acceptances, encouragement to graduate students, and even the job market. Alternatively, all things being equal, scholars may have been drawn to elections that seem free and fair more than to those that do not. But although this may explain the lack of attention to the Caucus region and parts of the Balkans, it certainly cannot explain all the variation. One potential factor might be that some countries are seen as inherently more comparable than others; note particularly that Latvia, Lithuania, Estonia, and Slovakia are all included in numerous comparative

---

[11]A reviewer suggested that one explanation for the trend might be the fact that Poles had been more active than most in trying to get work published in these journals. Although there is some evidence to support this statement, a cursory glance at the authors suggests that at least 60% of the articles on Poland were written by non-Polish authors. So even if we eliminated articles authored or coauthored by Poles, Poland would still clearly be the second most popular country for analysis.

articles, but each is the focus of only one single-country study (Ishiyama 1994, Clark 1995, Carpenter 1997, Stukuls 1997).

Finally, it is important to note that numerous countries have received little or no attention. Fourteen of the countries appeared in no more than one article; of these, eight appeared not a single time. Although it is understandable that no one is investigating elections in Turkmenistan or Uzbekistan owing to the lack of democratic evolution in these countries, numerous countries in this neglected group have conducted multiple elections in which voters have definitely made choices at the voting booth. Elections in places such as Georgia, Moldova, Azerbaijan, and Armenia may not be as free or fair as their counterparts in Central Europe, but these elections must still have something to offer social scientists.

Comparative Analysis

With the collapse of communism in the former Soviet Union and Eastern Europe, comparative political scientists were faced with an almost unprecedented opportunity. Over 25 states, having undergone similar political and economic experiences over at least the past four decades, were simultaneously facing the task of transition. For many of these states, elections and voting have played a crucial role in that process, both by installing democratic institutions and by providing the leadership of the governments that would undertake those transitions. Although there were undoubtedly important differences between the countries, the similarities in their collective political tasks may have outnumbered those in any other group of countries in the twentieth century. Nevertheless, as Table 1 demonstrates, the field of political science seems to have collectively shied away from the opportunity to pursue comparative research.

Of the 101 articles in the study, only 13 chose to compare countries. The old border between the former Soviet Union and East Central Europe seems to be remarkably intact, especially if we exclude the Baltic states (Latvia, Lithuania, and Estonia) from the former Soviet Union. Seven of the articles compare only countries from Eastern Europe (Barany & Vinton 1990, Ishiyama 1993, Pacek 1994, Mahr & Nagle 1995, Bielasiak 1997, Szelenyi et al. 1997, Fidrmuc 2000), one compares only Baltic countries (Pettai & Kreuzer 1999), one compares two Baltic countries and one Eastern European country (Harper 2000), and one compares

TABLE 1   How comparative are election studies?

Number of countries	Number of elections		
	Single	Multiple	Total
Single	61	27	88
Multiple	0	13	13
Total	61	40	101

Russia and Ukraine (Pammett 1996). The remaining three are the only articles in the entire database to compare countries from the non-Baltic former Soviet Union with countries from Eastern Europe (Ishiyama 1997, Moraski & Loewenberg 1999, Moser 1999a; although see also Bohrer et al 2000; Tucker 2000a, 2001).

It is also interesting to note that the percentage of articles employing comparative analysis would have dropped even further had I chosen to include only articles that focused on elections as a dependent variable. Of the 13 elections included in the study solely because elections functioned as an independent variable, four were comparative studies (Ishiyama 1993, Pammett 1996, Bielasiak 1997, Pettai & Kreuzer 1999). Without these articles, only 10% (9 out of 88 articles) of the database would have contained multiple-country studies.

Whereas multiple-country studies have been largely eschewed, multiple-election studies have been far more prevalent. Almost 40% of the articles looked at more than one election. Although the vast majority of the 27 multiple-election single-country studies focus on Russia (14) or Poland (5), it is possible to find articles that analyze more than one election across a number of countries, including Bosnia (Shoup 1997), the Czech Republic (Fule 1997, Turnovec 1997), Lithuania (Clark 1995), Romania (Mihut 1994), Ukraine (Birch 1995), and even Kyrgyzstan (Huskey 1995, Koldys 1997).

Types of Elections

I turn next to the question of which elections scholars have chosen to analyze. Table 2 examines the breakdown of the articles across national and local elections (defined here as an election at any subnational level, including the elections of governors, regional legislatures, city mayors, or even town or local administrators).

There are two important patterns. First, scholars have overwhelmingly chosen to focus on national elections. Despite my broad definition of "local" elections, only 10 out of 101 articles analyzed such elections. Moreover, none of these articles compared elections across countries. Second, and perhaps more surprisingly, every article that analyzed subnational elections exclusively did so using Russian elections. If this trend continues, then almost our entire understanding of local elections in the post-communist context is likely to be based on the Russian case. Certainly, there is room here for interesting comparative research on local elections in other post-communist countries.

TABLE 2   National elections get all the attention

	Local	National	Both	Total
Single country: Russia	8	42	0	50
All other articles	0	49	2[a]	51
Total	8	91	2	101

[a]Romania and Kyrgyzstan.

TABLE 3   Scholars are more interested in legislative elections

	Executive	Legislative	Referenda	Multiple	Total
Single country: Russia	14	31	1	4	50
All other articles	0	42	0	9	51
Total	14	73	1	13	101

In addition to local versus national considerations, elections can be categorized by their subjects of contestation. Table 3 breaks down the articles in the database into those focusing on the vote for executives, legislators, or referenda. Again, two clear patterns emerge. First, elections for legislators are receiving much more attention than elections for executives. Some of this may simply be because several of the countries in the study do not have elected presidents, so that there are more legislative elections to analyze. Nevertheless, this cannot explain all of the variation. Russia has had both presidential and parliamentary elections. Given the predominant importance of the president in Russia's strong presidential system, one would expect to find more articles written about Russian presidential elections than Russian parliamentary elections. Instead, over twice as many articles have been written about Russian parliamentary elections.[12] The Polish case is an even more stark example. Of the 25 articles in the database that analyze Polish elections in either a single-country study or a comparative framework, 22 examine legislative elections exclusively, 3 examine both legislative and executive elections (Pacek 1994, Bell 1997, Shabad & Slomczynski 1999), and none examine only Polish presidential elections.

The second point of concern in Table 3 is that, similarly to the national/local divide, all the articles that focus exclusively on presidential elections are about Russian presidential elections. The situation is somewhat more heartening in that nine articles consider both legislative and executive elections in countries other than Russia. Nevertheless, it is curious that all the authors who chose to focus exclusively on presidential elections did so in the Russian context.

The lack of interest in presidential elections is somewhat surprising, especially when one considers that the study of elections in the American politics subfield is dominated by studies of presidential elections. The fact that most of the Eastern European countries are parliamentary republics may explain much of the preoccupation with parliamentary elections in that region, although this logic clearly does not explain the pattern in Russia. Likewise, it cannot explain why presidential elections in Poland, which is a mixed parliamentary-presidential state, have

---

[12]Interestingly, though, the eight articles that analyzed Russian local elections (see Table 2) are evenly split: four focus on regional gubernatorial elections (Hahn 1997, McFaul 1997a, Solnick 1998, Belin 1997), and the other four examine regional legislative elections (Colton 1990, Helf & Hahn 1992, Slider 1996, Golosov 1999).

TABLE 4   Both quantitative and qualitative methods are popular

	Qualitative	Quantitative	Total
Single country, single election	33	28	61
Single country, multiple elections	14	13	27
Multiple countries, multiple elections	5	8	13
Total	52	49	101

received so little attention. Perhaps it is intrinsically more interesting to sort out political parties in a new democracy than to study individual candidates who may run for election as independents. Alternatively, the predominance of studies of legislative elections outside of the Russian case may reflect the lack of attention paid to regions with powerful elected presidents, such as the Caucus region.

Finally, it is worth noting that only one article in the entire database attempts to explicitly compare the results of both presidential and parliamentary elections in multiple countries (Pacek 1994).[13]

Methods of Analysis

A final question concerns the methods that scholars have employed to study post-communist elections. Table 4 categorizes the 101 articles in the database on the basis of quantitative versus qualitative analysis. Both terms are open to interpretation; for this review, I have defined an article as quantitative if it either reports the results of statistical analysis or is primarily devoted to describing the results of a survey. I do not classify an article as quantitative if it merely reports public opinion polls as a supplementary form of analysis. Although the classification is obviously subjective, it does give us a sense of what proportion of articles are relying, at least in part, on quantitative analysis.

Table 4 contains two important findings. Most important, scholars are definitely taking advantage of both quantitative and qualitative research approaches. Moreover, there is no distinction between articles that focus exclusively on Russia and those that do not.[14] Given the history of Soviet and communist studies as a largely nonquantitative field, one might have expected researchers to be hesitant

---

[13]Pacek compares the effect of economic conditions on election results and turnout in four elections: one parliamentary election each in Poland, Bulgaria, and Czechoslovakia, and one Polish presidential election. My own work (e.g., Tucker 1999, 2000a), which is not included in the database, also spans this divide; it examines the effect of economic conditions on election results in Russia, Poland, Hungary, the Czech Republic, and Slovakia (two parliamentary elections from each country and two presidential elections from both Russia and Poland).

[14]Of the 50 articles that focus exclusively on Russia, 24 employ quantitative methods and 26 do not; of the remaining 51 articles, 25 use quantitative methods and 26 do not.

TABLE 5   Researchers take advantage of different sources of data

	National	Regional	Individual	Total
Single country, single election	0	14	14	28
Single country, multiple elections	0	11	2	13
Multiple countries, multiple elections	3	2	3	8
Total	3	27	19	49

to adapt the quantitative approaches long used in the study of elections and voting elsewhere. Conversely, one could imagine that analysts suddenly presented with new tools for analysis could get so caught up in using these new tools that they would abandon other important avenues of inquiry. Impressively, neither of these scenarios appears to have come to fruition, as scholars have chosen to apply both methods of study.

Table 4 also suggests a weak relationship between the methodology employed and the number of elections and countries studied. Generally speaking, comparative analysis is a little more likely than noncomparative analysis to rely on quantitative methods. Qualitative analysis is most frequently used in articles that examine a single election and is least frequently used in articles that examine multiple elections in multiple countries; single-country studies of multiple elections are in the middle. Nevertheless, this finding should not be overstated, as the proportions are fairly similar in any case and there is clear evidence of quantitative work in single-election studies and qualitative work in comparative studies.

Regarding the quantitative analyses, another interesting question concerns the type of data used in each article. Table 5 breaks down the 49 articles that employ quantitative analysis on the basis of the data used. Individual data come from surveys and are used to compare the vote choices or opinions of individuals.[15] Regional data are used in studies that either compare national election results disaggregated to a regional or precinct level or employ a systematic comparison of different regional election results.[16] National data are used in studies that compare the national election results for a party or candidate across different national elections; by definition, this category can only be applied to quantitative analysis from multiple elections, be it a time-series of election results from a single country or a cross-section of election results from multiple countries.

Table 5 leads to several interesting observations. Most striking is the predominance of cross-regional studies at the expense of cross-national studies in the

---

[15]One of the single-election articles used an elite survey as opposed to a mass survey, examining whether legislative voting behavior was affected by whether a Russian deputy had been elected on a party list or from a single-member district (Haspel et al. 1998).
[16]Of the 10 articles in the database that analyzed local elections, only three employed quantitative methods. Two of these compared results from regional elections across Russia (Solnick 1998, Golosov 1999), and one compared results from across Moscow (Colton 1990).

aggregate data category. In fact, 90% of the studies that use aggregate data relied on cross-regional data, whereas only 10% used cross-national analysis. Given the prevalence of quantitative studies using national data—especially in the economic voting sub-field—in the United States (Kramer 1971, Tufte 1975, Erikson 1989, MacKuen et al. 1992), other advanced industrialized democracies (Paldam 1991, Powell & Whitten 1993, Wilkin et al. 1997), and even Latin America (Remmer 1991), this finding seems baffling.

Nevertheless, in the context of the post-communist experience, it should not be so surprising. In no country are there enough data points to conduct a single-country time-series analysis across multiple elections. Cross-national analyses have to wrestle with the fact that the coding of basic categories such as "incumbents" across countries can be fraught with difficulties, not to mention problems with the comparability of explanatory variables. As an example, consider a study of economic voting. A cross-national statistical analysis including a series of Russian and Polish elections would have to assume that an unemployment statistic in Poland in 1991 measured the same thing as an unemployment statistic in Russia in 1999. A cross-regional statistical analysis, on the other hand, need only assume that an unemployment statistic in Russia in 1999 in Region A measured the same thing as an unemployment statistic in Russia in 1999 in Region B. In a region where questions persist concerning the reliability of data, especially in the earlier part of the decade, the second assumption is obviously easier to accept than the first.

Another explanation is that studies that employ national data must include multiple elections by definition, and, if single-country time-series analysis is not an option, this necessitates a study of multiple countries. Therefore, whatever factors have depressed the number of multiple-countries studies in general, as discussed above, are likely to have decreased the number of quantitative studies that employ national data as well.

A second interesting observation drawn from Table 5 is the variety in the popularity of survey data across comparative and noncomparative analyses. In single-election studies, survey data appear just as popular as aggregate data. In single-country multiple-election studies, however, survey data are much less popular than aggregate data, appearing in only 2 of the 13 quantitative studies. In multiple-country multiple-election studies, survey data appear more popular, although this impression is based on a small number of articles.

Though initially puzzling, these findings are not that surprising given the costs of acquiring survey data in an area of the world where researchers cannot simply download National Election Studies data from the web site of the ICPSR (Inter-University Consortium for Political and Social Research). Finding the time and funding to carry out one survey, let alone trying to repeat the same survey four years later, can be quite a burden to an individual researcher.[17] Therefore, it is not

---

[17]Indeed, it may even be easier to carry out the same survey in multiple countries—language difficulties notwithstanding—during a roughly similar time frame (e.g., Hungary, Slovakia, and the Czech Republic all had parliamentary elections during a six-month period in 1998) than to carry out another survey in the same country for another election.

surprising that most of the articles that used survey data commented on a single election. Regional data present a different picture. If one is willing to invest the time and effort to travel to the relevant national statistical office, then it is often not much more difficult to collect regional data over many years than it is for just one year. Although the quality of archives and libraries certainly differs between countries, the major investment of both time and money involves getting to the country in the first place.[18] By this logic, one would also expect little difference between the number of cross-regional studies that analyzed data from one election in a single country and the number that analyzed more than one election in a single country, but a large difference between the number of single-country and multiple-country studies that employ regional data. This is exactly what Table 5 reveals: 14 single-country single-election studies and 11 single-country multiple-election studies used regional data (for a total of 25 single-country studies), but only 2 articles used regional data from more than one country (Pacek 1994, Fidrmuc 2000; although see also Tucker 2000a, 2001).

Overall, though, Table 5 must be viewed in a similarly positive light to Table 4. Faced with new methodological opportunities, researchers who study elections and voting in post-communist countries have chosen to examine both aggregate and individual-level data, which can only be good for the development of the discipline. Analyses of individual and aggregate data can teach us different lessons, and it is encouraging to see scholars embracing both in their research.

Another interesting facet of the question of research methods can be found in Table 6. Table 4 illustrated an almost even split between the number of articles that employed quantitative analysis and those that did not. However, when we break these articles down by type of journal—area studies versus political science—this even split disappears. As Table 6 demonstrates, there is a much larger proportion of quantitative work on post-communist elections and voting in the political science journals (70%) than in the area studies journals (43%). One possible explanation could be that post-communist area studies journals probably have a history of publishing relatively qualitative work owing to the nature of Soviet Studies, and perhaps this bias has lingered into the post-communist era. Likewise, one might expect that general political science journals that have historically published quantitative work on American elections might be more comfortable publishing work on elections in new democracies that looks familiar; quantitative analysis might be a step in that direction.

Disaggregating the data to the level of the individual journal, however, suggests that the much of the explanation may lie with the journals themselves. Within the area studies journals, qualitative articles predominate in three journals

---

[18]The acquisition of language skills is a similar investment: Once a researcher has acquired the skill to translate data in one country, it is not costly to translate data from other years. Moving on to another country, however, can be much more difficult. Although more data are available in English as time goes by, this availability is by no means universal. In particular, Russia continues to publish its election results and regional statistical yearbook in Russian.

TABLE 6   Area studies journals are less likely to feature quantitative work

	Qualitative	Quantitative	Total
Area studies journals[a]	46	35	81
Political science journals[a]	6	14	20
Total	52	49	101

[a]Classification of journals by type can be found in footnote 2.

(*Communist and Post-Communist Studies*, *Demokratizatsiya*, and *Problems of Post-Communism*) and quantitative articles in two other journals (*Post-Soviet Geography and Economics* and *Post-Soviet Affairs*), while the remaining three have almost an even split. Although there are many fewer articles from the general political science journals, there is also evidence of journal preferences. One journal (*Comparative Politics*) published three qualitative articles and no quantitative articles, whereas three other journals (*American Political Science Review*, *Comparative Political Studies*, and *World Politics*) published only quantitative articles (two, three, and one respectively). In addition, *Electoral Studies* published five quantitative articles and only one qualitative article, although it is worth noting that this pattern would have changed greatly had I included articles from the "Notes on Recent Elections" section in that journal.

Why particular journals might prefer quantitative or qualitative studies of elections is another question, and there may be selection bias at work as the authors decide where to send their papers. Still, such findings beg the question of whether this pattern is limited to articles on elections and voting or whether it is present in other fields. Regardless of its cause, it remains an interesting pattern and one that merits watching as the field continues to develop.

A final interesting aspect of the qualitative/quantitative divide is highlighted in Table 7. Based on a very crude coding rule—whether or not the author's name suggested that he or she could be a citizen of one of the post-communist countries in the study—I broke down all the articles into three categories: only author(s) from post-communist countries; only author(s) who were *not* from post-communist countries (almost all of these were from Western countries, so for simplicity I will refer to them as Western authors); and collaborative works involving at least one author

TABLE 7   Is there a diffusion of quantitative methods from West to East?

	Qualitative	Quantitative	Total
Post-communist author(s)	17	6	23
Non-post-communist author(s)	32	33	65
Collaborative (at least one of each)	3	13	13
Total	52	49	101

from each of the groups. Although I am confident that a more rigorous coding rule would reveal shortcomings in my simple coding scheme, there are nevertheless distinct patterns in the table that would survive a recoding of a number of data points.

Of the three categories, articles written only by post-communist authors are by far the most likely to fall into the qualitative category. Whereas Western authors utilize quantitative and qualitative methods at a practically even rate (thus mimicking the database as a whole), post-communist authors are almost three times more likely to employ qualitative than quantitative methods. However, when post-communist authors collaborate with Western authors, the resulting work is much more likely to be quantitative than it is to be qualitative; of the 13 articles that fall into this category, 10 are quantitative.

One possible explanation for this pattern is that we are witnessing a diffusion of quantitative methods developed in the West for studying Western elections to non-Western academics through collaborative work. Clearly, work written by post-communist authors without collaboration with a Western author is much less likely to be quantitative than if there is collaboration. There are multiple means by which this diffusion may be taking place, but one must be the fact that post-communist citizens are both studying and teaching at Western academic institutions, which would obviously increase the likelihood of collaboration with Western colleagues. Another may be that Western academics are actively seeking collaboration with post-communist authors, not necessarily limited to those who are already studying or working in Western countries. Although the percentage of such collaborative work is still low (13% of the articles in the database), it is encouraging to see that it is occurring. That being said, it is important to note that 10 of the 13 collaborative articles examined Russian elections; of the remaining three, two focused on Poland, one on Poland and Hungary. Still, the fact that over one third of the articles in the database have at least one post-communist author is interesting, as it shows that although the field may still be dominated by Western authors, theirs are not the only voices being heard.[19] It would be interesting to learn the corresponding figures for other regions of the world.

WHAT ARE WE STUDYING ABOUT ELECTIONS AND VOTING?

Having explored how the subfield of elections and voting in post-communist democracies conducts research, I now address the question of what scholars are studying in their research on elections and voting. This section is divided into three

---

[19]One other interesting finding regarding the authorship of articles concerns the propensity of collaboration within the two categories. Whereas slightly under a third of the Western-only articles had at least two authors (20 out of 65), only one (Mateju & Vlachova 1998) of the 23 post-communist-only pieces was collaborative. So for the time being, it appears that the post-communist authors are much more interested in collaborating with Western authors than with other post-communist authors.

parts. First, I look at the cases in which elections function as explanatory variables and examine what they are being used to explain. Next, I turn to the vast majority of the articles in the database in which election results and voter choices are the dependent variables of the studies. I conclude with a short discussion of a small number of articles in the database in which elections function as a dependent variable but the outcome of the election is not what the author is interested in explaining.

Elections as Independent Variables

It was previously noted that 13 articles are included in the database exclusively because elections function as a primary independent variable in those articles. In 11 other articles elections function as both an independent and dependent variable, resulting in a total of 24 articles in which elections play a role as an explanatory variable.

What do authors use elections to explain? Most articles can be placed into one of two general categories. Either the election is invoked for its effect on the overall success or failure of democracy (or democratic consolidation) or the election is used to explain developments in the party system.

In the first category, one finds several articles on elections that took place in the first half of the decade, all of which have a roughly similar theme. The basic argument is that despite some hiccups in the process, the occurrence of the election (or series of elections) demonstrates that pluralism and democracy are indeed emerging. One finds this type of article across numerous countries, including Ukraine (Bojcun 1995), Romania (Mihut 1994), Lithuania (Clark 1995), and Russia (Sakwa 1996). One also finds the opposite argument: Despite the presence of a democratic election, and indeed victory by the democratic candidate, the election should not be interpreted to mean that democratic consolidation has taken place (Brovkin 1997). Two articles look for insight into the future success of Russian democracy by examining gubernatorial elections: Solnick (1998) assesses whether the 1996–1997 round of gubernatorial elections reveal that local democracy is being overrun by either a powerful center or powerful regional bosses (he finds that neither is the case), and Hahn (1997) comments on the likelihood of these same elections leading to further disintegration in the country (he concludes that they will not). One other interesting article examines not the results of an individual election but rather whether people in Ukraine and Russia see elections as having any inherent meaning in their lives and the effect of this attitude on the likelihood of democratic development in those countries (Pammett 1996).

The second type of article that uses elections as an explanatory variable examines the effect of an election or elections on the development of political parties and the party system. One common approach is to look at a series of early elections, asking how these elections have affected the emergence of a post-communist party system in that particular country or countries (Ishiyama 1993, Millard 1994b, Bielasiak 1997, Pettai & Kreuzer 1999). Other articles look at a specific election (or election cycle), asking how it will change the nature of the party system in that country (Zubek 1993, Koldys 1997, Szczerbiak 1999, McFaul 2000). In the Russian case, some authors have used elections and electoral rules in an attempt to explain the failure of Russian political parties to consolidate (Moser 1995, Clark 1999), although others provide a more optimistic outlook (Sakwa 1995, McFaul 2000). In addition, one article focuses on the effects of an election defeat on the evolution of a particular party, in this case the Hungarian Socialist Party (Agh 1995).

Falling into neither of the two general categories, a final set of articles examines whether aspects of the previous legislative election affect how Russian legislators subsequently vote in the parliament (Remington & Smith 1996, Haspel et al. 1998, Treisman 1998).

Elections as Dependent Variables

The vast majority of the articles in the database (88 out of 101) attempt to explain some aspect of election results or individual voting decisions. It is possible to very roughly divide these "dependent variable" articles into three distinct (but not entirely exclusive) categories. First, there are articles that primarily focus on explaining what happened in a particular election. These articles aim to communicate who won and lost the election and why. I refer to these articles as "election centered." A closely related type of article, which I label "party centered," tries to explain the success or failure of a particular party in an election or series of elections. The final type of article is interested not only in explaining election results but also in using those results to shed light on a particular topic of interest in the political science literature. Although some articles are much more explicit about this task than others, they all share the common feature of trying to draw conclusions that will be of interest beyond the confines of the particular election(s) and parties being analyzed. I refer to such articles as "hypothesis centered." Below, I address each of the three types of articles in turn.

Before turning to the examples, it is important to note that the classification proposed above is not intended to privilege any of the types of articles at the expense of the others. There is nothing inherently better or worse about election-, party-, or hypothesis-centered articles, and all three have clearly enhanced our understanding of elections and voting in post-communist countries.

ELECTION-CENTERED ARTICLES   An election-centered article is primarily concerned with trying to answer the question, "What determined the results of election X?" Accordingly, almost all of the articles that fall into this category are single-country single-election studies.

Election-centered articles come in two varieties. Quantitative election-centered articles tend to throw a lot of independent variables—often including various measures of demographics, socioeconomic status, subjective and objective economic indicators, and social, political, and economic attitudes—into a statistical analysis of the election results or vote choice. In general, aggregate-level studies have fewer variables than micro-level studies relying on survey data, but the overall approach is similar. Authors use these analyses to comment on the type of support enjoyed by the various political parties and candidates and/or the major factors underlying the voting decisions of individuals. Examples include articles on Ukraine (Wilson & Birch 1999), Poland (Wade et al. 1994, Chan 1995), and Russia (Wyman et al. 1994, Rose et al. 1997).

Qualitative election-centered articles are distinguished by a different pattern, although the general goal of providing insight into a given election remains the same. These articles always focus on the actions of the political parties and candidates competing in the election. The emphasis usually includes a systematic look at how the parties have run their campaigns and the types of voters they have attempted to target, but it may also extend to a wide variety of factors, such as policies pursued in the legislature or government, development of internal party decision-making structures, and public behavior of key party leaders. In addition, most qualitative election-centered articles contain at least a cursory description of the electoral system, if not a more explicit attempt to link electoral laws to election outcomes. In addition, many of these articles address other issues that may have influenced the outcome of the election, including economic conditions, underlying socioeconomic cleavages, and the degree to which the election may have been free and fair. Examples include articles focused on several different countries, such as Poland (Olson 1993, Millard 1994a), Hungary (Racz & Kukorelli 1995), Ukraine (Bojcun 1995), Bosnia (Shoup 1997), and Russia (Zlobin 1994, McFaul 1996, White et al. 1997b, Oates 2000).

PARTY-CENTERED ARTICLES   Party-centered articles aim to explain why a particular party fared the way it did, either in an individual election or across a series of elections. The most popular variety of the party-centered article attempts to explain how communist successor parties have fared in post-communist elections. Two articles address this in a comparative vein, and both conclude that the key explanatory variable in distinguishing between the relative success of post-communist parties across countries is the nature of the party itself and the type of strategy it pursues (Mahr & Nagle 1995, Ishiyama 1997). The same point is emphasized in single-country studies of the post-communist Party of Democratic Socialism in Germany (Olsen 1998) and Party of the Democratic Left in Poland (Curry 1995); see Wade et al. (1995) for a more demographic-based approach. In the Russian context, the debate often concerns whether the success of the Communist Party of the Russian Federation really represents a preference for a return to communism or whether the party has managed to morph itself into something new (Tsipko 1996, Urban 1996).

There are also party-centered articles focused on other parties, although the ones in the database are primarily limited to the Polish and Russian cases. Two articles examine Solidarity's stunning victory in the 1989 Polish parliamentary election; both concluded that a vote for Solidarity was a vote against the communists and predicted that the coalition of disparate groups under its umbrella would not last long (Heyns & Bialecki 1991, Zubek 1991). In Russia, scholars have tried to understand how Boris Yeltsin could manage to win the 1996 elections (Brovkin 1997, Brudny 1997) and why pro-reform liberals have done so poorly in parliamentary elections (Tsygankov 1995, Fish 1997). Finally, a recent article tracks the meteoric rise of Unity in the run up to the 1999 Russian Duma elections (Colton & McFaul 2000).

HYPOTHESIS-CENTERED ARTICLES   Hypothesis-centered articles are distinguished by an attempt to more directly link the analysis of an election or voting to a thematic question, usually with a strong connection to the general political science literature. Although the articles do not necessarily use the terminology of hypothesis testing, they do consider whether the subject of analysis provides evidence concerning a larger question about the nature of elections and voting. The three most popular topics that authors have attempted to address using post-communist countries as case studies are the influence of underlying societal cleavages in determining election results, the effect of economic conditions on electoral outcomes, and the impact of electoral institutions on elections.

I turn first to articles that consider whether election results are a function of underlying societal cleavages. In a way, all of these articles are looking for evidence to refute a null hypothesis that claims post-communist societies are so chaotic and filled with uncertainty that there will be no coherent patterns in elections and voting. Cleavages are important in political science because of their relationship to overall political stability and the development of party systems. In addition, much of the theoretical work on voting in advanced democracies depends on the presence of clear cleavages in society.

In general, the literature on elections and voting in post-communist countries offers a fairly consistent "yes" as an answer to the question of whether societal cleavages exist and can be recognized through voting patterns and election results. Beyond this minimal consensus, though, lie numerous suggestions as to where these cleavages are located.[20] Many have chosen to look toward traditional socioeconomic cleavages such as urban/rural splits, generational effects, and class (Kopstein & Richter 1992; Clem & Craumer 1995c, 1997; Wyman et al. 1995; Szelenyi et al. 1997; Moser 1999b). Other scholars have looked beyond socioeconomic considerations to cleavages based on factors such as geography (Wade et al. 1995, Hough 1998), ethnicity (Birch 1995), center-periphery conflict (Wyman et al. 1995, O'Loughlin et al. 1996), degree of religiosity (Jasiewicz 1993), and a contemporary-versus-traditional conflict (Gershanok 1996). Some studies have also addressed a cleavage that may be peculiar to transition countries, which is the attitude of voters toward political and economic reform (Clem & Craumer 1993, Powers & Cox 1997, Shabad & Slomczynski 1999).

Another subfield of the general voting literature that has attracted a great deal of attention from those studying elections and voting in post-communist countries is economic voting; as my own work falls into this category I include it in

---

[20]Indeed, the question of whether these cleavages should be located in the same place in different post-communist countries has itself become a subject of argument; see O'Loughlin et al. (1996) for a good summary of this debate.

the following discussion as well. In almost all of the election- and party-centered articles mentioned above, the state of the economy is considered as a potential explanatory variable; likewise, in the hypothesis-centered category, many of the cleavage-centered approaches use socioeconomic variables to help identify cleavages. However, some scholars have decided to place economic voting at the center of their analysis. Not surprisingly, all articles in the database in this category use quantitative analysis. The topic has been explored through both comparative and single-election analyses relying on both individual level-data (Colton 1996a, Mason & Sidorenko-Stephenson 1997, Powers & Cox 1997, Harper 2000) and aggregate-level data (Pacek 1994, Gibson & Cielecka 1995, Bell 1997, Fidrmuc 2000; Tucker 2000a, 2001).

To date, the primary motivating question for most studies has been whether the economy affects election results and voting behavior. Interestingly, there seems to be a divergence in the answer to this question between the macro-level work, which generally supports the conclusion that economic conditions affect election results, and the micro-level work, which tends to minimize the importance of economic considerations in affecting individual vote choices, especially relative to other factors (although see Mason & Sidorenko-Stephenson 1997). My suspicion is that this distinction is largely driven by the nebulous nature of the question. How exactly does one measure whether the economy matters? In micro-level studies, analysts have a wide range of additional variables that they can throw into the regression, such as evaluation of democratic reform (Harper 2000), assessment of the communist past (Powers & Cox 1997), and partisan affinity and issue preferences (Colton 1996). As these other variables also matter, they tend to affect the size and significance of the coefficients of the economic variables (see Colton 1996 for an explicit comparison of economic models with and without these other factors). In the macro-level analyses, it is much harder to find data on political variables, so the analyses are largely restricted to economic and demographic variables. Because the economic variables have turned out to have effects across numerous studies, authors tend to conclude that the economy matters.

Although it may be that the inherent nature of the analyses will continue to lead to different conclusions, more explicit attention to what is being tested and claimed would help. Testing to see whether economic conditions affect election results is clearly not the same thing as arguing that economic conditions completely determine election results. Likewise, testing to see if economic conditions affect certain types of parties in the manner in which a hypothesis predicts they will is not the same as testing to see whether economic conditions have the same magnitude of effect on all parties of a particular type. As we move away from the general question of whether the economy matters to examining in detail how it matters, micro- and macro-level studies may be able to complement each other more easily. Explicit consideration of the substantive effect of results may also allow more common dialogue across various studies, since it is possible in both micro- and macro-level studies. For example, Powers & Cox (1997, p. 628, Figure 2) report the change in the predicted probability of individuals supporting different parties as economic evaluations shift, while Tucker (2001, p. 321, Table 3) reports on the change in the predicted vote share for each party in an average region following comparable economic shocks.

Cutting across the micro-macro divide, however, is a different pattern. Single-election studies almost always focus on the question "how has the economy affected the vote for the parties that contested this particular election?" This is not to say that the authors do not have a priori expectations, but they are by and large couched in the particular circumstances of that country and tend to remain more implicit than explicit (although see Powers & Cox 1997). Although one can certainly find similarities in these expectations across articles, the authors are less concerned with the generalizable implications of their findings than with what has been learned about the effect of the economy on that particular election. Comparative analyses, however, are likely to be much more explicit in presenting general hypotheses about which types of parties—irrespective of country—the economy is likely to affect. Although the categories differ from study to study, the conclusions are all able to speak to the more general question of how economic conditions affect election results and voting in the post-communist context (Pacek 1994, Fidrmuc 2000, Harper 2000, Tucker 2000a).

As the study of economic voting in post-communist countries moves forward, it would be encouraging to see the trend toward more general models of economic voting in post-communist countries continue. This does not mean that we should eschew single-election studies but rather that we should strive toward a common theoretical framework in terms of which we can discuss either single-country or comparative work. To accomplish this, it may prove useful to be more explicit about the theoretical links between our hypotheses and existing economic voting models from established democracies, while remaining conscious of the factors that differentiate the post-communist context. Doing so may help the field move away from a series of individual hypotheses that vary from author to author toward a more unified theoretical approach, although the fact that all four studies mentioned above chose to use different general categories illustrates that this will not happen overnight.

Additionally, after a decade of work, it may be safe to move beyond the simple question of whether the economy matters. Clearly it does, and clearly it is not the only factor that matters. Therefore, we can now begin to ask the more interesting question of exactly *how* the economy affects election results and voting. Up until now, most generalizable work in this regard has focused on the question of what types of parties are affected by economic conditions and the direction of this effect (e.g., are they helped or hurt by better economic conditions?). Not surprisingly, incumbents have attracted the lion's share of attention, but other categories of parties have also been examined, including new-regime and old-regime parties (Tucker 2000a), reformist, nationalist, and left-wing parties (Fidrmuc 2000), post-communist parties (Harper 2000), and opposition and extreme-opposition parties (Pacek 1994). This attention to categories other than incumbents may prove especially valuable given that the two most broadly comparative studies both found that economic conditions did not affect incumbents in the manner the received wisdom would have us expect nearly as consistently as they affected other categories of parties (Tucker 1999, 2000a; Fidrmuc 2000).

Perhaps even more intriguingly, the post-communist cases hold open the possibility of contributing to an emerging literature that predicts variation in the effect of economic conditions, or, in other words, when economic conditions should be expected to have a stronger or weaker effect on election results and voting (e.g., Powell & Whitten 1993, Wilkin et al. 1997). Two articles that appeared in print after the closing date for the database tackle this question in regard to incumbent parties. Tucker (2001) predicts that economic conditions will have a greater effect on the election results for the primary incumbent in governing coalitions than on other incumbents; Duch (2002) predicts that economic conditions will have a greater effect on the choice to vote for incumbent parties as citizens become more informed about how democratic institutions function. Both authors present empirical support for their propositions, the former using aggregate-level data and the latter survey data. Taking the same idea in a different direction, I have elsewhere considered the effect of electoral and governing institutions on the relative impact of economic conditions on election results across different elections (Tucker 2000b).

Several authors have also used the post-communist experience to contribute to debates over the effect of electoral institutions and rules on election outcomes. Two articles explore the familiar debate over whether single-member districts reduce the number of effective political parties. In a single-country study of Hungary, Gabel (1995) finds support for the consensus view that fewer parties emerge from single-member districts than proportional representation districts. In a comparative study of six countries, though, Moser (1999a) comes to the opposite conclusion, arguing that single-member district elections do not necessarily reduce the number of political parties in the parliament. Other articles trace the effect of electoral rules more generally on the number of parties that successfully enter the parliament (Zubek 1993, Clark 1999, Moraski & Loewenberg 1999). Employing a slightly different approach, Colton (1996b) explicitly contrasts the effect of the winner-take-all nature of presidential elections with parliamentary elections lacking that feature in Russia. Finally, several articles test the effect of electoral rules on other aspects of elections that are discussed in the following section (Ishiyama 1994, Turnovec 1997, Golosov 1999).

Although space limitations prohibit going into much detail, numerous additional themes in political science have been addressed by articles in the database. One question of interest, especially in the post-Soviet cases, has been the relative influence of unfair election practices, ranging from the manipulation of local election administration by old party *nomenklatura*, violations of campaign spending rules, and control over the media (Helf & Hahn 1992, Huskey 1995, Slider 1996, Brovkin 1997) to outright fraud in determining election results (Filipov & Ordeshook 1997, Hough 1998). Another topic of interest has been electoral turnout, including variation across countries (Pacek 1994, Bohrer et al. 2000), elections (Myagkov et al. 1997), and regions (Wade et al. 1994; Clem & Craumer 1995b, 1997). Two other studies use turnout as an independent variable for explaining the party vote in Poland in 1991 (Heyns & Bialecki 1991, Wade et al. 1995). Finally, a number of interesting articles have explored geographic influences on election results (Clem & Craumer 1993, 1995a; O'Loughlin et al. 1996, O'Loughlin & Kolossov 1997, Hough 1998, Hinich et al. 1999).

OTHER DEPENDENT VARIABLES   Not all of the articles in the database that treat elections as a dependent variable attempt to explain election results or voting decisions. Additional topics include the translation of votes into seats (Turnovec 1997), the nominating strategies of parties (Ishiyama 1994), the decision of candidates to run with or without party affiliations (Moser 1999b), the relative success of candidates with party affiliation (Golosov 1999), and the stability of voting patterns across elections (Fule 1997, Myagkov et al. 1997). Finally, one article in the database analyzes the different types of campaign posters produced by competing political organizations in the 1993 Latvian parliamentary elections (Stukuls 1997).

CONCLUDING THOUGHTS

As the study of elections and voting in post-communist countries heads into its second decade, it faces both challenges and opportunities. Of all the aspects of the post-communist experience, elections and voting may be the most directly tied to a large existing literature in the field of political science. Therefore, studies of elections and voting in post-communist countries are not merely one facet of post-communist area studies but rather are part of a general political science literature. To make a contribution to this literature, however, will require a continued effort. Given the dearth of articles from the field in major political science journals and the lack of books published by university presses, it is clear that we need to be more aggressive in engaging questions that are of interest to the broader political science community. The trick is to do this without sacrificing the understanding of political dynamics inside these countries that comes from more focused study of individual elections and parties.

One option is to pursue research that strives to more explicitly link analyses of post-communist elections and voting to broader themes in the literature. Even if the purpose of an article is to shed light on a particular election, it is possible to simultaneously engage theoretical issues. Many studies have already proved this task manageable, especially in the areas of societal cleavages, economic voting, and electoral institutions. Another solution may be a renewed focus on comparative analysis. As noted above, most of the work in this field has focused on a single country. Comparative analysis may be able to speak more directly to the discipline as a whole by presenting evidence that is less closely tied to individual countries and circumstances. Although it surely would have been a mistake to rush into comparative analysis without understanding dynamics in individual countries, the field may now be reaching a point where the numerous single-country studies have provided a sufficient base upon which to build more comparative work.

This leads, however, to what might be the most serious issue facing the field, which is the preponderance of articles on Russia and Poland. We can take several steps to address this situation. The first, and probably most obvious, is to continue to encourage work on other post-communist countries. But because the pattern is probably unlikely to change greatly in the near future, we should be more conscious of the imbalance and avoid the temptation to generalize from one case when it is not warranted. Another, perhaps counterintuitive, approach is to continue to encourage work on Russia and Poland, but to place this work in a more explicitly comparative framework. By including these countries in comparative studies, we can both take advantage of the wealth of knowledge that is accumulating around them and see how they compare to other countries, thus gaining a better sense of when it is legitimate to generalize from the Polish and Russian experience and when it may not be.

Another way to break out of this seeming dependence on the Russian case may be for researchers to follow in the footsteps of the successful East-West collaboration on studies of Russian elections. As was noted above, 10 of the 13 articles in the database that included at least one post-communist and one Western author focused on Russia. Obviously, this pattern reflects the prevalence of contacts and relationships between Western and Russian academics. One way to encourage collaborative work on non-Russian elections—and indeed more work in general on non-Russian elections—must be for Westerners writing in this field to try to develop similar contacts and relationships with post-communist academics and institutions in countries besides Russia.[21] Although normally beyond the purview of a review article, I think it is worth noting that this is an area in which funding and grant-giving institutions could play important roles in helping the field to develop. Imagine what could be gained from an annual conference, rotating among post-communist countries, that paired local social scientists and Western academics to produce joint studies of post-communist elections. Not only could such contacts lead to an increase in work on specific post-communist countries, but it might get the whole community of scholars thinking about what could be learned about elections and voting in post-communist countries generally.

---

[21]There are certainly institutions in post-communist countries where researchers are already studying elections and voting in their own (and other post-communist) countries. Even in my own field work, I have met academics engaged in such research at the Institute for Social Studies at the University of Warsaw, the Institute of Philosophy and Sociology in the Polish Academy of Sciences, Central European University in Budapest, the Institute of Sociology in the Academy of Social Sciences in Prague, and the Institute for Sociology in the Slovak Academy of Sciences.

Although it is clear that Westerners and Russians have managed to start this process already, it is possible that a little money in the right place now could build similarly fruitful partnerships in the rest of the post-communist world, which could play a crucial role in the development of the field.

I would like to close with another exhortation for collaborative efforts. Not only do Western authors and post-communist authors have much to learn from one another, but those who study Western elections and post-communist elections must have much to teach each other as well. As the study of Western, and in particular American, elections can provide a reservoir of theoretical and methodological insights for those interested in post-communist elections—preventing us from having to reinvent the wheel in many cases—it is likewise true that post-communist elections can present a host of new empirical data and theoretical questions for existing debates. There are many potentially valuable synergies between work on elections and voting in new post-communist democracies and similar literatures in more established democracies. Anyone who has ever wondered how electoral institutions affect electoral outcomes should be thrilled by the possibility of having so many new sets of electoral rules appear simultaneously. Scholars who have bemoaned the lack of survey data during the early days of voting in the United States can finally have an opportunity to test how voters behave in initial rounds of competitive elections. Theories of economic voting that have primarily been tested in relatively stable economic settings can be analyzed in (and modified for) a context of much more extreme change. Moreover, the opportunities for comparative research may be unprecedented. So just as I have suggested that those who write on elections and voting in post-communist countries ought to try to contribute to the general theoretical literature, I also urge those who study elections and voting in more advanced democracies to give a long hard look at the post-communist cases and the emerging literature in this field.[22] It is hoped that this article can serve as a springboard to such collaborative interest.

Although important challenges remain, there are many achievements of which the subfield of elections and voting in post-communist countries should be proud. Faced with a brand-new subject for analysis, scholars have eagerly rushed to the fill the void and employed a wide variety of methodological tools in doing so. And although a large amount of attention continues to be focused on Russia, scholars are clearly branching out and considering multiple post-communist experiences. At the same time, we are beginning to actively embrace questions of interest to those who are not area specialists, demonstrating that there may be much for mainstream political science to learn from the study of post-communist elections and voting.

---

[22]Consider, for example, a two-day conference. On the first day, those who study elections in established democracies could present papers and those who study elections in post-communist countries could serve as discussants; on the second day, they would reverse roles. This would probably be extremely illuminative to all participants.

The *Annual Review of Political Science* is online at http://polisci.annualreviews.org

LITERATURE CITED

Agh A. 1995. The experience of the first demo-cratic parliaments in East Central Europe. *Communist Post-Communist Stud.* 28(2): 203–14

Barany ZD, Vinton L. 1990. Breakthrough to democracy: elections in Poland and Hungary. *Communist Post-Communist Stud.* 23(2): 191–212

Belin L. 1997. Russia's 1996 gubernatorial elections and the implications for Yeltsin. *Demokratizatsiya* 5(2):165–83

Belin L, Orttung RW. 1997. *The Russian Parliamentary Elections of 1995: The Battle for the Duma.* Armonk, NY: Sharpe

Bell J. 1997. Unemployment matters: voting patterns during the economic transition in Poland, 1990–1995. *Eur.-Asia Stud.* 49(7): 1263–91

Benoit K. 1998. *The causes and effects of electoral systems (in Hungary).* PhD thesis. Harvard Univ.

Bielasiak J. 1997. Substance and process in the development of party systems in East Central Europe. *Communist Post-Communist Stud.* 30(1):23–44

Birch S. 1995. Electoral behaviour in western Ukraine in national elections and referendums, 1989–91. *Eur.-Asia Stud.* 47(7):1145–76

Birch S. 1998. *The social determinants of electoral behaviour in Ukraine,* 1989–1994. PhD thesis. Univ. Essex

Birch S. 2000. *Elections and Democratization in Ukraine.* New York: St. Martin's

Bohrer R, Pacek AC, Radcliff B. 2000. Electoral participation, ideology, and party politics in post-communist Europe. *J. Polit.* 62(4):1161–72

Bojcun M. 1995. The Ukrainian parliamentary elections in March–April 1994. *Eur.-Asia Stud.* 47(2):229–49

Brader T, Tucker JA. 2001. The emergence of mass partisanship in Russia, 1993–96. *Am. J. Polit. Sci.* 45(1):69–83

Brovkin V. 1997. Time to pay the bills: presidential elections and political stabilization in Russia. *Prob. Communism* 44(6):34–42

Brudny YM. 1997. In pursuit of the Russian presidency: why and how Yeltsin won the 1996 presidential election. *Communist Post-Communist Stud.* 30(3):255–75

Bunce V. 2001. Democratization and economic reform. *Annu. Rev. Polit. Sci.* 4:43–65

Carpenter M. 1997. Slovakia and the triumph of nationalist populism. *Communist Post-Communist Stud.* 30(2):205–20

Chan K. 1995. Poland at the crossroads: the 1993 general election. *Eur.-Asia Stud.* 47(1):123–45

Chan K. 1998. The Polish general election of 1997. *Elect. Stud.* 17(4):561–67

Clark T. 1995. The Lithuanian political party system: a case study of democratic consolidation. *East Eur. Polit. Soc.* 9(1):41–62

Clark W. 1999. The Russian state Duma: 1993, 1995, and 1999. *Prob. Communism* 46(6):3–11

Clem R, Craumer PR. 1993. The geography of the April 25 (1993) Russian referendum. *Post-Sov. Geogr. Econ.* 34(8):481–96

Clem R, Craumer PR. 1995a. The geography of the Russian 1995 parliamentary election: continuity, change, and correlates. *Post-Sov. Geogr. Econ.* 36(10):587–616

Clem R, Craumer PR. 1995b. The politics of Russia's regions: a geographical analysis of the Russian election and constitutional plebiscite of December 1993. *Post-Sov. Geogr. Econ.* 36(2):67–86

Clem R, Craumer PR. 1995c. A rayon-level analysis of the Russian election and constitutional plebiscite of December 1993. *Post-Sov. Geogr. Econ.* 36(8):459–75

Clem R, Craumer PR. 1997. Urban-rural voting differences in Russian elections, 1995–1996: a rayon-level analysis. *Post-Sov. Geogr. Econ.* 38(7):379–95

Colton TJ. 1990. The politics of democratization: the Moscow election of 1990. *Post-Sov. Aff.* 6(4):285–344

Colton TJ. 1996a. Economics and voting in Russia. *Post-Sov. Aff.* 12(4):289–318

Colton TJ. 1996b. From the parliamentary to the presidential election: Russians get real about politics. *Demokratizatsiya* 4(3):371–79

Colton TJ. 2000a. *Parties, citizens, and democratic consolidation in Russia.* Presented at Ten Years after the Collapse of the Soviet Union: Lessons and Perspectives, Oct. 13–14, Princeton, NJ. 46 pp.

Colton TJ. 2000b. *Transitional Citizens: Voters and What Influences Them in the New Russia.* Cambridge, MA: Harvard Univ. Press

Colton TJ, Hough JF, eds. 1998 *Growing Pains: Russian Democracy and the Election of 1993.* Washington, DC: Brookings Inst.

Colton TJ, McFaul M. 2000. Reinventing Russia's party of power: "Unity" and the 1999 Duma election. *Post-Sov. Aff.* 16(3):201–24

Curry J. 1995. Elected communists in Poland. *Prob. Communism* 42(1):46–50

Duch R. 2002. A developmental model of heterogeneous economic voting in new democracies. *Am. Polit. Sci. Rev.* 95(4):895–910

Erikson RS. 1989. Economic conditions and the presidential vote. *Am. Polit. Sci. Rev.* 83(2):567–73

Fidrmuc J. 2000. Economics of voting in post-communist countries. *Elect. Stud.* 19(2/3):199–217

Filipov M, Ordeshook PC. 1997. Who stole what in Russia's December 1993 elections. *Demokratizatsiya* 5(1):36

Fish MS. 1997. The predicament of Russian liberalism: evidence from the December 1995 parliamentary elections. *Eur.-Asia Stud.* 49(2):191–220

Fule E. 1997. Changes on the Czech political scene. *Elect. Stud.* 16(3):341–47

Gabal I, ed. 1996. *The 1990 Election to the Czechoslovakian Federal Assembly: Analyses, Documents and Data.* Berlin: Sigma

Gabel MJ. 1995. The political consequences of electoral laws in the 1990 Hungarian elections. *Comp. Polit.* 27(2):205–14

Gelman V, Golosov G, eds. 1999. *Elections in Russia, 1993–1996: Analyses, Documents and Data.* Berlin: Sigma

Gershanok G. 1996. Cats and mice: the presidential campaign in the Russian heartland. *Demokratizatsiya* 4(3):349–57

Gibson J, Cielecka A. 1995. Economic influences on the political support for market reform in post-communist transitions: some evidence from the 1993 Polish parliamentary elections. *Eur.-Asia Stud.* 47(5):765–85

Golosov G. 1999. From Adygeya to Yaroslavl: factors of party development in the regions of Russia, 1995–1998. *Eur.-Asia Stud.* 51(8):1333–65

Hahn J. 1997. Regional elections and political stability in Russia. *Post-Sov. Geogr. Econ.* 38(5):251–63

Harper M. 2000. Economic voting in postcommunist Eastern Europe. *Comp. Polit. Stud.* 33(9):1191–227

Haspel M, Remmington T, Smith S. 1998. Electoral institutions and party cohesion in the Russian Duma. *J. Polit.* 60(2):417–39

Helf G, Hahn J. 1992. Old dogs and new tricks: party elites in the Russian regional elections of 1990. *Slav. Rev.* 51(3):511–30

Heyns B, Bialecki I. 1991. Solidarnosc: reluctant vanguard or makeshift coalition? *Am. Polit. Sci. Rev.* 85(2):351–70

Hinich M, Khmelko V, Ordeshook P. 1999. Ukraine's 1998 parliamentary elections: a spatial analysis. *Post-Sov. Aff.* 15(2):149–85

Hough JF. 1998. The political geography of European Russia: republics and oblasts. *Post-Sov. Geogr. Econ.* 39(2):63–95

Huskey E. 1995. The rise of contested politics in Central Asia: elections in Kyrgyzstan, 1989–90. *Eur.-Asia Stud.* 47(5):813–33

Ishiyama J. 1993. Founding elections and the development of transitional parties: the cases of Estonia and Latvia, 1990–1992. *Communist Post-Communist Stud.* 26(3):277–99

Ishiyama J. 1994. Electoral rules and party nomination strategies in ethnically cleaved societies: the Estonian transitional election of 1990. *Communist Post-Communist Stud.* 27(2):177–92

Ishiyama J. 1997. The sickle or the rose? Previous regime types and the evolution of the ex-communist parties in post-communist politics. *Comp. Polit. Stud.* 30(3):299–330

Jasiewicz K. 1993. Polish politics on the eve of the 1993 elections: toward fragmentation or pluralism? *Communist Post-Communist Stud.* 26(4):387–411

Jones-Luong P. 1998. *Ethno-politics and institutional design: explaining the establishment of electoral systems in post-Soviet central Asia.* PhD thesis. Harvard Univ.

Karasimeonov G, ed. 1997. *The 1990 Election to the Bulgarian Grand National Assembly and the 1991 Election to the Bulgarian National Assembly: Analyses, Documents and Data.* Berlin: Sigma

King G, Keohane R, Verba S. 1994. *Designing Social Inquiry: Scientific Inference in Qualitative Research.* Princeton, NJ: Princeton Univ. Press

Klingemann H-D, Mochmann E, Newton K, eds. 2000. *The 1990 Election to the Hungarian National Assembly: Analyses, Documents and Data.* Berlin: Sigma

Koldys G. 1997. Constraining democratic development: institutions and party system formation in Kyrgystan. *Demokratizatsiya* 5(3): 351–75

Kopstein J, Richter K-O. 1992. Communist social structure and post-communist elections: voting for reunification in East Germany. *Communist Post-Communist Stud.* 25 (4):363–80

Kramer GH. 1971. Short-term fluctuations in U.S. voting behavior: 1896–1964. *Am. Polit. Sci. Rev.* 65:131–43

Krejcí O. 1995. *History of Elections in Bohemia and Moravia.* Boulder, CO: East Eur. Monogr.

Krupavicius A. 1997. Notes on recent elections: the Lithuanian parliamentary elections of 1996. *Elect. Stud.* 16(4):541–75

Lentini P, ed. 1995. *Elections and Political Order in Russia: The Implications of the 1993 Elections to the Federal Assembly.* Budapest/New York: Cent. Eur. Univ. Press

MacKuen MB, Erikson RS, Stimson JA. 1992.

Peasants or bankers? The American electorate and the U.S. economy. *Am. Polit. Sci. Rev.* 86(3):507–611

Mahr A, Nagle J. 1995. Resurrection of the successor parties and democratization in East-Central Europe. *Communist Post-Communist Stud.* 28(4):393–409

Mason DS, Sidorenko-Stephenson S. 1997. Public opinion and the 1996 elections in Russia: nostalgic and statist, yet pro-market and pro-Yeltsin. *Slav. Rev.* 56(4):698–717

Mateju P, Vlachova K. 1998. Values and electoral decisions in the Czech Republic. *Communist Post-Communist Stud.* 31(3):249–69

McFaul M. 1996. Russia's 1996 presidential elections. *Post-Sov. Aff.* 12(4):318–50

McFaul M. 1997a. Russian electoral politics after transition: regional and national assessments. *Post-Sov. Geogr. Econ.* 38(9):507–49

McFaul M. 1997b. *Russia's 1996 Presidential Election: The End of Polarized Politics.* Stanford, CA: Hoover Inst.

McFaul M. 2000. Russia's 1999 parliamentary elections: party consolidation and fragmentation. *Demokratizatsiya* 8(1):5–23

Mihut L. 1994. The emergence of political pluralism in Romania. *Communist Post-Communist Stud.* 27(4):411–22

Millard F. 1994a. The Polish parliamentary election of September, 1993. *Communist Post-Communist Stud.* 27(3):295–313

Millard F. 1994b. The shaping of the Polish party system, 1989–93. *East Eur. Polit. Soc.* 8(3):467–94

Miller AH, Klobucar TF. 2000. The development of party identification in post-Soviet societies. *Am. J. Polit. Sci.* 44(4):667–86

Moraski B, Loewenberg G. 1999. The effect of legal thresholds on the revival of former communist parties in East-Central Europe. *J. Polit.* 61(1):151–70

Moser R. 1995. The impact of the electoral system on post-communist party development: the case of the 1996 Russian parliamentary elections. *Elect. Stud.* 14(4):337–98

Moser R. 1999a. Electoral systems and the number of parties in postcommunist states. *World Polit.* 51(3):359–84

Moser R. 1999b. Independents and party formation: elite partisanship as an intervening variable in Russian politics. *Comp. Polit.* 37(2):147–66

Moser RG. 2001. *Unexpected Outcomes: Electoral Systems, Political Parties, and Representation in Russia.* Pittsburgh, PA: Univ. Pittsburgh Press

Myagkov M, Ordeshook P, Sobyanin A. 1997. The Russian electorate, 1991–1996. *Post-Sov. Aff.* 13(2):134–66

Oates S. 1998. *Voting behavior and party development in new democracies: the Russian Duma elections of 1993 and 1995.* PhD thesis. Emory Univ.

Oates S. 2000. The 1999 Russian Duma elections. *Problems of Post-Communism* 47(3): 3–14

O'Loughlin J, Kolossov V, Vendina O. 1997. The electoral geographies of a polarizing city: Moscow, 1993–1996. *Post-Sov. Geogr. Econ.* 38(10):567–600

O'Loughlin J, Shin M, Talbot P. 1996. Political geographies and cleavages in the Russian parliamentary elections. *Post-Sov. Geogr. Econ.* 37(6):355–85

Olsen J. 1998. Germany's PDS and varieties of post-communist socialism. *Prob. Communism* 45(6):42–52

Olson D. 1993. Compartmentalized competition: the managed transitional election system of Poland. *J. Polit.* 55(2):415–41

Pacek A. 1994. Macroeconomic conditions and electoral politics in East Central Europe. *Am. J. Polit. Sci.* 38(3):723–44

Paldam M. 1991. How robust is the vote function? A study of seventeen nations over four decades. In *Economics and Politics: The Calculus of Support*, ed. H Norpoth, MS Lewis-Beck, J-D Lafay, pp. 9–31. Ann Arbor: Univ. Mich. Press

Pammett J. 1996. The meaning of elections in transitional democracies: evidence from Russia and Ukraine. *Elect. Stud.* 15(3):363–81

Perepechko AS. 1999. *Spatial change and continuity in Russia's political party system: comparison of the constituent assembly elec-*

tion of 1917 and parliamentary election of 1995. PhD thesis. Univ. Washington

Pettai V, Kreuzer M. 1999. Party politics in the Baltic states: social bases and institutional contest. *East Eur. Polit. Soc.* 13(1):148–89

Powell GB, Whitten GD. 1993. A cross-national analysis of economic voting: taking account of the political context. *Am. J. Polit. Sci.* 37(2):391–414

Powers DV, Cox JH. 1997. Echoes from the past: the relationship between satisfaction with economic reforms and voting behavior in Poland. *Am. Polit. Sci. Rev.* 91(3):617–33

Racz B, Kukorelli I. 1995. The second generation post-communist elections in Hungary in 1994. *Eur.-Asia Stud.* 47(2):251–79

Remington TF, Smith SS. 1996. Political goals, institutional context, and the choice of an electoral system: the Russian parlimentary election law. *Am. J. Polit. Sci.* 40(4):1253–79

Remmer KL. 1991. The political impact of economic crisis in Latin America in the 1980s. *Am. Polit. Sci. Rev.* 85(3):777–800

Rose R. 1998. Negative and positive party identification in post-communist countries. *Elect. Stud.* 17(2):217–34

Rose R, Tikhomirov E, Mishler W. 1997. Understanding multi-party choice: the 1995 Duma election. *Eur.-Asia Stud.* 49(5):799–823

Sakwa R. 1995. The Russian elections of December 1993. *Eur.-Asia Stud.* 47(2):195–227

Sakwa R. 1996. *The Communist Party of the Russian Federation and the Electoral Process.* Glasgow: Cent. Stud. Public Policy Univ. Strathclyde

Shabad G, Slomczynski K. 1999. Political identities in the initial phase of systemic transformation in Poland: a test of the tabula rasa hypothesis. *Comp. Polit. Stud.* 32(6):690–723

Shoup P. 1997. The elections in Bosnia and Herzegovina: the end of an illusion. *Prob. Communism* 44(1):3–15

Slider D. 1996. Elections to Russia's regional assemblies. *Post-Sov. Aff.* 12(3):243–64

Solnick S. 1998. Gubernatorial elections in

Russia, 1996–1997. *Post-Sov. Aff.* 14(1):48–80

Stegmaier MA. 2000. *Voting behavior during economic and political transitions: the case of post-communist East Central Europe (Hungary, Poland, Czech Republic).* PhD thesis. Univ. Iowa

Stukuls D. 1997. Imagining the nation: campaign posters of the first postcommunist elections in Latvia. *East Eur. Polit. Soc.* 11(1):131–54

Szczerbiak A. 1999. Interests and values: Polish parties and their electorates. *Eur.-Asia Stud.* 51(8):1401–32

Szelenyi I, Fodor E, Hanley E. 1997. Left turn in postcommunist politics: bringing class back in? *East Eur. Polit. Soc.* 11(1):190–224

Tóka G, ed. 1995. *The 1990 Election to the Hungarian National Assembly: Analyses, Documents and Data.* Berlin: Sigma

Treisman D. 1995. *Fiscal transfers, voting behavior, and national integration in post-Soviet Russia.* PhD thesis. Harvard Univ.

Treisman D. 1998. Dollars and democratization: the role and power of money in Russia's transitional elections. *Comp. Polit.* 31(1):1–19

Tsipko A. 1996. Why Gennady Zyuganov's communist party finished first. *Demokratizatsiya* 4(2):185–200

Tsygankov A. 1995. Russia: strategic choices facing Democrats. *Prob. Communism* 42(2):49–53

Tucker JA. 1999. *Reconsidering economic voting: party type vs. incumbency in transition countries.* Presented at 1999 Ann. Meet. Am. Polit. Sci. Assoc., Sept. 2–5, 1999, Atlanta, GA

Tucker JA. 2000a. *It's the economy, comrade! Economic conditions and election results in post-communist Russia, Poland, Hungary, Slovakia, and the Czech Republic from 1990–96.* PhD thesis. Harvard Univ.

Tucker JA. 2000b. *Taking account of the institutional effect: how institutions mediate the effect of economic conditions on election results in five post-communist countries.* Presented at 2000 Ann. Meet. Am. Polit. Sci. Assoc., Aug. 31–Sep. 3, 2000, Washington, DC

Tucker JA. 2001. Economic conditions and the vote for incumbent parties in Russia, Poland, Hungary, Slovakia, and the Czech Republic from 1990–1996. *Post-Sov. Aff.* 17(4):309–31

Tufte ER. 1975. Determinants of the outcomes of midterm congressional elections. *Am. Polit. Sci. Rev.* 69(3):812–26

Turnovec F. 1997. Votes, seats and power: 1996 parliamentary election in the Czech Republic. *Communist Post-Communist Stud.* 30(3):289–305

Tworzecki H. 1994. *The political consequences of the cleavage structure: the bases of party support in post-1989 Poland.* PhD thesis. Univ. Toronto

Tworzecki H. 1996. *Parties and Politics in Post-1989 Poland.* Boulder, CO: Westview

Urban J. 1996. The communist movement in post-Soviet Russia. *Demokratizatsiya* 4(2):173–84

Wade L, Groth A, Lavelle P. 1994. Estimating participation and party voting in Poland: the 1991 parliamentary elections. *East Eur. Polit. Soc.* 8(1):94–121

Wade L, Lavelle P, Groth A. 1995. Searching for voting patterns in post-communist Poland's Sejm elections. *Communist Post-Communist Stud.* 28(4):411–25

White S, Rose R, McAllister I. 1997a. *How Russia Votes.* Chatham, NJ: Chatham House

White S, Wyman M, Oates S. 1997b. Parties and voters in the 1995 Russian Duma election. *Eur.-Asia Stud.* 49(5):767–98

Whitefield S, Evans G. 1999. Class, markets, and partisanship in post-Soviet Russia: 1993–96. *Elect. Stud.* 18:155–78

Wilkin S, Haller B, Norpoth H. 1997. From Argentina to Zambia: a world-wide test of economic voting. *Elect. Stud.* 16(3):301–16

Wilson A, Birch S. 1999. Voting stability, political gridlock: Ukraine's 1998 parliamentary elections. *Eur.-Asia Stud.* 51(6):1039–68

Wyman M. 1997. The Russian elections of 1995 and 1996. *Elect. Stud.* 16(1):79–85

Wyman M, Miller B, White S, Heywood P.

1994. The Russian elections of December 1993. *Elect. Stud.* 13(3):254–71

Wyman M, White S, Miller B, Heywood P. 1995. Public opinion, parties and voters in the December 1993 Russian elections. *Eur.-Asia Stud.* 47(4):591–614

Wyman M, White S, Oates S, eds. 1998. *Elections and Voters in Post-Communist Russia.* Cheltenham, UK: Elgar

Zlobin N. 1994. Finita la comedia? *Demokratizatsiya* 2(2):173–76

Zubek V. 1991. The threshold of Poland's transition: 1989 electoral campaign as the last act of a united Solidarity. *Stud. Comp. Communism* 24(4):355–76

Zubek V. 1993. The fragmentation of Poland's political party system. *Communist Post-Communist Stud.* 26(1):47–71

Annu. Rev. Polit. Sci. 2002. 5:305–31
DOI: 10.1146/annurev.polisci.5.112701.184858
Copyright © 2002 by Annual Reviews. All rights reserved

CORPORATISM: The Past, Present, and Future of a Concept

Oscar Molina and Martin Rhodes

Department of Social and Political Science, European University Institute, 50016 San Domenico di Fiesole, Florence, Italy; e-mail: oscar.molina@iue.it, martin.rhodes@iue.it

Key Words economic policy, industrial relations, bargaining, social pacts

■ **Abstract** Following a period of almost obsessive academic attention in the 1980s, in the early 1990s the concept of corporatism fell from favor, as its explanatory powers appeared to wane and the Keynesian welfare systems under which it had flourished apparently fell into decline. In the late 1990s, a new interest in corporatism emerged, in line with new patterns of concertation and corporatist behavior in some unexpected places—countries in which the institutional basis for collaborative, bargained methods of policy making and conflict resolution seemed distinctly unpromising. We review the extensive literature on corporatism since the 1970s and consider its applicability in the contemporary period. We argue that an excessively structural-functionalist interpretation of corporatism led many wrongly to predict its demise as a form of policy making, and that an understanding of its persistence and new manifestations today must resurrect and strengthen some early, recently neglected insights into processes of political exchange.

INTRODUCTION

When Schmitter asked, "Still the century of corporatism?" in the title of his seminal 1974 article, the answer seemed to be a definite "yes." Many of the countries of Western Europe had developed complex and enduring forms of interest representation and intermediation that appeared to warrant a revision of how we understood the workings of democratic polities. Alongside party systems and parliamentary politics, we had also to understand the equally important contribution to governance made by networks linking government with interest organizations, many of which had quasi-public status as key actors in policy making (Offe 1981). Although the Scandinavian countries and Austria provided the most compelling examples of this type of polity, other nations contained less complete but nevertheless important elements of neo-corporatist bargaining as integral parts of their systems of government.

But almost a quarter of a century later, two seasoned analysts of European economic policy and industrial relations argued that "there is no reason to doubt that, as a strategic program for the resolution of employment issues, neo-corporatism

1094-2939/02/0615-0305$14.00

305

is moribund—defeated on the ground by the actual evolution of employment relations before reluctant abandonment by its academic proponents" (Grahl & Teague 1997, p. 418). According to this view, the corporatism concept had outlived its utility, for in a neoliberal world of freer markets and welfare state retrenchment, the practice of corporatist policy making was bound to disappear. In reality, though, reports of the death of corporatism were greatly exaggerated. Employment issues (wage bargaining and labor market regulation) continued to be at the center of the still highly coordinated Scandinavian and Austrian industrial relations systems; meanwhile, new "social pacts" had sprung up across Europe from the late 1980s onward, specifically to deal with new turbulence and new challenges in the economic environment. Even the founding fathers of corporatist studies mistakenly assumed that if the structures on which corporatism had been based were eroded (i.e., Keynesian policy making and Fordist industrial organization), then corporatist behavior and patterns of governance would also disappear (e.g., Schmitter & Streeck 1991).

In the core sections of this article, we attribute this error of analysis to the ways in which the concept of corporatism was developed from the 1970s onward. Although originally endowed with both structural and procedural significance as a system *and* a process of decision making (albeit by different authors and streams of inquiry), by the 1980s and 1990s, corporatism as an evolutionary form of governance—and especially as a mode of macro policy making—was being neglected. Instead, there was an emphasis at the macro level on corporatism as a "system" and its degree of association with certain kinds of economic performance, as well as a concentration at meso levels on ever more detailed empirical investigations of the sectoral arena of policy making. Thus, political scientists were caught unawares—both empirically and conceptually—in the mid-1990s, when macro policy concertation (i.e., forms of routinized bargaining between governments, employers, and trade unions) reemerged. Responding to this new reality requires new attention to corporatism as a macropolitical phenomenon. Also needed, as we suggest toward the end of this article, are a revival and reinterpretation of a now neglected part of the corporatist literature—that devoted to the modes and modalities of political exchange.

A BRIEF HISTORY

Since it first entered the academic lexicon and debate, the term corporatism has been characterized by ambiguity, imprecision, and a liberal, rather undisciplined usage. This has been because of its initial ideological connotations (connected to twentieth-century fascism), its gradual (and at times fashion-driven) adoption to explain diverse phenomena, and its application to very different time periods and countries. Despite great attempts to clarify the term (e.g., Nedelman & Meier 1977, Lehmbruch 1979, Panitch 1980, Williamson 1989), corporatism became a multipurpose concept. Its elasticity has ensured its popularity; but simultaneously its power to explain or even characterize political systems and processes has been diluted.

Historically, the use of the term corporatism had a strong normative and ideological component, adopted by fascist and communist ideologues and activists for widely divergent reasons, but having at its core the advocacy of an institutional relationship between systems of authoritative decision making and interest representation. Accordingly, the term became synonymous with the structures of a strong and dominant state. After World War II, the work of Shonfield (1965) marked the renaissance of corporatism as a theoretical concept. He provided empirical evidence supporting the validity of Manoïlesco's (1934) argument, which predicted the gradual "corporatization" of western capitalist economies. Shonfield observed that, in order to attain a high level of macroeconomic performance within the Keynesian framework, modern economies had promoted processes, including state planning, in which

> the major interest groups are brought together and encouraged to conclude a series of bargains about their future behavior, which will have the effect of moving economic events along the desired path. The plan indicates the general direction in which the interest groups, including the state in its various guises, have agreed that they want to go. (Shonfield 1965, p. 231)[1]

The explosion in academic interest in corporatism that took place in the 1970s was accompanied by efforts to endow the concept with greater precision. Accordingly, a basic differentiation was introduced between the old "state corporatism" and the "new" or "neo" societal corporatism. The work of Schmitter (1974) marked an academic milestone in this conceptual evolution. He clearly defined neo-corporatism as a form of interest representation distinct from pluralism, statism, and syndicalism. At around the same time, Lehmbruch (1977, 1979) put greater emphasis on neo-corporatism as a form of policy making in which concertation assumed central importance.[2] Despite these differences, the common concern of both was in understanding the continuous and structured participation of interest organizations in policy-making and other stages of the policy process, especially policy implementation (Williamson 1985).

During the 1970s, corporatism acquired the status of a social science model—an "approach, an intellectual framework, a way of examining and analyzing corporatist political phenomena across countries and time periods" (Wiarda 1997, p. 23). Corporatism, it seemed, would offer an overarching and coherent method for understanding the working of economies and societies. At the same time, there occurred a shift in the locus of corporatist literature from political theory to political economy. This shift was provoked by the large divergences observed in the responses

---

[1]In this view, the macroeconomic framework and economic conditions were very important in determining the existence of corporatist institutions and policy making. Many of the "evolutionary" corporatist authors argued that the gradual consolidation of Keynesianism is a major explanatory factor for the transition from pluralism to corporatism (Manoïlesco 1934, Beer 1956, Shonfield 1965). Similarly, Harrison (1980) argued that this transition was driven by technological, social, and macroeconomic factors.

[2]Lehmbruch sees corporatism as an institutional pattern of policy formation in which large interest organizations cooperate with each other and with public authorities not only in the articulation and even intermediation of interests, but also in the authoritative allocation of values and the implementation of policies.

and performance of economies during the oil crisis of the 1970s. Corporatist theory might, it seemed, offer considerable insights into the success or failure of those responses, and in particular into the economic steering capacity of governments.

The separation between the two conceptions of neo-corporatism elaborated by Schmitter and Lehmbruch became "official" with Schmitter's (1982) distinction between "neo-corporatism 1" (a structure of interest representation) and "neo-corporatism 2" (a system of policy making). Henceforth, the character of the actors involved in the decision-making process and the nature of their relations with the state became the principal means of distinguishing a corporatist from a pluralist system of representation. At the same time, they became the keys for establishing a link between institutional configurations, policy making, and the character of policies and policy outcomes. The positions of Crouch and Martin were representative of the two main points of view in this debate. Crouch (1983) located the difference between pluralism and corporatism in the nature of the actors involved and in their internal organization, rather than in their role in the policy machinery. Martin (1983) argued instead that "what is at stake in the distinction between pluralism and corporatism is the extent to which organized groups are integrated into the policy-making arenas of the state." This fundamental insight was subsequently downplayed in the literature.

The proliferation of neo-corporatist studies in the 1980s took two main directions. First, greater efforts were made to analyze the relationship between certain neo-corporatist institutional configurations and their respective policy systems, and the ways in which these distinguished them from pluralist systems of representation and decision making. Second, there were attempts to increase and improve the empirical evidence of neo-corporatism in practice, as well as to find a relationship between neo-corporatism and macroeconomic performance.

At the same time, there were two closely connected developments in the application of the concept. First, the subconcept of meso-corporatism (Wassenberg 1982) was developed to examine the role of collective actors, not as peak class associations (as in the prior literature) but as organizations that cluster around and defend the specific interests of sectors and professions. Their relationships of power dependence with state agencies could be monopolistic and exclusive, but not necessarily tripartite in the manner of, say, peak employers and labor organizations in their role as incomes policy partners (Cawson 1986). Second, the concept of private interest government was developed to refer to the collective, private self-regulation of industry, with different degrees of assistance from the state, as a possible policy alternative to either market liberalism or state interventionism (Streeck & Schmitter 1985).

Thus, the 1970s literature served to define corporatism more clearly, as well as to introduce greater clarity into the debate; the 1980s saw a more extensive empirical application and diffusion of the concept. But by the early 1990s, a new variant of the literature began to focus more speculatively on the fate of neo-corporatism amid the new economic turbulence of the time—and, in particular, the so-called decline of Keynesianism. Numerous writers proclaimed the extinction of the neo-corporatist "beast." Corporatism, it was argued, would be eroded from below, as technological change and the decline of heavy industry undermined the foundations of old-style European industrial relations. It would also be incapacitated from above, as looser labor markets and a shift in the balance of power from unions to employers rendered tripartite macropolitical bargaining less useful (see among others Schmitter 1989, Gobeyn 1993).

However, predictions of the death of corporatism were not entirely borne out by subsequent developments. First, as Wiarda (1997, p. 180) argues, there was an evolution in the form of neo-corporatism. In its early years, neo-corporatist analysis was mainly concerned with tripartite relations between labor, business, and the state. It dealt with such issues as wages, production, social programs, labor benefits, and the like; it was associated with the early or intermediary stages of postwar industrialism. During the 1980s, there was in some countries a decline in this older neo-corporatism and the emergence of new forms of neo-corporatist decision making in the postindustrial policy arenas of education, health care, welfare, and environmentalism. This change involved not merely newer issues but also new corporatized actors.

But at the same time, older, traditional corporatist structures and relationships were being adapted, rather than abandoned, in those countries where they were always most important (e.g., Austria and Scandinavia) in order to address the "older" employment and social issues that were of renewed concern. Moreover, the 1980s and 1990s witnessed the emergence of such structures and relationships, albeit in less embedded and institutionalized form, in many other European countries. To varying degrees, the Netherlands, Ireland, Portugal, Italy, and Spain have all implemented social pacts, based on peak-level concertation, to adapt to new economic policy challenges. These included new competitive demands stemming from the creation of the European single market and from the urgent necessity of bringing debts, deficits, and inflation under control for membership in the economic and monetary union. Since the mid-1990s, several authors have paid attention to these experiences (Fajertag & Pochet 1997, 2000; Traxler 1997; Rhodes 1998; Regini 1999; Goetschy 2000; Negrelli 2000). The "return" of neo-corporatism has led another group of scholars to analyze its cyclical nature and the reasons for its rise, demise, and resurgence (Schmitter & Grote 1997). The new wave of concertation has also revived discussions of the relationship between these new forms of corporatism and their antecedents. However, the theoretical analysis of this new wave of corporatism remains underdeveloped—largely because of the problems of application that have long afflicted the concept.

PROBLEMS OF APPLICATION

In the 1980s and 1990s, the study of corporatism followed two main paths. The first was the study of corporatism as a political phenomenon, which elaborated on Schmitter's and Lehmbruch's respective characterizations of corporatism as a system of representation and a process of policy making. The second, which was related but assumed a distinct place in the literature, focused on the systemic effects of corporatist institutions. This literature became methodologically separate from the first. Whereas the first path of study explored the varieties of corporatism across different countries (and sectors), the second concentrated on the links between systemic features and socioeconomic outcomes.

The first path was by and large a response to the criticism that neo-corporatist theory lacked strong empirical evidence to support its claim that corporatism was genuinely distinct from pluralism (Almond 1983, Jordan 1984). Thus, much subsequent work consisted of case studies presenting qualitative evidence on the representation of organized interests and their participation in decision-making structures. Following Cawson (1986), the three main interpretations of "corporatism" in this period can be identified as follows:

1. A specific form and process of interest intermediation; a distinctive way in which interests are organized and interact with the state (e.g., Schmitter 1974, Grant 1985).

2. A differentiated model of policy making with the intervention of social partners, and potentially a novel system of political economy different from capitalism and socialism (Winkler 1976, Lehmbruch 1977).

3. A different form of state within democratic and capitalist societies, emerging alongside and then dominating the traditional parliament-centered political system.

The problems in the application of the concept lies precisely in these very different uses of the term. Not only has "corporatism" been used to characterize all three major elements of political systems—i.e., polity (structures and institutions), politics (processes and mechanisms), and policy (outcomes), but it has also been applied to numerous levels of the polity (the national economy, specific policy arenas, subnational governance, and industrial sectors) in very different national contexts.

As for the second path of study, the imprecision, yet clear utility, of the concept triggered efforts to provide more rigorous quantitative indicators of its existence (Coevers & van Veen 1995, Mitchell 1996). Kenworthy (2000) identifies four categories of work in this area:

1. Studies of interest groups, concerned with the centralization, concentration, and density of labor and business organizations (Schmitter 1981, Cameron 1984, Wallerstein et al. 1997, Hicks & Kenworthy 1998).

2. Studies of wage setting, focusing on the centralization, coordination, and coverage of collective bargaining (Cameron 1984, Bruno & Sachs 1985, Calmfors & Drifill 1988, Soskice 1990, Layard et al. 1991, Nickell 1997, Wallerstein et al. 1997, Hall & Franzese 1998, Traxler & Kittel 2000).

3. Studies of interest group participation in policy making (Lehmbruch 1984; Compston 1997, 1998).

4. Studies of political-economic consensus and strike rates (Keman 1984, Paloheimo 1984, Katzenstein 1985, McCallum 1986, Crepaz 1992).

As mentioned, most of these studies were devoted to the analysis of corporatist structures and systems rather than processes. Many pointed to the benefits of corporatist policy making and structures for macroeconomic performance. The adjustment of European economies to the economic crisis of the 1970s provided an excellent opportunity for assessing these effects. The need to contain inflation rates in order to safeguard competitiveness increased the importance of wage and incomes policies (Chater et al. 1981, Boyer & Dore 1995). The differences observed in the ability of certain countries to achieve wage restraint, make it compatible with monetary policy, and offset rising unemployment were explained institutionally. With the help of the quantitative indicators and rankings elaborated, most authors concluded that a positive relationship existed between macroeconomic performance and the degree of corporatism (Flanagan et al. 1983, Pekkarinen et al. 1992, Scharpf 1997). Corporatist countries were deemed more successful in terms of inflation control, employment performance, and adjustment in periods of crisis than less corporatist or noncorporatist ones (Kurzer 1991, Western 1991, Crepaz 1992). There was considerable empirical evidence for a strong and positive correlation between such "cooperative economies" and high rates of productivity and investment growth, whereas "conflictual" economies (conventionally including Canada, the United States, and Great Britain) traditionally lagged behind in both (Gordon 1996).

But in recent years, much work has gone into reassessing this relationship, especially after a decade of neoliberal policies and the apparent erosion of corporatist structures (Therborn 1998, Glyn 2001). This literature suggests that neo-corporatist theory was ill-prepared to explain the new economic developments of the 1990s. Analyzing eight small countries, Woldendorp (1997) showed that countries ranking higher in neo-corporatist scales do not, as a rule, perform better than countries ranking lower. Flanagan (1999, p. 1171) found that the indicators of corporatism constructed in the 1980s have little ability to explain macroeconomic performance in the 1990s. He argues that neo-corporatist theory has to develop more carefully the relationship between changes in the macroeconomic context and the capacity of corporatist institutions and arrangements to adjust. Hemerijck (1995) was one of the first to provide a detailed study (of the Dutch case) into how positive corporatist stability could degenerate into negative immobility, demanding a critical shift in institutional arrangements if the responsiveness and potential for innovation in the system were to be regained.

Seeking a better understanding of the differences in macroeconomic performance in the post-Keynesian era of non-accommodating monetary policy, certain authors began to include the monetary regime as a variable that interacted with neo-corporatist institutions (Cukierman & Lippi 1998, Hall & Franzese 1998, Iversen & Soskice 1998, Iversen 1999, Iversen et al. 2000). They have focused on the relationship between coordinated bargaining and central banks, arguing that the key to effective wage and labor-cost setting is coordination among actors and an emphasis on cost containment rather than on centralization and elaborate redistributive goals (Iversen 1999). Crouch (2001) suggests that such "organized decentralization"—to use Traxler's (1995) term—might prove to be a "new" (but unusual) form of neo-corporatism, in which representative organizations accept a role of restraining their members, a role that would also prove more appropriate for an era of global restructuring and monetary discipline than a disorganized *and* decentralized neoliberal alternative.

This shift in the literature represented a first attempt to deal with the fact that neo-corporatist bargaining and institutions were clearly surviving and adjusting, not collapsing. Analysts had to make a sudden retreat from confident predictions of corporatist demise and assumptions concerning a new phase of "conservative convergence"[3] to a more cautious study of corporatist redeployment. This retreat and subsequent equivocation about the direction of corporatist developments revealed a problem not in neo-corporatist theory as such (as we suggest below, it had always contained the tools for understanding evolutionary change) so much as in the ways it had been developed in the 1980s. Broadening the agenda had provided considerable clarification of what was meant by corporatism, as well as an appreciation of its consequences for policy, but there remained a gap in our understanding of the mechanisms or processes that linked institutional structures with outcomes (Williamson 1989, pp. 18–19). There was thus a tendency to underplay the refinement of what we might term the operation of corporatism, i.e., the relationship between the corporatist polity and corporatist policies.

To put it another way, there was a failure to focus on the role and characteristics of corporatist politics.[4] Scholars regarded a particular set of formal policy-making practices as neo-corporatist (social pacts, tripartite negotiations at national or peak level, and forms of concertation) but offered few insights into how these functioned or adjusted over time (Parsons 1988). As Flanagan (1999, p. 1156) argued, discussions on corporatism had neglected the micro foundations of decision making within interest organizations and the government, effectively assuming identical preferences among all members or an absence of democratic processes for resolving internal conflicts. As a result, the corporatist literature lacked precision on the process and outcome of bargaining among interest groups.

Thus, it is not surprising that the "dysfunctionality" of corporatist arrangements and practices for capitalism was emphasized at the expense of understanding how "functionality" might evolve. In responding to a literature that more or less agreed that the demise of Swedish centralized wage bargaining in the 1980s heralded the

---

[3]See Gerlich et al. (1988) for a critique of this trend based on the Austrian case.

[4]One of the few attempts to correct this problem came from Cawson (1986), who rejected Schmitter's (1982) distinction between corporatism and concertation and Cox's (1982) distinction between state corporatism and pluralism [see also the debate between Cox (1988) and Cawson (1988)]. In Cawson's view, both Schmitter and Cox tried to draw a clear distinction between the political form of the state and the nature of policy making, when in practice no such distinction can be made.

end of corporatism everywhere (if it could not survive postindustrial pressures in its "homeland," how could it be feasible elsewhere?), Wallerstein & Golden (2000, pp. 134–35) had to remind us that the adaptability of corporatism as a process depends primarily on politics, not technological determinism:

> Any lasting system of wage setting must be responsive to changes in the economic environment. Adjustments in the distribution of wages and benefits, however, do not necessarily require abandoning centralized bargaining. Whether or not employers and unions are willing to cooperate in modifying central agreements to accommodate changes in technology and in market conditions depends on the political relationships that exist within and between the unions and employers' confederations.

At the end of the 1990s, then, several questions remained unresolved, or at least unclear in the literature. How does corporatism evolve? How can we relate changing corporatist processes to changing corporatist structures? If indeed there has been a return to neo-corporatism after the premature announcement of its death in the 1980s, on what institutional basis has this occurred? What are the traits that differentiate it from past forms and experiences? Or to put it another way, what has been the political logic behind processes of concertation in the last decade?

CONTEMPORARY CORPORATISMS

As suggested above, the corporatist literature in the 1980s and 1990s was ill-prepared to answer these questions and initially responded with a structural-functionalist interpretation of change. Schmitter (1989) suggested that the erosion of traditional neo-corporatist structures lay behind the extinction of processes of concertation and macropolitical bargaining (see also Gobeyn 1993, Walsh 1995). The challenges posed to unions (Crouch 2000) and the neoliberal character of economic policies during the 1990s (Glyn 2001) had undermined the structural conditions upon which neo-corporatism had been based and developed (Schmitter 1974). Lash & Urry (1987) and Regini (1995) argued that neo-corporatist institutions were degenerating in the transition to post-Fordism and would recompose on a more flexible, decentralized basis, demanding that our analytical ttention be redirected to the micro and meso (or local and company) levels of concertation between employers and employees.

Schmitter & Streeck (1991) maintained that a combination of the business cycle effect (lower growth and higher unemployment) and European integration would remove the logic underpinning successful corporatism. While looser labor markets would empower employers, an integrated European economy, with less room for discretionary national economic policies, would reduce the incentives for unions to organize collectively and deliver wage restraint in return for package deals or side payments. Gobeyn (1993, p. 20) asserted bluntly that "contemporary economic realities . . . make corporatism largely unnecessary. Market

forces alone can presently achieve labor discipline and wage demand moderation."
Kurzer (1993, pp. 244–45) concluded from a study of European economies that
social concertation was no longer feasible: "[H]igh capital mobility and deepening
financial integration prompt governments to remove or alter institutions and practices objectionable to business and finance" (for a survey and critique, see Rhodes
2001b).

The alleged decline of neo-corporatism was thus interpreted with the same
structuralist logic that was frequently used to explain its ascendancy—a tendency
already criticized in the mid-1980s by Regini (1984). If the rise of the Keynesian
paradigm had created the incentives and need for inclusive and negotiated forms
of economic management, the end of the Keynesian golden age of capitalism had
removed them. But the institutional bias in (neo) corporatist theory meant that all
of these explanations underplayed actors' rational calculation of their interests and
objectives in creating corporatist institutions. The relationship between forms of
neo-corporatist intermediation and processes was all too readily regarded as uni-
directional; in order to have peak-level social dialogue, social pacts, or macropolitical bargaining it was necessary to have traditional neo-corporatist structures.[5]
Those structures, in turn, were linked to a particular phase of the postwar political
economy. To the extent that there has been any revisionism in the literature, it
has often been in the direction of class or class-fraction–based explanations (e.g.,
Iversen et al. 2000). These retain, however, a deterministic bias that leaves little
room for political contingency.

Does the literature on the return of corporatism provide us with an analytical
way forward? The economic crisis of the early 1990s, which coincided with the
first stages of European Monetary Union (EMU), obliged European governments
to adjust their economies and institutions, which produced a proliferation of new
forms of concertation and tripartite social dialogue (*International Labour Review*
1995; Visser & Hemerijck 1997; Rhodes 1998, 2001a; Crouch 1999; Pochet 1999;
Pérez 1999). Schmitter & Grote (1997) present several plausible explanations for
the "return" (and apparent cyclical character) of neo-corporatism, including the
economic business cycle and Hirschman's notion of shifting involvements. But
they find no single satisfactory answer beyond the apparent destiny of certain
types of system to keep up the search for bargained, consensus-based solutions.
Other authors look for an explanation in the specific context of the 1990s. Traxler
(1995) and Traxler et al. (2001) argue that a shift from classic to "supply-side"
or "lean" corporatism has been driven by the shift from Keynesian economic
policy to a non-accommodating monetary regime under the Maastricht Agreement
and EMU. Rhodes (1998, 2001a) argues that concertation through a model of
"competitive" neo-corporatism has been the response of European welfare states
to increasing economic internationalization and accentuated economic integration
in Europe. Others (Fajertag & Pochet 1997, Pochet 1998, Pochet & Fajertag 2000)

---

[5]However, Schmitter (1989, p. 64) does accept that although neo-corporatist associabil-
ity and concertative policy making are empirically interrelated, they are not necessarily
covariant.

trace the changing nature of the external context of new social pacts from the early phases of EMU (when the issue of pay restraint became central) to the more recent period when labor costs and pension reform have risen to the top of the policy-making agenda.

In stressing the functional appropriateness of new forms of corporatist experimentation, such interpretations draw the opposite conclusion from the literature on corporatist decline. Although the latter saw globalization, deindustrialization, and new post-Fordist production paradigms as undermining forces, perhaps there was also something in this turbulent environment that triggered the search for new modes of concertation. This interpretation suggested, in turn, the possibility of an evolutionary, transformative understanding of corporatism, rather than one that saw it as cyclical but essentially unchanging.

We argue that to identify neo-corporatism with a stable combination of Keynesianism and Fordism is to underestimate the capacity of actors to seek and sustain its benefits in more difficult times (Rigby & Serrano 1997, Martin & Ross 1999, Rigby et al. 1999, Crouch 2000). The work of Crepaz (1992) suggested, by contrast, that if neo-corporatist systems were functional for delivering better macroeconomic performance in the 1960s and 1970s, such systems might also have the capacities and internal flexibility to deliver similar outcomes under different conditions. Traxler (1998) advances this functional but evolutionary view for the Austrian case. The advantages of a concerted approach to adjustment are also outlined by Visser & Hemerijck (1997), who see a renewal of corporatism (on a much more flexible basis than hitherto) in the Dutch case as the outcome of a search for greater stability and predictability in a competitive and turbulent environment. Based on the Danish example, Blom-Hansen (2001) explains the return (or rather survival) of concertation as a governmental strategy to guarantee continuity in policies, which, if agreed on through concerted pacts, are much less likely to be changed because of a loss of legitimation.

Nevertheless, a functional, systemic explanation of new corporatist experiments may be as inadequate, on its own, as past attempts to link corporatism with Keynesianism. We accept that economic conditions are important. The high unemployment rates and slack labor markets of European economies since the 1980s have pushed issues of employment and labor market regulation to the top of the political agenda. The conditions imposed on access to EMU made budget deficit reduction a central feature of member-state policy and have limited the resources available for traditional distributive politics and side-payments. The EMU macroeconomic framework also entails the loss of independent national exchange rate policies and the creation of a central monetary authority with an inflation target, which makes wage costs a key component of macroeconomic adjustment and a major determinant of labor market performance. Accordingly, three issues have figured in processes of concertation during the 1990s: pay discipline, labor market flexibility, and the restructuring of social security programs.

Thus, many works have studied the impact of EMU on industrial relations and collective bargaining institutions (e.g., Kauppinen 1998, Pochet 1998, Wallerstein 1998, Crouch 1999, Martin 1999, Traxler 1999). The change in the macroeconomic as well as institutional framework has led some to renew the study of the relationship between institutions and macroeconomic performance (Calmfors 1998, Iversen 1999, Soskice 1999). In most studies, it is implicitly assumed that social pacts and the return to forms of concertation are the "second-best" choices of actors responding to external pressures, seeking new positive-sum solutions between particularistic goals and certain shared macroeconomic objectives. In those cases where EMU and its stringent conditions posed serious challenges to the economy (this is the case of peripheral countries: Italy, Spain, Greece, Portugal, and Ireland), social pacts have also served to legitimize and to make socially acceptable the sacrifices required by adjustment to the single currency.

But although these contextual changes may help explain the presence of new incentives for governments, employers, and unions to engage in concertation, they do not in themselves explain how or why attempts at concertation achieved greater or lesser degrees of success in different countries. For although there is agreement on the renewed importance of concertation, there have been few serious and systematic attempts to explain why this has occurred and how it has been possible. We argue that understanding the return to neo-corporatism in the 1990s (both in terms of the redeployment of existing corporatisms and the emergence of new versions) requires greater emphasis on the goals and strategic behavior of actors than on institutions and systemic variables (Therborn 1992). It is therefore important to note the differences in actors' perceptions and political resources.

As far as the role of actors is concerned, the main points to highlight with regard to the corporatisms of the contemporary period are as follows:

1. The state plays an active role in negotiations. In some cases, the government has intervened simply as a third actor. In others, it has pressured unions and employers to come together. In most cases, it has been responsible for steering the bargaining process (Pochet & Fajertag 2000). Pekkarinen predicted this development in the early 1990s in suggesting that the gradual erosion of those institutions traditionally supporting neo-corporatism would increase the importance of public authorities. These would "replace, reinforce, or supplement private, centralized wage bargaining with various kinds of official intervention" (Pekkarinen 1992, pp. 18–19).

2. The "balance between the negotiating partners has shifted substantially as compared with the situation prevailing when the pacts of the 1960s and 1970s were signed" (Pochet & Fajertag 2000, p. 18). The fragmentation or weakening of the trade union movement in most of Europe over the past 20 years has weakened unions' position vis-à-vis employers and governments. Accordingly, negotiations and the political exchange involved have also been shaped by new asymmetries in the objectives and action capacities of the different actors.

3. In the presence of these new asymmetries, the centralization and extensive associational coverage of the peak interest organizations of capital and labor may not be the sine qua non of successful corporatism at all (and probably

never was, outside of Sweden and Austria). Instead, the flux of corporatist structures will bring with it a change in the processes of bargaining, rather than their disappearance. In certain contexts, new and flexible forms of concertation may actually be more successful when unions are less centralized and less embedded in the workplace. Thus, it is precisely the strength of the German unions that has enabled them to resist government overtures to negotiate labor market reforms that their weaker Dutch counterparts have been able to embrace (e.g., Ebbinghaus & Hassel 2000).

But these changed perceptions and behavior are explainable only if we focus on the underlying process of political exchange within the new social pacts:

1. Recently, neo-corporatist concertation has not been centered on the distribution of financial resources among participating actors; the economic surplus that had facilitated compromises via side payments in the past was simply absent or was heavily restricted (Schmitter 1989, p. 70). Instead, concertation has focused on the establishment of adequate institutional frameworks for macroeconomic management and microeconomic (supply-side) reform.

2. In practice, therefore, the new social pacts no longer stem principally from an incomes policy commitment, in return, say, for an increase in the social wage, as in traditionally conceived neo-corporatism. Instead, they stem first from the unions' acceptance of pay restraint in return for an undertaking by the public authorities and employers to promote employment creation (Fajertag & Pochet 1997). A second key component of the trade-off is the opportunity for the unions to help reform the welfare state via changes that span the labor market, social security, and industrial relations. This is especially important when the social partners administer social insurance schemes. Thus, the process of exchange has also had a participation component, i.e., pay restraint in exchange for enhanced involvement in policy making and institutional design (see Traxler 1997 for an extended discussion).

3. Given the cross-party nature of welfare reform projects in many European countries, the dependence of corporatist concertation on Left governments has been replaced by a new pragmatism with regard to macroeconomic management and micro-policy reform, making newer forms of corporatism "rather neutral to government composition" (Traxler et al. 2001, p. 302).

4. Looking at the general experience of changes introduced in industrial relations systems, we observe a tendency to strike a balance between the need for competitiveness and flexibility on the one hand and the need for macroeconomic stability on the other. This balance has been sought (sometimes successfully, sometimes not) via processes of articulated decentralization, in other words, by increasing the importance of sectoral bargaining at the national level while reinforcing and strengthening company-level institutions. As discussed below, this process has contributed to the "network" character of contemporary corporatisms.

5. There has been an extension of the issues covered by social pacts and agreements. Accordingly, macropolitical bargaining has not been restricted to the negotiation of (short-term) incomes policies but has also involved the introduction of (longer-term) institutional reforms. As Hassel & Ebbinghaus argue (2000, p. 35), this is because "concerted social policy reform is more than a means to facilitate wage moderation; it is also an *end* in itself." Rising social contributions linked to increasing social expenditure can counteract the positive effect of wage agreements, and thus social security reform necessarily becomes a key part of the wages-and-competitiveness equation. The linking together of issue areas in this way has favored the conclusion of agreements, for the greater the number of topics included in the negotiations, the greater is the chance of finding a compromise through "generalized political exchange" and trade-offs (Crouch 1990)—a point we return to below.

6. There has been a tendency for the most enduring social pacts (for example, those of Ireland and Portugal) to be the subject of constant renegotiation. This is partly because of their extension to new issues (and sometimes new partners) in line with changing pressures for reform. But it is also because, in the absence of traditional institutional prerequisites, an iterative process can help consolidate concertation and embed it in institutions and behavior. A strong process may compensate for a lack of traditional corporatist prerequisites in countries where organizational structures are weak and fragmented.

Compared with the institutionally embedded, traditional corporatisms of Austria and Scandinavia, these new bargains are simultaneously more flexible and, in some cases, more ambitious. They are more susceptible to periodic breakdown and renewal, but even if they are not embedded in Keynesianism, they are often just as central to the macromanagement and steering of the economy. They are also much more clearly process dependent to the extent that the process (as a means of policy development as well as conflict resolution) also becomes an objective of reform. Not only the content but also the process can be the subject of negotiation, as new policy linkages are made and as partners enter and leave to express approval or disapproval of particular reforms.

As argued by Traxler (1997, p. 35), there are two prerequisites for political exchange in the process of concluding social pacts: in terms of content, there must be a settlement (or at least suspension) of the conflict of distribution between capital and labor; and in terms of procedures, there must be a reciprocal allocation of representational and organizational privileges among the social partners. It is precisely when concertation involves the distribution of concessions and sacrifices rather than economic surpluses (as has tended to be the case for the 1990s) that procedural topics gain significance. These give the partners the opportunity to exchange representational and organizational privileges as compensation for material concessions and thus enhance the chances of building a compromise.

An extension of this way of thinking interprets social pacts and their ensuing reforms and institutional changes within ongoing deliberative processes of learning (Hemerijck & Schludi 2000, Teague 2000). The endeavor to modernize economic and social governance structures has intensified policy learning and transfer across the European Union's member states (Teague 2000, p. 447). Thus, the reshaping of employment systems is not only about the diffusion of market-oriented reforms but also about a new wave of interactions between economic and social actors committed to updating traditional welfare states. As Hemerijck & Schludi (2000) argue, policy adjustment under these conditions, with increasingly dense linkages between policy areas and with greater attention to policy sequencing, should be understood as a dynamic political process of trial and error and of puzzling about reform. Policy adjustment in many European countries is now best portrayed as a system-wide search for new, economically viable, politically feasible, and socially acceptable policy mixes in which distributive trade-offs, defined via various forms of concertation, still play a critical role.

Social pacts and macropolitical bargaining in the 1990s therefore differ in several important respects from the neo-corporatist concertation of the 1960s and 1970s—or at least from common assumptions about how those systems functioned.[6] These differences relate especially to procedures and content and the ways in which these are subject to political exchange. Thus—just as Nedelman & Meier (1977) recommended for the analysis of "traditional" neo-corporatism— our understanding of corporatism in the contemporary period should be less concerned with the structural nature of the phenomenon (or with misleading structural-functionalist arguments about the possibility of its occurrence) than with the processes and procedures of political exchange. In terms of Schmitter's (1982) characterization, our focus should shift from "neo-corporatism 1" (the structure of interest representation) to "neo-corporatism 2" (the system of policy making).

Our key point, however, is that one crucial element remains constant in both past and present manifestations of corporatism—the existence of political exchange. Counter to the basic intuition that informed the "demise of corporatism" literature, political exchange is still viable in the contemporary period—even if the currency of that exchange has been altered (many would say "devalued"). And because political exchange is possible, so too is macro-level concertation in various forms. The problem lies in the use and adaptation of the tools we already have for analyzing and understanding it.

REFINING AND REDEPLOYING THE CONCEPT OF CORPORATISM

A common characteristic of the literature that deals with the link between neo-corporatist systems and policy outcomes has been the use of structural features and "favorable contexts." Thus, given the pressures generated by globalization,

---

[6]As Nedelman & Meier (1977, pp. 48–56) argued, even the Swedish corporatism of the 1970s was much more dynamic, fluid, and shifting in its organizational basis and "interaction constellation" than Schmitter's original conception of societal corporatism allowed for. For similar arguments relating to Norway and Austria, see Lehmbruch (1984) and Gerlich et al. (1988).

economic integration (EMU), tertiarization, etc., it was argued that neo-corporatist structures have been eroded and can no longer yield the benefits they delivered in previous decades. But as we have begun to suggest, behind this alleged misfit between corporatism and economic development in the 1990s, there is an implicit consideration of corporatism as a structure, rather than as a policy-making process. "Neo-corporatism 1" had triumphed over "Neo-corporatism 2." In the light of developments during the past decade, this approach clearly suffers from several important shortcomings.

First, an emphasis on structure proceeds from a static view of corporatism. But this approach is justified neither by the historical nor the cross-country diversity of the western capitalist world. Instead, if we think of corporatism from an evolutionary point of view, we can endow it with the capacity to adapt to a changing environment and find substitutes to those structural conditions that apparently no longer exist (Flanagan 1999). In this sense, the increasing intervention of the government in the corporatist developments of the 1990s should not be seen as a sign of weakness in the system (Pochet 1998, 1999). Nor should the search for new, less centralized (although still coordinated) systems of wage bargaining be seen as the end of corporatism. They should rather be understood as the search for new ways of maintaining the positive benefits that corporatist approaches provide.

As recognized by Hemerijck & Schludi (2000, p. 208) in their analysis of effective policy responses in the 1990s,

> many of the countries that have successfully pursued a coordinated strategy of wage restraint could not rely on the traditional prerequisites, such as the strong, centralized, hierarchically ordered interest associations, of 1970s neo-corporatism.

What they relied on, instead, was institutional adaptation and the discovery of a "new politics" of corporatism, with a different set of trade-offs and innovations in the process of political exchange. What we need to understand is the nature of this change. Those who predicted the demise of corporatism did so because they thought that political exchange was no longer possible. In fact, as we have argued above, the "currency" available for exchange did not disappear but rather changed. Thus, if political exchange was still possible, so too was concertation; and as we argue below, if there is scope for concertation—even in the form of sporadic social pacts—there is also scope for the institutional embedding of such practices.

Second, if instead of conceiving of corporatism as a system we approach it as a specific form of policy making, then the structural argument linking the possibility of corporatism with a particular moment of postwar Keynesianism loses much of its validity. For although it is true that some of the structures usually linked to corporatism have been eroded, we cannot conclude that a certain system has ended or that certain forms of policy making are redundant. In order to test whether in the 1990s corporatism really stopped yielding the benefits it had previously delivered, or whether indeed the nature of those benefits has changed, it would be appropriate to look to the procedural aspects of corporatism rather than just its structural components.

Once we leave aside the purported structurally necessary conditions for corporatism, what we are left with is the nature of corporatism as a process—and the need to conceptualize the politics of corporatism much more thoroughly. This perception is not a new one. Bull (1992, p. 256), among others, argued that the value of any corporatist ideal-type based on structural factors is likely to be limited because of the nature of the dynamics at the heart of the neo-corporatist process, i.e., political exchange. More recently, Siaroff (1999), in an attempt to marry structure and dynamic processes, distinguished four key elements of an ideal-type corporatist political economy: (*a*) structural features, mainly the characteristics of interest groups (degree of unionization, internal organization, concentration of representation, encompassment, etc.); (*b*) functional roles, i.e., the integration of labor and business organizations into the decision-making process; (*c*) behavioral patterns, i.e., the role of political exchange as a means of attaining consensus in policy making); and (*d*) favorable contexts, such as a tradition of consensual politics, a long-term political role of or even dominance of a united social democratic party, or high expenditure on social programs. Obviously, not all of these ideal-type features will be found in all real-world systems, most of which will contain a complex mix of them all. As we argued above, (*b*) and (*c*) may be present without a full complement of either (*a*) or (*d*).

We suggest two ways forward: (*a*) refocusing our inquiry on the process of political exchange and (*b*) adopting the notion of integration as central to our understanding of how exchange can contribute to a new structuring of policy-making systems. Once again, placing political exchange at the core of the corporatist policy-making process is far from new. In the mid-1980s, both Lehmbruch (1984) and Regini (1984) began to introduce the concept of "political exchange" as a means of producing a more dynamic account of the phenomenon. Shortly thereafter, Cawson (1986, p. 38) offered a definition of corporatism as

> a specific socio-political process in which organizations representing monopolistic functional interests *engage in political exchange* with state agencies over public policy outputs which involves those organizations in a role which combines interest representation and policy implementation through delegated self-enforcement.

Somewhat later, Crouch (1990) developed an empirical analysis of corporatism based on "generalized political exchange". This, in turn, was an extension of Pizzorno's (1977) classic distinction between collective bargaining, a political manifestation of market exchange, and political exchange, a process based on functional interdependence and mutual interest among actors (for an early theoretical critique, see Mutti 1982). The notion of generalized political exchange broadens the scope of the concept of political exchange from the labor market or industrial relations to policy-making processes in general. However, both Cawson and Crouch were thinking of monopolistic or all-encompassing organizations. Thus, Crouch considers generalized political exchange a function of high levels of union strength and the existence of centralized organizations of both capital and labor. But can the idea of generalized political exchange be applied under other conditions?

We argue that it is possible to use exchange relations as a means of recognizing and understanding the existence and operation of corporatist policy making, even—and especially—in the absence of the traditional structural prerequisites.[7] For amid greater uncertainty, the nature of political exchange will be more complex and subject to shifting interpretations by actors. Marin's (1990a, p. 40) definition is helpful here in thinking of political exchange as forms of mutually contingent, macropolitical and noneconomic transaction between autonomous, organized, collective actors with divergent/competitive/antagonistic but functionally interdependent interests, the binding character of which cannot be based on law and contract. The work of Marin is also important in linking the concept of political exchange with policy network analysis. Policy networks have not only been theoretically conceived as a specific form of interest intermediation or governance (Mayntz & Scharpf 1995, Scharpf 1997) but also as an analytical framework (Kenis & Schneider 1991). By combining the two, we can link complex processes of political exchange to the institutional settings in which they take place.

The process of exchange itself can occur in different institutional settings as networks evolve. Exchange can also beget institutions, as rules and norms of behavior accumulate and accrete over time. Following Marin, we can argue that whereas elementary political exchange (e.g., basic forms of wage bargaining) can take place in weakly institutionalized contexts, generalized political exchange requires a hierarchy of rules ("calculated rigidity" in Marin's terminology). And this is why the linking together of diverse policy domains in weakly institutionalized social pacts can help sustain those pacts over time, for the generalization of exchange will in and of itself generate new relations of dependence and mutual commitment—and a form of institutional hierarchy and rigidity. Thus, even in the "lean" corporatisms of contemporary, post-Keynesian Europe, actors interact within a set of interdependent and hierarchically ordered policy fields or games—and the degree of that interdependence and order can ebb and flow (cf. Traxler et al. 2001). For as well as evolving and acquiring institutional presence and durability, rules and norms can also devolve and become dysfunctional, if the intensity of exchange between actors decreases or if corporatist stability degenerates into sclerosis and immobility—a development to which environmental changes will also contribute.

Understanding corporatism as a variable and constantly evolving phenomenon allows us to understand how social pacts may fade away or, as is sometimes the case in contemporary Europe, how they gradually shift from being temporary emergency solutions to acquiring the status of formal or quasiformal subsystems of policy making. A focus on how actors' perceptions and behavior relate to—but are certainly not determined by—external pressures also allows us to understand

---

[7]Again, this insight is not new—merely underdeveloped in the contemporary literature. As Regini (1984, p. 141) advised, "Further research should focus on the variability of the conditions for political exchange ... rather than on the supposed organizational or institutional prerequisites, which, for all their importance in some situations, may be shown to be neither necessary nor sufficient in others."

the redeployment of traditional corporatisms in countries such as Sweden and Austria. As recently argued by Stephens (2000), an analysis that focuses on the perceptions and behavior of unions and employers and the power relations between them provides a better understanding of recent developments in Scandinavian corporatism than one in which structure on its own (e.g., increasing organizational diversity) plays the central role.

The concept of integration is also useful here for understanding the extent to which exchange becomes politically embedded—or in some instances less embedded—over time. It also helps us to "bring structure back in." Narrowly defined, integration is equivalent to the acceptance by the public authorities of an active role for social partners in the policy-making process. The broader view, which Siaroff (1999, p. 189) presents as an alternative paradigm to corporatism, defines it as a

> long-term co-operative pattern of shared economic management involving the social partners and existing at various levels such as plant-level management, sectoral wage bargaining, and joint shaping of national policies in competitiveness-related matters (education, social policy, etc).

We suggest that, rather than replacing corporatism, the concept of integration can be used to enrich our understanding of how corporatism works and evolves. Treu (1992) provides a useful extension of an argument originally developed by Lehmbruch (1984, pp. 66–74), who sought to show how the instutionalization of corporatist systems occurred along two dimensions—the vertical (the pattern of participation of social actors in policy making and implementation) and the horizontal (the pattern of concertation between social actors and government). Treu distinguishes integration from less developed forms of concertation in processes of consultation and collective bargaining. Collective bargaining corresponds to the simple exchange required for government policies to be implemented and effective, without giving social partners policy-making power. Consultation simply provides social partners with access to information, whereas integration gives them real influence over policy design.

Treu further distinguishes between quantitative and qualitative integration. Whereas quantitative integration refers to the number of partners involved, qualitative integration has both horizontal and vertical features. Qualitative integration varies horizontally in terms of the number of policy areas that are linked together in processes of concertation. The greater the number and relevance of policy areas— and by implication the greater the scope for "generalized exchange"—the higher will be the degree of integration. Qualitative integration also varies vertically in terms of the capacity of actors to influence the policy process from policy design through implementation, often via the delegation of authority from the state. So, although Regini (2000, pp. 160–62) distinguishes between political exchange and the delegation of authority as separate phenomena (arguing that whereas the former was characteristic of classic forms of corporatism, delegation is more important in recent social pacts), in reality the delegation of power and influence has always been part of the process of exchange.

Anyone who has tried to understand the fluid and shifting systems and levels of concertation that have emerged around Europe in the past decade or so will appreciate the contribution that these tools of analysis can make. Tracing the evolution of those systems along the dimensions of quantitative and qualitative integration (with special attention to the latter's horizontal and vertical characteristics) provides more than a means of static cross-national comparison. With due attention to the nature of political exchange involved, it also allows a better understanding of the dynamics and evolution of corporatist governance—of how the process of exchange can build and transform institutional frameworks and the nature of institutional "embeddedness" under different circumstances. It is also, crucially, a means of avoiding futile disputes over whether a system is corporatist or not and whether concertation is the equivalent of corporatism or is a weaker, less institutionalized subcategory.

Instead, there exists an array of corporatist phenomena, ranging from the intensive to the extensive and from the highly to the weakly integrated, encompassing manifestations that are horizontally inclusive or exclusive and vertically shallow or deep. Particular instances of corporatism do not remain static; they evolve along these dimensions, as witnessed by developments in many European countries over the past decade or so. Although that evolution is clearly driven in part by external pressures, a genuine understanding of corporatist development must focus on the internalization of environmental constraints and opportunities in the politics of corporatist concertation and in relations between the actors in the system.

Empirical evidence of the ways in which particular industrial regimes move along a "corporatist trajectory," with varying degrees of qualitative and quantitative integration, has been provided by numerous authors, and several studies have begun to illustrate that social pacts and the most recent (post 1980s) era of corporatism can best be understood in terms of a networked form of governance. Based on a study of the Dutch case, Hemerijck has provided one of the best illustrations to date of how corporatist relations can generate innovation or stasis in policy making, depending on the dynamics of societal support or institutional integration, with change taking place at "critical junctures" (Hemerijck 1995, p. 197). His "dynamic model" provides useful lessons for understanding other cases in which classic forms of corporatism have survived the crisis of Keynesianism and have been reconfigured as more complex, flexible, and networked varieties of economic governance.

At a more general and comparative level, Traxler et al. (2001) have shown how labor-relations regimes can shift backward and forward over time from what they call "classic" to "lean" corporatism, via intermediary, heterogeneous stages, depending on levels of centralization, coordination, and participation in bargaining. They make a strong case for contrasting classic corporatism, as a hierarchical system of governance solidly embedded in systems of Keynesian demand management, with a more recent "lean" variety, which, in line with our argument above, they portray as a "distinct governance mode beyond hierarchy and market, something that is widely understood as the constituent property of a network."

Weaker levels of bargaining governability in such systems are substituted by an external straightjacket—tough monetary policy (Traxler et al. 2001, p. 301).

We would simply stress that classic corporatism, as argued, for example, by Lehmbruch (1984), was also a networked form of governance, albeit one with different properties from more contemporary varieties. Equally, we suggest that, far from being "beyond hierarchy," social pacts and recent examples of "lean" or "supply-side" corporatism also depend for their successful operation on a degree of hierarchy and institutional integration. In itself, a hard monetary policy as the external "functional equivalent" of internal, hierarchical discipline is insufficient for explaining the survival of such experiments. This is especially so when, as is often the case, they link, in a form of generalized political exchange, productivity goals (supply-side modernization) with distributional package deals (covering incomes policies, pensions, and social security reform). The relationship between the productivity and distributional coalitions within such pacts is complex, and tension between the two is a constant source of instability (Rhodes 2001a). Without hierarchy and integration—linking levels of bargaining and involving strong commitments (and exchange) between social partners and government—the new "networked" forms of corporatism could hardly be sustained.

CONCLUSION

This article began with a survey of the main streams in the corporatist literature and argued that although it is rich and extensive, by the 1980s and 1990s there had been a manifest failure to find new ways of exploring contemporary reality. The political branch of corporatist studies had either reached a dead end in its attempts to define the nature of the phenomenon, or had proliferated, but simultaneously dissipated itself, in ever more detailed sectoral case study research. At the same time, the political economy branch had exhausted its capacity for measuring corporatism and equating corporatist systems with certain types of economic performance. Although large-scale, cross-national studies of this type have imparted important insights—especially of a historical nature when quantitative work has been linked to complex narratives (e.g., Hicks 1999, Swank 2002)—there have been diminishing returns on investment in such exercises (Woldendorp 1997, Flanagan 1999). Most important for our argument, neither branch has been well adapted to the task of explaining the developments of the 1980s and 1990s.

We have not presented a new theory in their stead. Nor have we attempted to redefine the concept of corporatism. We have rather argued for a resurrection, reassessment, refinement, and application of certain tools of analysis, derived in particular from theories of political exchange, that have long been present in the corporatist literature as a third branch of the study that has withered on the tree. From Lehmbruch (1977) and Pizzorno (1977) through Martin (1983) to Cawson (1986) and the work of Crouch and especially Marin in the early 1990s, there has been a deep concern with corporatism as complex process of political exchange that we believe is highly relevant for understanding the contemporary period.

This is particularly so because of the less formal, less institutionalized, and less predictable nature of the new types of corporatist concertation. Their structures and actors should be understood in terms of networks; their logics in terms of the processes that underpin them; their fate in terms of the evolution of integration and the changing "currency" of exchange. To date, with few exceptions (e.g., Traxler 1997, Regini 1999, Hassel & Ebbinghaus 2000), those who have begun studying the new neo-corporatisms or systems of concertation of the late twentieth and early twenty-first centuries have barely moved beyond description and speculation. If we go back to some of the earlier insights in the neo-corporatist literature that have recently been neglected, our attempts to understand contemporary corporatist practices and experimentation can be enriched.

The *Annual Review of Political Science* is online at http://polisci.annualreviews.org

LITERATURE CITED

Almond G. 1983. Corporatism, pluralism and professional memory. *World Polit.* 35:245–60

Beer S. 1956. Pressure groups and parties in Britain. *Am. Polit. Sci. Rev.* 50:1–23

Blom-Hansen J. 2001. Organized interests and the state: a disintegrating relationship? Evidence from Denmark. *Eur. J. Polit. Res.* 39 (3):391–416

Boyer R, Dore R. 1995. *Les Politiques des Revenues in Europe.* Paris: La Découverte

Bruno M, Sachs J. 1985. *Economics of Worldwide Stagflation.* Cambridge, MA: Harvard Univ. Press

Bull M. 1992. The corporatist ideal-type and political exchange. *Polit. Stud.* 40:255–72

Calmfors L. 1998. Macroeconomic policy, wage-setting and employment—what differences does the EMU make? *Oxf. Rev. Econ. Policy* 14(3):125–51

Calmfors L, Driffill J. 1988. Bargaining structure, corporatism and macroeconomic performance. *Econ. Policy* 6:13–61

Cameron D. 1984. Social democracy, corporatism, labour quiescence and the representation of economic interests in advanced capitalist society. See Goldthorpe 1984, pp. 143–78

Cawson A. 1986. *Corporatism and Political Theory.* London: Blackwell

Cawson A. 1988. In defence of the New Testament: a reply to Andrew Cox, "The Old and New Testaments of corporatism." *Polit. Stud.* 36:309–15

Chater R, Dean A, Elliot R. 1981. *Incomes Policy.* Oxford, UK: Clarendon

Coevers F, van Veen T. 1995. On the measurement of corporatism. *Labour* 9(3):423–42

Compston H. 1997. Union power, policy making and unemployment in Western Europe, 1972–1993. *Comp. Polit. Stud.* 30:732–51

Compston H. 1998. The end of national policy concertation? Western Europe since the Single European Act. *J. Eur. Public Policy* 5(3):507–26

Cox A, ed. 1982. *Politics, Policy and the European Recession.* London: Macmillan

Cox A. 1988. The Old and New Testaments of corporatism: Is it a political form or a method of policy-making? *Polit. Stud.* 36:294–308

Crepaz ML. 1992. Corporatism in decline? An empirical analysis of the impact of corporatism on macroeconomic performance and industrial disputes in 18 industrialized economies. *Comp. Polit. Stud.* 25(2):139–68

Crouch C. 1983. Pluralism and the new corporatism: a rejoinder. *Polit. Stud.* 31:452–60

Crouch C. 1990. Generalised political exchange in industrial relations in Europe during the twentieth century. See Marin 1990b, pp. 68–116

Crouch C, Traxler F, eds. 1995. *Organized Industrial Relations in Europe: What Future?* Aldershot, UK: Avebury

Crouch C. 1999. National wage determination and European Monetary Union. In *After the Euro: Shaping Institutions for Governance in the Wake of European Monetary Union*, ed. C Crouch, pp. 203–26. Oxford, UK: Clarendon

Crouch C. 2000. The snakes and ladders of twenty-first-century trade unionism. *Oxf. Rev. Econ. Policy* 16(1):70–83

Crouch C. 2002. The Euro and labour market and wage policies. In *European States and the Euro*, ed. K Dyson. Oxford, UK: Oxford Univ. Press. In press

Cukierman A, Lippi F. 1998. *Central bank independence, centralization of wage bargaining, inflation and unemployment.* Disc. Pap. 1847. Cent. Econ. Policy Res.

Ebbinghaus B, Hassel A. 2000. Striking deals: concertation in the reform of European welfare states. *J. Eur. Public Policy* 7(1):44–62

Fajertag G, Pochet P, eds. 1997. *Social Pacts in Europe.* Brussels: Eur. Trade Union Inst./ Obs. Soc. Eur.

Fajertag G, Pochet P, eds. 2000. *Social Pacts in Europe: New Dynamics.* Brussels: Eur. Trade Union Inst./Observatoire Soc. Eur.

Flanagan R. 1999. Macroeconomic performance and collective bargaining: an international perspective. *J. Econ. Lit.* 37:1150–75

Flanagan R, Soskice D, Ulman L. 1983. *Unionism, Economic Stabilization and Incomes Policies: European Experience.* Washington: Brookings Inst.

Gerlich P, Grande E, Müller WC. 1988. Corporatism in crisis: stability and change of social partnership in Austria. *Polit. Stud.* 36:209–33

Glyn A, ed. 2001. *Social Democracy in Neoliberal Times. The Left and Economic Policy since 1980.* New York: Oxford Univ. Press

Gobeyn MJ. 1993. Explaining the decline of macro-corporatist political bargaining struc-

tures in advanced capitalist societies. *Governance* 6(1):3–22

Goetschy J. 2000. The European Union and national social pacts: employment and social protection put to the test of joint regulation. See Fajertag & Pochet 2000, pp. 41–60

Goldthorpe J, ed. 1984 *Order and Conflict in Contemporary Capitalism.* Oxford, UK: Clarendon

Gordon DM. 1996. Conflict and cooperation: an empirical glimpse of the imperatives of efficiency and redistribution. *Polit. Soc.* 24 (4):433–56

Grahl J, Teague P. 1997. Is the European social model fragmenting? *New Polit. Econ.* 2(3):405–26

Grant W. 1985. *The Political Economy of Corporatism.* New York: St. Martin's

Hall P, Franzese R. 1998. Mixed signals: central bank independence, coordinated wage bargaining and European Monetary Union. *Int. Org.* (52):505–35

Harrison RJ. 1980. *Pluralism and Corporatism: The Political Evolution of Modern Democracies.* London: Allen & Unwin

Hassel A, Ebbinghaus B. 2000. *Concerted reforms: linking wage formation and social policy in Europe.* Presented at Int. Conf. Europeanists, 12th, Chicago, Mar. 30–Apr. 1

Hemerijck A. 1995. Corporatist immobility in the Netherlands. See Crouch & Traxler 1995, pp. 183–226

Hemerijck A, Schludi M. 2000. Sequences of policy failures and effective policy responses. In *Welfare and Work in the Open Economy*, Vol. I, *From Vulnerability to Competitiveness*, ed. F Scharpf, V Schmidt, pp. 125–228. Oxford, UK: Oxford Univ. Press

Hicks A. 1999. *Social Democracy and Welfare Capitalism: A Century of Income Security Politics.* Ithaca/London: Cornell Univ. Press

Hicks A, Kenworthy L. 1998. Cooperation and political economic performance in affluent democratic capitalism. *Am. J. Soc.* 103(6): 1631–72

International Labour Review. 1995. Perspectives: experiences of social pacts in Western Europe. *Int. Labour Rev.* 134(3):401–26

Iversen T. 1999. *Contested Economic Institutions. The Politics of Macroeconomics and Wage Bargaining.* Cambridge, UK: Cambridge Univ. Press

Iversen T, Pontusson J, Soskice D. 2000. *Unions, Employers, and Central Banks.* Cambridge, UK: Cambridge Univ. Press

Iversen T, Soskice D. 1998. *Central bank—trade unions interactions and the equilibrium rate of unemployment.* Disc. Pap. FS I 97–308. Berlin: Wissenschaftszentrum

Jordan G. 1984. Pluralistic corporatisms and corporate pluralism. *Scand. Polit. Stud.* 7: 137–51

Katzenstein P. 1985. *Small States in World Markets.* Ithaca, NY: Cornell Univ. Press

Kauppinen T, ed. 1998. *The Impact of EMU on Industrial Relations in Europe.* Helsinki: Finn. Ind. Rel. Assoc.

Keman H. 1984. Politics, policies, and consequences: a cross-national analysis of public policy formation in advanced capitalist democracies (1967–1981). *Eur. J. Polit. Res.* 12:1147–70

Kenis P, Schneider V. 1991. Policy networks and policy analysis: scrutinising a new analytical box. In *Policy Networks: Empirical Evidence and Theoretical Considerations,* ed. B Marin, R Mayntz, pp. 25–59. Frankfurt: Campus Verlag

Kenworthy L. 2000. *Quantitative indicators of corporatism: a survey and assessment.* Disc. Pap. 00/4. Cologne: Max Planck Inst. Ges.schaftsforsch.

Kurzer P. 1991. Unemployment in open economies: the impact of trade, finance and European integration. *Comp. Polit. Stud.* 24 (1):3–30

Kurzer P. 1993. *Business and Banking: Political Change and Economic Integration in Western Europe.* Ithaca/London: Cornell Univ. Press

Lash S, Urry J. 1987. *The End of Organized Capitalism.* Oxford, UK: Polity

Layard R, Nickell S, Jackman R. 1991. *Unemployment: Macroeconomic Performance and the Labour Market.* New York: Oxford Univ. Press

Lehmbruch G. 1977. Liberal corporatism and party government. *Comp. Polit. Stud.* 10(1): 91–126

Lehmbruch G. 1979. Concluding remarks: problems for research on corporatist intermediation and policy making. See Schmitter & Lehmbruch 1979, pp. 299–310

Lehmbruch G. 1984. Concertation and the structure of corporatist networks. See Goldthorpe 1984, pp. 60–80

Manoïlesco M. 1934. *Le Siècle du Corporatisme.* Paris: Felix Alcan

Marin B. 1990a. Introduction: generalised political exchange. Governance and generalised exchange. See Marin 1990b, pp. 13–35

Marin B, ed. 1990b. *Governance and Generalised Exchange. Self-Organising Policy Networks in Action.* Frankfurt: Campus Verlag

Martin R. 1983. Pluralism and the new corporatism. *Polit. Stud.* 31:86–102

Martin A. 1999. *Wage bargaining under EMU: Europeanisation, re-nationalisation or Americanisation.* Disc. pap. DWP 99.01.03. Harvard Univ., Cent. Eur. Stud.

Martin A, Ross G, eds. 1999. *The Brave New World of European Labour. European Trade Unions at the Millennium.* New York: Berghahn Books

Mayntz R, Scharpf F. 1995. *Gesellschaftliche Selbstregelung und Politische Steuerung.* Frankfurt am Main: Campus Verlag

McCallum J. 1986. Unemployment in the OECD countries in the 1980s. *Econ. J.* 96: 942–60

Mitchell N. 1996. Theoretical and empirical issues in the comparative measurement of union power and corporatism. *Br. J. Polit. Sci.* 26(3):419–28

Mutti A. 1982. Lo scambio politico nelle relazione industriali. *Stato Mercat.* 5:295–320

Nedelman B, Meier K. 1977. Theories of contemporary corporatism; static or dynamic? *Comp. Polit. Stud.* 10(1):39–60

Negrelli S. 2000. Social pacts in Italy and Europe: similar strategies and structures; different models and national stories. See Fajertag & Pochet 2000, pp. 85–112

Nickell S. 1997. Unemployment and labour market rigidities: Europe versus North America. *J. Econ. Persp.* 11(3):55–74

Offe C. 1981. The attribution of public status to interest groups: observations on the West German case. In *Organizing Interests in Western Europe*, ed. S Berger, pp. 123–58. Cambridge, UK: Cambridge Univ. Press

Paloheimo H. 1984. Distributive struggle and economic development in the 1970s in developed capitalist countries. *Eur. J. Polit. Res.* 12:171–90

Panitch L. 1980. Recent theorizations of corporatism: reflections on a growth industry. *Br. J. Soc.* 31(2):159–87

Parsons S. 1988. On the logic of corporatism. *Polit. Stud.* 36:515–23

Pekkarinen J. 1992. Corporatism and economic performance in Sweden, Norway and Finland. In *Social Corporatism: A Superior Economic System?* ed. J Pekkarinen, M Pohjola, B Rowthorn, pp. 298–337. Oxford, UK: Clarendon

Pérez S. 1999. *The resurgence of national social bargaining in Europe: explaining the Italian and Spanish experiences*. CEACS Work. Pap. 1999/130. Madrid: Inst. Juan March Estud. Invest.

Pizzorno A. 1977. Scambio politico e identità colletiva nel conflitto di classe. *Riv. It. Sci. Polit.* 7(2):165–98

Pochet P. 1998. Les pactes sociaux en europe dans les années 1990. *Soc. Trav.* (2):173–90

Pochet P, ed. 1999. *Monetary Union and Collective Bargaining in Europe*. Brussels: PIE-Peter Lang

Pochet P, Fajertag G. 2000. A new era for social pacts in Europe. See Fajertag & Pochet 2000, pp. 9–40

Regini M. 1984. The conditions for political exchange: How concertation emerged and collapsed in Italy and Great Britain. See Goldthorpe 1984, pp. 124–42

Regini M. 1995. *Uncertain Boundaries. The Social and Political Construction of European Economies*. Cambridge, UK: Cambridge Univ. Press

Regini M. 1999. Between de-regulation and social pacts. The responses of European economies to globalisation. *Polit. Soc.* 28:5–33

Regini M. 2000. *Modelli di Capitalismo. Le Risposte europee alla Sfida della Globalizzazione*. Roma-Bari: Ed. Laterza

Rhodes M. 1998. Globalisation, labour markets and welfare states: a future of "competitive corporatism"? In *The Future of European Welfare: A New Social Contract*, ed. M Rhodes, Y Mény, pp. 178–203. London: Macmillan

Rhodes M. 2001a. The political economy of social pacts: "competitive corporatism" and European welfare state reform. In *The New Politics of the Welfare State*, ed. P Pierson, pp. 165–96. Oxford, UK: Oxford Univ. Press

Rhodes M. 2001b. Globalization, welfare states, and employment: Is there a European "Third Way"? In *Unemployment in the New Europe*, ed. N Bermeo, pp. 87–118. Cambridge, UK: Cambridge Univ. Press

Rigby M, Serrano R. 1997. *Estrategias Sindicales en Europa: Convergencias o Divergencias*. Madrid: Com. Econ. Soc.

Rigby M, Smith R, Lawlor T. 1999. *European Trade Unions. Change and Response*. London: Routledge

Scharpf F. 1997. *Games Real Actors Play. Actor-Centered Institutionalism in Policy Research*. Boulder, CO: Westview

Schmitter P. 1974. Still the century of corporatism? *Rev. Polit.* (36):85–131

Schmitter P. 1981. Interest intermediation and regime governability in contemporary Western Europe and North America. In *Organizing Interests in Western Europe*, ed. S Berger, pp. 285–37. New York: Cambridge Univ. Press

Schmitter P. 1982. Reflections on where the theory of neo-corporatism has gone and where the praxis of neo-corporatism may be going. In *Patterns of Corporatist Policy Making*, ed. G Lehmbruch, P Schmitter, pp. 259–79. London: Sage

Schmitter P. 1989. Corporatism is dead! Long live corporatism! *Gov. Oppos.* 24:54–73

Schmitter P, Grote J. 1997. Sisifo corporatista: passato, presente e futuro. *Stato Mercat.* 50: 183–215

Schmitter P, Lehmbruch G. 1979. *Trends Towards Corporatist Intermediation.* Beverly Hills, CA: Sage

Schmitter P, Streeck W. 1991. From national corporatism to transnational pluralism. *Polit. Soc.* 19(2):133–64

Shonfield A. 1965. *Modern Capitalism: the Changing Balance of Public and Private Power.* Oxford, UK: Oxford Univ. Press

Siaroff A. 1999. Corporatism in 24 industrial democracies: meaning and measurement. *Eur. J. Polit. Res.* (36):175–205

Soskice D. 1990. Wage determination: the changing role of institutions in advanced industrialized countries. *Oxf. Rev. Econ. Policy* 6(4):36–61

Soskice D. 1999. *The political economy of EMU. Rethinking the effects of monetary integration on Europe.* Disc. pap. FS I 99–302. Berlin: Wissenschaftszentrum

Stephens JD. 2000. *Is Swedish corporatism dead? Thoughts on its supposed demise in the light of the abortive "alliance for growth" in 1998.* Presented at Int. Conf. Europeanists, 12th, Chicago, Mar. 30–Apr. 1

Streeck W, Schmitter P, eds. 1985. *Private Interest Government: Beyond Market and State.* London: Sage

Swank D. 2002. *Global Capital, Political Institutions, and Policy Change in Developed Welfare States.* Cambridge, UK: Cambridge Univ. Press

Teague P. 2000. Macroeconomic constraints, social learning and pay bargaining in Europe. *Br. J. Ind. Relat.* 38(3):429–52

Therborn G. 1992. Lessons from corporatist theorizations. In *Social Corporatism: A Superior Economic System?* ed. J Pekkarinen, M Pohjola, B Rowthorn, pp. 24–43. Oxford, UK: Clarendon

Therborn G. 1998. Does corporatism really matter? The economic crisis and issues of political theory. *J. Public Policy* 7(3):259–84

Traxler F. 1995. Farewell to labour market asso-

ciations? Organized versus disorganized decentralization as a map for industrial relations. See Crouch & Traxler 1995, pp. 3–19

Traxler F. 1997. The logic of social pacts. See Fajertag & Pochet 1997, pp. 27–35

Traxler F. 1998. Collective bargaining in the OECD: developments, preconditions and effects. *Eur. J. Ind. Relat.* 4(2):207–26

Traxler F. 1999. Wage-setting institutions and European Monetary Union. In *The Role of Employers' Associations and Labour Unions in the EMU. Institutional Requirements for European Economic Policies,* ed. G Huemer, M Mesch, F Traxler, pp. 115–36. Aldershot, UK: Ashgate

Traxler F, Blaschke S, Kittel B. 2001. *National Labour Relations in Internationalized Markets: A Comparative Study of Institutions, Change, and Performance.* Oxford, UK: Oxford Univ. Press

Traxler F, Kittel B. 2000. The bargaining system and performance. A comparison of 18 OECD countries. *Comp. Polit.* 33(9):1154–90

Treu T. 1992. *Participation in Public Policy-Making. The Role of Trade Unions and Employers' Associations.* Berlin: de Gruyter

Visser J, Hemerijck A. 1997. *A Dutch Miracle: Job Growth, Welfare Reform and Corporatism in the Netherlands.* Amsterdam: Amsterdam Univ. Press

Wallerstein M. 1998. The impact of economic integration on European wage-setting institutions. In *Forging an Integrated Europe,* ed. B Eichengreen, pp. 185–207. Ann Arbor: Univ. Mich. Press

Wallerstein M, Golden M. 2000. Wage setting in the Nordic countries. In *Unions, Employers and Central Banks: Macroeconomic Coordination and Institutional Change in Social Market Economies,* ed. T Iversen, J Pontussen, D Soskice, pp. 107–36. Cambridge, UK: Cambridge Univ. Press

Wallerstein M, Golden M, Lange P. 1997. Unions, employers' associations and wage-setting institutions in Northern and Central

Europe, 1950–1992. *Ind. Labor Relat. Rev.* 50(3):379–401

Walsh J. 1995. Convergence or divergence? Corporatism and the dynamics of European wage bargaining. *Int. Rev. Appl. Econ.* 9(2):196–91

Wassenberg A. 1982. Neo-corporatism and the quest for control: the cuckoo game. In *Patterns of Corporatist Policy Making*, ed. G Lehmbruch, P Schmitter, pp. 83–108. London: Sage

Western B. 1991. A comparative study of corporatist development. *Am. Soc. Rev.* 56:283–94

Wiarda H. 1997. *Corporatism and Comparative Politics. The Other Great Ism.* New York: Sharpe

Williamson P. 1985. *Varieties of Corporatism: Theory and Practice.* Cambridge, UK: Cambridge Univ. Press

Williamson P. 1989. *Corporatism in Perspective: An Introductory Guide to Corporatist Theory.* London: Sage

Winkler J. 1976. Corporatism. *Eur. J. Soc.* (17): 100–36

Woldendorp J. 1997. Neo-corporatism and macroeconomic performance in eight small West European countries. *Acta Polit.* 32: 49–79

Annu. Rev. Polit. Sci. 2002. 5:333–67
DOI: 10.1146/annurev.polisci.5.011002.115655
Copyright © 2002 by Annual Reviews. All rights reserved

LANDMARKS IN THE STUDY OF CONGRESS SINCE 1945*

Nelson W. Polsby and Eric Schickler

*Department of Political Science, 210 Barrows Hall, University of California at Berkeley,
Berkeley, California 94720; e-mail: nwpolsby@socrates.berkeley.edu,
schick@socrates.berkeley.edu*

Key Words legislative behavior, responsible parties, rational choice, House of
Representatives, Senate

■ **Abstract** This paper traces the course of inquiry on the U.S. Congress from 1945
to the present day, noting antecedents in the work of Woodrow Wilson, and through
Wilson, of Walter Bagehot. Since 1945, the study of Congress has gone through an
anglophile responsible-party phase, championed especially by William Yandell Elliott
at Harvard, followed by a sociologically oriented legislative-behavior phase, identified
in one generation with Lewis Anthony Dexter, Stephen K. Bailey, David Truman, and
especially Ralph K. Huitt at Wisconsin, and in the next generation with Richard Fenno,
Charles O. Jones, Donald R. Matthews, and H. Douglas Price, among others. A third,
contemporary intellectual orientation is identified most strongly with rational choice
scholars, especially from the University of Rochester. The agenda of political science
is formed not only by the literature but by events. Hence, the congressional reforms
of the 1970s were influential in shaping the literature, as were such organizational
innovations as the Congressional Fellowship Program and the Study of Congress, both
projects of the American Political Science Association.

INTRODUCTION

The social sciences have rarely been considered fit for study as intellectual history.[1]
This, we think, will be a temporary phenomenon in light of the prodigious growth of
this luxuriant branch of learning since World War II; its exfoliation into specialties
and subspecialties; its expression in university departments and research institutes,
and schools of thought; its intellectual trends and hot spots, texts and syntheses,
blind alleys and fruitful innovations. Sooner or later, perhaps a generation from
now, scholars will want to look at the growth and diversification of modern social

---

*Prepared for delivery at the 2001 Annual Meeting of the American Political Science
Association, San Francisco, CA, August 30–September 2, 2001. In writing this essay, we
have drawn freely on our earlier work (Polsby 1984, 1990, 1998; Schickler 2001a).
[1]Honorable exceptions include Hughes (1976) and Hyman (1962).

333

scientific knowledge as a cultural artifact—or as many cultural artifacts. For the moment, we may be too close to the origins to be able to sort things out properly. But we can prepare the ground.

This paper traces some of the lines of intellectual influence that helped to form a significant portion of the literature on the U.S. Congress from the end of World War II to the present day. (We exclude here the literature on congressional elections, which is important in its own right.) In the subspecialty of political science known as congressional studies, there was a sharp upturn after World War II in the number and quality of books and articles that focused on the political behavior of Congress rather than its legal or constitutional powers, its administrative machinery, or its alleged inadequacies as a vessel of responsible party government.[2]

THE ANGLOPHILE "RESPONSIBLE PARTY" TRADITION

The most significant intellectual influence on prewar congressional studies was Walter Bagehot, whose *The English Constitution* (1867) inspired Woodrow Wilson to write *Congressional Government* (1885), later his Johns Hopkins doctoral dissertation. (For a thorough account of the writing of this book, see Link 1968, 4:6–13.) Wilson found the committee-dominated, decentralized Congress of the 1880s to be deficient when compared with what he understood to be the more disciplined British system. To Wilson and numerous academic successors, America suffered from a lack of responsible parties. Instead of programmatic parties that offered coherent platforms to the public, which were then implemented by the government, the U.S. system was characterized by separation between Congress and the President and by a lack of accountable leadership within the legislative branch. As a rough measure of the unempirical spirit of the time, contemporary readers still find it remarkable that Wilson was able to say to his fiancée that he wrote this influential work—which he styled a critique of "literary" theories of congressional activity—without once traveling the 40 miles from Baltimore to observe Congress directly (Link 1968, vol. 3, letter of Jan. 22, 1885). Those who followed in his footsteps, on the whole, even when they maintained Wilson's strong prescriptive (and anglophile) orientation, have more frequently availed themselves of the opportunity to study Congress in the flesh before pronouncing judgment.

An important academic successor of Wilson's was William Y. Elliott (1896–1979), an Oxford D. Phil., Rhodes Scholar, and Balliol College man, who, in addition to a long and fruitful university career (especially at Harvard, 1925–1963), served as a senior staff member of the House Committee on Foreign Affairs in the Republican-controlled 80th Congress. Elliott's book *The Need for Constitutional Reform* (1935) was written a decade before his most intensive congressional service and exemplifies the prescriptive mode that dominated prewar congressional studies. In the immediate postwar period, two Elliott doctoral students, Holbert N.

---

[2]Good examples of the earlier style include Galloway (1946), Griffith (1951), Burns (1949), and Kefauver & Levin (1947).

Carroll and H. Bradford Westerfield, wrote excellent dissertations on Congress and foreign affairs (Westerfield 1955, Carroll 1958).[3] Both were primarily empirical, not prescriptive, in their approach. In his thorough survey of House involvement in foreign affairs, Carroll was especially alert in noting the growing importance of the House-dominated appropriations process in boosting congressional influence on U.S. foreign policy in the postwar years. Westerfield ultimately rejected the party-responsibility model of his mentor in tracing what became of congressional bipartisanship in foreign affairs between the Pearl Harbor attack and the Korean War.

SOCIOLOGICALLY ORIENTED RESEARCH: THE FIRST GENERATION

In some ways, Arthur Maass (Harvard Ph.D., 1949) became Elliott's successor in the Harvard Department. The book he wrote late in his career, *Congress and the Common Good* (Maass 1983), summarized a quarter century of teaching. In it, he made a strong argument in defense of Congress as an institution embodying a meaningful conception of the common good, in dialogue with the literature that characterized American political institutions as arenas for the expression of group interests. This brought to the study of Congress a dispute that had preoccupied students of American political parties for half a century.[4] "The focus throughout," he said, making a distinction that by the 1980s seemed anachronistic, "is institutional, not political behavior" (Maass 1983, p. vii). Like Wilson and Elliott, Maass combined the study of Congress with an abiding interest in public administration. One of Maass's doctoral students, John Johannes (Ph.D., 1970), wrote a book on the management of congressional casework (Johannes 1984). Another, Joseph Cooper (Ph.D., 1961) has recently achieved broad recognition as a pioneer in uncovering the historical roots of contemporary congressional organization (see especially Cooper 1970).

The largest group of scholars to display the new empirical focus were either political scientists who had been associated with the Congressional Fellowship Program of the American Political Science Association (such as Brad Westerfield, who was in the first class of Fellows in 1953), or were students of Ralph Huitt (1913–1986) at the University of Wisconsin.

In any account of the professional study of Congress, the Congressional Fellowship Program of the American Political Science Association (APSA) deserves more than passing attention. It was an institutional invention of considerable ingenuity. The idea was to mimic in a congressional setting the clerkships that appellate judges gave to promising graduates of law schools, affording young political scientists hands-on experience in the legislative branch in a pre-CSPAN time when

---

[3]See also Dahl (1950), which takes as its main problem the extent to which Congress is capable of pursuing a rational and responsible foreign policy.

[4]Perhaps the work on Congress in this era most focused on legislative process as competition among groups was Gross (1953).

the public had limited regular access to Congress and very little knowledge of its routines. The program from the start included journalists as well. Members of Congress who might see little value in getting to know young scholars would have no difficulty in appreciating the benefits of acquaintance with a new generation of reporters on mutually beneficial terms. Piggy-backing on the higher status of journalists in the nation's capital, many generations of political scientists have undertaken close participant observation of members, their offices, and their committees under APSA's nonpartisan auspices. Over 1800 men and women early in their careers have passed through the program. At first these were predominantly American political scientists and journalists; later, civil servants and health policy specialists from medical schools were added to the mix, as were foreign scholars and journalists. Research political scientists have always been a minority of the population—less than one third—but it is doubtful that funding could ever have been found to support political scientists alone.

Although the fraction of Fellows who have been political scientists is not over-whelming, the program, in nearly half a century of existence, has had a profound impact on the intellectual agendas of many able researchers who have contributed enormously to the empirical study of Congress. (Table 1 lists roughly a tenth of the political scientists who have participated in the program.) The number of books and articles on all aspects of Congress written by members of this group is, of course, very impressive. Some of these scholars had already committed themselves to the study of Congress before they became Fellows, but many had not. Both subgroups found their horizons extended and their agendas transformed by the experience of working on Capitol Hill.

A decade after the Congressional Fellowship Program was begun, APSA intervened significantly once again in congressional studies by soliciting and receiving a grant from the Carnegie Corporation to sponsor what was called a Study of Congress. This large undertaking (1964–1969) was put in the charge of Ralph K. Huitt, who had already emerged as a major influence in the training of congressional scholars.[5] Rather than conduct one consolidated inquiry in the style of Gunner Myrdal's *An American Dilemma* (1944), Huitt decided to spread the project

---

[5]Huitt's doctoral students at Wisconsin included Charles O. Jones, Samuel C. Patterson, John W. Kingdon, Charles Backstrom, Lawrence Pettit, John Bibby, and Dale Vinyard. Despite Huitt's long absence from teaching (1965–1978) while he worked in Washington as Assistant Secretary of Health, Education and Welfare and Executive Director of the National Association of Universities and Land Grant Colleges, he created something close to a Wisconsin dynasty in congressional studies. Consider his student Samuel C. Patterson, whose main impact as a scholar was in comparative legislative studies rather than as a specialist in Congress alone. Patterson was a founder of *Legislative Studies Quarterly*, the leading journal in the field; coauthor of an important text, *The Legislative Process in the United States* (Patterson & Jewell 1966); and, in a lengthy teaching career at the University of Iowa and Ohio State University, was himself mentor to several congressional scholars (Huitt's academic grandchildren), notably David W. Brady, Garrison Nelson, John Alford, and John Hibbing. We mention below some of the contributions of Kingdon, Hibbing, Brady, and Jones.

TABLE 1 A partial list of political scientists who were APSA
Congressional Fellows

Abraham Holtzman, 1953	Barbara Sinclair, 1973
Harry H. Ransom, 1953	James A. Thurber, 1973
Marvin Harder, 1954	Lawrence C. Dodd, 1974
Charles L. Clapp, 1955	John W. Ellwood, 1974
H. Douglas Price, 1956	Bruce I. Oppenheimer, 1974
Alan Fiellen, 1957	Catherine Rudder, 1974
Joyce M. Mitchell, 1957	Marcia Lynn Whicker, 1974
William C. Mitchell, 1957	Richard J. Born, 1975
James A. Robinson, 1957	Burdett Loomis, 1975
Eddie N. Williams, 1958	Henry Kenski, 1975
Daniel M. Berman, 1959	David J. Vogler, 1975
Robert Gilpin, 1959	Jo Freeman, 1978
Alan Rosenthal, 1959	Charles N. Tidmarch, 1978
Raymond E. Wolfinger, 1959	Gary Copeland, 1979
Alton Frye, 1961	Steven S. Smith, 1980
John S. Saloma, 1961	David Kozak, 1981
Lewis A. Froman, Jr., 1963	Paul C. Light, 1982
Irwin Gertzog, 1963	Hanes Walton, Jr., 1983
John F. Manley, 1963	Christopher Deering, 1984
D. Alan Heslop, 1967	Richard Hall, 1987
David R. Mayhew, 1967	Thomas Kazee, 1987
Marie–France Toinet, 1968	Paul S. Herrnson, 1989
Hugh Heclo, 1969	Mark A. Peterson, 1990
Thomas E. Mann, 1969	Lyn Ragsdale, 1990
Norman J. Ornstein, 1969	Daniel Wirls, 1993
Karl T. Kurtz, 1970	Forrest Maltzman, 1994
Charles S. Bullock, 1971	Nicol C. Rae, 1995
Stanley Bach, 1972	Daniel Palazzolo, 1996
Glenn R. Parker, 1972	Diana Dwyer, 1997
David W. Rohde, 1972	Ben Highton, 1998
Ada Finifter, 1973	

out and support a number of members of the generation junior to him nationwide. (Works published under the auspices of the Study of Congress include Froman 1967, Polsby 1968, Polsby et al. 1969, Jones 1970, Manley 1970, Ogul 1976, and Patterson 1970.) When Huitt took up his administrative duties in Washington, Robert L. Peabody became Associate Director of the Study of Congress.

Huitt's own scholarship played a strong role in giving the Study of Congress intellectual guidance. In particular, he had developed a preference for hands-on empirical study and close observation. Although Huitt never wrote a book,[6] his grasp of the nuances and the realities of congressional politics was exceptional, and his teaching was frequently spellbinding.

Four remarkable articles in *The American Political Science Review* (*APSR*) between 1954 and 1961 constitute the heart of Huitt's scholarly output.[7] He asked (Huitt & Peabody 1969, p. vii), "Why should not Congress be studied as a legislature, and the behavior of its members analyzed against the institutional demands of the legislative process?" Today we might describe the endeavor as an attempt to assimilate Congress to organization theory.

The earliest of his *APSR* articles on Congress, a case study of a congressional committee (Huitt 1954), was concerned with "inventing a way to study the U.S. Congress from a library in Madison, Wisconsin." Not the optimal locale, Huitt thought, for understanding a living, breathing institution: "It looked as if I might never get away from there" (Huitt & Peabody 1969, p. viii). Fortune smiled in the form of a Ford grant (1953–1954) and a significant professional connection: Huitt, a Texan with a University of Texas Ph.D., landed what was in effect a senior internship in the office of Senator Lyndon Johnson of Texas through the intervention of Johnson's childhood friend, Professor Emmette Redford of the University of Texas Political Science Department. Johnson had just become the Senate Democratic leader. Huitt made the most of this connection, as well as a 1958 stint as legislative assistant to Senator William Proxmire of his adopted state of Wisconsin. These experiences enabled Huitt to write with confidence about the ways in which two very different personalities, differently situated in the organization, shaped their careers and adapted to the web of organizational norms and practices that defined the Senate as an institution (see Huitt 1961a,b). And they strongly reinforced Huitt's conviction that understanding Congress required inquiry into the way the institution looked to its inhabitants, not merely to academic outsiders. This constituted a sharp break with the tradition of measuring Congress by the yardstick of responsible party government, as in the British model that had dominated the field since Woodrow Wilson's day.

The last great landmark of the older tradition, marking a transition to the newer approach, was Stephen K. Bailey's *Congress Makes a Law* (1950).[8] This careful

---

[6]His work on Congress, collected posthumously, makes a very interesting book (Huitt 1990). An earlier, less complete assembly of his work can be found in Huitt & Peabody (1969).

[7]Three are discussed below; the fourth (Huitt 1957) addressed the politics behind the celebrated 1952–1953 controversy surrounding the decision of Senator Wayne Morse to leave the Republican party and seek committee assignments from the whole Senate.

[8]Winner of APSA's Woodrow Wilson Prize in 1950, Bailey (Harvard Ph.D., 1948) had also been a Rhodes Scholar at University College, Oxford, in 1939 and a tutee of, among others, Harold Wilson. At the time of publication, Bailey (1916–1982) was on the faculty of Wesleyan University, which had no graduate students in political science. While at Wesleyan, Bailey took a great interest in practical politics, and he served as Mayor of

and evocative case study of the passage of the Employment Act of 1946 required 400 interviews. Huitt appreciated Bailey's interest in "what went on in the two houses where an intellectual's dream of a national commitment to full employment was converted into a bill that could pass. The idea of paying attention to what legislatures do was revolutionary, and legislative scholarship was never quite the same after that." But, Huitt continued, "The revolution was not complete. Bailey's frame of theory was not the legislature itself but something called 'a responsible two-party system' which seemed important at the time" (Huitt & Peabody 1969, p. vii).[9]

Although Bailey had few students, he had many followers, especially in the creation of a pedagogical tradition. If there is something like a "textbook Congress," it is embodied in the large number of books, written as texts, that follow in Bailey's footsteps by describing in detail the process by which a particular law is enacted. (Examples include Berman 1962, Bendiner 1964, JP Harris 1964, Bibby & Davidson 1967, Eidenberg & Morey 1969, RA Harris 1969, Peabody et al. 1972, Redman 1973, Brezina & Overmyer 1974, Reid 1980, Birnbaum & Murray 1987, Martin 1994, and Elving 1995.) To the best of our knowledge, nobody has attempted a propositional inventory that examines this formidable body of reportage synoptically. If it were attempted, perhaps we could claim to have glimpsed the textbook Congress.

Two other contemporaries of Huitt's wrote important works incorporating the study of Congress into the discipline-wide movement focusing on political behavior, but neither of them produced many students. David Truman (b. 1913) was a major figure in political science from the publication of his *The Governmental Process* (1951), early in his career. *The Congressional Party: A Case Study* (Truman 1959) portrayed the ways in which the political parties organized the work of the eighty-first Congress (1949–1951). The idea was to seek hard empirical measures—especially through the analysis of roll calls—to assess the actual impact of parties on the life of an institution alleged to be lacking (by standards of the time) in party responsibility. Truman (1959) found more structure than the prescriptive literature of the day presumed existed.[10] This added meaningful detail to an emerging portrait of Congress as an autonomous institution that was important in its political system despite its lack of resemblance to the Westminster model. This book was Truman's last significant scholarly effort before he became a senior member of the administration at Columbia University and later President of Mount Holyoke College. His departure from the world of scholarly endeavor

---

Middletown, Connecticut (1952–1954) before moving on to Princeton in 1954 and then to Syracuse in 1959, where he became Dean of the Maxwell School of Citizenship. Later he taught at the Harvard (graduate) School of Education.

[9]Bailey never relinquished his strong preference for responsible parties (Bailey 1959, 1966).

[10]Another early example of an empirical study of party voting is Julius Turner's *Party and Constituency: Pressures on Congress* (1951). Turner analyzed party cohesion on roll-call voting in selected Congresses from 1921 to 1944. Like Truman, he found evidence of substantial partisanship, though with considerable variation across issue areas.

in American politics deprived the field of one of its sharpest minds and one of its most generous teachers.

Lewis Anthony Dexter (1915–1995) was an immensely prolific maverick. Although his B.A. from the University of Chicago was dated 1935, his sociology Ph.D. from Columbia was delayed until 1960 because of a conflict with his supervisory committee. He never stayed long enough at one teaching job to accumulate a body of students, but his writings about Congress, many of them employing a quasi-anthropological style of observation and exhaustive interviewing, were held in very high esteem by the next cohort of scholars, who passed his unpublished manuscript (which later was accepted as his doctoral dissertation), "Congressmen and the People They Listen to,"[11] around among themselves samizdat-style or excavated his early articles in out-of-the-way journals (Dexter 1957, 1960/1961).

Dexter was interested in how congressional organization constrained the attention patterns of members of Congress. Ignorance of these constraints handicapped outsiders in their attempts to influence outcomes. It was no use, Dexter pointed out, attempting to put heat on members of the wrong committee, or approaching the right committee after it had decided the issue. Dexter collected a tremendous fund of political lore, which he frequently published in an unprocessed form. His work created the impression that Congress was a complicated, contingent world containing a vast variety of possible narratives. For example, Dexter propounded the highly fruitful idea that the congressional district was best understood as a social-psychological construct in the mind of the member of Congress, an archipelago embedded in the population located within the district's geographical boundaries. This explained, among other things, why two senators from the same party and the same state might behave differently and see their representational roles differently, yet both survive comfortably, and why the same district might be well represented successively by members of different parties.

SOCIOLOGICALLY ORIENTED RESEARCH: THE SECOND GENERATION

By the 1960s, the empirical study of Congress had begun to flourish and develop in a number of different directions. Three articles appeared in a single issue of *APSR*, all written by University of Wisconsin scholars: Huitt's (1961a) classic on Lyndon Johnson's Senate leadership; an utterly persuasive article by Huitt's doctoral student Charles O. Jones (1961) on the House Agriculture Committee and the way it organized to serve agricultural interests nationwide; and a pathbreaking examination of the hitherto mysterious committee-assignment process in the House by a recent Wisconsin Ph.D., Nicholas Masters (1961).[12]

---

[11]A condensed version was later incorporated into Bauer et al. (1963), which won the APSA Woodrow Wilson Prize in 1963 (see also Dexter 1969).

[12]Although Masters' article was clearly influenced by Huitt's approach to the study of Congress, he wrote his Ph.D. thesis at Wisconsin with David Fellman. Later in his career,

These and other contributions—especially on the House of Representatives—reflected an important turn in the study of Congress. It was possible in short order for one of us, with Robert L. Peabody, to put together a book of readings on the House that for a time captured an enthusiastic market and ultimately went through four editions, thanks to "an extraordinary reawakening of scholarly interest in the U.S. House of Representatives" (Peabody & Polsby 1963).

One reason we felt justified in concentrating on the House was that the Senate was so much better covered in the newspapers. Senators were well-known public figures. Indeed, in the 1950s Senators Estes Kefauver and Joseph McCarthy had become household names, and the committees associated with each were the subjects of much attention in the news media. Several senators contested for the presidential nomination of 1960, and both major parties that year nominated candidates from the Senate.

In the world of scholarship there were also the articles of Ralph Huitt, and a book by Donald R. Matthews (b. 1924) of the University of North Carolina, *U.S. Senators and Their World* (1960) that dominated the field. In particular, Matthews' chapter headed "Folkways of the Senate" (also an article, Matthews 1959) codified a great deal of what we thought we were learning in a less systematic way from Dexter and from the news media about how the Senate operated. It proved to be of great utility to have the norms that seemed to be so influential in the lives of senators spelled out and fortified by substantial independent research.

Matthews (Princeton Ph.D., 1953) had previously indicated a deep interest in a sociological approach to politics with his dissertation, "U.S. Senators: A Study of the Recruitment of Political Leaders." An adaptation focused on theoretical issues, *The Social Background of Political Decision-Makers* (Matthews 1954), was published in a very successful series edited by his mentor Richard Snyder, who later at Northwestern also inspired James A. Robinson's study of the *House Rules Committee* (1963) and numerous other writings by Robinson on Congress.

The productivity of the next generation of congressional scholars is so voluminous as nearly to preclude compact summary. But the work of one scholar achieved special prominence. In the more than 200 years since the founding of the American nation no scholar has contributed more to the understanding of the U.S. Congress than Richard F. Fenno, Jr. (b. 1926). Fenno began with what turned out to be a diversion from his career-long scholarly focus: a very successful Harvard dissertation (under W. Y. Elliott) on the president's cabinet that he later turned into a book (Fenno 1959). From that point onward, Fenno has devoted himself single-mindedly to the study of the U.S. Congress, an effort that now encompasses 14 books (Munger & Fenno 1962; Fenno 1966, 1973, 1978, 1982, 1989, 1990a,b, 1991a,b, 1992, 1996, 1997, 2000). It hit an early high point with the magisterial *Power of the Purse* (Fenno 1966), a detailed portrait of the congressional appropriations

---

Masters became a senior staff member on the House Budget Committee and the key access point for John Gilmour's book *Reconcilable Differences? Congress, the Budget Process, and the Deficit* (1990).

process, starring the House Appropriations Committee as that institution existed during the period 1947–1965. In this book, Fenno offers a distinctive and useful vocabulary for the discussion of Congress: a focus on internal structure, on the interplay between committee loyalties and party loyalties, and on the development of norms of behavior and role expectations tied to committee service. Fenno shows how these norms and roles affect actual public policy—votes on the floor of the House, dollars and cents in the federal budget. Fenno's extraordinary sensitivity as a field worker, the clarity of his thinking about ethical, methodological, strategic, and substantive issues that were puzzling us all, his capacity to make something theoretically interesting out of raw political experience, and his friendly availability as a colleague soon made him signally influential among Congress watchers. Moreover, he got fascinating results.

Half a decade before *The Power of the Purse* came out, it was clear that Fenno was onto something. His congressional section of *National Politics and Federal Aid to Education* (Munger & Fenno 1962) was a tidy case study. But it was his paper, "The House Appropriations Committee as a Political System: The Problem of Integration," first given at an APSA convention, then published as an *APSR* article, that caught the attention of Congress watchers and established his influence among them (Fenno 1962).

The rejuvenation of the Rochester department where Fenno taught also played a significant role in multiplying his influence. Among the contemporary scholars of Congress who passed through Fenno's seminars over the years have been Theodore Anagnoson, Peter Aranson, John Blydenburgh, Morris Fiorina, Linda Fowler, Keith Krehbiel, James Murphy, Keith Poole, Lynda Powell, David Rohde, Kenneth Shepsle, Barbara Sinclair, Richard Smith, John Stolarek, Theodore Westen, Peter Wissel, Jack Wright, and Diana Yiannakis. Political scientists will recognize many of these as significant contributors to the literature.

By the time *Congressmen in Committees* came along, the Fenno hallmark was well established (Fenno 1973). This book took as its task the explanation of variations in the styles and performance characteristics of congressional committees. Committees, in Fenno's analysis, embody to different degrees the varying goals that members of Congress bring to their work: the desire for reelection, the desire to make good policy, the desire to exercise influence in Washington. The aggregation of these goals, filtered through various environmental constraints, produces different strategic premises, decision-making processes, and public policy results.

Home Style (Fenno 1978) follows logically from *Congressmen in Committees*. If how committees behave is in some measure the reflection of members' needs and goals, then it becomes important to reach backward into the environments from which members, in all their variety, spring. *Home Style* explores the terrain out of which members of Congress come and discusses the dilemmas that congressmen face in reconciling the disparate and often conflicting demands, values, and perceptions of home and the distant congressional workplace. It was in connection with research for this book that Fenno noticed that although congressmen are nearly everywhere popular with their own constituents, Congress as a collective entity is low in popularity. In response, he discovered, congressmen frequently succumb to the temptation to run against Congress, a plausible solution to the conundrum now sometimes known as Fenno's paradox.[13]

Like most professional students of Congress, through the early years of his career Fenno gave more of his time and affection to the House of Representatives than the Senate. The House, as we all know, is more open to observation. It is more complex in its structure, more difficult to predict in its outcomes, and altogether a more satisfying object of study. Fenno's more recent work, however, has gone a long way toward redressing the imbalance (see, e.g., Fenno 1986).

By the time Fenno was ready to tackle the Senate, he had established a style of work and had discovered an overarching problem. These interacted to influence his work product. The problem was turning the study of representation in a large-scale society into an empirical inquiry. The method was close observation of elected officials one by one as they constructed their own treaties with their constituents back home, educating constituents on the constraints that they faced as public servants in Washington and learning constituent demands and requirements. A companion challenge for senators and representatives was finding a niche in the legislative institution that allowed them room to pursue activities that satisfied their varied goals of survival, public service, and political influence and that they could explain to their constituents.

Fenno got to know a dozen or so senators very well over the years, and he wrote absorbing books about five: Mark Andrews of North Dakota as he, quite unexpectedly, failed to be reelected to the Senate; John Glenn of Ohio as he leveraged a position in the Senate (and his fame as an astronaut) into a presidential candidacy; and Pete Domenici of New Mexico, Arlen Specter of Pennsylvania, and Dan Quayle of Indiana as they managed their senatorial careers, coping with minority status, the workings of the seniority system, the resources of a committee chairmanship, and other contingencies of Washington life.

In another book, Fenno (1996) distilled a great deal of what he was learning about the interface between politicians and voters by closely following the campaigns of 20 senatorial candidates. And in still another, switching back to the House of Representatives, he contrasted two members of Congress from Georgia—one from the 1970s, the other from the 1990s—to illustrate how styles of representation have changed with the changing political demographics of the South (Fenno 2000). More and more, it seems, Fenno's intense interest in the practical tasks of representation require detailed observation of the ways in which individual members of Congress cope with a cluster of challenges set by the social facts of American

---

[13]Fenno's paradox raises the topic of public distrust, and the study of public disapproval of Congress has been a recent growth area (see Hibbing & Thiess-Morse 1995, Cooper 1999, Uslaner 1993).

democracy: large electorates at a great distance from the capital, with mass media and political parties as important competing sources of intermediation.

Fenno was senior member of a cohort of congressional scholars that frequently crossed paths on Capitol Hill. "We met in the early 1960's," he wrote, "as members of a small group of young political scientists who came together to share the excitement of our budding research on Congress. We got a grant [from the Social Science Research Council] to get together periodically in Washington to take members of Congress to dinner and talk about how to study Congress. There were eight of us—Doug [Price], Chuck Jones, Nelson Polsby, Bob Peabody, Milt Cummings, Randall Ripley, Joe Cooper and myself—'The Boys of Congress'" (Fenno 1998).

Among this group, Fenno's work takes up the most space on the bookshelf. The work of Hugh Douglas Price takes up the least (1975, 1998).[14] His influence was extremely important, however, magnified by the good communications that generally prevailed among students of Congress in his generation and by his generosity as a colleague. Price was a gifted student of V.O. Key, and showed Key's triple-threat talent: keen historical curiosity, statistical facility, and the imagination to put together compelling explanations of institutional behavior combining both.

Price's trenchant comments on the emerging literature, his observations on the growth of legislative professionalism, his creative leap that linked trends in electoral politics with the entrenchment of seniority in the early twentieth century, all had a tremendous impact on his colleagues. This was true even though he rarely wrote down an argument in full. We students of Congress passed his occasional papers among ourselves and treasured his remarks at chance meetings and at conferences. He involved himself actively as a cheerleader and kibitzer in the intellectual life of his colleagues. Fenno remembers:

> When I was finishing my 1960s manuscript on the politics of the appropriations process, Doug came over to Rochester from Syracuse and spent a long day— into the night—at the house critiquing the manuscript and talking about it. It was an incredibly helpful and stimulating day. And it was his idea—not mine. In the 1990s, when I sent him a copy of my book on Dan Quayle and, again, the one on Mark Andrews, he responded with scattergrams showing me how I could have clarified my distinction between the partisan and personal components of their support. In both cases, he had spent a day in the library, he said, collecting the necessary data. Accompanying the Andrews scattergram was an elaborate causal analysis, recreating the book's entire argument with boxes and arrows—a typical Price effort to help you think about a complex set of relationships. He had an uncanny ability to see where your argument was going and where it could be improved (Fenno 1998, p. xiv).

---

[14]A bibliography and a collection of most of his work on Congress, issued, sadly, two years after he died, appears in *Explorations in the Evolution of Congress* (Price 1998).

Two of Price's doctoral students wrote significant works on Congress: John Manley (Syracuse Ph.D., 1967) and Elaine Swift (Harvard Ph.D., 1989) (see Manley 1970, Swift 1996).

Whereas Fenno was his generation's preeminent hedgehog, knowing and concentrating on one big thing, Charles O. Jones was the great fox, a scholar whose contributions span such diverse topics as public policy and its analysis, the presidency, political parties, and the separation of powers, as well as Congress. Jones combines tremendous range with great modesty. It is his style to advance knowledge along many fronts but never to claim exclusive turf anywhere; hence, there is a tendency not to associate his name with any single magnum opus. But his presence is especially important in at least three endeavors. First, he is the leading academic student of the Republican party (see Jones 1964, 1965, 1970). Second, his book *Clean Air* (Jones 1975), which covers multiple levels of governmental and political activity, and describes a policy process that transformed the city of Pittsburgh, is a major and an exemplary work of policy analysis. Third, his work on the separation of powers has made the most thorough and the most powerful case against those comparativists who mistakenly describe the United States as a presidential system of government (Jones 1994, 1995).[15]

Only a deeply committed congressional scholar would be likely to acquire the intellectual ammunition to sustain this argument. The depth of Jones' engagement in the study of Congress is most apparent in his highly original textbook (1982), which synthesizes enormous amounts of material and combines it felicitously with the results of decades-long personal study, field work, and research.

Jones identifies himself as a student of political institutions primarily because these institutions make policy; hence, for most of his students at (successively) the Universities of Arizona, Pittsburgh, Virginia, and Wisconsin, the study of Congress has been incidental to the study of the public policies that have been the focus of their work. But there are a few exceptions, notably Randall Strahan (University of Virginia Ph.D., 1986) and Daniel Palazzolo (University of Virginia Ph.D., 1989), who have written on Congress directly (Strahan 1990; Palazzolo 1992, 1999).

In the 25 years from the end of World War II to the early 1970s, scholarship on Congress displayed five notable features:

1. A turn away from the issue of party responsibility as the great organizing theme of congressional studies and an embrace of the spirit of the behavioral movement, which brought political science closer to the other social sciences in its methods and concerns. For congressional studies, this meant measuring the performance of Congress against the requirements of an autonomous legislative body whose members had important representational

---

[15]Peterson (1990) is an excellent companion to Jones's study. Peterson uses a random sample of 299 presidential domestic legislative proposals to investigate the institutional and political conditions under which Congress accepts, modifies, or rejects presidential initiatives.

responsibilities and which collectively had significant independent impact on the making of public policy.

2. Numerous individual studies of work groups within Congress, notably committees (Peabody 1963, Robinson 1963, Manley 1970, Fenno 1966) and state delegations [Truman 1959, Fiellen 1962, Deckard (Sinclair) 1972], and in studies of the politics of internal management, especially narratives describing party leadership struggles and the strategic principles that dominated these significant events (especially "inside" versus "outside" strategies) (Polsby 1963, Peabody 1976).

3. A proliferation of sequential narratives portraying the complicated processes through which specific individual bills were transformed into laws.

4. Studies characterizing the institutional structures and historical development of the House and Senate, providing individual treatments of each. For the first time, the House and Senate began to emerge as distinct entities in the scholarly literature as befits their independent standing in the Constitution.[16]

5. Increasing opportunity to study the bloc structure of Congress as reflected in roll calls on the floor, and to track the ways in which Congress gratified or failed to gratify presidential requests. (Such information became available with the emergence of adequate publicly available record keeping, largely thanks to the *Congressional Quarterly* organization, but also owing to public-spirited scholars located in the Congressional Research Service of the Library of Congress.) The information could be considered in the aggregate or by tracking the performance of individuals, and could be used not only to monitor policy outcomes but also to follow the decision making (or cue-taking) of individual members (see Kingdon 1973, Matthews & Stimson 1975).

Two books by David Mayhew (Harvard Ph.D., 1964) illustrate the expansion of the possibilities for study during the postwar era. His first book was his doctoral dissertation, *Party Loyalty among Congressmen: The Difference between Democrats and Republicans, 1947–1962* (Mayhew 1966), a highly creative roll-call study. Mayhew demonstrated that Democrats and Republicans behave differently toward the interest groups that make up their core constituencies. Democrats, he found, always vote to sustain their constituent interests; Republicans tend to vote on principled grounds even against their constituents and allies.

---

[16]See Truman's *The Congress and America's Future* (1965), an American Assembly volume. Separate chapters address the internal distribution of influence in the House (Fenno 1965, pp. 52–76) and in the Senate (Huitt 1965, pp. 77–101). Only one text, to our knowledge, deals with the two branches of Congress separately. See Polsby's *Congress and the Presidency* (1964, 1971, 1975, 1986).

Later, in *Congress: The Electoral Connection* (1974),[17] Mayhew executed one of the first—and still one of the best—rational choice studies of Congress, parsimoniously asking how members would logically behave if they were obsessed only with the goal of assuring their reelection. He deduces that in such circumstances, members would do a lot of what we observe them doing: position-taking, credit-claiming, and advertising. The assumption of pure reelection-mindedness yields less-good predictions of congressional organization, but the exercise was by any reasonable standard a tremendous success. Because of the compactness of the argument, Mayhew's landmark has not really been superseded, even though it was thoughtfully amended by Fenno's addition of more motives for members—influence in Congress, good public policy, ambition for further office—in connection with his study of variations in committee organization and behavior (Fenno 1973).

These contributions of Fenno and Mayhew marked a transition in congressional scholarship. The sociological style characteristic of most work in the 1950s and 1960s (including Fenno's own early work) gave way to a focus on individual members' goal-oriented behavior. Three themes have emerged as particularly significant in the ensuing decades. First, scholars have devoted considerable energy to understanding the major reforms adopted by Congress in the 1970s. Both the reform era itself and the contours of the so-called "post-reform" Congress have been major topics of debate. Second, the rise of rational choice approaches in the discipline at large has sparked a new focus on the design and effects of legislative institutions. Scholars ask to what extent congressional organization serves the interests of three sorts of aggregated actors: cross-party distributive coalitions, the majority party, and floor majorities. A major animating issue has been whether the majority party is able to use its agenda control to pull policy outcomes toward the party median and away from the median of the whole House. Third, historically oriented scholars have traced changes in congressional institutions over time,

---

[17]This book grew directly out of Mayhew's experience as an APSA Congressional Fellow. In neither this book nor his first, as it happens, did Mayhew employ the highly individual and labor-intensive technique of investigation that became his hallmark: framing a big issue and then creating a dataset designed expressly to resolve the issue by ransacking the library for newspaper and textbook coverage of relevant historical examples. *Divided We Govern* (Mayhew 1991) shows that national government divided between the major parties is roughly as productive as government united under the leadership of a single party. *Placing Parties in American Politics: Organization, Electoral Settings, and Government Activity in the Twentieth Century* (Mayhew 1986) assesses each state's level of party organization, tracing variation to geographically rooted traditions and showing that states with a high level of party organization tend to have lower state expenditures relative to their income level. *America's Congress: Actions in the Public Sphere, James Madison through Newt Gingrich* (Mayhew 2000) shows the distribution of "significant" member actions throughout American history and relates the propensity to perform such actions to several theoretically relevant variables (party, seniority, and so on).

using history both as a source of data to test existing theories and as a source of new theories. Beyond these three substantive themes, a fourth important development has been the emergence of several extensive datasets on congressional behavior and history that have provided a windfall for Congress scholars.

THE INFLUENCE OF CONGRESSIONAL REFORM

The 1970s reforms of Congress instigated the sort of broad-scale institutional change that comes at most once in a generation. As a result, many leading congressional scholars focused their attention on uncovering the sources, short-term effects, and long-term implications of these changes. In contrast to the early scholarship on the Legislative Reorganization Act of 1946, which tended to measure reform by the yardstick of whether it would bring about responsible party government (see, e.g., Galloway 1946), this new scholarship was more interested in understanding the goals of the reformers themselves and in assessing the complicated factional politics that shaped their prospects for success. *On Capitol Hill* (1972), by John Bibby (Wisconsin Ph.D., 1963) and Roger Davidson, a detailed account of the passage of the Legislative Reorganization Act of 1970, highlighted how disaffected liberal Democrats and backbench Republicans were able to coalesce behind a set of reforms intended to challenge the power of conservative southern chairmen (see also Schickler et al. 2001). Davidson went on to conduct careful studies of many of the key reforms of the 1970s and, working with Walter Oleszek, offered a theoretical model that distinguished between "adaptive" innovations that respond to pressures from the environment and "consolidative" changes that are prompted by internal conflicts (Davidson & Oleszek 1976, 1977).[18]

But Davidson and his coauthors were by no means alone in examining these reforms. In a series of papers written in the 1970s, David Rohde and Norman Ornstein analyzed the Reorganization Act of 1970, the subcommittee bill of rights, and the attack on seniority, among other changes (Ornstein 1975; Ornstein & Rohde 1974, 1977, 1978; Rohde 1974). Rohde's efforts were helped, no doubt, by his APSA Congressional Fellowship, which placed him in the office of one of the Democratic reformers and afforded him an unusually close view of the maneuvering that entered into adoption of the subcommittee bill of rights. Ornstein, who began his Washington career as an APSA Fellow, has carved out a nearly unique specialty as a locally based authority on trends in congressional politics, and as an explainer of these trends to the national press corps, founded on a thorough grounding in political science research.

---

[18]Davidson (Columbia Ph.D., 1963) moved from academic political science to the Library of Congress and back to academia again. Oleszek (SUNY, Albany, Ph.D., 1968) is one of a significant corps of congressional scholars who have made their careers at the Library and made the Library an important resource for the entire discipline. Others include Louis Fisher, Ronald Moe, Stanley Bach, Richard Beth, and the late Walter Kravitz.

Among the reforms, the overthrow of the seniority system for selection of chairmen prompted extensive studies. One of the first, by Barbara Hinckley, explored why Democrats deposed three barons in 1975. Hinckley argued that three characteristics made these chairmen inviting targets to newly assertive liberal Democrats: their advanced age, "southernness," and the presence of an acceptable challenger (Hinkley 1976). Other studies focused on how the challenge to seniority affected internal committee operations, often finding that the effects, at least in the short term, were not great (Rieselbach & Unekis 1981/1982). A third wave of studies focused on how the seniority overthrow affected the party system, typically finding that the reforms increased the loyalty of the remaining chairmen and therefore enhanced the strength of the Democratic majority (Crook & Hibbing 1985, Rohde 1991).

The reforms of the 1970s also fostered new efforts at synthesis, notably Dodd & Oppenheimer's *Congress Reconsidered* (1977), which brought together a series of chapters by many hands probing the meaning of the recent transformation. Now in its seventh edition, this series continues to promote the cumulation and spread of knowledge by serving as an easily accessible and lively compendium of research that addresses both recent changes and longer-term trends.

The initial literature on the 1970s reforms tended to emphasize decentralizing trends: the empowering of subcommittees, the opening of committee deliberations to the public, and challenges to the seniority system.[19] These early accounts also noted the party-building potential of such reforms as granting to the Speaker control of assignments to the House Rules Committee and making chairmen more accountable to the majority party caucus (see, e.g., Dodd 1977, 1979; Oppenheimer 1977; Ornstein & Rohde 1978; Sundquist 1981). In the 1980s, as the decline in the number of southern Democrats helped the majority party to become more internally unified and as party leaders began to use their powers more aggressively, these party-building changes became more prominent in accounts of the lasting implications of the reform era. The "post-reform" Congress was not the wide-open, fragmented, individualistic world depicted by Mayhew in 1974; rather, it was characterized by increasingly active parties, a surprisingly centralized budget process (Schick 1980, Gilmour 1990), and omnibus bills that placed a premium on coordination (Krutz 2001). Once again, Davidson, Rohde, and Dodd & Oppenheimer were among the first to chart the development of the post-reform Congress (Davidson 1988, 1992; Dodd & Oppenheimer 1989; Rohde 1991). They were joined by, among others, Barbara Sinclair, who drew upon her extraordinary access to House Democratic leader Jim Wright's office to offer an array of new data and new insights into leadership strategies and activities (see especially Sinclair 1983, 1995).

In studying both the 1970s reforms and the transition to the post-reform Congress, one of the key moves was to focus on House rules and procedures

---

[19]Another stream of literature considered the major expansion in committee and personal staff that coincided with the reform era (Fox & Hammond 1977, Kofmehl 1977, Malbin 1980). The increase in committee staffing began with the Legislative Reorganization Act of 1946 but picked up steam once again in the 1970s.

as indicators that could be used to reveal important changes. One of the pioneers of this approach was Steven S. Smith of the University of Minnesota. Working with Stanley Bach, Smith traced the development of the restrictive rules that have increasingly come to structure the consideration of legislation on the House floor (Bach & Smith 1988; see also Bach 1990). The details of such "special rules," once an obscure subject even to most scholars, have in recent years become a major topic of empirical and theoretical work (see Sinclair 1994, Dion & Huber 1996, Krehbiel 1997). Smith has also influenced the field through his Ph.D. students, who have demonstrated a keen interest in the intersection of partisan calculations, congressional rules and procedures, and committee organization. The result has been several noteworthy studies of congressional institutions, including an analysis of rules concerning minority rights in the House (Binder 1997), a study of committee politics (Maltzman 1997), and an exploration of Speaker Joe Cannon's committee assignments (Lawrence et al. 2001).[20]

RATIONAL CHOICE AND THE "NEW INSTITUTIONALISM"

The classic studies by Mayhew and Fenno in the mid-1970s were partly inspired by the shift in the discipline at large toward rational choice models of politics. The success of these studies and the Rochester-led dissemination of new skills, adapting for political science a style of work that had proved so effective in economics, led to one of the main growth areas in congressional scholarship over the past 25 years.

Three main branches of this work are worth distinguishing. One branch explores a question raised but not fully answered by Mayhew: In a world of self-interested, reelection-seeking members, each of whom has incentives to spend time on casework, particularistic credit-claiming, and position-taking, how does it happen that Congress actually produces major legislation that offers general, rather than particularistic, benefits? More broadly, under what conditions will self-interested legislators have incentives to work hard to produce broad legislation? Mayhew's student at Yale, R. Douglas Arnold, offers the most thorough treatment of the first question in *The Logic of Congressional Action* (Arnold 1990). Arnold focuses on members' need to respond to voters' "potential preferences" (which often place value on general benefits) and on coalition leaders' ability to manipulate the visibility of member actions such that these potential preferences become more salient. Richard L. Hall at the University of Michigan has offered one of the key analyses of the second issue; *Participation in Congress* (Hall 1996) combines a wealth of new data on committee operations with a theoretical exploration of the conditions under which members will have incentives to participate in legislative work (see also Wawro 2000). Hall finds that the division of labor in Congress is not "authoritatively imposed" but rather "bubbles up" from individual choices about how to

---

[20]This article's findings were anticipated by Polsby et al. (1969).

allocate one's time (Hall 1996, p. 10). Even within specialized subcommittees, the set of active participants is rarely more than half the members, and this set shifts dramatically across bills.

Closely related to the scholarship on members' incentives to perform legislative work, another stream of rational choice work has explored the extent to which Congress influences policy implementation by the bureaucracy. This enduring theme in congressional studies dates back to the post–World War II studies by Hyneman (1950), Harris (1964), and Ogul (1976), with important elaborations in the work of Dodd & Schott (1979), Arnold (1979), and most recently Aberbach (1990). Morris Fiorina's *Congress: Keystone of the Washington Establishment* (1977) was an early rational choice work to consider the question of Congress's relationship to the bureaucracy. In the tradition of studies describing "iron triangles," "subgovernments," or "policy networks" (see, e.g., Freeman 1955, Heclo 1978), Fiorina argues that members of Congress and bureaucrats enjoy a symbiotic relationship. In his account, members pass vague laws that delegate tremendous discretion to federal agencies. The agencies then draft extensive rules and regulations to put the laws into practice, which inevitably annoy some groups of citizens, who routinely turn to their representative in Congress for help. The member gains political credit for intervening on behalf his constituents, even as the bureaucracy continues to enjoy considerable discretion. The result is not necessarily good or coherent policy, but it does promote the electoral interests of members and the career interests of bureaucrats. Numerous studies have ensued modeling mechanisms by which Congress influences bureaucratic decision making and debating the extent to which Congress and the President control the bureaucracy (see, e.g., Fiorina 1981; Weingast & Moran 1983; McCubbins & Schwarz 1984; McCubbins et al. 1987; Moe 1987, 1990; Ferejohn & Shipan 1990; Wood & Waterman 1991).

The third branch of rational choice work is commonly assigned to a genre called "new institutionalism." Though it draws upon earlier congressional scholarship, this literature owes a good deal to social choice theory. This theory suggests that when individuals or institutions must make complicated choices involving policy options that cannot be placed along a single evaluative dimension, the probability that any single policy proposal will be able to defeat all other alternatives in pairwise majority voting becomes vanishingly small (Plott 1967). In the absence of a single equilibrium point, political outcomes may be expected to wander chaotically or to "cycle" uncertainly among alternative possibilities (McKelvey 1976). Yet observers had seldom criticized congressional politics for giving rise to evershifting outcomes; to the contrary, excessive policy stability had far more often been the concern (Tullock 1981).

Kenneth Shepsle and Barry Weingast argued that congressional institutions could resolve the puzzle of theoretical instability juxtaposed with real-world policy stability (Shepsle 1979, Shepsle & Weingast 1981). The basic claim was that the committee system restricts policy making to a single issue dimension at a time. This cuts off the lifeblood of cycling. The principal mechanisms, built into congressional rules, were committees' monopoly proposal powers, plus House germaneness rules restricting floor amendments.

This work led scholars to explore further effects of congressional institutions. The main claim emerging from the Shepsle-Weingast approach is that committees tend to consist of members with a high demand for the policies in their jurisdiction and that congressional rules and procedures give such committees dominance over policy making within their domain. This claim tracks well with earlier committee studies that had come to much the same conclusion (e.g., Jones 1961). A further implication explored by the newer literature is that the committee system provides an enforcement mechanism for a giant institutional "logroll" in which members trade influence with one another, gaining power in the policy area they care most about (which, by assumption, is the jurisdiction covered by their committee), while sacrificing the ability to determine policy in areas less salient to them (see Weingast & Marshall 1988).

This line of argument (called a distributive model) has given rise to a spirited debate over whether committees are, in fact, composed of high-demanders (see, e.g., Krehbiel 1991 and Adler & Lapinski 1997) and whether congressional rules do, in fact, grant committees monopoly proposal power.[21] In recent years, two major theoretical perspectives within the "new institutionalism" genre have challenged distributive models: informational theory and majority-party government models.

Whereas distributive models focus on members' gains from trade, informational models suggest that legislative institutions are designed to help members reap gains from specialization. The foundation for the informational approach emerged from a series of papers by Keith Krehbiel and Thomas Gilligan in the late 1980s, but the theory's most definitive statement and empirical assessment is in Krehbiel's *Information and Legislative Organization* (1991; see also Gilligan & Krehbiel 1987, 1989, 1990; King 1997). Krehbiel argues that committees are not autonomous entities but agents of the institution as a collective entity, supplying information that reduces individual legislators' uncertainty about the consequences of diverse proposed bills. The institution creates committees that are representative of its own policy preferences, because representative committees are most likely to specialize and to transmit their information to the whole House. Krehbiel finds that committees are in general ideologically representative of the whole, and that representative, specialized committees are more likely to be granted protection from amendments when legislation is considered on the floor. Krehbiel's second book, *Pivotal Politics: A Theory of U.S. Lawmaking* (1998), builds upon the majoritarian logic of the first, but adds supermajority institutions (i.e., the Senate cloture rule, presidential veto) and shows that several broad patterns in U.S. lawmaking can be accounted for through a nonpartisan model incorporating these features.

A third branch of the new institutionalism shifts the focus from committees to parties. In the formulation of Cox & McCubbins (1993), majority party members

---

[21]A precursor to distributive models, which emphasizes self-selection onto committees, is Shepsle (1978). On committee gatekeeping power, see Krehbiel (1987, 1991).

are united by their stake in the value of their common party label. To safeguard that label, the majority party establishes House institutions that provide it with built-in advantages throughout the legislative process. The majority party constitutes a "cartel" that uses the rule-making power of the House to bias the legislative process in its favor. Hence, committees are agents of the party.[22]

In contrast to Cox & McCubbins' portrayal of a consistent, strong bias in favor of the majority party, Rohde's conditional party government model emphasizes variations over time in party strength. Rohde (1991) argues that party government depends on the degree of majority party unity on the major agenda items confronting Congress, and on the level of polarization between the majority and minority parties. Subsequent studies have both challenged and refined the conditional party government approach, fostering one of the more spirited sets of debates in congressional studies.[23] One key issue is how to measure party unity (referred to as homogeneity) and polarization without resorting to the same roll-call votes that are themselves measures of the dependent variable, party strength. Another is how to distinguish the effects of members' preferences from the effects of their party affiliation, given that partisan theory suggests that preference measures are themselves contaminated by party effects (see Krehbiel 2000, McCarty et al. 2001, Snyder & Groseclose 2000).

In addition to focusing attention on the effects of congressional institutions, new institutionalist works raise important questions concerning the sources of congressional organization. These questions are perhaps most pressing for distributive theory, given its assumption of a multidimensional policy space. Why does the House abide by a specific allocation of agenda power to committees when there will generally be a majority of members who would benefit, at least in the short run, by reneging—for example, by changing committee jurisdictions or by overturning committee gatekeeping? (For one effort to tackle this problem, see Shepsle 1986.) At a broader level, under what conditions will distributive, partisan, or informational rationales take on a predominant role in influencing institutional design? Although such issues have been addressed through different types of work, they are particularly suited to historical approaches, which examine variations in institutions across time.

CONGRESSIONAL HISTORY

The volume of congressional scholarship that adopts a historical approach has increased dramatically in recent years. This trend does not imply that earlier scholarship ignored history. Indeed, congressional scholarship of the 1960s and 1970s contains numerous historical works that have had a lasting impact on the field. Jones

---

[22]Kiewiet & McCubbins (1991) argue that the House Appropriations Committee is the agent of the majority party caucus.

[23] Krehbiel (1993, 1998) has been the most forceful critic. For refinements and elaborations on the conditional party government perspective, see Aldrich & Rohde (1998, 2000).

(1968) used historical evidence concerning the Cannon speakership (1903–1911) to illuminate the battle to limit Howard Smith's power as Rules Committee chairman in the early 1960s. This comparison provided an early foundation for the conditional party government literature that became prominent two decades later. Polsby (1968) traced changes in a diverse array of indicators showing increased organizational boundedness, internal complexity, and universalistic internal decision making across nearly two centuries of congressional history. The finding that many of these indicators of institutionalization "took off" in the 1890–1910 period helped make that era one of the most studied by scholars of congressional history.

The literature on party leadership in the 1960s and 1970s includes such historically oriented work as Jones's classic, *The Minority Party in Congress* (1970; see also Ripley 1969, the companion work from the *Study of Congress* series). A major component in the literature on congressional committees was a lively discussion concerning the origins of legislative professionalism and seniority (see Abram & Cooper 1968, Polsby et al. 1969, Price 1975, Budgor et al. 1981). Even the reforms of the 1970s led some scholars, most notably Larry Dodd, to consider recent developments within a broader historical framework. Dodd (1977) offered a cyclical model of congressional change rooted in the tension between individual members' drive to exercise power and the institution's policy-making capacity.

Joseph Cooper's 1960 doctoral dissertation, published as *Congress and Its Committees* (1988), was a far-reaching investigation of the origins and development of the House committee system that not only supplied a rich information base for subsequent studies but also provided an institutionalist perspective that anticipated important elements of the informational theory of committees. (Several other articles and monographs grew out of the research; see, e.g., Cooper 1970.) Cooper's dissertation previewed his approach in subsequent research on Congress, combining meticulous study of the historical record with insights derived from organization theory, and later rational choice theory, to gain a better understanding of institutional capacity and performance. A particularly nice example is Cooper & Young (1989), which provides a nuanced analysis of the origins of the modern bill introduction process.

David W. Brady, in his published dissertation *Congressional Voting in a Partisan Era* (1973), adopted the literature on institutionalization as his point of departure. In sharp contrast to the individualistic 1970s, Brady found considerable evidence that the two Congresses of the McKinley era (1897–1901) were characterized by party government. Althoff & Brady (1974) extended the analysis to cover the 1890–1910 period, finding once again considerable evidence that parties dominated the congressional scene. Brady's early work hearkened back to the earlier literature on party government by providing a glimpse into what a system of "responsible party government" actually looks like. Brady et al. (1979) traced the decline in party voting from its height at the turn of the century to its low levels in the contemporary era. Brady's later book, *Critical Elections and Congressional Policy-Making* (1988), draws upon realignment theory in offering a broad-scale account of the (rare) conditions under which both party government and major policy changes happen.

The article "Institutional Context and Leadership Style: The House from Cannon to Rayburn" (Cooper & Brady 1981a) did much to set the agenda for historically oriented scholarship over the next two decades.[24] Cooper & Brady outlined a "contextual" theory of party leadership that highlighted the role of constituency characteristics and electoral institutions (e.g., partisan control of nominations) in explaining party strength in Congress. Using census data on manufacturing and agriculture from the 1880s to the 1910s, they showed that aggregate levels of party voting in Congress tracked changes in party polarization at the constituency level. The centralization of power under Speakers Thomas Reed and Joseph Cannon in the 1890–1910 era thus reflected constituency cleavages more than the personal characteristics of the leaders themselves.[25] The relative weakness of party leaders in more recent times reflects the huge gap between southern and northern Democrats' constituencies, and parties' weakness in the nominations process, rather than the failings of individual leaders. In addition to presaging later research described as conditional party government, this article suggested the potential for using historical data to illuminate the interplay between individual leadership and congressional institutions.

Recent work on congressional history is distinguished by its engagement with emerging literature on other American political institutions that flies the banner of "American political development" (APD). Among the best examples of APD research that focus on Congress are Hansen's (1991) exploration of the development of the close relationship between congressional committees and farm interest groups, Kernell & MacDonald's (1999) analysis of Congress's role in initiating changes in the postal service, Sanders' (1999) study of how congressional agrarians drove state development in the progressive era, and Stewart's (1989) innovative analysis of budget reform politics. With these and a few other notable exceptions, Congress scholars have for the most part focused on the internal dynamics of congressional institutions, but they have not linked those developments to the major transformations in the scale of the national government or the powers of the other branches.[26]

---

[24]A second article (Cooper & Brady 1981b) calls for increased attention to the study of congressional history and suggests several ways to make such studies more systematic and theoretically informed. See also the comments on this article by Patterson (1981) and Polsby (1981).

[25]Brady had focused on constituency characteristics in his earlier work, and he has built upon this argument in subsequent research on the House and Senate (see, e.g., Brady et al. 1989, Brady & Epstein 1997). For a somewhat different account of the Reed-Cannon era, see Schickler (2001b, ch. 2).

[26]Swift's (1996) book on the Senate, though focused on internal dynamics, links with broader themes of democratization in the APD literature, as does Rothman (1966). Bensel's (1984, 2000) ongoing research on sectionalism is a further example of APD research that has also contributed to our understanding of Congress. Poole & Rosenthal (1997) have related internal institutional politics to broader political outcomes. Mayhew (2000) also offers an innovative approach to linking congressional politics to American political development, broadly construed.

Recent work on congressional history also differs from earlier research in its emphasis on testing rational choice theories of congressional institutions. Books by Stewart (1989), Dion (1997), and Binder (1997), as well as Jenkins' (1999) comparison of the U.S. and Confederate Congress, each used historical data as a new basis to evaluate and refine rational choice models that had been developed with the contemporary Congress in mind. This was not the sole goal of any of these studies, but it nonetheless was a contribution of each (see also Schickler 2000, 2001; Jillson & Wilson 1994).

Earlier historical work on Congress also engaged in theoretical debates; but the theories at issue have changed from those derived from sociology and organization theory to those rooted in assumptions about individual maximizing. The turn to rational choice is less a distinctive feature of recent historical research than an outgrowth of broader currents in the field. Just as analyses of the present-day Congress are often framed in terms of rational choice models, so is much of the historically oriented research.

Another feature of today's scholarship is explicit awareness of the goal of introducing a historical dimension in understanding congressional politics. One result has been an outpouring of conferences and panels at political science conventions that address historical themes.[27] Another is that cumulation of knowledge is facilitated, as scholars with different methodological skills (quantitative, game theoretic, and qualitative) and different theoretical assumptions (rational choice, historical institutionalist, etc.) are reading one another's work and learning from it.

THE INFRASTRUCTURE OF RESEARCH

A final development that has contributed to the cumulation of knowledge has been the expansion in the infrastructure of research. As described above, the APSA congressional fellowship and "Study of Congress" were critical early innovations fostering a research community. Another significant development occurred with the founding of *Legislative Studies Quarterly*, which for more than a quarter century has served as a valuable outlet for research on Congress. Perhaps the most striking aspect of this expanding infrastructure has been the compilation and distribution of new datasets that measure theoretically relevant variables across an extensive time span. *Congressional Quarterly* has played an important role in compiling and promoting the dissemination of data, including measures of party unity, presidential support, lists of key votes, and so on. This journal has provided a consistent information base for scholars since the 1950s. The vast range of

---

[27]In 1985–1986, shortly before the increase in the volume of work on congressional history, the Center for Advanced Studies in the Behavioral Sciences hosted a year-long congressional history working group that consisted of Allan G. Bogue, David W. Brady, Nelson W. Polsby, and Joel H. Silbey. This group produced one joint product (Bogue et al. 1986) and three individually authored books (Brady 1988, Bogue 1989, Silbey 1991).

information presented in the *Almanac of American Politics* (since 1972), *Politics in America* (since 1999), and *Vital Statistics on Congress* (since 1980) has also been enormously useful for scholars. One of the most widely used of the new datasets has been Poole & Rosenthal's (1991, 1997) NOMINATE scores, which estimate Congress members' ideal points in a two-dimensional space. Poole & Rosenthal have computed these scores (and several variants thereof) for all Congresses from 1789 to the present. It is especially noteworthy that Poole & Rosenthal have freely distributed the scores to all interested scholars and have developed and distributed the VOTEVIEW software to make it especially easy for scholars to examine how individual roll calls map onto the two NOMINATE dimensions. The result has been an outpouring of studies that share a common set of measures and assumptions.[28]

In addition to Poole & Rosenthal, several other scholars have contributed major data-collection efforts to the field. Mayhew's (1991) compilation of major laws enacted in the post–World War II era not only served as the dependent variable in his study of the effects of divided government, but also served as a linchpin of numerous subsequent studies of the same and related issues (e.g., this dataset is one of the main dependent variables in Krehbiel 1998). Another important example is the congressional hearings project undertaken by Bryan Jones, Frank Baumgartner, Valerie Hunt, and Michael Rosensteihl. Jones and his colleagues have constructed an impressive dataset with information on all hearings from 1947 through the mid-1990s and have made these data available to the public (http://depts.washington.edu/ampol/hearings.shtml). A third example is "Histor ical Congressional Standing Committees, 1st to 79th Congresses, 1789–1947" by David Canon, Garrison Nelson & Charles Stewart (http://web.mit.edu/17.251/www/data_page.html). And these are by no means the only major datasets that have been contributed to the profession. Such data collection and dissemination efforts put congressional scholarship on a firmer footing than it was in Woodrow Wilson's day.

IN CONCLUSION

In this paper, we have concentrated on contributions made to the study of Congress by professional political scientists since 1945 and on the evolution of this literature over half a century. We are conscious, however, that the political science literature exists side by side with—and in many respects draws nourishment from—biographies, memoirs, and journalistic accounts of Congress and its members. There is no way to make a satisfactory short list of examples, but they would include Barry (1989), Biggs & Foley (1999), Bolling (1965), Cohen (1999), Evans &

---

[28]This is not to say that NOMINATE scores are without critics. For an alternative methodology for estimating ideal points, see Heckman & Snyder (1997). The Summer 2001 special issue of *Political Analysis* offers an extremely useful set of articles that indicate the present state of the art of estimation of legislators' preferences.

Novak (1966), Farrell (2001), Hardeman & Bacon (1987), Jacobs (1995), MacNeil (1963), Miller (1972), Patterson (1972), DE Price (1992), Voorhis (1948), White (1957), and Zelizer (1998). In addition, important contributions to congressional news and congressional lore are now available twice weekly from the Capitol Hill newspapers *Roll Call* and *The Hill.* More than a few of these works are of very high quality and deserve extended consideration in their own right, as does the formidable literature on congressional elections, to which so many of our colleagues have contributed significantly.

This survey of work over a protracted period has given us an opportunity to appreciate the development of clusters of activity, especially at Harvard in the immediate postwar era, then at Wisconsin over most of the span covered in this report, and later at Rochester. In political science, a discipline in which communication among scholars is not tightly articulated, a casual examination of the scholarly enterprise at any given time might well miss the extent to which forward movement has been provided by such mentors as Ralph K. Huitt at Wisconsin or William Y. Elliot at Harvard, by such organizational innovations as the two APSA projects or the creation, principally by William Riker, of the Rochester political science department.[29]

Our historical survey demonstrates the profound impact of exemplary scholarship, not only for its individual virtues but also as it resonates through the later work of students and successors. In the study of Congress, an academic community, though loosely bounded, does exist, providing good conversation, intellectual standards, problems, solutions, and suggestions for further inquiry.

An exercise of this sort can also teach us how political scientists find and shape their research agendas. The literature on Congress was for many years deeply influenced by the discipline-wide preoccupation with responsible parties on the British model. In the next stage, congressional research reflected wider concerns with the study of political behavior and social organization. More recently, rational choice approaches have entered the picture. Clearly, what happens in political science at large has guided the study of Congress.

That is perhaps half the story. The other half recognizes the importance of political events in generating research questions. Right in the middle of the period covered in this survey, Congress undertook significant reform, and changed in other ways that attracted the attention of scholars. We suppose that disciplines seeking to cumulate knowledge follow the inner logic of their own literature more frequently than they respond to events, but we do not think that attentiveness to events in shaping a research agenda precludes cumulativeness in a discipline. In any case, this hybrid character, responding both to priorities emerging in the literature and to changes in the political world, is what we observe in the study of Congress over the past half century.

---

[29]Although Fenno has been the leading congressional scholar in the Rochester department over the past 40 years, Riker (e.g., 1962, 1986) has also had a lively interest in Congress and its history.

ACKNOWLEDGMENTS

We acknowledge with thanks the superb assistance of Keith W. Smith, Casey B.K. Dominguez, and Kathryn Pearson. We also thank Gerhard Loewenberg, Larry Dodd, Richard Fenno, Morris Fiorina, Keith Krehbiel, David Mayhew, and Brad Westerfield for their helpful comments.

The *Annual Review of Political Science* is online at http://polisci.annualreviews.org

LITERATURE CITED

Aberbach JD. 1990. *Keeping a Watchful Eye: The Politics of Congressional Oversight.* Washington, DC: Brookings Inst.

Abram M, Cooper J. 1968. The rise of seniority in the House of Representatives. *Polity* 1:52–85

Adler S, Lapinski J. 1997. Demand-side theory and congressional committee composition: a constituency-characteristics approach. *Am. J. Polit. Sci.* 41:895–919

Aldrich JH, Rohde DW. 1998. *Measuring conditional party government.* Presented at Annu. Meet. Am. Polit. Sci. Assoc., Chicago, IL, April

Aldrich JH, Rohde DW. 2000. The consequences of party organization in the House: theory and evidence on conditional party government. In *Polarized Politics: Congress and the President in a Partisan Era*, ed. JR Bond, R Fleisher, pp. 31–72. Washington, DC: CQ Press

Almanac of American Politics. 1972–Present. New York: EP Dutton

Althoff P, Brady DW. 1974. Party voting in the U.S. House of Representatives, 1890–1910: elements of a responsible party system. *J. Polit.* 36:753–75

Arnold RD. 1979. *Congress and the Bureaucracy: A Theory of Influence.* New York: Yale Univ. Press

Arnold RD. 1990. *The Logic of Congressional Action.* New Haven, CT: Yale Univ. Press

Bach S. 1990. Suspension of the rules, the order of business, and the development of congressional procedure. *Legis. Stud. Q.* 15: 49–63

Bach S, Smith SS. 1988. *Managing Uncertainty in the House of Representatives.* Washington, DC: Brookings Inst.

Bagehot W. 1867. *The English Constitution.* London: Chapman & Hall

Bailey SK. 1950. *Congress Makes a Law.* New York: Columbia Univ. Press

Bailey SK. 1959. *The Condition of Our National Political Parties.* New York: Fund for the Republic

Bailey SK. 1966. *The New Congress.* New York: St. Martin's

Barry J. 1989. *The Ambition and the Power.* New York: Viking

Bauer R, deSola Pool I, Dexter LA. 1963. *American Business and Public Policy.* New York: Atherton

Bendiner R. 1964. *Obstacle Course on Capitol Hill.* Toronto: McGraw-Hill

Bensel R. 1984. *Sectionalism and American Political Development.* Madison: Univ. Wisc. Press

Bensel R. 2000. *The Political Economy of American Industrialization.* New York: Cambridge Univ. Press

Berman DJ. 1962. *A Bill Becomes a Law: The Civil Rights Act of 1960.* New York: Macmillan

Bibby JF, Davidson R. 1967. *On Capitol Hill: Studies in the Legislative Process.* New York: Holt, Rinehart & Winston

Bibby JF, Davidson RH. 1972. *On Capitol Hill.* Hinsdale, IL: Dryden

Biggs JR, Foley T. 1999. *Honor in the House: Speaker Tom Foley.* Pullman, WA: Washington State Univ. Press

Binder S. 1997. *Minority Rights, Majority Rule*. Cambridge, UK: Cambridge Univ. Press

Birnbaum JH, Murray AS. 1987. *Showdown at Gucci Gulch*. New York: Random House

Bogue AG. 1989. *The Congressman's Civil War*. New York: Cambridge Univ. Press

Bogue AG, Brady DW, Polsby NW, Silbey JH. 1986. *The Stabilization of the 20th Century Congress: New Evidence on Change in the American Political Universe*. Stanford, CA: CASBS

Bolling R. 1965. *House Out of Order*. New York: Dutton

Brady DW. 1973. *Congressional Voting in a Partisan Era*. Lawrence: Kansas Univ. Press

Brady DW. 1988. *Critical Elections and Congressional Policy–Making*. Stanford: Stanford Univ. Press

Brady DW, Brody R, Epstein E. 1989. Heterogeneous parties and political organization: the U.S. Senate, 1880–1920. *Legis. Stud. Q.* 14:205–23

Brady DW, Cooper J, Hurley P. 1979. The decline of party in the House of Representatives. *Legis. Stud. Q.* 4:381–407

Brady DW, Epstein D. 1997. Intraparty preferences, heterogeneity, and the origins of the modern Congress. *J. Law Econ. Organ.* 13:26–49

Brezina DW, Overmyer A. 1974. *Congress in Action*. New York: Free

Budgor J, Capell EA, Flanders DA, Polsby NW, Westlye MC, Zaller J. 1981. The 1896 election and congressional modernization. *Soc. Sci. Hist.* 5:53–90

Burns JM. 1949. *Congress on Trial*. New York: Harper

Carroll HN. 1958. *The House of Representatives and Foreign Affairs*. Pittsburgh, PA: Univ. Pittsburgh Press

Cohen RE. 1999. *Rostenkowski: The Pursuit of Power and the End of the Old Politics*. Chicago: Ivan R. Dee

Cooper J. 1970. *The Origins of the Standing Committees and Development of the Modern House*. Houston, TX: William Marsh Rice Univ. Press

Cooper J. 1988. *Congress and Its Committees: A Historical Approach to the Role of Committees in the Legislative Process*. New York: Garland

Cooper J, ed. 1999. *Congress and the Decline of the Public Trust*. Boulder, CO: Westview

Cooper J, Brady DW. 1981a. Institutional context and leadership style: the House from Cannon to Rayburn. *Am. Polit. Sci. Rev.* 75:411–25

Cooper J, Brady DW. 1981b. Toward a diachronic analysis of Congress. *Am. Polit. Sci. Rev.* 75:988–1006

Cooper J, Young CD. 1989. Bill introduction in the nineteenth century: a study of institutional change. *Legis. Stud. Q.* 14:67–105

Cox G, McCubbins M. 1993. *Legislative Leviathan: Party Government in the House*. Berkeley: Univ. Calif. Press

Crook SB, Hibbing JR. 1985. Congressional reform and party discipline. *Br. J. Polit. Sci.* 15:207–26

Dahl RA. 1950. *Congress and Foreign Policy*. New York: Harcourt Brace

Davidson RH. 1988. The new centralization on Capitol Hill. *Rev. Polit.* 50:345–64

Davidson RH. 1992. The emergence of the postreform Congress. In *The Postreform Congress*, ed. RH Davidson, pp. 3–24. New York: St. Martin's

Davidson RH, Oleszek WJ. 1976. Adaptation and consolidation: structural innovation in the U.S. House of Representatives. *Legis. Stud. Q.* 1:37–65

Davidson RH, Oleszek WJ. 1977. *Congress Against Itself*. Bloomington: Indiana Univ. Press

Deckard B. 1972. State party delegations in the U.S. House of Representatives: a comparative study of group cohesion. *J. Polit.* 34:199–222

Dexter LA. 1957. The representative and his district. *Hum. Organ.* 16:2–13

Dexter LA. 1960/1961. When the elephant fears to dance among the chickens: business in politics? The case of du Pont. *Hum. Organ.* 19:188–94

Dexter LA. 1969. *The Sociology and Politics of Congress*. Chicago: Rand McNally

Dion D. 1997. *Turning the Legislative Thumb-screw*. Ann Arbor: Univ. Mich. Press

Dion D, Huber JD. 1996. Procedural choice and the House Committee on Rules. *J. Polit.* 58:25–53

Dodd LC. 1977. Congress and the quest for power. See Dodd & Oppenheimer 1977, pp. 269–307

Dodd LC. 1979. The expanded roles of the House Democratic whip system: the 93rd and 94th Congresses. *Congr. Stud.* 7:27–46

Dodd LC, Oppenheimer BI, eds. 1977. *Congress Reconsidered*. New York: Praeger

Dodd LC. 1986. The cycles of legislative change: building a dynamic theory. In *Political Science: The Science of Politics*, ed. HF Weisberg, pp. 82–104. New York: Agathon

Dodd LC. 1987. Woodrow Wilson's *Congressional Government* and the modern Congress: the "universal principle" of change. *Congr. Presidency* 14:33–49

Dodd LC, Oppenheimer BI. 1989. Consolidating power in the House: the rise of a new oligarchy. In *Congress Reconsidered*, ed. LC Dodd, BI Oppenheimer, pp. 39–64. Washington, DC: CQ Press

Dodd LC, Schott RL. 1979. *Congress and the Administrative State*. New York: Wiley

Eidenberg E, Morey R. 1969. *An Act of Congress: The Legislative Process and the Making of Education Policy*. New York: Norton

Elliott WY. 1935. *The Need for Constitutional Reform*. New York: Whittlesey House, McGraw-Hill

Elving RD. 1995. *Conflict and Compromise: How Congress Makes the Law*. New York: Simon & Schuster

Evans R, Novak R. 1966. *Lyndon B. Johnson: The Exercise of Power*. New York: New Am. Library

Farrell J. 2001. *Tip O'Neill*. Boston: Little, Brown

Fenno RF. 1959. *The President's Cabinet: An Analysis in the Period from Wilson to Eisenhower*. New York: Vintage Books

Fenno RF. 1962. The House Appropriations Committee as a political system: the problem of integration. *Am. Polit. Sci. Rev.* 56:310–24

Fenno RF. 1965. The internal distribution of influence: the House. In *The Congress and America's Future*, ed. DB Truman, pp. 63–90. Englewood Cliffs, NJ: Prentice-Hall

Fenno RF. 1966. *The Power of the Purse: Appropriations Politics in Congress*. Boston: Little, Brown

Fenno RF. 1973. *Congressmen in Committees*. Boston: Little, Brown

Fenno RF. 1978. *Home Style: House Members in Their Districts*. Boston: Little, Brown

Fenno RF. 1982. *The United States Senate: A Bicameral Perspective, Studies in Political and Social Processes*. Washington, DC: Am. Enterp. Inst.

Fenno RF. 1986. Adjusting to the U.S. Senate. In *Congress and Policy Change*, ed. GC Wright, LN Reiselbach, LC Dodd, pp. 123–47. New York: Agathon

Fenno RF. 1989. *The Making of a Senator: Dan Quayle*. Washington, DC: CQ Press

Fenno RF. 1990a. *The Presidential Odyssey of John Glenn*. Washington, DC: CQ Press

Fenno RF. 1990b. *Watching Politicians: Essays on Participant Observation*. Berkeley, CA: IGS Press

Fenno RF. 1991a. *The Emergence of a Senate Leader: Pete Domenici and the Reagan Budget*. Washington, DC: CQ Press

Fenno RF. 1991b. *Learning to Legislate: The Senate Education of Arlen Specter*. Washington, DC: CQ Press

Fenno RF. 1992. *When Incumbency Fails: The Senate Career of Mark Andrews*. Washington, DC: CQ Press

Fenno RF. 1996. *Senators on the Campaign Trail: The Politics of Representation*. Norman: Univ. Oklahoma Press

Fenno RF. 1997. *Learning to Govern: An Institutional View of the 104th Congress*. Washington, DC: Brookings Inst.

Fenno RF. 1998. Introduction. In *Explorations in the Evolution of Congress*, ed. HD Price, pp. xiii–xv. Berkeley, CA: IGS Press

Fenno RF. 2000. *Congress at the Grassroots:*

Representational Change in the South. Chapel Hill: Univ. N. Carol. Press

Ferejohn J, Shipan C. 1990. Congressional influence on bureaucracy. *J. Law Econ. Organ.* 6:S1–S20

Fiellen A. 1962. The functions of informal groups in legislative institutions. *J. Polit.* 24:72–91

Fiorina MP. 1977. *Congress: Keystone of the Washington Establishment.* New Haven, CT: Yale Univ. Press

Fiorina MP. 1981. Congressional control of the bureaucracy: a mismatch of incentives and capabilities. In *Congress Reconsidered,* ed. LC Dodd, BI Oppenheimer, pp. 332–48. Washington, DC: CQ Press

Fox HW, Hammond SW. 1977. *Congressional Staffs.* New York: Free

Freeman JL. 1955. *The Political Process.* Garden City, NJ: Doubleday

Froman LA. 1967. *The Congressional Process: Strategies, Rules and Procedures.* Boston: Little, Brown

Galloway GB. 1946. *Congress at the Crossroads.* New York: Crowell

Gilligan TW, Krehbiel K. 1987. Collective decision-making and standing committees. *J. Law Econ. Organ.* 3:287–335

Gilligan TW, Krehbiel K. 1989. Collective choice without procedural commitment. In *Models of Strategic Choice in Politics,* ed. PC Ordeshook, pp. 295–314. Ann Arbor: Univ. Mich. Press

Gilligan TW, Krehbiel K. 1990. Organization of informative committees in a rational legislature. *Am. J. Polit. Sci.* 34:531–64

Gilmour J. 1990. *Reconcilable Differences? Congress, the Budget Process, and the Deficit.* Berkeley: Univ. Calif. Press

Griffith E. 1951. *Congress, Its Contemporary Role.* New York: New York Univ. Press

Gross B. 1953. *The Legislative Struggle.* New York: McGraw-Hill

Hall RL. 1996. *Participation in Congress.* New Haven, CT: Yale Univ. Press

Hansen JM. 1991. *Gaining Access: Congress and the Farm Lobby, 1919–1981.* Chicago: Univ. Chicago Press

Hardeman DB, Bacon D. 1987. *Rayburn, a Biography.* Austin, TX: Texas Monthly Press

Harris JP. 1964. *Congressional Control of Administration.* Washington, DC: Brookings Inst.

Harris RA. 1969. *The Fear of Crime.* New York: Praeger

Heckman JJ, Snyder JM. 1997. Linear probability models of the demand for attributes with an empirical application to estimating the preferences of legislators. *RAND J. Econ.* 28:S142–S89

Heclo H. 1978. Issue networks and the executive establishment. In *The New American Political System,* ed. A King, pp. 87–124. Washington, DC: Am. Enterp. Inst.

Hibbing JR, Thiess-Morse E. 1995. *Congress as Public Enemy: Public Attitudes Toward American Political Institutions.* Cambridge, UK: Cambridge Univ. Press

Hinckley B. 1976. Seniority 1975: old theories confront new facts. *Brit. J. Polit. Sci.* 6:383–99

Hughes HS. 1976. *Consciousness and Society.* New York: Octagon

Huitt RK. 1954. The congressional committee: a case study. *Am. Polit. Sci. Rev.* 48:340–65

Huitt RK. 1957. The Morse committee assignment controversy: a study in Senate norms. *Am. Polit. Sci. Rev.* 51:313–29

Huitt RK. 1961a. Democratic party leadership in the Senate. *Am. Polit. Sci. Rev.* 55:331–44

Huitt RK. 1961b. The outsider in the Senate: an alternative role. *Am. Polit. Sci. Rev.* 55:566–75

Huitt RK. 1965. The internal distribution of influence: the Senate. In *The Congress and America's Future,* ed. DB Truman, pp. 91–117. Englewood Cliffs, NJ: Prentice-Hall

Huitt RK. 1990. *Working Within the System.* Berkeley, CA: IGS Press

Huitt RK, Peabody RL. 1969. *Congress: Two Decades of Analysis.* New York: Harper & Row

Hyman SE. 1962. *The Tangled Bank.* New York: Athenaeum

Hyneman CF. 1950. *Bureaucracy in a Democracy.* New York: Harper

Jacobs J. 1995. *A Rage for Justice*. Berkeley: Univ. Calif. Press

Jenkins JA. 1999. Examining the bonding effects of party: a comparative analysis of roll call voting in the U.S. and Confederate Houses. *Am. J. Polit. Sci.* 43:1144–65

Jillson CC, Wilson R. 1994. *Congressional Dynamics: Structure, Coordination, and Choice in the First American Congress, 1774–1789*. Stanford, CA: Stanford Univ. Press

Johannes J. 1984. *To Serve the People: Congress and Constituency Service*. Lincoln: Univ. Nebraska Press

Jones CO. 1961. Representation in Congress: the case of the House Agriculture Committee. *Am. Polit. Sci. Rev.* 55:358–67

Jones CO. 1964. *Party and Policy-Making: The House Republican Policy Committee*. Rutgers, NJ: Rutgers Univ. Press

Jones CO. 1965. *The Republican Party in American Politics*. New York: Macmillan

Jones CO. 1968. Joseph G. Cannon and Howard W. Smith: an essay on the limits of leadership in the House of Representatives. *J. Polit.* 30:617–46

Jones CO. 1970. *The Minority Party in Congress*. Boston: Little, Brown

Jones CO. 1975. *Clean Air: The Policies and Politics of Pollution Control*. Pittsburgh, PA: Univ. Pittsburgh Press

Jones CO. 1982. *The United States Congress: People, Place and Policy*. Homewood, IL: Dorsey

Jones CO. 1994. *The Presidency in a Separated System*. Washington, DC: Brookings Inst.

Jones CO. 1995. *Separate but Equal Branches: Congress and the Presidency*. Chatham, NJ: Chatham House

Kefauver E, Levin J. 1947. *A Twentieth Century Congress*. New York: Duell, Sloan & Pearce

Kernell S, McDonald MP. 1999. Congress and America's political development: the transformation of the post office from patronage to service. *Am. J. Polit. Sci.* 43:792–811

Kiewiet RD, McCubbins MD. 1991. *Logic of Delegation*. Chicago: Univ. Chicago Press

King D. 1997. *Turf Wars: How Congressional Committees Claim Jurisdiction*. Chicago: Univ. Chicago Press

Kingdon JW. 1973. *Congressmen's Voting Decisions*. New York: Harper & Row

Kofmehl K. 1977. *Professional Staffs of Congress*. West Lafayette, IN: Purdue Univ. Press

Krehbiel K. 1987. Why are congressional committees powerful? *Am. Polit. Sci. Rev.* 81:929–35

Krehbiel K. 1991. *Information and Legislative Organization*. Ann Arbor: Univ. Mich. Press

Krehbiel K. 1993. Where's the party? *Br. J. Polit. Sci.* 23:235–66

Krehbiel K. 1997. Restrictive rules reconsidered. *Am. Polit. Sci. Rev.* 44:919–44

Krehbiel K. 1998. *Pivotal Politics: A Theory of U.S. Lawmaking*. Chicago: Univ. Chicago Press

Krehbiel K. 2000. Party discipline and measures of partisanship. *Am. J. Polit. Sci.* 44:212–27

Krutz GS. 2001. *Hitching a Ride: Omnibus Legislation in the U.S. Congress*. Columbus: Ohio State Univ. Press

Lawrence ED, Maltzman F, Wahlbeck PJ. 2001. The politics of Speaker Cannon's committee assignments. *Am. J. Polit. Sci.* 45:551–62

Link AS, ed. 1968. *The Papers of Woodrow Wilson*. Princeton, NJ: Princeton Univ. Press

Maass A. 1983. *Congress and the Common Good*. New York: Basic Books

MacNeil N. 1963. *Forge of Democracy: The House of Representatives*. New York: D. MacKay

Malbin MJ. 1980. *Unelected Representatives: Congressional Staff and the Future of Representative Government*. New York: Basic Books

Maltzman F. 1997. *Competing Principals: Committees, Parties, and the Organization of Congress*. Ann Arbor: Univ. Mich. Press

Manley JF. 1970. *The Politics of Finance: The House Committee on Ways and Means*. Boston: Little, Brown

Martin JM. 1994. *Lessons from the Hill*. New York: St. Martin's

Masters NA. 1961. Committee assignments in

the House of Representatives. *Am. Polit. Sci. Rev.* 55:345–57

Matthews DR. 1954. *The Social Background of Political Decision-Makers*. Garden City, NJ: Doubleday

Matthews DR. 1959. The folkways of the United States Senate: conformity to group norms and legislative effectiveness. *Am. Polit. Sci. Rev.* 53:1064–89

Matthews DR. 1960. *U.S. Senators and Their World*. Chapel Hill: Univ. N. Carol. Press

Matthews DR, Stimson JA. 1975. *Yeas and Nays: Normal Decision-Making in the U.S. House of Representatives*. New York: Wiley

Mayhew DR. 1966. *Party Loyalty among Congressmen: The Difference between Democrats and Republicans, 1947–1962*. Cambridge, MA: Harvard Univ. Press

Mayhew DR. 1974. *Congress: The Electoral Connection*. New Haven, CT: Yale Univ. Press

Mayhew DR. 1986. *Placing Parties in American Politics: Organization, Electoral Settings, and Government Activity in the Twentieth Century*. Princeton, NJ: Princeton Univ. Press

Mayhew DR. 1991. *Divided We Govern*. New Haven, CT: Yale Univ. Press

Mayhew DR. 2000. *America's Congress: Actions in the Public Sphere, James Madison through Newt Gingrich*. New Haven, CT: Yale Univ. Press

McCarty N, Poole K, Rosenthal H. 2001. The hunt for party discipline. *Am. Polit. Sci. Rev.* 95: 673–88

McCubbins M, Noll R, Weingast B. 1987. Administrative procedures as instruments of political control. *J. Law Econ. Organ.* 3:243–77

McCubbins M, Schwarz T. 1984. Congressional oversight overlooked: police patrols versus fire alarms. *Am. J. Polit. Sci.* 28:165–79

McKelvey RD. 1976. Intransitivities in multidimensional voting models and some implications for agenda control. *J. Econ. Theory* 12:472–82

Miller C. 1972. *Member of the House*, ed. JW Baker. New York: Scribner

Moe T. 1987. An assessment of the positive theory of congressional dominance. *Legis. Stud. Q.* 12:475–520

Moe T. 1990. Political institutions: the neglected side of the story. *J. Law Econ. Organ.* 6:S213–S54

Munger FJ, Fenno RF. 1962. *National Politics and Federal Aid to Education: The Economics and Politics of Public Education*. Syracuse, NY: Syracuse Univ. Press

Myrdal G. 1944. *An American Dilemma*. New York: Harper

Ogul MS. 1976. *Congress Oversees the Bureaucracy: Studies in Legislative Supervision*. Pittsburgh, PA: Univ. Pittsburgh Press

Oppenheimer BI. 1977. The Rules Committee: new arm of the leadership in a decentralized House. See Dodd & Oppenheimer 1977, pp. 96–116

Ornstein NJ. 1975. Causes and consequences of congressional change. In *Congress in Change*, ed. NJ Ornstein, pp. 88–114. New York: Praeger

Ornstein NJ, Rohde DW. 1974. *The strategy of reform: recorded teller voting in the U.S. House of Representatives*. Presented at Annu. Meet. Midwest Polit. Sci. Assoc., Chicago, IL

Ornstein NJ, Rohde DW. 1977. Shifting forces, changing rules, and political outcomes. In *New Perspectives on the House of Representatives*, ed. RL Peabody, NW Polsby, pp. 186–270. Chicago: Rand McNally

Ornstein NJ, Rohde DW. 1978. Political parties and congressional reform. In *Parties and Elections in an Antiparty Age*, ed. J Fishel, pp. 280–94. Bloomington: Univ. Indiana Press

Palazzolo D. 1992. *The Speaker and the Budget: Leadership in the Post-Reform House of Representatives*. Pittsburgh, PA: Univ. Pittsburgh Press

Palazzolo D. 1999. *Done Deal? The Politics of the 1997 Budget Agreement*. New York: Chatham House

Patterson JT. 1972. *Mr. Republican: A Biography of Robert A. Taft*. Boston: Houghton Mifflin

Patterson SC. 1970. The professional staffs of congressional committees. *Admin. Sci. Q.* 15:22–37

Patterson SC. 1981. Understanding Congress in the long run: a comment on Joseph Cooper and David W. Brady, "toward a diachronic analysis of congress." *Am. Polit. Sci. Rev.* 75:1007–9

Patterson SC, Jewell M. 1966. *The Legislative Process in the United States*. New York: Random House

Peabody RL. 1963. The enlarged Rules Committee. In *New Perspectives on the House of Representatives*, ed. RL Peabody, NW Polsby, pp. 129–66. Chicago: Rand McNally

Peabody RL. 1976. *Leadership in Congress: Stability, Succession, and Change*. Boston: Little, Brown

Peabody RL, Berry JM, Frasure WG, Goldman J. 1972. *To Enact a Law: Congress and Campaign Financing*. New York: Praeger

Peabody RL, Polsby NW, eds. 1963. *New Perspectives on the House of Representatives*. Chicago: Rand McNally

Peterson M. 1990. *Legislating Together: The White House and Capitol Hill from Eisenhower to Reagan*. Cambridge, MA: Harvard Univ. Press

Plott CR. 1967. A notion of equilibrium and its possibility under majority rule. *Am. Econ. Rev.* 57:787–806

Politics in America. 1999–Present. Washington, DC: CQ Press

Polsby NW. 1963. Two strategies of influence. In *New Perspectives on the House of Representatives*, ed. RL Peabody, NW Polsby, pp. 237–72. Chicago: Rand McNally

Polsby NW. 1964, 1971, 1975, 1986. *Congress and the Presidency*. Englewood Cliffs, NJ: Prentice Hall

Polsby NW. 1968. The institutionalization of the House of Representatives. *Am. Polit. Sci. Rev.* 62:144–68

Polsby NW. 1981. Studying Congress through time: a comment on Joseph Cooper and David Brady, "toward a diachronic analysis of Congress." *Am. Polit. Sci. Rev.* 75:1010–12

Polsby NW. 1984. The contributions of President Richard F. Fenno, Jr. *PS* 17:778–81

Polsby NW. 1990. Foreword. In *Working within the System*, RK Huitt. Berkeley: IGS Press

Polsby NW. 1998. Foreword. In *Explorations in the Evolution of Congress*, HD Price. Berkeley: IGS Press

Polsby NW, Gallaher M, Rundquist BS. 1969. The growth of the seniority system in the U.S. House of Representatives. *Am. Polit. Sci. Rev.* 63:787–807

Poole KT, Rosenthal H. 1991. Patterns of congressional voting. *Am. J. Polit. Sci.* 35:228–78

Poole KT, Rosenthal H. 1997. *Congress: A Political-Economic History of Roll Call Voting*. New York: Oxford Univ. Press

Price DE. 1992. *The Congressional Experience: A View from the Hill*. Boulder, CO: Westview Press

Price HD. 1975. Congress and the evolution of legislative professionalism. In *Congress in Change*, ed. NJ Ornstein, pp. 2–23. New York: Praeger

Price HD. 1998. *Explorations in the Evolution of Congress*. Berkeley, CA: IGS Press

Redman E. 1973. *The Dance of Legislation*. New York: Simon & Schuster

Reid TR. 1980. *Congressional Odyssey*. San Francisco: WH Freeman

Rieselbach LN, Unekis JK. 1981/1982. Ousting the oligarchs. *Congress and the Presidency* 9:83–117

Riker W. 1962. *The Theory of Political Coalitions*. New Haven, CT: Yale Univ. Press

Riker W. 1986. *The Art of Political Manipulation*. New Haven, CT: Yale Univ. Press

Ripley RB. 1969. *Majority Party Leadership in Congress*. Boston: Little, Brown

Robinson JA. 1963. *House Rules Committee*. Indianapolis, IN: Bobbs-Merrill

Rohde DW. 1974. Committee reform in the House of Representatives and the subcommittee bill of rights. *Ann. Am. Acad. Polit. S.S.* 411:39–47

Rohde DW. 1991. *Parties and Leaders in the Postreform House*. Chicago: Univ. Chicago Press

Rothman D. 1966. *Politics and Power: The United States Senate*. Cambridge, MA: Harvard Univ. Press

Sanders E. 1999. *Roots of Reform: Farmers, Workers, and the American State, 1877–1917*. Chicago: Univ. Chicago Press

Schick A. 1980. *Congress and Money*. Washington, DC: Brookings Inst.

Schickler E. 2000. Institutional change in the House of Representatives, 1867–1998: a test of partisan and ideological power balance models. *Am. Polit. Sci. Rev.* 94:269–87

Schickler E. 2001a. Congressional history: new branches on mature trees. *Legis. Stud. Sect. News. Exten. Remarks*

Schickler E. 2001b. *Disjointed Pluralism: Institutional Innovation and the Development of the U.S. Congress*. Princeton, NJ: Princeton Univ. Press

Schickler E, McGhee E, Sides J. 2001. *Remaking the House and Senate: personal power, ideology, and the 1970s reforms*. Presented at Annu. Meet. Midwest Polit. Sci. Assoc., Chicago, IL

Shepsle KA. 1978. *The Giant Jigsaw Puzzle: Democratic Committee Assignments in the Modern House*. Chicago: Univ. Chicago Press

Shepsle KA. 1979. Institutional arrangements and equilibrium in multidimensional voting models. *Am. J. Polit. Sci.* 23:27–59

Shepsle KA. 1986. Institutional equilibrium and equilibrium institutions. In *Political Science: The Science of Politics*, ed. H Weisberg, pp. 51–81. New York: Agathon

Shepsle KA, Weingast B. 1981. Structure-induced equilibrium and legislative choice. *Public Choice* 37:503–29

Silbey JH. 1991. *The American Political Nation 1838–1893*. Stanford, CA: Stanford Univ. Press

Sinclair B. 1983. *Majority Leadership in the U.S. House*. Baltimore/London: Johns Hopkins Univ. Press

Sinclair B. 1994. House special rules and the institutional design controversy. *Legis. Stud. Q.* 19:477–94

Sinclair B. 1995. *Legislators, Leaders, and Lawmaking*. Baltimore/London: Johns Hopkins Univ. Press

Snyder JN, Groseclose T. 2000. Estimating party influence in congressional roll call voting. *Am. J. Polit. Sci.* 44:193–211

Stewart CH. 1989. *Budget Reform Politics: The Design of the Appropriations Process in the House of Representatives, 1865–1921*. New York: Cambridge Univ. Press

Strahan R. 1990. *New Ways and Means: Reform and Change in a Congressional Committee*. Chapel Hill: Univ. N. Carol. Press

Sundquist JL. 1981. *The Decline and Resurgence of Congress*. Washington, DC: Brookings Inst.

Swift EK. 1996. *The Making of an American Senate: Reconstitutive Change in Congress, 1787–1841*. Ann Arbor: Univ. Mich. Press

Truman DB. 1951. *The Governmental Process*. New York: Knopf

Truman DB. 1959. *The Congressional Party: A Case Study*. New York: Wiley

Truman DB, ed. 1965. *The Congress and America's Future*. Englewood Cliffs, NJ: Prentice Hall

Tullock G. 1981. Why so much stability? *Public Choice* 37:189–202

Turner J. 1951. *Party and Constituency: Pressures on Congress*. Baltimore, MD: Johns Hopkins Univ. Press

Uslaner EM. 1993. *The Decline of Comity in Congress*. Ann Arbor: Univ. Mich. Press

Vital Statistics on Congress. 1980–Present. Washington, DC: Am. Enterp. Inst.

Voorhis J. 1948. *Confessions of a Congressman*. Garden City, NJ: Doubleday

Wawro G. 2000. *Legislative Entrepreneurship in the U.S. House of Representatives*. Ann Arbor: Univ. Mich. Press

Weingast B, Marshall W. 1988. The industrial organization of Congress. *J. Polit. Econ.* 96:132–63

Weingast B, Moran M. 1983. Bureaucratic discretion or congressional control? Policy-making by the FTC. *J. Polit. Econ.* 91:765–800

Westerfield HB. 1955. *Foreign Policy and Party*

Politics: Pearl Harbor to Korea. New Haven, CT: Yale Univ. Press

White WS. 1957. *Citadel: The Story of the U.S. Senate.* New York: Harper

Wilson W. 1885. *Congressional Government.* Boston: Houghton, Mifflin

Wood BD, Waterman RW. 1991. The dynamics of political control of the bureaucracy. *Am. Polit. Sci. Rev.* 85:801–28

Zelizer JE. 1998. *Taxing America: Wilbur D. Mills, Congress and the State, 1945–1975.* Cambridge, UK: Cambridge Univ. Press

Annu. Rev. Polit. Sci. 2002. 5:369–421
DOI: 10.1146/annurev.polisci.5.112801.080924
Copyright © 2002 by Annual Reviews. All rights reserved

ELECTORAL AND PARTISAN CYCLES IN ECONOMIC POLICIES AND OUTCOMES

Robert J. Franzese, Jr.

*Department of Political Science, University of Michigan, Ann Arbor, Michigan 48106;
e-mail: franzese@umich.edu*

Key Words political business cycles, electioneering, partisan theory, political economy

■ **Abstract** Policy makers in democracies have strong partisan and electoral incentives regarding the amount, nature, and timing of economic-policy activity. Given these incentives, many observers expected government control of effective economic policies to induce clear economic-outcome cycles that track the electoral calendar in timing and incumbent partisanship in character. Empirics, however, typically revealed stronger evidence of partisan than of electoral shifts in real economic performance and stronger and more persistent electoral and partisan shifts in certain fiscal, monetary, and other policies than in real outcomes. Later political-economic general-equilibrium approaches incorporated rational expectations into citizens' and policy makers' economic and political behavior to explain much of this empirical pattern, yet critical anomalies and insufficiencies remain. Moreover, until recently, both rational- and adaptive-expectations electoral-and-partisan-cycle work underemphasized crucial variation in the contexts—international and domestic, political and economic, institutional, structural, and strategic—in which elected partisan incumbents make policy. This contextual variation conditions policy-maker incentives and abilities to manipulate economic policy for electoral and partisan gain, as well as the effectiveness of such manipulation, differently across democracies, elections, and policies. Although relatively new, research into such context-conditional electoral and partisan cycles seems to offer much promise for resolving anomalies and an ideal substantive venue for theoretical and empirical advancement in the study of political economy and comparative democratic politics more generally.

INTRODUCTION

In democracies, voters elect the key economic policy makers or elected officials appoint them. In these elections, *ceteris paribus*, voters prefer candidates whom they expect, perhaps based on recent experience, will deliver them greater material well-being, perhaps through better aggregate economic performance. Thus, incumbents have powerful incentives to improve voters' economic fortunes, or to signal or feign ability to do so. Moreover, these incentives will sharpen near election time if voters weight the recent past more heavily than the distant past, which they may do myopically or rationally. Furthermore, candidates wage and voters adjudicate these electoral contests in partisan terms. Competing parties cultivate strong ties to differing segments of the voting public and nurture reputations for policy making that favors those segments and their ideological precepts. Parties and voters alike greatly value these partisan ties and reputations, so incumbents generally conduct recognizably distinct partisan policies, which might yield appreciably distinct macroeconomic outcomes.

Political economists have long recognized democratic policy makers' strong electoral and partisan motivations regarding the degree, nature, and timing of economic-policy activity (Nordhaus 1975, Hibbs 1977, Tufte 1978).[1] Given governmental control of effective economic policies, they argued, partisan electoral competition induces observable, regular cycles of electoral-calendar timing and incumbent-partisan nature in economic policies and outcomes. Empirical work, however, typically uncovered stronger evidence of partisan than of electoral cycles in real economic performance, and it found stronger and more persistent electoral and partisan shifts in certain monetary, fiscal, and other policies than in real outcomes. Subsequent general-equilibrium political-economy models of electoral and partisan cycles (Alesina 1987, 1988; Chappell & Keech 1988; Rogoff & Sibert 1988; Rogoff 1990; Alesina & Rosenthal 1995; Alesina et al. 1997)[2] added rational expectations to citizen and policy-maker political and economic behavior, which can explain some of this empirical pattern; yet critical anomalies and insufficiencies remain. For example, patterns and magnitudes of certain cycles of policies and outcomes do not accord well with each other and/or fail to follow known contextual variation in policy makers' policy incentives, control, or maneuverability (see, e.g., Drazen 2001; Franzese 2000, 2002a).

Both rational- and adaptive-expectations political-cycle studies typically underemphasized crucial variation in the (a) international and domestic, (b) political-economic, and (c) institutional, structural, and strategic contexts in which elected, partisan incumbents make policy. Below, the simple term "context" or "contextual" frequently stands for all these contexts; the reader should not forget this central theme: The magnitude, regularity, and content of electoral and partisan

---

[1] A fuller list of this first wave might begin with Schumpeter (1939) and Kalecki (1943) and add Ben-Porath (1975), Lindbeck (1976), Mosley (1976, 1978), MacRae (1977), Frey & Schneider (1978a,b), McCallum (1978), Chappell & Peel (1979), Golden & Poterba (1980), Beck (1982a, 1987), and Lachler (1982) on electoral cycles; on partisan cycles, refer to Beck (1982b,c), Alt (1985), Hibbs (1986, 1987a,b, 1992, 1994), and Havrilesky (1987). For reviews, see Alt & Chrystal (1983) and Willett (1988).

[2] Add to these Cukierman & Meltzer (1986), Nordhaus (1989), Terrones (1989), Ellis & Thoma (1991a,b, 1995), Alesina & Roubini (1992), Alesina et al. (1992, 1993a, 1997), Garfinkel & Glazer (1994), Alesina & Rosenthal (1995), Sieg (1997), Lohmann (1998, 1999), Carlsen & Pedersen (1999), Faust & Irons (1999), Gonzalez (1999a,b, 2000), Cusack (2000), and Heckelman (2001). For reviews, see Paldam (1997), Gärtner (2000), Persson & Tabellini (1990, 1994, 2000, 2001), Drazen (2000, 2001), and Olters (2001).

cycles will vary with the contexts reflected in differing combinations of conditions (*a*), (*b*), and (*c*). For example, in small, open economies, domestic policy makers may retain less autonomy over some policies, or some policies may be less economically effective, so that electoral and partisan cycles in those policies and outcomes are less pronounced than in larger, less-exposed economies. Some polities, moreover, concentrate policy-making control in fewer, more disciplined partisan actors, which may induce sharper political cycles in, e.g., Westminsterian than in other democracies. Furthermore, some policies may have more effect and so be more useful and so more used for electoral or partisan purposes, and this too varies with institutional, structural, or strategic context. For instance, the political benefits of demographic versus geographic targeting of spending may vary by electoral system, e.g., single-member plurality or proportional representation. As reviewed below, these and other contextual variations condition policy makers' incentives and abilities to manipulate policies and outcomes for electoral and partisan gain, and modify the political and economic efficacy of such manipulation, in manifold ways—which scholars can model, and increasingly have modeled, fruitfully—across democracies, elections, and policies.[3]

Although in infancy, research into context-conditional electoral and partisan cycles in policies and outcomes seems to offer much promise in redressing lingering anomalies and insufficiencies. This work provides an ideal venue for furthering recent theoretical and empirical advances in comparative and international political economy—specifically, the positive political economy of macroeconomic policy and, generally, comparative democratic institutions and policy making. Several recent books (e.g., Keech 1995, Boix 1998, Garrett 1998, Iversen 1999, Clark 2002, Franzese 2002a) show, for example:

- How developed democracies' postwar commitments to the Keynesian welfare state—i.e., some degree of social insurance, public goods and services provision, and macroeconomic management by fiscal, monetary, and wage/price-regulatory policy—evolved differently, depending on international and domestic political-economic institutional, structural, and strategic setting;

- How policy-maker recourse to *macro*economic policies to fulfill such commitments became increasingly constrained by their own expansion and rising international exposure and so faded relative to *micro*economic policies of public investment and tax structure;

- How choices among forms of these institutional and policy-paradigm changes manifest as and are determined by partisan electoral and governmental conflict.

Meanwhile, studies of how electoral and governmental institutions shape democratic politics have also advanced greatly. Such studies have elucidated electoral

---

[3]These moves toward explicit theories of institutional, structural, and strategic-contextual conditional policy making may begin to answer the complicating considerations Alt & Woolley (1982) raised two decades ago.

systems, representation, and competition (e.g., Cox 1997); coalition formation (e.g., Laver & Shepsle 1996); divided government and shared policy control (e.g., Tsebelis 2002); and myriad other issues in delegation and agency, common pools, regulation and oversight, etc. Finally, recent developments in macroeconomic modeling of political economy offer a coherent theoretical framework in which to study institutionally and interest-structurally conditioned political and economic effects of economic policy and the democratic choice thereof (e.g., Drazen 2000, Persson & Tabellini 2000, Grossman & Helpman 2001).

All this progress opens exciting opportunities for merging such insights to study how international and domestic political-economic conditions, institutions, and interest structures interact to determine electoral- and partisan-motivated economic policy making in democracies. The key factors that vary across policies, countries, and time to produce such interactive contextual effects include:

- The nature and relative, effective intensity of popular demands for economic policy and outcomes;
- The nature and relative, effective intensity of policy makers' reelection and partisan incentives;
- The inter-, intra-, and extra-governmental allocation of policy-making control across multiple actors;
- Policy maneuverability and efficacy.

Some examples of variation are as follows:

1. Relative, effective electoral demand for redistribution may depend on who votes and in what numbers, which in turn depends partly on electoral institutions (e.g., Franzese 2002a, ch. 2), which suggests that electoral and partisan cycles will stress transfers more in some political economies than others.

2. Incumbents' incentives to electioneer may rise with expected closeness of elections (e.g., Wright 1974; Tufte 1978; Frey & Schneider 1978a,b; Golden & Poterba 1980; Schultz 1995; Price 1998) and fall with the number of elected policy makers sharing control (e.g., Alt 1985, Goodhart 2000).

3. Incumbents' autonomy to manipulate monetary policy for electoral or partisan purposes, and the effectiveness of doing so, may depend on central bank independence, exchange-rate regime, and international exposure (e.g., Bernhard & Leblang 1999, 2002; Franzese 1999, 2002b; Oatley 1999; Boix 2000; Clark & Hallerberg 2000; Clark 2002; Leblang & Bernhard 2000a,b).

4. Maneuverability, economic efficacy, and political utility may vary across policies and across polities (e.g., Pommerehne et al. 1994, Keech 1995) depending on domestic economic institutions (e.g., Alvarez et al. 1991, Beck et al. 1993), on accumulated prior obligations (e.g., Blais et al. 1993, 1996; Franzese 2002a, ch. 3), or on international or domestic monetary-policy institutions or commitments (e.g., Oatley 1999; Clark 2002; Franzese 1999, 2002b).

TABLE 1   Classification of political-business-cycle theories*

Motivations	Expectations and Evaluations	
	Adaptive, retrospective	**Rational, prospective**
Office-seeking	Tufte (1978), Nordhaus (1975)	Rogoff & Sibert (1988), Rogoff (1990)
Partisan	Hibbs (1977, 1987a,b)	Alesina (1987, 1988), Alesina & Rosenthal (1995), Alesina et al. (1997)

*Classification scheme adopted from Alesina (1988).

Electoral and partisan cycles in economic policies and outcomes offer an ideal forum for exploring such institutional, structural, and strategic-contextual interactions. The forum is ideal because, in all democracies,

- all policy makers and policies ultimately must survive electoral evaluation (directly for elected policy makers, indirectly for appointed, bureaucratic, and other nongovernmental policy makers); and

- all electoral competition manifests as partisan representative democracy, in which all parties must develop, adapt, and maintain ideological reputations to survive and thrive.

Therefore, electoral and partisan cycles in policies and outcomes should emerge in all democracies, but to degrees and in characters heavily conditioned by multiple interactions among international and domestic political-economic institutional, structural, and strategic conditions.

This review of classical and modern studies of political business cycles, i.e., electoral and partisan cycles in economic policies and outcomes,[4] follows Alesina's (1988) useful organization of models. That classification is based on whether voters evaluate candidates retro- or prospectively, whether economic actors have adaptive or rational expectations, and whether policy makers have opportunistic (office-seeking) or partisan motivations (Table 1). This review, however, stresses implications of these alternative theoretical foundations for economic policy making as well as for outcomes. It first surveys classic Nordhaus (1975)/Tufte (1978) models of electoral outcome cycles, which assume that policy makers are office-seeking and that citizens form adaptive expectations and retrospective evaluations. They argue that such conditions produce regular pre-electoral surges in stimulatory macroeconomic policies, which spur real economic improvement as

---

[4]This paper generally avoids the term political business cycles so as to distinguish explicitly and clearly electoral cycles from partisan cycles, and policy cycles from outcome cycles. As used here, "political" means "electoral and/or partisan."

elections near and defer any resulting adverse real or nominal effects to incur after the election. As reviewed next, Tufte (1978) stresses electoral cycles in directly manipulable policies and outcomes, such as transfer payments, more than in broader macroeconomic policies and outcomes, and introduces (albeit with little elaboration) several reasons electoral-cycle magnitude or content may vary across democracies, elections, and policies. Next discussed is Rogoff & Sibert's (1988) and Rogoff's (1990) concept of "incumbent competence," which reproduces, in their models (and similar ones, e.g., Persson & Tabellini 1990), electoral cycles in economic policies and outcomes if voters and economic actors apply rational foresight. The review then surveys parallel developments in partisan theory: Hibbs' (1977, 1987a,b) foundational contribution, then the introduction of election-induced surprises in government partisanship, and so in policy, which reproduces at least short-term economic-outcome cycles from partisan policy cycles (Alesina 1987, 1988; Alesina & Rosenthal 1995; Alesina et al. 1997). Relevant empirical contributions are surveyed throughout, noting theoretical strengths and lingering anomalies or insufficiencies. The last section surveys some of the recent research on international and domestic political-economic institutional, structural, and strategic contextual conditioning of electoral and partisan cycles in economic policies and outcomes, which may begin to redress these shortcomings.

ELECTORAL CYCLES (OFFICE-SEEKING POLICY MAKERS)

Adaptive, Retrospective Citizens

ECONOMIC-OUTCOME CYCLES   Nordhaus's "The Political Business Cycle" (1975) considered how incumbents might use monetary policy to leverage an exploitable Phillips curve[5] to buy votes from myopic voters. Although originally, and usually subsequently, stated in monetary-policy terms, the logic of models that assume adaptive, retrospective citizens and office-seeking policy makers (see also Lindbeck 1976, MacRae 1977, Tufte 1978, and footnote 1) extends easily to macroeconomic policy generally.[6]

1. Economic actors have adaptive expectations (i.e., their expectations of current policy are based on past policy), so an expectations-augmented Phillips curve characterizes the economy (i.e., unexpected stimulatory policies spur the real economy: growth and employment).

2. Voters favor incumbents who preside over low inflation and high growth and employment, and they discount recent outcomes less than distant ones in their retrospective evaluations.

---

[5]The Phillips curve reflects the empirical relationship between nominal (e.g., inflation) and real (e.g., unemployment) outcomes. Early electoral-cycle theories built from a macroeconomic theory that a stable negative relationship existed between the two, which policy makers could exploit to trade higher inflation for lower unemployment and vice versa.
[6]Drazen (2001) shows, more fully and formally, how aspects of the logic extend to partisan and electoral fiscal policy with fully rational economic actors, voters, and politicians.

3. Incumbent policy makers (*a*) seek reelection and (*b*) control Phillips-curve stimulatory policies.

Under these assumptions, incumbents will conduct stimulatory policy to improve real outcomes (e.g., output, income, employment) in pre-electoral periods and shift to contractionary policy after the election to combat the resulting inflation and to prepare to stimulate again for the next election. Applying Tufte's (1978) murder-mystery terms, points 2 and 3*a* create the "motive," point 1 creates the "opportunity," and point 3*b* creates the "weapon" for incumbents to electioneer.

Point 2 of all office-seeking models—that incumbents benefit from presiding over favorable macroeconomic outcomes—has plentiful, unequivocal support. Kramer (1971), Stigler (1973), Tufte (1978), Arcelus & Meltzer (1975), Bloom & Price (1975),[7] Fair (1978, 1982, 1988), and Hibbs (1987a) all find clearly that incumbent parties in U.S. presidential elections win more votes, *ceteris paribus*, with economic growth higher (tightest relationship), inflation lower, and unemployment lower (weakest). Tufte (1975, 1978) finds similar though smaller and weaker relations of economic conditions to U.S. congressional incumbent votes. Lewis-Beck (1988) shows generally strong support for these relations in Germany, France, Italy, Spain, and the United Kingdom, as does Madsen (1980) in Denmark, Norway, and Sweden. Alesina et al. (1993b) and Alesina & Rosenthal (1995) also find U.S. presidential and congressional incumbent vote-shares tightly and mildly related, respectively, to recent past economic performance; notably, however, they find that voters reward/punish incumbents consistently with naïve, rather than rational, retrospective voting. Others find similarly strong links between incumbents' electoral success and presiding over highly visible and popular macroeconomic policies (e.g., Brender 1999 regarding fiscal policy, specifically deficit reduction). Indeed, "economic voting" seems nearly as reliable across democracies as Duverger's law and the relationship of district magnitudes and numbers to proportionality. So empirically secure is Tufte's "motive" for electoral cycles that scholars have moved to explore how institutional-structural context modifies economic voting, which is itself fully accepted. One highly influential study (Powell & Whitten 1993) finds that voters reward/punish disciplined one-party governments more than multiparty or undisciplined ones for macroeconomic outcomes. By similar logic, scholars might expect voters to hold central governments more tightly accountable for macroeconomic outcomes in unitary systems than in federal systems, which would imply sharper incumbent incentives to electioneer in disciplined, single-party-government, and unitary systems than in others. *Electoral Studies* (2000) offers two full issues of reviews and extensions of these and related advances in economic voting, many of which also suggest context-conditional electoral cycles.

Contrarily, evidence for opportunistic, office-seeking electoral cycles in outcomes, especially real outcomes, is weaker. As Alt & Chrystal (1983, p. 125)

---

[7]Interestingly, Bloom & Price (1975) find voters asymmetrically rewarded incumbents less for economic booms than they punished them for busts.

remark, "no one could read the political business cycle literature without being struck by the lack of supportive evidence." Alesina and colleagues[8] conclude similarly that evidence from the United States or OECD democracies offers inconsistent support for electoral policy cycles and very little support for electoral outcome cycles, especially in real outcomes. Hibbs (1987a) also doubts electoral cycles, arguing that U.S. presidents require popular support consistently, not just around elections, to pass their agendas through Congress.

Although these partisan-theory protagonists are the sharpest critics, Nordhaus (1975) also finds significantly more pre- (post-) election years of falling (rising) than of rising (falling) unemployment in only 3 of 9 countries during 1947–1972. However, the relative significance[9] of these comparisons could support a view that closely contested elections, strong and unified executives, and domestic policy autonomy induce the strongest electoral outcome cycles. Thus, some suggestion of conditionality existed from the beginning. Tufte (1978), studying cycles especially in real disposable income, but also in inflation and unemployment, sees greater support in U.S. data and some in a simple cross-national study, but Alt & Chrystal (1983, pp. 120–22) sharply question many of his results, especially regarding U.S. real outcomes. They allow, "Not all of Tufte's evidence can or should be discredited. Sometimes there is observable evidence of a cycle and sometimes not." They suggest this irregularity in electoral cycles might support Mosley's (1976) "satisficing" theory of electioneering, in which public demand and hence policy-maker action on the economy heighten only when key political-economic conditions breach voters' attention filters. Mosley (1978) finds some support for this, an early, simple alternative to later, sophisticated rational-expectations "competence-signaling" models of sporadic electoral cycles (see below).

In a wider view, evidence for classic electoral cycles in economic outcomes is certainly mixed, but less uniformly unfavorable. Paldam (1979, 1981), Golden & Poterba (1980), MacRae (1981), Haynes & Stone (1988, 1989, 1990, 1994), Willett (1988), Grier (1989), Klein (1996), and Schuknecht (1996) all find some signs of outcome cycles, Haynes & Stone most favorably and stridently. Others find weaker signs or none at all (Lachler 1978, 1982; McCallum 1978; Beck 1982a, 1987; Thompson & Zuck 1983; Ahmad 1983; Lewis-Beck 1988; also Alt, Hibbs, and Alesina and colleagues, discussed above). McCallum (1978) explores the relation of unemployment to U.S. electoral cycles and concludes that a variable indicating electoral-cycle phase adds no explanatory power to autoregressive models of unemployment. Lachler (1978, 1982), Beck (1982a, 1987), Ahmad (1983), and Thompson & Zuck (1983) reach similar conclusions regarding U.S. real-outcome cycles. MacRae (1981), contrarily, reports some supportive evidence, especially

---

[8]Alesina & Sachs (1988), Alesina & Roubini (1992), Alesina et al. (1992, 1993a,b, 1997), Alesina & Rosenthal (1995).
[9]United States $p \approx 0.011$, New Zealand $p \approx 0.029$, Germany $p \approx 0.090$, France $p \approx 0.254$, Sweden $p \approx 0.387$, United Kingdom $p \approx 0.623$, Australia $p \approx 0.696$, Japan $p \approx 0.696$, Canada $p \approx 0.867$.

in the Kennedy and Johnson administrations. Golden & Poterba (1980) find some (though weak) signs of real cycles in the United States, as does Paldam (1979, 1981) comparatively. However, Haynes & Stone (1988, 1989, 1990, 1994) insist that many previous studies mis-specify, and so obscure or understate, electoral cycles by mistakenly creating indicators for some pre-electoral quarters, whereas true U.S. electoral cycles, e.g., cover 16 quarters. Any electioneering policies, and so any electoral outcome cycle, would surely follow a smoother path than any simple election-period dummies could well approximate.[10] In autocorrelation, spectral density, and sine-wave analyses of four-year inflation and unemployment cycles, Haynes & Stone's three-equation model of Phillips curve, aggregate demand, and macroeconomic-policy reaction function uncovers strong evidence of four-year unemployment and inflation patterns in U.S. 1951–1980 data, with peaks and troughs that seem consistent with the presidential election cycle. Grier (1989) and Klein (1996) reanalyze U.S. data differently but also find encouraging signs of a real-economic electoral cycle. In all cases, evidence of inflation (and other nominal-outcome) increases around or after elections was the strongest of the electoral-*outcome*-cycle results. (See also Edwards 1993 and Remmer 1993 on inflation and other monetary cycles in developing countries.)

Finally, some recent studies extend the outcome purview of electoral-cycle theory to the financial markets that Tufte (1978) mentioned briefly. Bernhard & Leblang (1999), for example, consider whether election timing and exchange-rate regime choice correlate in parliamentary democracies but find no statistically significant relationship. Leblang & Bernhard (2000b) argue that economic actors make probabilistic assessments of the likelihood that a government will end by election or dissolution. The authors compare the probability to the actual event and find speculative attacks more likely when the political surprise is greater. Leblang (2002) finds that speculative attacks on developing-country currencies are also more likely during periods surrounding elections. Bernhard & Leblang (2002) argue that events beyond election day offer information to actors. They identify three periods that contain key political information: the campaign period from election announcement to election day, the post-election negotiation period

---

[10]To this concern, Franzese (2002a) adds the following observations. First, many studies paid insufficient attention to the timing of elections within years and relative to fiscal years. Second, U.S. electoral-cycle studies often use seasonally adjusted data, which, with one third of the Senate and the whole House of Representatives elected every second November and the President every fourth, likely purged about $(1/3)^*(1/3)^*(1/2) + (1/3)^*(1/2) + (1/3)^*(1/4) = 1/18 + 1/6 + 1/12 = 11/36 \approx 30.5\%$ of electoral cycles *before estimation*. Third, for this and several other political-institutional reasons (see below), U.S. electoral cycles, on which most studies focused, should be empirically smallest and so hardest to uncover in the data. Fourth, with challengers, post-election years should be at least as stimulatory, and more consistently so, than pre-election years (see below). He thus concludes that previous failure to find electoral cycles may be more condemning of the empirical than the theoretical constructs of these studies. However, Franzese's theories and empirics address policy cycles more directly than outcome cycles.

from election day until the cabinet forms, and the dissolution period when cabinet membership reshuffles. They find greater biases in forward exchange rates during these periods. Leblang & Bernhard (2000a) find, using a GARCH framework, that these periods also correlate with greater exchange-rate variability.

Alesina and colleagues (see footnote 8) champion the opposite side. Alesina & Roubini (1992), e.g., examined political cycles in quarterly observations on 18 OECD democracies. Their base models, essentially maintained in later work, regress growth on some lags, a control for world growth, and an indicator for $N-1$ quarters preceding an election, experimenting with $N = \{4, 6, 8\}$ and estimating country by country. They find, in sum, no support for office-seeking electoral real-outcome cycles, whereas inflation tends to increase after elections. Pre-electoral stimulatory policies would increase inflation, which, they argue, might support Rogoff's (1990) model of political budget cycles.[11] As one could infer from Drazen (2001), though, virtually any pre-electoral fiscal activism, Rogoff-type or not, would spur post-electoral inflation. Alesina & Roubini (1992) also report, citing other studies, strong evidence of Nordhaus/Tufte cycles in certain policy in-struments, notably in transfers. Alesina et al. (1992, 1993a) similarly analyze a like dataset and, again, find little sign of pre-electoral *real* outcome cycles (i.e., cycles in unemployment or growth), but some evidence of monetary expansion around, fiscal loosening before, and inflation increases after elections. Later work (Alesina et al. 1993b, Alesina & Rosenthal 1995, Alesina et al. 1997) enhances the econo-metric sophistication of rational-partisan-cycle empirical models (see below) but does not essentially alter the electoral-cycle empirical models, samples, or findings.

On balance, then, the empirical literature uncovers some possible, but incon-sistent and weak, evidence for electoral cycles in macroeconomic outcomes, with evidence for cycles in real variables generally weakest (but not wholly absent). Inflation and other nominal outcomes (such as exchange rates) seem more clearly to rise around or after elections, although the regularity and magnitude of this ten-dency may have varied across countries (see Drazen 2001, sect. 3.3). Contrarily, electoral cycles in certain economic policies, and especially in direct transfers, appeared stronger and more regular, both statistically and substantively [see be-low; Alt & Chrystal (1983), Schneider & Frey (1988), Nordhaus (1989), Paldam (1979, 1997), Drazen (2001), and Block (2001b) provide further useful reviews]. Moreover, evidence that voters evaluate incumbents on past economic performance (apparently myopically) unequivocally supports the existence of Tufte's "motive." Economists, therefore, have naturally sought explanation for this pattern of mixed support—stronger for nominal than real electoral outcome-cycles and strongest for electoral policy cycles—in Tufte's "opportunity," i.e., in the proposition that citizens hold adaptive expectations, producing an exploitable Phillips curve (see

---

[11]Alesina & Roubini (1992) also find temporary partisan differences in output and unem-ployment (as well as permanent differences in inflation, as Alesina's rational partisan theory implies), and no evidence of permanent partisan differences in unemployment or output (as Hibbs' partisan theory implies; see below).

below). This review will suggest that slippage is as likely to emerge from the implicit assumption in most empirical work that all incumbents seek re-election equally in all elections and that they all equally control policies that are equally effective in pursuing those aims. Theoretically and substantively, contrarily, incumbents' desire for re-election, their control over policies, and the effectiveness of those policies will vary contextually from one election to another. First, let us consider the theories and evidence regarding electoral cycles in economic policies.

ECONOMIC-POLICY CYCLES   In addition to electoral economic-outcome cycles, Tufte's *Political Control of the Economy* (1978) also stresses incumbent electioneering of the character and timing of economic policy. En route, Tufte presages several conditional electoral-cycle arguments that view the incentive, ability, and efficacy to electioneer as varying across policies, elections, and democracies. "The single most important fact about politicians is that they are elected. The second . . . is that they usually seek reelection . . ." (Tufte 1978, p. xi). "[This] simple fact of competition, especially when competition is informed by political ideology, explains a great deal of what goes on in the political world and . . . in important parts of the economic world also" (p. xiv). Tufte expands the notion, long and widely held by voters, pundits, and politicians, that incumbents benefit electorally from recent favorable macroeconomic conditions—see, e.g., Brougham's complaint about his competitor Pitt's "damned spurts in the nick of time" (p. 3)[12]—to argue that "incumbents may seek to determine the *location* and the *timing* of economic benefits in promoting the fortunes of [themselves], their party, and friends" (p. 4).

Tufte characterizes this electoral cycle as a murder mystery. To electioneer, a candidate, like a murderer, must have motive, opportunity, and weapon. Motive: Incumbent politicians desire re-election and believe that delivering strong pre-election economic conditions to voters will achieve it. That is, "economic movements in the months immediately preceding an election can tip the balance and decide the outcome of the election," and, because the electorate rewards or punishes incumbents for material gains or losses, "short-run spurts . . . in months immediately preceding an election benefit incumbents" (Tufte 1978, p. 9).[13] Opportunity: Tufte assumes incumbents control macroeconomic policies that can exploit Phillips-curve relations between nominal and real outcomes and various other discretionary policies that can target and time economic benefits to voters around elections. Such policy control and outcome manipulability provide ample opportunity. Weapon: As incumbents aim to deliver carefully timed economic benefits

---

[12]The full quotation is, "A Government is not supported a hundredth part so much by the constant, uniform, quiet prosperity of the country as by the damned spurts Pitt used to have just in the nick of time," to which add Reagan's "Are you better off now than you were four years ago?" and Clinton's "It's the economy, stupid!"

[13]Nixon's memoirs, for example, are particularly candid in attributing Republican losses in 1954 and 1958, as well as his own 1960 loss, to economic slumps that bottomed near the election.

to key voters, they prefer easily maneuverable policy instruments that can deliver timed and clearly palpable and attributable (to incumbents) economic benefits to large numbers or specific groups of voters. This, Tufte notes, suggests transfers (e.g., social security, veterans' benefits, or other direct payments),[14] tax cuts or delayed hikes, certain types of spending increases or delayed cuts (especially public works), and public hiring or delayed firing. Notably, adaptive expectations and Phillips-curve exploitability are largely irrelevant to citizen receipt of benefits from such policies. Indeed, some of Tufte's strongest evidence, and that best-replicated later across many countries and time periods, involves electoral cyclicality in economic policies, especially transfers but also other fiscal and monetary policies (see, e.g., Wright 1974; Ben-Porath 1975; Maloney & Smirlock 1981; Beck 1987; Ames 1987; Alesina 1988; Keech & Pak 1989; Sheffrin 1989; Alesina & Roubini 1992; Alesina et al. 1992, 1997; Krueger & Turan 1993; Schultz 1995; Fouda 1997; Price 1998; Brender 1999; Franzese 1999, 2002a,b; Gonzalez 1999a,b, 2000; Moyo 1999; Schuknecht 1999, 2000; Khemani 2000; Shi & Svensson 2001; Block 2001a,b; Block et al. 2001; Harrinvirta & Mattila 2001; Clark 2002).

Tufte also argues, though, that accelerating real-disposable-income growth could serve as a reasonable summary indicator of electioneering across a range of policies. On this point, as noted above, evidence serves him and successors less well. Only 8 of 15 election years in Tufte's sample saw accelerating real-disposable-income growth per capita. He suggests excluding the "abnormally" fiscally conservative Eisenhower administration, which was indeed an exceptional period statistically ($p \approx 0.026$), leaving 8 of 11. However, echoing the emerging theme of this review, Eisenhower's exceptionality suggests conditional electoral cycles, and so begs a systematic theory to explain how current political climate or incumbents' beliefs might alter predicted electoral cycles. Tufte also claims higher average unemployment rates 12 to 18 months before presidential elections (1946–1976) than around them (Tufte 1978, Figure 1–2), but this too received only weak and problematic (see Alt & Chrystal 1983) support. Less questionably, his content analysis of 1946–1969 State of the Union addresses shows that social-welfare and allocative policies are the second most prominent issues mentioned (behind foreign policy) and that their prominence rises over presidents' first terms, dominating by year four; the pattern repeats, but less starkly, in second terms. Likewise, Tufte notes, correctly though vaguely, that stock and financial markets are notoriously attentive to election-year politics, a theme to which Leblang & Bernhard (2000a,b) and Bernhard & Leblang (2002), among others, address more thorough and sophisticated attention. Thus, again, evidence that electioneering matters and that electoral policy cycles occur seems robust; evidence of real-outcome cycles seems less so.

Tufte also reports strong evidence for "credit-taking" and "kyphosis" in election-year policy making (Tufte 1978, Figures 2.1–7). ("Kyphosis" refers to the heaping of random outcomes around some value or, as here, around some time.) "The

---

[14]Clinton's last State of the Union address ("Save social security first!") suggests continued validity for this focus on transfers.

quickest way to . . . [accelerate growth in] real disposable income is to mail more people larger checks; i.e., for transfer payments to increase" (p. 29). Indeed, 9 of 13 social security payment increases from September 1950 to June 1976 occurred in even-number (i.e., presidential-election) years (Tufte 1978, Table 2–1), and 8 of 9 within-year payment increases were in even-number years (Table 2–1). Since 1954, moreover, notice of the increase has come with a signed presidential message (Tufte 1978, Figure 2–1) lest anyone misallocate credit. Moreover, within-year benefit hikes usually occur in September and within-year tax hikes in January (Tufte 1978, Figure 2–2), and U.S. elections occur in November of course. The book overflows with examples of incumbents "making an election-year prank of the social security system and payroll tax" (p. 143).[15] Although Alt & Chrystal (1983) find some of these tales exaggerated, Congress likely did enact automatic (COLA) increases partly in response to voter concern, after 1972's shenanigans, over kyphotic and other electioneering tendencies. Yet, even so, the new system collects social security taxes starting in January and continuing until the year's requirement is fulfilled, which for many voters precedes November; and, in 1978, after COLA provisions had restrained discretionary social security increases, Congress shifted fiscal years from July 1–June 30 to October 1–September 30. (Spending tends to heap at fiscal-year changes. It rises near the end of the year, as agencies strive to spend remainders, and again near the start of the year, with new programs.) Tufte notes in this context that incumbents can apply the influence of their office to adjust bureaucratic collection and disbursement processes to induce electoral kyphosis without new legislation. The subtlety in implementation yet palpability and "attributability" in receipt of such schedule-shifting electioneering, he argued, places it among office-seekers' preferred tools. Moreover, powerful presidents can more effectively entice bureaucracies to shift timing, implying that more-popular presidents can induce more kyphosis, which again suggests context-conditional electoral cycles.[16]

Tufte also considers electoral cycles in endogenous election timing, which has its own large literature, only briefly covered here (e.g., Chappell & Peel 1979; Lachler 1982; Ito & Park 1988; Ito 1990; Balke 1991; Cargill & Hutchinson 1991; Ellis & Thoma 1991b; Alesina et al. 1993a; Chowdhury 1993; Smith 1996, 2000; Heckelman & Berument 1998; Reid 1998; Heckelman 2001). He notes that, where incumbents can call early elections, policy makers might more easily schedule elections to coincide with economic expansions than vice versa (Tufte 1978, fn. 16, p. 14). In fact, Chapter 3 suggests that, as the economies of the

---

[15]Veterans' payments also tend to peak in the fourth quarter of election years (Tufte 1978, Figure 2–3). Normally, transfer payments peak in December (7 of 8 odd-number years; Tufte 1978, Figure 2–4), but in 4 of 7 even-number years, October or November was maximum (Tufte 1978, Figure 2–5). At the time of Tufte's research, social security checks arrived around the third day of the month; Tufte finds "octokyphosis" in 1964 and 1970, with elections early in the first week of November, and "novemkyphosis" in 1962 and 1972, with elections on November 6 and 7.

[16]This also suggests that, should scholars develop means to test the Rogoff (1990) implication that more-competent incumbents electioneer more, they will need to distinguish competence from popularity/bureaucratic influence.

developed democracies increasingly synchronize, elections elsewhere (almost all endogenous) would increasingly synchronize with U.S. elections (exogenous). Tufte noted, suggestively, that of the G7 nations only Italy saw greater growth in its own election years than in U.S. election years, and all saw more growth in their own election years than in non-election years (Tufte 1978, Table 3–1, Figure 3–1). From 1959–1970, 13 of 22 non-U.S. G7 elections occurred in odd years, but only 1 of 12 occurred in 1971–1976. However, in a later, more systematic analysis, Thompson & Zuck (1983) find little evidence of such synchronization. Ito & Park (1988) and Ito (1990) find strong evidence of strategic election timing in Japan, as do Alesina et al. (1993a), but the latter find little support for the idea elsewhere. Chowdhury's (1993) work on India, as well as most of the later, more comparative studies listed above, uncovered stronger support. The evidence for strategic election timing, particularly in India and Japan (which are dominant-party systems), raises another consideration. Early elections can occur because (*a*) incumbents opt to call them, which they may do when economic conditions are especially good, or (*b*) because coalition supporters abandon incumbents, which can force elections in some systems. Coalition partners might abandon government when economic conditions become especially bad, seeking to avoid the taint of presiding over recession. If this accurately describes the economic conditions that may conduce toward early elections, then the difference between election-year economic volatility and non-election-year economic volatility may be greater in countries with endogenous election timing than in countries with exogenous election timing. Furthermore, as this discussion clarifies, opportunistic election timing to "strong" economies should occur more regularly in single-party than in coalition governments (see also Smith 1996, 2000).

Thus, Tufte views incumbents as having several instruments for securing electoral advantage including fiscal and monetary policies to manipulate exploitable Phillips curves, more-direct transfers to large or strategic groups, policy timing, and election timing. Across policies and outcomes, he argues and offers suggestive evidence that manipulation of real disposable income per capita outranks that of unemployment among incumbents' preferred tools (Tufte 1978, p. 57), that incumbents prefer transfers to broad macroeconomic policy or outcome manipulation, and that they most prefer policy timing, or, in some settings, election timing. One can infer from Tufte, then, an electioneering Ramsey Rule: incumbents use all available policy tools for electoral gain in proportion to their utility toward that end.[17] This suggests (*a*) electoral cycles in composition as well as in amount of public activity, (*b*) more-prominent cycles in policies than in outcomes, (*c*) more-prominent cycles in some policies than others, and (*d*) that the amount and character of such policy-composition electioneering are institutionally, structurally, and strategic-contextually conditional (see also, e.g., Rogoff 1990, Mani & Mukand 2000, Chang 2001).

---

[17]The Ramsey Rule of public finance states that, with multiple revenue-generating instruments of positive and increasing marginal costs available to fund some task, using all the instruments in inverse proportion to their marginal costs is optimal.

Tufte (1978) mentions several other complications of the simple theory, some of which later conditional-electoral-cycles studies (reviewed further below) explore more closely. A single entity called an incumbent does not typically hold full economic policy-making control, for example. Therefore, to electioneer, policy makers (plural) may have to surmount (*a*) common-pool problems (e.g., Goodhart 2000), agency problems (e.g., Alt 1985), or veto-player problems (e.g., Franzese 2002a, ch. 3) in coalitions; (*b*) coordination problems between central banks and governments (e.g., Cusack 2000); or (*c*) other delegation and shared policy-making issues (e.g., Franzese 2002b). The degree of policy-maker discretion, moreover, varies across policies by international and domestic institutional-structural setting. Tufte mentions central-bank autonomy, global-economic exposure, and exchange-rate regime as key considerations, and these are central themes in later views of conditional electoral cycles (e.g., Bernhard & Leblang 1999, 2002; Franzese 1999, 2002b; Oatley 1999; Boix 2000; Clark & Hallerberg 2000; Leblang & Bernhard 2000a,b; Clark 2002). He also notes in this context (Tufte 1978, fn. 1, p. 69) the importance of reserve assets and, by implication, monetary and fiscal solvency more generally, to policy makers' maneuvering room for electioneering, presaging, e.g., Blais et al. (1993, 1996) and Franzese (2002a, ch. 3).[18] He also mentions that policy makers' and voters' beliefs about economic reality (and about others' beliefs) condition the policies most used for electioneering. Especially the economic voting side of recent literature elaborates this theme (e.g., Suzuki 1992). Tufte notes that incumbents may incur political costs if voters perceive them to be manipulating the economy opportunistically (1978, p. 23); given this cost, he speculates that the expected closeness of elections should augment electioneering incentives. This is an idea contemporaries and followers have often expanded theoretically and pursued empirically (Wright 1974, Frey & Schneider 1978a,b, Golden & Poterba 1980, Schultz 1995, Price 1998). Tufte also suggests that electioneering is asymmetric. In election years, governments defer some actions and hasten to perform others; they close military-bases in non-election years, start showcase programs in election years, generally delay or advance foreign-policy acts or appointments strategically, etc. Recent work stresses this policy asymmetry around elections regarding, for example, reform or exchange-rate policy in developing democracies (Frieden & Stein 2001) and tax cuts or spending hikes in developed democracies (e.g., Harrinvirta & Mattila 2001). Tufte's (1978) presidential-campaign case study illustrating the spiral of candidate promises and counter-promises to raise transfers (pp. 35–36) suggests a direct role for challengers in ratcheting electoral promises (p. 60) and provides the foundation for Franzese's (2002a, chs. 2–3) explanation of some of his findings. Tufte stresses most, though, that the political stakes—and so electioneering incentives and electoral-cycle sizes—vary systematically across elections. For U.S. policy makers, he argues, the stakes are highest in on-year presidential-congressional elections with incumbents seeking reelection, followed by on-year elections without incumbents, then off-year, and last non-election years.

---

[18]See also Tufte (1978, fn. 3, pp. 69–70) for an interesting commentary on the upshot by a contemporary British observer.

He finds (Tufte 1978, Table 1–3) that growth in real disposable income per capita supports this ranking. Later scholars have not thoroughly explored this likelihood that the number and importance of policy-making offices at stake varies by election.

Having demonstrated ample motive, means, and opportunity, Tufte (1978) eventually asks why electoral policy manipulation is not even greater and more regular than it is.[19] Essentially, he answered, because the conditions that particularly favor incumbent manipulation do not always obtain. This answer, upon elaboration, can serve to summarize the key conditional-electoral-cycle arguments that Tufte presages:

- *Expected closeness of election.* For voters to see incumbents as manipulating economic policy or, worse, the economy, for political gain is politically costly. Moreover, such manipulation may limit maneuverability for future policy actions or their efficacy. Therefore, incumbents will manipulate only in proportion to the value of buying a few marginal votes, e.g., only to the degree that they expect a close electoral contest.

- *Variable political stakes by election.* Where incumbents have greater and more unified stakes in an election, electioneering is more pronounced, e.g., more in elections contesting greater shares of powerful offices and to the degree that the incumbent is well-characterized as a unitary actor.

- *Shared policy control, conflict of interest among policy makers.* Several entities may share policy authority, e.g., under separation of powers, federalism, or bureaucratic (including central-bank) influence. If so, then problems of bargaining, agency, coordination, and collective action will dampen, or otherwise complicate, electioneering, especially insofar as these entities serve different constituencies.

- *Maneuvering room.* Prior policy and outcome legacies (e.g., debt or monetary reserves) and policy-making inertia/momentum limit current ability to electioneer in certain policies. For example, high accumulated debt or more policy-making veto players may hinder fiscal maneuverability.

- *Incumbent character, ideology, competence, and beliefs.* (These arguments are either vague or self-explanatory, depending on one's predilections.)

- *Varying issue saliency and policy efficacy.* Across elections and the electoral cycle, different outcomes will have greater saliency with voters, and different policies will be more accessible and effective in addressing those issues, depending on international and domestic political-economic institutional,

---

[19]Indeed, if voters so strongly reward positive economic performance, might not the opposition try covertly to sabotage the economy? Most analysts have not taken this possibility seriously; oppositions cannot affect the economy much anyway, and being caught in such cynicism is probably too devastating to risk. However, oppositions routinely do something like sabotage when they support legislation that harms the constituencies of incumbents, or resist legislation that benefits them. Thus, oppositions, like incumbents, choose far more direct and targeted tools than manipulation of the broad macroeconomy.

structural, and strategic context. This suggests conditional electoral cycles in policy composition.

■ *Endogenous election timing.* Election timing itself is another policy option in electioneering. This implies that other instruments are used less where election times are endogenous, and that the frequency of recourse to strategic election calling, and the conditions under which incumbents use this strategy, should also vary contextually.

Tufte (1978) also mentions several universal limits to political control of the economy from which scholars of conditional electoral cycles might derive hypotheses about the relative weights of different policies in electioneering. First, political control of the economy usually operates only at the margins rather than on the underlying structure of the economy; the aggregate of private-sector actions determines most economic conditions. Second, uncertain lead and lag times of policy implementation and the effects thereof, and third, mutual agreements to "depoliticize" some economic policies (e.g., collection and reporting of economic data)[20] limit access to or utility of some policies for electioneering. Economic theory imposes a fourth limit. Policy makers cannot easily ignore consensus among theoreticians (concerning free trade, no price floors or ceilings, etc.). Only strong political pressure can overcome such consensus, although well-organized groups, for example, may be able to apply sufficient pressure (Olson 1965, 1982). The Council of Economic Advisers gives economic consensus an institutionalized voice in the United States; similar institutions of varying influence exist in all democracies.[21]

---

[20]Tufte (1978) also cites central-bank independence in this context, but many would contest characterizing central banks as depoliticized.

[21]Tufte also enumerates and evaluates some potential costs of political control of the economy: stop-go economies; "making an election-year prank of the social security system and payroll tax" (1978, p. 143); myopic bias toward policies with immediate, highly visible benefits and deferred, hidden costs and away from policies with the opposite characteristics; special-interest biases toward policies with small costs on many and large benefits for few and away from the opposite; and replacement of economically optimal with politically optimal adjustment paths (p. 144). Tufte acknowledges all of these costs. He discounts Nordhaus' prediction that Phillips-curve exploitation implies "politically determined policy ... will have lower unemployment and higher inflation than is optimal," noting that the data indicate voters are strongly inflation-averse and know right-wing parties reduce inflation, so that they could simply elect the right if concerned about inflationary bias. He offers several prescriptions for these ills, of varying practical and philosophical interest: reduce incumbent flexibility in calling elections (although the Ramsey-Rule logic actually argues he should rather suggest increasing flexibility), randomize election dates, desynchronize electoral and fiscal calendars, raise public attention to and knowledge of electioneering, or dilute political control of economic policy. Tufte is highly critical of the depoliticization movement. He notes its "well-financed" arrival after the events of 1972 and calls proposed cures "obtuse" in removing economic policy from political control, one place where democratic ideals seem most realized in practice, merely to reduce the particular problem of election-year economics.

On these many theoretical complications, Alt & Chrystal comment (1983, p. 122), "Eclecticism is part of Tufte's problem." Their criticism refers to his tendency, perhaps reflecting the intellectual climate of his time or his near-exclusive single-country focus, to add these modifications to explain his data or examples entirely. That is, Tufte often applies such conditional argumentation to explain too much, so that "whatever happens can probably be interpreted as supporting one of [Tufte's arguments]" (Alt & Chrystal 1983, p. 122). A modern lens, however, naturally converts these ad hoc conditional hunches into theories of systematic variation in electoral-cycle magnitude or content that readily generate comparative hypotheses for empirical evaluation. Empirically, scholars should model or at least control for such conditionality (Alt & Woolley 1982). That is, each consideration that complicates the theory should, but generally does not, also complicate the empirical analyses. This omission may have contributed to the ad hoc sense and, via mis-specification, to the apparent empirical weakness. Some recent advances are discussed below, but first, consider the electoral policy-cycles evidence.

Since before Tufte (1978), empirical work has stressed not only that certain policies should expand or contract around elections, but that closer elections should generate more such electioneering. For instance, a cross-sectional analysis of federal government expenditures during the 1930s (Wright 1974) shows that states with more competitive presidential races (in past voting history) received higher shares of federal spending on average. Frey & Schneider propose a theory combining office-seeking and partisan (see below) motivations to argue that governments that expect lower odds of reelection will stress electoral aims relative to partisan aims more than those that expect better electoral showings. Vulnerable governments will therefore pursue "common" fiscal policies, ones "clearly preferred by a majority" of voters, prior to the election, but the victors become more ideologically motivated after the election. Frey & Schneider (1978a,b, 1979; see also Schneider & Frey 1988) find support for this theory in German, U.K.,[22] and U.S. data. Pommerehne & Schneider (1980) find Australian government expenditure and transfers (1960–1977) related positively, and total tax revenues negatively, to electoral vulnerability. Schultz (1995) returns to this theme, finding strong evidence of electoral cycles in U.K. transfers policy conditioned by expected closeness of elections; Price (1998) finds similar results in exploring his nonlinear modification of Schultz's argument.

Notably, when empirical specifications allow only unconditional electoral policy cycles, and/or fail to control electoral closeness, and/or analyze less-direct policies, the support for electoral policy-cycles is weaker, although still stronger than for electoral outcome-cycles. Alesina (1988), for example, finds some weak evidence of U.S. electoral cycles in transfers, as do Keech & Pak (1989) for veterans' payments, both of which more-direct policies than macroeconomic stimulus.

---

[22]Chrystal & Alt (1981) and Alt & Chrystal (1983) note that a permanent-public-income hypothesis could also explain Frey & Schneider's (1978b) U.K. results. Ahmad (1983) suggests Frey & Schneider unduly neglect economic conditions.

Maloney & Smirlock (1981) find that non-defense spending rises somewhat when new presidents take office, controlling for unemployment gaps; this suggests that spending is slightly more Keynesian in election years. Golden & Poterba (1980), contrarily, find electoral-cycle indicators and presidential popularity unimportant or insignificant determinants of budget surpluses. That is, their monetary- and fiscal-policy models reveal correctly signed but insignificant coefficients on electoral-cycle indicators, and their transfers models do not find the expected correlations with the electoral cycle. Hicks & Swank (1992) find welfare spending in OECD democracies during 1960–1982 insignificantly correlated with pre-electoral indicators but highly responsive to participation rates, which may suggest conditionality. Thus, the evidence for electoral transfers-cycles is not unquestionable but is mostly strong and favorable, especially considering the electoral-cycle specification weaknesses that Haynes & Stone (1988, 1989, 1990, 1994; see also footnote 10) stress, which persist here, and especially when empirical models allow cycles to be conditional on expected closeness.

As already noted, Alesina and colleagues (footnote 8) report monetary expansion around, fiscal laxity before, and inflation surges after U.S. or OECD-country elections. Grier (1987, 1989) and, less certainly, Sheffrin (1989) also report U.S. electoral monetary cycles. Beck (1987) finds higher U.S. money growth around elections, yet no electoral cycle in monetary reserves or the Federal Fund rate, which suggests that fiscal and other policies more than monetary activism induce monetary and inflation cycles, at least in the United States. As elaborated below, Franzese (1999, 2002a,b) finds highly context-conditional post-electoral inflation surges as well as pre- and post-electoral transfers and debt surges (transfers stronger) in OECD data. Clark & Hallerberg (2000), Hallerberg (2002), and Hallerberg et al. (2001) also find context-conditional electoral cycles in, respectively monetary policy, fiscal policy, and both. Meanwhile, in developing democracies, scholars almost uniformly discover electoral cycles in many different policies (e.g., Ben-Porath 1975, Ames 1987, Edwards 1993, Krueger & Turan 1993, and Remmer 1993 find mixed support; for reviews, see Schuknecht 1996, 1999, 2000; Fouda 1997; Brender 1999; Gonzalez 1999a,b, 2000; Moyo 1999; Grier & Grier 2000; Khemani 2000; Shi & Svensson 2001; Block 2001a,b). Block et al. (2001) offers a review. This pattern of support—almost unassailable for direct-transfers cycles, also strong in other policies and in inflation around or after elections, and weakest in real-outcome cycles—seems to favor Drazen's (2001) proposed active-fiscal-policy version of rational electoral and partisan cycles. That pattern and the remarkably strong support from developing democracies also suggest context-conditional cycles rather than fixed-magnitude, fixed-content cycles.

Rational, Prospective Citizens

ECONOMIC POLICY AND OUTCOME CYCLES   Viewing this pattern of electoral-cycle evidence—stronger in policies, especially more-direct ones, and stronger in nominal than in real outcomes—economists, as noted above, naturally questioned the assumption of adaptive expectations and exploitable Phillips curves (i.e., Tufte's "opportunity"). Economists observed that electoral cycles in these models consistently fool voters and economic actors (violating Lincoln's famous adage), yet voters can easily foresee elections and policy-maker incentives. Thus, electoral cycles should not exist or should have no real effects if voters and economic actors are rationally foresighted. Before proceeding on that basis, however, note that if some economic actors apply adaptive expectations, then exploitable Phillips curves will exist in proportion to their share of the economy. Likewise, if some voters evaluate incumbents retrospectively, their vote share gauges incumbents' incentives to leverage these Phillips curves to buy votes. Moreover, as next elaborated, if some performance-affecting incumbent characteristics persist over time and if voters cannot fully observe these characteristics, even rational prospective actors will evaluate retrospectively. Therefore, if, as many believe, some actors are more fully rational or informed than others (and other model assumptions hold), classical electoral-outcome-cycle models should have some, albeit irregular[23] or muted, validity.

In rational-expectations electoral-cycle models (Cukierman & Meltzer 1986; Rogoff & Sibert 1988; Rogoff 1990; Ellis & Thoma 1991a; Sieg 1997; Heckelman & Berument 1998; Lohmann 1998, 1999; Carlsen 1999; Faust & Irons 1999; Gärtner 1999; Gonzalez 1999a,b, 2000; for review articles or textbook treatments, see Nordhaus 1989, Terrones 1989, Alesina et al. 1997, Paldam 1997, Gärtner 2000, Persson & Tabellini 1990, 1994, 2000, 2002; Drazen 2000, 2001; Olters 2001), elected policy makers enjoy some information advantages over voters, possess some outcome-affecting characteristics that persist over time, and control some policies with which they can leverage their advantages to signal or to feign beneficial characteristics. In one model (Rogoff & Sibert 1988), incumbents of varying "competence," defined as the efficiency with which they finance fixed public spending, can lower taxes before an election to signal or feign high competence, using less-visible borrowing or seignorage to cover any shortfall until after elections. Crucially, voters cannot observe competence directly but know it to persist and to be policy-maker specific. Under certain assumptions and parameterizations, this induces pre-electoral tax cuts and post-electoral inflation or debt hikes, not from very low-competence policy makers, but increasingly over the middle-competence range and then decreasingly at higher competence levels.

In another model (Persson & Tabellini 1990), incumbents have information advantages over voters regarding exogenous macroeconomic shocks and control policies that can counteract such shocks. Some policy makers manage macroeconomic policies more competently, achieving greater real stabilization at lower nominal cost (inflation), and such competence persists but is unknown to voters. Under these conditions, prospective voters rationally evaluate incumbents retrospectively, preferring those who have recently delivered above-average mixtures of inflation and stabilization because (by Bayes' Law) the probability of

---

[23]That is, mixed-strategy equilibria involving random incumbent electioneering may exist.

high-competence incumbents given recent strong performance is greater. Thus, voters expect better real outcomes if they reelect incumbents than if they elect random, unproven (i.e., expected average-competence) challengers. Accordingly, incumbents would like to signal or to feign competence with stimulatory policies around elections, and either all incumbents will electioneer in this way ("pooling equilibrium") or only the more competent will ("separating equilibrium").

In a third model (Rogoff 1990), incumbents of varying competence in converting public revenues into valued spending control more-visible public consumption and less-visible public investment. Again, under certain informational conditions, incumbents shift budgetary composition toward current consumption as elections near, in order to signal or feign competence; and, again, either pooling or separating equilibria obtain, with all or only competent incumbents electioneering. Rogoff (1990) also notes usefully that competence in such models might reflect the match of a policy maker's worldview to the political-economic relations governing reality, and that this effectiveness of match between worldview and reality is the policy-maker-specific quality that persists over time.

As others (e.g., Alesina et al. 1997; Drazen 2000, 2001; Persson & Tabellini 2000) have also summarized, the main observable difference between rational-expectations-equilibrium electoral cycles and the Nordhaus (1975)/Tufte (1978) variety of electoral cycles is that the former model predicts smaller and less regular cycles, especially in real outcomes. This could fit the stylized facts discussed above, as those reviewers noted. However, determining whether the comparative-historical record exhibits the correct degree of "smaller, less regular" cycles, even if that degree were theoretically known, would be empirically difficult. Moreover, many conditional-cycle considerations also imply less-regular, smaller electoral cycles, especially in an empirical record generated by studies that did not allow such conditionality. Likewise, another distinguishing feature of equilibrium electoral-cycle models, namely that the magnitudes and natures of electoral cycles depend on incumbent competency, many may believe unobservable. (Recent advances in gauging challenger quality in studies of campaign-money effects on election outcomes might help.) In a rare direct analysis, Alesina et al. (1993b) conclude that the correlations of economic shocks across administrations required for retrospective voting to be rational do not obtain in the U.S. political economy.

In sum, the evidence does not contradict rational-expectations competence-signaling theories of electoral cycles in economic policies and outcomes, and these cycles do seem less regular and smaller than naive classical models suggest. However, voter evaluations do not seem consistent with the rational retrospections that underlie these models, and conditional-cycles theories—which either rational or myopic models could incorporate consistently but generally do not—also predict smaller, irregular cycles or cycles that seem smaller or irregular if empirical models specify them, as most do, unconditionally. Most political economists, moreover, probably view the empirical world as populated by actors with varying information and rationality, which, as noted at the start of this section, likewise implies smaller and irregular cycles in either classical or rational-expectations settings.

Thus far, therefore, the stronger case for general-equilibrium electoral-cycles models is more theoretical than empirical. It shows how to reconcile observed cycles with rational expectations but does not demonstrate that rational expectations explain observed cycles.

Further Discussion of Electoral Cycles

This review finds that claims of insufficient empirical support for the existence of electoral cycles condemn empirical specifications at least as much as the theory itself. Voters' rational expectations and prospective evaluations probably do limit the degree to which incumbents manipulate economic policies—and, *a fortiori*, outcomes—for electoral advantage. Moreover, although important economic issues may hinge on whether theories fully or only partly incorporate rational expectations, from a political-economy perspective, this is only one limitation on such opportunism, and perhaps neither the most important nor the most interesting. (Exploring the economic issues surrounding rational expectations directly, rather than simultaneously with the various political-cycle theories to be tested, might prove more productive.) As stated above, the capacity for, incentives for, and effects of electioneering should vary predictably across policies depending on context—international and domestic, political and economic, institutional, structural, and strategic context. In this light, competence-signaling models mainly offer further conditionality worthy of study if difficult to evaluate empirically.

Before discussing such context-conditional electoral cycles further, the next section reviews partisan models. Some issues, having been covered above, are addressed only briefly. First, one key issue underemphasized in electoral-cycle models demands attention.

Challengers play only the most indirect roles in all these models. Higher-quality challengers, for example, must lead incumbents to expect closer elections, so the mostly empirically supported prediction that closer elections generate more electioneering (Wright 1974, Tufte 1978, Frey & Schneider 1978a,b, Golden & Poterba 1980, Schultz 1995, Price 1998) also suggests that greater electoral manipulations will occur in elections with higher-quality challengers and in systems that generally produce such challengers. Likewise, higher challenger quality should modify incumbent incentives to signal competence, although the way the incentives change depends heavily on the exact informational assumptions.[24] Franzese (2002a) finds, for instance, that electioneering in transfers and in deficits occurs both the year before and the year after elections—in fact, electioneering is more pronounced and more certain the year after. Noting Tufte's (1978) observation that electoral campaigns often involve incumbent and challenger counter-promises of largesse, he suggests that the role of challengers may explain this. Incumbents can fulfill

---

[24]The typical result that more-competent incumbents electioneer more, being better able to distinguish themselves from challengers (whom voters in these models can only expect to be average), actually suggests that more-competent challengers incite *less* electioneering. This may offer some empirical leverage on (and does not bode well for) competence-signaling models.

their pre-electoral promises and therefore must do so to maintain credibility; winners can and almost always do likewise[25] for like reasons; and, *ceteris paribus*, candidates who promise more with greater credibility will win. Therefore, the pool of pre-electoral policy makers will contain some incumbents who promised and/or delivered too little, or whose promises were insufficiently credible, and who therefore lost; whereas the pool of post-electoral policy makers will contain winners (returning incumbents and entering challengers) who promised, and so now must enact, greater largesse. The election serves as a filter for credibility × promised largesse. Thus, especially if newly seated governments are most productive (another empirical regularity), post-electoral electioneering will be greater and more certain than pre-electoral. Note, finally, that this too could explain some weaknesses in many early studies, which compared only pre-electoral periods to all others, including immediate post-election periods. It could also explain the generally stronger findings for inflation cycles than other outcomes.

PARTISAN CYCLES (POLICY-SEEKING POLICY MAKERS)

Adaptive, Retrospective Citizens

ECONOMIC-OUTCOME CYCLES   As with electoral-cycle theory, the basic tenets of partisan theory are simple. Candidates contest and voters adjudicate elections in partisan terms. The competing parties cultivate strong ties to different groups of voters and nurture reputations for policy making that favors those groups and accords with their ideologies. Parties and voters value these partisan reputations and ties, so incumbents conduct recognizably distinct partisan policies, yielding appreciably distinct economic outcomes. However, given Downs' (1957) famous result that two-party electoral competition causes platforms and policies to converge on the preferences of the median voter, scholars must first demonstrate that parties pursue differing outcomes, and that this translates into enacting differing policies in office.

Tufte (1978) argued that electoral calendars set the schedules and timing of policy but partisanship and ideology set its substance. Parties of the right favor low taxes, low inflation, and modest, balanced budgets; they oppose equalization and accept higher unemployment more willingly than inflation. Parties of the left favor equalization, low unemployment, and larger budgets with less emphasis on balance; they accept inflation more willingly than unemployment. In Tufte's judgment, 1976 U.S. Democrat and Republican platforms contrasted more than public opinion on economic issues, and the 1944–1964 platforms differed more on economic and labor issues than on foreign affairs, agriculture, defense, natural resources, and even civil rights. (Voters were divided similarly, though less sharply.)[26] Concern over inflation and unemployment, in particular, is highly cyclical and common to all voters, but persistent partisan differences are evident

---

[25]Pomper (1971), Rose (1980), Alt (1985), and Gallagher et al. (1995, ch. 13) all report strong electoral-promise redemption.

[26]Even typographic style and how best to misquote the Founding Fathers differ between parties (Tufte 1978, fn. 3, p. 73).

(Tufte 1978, Figure 4–1). His analyses of *Economic Reports of the President* and *Annual Reports of the Council of Economic Advisors* (Tufte 1978, Table 4.2–4) also show recognizable partisan patterns in the frequencies of dire references to inflation or unemployment. These divergent party views, he argues, are rooted in their supporters' socioeconomic differences (Tufte 1978, pp. 84–85, Table 4–5). He concludes that party ideologies and platforms differ; voters recognize and act on these differences; and parties generally fulfill their promises (Tufte 1978, p. 90).[27]

Hibbs' partisan theory (1977, 1986, 1987a,b, 1992, 1994)[28] similarly distinguishes left- and right-party policy and outcome priorities, stressing their relative inflation or unemployment aversion:

> Avoidance of inflation and maintenance of full employment can be most usefully regarded as conflicting class interests of the bourgeoisie and proletariat, respectively, the conflict being resolvable only by the test of relative political power in society and its resolution involving no reference to an overriding concept of the social welfare. (Hibbs 1987a, p. 1, quoting Harry G. Johnson)

The main losers from unemployment and recessions, Hibbs (1987a) shows, are those at the low end of the occupational and income hierarchies; and the tax-and-transfer system only partly mitigates this. Specifically, he notes that unemployment is universally regarded as a key indicator of macroeconomic health and individual hardship. Its aggregate costs are obvious; unemployment implies a waste of human resources, which implies lost real output/income. Specifically, 1950–1983 U.S. data suggest 1% higher unemployment reduces output growth 2.1% (Hibbs 1987a, p. 50), which translated in 1987 to over $1,000 per household per year. (Hibbs also reports estimates that no more than 25% of this value returns to households as extra leisure.) More importantly, the divergent unemployment incidence over economic cycles across socioeconomic groups, especially class, race, and age, is striking. In 1960 (mild recession), 1970 (boom), and 1980 (recession), blue-collar exceeded white-collar unemployment by 5.1%, 3.4%, and 6.3%, respectively; minority exceeded white unemployment by 5.3%, 3.7%, and 6.9%, respectively; and unemployment among 20–24-year-olds exceeded that among 25–54-year-olds by 4.2%, 4.8%, and 6.1%, respectively (Hibbs 1987a, p. 53, Table 2.3).[29] Hibbs documents also the high individual costs of unemployment, and cites Brenner (1973, 1976) empirically linking unemployment rates to multifarious psychological, social, and medical problems that include family tensions, stress, mental health, suicide, homicide and other crime, and cardiovascular and

[27]By Pomper's (1971) estimate, presidents fulfill an average 84% of their party's economic-policy platform promises.
[28]Hibbs 1977 introduces; 1987a most thoroughly expounds; 1986, 1987b, 1992, and 1994 extend and review.
[29]Unemployment is also, but less, gender distinct. Higher female unemployment risk vanishes when the analysis controls for occupation, meaning that gender bias in unemployment risk stems directly from gender bias in occupational access or preferences.

renal disease. (Brenner's summary estimate is that 1% higher unemployment yields 30,000 more deaths per year.) Finally, Hibbs (1987a, pp. 57–61) shows that the tax-and-transfer system partly mitigates unemployment costs, replaces more lost income for lower income groups than higher, and, above the poverty line, functions about equally well for minorities and whites. Although it works less well for minorities below the poverty line and less well for female than for male heads of households, it otherwise generally does (or did) exactly what its designers intended. The tax-and-transfer system probably also has some of the detrimental side effects its opponents have decried, but claims that it has failed its primary mission are demonstrably false. In sum, unemployment severely harms the aggregate economy, and workers, minorities, and youth face more severe and more severely cyclical unemployment risks.

Contrarily, there is almost no evidence that inflation rates per se, short of hyperinflation and distinct from relative-price movements and inflation variability, harm any aggregate real outcome. Hibbs (1987a, pp. 90–98) and many others find no evidence that inflation affects average personal tax rates or aggregate real tax revenues, aggregate real growth, or aggregate investment or savings (which suggests that the substitution and income effects of inflation tend roughly to cancel). Nor do they find that inflation shifts private investment from nonresidential to housing (Hibbs 1987a, pp. 107–17). Even inflation's distributional effects are generally small compared with unemployment's (Hibbs 1987a, pp. 77–89). Inflation may (statistically insignificantly) shift some income from the top two quintiles to the bottom two, but only appreciably harms the wealthiest 1%–5% of the population, presumably as asset holders. Indeed, the only strong deleterious effects of inflation appear in capital returns, profitably, and stock returns (Hibbs 1987a, pp. 98–107). Thus, notes Hibbs, popular aversion to inflation is largely psychological and/or arises from confusion of aggregate (nominal) with relative (real) price changes,[30] perhaps both partisan abetted. In sum (Hibbs 1987a, pp. 72–77), the main real aggregate costs of inflation arise from policy makers' reactions against it. At least in the postwar United States, these costs follow an empirical rule of 1% unemployment above the natural rate for one year reducing inflation by about 0.5%. Distributional effects, though generally small, appreciably affect only the wealthiest.

Therefore, objectively, the upper middle and especially the upper classes have relatively more to fear from inflation and less from unemployment than do the lower middle and especially the lower classes. The relevant comparison for partisan theory is that the ratio of unemployment aversion to inflation aversion among the lower class exceeds that ratio among the upper class. All classes surely dislike both unemployment and inflation, and one need not establish that either the lower or upper

---

[30]If aversion to inflation arises from the confusion of aggregate and relative price changes, then this aversion should be strongest in countries where the oil crises, which were relative-price shocks, caused more severe real costs along with inflation. Oil importers (e.g., Japan, most of Europe, the United States) should have more inflation-averse voters than do oil exporters (e.g., Norway, the United Kingdom, Canada).

class suffers more from either outcome, but rather that lower/middle classes fear unemployment relative to inflation more than upper/middle classes do. Moreover, the relevant comparison is their actual distaste for unemployment and inflation, i.e., their perceived and not necessarily their objective costs from these two evils.

Hibbs (1987a, pp. 127–38, Figures 4.1–4.3) shows that economic issues, most prominently inflation and unemployment, typically dominate popular responses to Gallup's "most important problem today" question, although international and defense and/or domestic political and social issues occasionally surpass them. Further, Hibbs demonstrates that inflation and unemployment concerns respond to objective economic conditions intuitively. More crucially, he shows how relative inflation/unemployment concern varies across electoral groups, with Democratic, blue-collar, lower-income voters more unemployment-averse and less inflation-averse than Republican, white-collar, higher-income voters (Hibbs 1987a, pp. 138–41, Figures 4.5–4.7, Table 4.1). Thus, actual aversions to as well as objective costs of inflation and unemployment exhibit the required relativity.

Finally, Hibbs (1987a, pp. 142–84) shows that popular support for the U.S. president and his party depends on current, past, and perhaps anticipated future performance. He reports obvious partisan patterns in preferences for specific presidents, and several ancillary results regarding lag structures, weights on the degrees to which voters compare current incumbent performance to that of past administrations or to that of past administrations of the same party,[31] honeymoons, and responses to events such as the Vietnam War and Watergate. His crucial finding is that Democrats penalize incumbents 1.1 times as much for unemployment as for inflation, whereas Republicans and Independents punish them only .65 and .49 times as much for unemployment as for inflation (Hibbs 1987a, p. 177). In sum, different groups of voters suffer disproportionately from unemployment or inflation; public perceptions reflect this objective difference; and popular and electoral approval of incumbents follow the same pattern, producing differing partisan incentives to combat unemployment or inflation.

Hibbs (1987a) suggests that scholars view the above relations as reflecting popular demand for economic policies and outcomes. These relations provide Tufte's (1978) "motive," discussed above regarding electoral economic-outcome cycles, for partisan economic-outcome cycles; an exploitable Phillips curve again provides opportunity and weapons. For supply (i.e., the policy motives derived from demand), Hibbs argues policy makers seek to maintain comfortable support levels during their terms, to maximize votes at election time, and to serve their core constituencies' ideological and distributional goals. Constraints on these pursuits, mentioned but not elaborated by Hibbs, include central bank autonomy, executive-legislative relations, federalism, and economic structure and conditions

---

[31]Hibbs shows how to estimate empirical answers to some very precise questions regarding the electorate's reaction to economic outcomes: the rate at which voters discount past performance, the degrees to which voters compare incumbents to the performance of their party's past administrations or to which they compare the current to all past administrations, and the relative weights on unemployment and inflation.

(e.g., Phillips-curve shapes, international institutions, global shocks). For weapons, Hibbs notes four basic options: monetary policy, fiscal policy, direct controls, and rhetorical persuasion. He stresses the first two. Rhetorical persuasion, though cheap and easy and therefore commonly used by policy makers, is relatively ineffective. Policy makers rarely resort to direct controls because they find them more costly and difficult to use (conflicting starkly with academic consensus), and their effectiveness is uncertain. Monetary policy and fiscal policy are more promising weapons. In the "new Keynesian" perspective, they can and do have sizable short-run impacts, although the government cannot do much about long-run conditions except through public investment (e.g., in education).[32]

Working from a roughly new-Keynesian basis, Hibbs' central arguments are that the two most important political influences on macroeconomic policy are partisanship and electoral incentives, and that partisanship is the more potent.

> The economic interests at stake during inflations and recessions, the ways in which class-related political constituencies perceive their interests and respond in the opinion polls and in the voting booth to macroeconomic fluctuations, and the ways in which economic interests, preferences, and priorities of political constituencies are transmitted to macroeconomic policies and outcomes observed under the parties are the main themes of [partisan theory]. (Hibbs 1987a, p. 2)

Specifically, left parties seek, and will accept higher inflation to get, lower unemployment and higher growth; right parties seek, and will tolerate higher unemployment and lower growth to obtain lower inflation. Left parties will also expend greater effort toward equalization than right parties. Hibbs acknowledges that stable, long-run inflation-unemployment tradeoffs may not exist but stresses that stabilizing inflation and supporting low unemployment (and high growth) are often conflicting goals.

> Faced with demand shifts, supply shocks, labor-cost push, and other inflationary events, political administrations repeatedly have been forced to choose between accommodating inflationary pressures by pursuing expansive monetary and fiscal policies, thereby foregoing leverage on the pace of price rises in order to preserve aggregate demand and employment, and leaning against such pressures by tightening spending and the supply of money and credit, thereby slowing the inflation rate, at the cost of higher unemployment and lower growth. (Hibbs 1987a, p. 2)

Estimating partial-adjustment models from U.S. data, Hibbs (1977, 1987a) shows roughly long-run 1.5%–2% higher unemployment and 5.3%–6.2% lower real growth under Republicans than Democrats (1987a, p. 225, Table 7.3). Democratic

---

[32]Economic models with certain combinations of multiple non-competitive markets, e.g., non-competitive labor and product markets, and/or with nominal contracts ("sticky" wages and/or prices) or other nominal rigidities can support new-Keynesian (as opposed to neoclassical) models (with much debate about how short is the short run, etc.).

administrations contributed about three fifths of the 1948–1978 reduction in 20/40 (the ratio of top to bottom-two quintiles shares) income inequality (1987a, p. 242, Table 7.6). Beck (1982b) raises some methodological and empirical concerns about these magnitudes, finding that Hibbs' (1977) results exaggerate differences between U.S. parties by about one third and that unemployment was actually higher under some Democrats than some Republicans (Hibbs 1983 replies), but Hibbs' basic conclusions emerge unscathed. Haynes & Stone (1994) also find partisan outcome cycles in the United States, again stressing that typical dummy-variable specifications assume more discrete policy and outcome shifts than are empirically likely, which may obscure actual cycles and, here, cloud comparisons of traditional and rational partisan theories (see below). Hibbs (1987b, 1992, 1994) finds appreciably distinct economic outcomes under left and right governments not only in the United States but also in broader samples of OECD democracies, as does Paldam (1989). Alesina and colleagues (footnote 8) concur on the existence of both U.S. and OECD partisan outcome cycles (see below). Alt (1985), Alvarez et al. (1991), and Beck et al. (1993) find partisan patterns in unemployment or growth in OECD countries that depend on institutional and strategic context (see below). In sum, evidence for partisan outcome cycles of worsening nominal and improving real and distributional outcomes under left governments generally emerges readily from U.S. and comparative data, although Clark and colleagues[33] find that more-sophisticated conditional-cycle explorations favor electoral more than partisan models (see below).

ECONOMIC-POLICY CYCLES   A mammoth empirical literature addresses various aspects of partisan policy. For example, Imbeau et al. (2001) offer meta-analysis of 43 of over 600 publications they uncovered from, among other sources, Bartolini et al.'s (1998) database of 11,500 studies of European parties and party systems. Hibbs (1987a, p. 249, Table 7.7) finds that U.S. fiscal policy (cyclically adjusted deficits controlling for wars) and monetary policy (M1 money-supply growth) track presidential partisanship (and, to a lesser degree, House and Senate partisanship), consistent with the outcome effects he has noted. Alesina and colleagues (footnote 8) likewise interpret the partisan monetary and fiscal cycles they find in U.S. and OECD postwar samples as capable of producing the outcome effects predicted by rational partisan theory (although others note some anomalies in this regard; see below). However, as one might expect with so many samples, methodologies, and specifications, the wider empirical record is mixed. In Imbeau et al.'s (2001) meta-analysis, 37 of the 43 studies address economic policy, spanning welfare, education, health, social security, privatization, intervention, public-employment, spending, revenue, debt, deficit, and other economic policies to yield 545 correlations or regression coefficients. (Imbeau et al. graciously posted their IDEOPOL data to http://www.capp.ulaval.ca/bases/bd6.htm.) Of these, 395 (72.5%) sign as standard partisan theory predicts, with 135 (24.8%) significant at $p \leq .10$; 145 (26.6%)

---

[33]Clark et al. (1998), Clark & Hallerberg (2000), Hallerberg et al. (2001), Clark (2002), Clark et al. (2002).

have wrong sign, 45 (8.3%) significantly; 5 (0.9%) report no relation. Overall, this is a fair record, considering the simplicity of many of these studies (e.g., 58% bivariate). Moreover, as the Imbeau et al. (2001) study clarifies statistically, the strongest evidence of partisan policy effects comes from multivariate analyses[34] of post-1973 samples, examining government "size" in terms of revenue, spending, employment (especially), or social welfare effort (to a lesser extent). Such results may suggest that partisan cycles, like electoral cycles, follow a Ramsey Rule, with preferences for certain policies and a high degree of context dependence.

Wilensky (1976, 1981) finds many but often insignificant bivariate correlations of partisanship with various social, welfare, or fiscal policies in 19 OECD countries during 1965–1971. Hewitt (1977) finds slightly stronger signs of partisan effects on redistribution with controls in 17 OECD countries during 1962–1974. Cameron (1978) finds mildly or nearly significant partisan effects on total public revenues in an early cross-section, and an early time-series study by Pommerehne & Schneider (1980) finds Australian Liberal (right) and Labor (left) parties in 1960–1977 pursuing partisan spending and tax policies. Hicks & Swank (1984a,b) find stronger partisan cycles in social and welfare policies than in fiscal budgetary policies, and Swank (1988) finds that left parties spent more than right and center parties in the 1960s but less than center in the 1970s. Finally, perhaps most prolifically and representatively, Castles and colleagues report fully 183 correlations and regression coefficients relating partisanship to social, education, welfare, health, and total spending, of which 166 (90.7%) have correct sign, 57 (31.1%) significantly so, and 16 (8.7%) have incorrect sign, 2 (1.1%) significantly so (Castles & McKinlay 1979a,b; Borg & Castles 1981; Castles 1981, 1982, 1986, 1989). Thus, first, the early record shows the strongest partisan ties to total spending or revenues, and stronger ties to social or welfare policies than to fiscal-deficit policy. Second, the motif of correct signs and near significance might suggest insufficient sample size or variation, inappropriate or inadequate controls, or mis-specification of a conditional relationship as unconditional;[35] or it might simply indicate that partisan policy differences are weak, as Clark and colleagues hold (footnote 33).

Later studies, often more sophisticated and including more post-1973 data in time-series cross-section form, are typically stronger, especially regarding government size. The strongest incorporate systematic institutional, structural, or context conditional predictions (see below). For example, like Cameron (1978) but stronger, Huber et al. (1993) find long-term left governance associated with government size, as do Blais et al. (1993, 1996), conditional on outstanding debt. Cusack et al. (1989) finds strong partisan effects on public employment. More recently, Persson (1999, 2002) and Persson et al. (2000) offer further broad

---

[34]Multivariate analysis probably serves as a proxy for appropriate methodological and specification sophistication.

[35]Many critics suspect this mis-specification, or at least suspect that a conditional relationship was modeled as incorrectly or insufficiently conditional. The frequent resort to time-period-specific effects, for example, only imperfectly proxies for more systematic institutional, structural, strategic conditionality.

support for partisan government size and macro-policy effects. For the United States, Beck (1982c) and Chappell et al. (1993) find partisan monetary effects via federal appointments. Several others (e.g., Jonsson 1995; Simmons 1996; Oatley 1999; Franzese 1999, 2002b) find partisan monetary policies in wider samples, conditional on domestic and international institutional and structural context (see below). Innovatively, Boix (1998) finds intuitive partisan differences in several supply-side policies (active labor market, privatization policies, etc.). Franzese (2002a) reports nearly significant partisan effects on transfers, even when controlling for median-voter income. He also finds significant partisan deficit effects, but those predicted by simple partisan theory emerge only in specific, extreme, and somewhat rare strategic contexts. Cusack (1997) finds partisan influences on public spending, which increasing international-economy linkages have weakened but not severed. Contradicting naive views that the left are unconditional deficit producers and the right are unconditional surplus producers, Cusack (1999) demonstrates that left governments use fiscal policy countercyclically and right governments use it procyclically—styles that conform to their respective supporters' interests—and that this difference, too, has weakened with increasing international exposure. Cusack (2000) finds partisan government fiscal and monetary policy, with which central banks coordinate under right but not left governments (see also Sieg 1997, Vaubel 1997). Garrett (1995, 1998), Swank (1992), and Hallerberg & Basinger (1998) study partisan effects on government's relative reliance on capital, income, and consumption taxation, finding that the left favors income over consumption taxation, but also, counterintuitively, that international exposure has induced greater capital-tax cuts from the left. Clark and colleagues (footnote 33) are more pessimistic. Even though they allow conditionality on various combinations of central-bank autonomy, exchange-rate regimes, and capital mobility, they can unearth little evidence of partisan monetary or fiscal policy, especially any simple relationship between left governments and budget deficits. As the above survey shows, many now share some of this skepticism (see also Alesina & Perotti 1995a,b, Hahm 1996, Hahm et al. 1996, Ross 1997, Boix 2000).

In general, the U.S. and comparative evidence most strongly supports partisan effects on the size of government, in terms of public employment, revenue, or spending. It also moderately supports partisan distinctions in some specific policy areas, namely social and welfare, tax-structure, and monetary policy. The evidence offers considerably less support for naive views of the left (right) as unconditional deficit (surplus) producers. In all cases, and perhaps especially in monetary and fiscal-deficit policies, the evidence seems to suggest that partisan governments' recourse to these policies depends heavily on their international and domestic political-economic institutional, structural, and strategic context. (See Schmidt 1997 for an early, partial review.)

Rational, Prospective Citizens

ECONOMIC POLICY AND OUTCOME CYCLES   In contrast to electoral cycles, no particular empirical puzzle motivated the introduction of rational expectations into partisan theory. As shown above, the evidence was solid for partisan cycles in real and nominal outcomes and sufficient if not unequivocal for some policy cycles that could produce those outcomes. Alesina's (1987, 1988) seminal "rational partisan theory" filled more-pressing theoretical needs, providing a framework logically coherent with modern rational-expectations economics, the central tenet of which is that fully expected macroeconomic policies, such as those assumed by traditional electoral or partisan policy-cycle models, are ineffective.

Alesina & Rosenthal (1995) and Alesina et al. (1997) collect and advance their 15 years of research (footnote 8) on the effects of democratic politics, i.e., primarily of central-government elections and partisanship, on macroeconomic policies and performance. These books examine "how the timing of elections . . . [and] the ideological orientation of governments . . . influence unemployment, economic growth, inflation, and various monetary and fiscal policy instruments" (Alesina et al. 1997, p. 1) in developed capitalist democracies. Alesina and colleagues contrast (*a*) "opportunistic" models of electoral cycles, in which politicians are motivated primarily by the desire to retain office and care little about policies or outcomes per se, with (*b*) models of partisan cycles, in which politicians do care about policies and outcomes and exhibit strong partisan ideological differences. (They recognize, of course, the possibility that politicians care about both.) Within each of these types, they distinguish between (*a*) first-generation models, which relied on stable, exploitable Phillips curves and relatively naive voters with nonrational expectations, and (*b*) subsequent iterations, which emphasize the rational expectations of all economic and political actors.

Alesina and colleagues have examined aggregate political and economic data over the postwar period from the United States separately and from many OECD countries together (including the United States). They conclude that the evidence remarkably consistently favors the later, rational-expectations models; that it indicates strong partisan effects but few discernible election-year effects on macroeconomic outcomes; and that it suggests both election and partisan effects on macroeconomic policies. Subsidiarily, they find that partisan policy and outcome effects are clearer in two-party/bloc than in multi-party/bloc systems; that governments in two-party/bloc systems adjust fiscally to deficit-inducing shocks more quickly than irregularly alternating coalition governments do; and that the net economic benefits of credibly delegating monetary authority to conservative policy makers (e.g., central-bank independence) are larger than would be expected in the absence of electoral and partisan policy-making cycles. The empirical case, however, may be less unambiguous than they claim.

In Chapters 2 and 3, Alesina et al. (1997) summarize the rational-expectations (RE) and non-RE versions of electoral- and partisan-cycle theories. In non-RE electoral theory, policy makers control policies that can exploit a stable Phillips curve, and voters naively and myopically reward incumbents who preside over strong economies (high growth, low inflation and unemployment). Policy makers thus regularly attempt to time their use of fiscal and monetary policies to exploit the delay between expansionary policies and inflationary consequences to secure high growth and low unemployment and inflation before elections, with a post-election inflationary effect. In RE versions, Phillips curves and voters are less exploitable. Instead, policy makers achieve similar electoral effects by exploiting (*a*) differences in the timing with which various policies become clear to rational voters and (*b*) private information on their own competence (e.g., their ability to provide more public goods at less tax cost). If competence is random but policy-maker specific and persistent over time, voters will reelect incumbents who have recently shown competence. If voters can see some the benefits of some public policies before they can evaluate their full costs, then incumbents will try to signal or feign competence by providing more such public goods at lower taxes before elections, delaying the costs (inflation, other tax increases, or reduced spending) until after elections, when the relevant information will reach voters.

The implications of RE and non-RE opportunistic theory are similar, except that voter rationality will limit the size, regularity, or duration of electoral cycles in the RE version relative to non-RE version. In non-RE partisan theory, left policy makers target higher growth and lower unemployment and tolerate higher inflation than those of the right, who prefer the opposite. With exploitable Phillips curves, policy makers use their policy control to shift economic outcomes in the desired direction during their term. In RE partisan theory, only unexpected monetary and fiscal policy can create such real-economic effects, so when left (right) governments are elected, to the degree this was not completely foreseen, growth, employment, and inflation rise (fall). However, as time elapses, new economic actors can agree to new price and wage contracts expecting the higher (lower) inflation, so growth and employment return to their natural rates, while inflation remains higher (lower). Thus, Alesina et al. (1997) claim that RE and non-RE versions of partisan theory differ primarily in whether the real effects of partisan shifts in government persist or fade over the term of the government.

In an interesting political extension, Alesina & Rosenthal (1995) show how U.S. voters can leverage the division of policy control between presidents and Congress to achieve actual policies intermediate between the two parties' ideals. In on-year elections, voters can only base their balancing on expected presidential winners and congressional medians. In off-year elections, with presidential uncertainty resolved, they can balance with congressional votes more effectively, inducing the oft-noted midterm congressional losses of the president's party.

In seasonally adjusted, quarterly U.S. data on macroeconomic outcomes from 1947 through 1993, Alesina et al. (1997) find that an indicator equal to 1 (–1) in the first few quarters[36] of Republican (Democratic) administrations, and 0 after, empirically dominates a traditional indicator equal to 1 (–1) over whole administrations. They interpret the former specification as representing the shorter-term real effects in the RE model of the unexpected component of post-election policy. Inflation, contrarily, is permanently higher under left than under right governments in both the RE and non-RE models, and the data support that too. The empirical

---

[36]They report that results for 6 quarters versus 4 and 8 quarters differ little. The indicators are lagged 1 quarter for growth and 2 quarters for unemployment to reflect delays in outcome responses to policies.

dominance of the short-term dummy seems indisputable; yet the strong conclusion for RE models on this basis carries caveats.

First, the substantive difference in their reported results is not great (see Franzese 2000). Second, more important, rational expectations are not the only explanation for the shorter duration of partisan effects. As Alesina et al. (1997, p. 62) note themselves,

> Democratic administrations, which are expansionary in the first half, observe by midterm a significant increase in the inflation rate. Because a high inflation rate may become a significant electoral liability, Democratic administrations contract the economy so that by the election year one observes a growth slowdown and a reduction in the inflation rate. Conversely, Republican administrations that had anti-inflationary recessions in their first half pursue low inflation and accelerating growth in the second half, a combination that may give them an electoral benefit.

In either RE or non-RE models, the described policy pattern, which would result from the midterm balancing that they predict for example, would yield the shorter-term outcome pattern. "Honeymoon effects," the historically greater ability of administrations to enact policy changes in their first few months than later, would also produce this pattern under either theory. So would any diminishing returns from stimulation and anti-inflation policies. Third, and worst for RE partisan theories, Alesina et al. (1997, p. 87) report substantively and statistically stronger real-growth partisan cycles before 1972, the Bretton Woods (fixed exchange-rate) era, than after; yet they also find that the inflation differences across right and left administrations emerged only after 1972 (p. 90). Since RE partisan theory holds that the inflation surprises induced by elections cause the short-term real partisan cycles, this is suspicious.

Meanwhile, they report little to no evidence of low unemployment ($\tilde{t} \approx 1.15$) or higher growth (wrong sign, $\tilde{t} \approx -.58$) before elections or of higher inflation after elections ($\tilde{t} \approx +.31$). Unfortunately, they do not report results with controls for real-supply shocks, nor do they attempt to distinguish pre– from post–Bretton Woods eras, as they did for the partisan theories. As noted above, Clark and colleagues (footnote 33) find stronger electoral outcome cycles with these refinements, and Alesina and colleagues (footnote 8) themselves find stronger post-electoral inflation cycles in such studies, as do several others who allow such conditional inflation cycles (see below). Seasonally adjusted data are also somewhat problematic in the United States, since the occurrence of congressional elections every other November and presidential elections every fourth November could reduce the size of U.S. electoral effects by 25% to 50% (depending on adjustment method).

In U.S. policy, Alesina et al. (1997) explore money growth, nominal-interest rates, budget deficits, and transfers. They find weak evidence of partisan differences in money growth ($\tilde{t} \approx 1.1$–1.2), though stronger in a 1949–1982 sample ($\tilde{t} \approx$ 1.8–2.4), and stronger evidence of partisan differences in nominal-interest rates

($\tilde{t} \approx 2.2$–3.3).[37] They again find little sign of pre-electoral effects on monetary policy ($t < 0.5$ in all cases). However, they do not report differences by exchange-rate regime and, oddly, they lag the partisan indicator 2 quarters. The latter seems problematic because they assume real effects to lag 1–2 quarters and to arise from the gap between expected and actual nominal outcomes or policies. Empirically, the real effect emerges *before* monetary-policy or inflation changes, suggestive of Drazen's (2001) active-fiscal/passive-monetary cycles (see also Beck 1982c, 1987; Berger & Woitek 1987, 2002).[38] Furthermore, if Bretton Woods dampened partisan differences in monetary policy, as their and others' results suggest, then their stronger 1949–1982 (than post 1982) monetary-policy results indicate a narrow window of distinct partisan U.S. monetary policy, only or primarily during 1973–1982. Finally, Alesina et al. (1997) find little pre-electoral effect on deficits ($\tilde{t} \approx .3$) or transfers ($\tilde{t} \approx .4$–.7), and little partisan effect on transfers ($\tilde{t} \approx .7$), although these reduce data to fiscal years rather than quarters and ignores post-electoral effects. However, they do find statistically significant effects of right administrations in increasing deficits ($\tilde{t} \approx 2.1$).[39]

Alesina et al. (1997, chs. 2 and 3; see also footnote 8) clearly establish that the real effects of partisan U.S. administrations follow a short-term pattern, but the RE explanation for that pattern is less fully established by this evidence than the authors claim. First, little substantive difference emerges in the estimated effects. Second, many other explanations for short-term patterns are at least as consistent with evidence and intuition (including at least one of their own). Third, based on Alesina et al.'s own evidence, the monetary- and fiscal-policy pattern, especially across pre– and post–Bretton Woods samples, cannot explain the outcome pattern within the RE framework. Likewise, the lack of evidence for either outcome or policy effects of U.S. elections is weakened by the failure to consider exchange-rate regimes, by the seasonal adjustment of the outcome data, and by the complete ignoring of congressional elections (fiscally, Congress is at least as influential as the president). Moreover, others have shown (see above) that electoral effects occur when incumbents are willing to risk being caught at such cynical maneuvering, i.e., when elections are expected to be close; and that electoral effects occur immediately before as well as after elections. The latter could

---

[37]This difference may reflect higher risk premia for left administrations, rather than a policy-tool choice.

[38]Even ignoring the timing issues, the Phillips-curve slopes needed to produce the estimated partisan real cycles from the estimated monetary surprises are larger than many believe likely (gratitude to J. Londregan for this insight).

[39]This last apparently stems solely from the Reagan and Bush I administrations, regarding which the authors point to theories that predict right governments will increase debt to reduce future left governments' fiscal maneuverability. Early empirical indications for such theories are not promising, though. Franzese (2002a) finds statistically significantly the opposite of what those theories predict.

reflect continuing differences between calendar-year-measured electoral data and fiscal-year-measured economic data, or policy-implementation momentum, or the impact of challengers, whom both RE and non-RE opportunistic theories ignore (Franzese 2002a). Thus, the absence of electoral-cycle findings likely reflects the inadequacies of the political theory underlying these empirical versions of the broader theoretical models as much as it reflects any actual absence of electoral effects.

Alesina et al. (1997, ch. 5) also consider that RE partisan theory predicts partisan real-outcome effects to be proportional to the surprise of the election outcome. (This point was originally explored empirically in an unpublished paper by Hibbs, Carlsen, and Pedersen, which eventually became Carlsen & Pedersen 1999.) Cleverly applying option-pricing theory to measure the electoral surprise, Alesina et al. find that measure to correlate with unemployment in monthly U.S. data, most strongly when using 24- to 36-month-long surprise measures ($\tilde{t} \approx 3.5$–3.8). They consider this correlation conclusive support for their theory, but again, one may remain agnostic. First, the longer-duration finding further diminishes the substantive difference between RE and non-RE versions. Second, they test these surprise measures only against their absence—i.e., the alternative hypothesis is zero partisan effect—rather than exploring whether the surprise measurement improves on the simple indicator. Moreover, the separate results reported for the surprise measure and for the permanent-partisan-effect measure say little about which dominates because the shift to monthly data for the former triples the sample and so would yield higher t statistics in many circumstances. Third, the theory actually states that the degree of electoral surprise multiplied by the expected difference in inflation between incumbent and challenger produces the real effects. The empirical model implicitly assumes that difference to be equal in all U.S. elections. This is false, of course, and produces biased estimates if, for example, the probability of victory for the left or right relates to the ideological distance between them, which it would in any reasonable model (including, e.g., Alesina & Rosenthal 1995). The direction of the bias is hard to predict, and the small number of presidential elections in the sample suggests that the impact on estimated results could have been large. Poole (http://k7moa.gsia.cmu.edu/default.htm) offers data from congressional voting records of most presidential candidates, which one could use to derive the requisite incumbent-challenger distance measures. Fourth, the complications noted above—e.g., the missing policy links behind the observed outcome cycles and the effects of congressional influence and exchange regime—also plague this estimation. The results are perhaps supportive but warrant more-cautious conclusions.

Alesina et al. then (1997, ch. 6 and 7) return to the dummy-variable specification to explore partisan and electoral cycles in outcomes and monetary and fiscal-budget policies in a broader sample of OECD democracies. They again find no evidence of pre-electoral growth or unemployment effects, although now some post-electoral inflation effects emerge, and again they find that shorter-term partisan cycles dominate longer-term ones.[40] They also find the strongest partisan effects in two-party/bloc countries, as is intuitive in any partisan model (see, e.g., Powell 1982, Alt 1985), as well as some indication of pre-electoral tax manipulation and weaker evidence of pre-electoral spending manipulation. Most reasons for cautious interpretation mentioned above recur here, plus some new ones. For example, Alesina et al. (1997, p. 196) find no significant partisan effects on real interest rates, which implies that real effects of partisan monetary-policy differences must originate in wage rigidity and differences between expected and actual inflation. Yet, partisan inflation differences are statistically weak and are concentrated in a post–Bretton Woods/pre–European Monetary Union window, whereas partisan real-outcome differences are not. Policy effects consistent with producing RE partisan cycles again do not emerge whereas short-term real partisan cycles do, so the source of the latter remains in doubt.

Next, Alesina et al. (1997, ch. 8) extend the standard theory of how central bank "independence" (CBI), i.e., autonomy plus conservatism, reduces the inflation biases of discretionary monetary-policy control but raises output variation by sacrificing the use of monetary-stabilization policies. They show that, since CBI also mitigates partisan monetary cycles, which are destabilizing, the theoretically expected correlation of CBI and output variability is ambiguous. They conclude that CBI should lower inflation, at no on-average real costs, as usual in the standard model, but with less output-variability cost than typically simplified versions of that model predict. Here, though, they offer no evidence to support their claim that the way CBI reduces electoral and partisan variance in monetary policy explains the lack of CBI correlation with output variability. The cited evidence for the lack of real effects of CBI emerges from mere cross-sectional correlations of postwar-average real outcomes with postwar-average CBI in 18–21 OECD countries. Insignificance of simple correlations in such samples hardly establish that the true effects are zero in all contexts.

Most important, strong theoretical and empirical challenges to the CBI model from which this claim derives have recently emerged. First, the political authorities who might delegate monetary policy to conservative agents also dislike inflation. If the governments also control structural-reform policies that have real benefits, which would lower discretionary inflation biases, then delegation to conservative monetary agents diminishes the incentives of the political principals to undertake such structural reforms and thus has real RE-equilibrium effects on average. Second, the standard model inconsistently assumes policy makers dislike inflation although no other economic actor does. If any sizable private actor also dislikes

---

[40]Alesina & Roubini (1992), following a similar procedure but estimating the models country by country, find seven coutries favorable to RE partisan theory (the United States, Australia, Denmark, Germany, France, New Zealand, and the United Kingdom); seven others have insignificantly correct sign; and two (Canada and Italy) show no significant coefficients in any regressions.

inflation, then CBI has real effects in equilibrium. Third, CBI alters the real- and relative-wage effects of nominal-wage increases differently; and fourth, like-wise, the effect of CBI on optimal nominal settlements differs across traded and public sectors. Either of these differences will induce on-average real effects of CBI. Fifth, if CBI affects domestic- and import-price inflation differently, this is a relative-price and therefore real-equilibrium effect. Franzese (2002c) reviews these emerging critiques, most of which indicate that CBI's real effects vary with labor-market institutional structure. The available data, queried in a way that allows the real effects of CBI to vary with institutional structure, supports such critiques. Postwar-average cross sections would miss this evidence (Franzese 2002c).

Last, Alesina et al. (1997) explore the effects of single-party versus coalition governments and of government partisanship on public debt. They find that coalition governments delay fiscal stabilization, whereas single-party governments adjust more quickly but produce sharper partisan fiscal cycles (see also, e.g., Powell 1982, Alt 1985, Roubini & Sachs 1989, Grilli et al. 1991). Thus, they find a trade-off between too little action with low variability and too much action with high variability. These results bring few caveats, except that the postwar OECD data also support many of the other (mostly noncompeting) political-economic explanations of public-debt evolution in developed democracies that Alesina et al. dismiss more lightly here. Alesina & Perotti (1995b) review these theories; Franzese (2002b, ch. 3) offers and empirical exploration.

In sum, Alesina and colleagues' (footnote 8) rational partisan theory and associated empirical work demonstrates important partisan effects on macroeconomic policies and outcomes. If it leaves the mechanisms and explanation for the form of these effects inconclusive, political economists may take that as an exciting challenge. Even electoral-cycle theory, which emerges scathed, retains cause for continued research. Alesina and colleagues (footnote 8) set the stage for political scientists to revisit these venerable theories. Rational-expectations (RE) revolutions rekindled economists' interest in political cycles and advanced the field greatly, but parallel advances in political theory were relatively neglected. Sadly, since Tufte and Hibbs, many political scientists seem to have thought the political side of electoral and partisan cycles resolved with only the incorporation of those RE advances remaining, which is false. For instance, policy makers have many policies at their disposal; they are differently constrained in the use of those policies by, for example, international (e.g., exchange-rate) and domestic (e.g., government-structure) institutions, and those policies are differently effective under these and other institutions (e.g., labor-market institutions, alternative configurations of capital mobility and exchange-rate fixity). Political scientists can, should, and are starting to offer further insights on what policies incumbents will manipulate for electoral and partisan purposes under what conditions. These early efforts are reviewed below, but first, let us consider other contributions to RE partisan theory.

Further Discussion of Partisan Cycles

Other empirical studies of RE partisan theory report more-mixed results. Sheffrin (1989), for example, finds signs of U.S. monetary cycles, but not significantly consistent with RE partisan theory in the United States or elsewhere. Klein (1996) estimates the duration of economic cycles from 100+ years of U.S. data and finds certain political events associated with ends of slumps and booms, consistent with, but not directly testing, RE partisan theory. Carlsen (1999) gauges nominal rigidities and electoral surprises, whose combined magnitude should track that of RE partisan cycles, and compares such measures directly with those analogously derived from Hibbs' partisan theory; the results are weakly positive for U.S. inflation cycles, supporting both versions. Carlsen (1998), though, finds negatively for U.S. real outcomes, and Carlsen & Pedersen (1999) report mixed results when comparing RE with classic partisan cycles. They find clear support for RE partisan cycles in the United Kingdom and some support in Canada and Australia, but U.S. data support standard partisan theory, and results in Sweden and Germany are inconclusive. Finally, Faust & Irons (1999) note that, whereas political econometricians routinely find presumed monetary-driven partisan and/or electoral cycles, macroeconometricians continue to debate the size, timing, and existence of monetary effects. Faust & Irons ask, therefore, whether (*a*) political-cycle models mis-specify and so mislead or (*b*) their results might indicate that elections and partisan shifts offer valid exogenous instruments for estimating monetary-policy real effects. They confirm Alesina and colleagues' (footnote 8) "distinctive first two years" result but find that it persists even when the analysis controls for partisan monetary policies, economic conditions, and other political effects. This finding suggests that perhaps election-induced monetary surprises do not cause the short-term nature of the cycle.

Others stress more-theoretical limitations in basic rational partisan theory. From the start, Rogoff (1988) questions why, if elections have such sizable real effects, bargainers could not simply defer signing contracts until after elections or sign election-outcome-conditional contracts. In fact, Garfinkel & Glazer (1994) find two-year or shorter contracts do exhibit post-electoral kyphosis in the United States. This contracting pattern suggests bargainers perceive sufficient electoral economic uncertainty to merit shifting contract schedules, but the bargainers' endogenous reaction that produces the contracting pattern also mutes the real cycles that electoral surprises in monetary policy can induce. Moreover, Ellis & Thoma (1991b) note that, because parliamentary governments may change at any time, not just at elections, partisan surprises are more continuous and irregular in parliamentary democracies. Ellis & Thoma (1995) find current-account, real-exchange-rate, and terms-of-trade cycles that support their model of open-economy parliamentary democracies. This could reflect cycles in international-oriented policies directly, but certain combinations of domestic-oriented monetary and fiscal policies could also generate these effects indirectly. Heckelman (2001) further develops a similar model wherein rational economic agents face uncertainty regarding the timing of elections and the party that will emerge victorious should an election occur. This continual electoral uncertainty also has real economic effects, but the size and direction of those effects depend on (*a*) which party holds power in the current and previous period, (*b*) time elapsed since the last election, and (*c*) party popularity. Here, left governments spur (and right governments dampen) real output throughout their electoral term, and these partisan differences increase until the next election. Adolph (2001) shows how strategic partisan government responses to conservative central bankers (monetary policy makers) and wage/price bargainers induce permanent partisan effects even in RE models. The mechanism operates through public-policy side payments that governments can offer bargainers to sway their settlements, depending on the central banker's conservatism. Drazen (2001), as noted above, questions the monetary-policy mechanism in RE partisan theory, showing how an active-fiscal/passive-monetary (AFPM) model can produce, with fully rational and prospective actors, policy and outcome cycles more consistent with the pattern of evidence sketched above.

In partisan cycles, as in electoral cycles, the incentives for, capacity for, and effects of "partisaneering" should vary predictably from policy to policy and across domestic and international, political-economic, institutional, structural, and strategic contexts.

CONDITIONAL ELECTORAL AND PARTISAN CYCLES IN ECONOMIC POLICIES AND OUTCOMES

To some significant degree in all modern democracies at all times, candidates compete in elections and voters evaluate them in partisan economic terms. Thus, partisan, elected policy makers have strong incentives to enact partisan and electorally motivated policies, aiming to produce outcomes that will buy votes and curry favor from their constituencies. Therefore, electoral and partisan cycles in policies and outcomes should be ubiquitous features of democratic policy making. As discovered throughout this review, however, electoral and partisan cycles in policies and outcomes tend to generate greatest theoretical interest and insight and to receive strongest empirical support when researchers recognize their context conditionality. This concluding section offers an overview of the issues surrounding such conditional electoral and partisan cycles.

We begin by parsing my statement that the incentives for, capacity for, and effects of electioneering or partisaneering should vary predictably from policy to policy across "domestic and international, political-economic, institutional, structural, and strategic contexts."

First, incentives to electioneer or partisaneer (Tufte's "motive") may vary predictably from policy to policy across domestic political institutional contexts. Some policies or outcomes can purchase votes or curry partisan favor more effectively than others, and how these policies or outcomes rank in such efficacy may vary with political-economic institutions, interest structures, and strategic context. Recall our Ramsey Rule that, subject to boundary conditions, partisan incumbents will use all effective instruments in proportion to their relative efficacy. This Ramsey Rule implies cycles of varying magnitude and regularity in all policies cum outcomes, as well as cycles in policy composition (e.g., Chang 2001) and outcome mixes (e.g., Tufte 1978). For example, we discovered above that incumbents seem more prone to manipulate direct transfers than macroeconomic policies, at least for electoral purposes, and perhaps more prone to manipulate the timing of policy implementation than policies themselves. Coalitions of incumbents may find it easier to influence timing than to change policy if the collective-action problems (e.g., Goodhart 2000) they must overcome to effect a timing change do not outweigh the veto-actor problems (e.g., Franzese 2002a, Tsebelis 2002) they must overcome to change policy. Moreover, where political-institutional systems produce unified, strong single-party governments (e.g., India, Japan, and perhaps the United Kingdom), the manipulation of election timing seems more accessible and effective than the manipulation of policies or of their timing (compare Thompson & Zuck 1983; Ito & Park 1988; Ito 1990; Alesina et al. 1993a; Chowdhury 1993; and Smith 1996, 2000). Likewise, general-interest redistributive policies such as transfers may better serve partisan and electoral goals in multi-member-district systems, but special-interest distributive policies such as public works might better serve those interests in single-member-district systems (see, e.g., Persson & Tabellini 2000, Chang 2001). Similarly, incentives to electioneer per se, and perhaps relative to the incentive to partisaneer (Schneider & Frey 1988), vary with features of strategic context, such as the expected closeness of elections (Wright 1974, Tufte 1978, Frey & Schneider 1978a,b, Golden & Poterba 1980, Schultz 1995, Price 1998). Any institutional, structural, or strategic conditions that reduce incumbents' effective electoral accountability (see, e.g., Powell & Whitten 1993) will also mute their incentives to manipulate (e.g., Shi & Svensson 2001). Electioneering and partisaneering incentives may also vary across elections, depending on the share of policy-making power at stake for incumbents and their allies (Tufte 1978). All democratic systems divide policy making among multiple elected (and nonelected, bureaucratic) actors. Thus, democratic systems that concentrate elections of important policy makers chronologically (e.g., Westminsterian systems) should induce sharper electoral and partisan cycles than systems that diffuse them (Powell 1982, Alt 1985, Goodhart 2000, Franzese 2002a). Scholars might also fruitfully explore conditionality upon interest structures or combinations of interest structures and the strategic context of such variation in electoral and partisan incentives. Hicks & Swank (1992), for example, find that policies depend on incumbent and opposition partisanship and strength. Franzese (2002a) also finds strategic-context-conditional partisan fiscal policies. Specifically, only the more electorally insecure right (left) run surpluses (deficits) that accord with naive views of partisan fiscal policies, and the fairly secure right (left) governments run deficits (surpluses). These results oppose one interesting strategic-debt theory

(Persson & Svensson 1989) and are orthogonal to another (Alesina & Tabellini 1990, Tabellini & Alesina 1990), but perhaps support a third (Aghion & Bolton 1990).

Without claiming that the above exhausts possible systematically conditional arguments regarding varying incentives, we proceed to consider variation in policy makers' abilities to manipulate policies or outcomes for electoral or partisan purposes. As reviewed above, equilibrium models of political cycles emphasize the severe limitations rational expectations imposes on affecting macroeconomic outcomes, especially real outcomes. To determine characteristics of political-economic environments that induce more forward-looking and better-informed citizens, therefore, suggests one possibility for systematic conditional argumentation, although probably a hard one to implement. Other central issues, better explored in the literature, surround the allocation of policy-making control across multiple actors and internal and external constraints on policy maneuverability. For example, Blais et al. (1993, 1996) show that prior accumulated debt limits partisan fiscal-policy maneuverability; Acosta & Coppedge (2001) show that degrees of unified incumbent power, as gauged by government seat-share and party discipline, augment maneuverability; and Corsetti & Roubini (1997) show that the private or public ability to borrow abroad likewise magnifies political deficit biases. Tsebelis (2002), meanwhile, elaborates how multiple veto-player policy makers with diverse preferences inherently limit policy maneuverability in general. In different ways, Alt (1985) and Franzese (2002a) explore the implications of such logic for fiscal policies under coalitional and divided governments (see also Roubini & Sachs 1989, Grilli et al. 1991, Alesina & Perotti 1996, Perotti & Kontopoulos 1998). Crucial here is that veto players do not cause policy (e.g., debt or spending) per se but rather retard its adjustment rate.[41] Beyond hysteresis, incumbent cohesion and strength, access to external resources, and veto-actor constraints, incumbents' abilities to manipulate policies hinge also on various delegation, agency, and bargaining issues in "multiple hands on the wheel" scenarios of shared or constrained policy control.[42] In monetary policy especially, many

---

[41]Methodologically, therefore, veto-actor measures should enter policy equations multiplicatively with adjustment parameters (e.g., lagged dependent variables), not linear-additively (see Franzese 2002a, ch. 3). That more veto players retard adjustment rates is also the logical contrapositive of Powell's (1982) argument, and the Alesina et al. (1997) evidence, that wholesale alternation political systems tend to act too much too often.

[42]Franzese (1999, 2002b) offers a useful empirical formulation for such scenarios, including probably all principal-agent relations. In abstract, specify the agent's policy-reaction function, $g(X)$, the principal's, $f(Z)$, and some function, $1 \geq h(I) \geq 0$, reflecting the theoretical arguments. These arguments will often stress institutional, structural, strategic contexts that determine the costs (monitoring, enforcement, opportunity, etc.) that the principal must pay to induce the agent to follow $f(Z)$ instead of $g(X)$. Then, in most strategic models, equilibrium policy will be $y = h(I) \cdot g(X) + \{1 - h(I)\} \cdot f(Z)$, which will be empirically estimable by nonlinear least-squares or maximum likelihood for sufficiently distinct I, X, and Z.

have considered whether and how central-bank autonomy, fixed exchange rates, and/or capital mobility may hinder domestic policy-maker autonomy or otherwise dilute the expression of electoral or partisan cycles in policies or outcomes (e.g., Lohmann 1992, 1997; Jonsson 1995; Simmons 1996; Boix 1998, 2000; Garrett 1998; Franzese 1999, 2002b; Oatley 1999; Way 2000; Clark and colleagues, see footnote 33). Hallerberg & von Hagen (1998) consider the similar implications of fiscal-policy contracts or delegation. These empirical models of electoral and partisan policy and outcome cycles that recognize such institutional and structural constraints on policy-maker maneuverability typically produce strong results. Franzese (1999), for example, finds not only that central-bank autonomy mitigates electoral or partisan inflation cycles (as do, e.g., Jonsson 1995, Simmons 1996, and Way 2000) but also that it mitigates in equal proportion the inflation effect of all other political-economic factors to which elected governments would respond but conservative central banks would not. Notice, finally, that policy-maker abilities to manipulate different policies will be differently constrained or abetted by the above considerations; thus (to invoke the Ramsey Rule again), one can expect that (*a*) electioneering and partisaneering instrument choice will vary accordingly and (*b*) policy- and outcome-compositional as well as policy- and outcome-level cycles will occur.

Again, the above hardly exhausts the set of systematic ways domestic and international political-economic institutions, interest structures, and strategic contexts may condition policy-maker abilities to partisan-electioneer. However, let us proceed to consider the systematic variation in effectiveness across policies and contexts. From the earliest political-cycle models (e.g., Tufte 1978, Hibbs 1977), scholars recognized that especially macroeconomic policies and outcomes can have varying efficacy as electioneering and partisaneering tools under differing international and domestic political-economic contexts. However, until recently, analysis was limited to comments that, for example, Phillips-curve slopes can vary and should induce varying magnitudes of electoral and partisan policy and outcome cycles if they do. Recently, scholars have considered how the conduct and effects of electoral and partisan policies might be conditioned by (*a*) labor-market organization and corporatism and (*b*) various combinations of international exposure, capital mobility, and exchange-rate fixity.

Alvarez et al. (1991) argue and show empirically that partisan governments produce differing outcome cycles depending on labor-organizational structure (i.e., corporatism), although they later (Beck et al. 1993) weaken some empirical claims. Simmons & Clark (1997), however, find fewer signs that corporatism modifies left-government relations to any of 24 economic policies. In analyzing variation in fiscal (deficits) and monetary (interest-rate) policies during 1965–1995 across OECD democracies, Boix (2000) considers partisan cycles potentially conditional on both labor-market and international institutional structures. He shows that parties have affected, separately and in interaction with labor-market organization, the conduct of fiscal and monetary policies. Still, their impact has varied over time, mostly as a function of financial liberalization and the exchange-rate regime.[43] Garrett (1998) also considers international constraints on partisan policies. He argues first that some policies are more market-subverting and others more market-supporting and second, with some empirical support, that international exposure constrains market-subverting more than market-supporting policies and may even foster the latter. In short, policies have differing effects, and thus are differentially used, under differing international institutional-structural conditions. Other authors stress that the effects of partisan or electoral fiscal, monetary, and other policies may depend on central-bank independence (CBI) (e.g., Cusack 2000) or on the combination of CBI and labor-market structure (e.g., Adolph 2001).

Clark and colleagues (see footnote 33) offer the fullest and most sustained studies of context-conditional electoral and partisan cycles. Clark et al. (1998) find that CBI and loss of national policy autonomy (i.e., fixed exchange and mobile capital) each constrain the occurrence of electoral real-outcome cycles in OECD countries, finding evidence for cycles only when neither constraint is present. Clark & Hallerberg (2000) argue that although Clark et al.'s (1998) constraints bind monetary policy, they do not constrain fiscal policy. They show that, when capital is mobile, electoral cycles in fiscal policy tend to occur only with fixed exchange rates (with or without an independent central bank). They also show that electoral cycles in monetary supply are likely only if neither of Clark et al.'s (1998)

---

[43]Monetary policy was stable and relatively similar across countries in the 1960s; it loosened considerably after the first oil shock but quickly tightened again in the early 1980s. Real interest rates peaked in the mid-1980s and then declined slowly. Fiscal policies became expansionary in the 1970s, but most OECD countries trended toward fiscal consolidation afterward. Within these overall trends, conservative governments generally pursued more restrictive macroeconomic policies, keeping real interest rates above the OECD average and, except for the mid-1970s/early 1980s and the mid-1990s, roughly balanced budgets. Social-democratic cabinets in corporatist countries generally implemented very similar monetary policies to conservative-led countries throughout the past three decades, with fiscal policies as tight as under conservative governments, except in the 1970s. At that time, these countries embraced strongly counter-cyclical budgetary measures to address the oil-shock–induced economic slump. Under socialist administrations in decentralized economies, which were less common before the mid-1970s, both monetary and fiscal policies became sharply expansionary in the 1970s. Keynesian demand management reversed in the 1980s, however. Real interest rates converged to the OECD average by the mid 1980s. Fiscal discipline took much longer to achieve and quickly waned with the recession of the early 1990s. The substantial cross-national variation in the 1970s, when partisan differences were significant, followed by the 1980s' rapid convergence, was rooted in the evolving international economy. Until the early 1980s, widespread capital controls and floating exchange rates provided policy makers considerable autonomy to respond to stagflation. As international financial markets grew exponentially and capital controls lost viability, the socialist-led Keynesian expansions of the 1970s became unfeasible by the mid 1980s.

constraints is present. They also find, as noted above, no support for partisan monetary or fiscal policy cycles, Mundell-Fleming[44] conditional or otherwise (contra, e.g., Oatley 1999). Hallerberg et al. (2001) show that the Clark & Hallerberg (2000) results hold also for post-transition Eastern European economies. Clark's (2002) book re-examines the Clark et al. (1998) data, expecting, from Clark & Hallerberg's (2000) game-theoretic reanalysis, that elections would have zero real effects only with independent central banks and flexible exchange rates (given mobile capital) because (with mobile capital) flexible exchange rates limit fiscal-policy effectiveness and an independent central bank controls monetary policy. Under every other combination of exchange rates and degrees of CBI (given mobile capital), survival-maximizing incumbents retain at least one instrument, so real cycles are likely (see Clark 2002, Table 29). Specifically, following Mundell-Fleming and assuming capital mobility, fixed exchange rates make fiscal policy effective and monetary policy ineffective, and leave independent central banks with few effective countervailing actions. With flexible exchange rates, fiscal policy is ineffective, but if the central-bank is dependent, incumbents can use monetary policy for pre-electoral expansion.[45]

In short, Clark and colleagues (footnote 33) might join in paraphrasing Twain: "Rumors of electoral-cycle theory's demise were greatly exaggerated." Similarly exaggerated, they might add, were rumors of partisan-cycle theory's unassailability. And that, in conclusion, may serve as a spirited call for comparative and international political economists to return to the venerable field of electoral and partisan cycles in economic policies and outcomes, a field rich with opportunities to explore how international and domestic, political and economic institutions, structures, and strategic contexts condition the conduct of democratic politics and policy making.

ACKNOWLEDGMENTS

With deepest gratitude to Jon Hanson for extremely able and helpful research assistance and to Bill Bernhard, Carles Boix, Eric C.C. Chang, Bill Clark, Tom Cusack, Allen Drazen, Mark Hallerberg, David Leblang, Thomas Pluemper, Duane Swank, and Chris Way for comments, suggestions, and other valuable input.

---

[44]The Mundell-Fleming conditions of international-economic theory indicate what combinations of capital mobility and exchange-rate regimes produce fiscal or monetary policy effectiveness.

[45]Clark (2002, ch. 3, 5) tests for partisan cycles in monetary and fiscal policy and macroeconomic outcomes, allowing the expected modifying effects of exchange-rate regime and CBI, and finds them insignificant.

The *Annual Review of Political Science* is online at http://polisci.annualreviews.org

LITERATURE CITED

Acosta AM, Coppedge M. 2001. *Political determinants of fiscal discipline in Latin America, 1979–1998.* Presented at Annu. Meet. Latin Am. Stud. Assoc., Sep. 5–8, Washington, DC

Adolph C. 2001. *Parties, unions, and central banks: an interactive model of unemployment in OECD countries.* Presented at Comp. Polit. Econ. Dev. and Less Dev. Ctries., May 4–5, Yale Univ., New Haven, CT, http://www.people.fas.harvard.edu/~cadolph/Adolph PUCB.pdf

Aghion P, Bolton P. 1990. Government debt and the risk of default: a political economic model of the strategic role of debt. In *Public Debt Management: Theory and Practice*, ed. R Dornbusch, M Draghi, pp. 315–45. Cambridge, UK: Cambridge Univ. Press

Ahmad KV. 1983. An empirical study of politico-economic interaction in the United States. *Rev. Econ. Stat.* 65(1):170–77

Alesina A. 1987. Macroeconomic policy in a two-party system as a repeated game. *Q. J. Econ.* 102:651–78

Alesina A. 1988. Macroeconomics and politics. *Nat. Bur. Econ. Res. Macroecon. Annu.* 3:13–61

Alesina A, Cohen G, Roubini N. 1992. Macroeconomic policies and elections in OECD democracies. *Econ. Polit.* 4(1):1–30

Alesina A, Cohen G, Roubini N. 1993a. Electoral business cycles in industrial democracies. *Eur. J. Polit. Econ.* 23:1–25

Alesina A, Londregan J, Rosenthal H. 1993b. A model of the political economy or the United States. *Am. Polit. Sci. Rev.* 87(1):12–33

Alesina A, Perotti R. 1995a. Fiscal expansions and adjustments in OECD countries. *Econ. Policy* 21:207–18

Alesina A, Perotti R. 1995b. *Political economy of budget deficits.* Int. Monet. Fund Staff Pap. 42

Alesina A, Perotti R. 1996. *Budget deficits and budget institutions.* Nat. Bur. Econ. Res. Work. Pap. 5556

Alesina A, Rosenthal H. 1995. *Partisan Politics, Divided Government, and the Economy.* Cambridge, UK: Cambridge Univ. Press

Alesina A, Roubini N. 1992. Political cycles in OECD economies. *Rev. Econ. Stud.* 59:663–88

Alesina A, Roubini N, Cohen G. 1997. *Political Cycles and the Macroeconomy.* Cambridge, MA: MIT Press

Alesina A, Sachs J. 1988. Political parties and business cycle in the United States. *J. Money Credit Bank.* 20:63–82

Alesina A, Tabellini G. 1990. A positive theory of budget deficits and government debt. *Rev. Econ. Stud.* 57:403–14

Alt JE. 1985. Political parties, world demand, and unemployment: domestic and international sources of economic activity. *Am. Polit. Sci. Rev.* 79(4):1016–40

Alt JE, Chrystal KA. 1983. *Political Economics.* Berkeley: Univ. Calif. Press

Alt JE, Woolley J. 1982. Reaction functions, optimization and politics: modeling the political economy of macroeconomic policy. *Am. J. Polit. Sci.* 26(4):709–40

Alvarez RM, Garrett G, Lange P. 1991. Government partisanship, labor organization, and macroeconomic performance. *Am. Polit. Sci. Rev.* 85:539–56

Ames B. 1987. *Political Survival.* Berkeley: Univ. Calif. Press

Arcelus F, Meltzer A. 1975. The effect of aggregate economic variables on congressional elections. *Am. Polit. Sci. Rev.* 69:1232–39

Balke NS. 1991. Partisanship theory, macroeconomic outcomes, and endogenous elections. *So. Econ. J.* 57:920–35

Bartolini S, Caramani D, Hug S. 1998. *Parties and Party Systems: A Bibliographic Guide to the Literature on Parties and Party Systems in Europe since 1945* (CD-ROM). London, UK: Sage

Beck N. 1982a. Does there exist a political

business cycle? A Box-Tiao analysis. *Public Choice* 38(2):205–12

Beck N. 1982b. Parties, administration, and American macroeconomic outcomes. *Am. Polit. Sci. Rev.* 76(1):83–93

Beck N. 1982c. Presidential influence on the Federal Reserve in the 1970s. *Am. J. Polit. Sci.* 26:415–45

Beck N. 1987. Elections and the Fed: Is there a political monetary cycle? *Am. J. Polit. Sci.* 31:194–216

Beck N, Katz JN, Alvarez RM, Garrett G, Lange P. 1993. Government partisanship, labor organization and macroeconomic performance: a corrigendum. *Am. Polit. Sci. Rev.* 87:945–48

Ben-Porath Y. 1975. The years of plenty and the years of famine—a political business. *Kyklos* 28(2):400–3

Berger H, Woitek U. 1997. Searching for political business cycles in Germany. *Public Choice* 91:179–97

Berger H, Woitek U. 2002. The German political business cycle: money demand rather than monetary policy. *Eur. J. Polit. Econ.* In press

Bernhard W, Leblang D. 1999. Democratic institutions and exchange-rate commitments. *Int. Org.* 53:71–97

Bernhard W, Leblang D. 2002. Democratic processes and political risk: evidence from foreign exchange markets. *Am. J. Polit. Sci.* In press

Blais A, Blake D, Dion S. 1993. Do parties make a difference? Parties and the size of government in liberal democracies. *Am. J. Polit. Sci.* 37(1):40–62

Blais A, Blake D, Dion S. 1996. Do parties make a difference? A reappraisal. *Am. J. Polit. Sci.* 40(2):514–20

Block S. 2001a. Does Africa grow differently? *J. Development Econ.* 65(2):443–67

Block S. 2001b. *Elections, electoral competitiveness, and political budget cycles in developing countries.* Fletcher School of Law and Diplomacy, Tufts Univ. Work. Pap. http://www.bu.edu/econ/ied/neudc/papers/Block-final.pdf

Block S, Ferree K, Singh S. 2001. Institutions, electoral competitiveness, and political business cycles in nascent democracies. Fletcher School of Law and Diplomacy, Tufts Univ. Work Pap., Medford, MA

Bloom H, Price H. 1975. Voter response to short-run economic conditions: the asymmetric effect of prosperity and recession. *Am. Polit. Sci. Rev.* 69:1240–54

Boix C. 1998. *Political Parties, Growth and Equality: Conservative and Social Democratic Economic Strategies in the World Economy.* Cambridge, UK: Cambridge Univ. Press

Boix C. 2000. Partisan governments, the international economy, and macroeconomic policies in OECD countries, 1964–93. *World Polit.* 53:38–73

Borg SG, Castles FG. 1981. The influence of the political right on public income maintenance expenditure and equality. *Polit. Stud.* 29(4):604–21

Brender A. 1999. *The effect of fiscal performance on local government election results in Israel: 1989–98.* Bank Israel Res. Dept. Disc. Pap. 99.04

Brenner MH. 1973. *Mental Illness and the Economy.* Cambridge, MA: Harvard Univ. Press

Brenner MH. 1976. *Estimating the Social Costs of National Economic Policy: Implications for Mental and Physical Health, and Aggression.* Washington, DC: Gov. Print. Off.

Cameron DR. 1978. The expansion of the public economy: a comparative analysis. *Am. J. Polit. Sci.* 72:1243–61

Cargill TF, Hutchinson MM. 1991. Political business cycles with endogenous election timing: evidence from Japan. *Rev. Econ. Stat.* 73:733–39

Carlsen F. 1998. Rational partisan theory: empirical evidence for the United States. *So. Econ. J.* 65:64–82

Carlsen F. 1999. Inflation and elections: theory and evidence for six OECD economies. *Econ. Inq.* 37:120–35

Carlsen F, Pedersen EF. 1999. Rational partisan theory: evidence from seven OECD countries. *Econ. Polit.* 11(1):12–32

Castles FG. 1981. How does politics matter? Structure or agency in the determination of public policy outcomes. *Eur. J. Polit. Res.* 9(2):119–32

Castles FG. 1982. The impact of parties on public expenditure. In *The Impact of Parties*, ed. FG Castles, pp. 21–93. Beverly Hills, CA: Sage

Castles FG. 1986. Social expenditure and the political right: a methodological note. *Eur. J. Polit. Res.* 14:669–76

Castles FG. 1989. Explaining public education expenditure in OECD nations. *Eur. J. Polit. Res.* 17(4):431–48

Castles FG, McKinlay RD. 1979a. Does politics matter? An analysis of the public welfare commitment in advanced democratic states. *Eur. J. Polit. Res.* 7:169–86

Castles FG, McKinlay RD. 1979b. Public welfare provision, Scandinavia and the sheer futility of the sociological approach to politics. *Br. J. Polit. Sci.* 9(2):157–71

Chang ECC. 2001. *Electoral budget cycles under alternative electoral systems.* Presented at Annu. Meet. *Am. Polit. Sci.* Assoc., Aug. 31–Sep. 2, San Francisco, CA

Chappell HW, Havrilesky TM, McGregor RR. 1993. Partisan monetary policies: presidential influence through the power of appointment. *Q. J. Econ.* 108:185–219

Chappell HW, Keech WR. 1988. The unemployment consequences of partisan monetary policy. *So. Econ. J.* 55(1):107–22

Chappell H, Peel D. 1979. On the political theory of the business cycle. *Econ. Lett.* 2:327–32

Chowdhury AR. 1993. Political surfing over economic waves: parliamentary election timing in India. *Am. J. Polit. Sci.* 37(4):1100–18

Chrystal KA, Alt JE. 1981. The criteria for choosing a politico-economic model of the United Kingdom. *Econ. J.* 91:730–36

Clark WR. 2002. *Capitalism Not Globalism: Capital Mobility, Central Bank Independence, and Political Control of the Economy.* Ann Arbor: Univ. Mich. Press

Clark WR, Hallerberg M. 2000. Mobile capital, domestic institutions, and electorally induced monetary and fiscal policy. *Am. Polit. Sci. Rev.* 94(2):323–46

Clark WR, Golder M, Golder S. 2002. *Fiscal policy and the democratic process in the European Union.* Work. Pap., Dep. Polit. Sci., NY Univ. http://homepages.nyu.edu/~mrg217/JEUP3.pdf

Clark WR, Reichert UN, Lomas SL, Parker KL. 1998. International and domestic constraints on political business cycles in OECD economies. *Int. Org.* 52(1):87–120

Corsetti G, Roubini N. 1997. Politically motivated fiscal deficits: policy issues in closed and open economies. *Econ. Polit.* 9:27–54

Cox GW. 1997. *Making Votes Count: Strategic Coordination in the World's Electoral Systems.* Cambridge, UK: Cambridge Univ. Press

Cukierman A, Meltzer A. 1986. A positive theory of discretionary policy, the cost of democratic government, and the benefits of a constitution. *Econ. Inq.* 24:367–88

Cusack T. 1997. Partisan politics and public finance. *Public Choice* 91:375–95

Cusack T. 1999. Partisan politics and fiscal policy. *Comp. Polit. Stud.* 32:464–86

Cusack T. 2000. *Partisanship in the setting and coordination of fiscal and monetary policies.* Presented at IPSA World Congr., Aug. 1–5, Quebec

Cusack T, Notermans T, Rein M. 1989. Political-economic aspects of public employment. *Eur. J. Polit. Res.* 17(4):471–500

Downs A. 1957. *An Economic Theory of Democracy.* New York: Harper-Row

Drazen A. 2000. *Political Economy in Macroeconomics.* Princeton, NJ: Princeton Univ. Press

Drazen A. 2001. The political business cycle after 25 years. *Nat. Bur. Econ. Res. Macroecon. Annu.* 2000

Edwards S. 1993. *The political economy of inflation and stabilization in developing countries.* Nat. Bur. Econ. Res. Work. Pap. 4319

Electoral Studies. 2000. Volume 19, Issues 2–3

Ellis CJ, Thoma MA. 1991a. Causality in political business cycles. *Contemp. Econ. Policy* 9(2):39–49

Ellis CJ, Thoma MA. 1991b. Partisan effects in economies with variable electoral terms. *J. Money Credit Bank.* 23:728–41

Ellis CJ, Thoma MA. 1995. The implications for an open economy of partisan business cycles: theory and evidence. *Eur. J. Polit. Econ.* 11:635–51

Fair R. 1978. The effect of economic events on votes for president. *Rev. Econ. Stat.* 60:159–72

Fair R. 1982. The effect of economic events on votes for president: 1980 results. *Rev. Econ. Stat.* 64:322–25

Fair R. 1988. The effect of economic events on votes for president: 1984 update. *Polit. Behav.* 10:168–79

Faust J, Irons J. 1999. Money, politics, and the post-war business cycle. *J. Monet. Econ.* 43:61–89

Fouda SM. 1997. Political monetary cycles and independence of the central bank in a monetary union: an empirical test for a BEAC Franc Zone member. *J. Afr. Econ.* 6(1):112–31

Franzese RJ. 1999. Partially independent central banks, politically responsive governments, and inflation. *Am. J. Polit. Sci.* 43(3):681–706

Franzese RJ. 2000. Review of Alberto Alesina and Nouriel Roubini with Gerald Cohen, *Political Cycles and the Macroeconomy. J. Policy Analysis Manage.* 19(3):501–9

Franzese RJ. 2002a. *Macroeconomic Policies of Developed Democracies.* Cambridge, UK: Cambridge Univ. Press

Franzese RJ. 2002b. *Multiple hands on the wheel: empirically modeling partial delegation and shared control of monetary policy in the open and institutionalized economy.* Dept. Polit. Sci., Univ. Mich., Ann Arbor. http://www-personal.umich.edu/~franzese/cb.fe.ie.pdf

Franzese RJ. 2002c. Strategic interactions of monetary policymakers and wage/price bargainers: a review with implications for the European common-currency area. *Empirica J. App. Econ. Econ. Policy* 28(1). In press

Frey BS, Schneider F. 1978a. An empirical study of politico-economic interaction in the United States. *Rev. Econ. Stat.* 60:174–83

Frey BS, Schneider F. 1978b. A politico-economic model of the United Kingdom. *Econ. J.* 88:243–53

Frey BS, Schneider F. 1979. An econometric model with an endogenous government sector. *Public Choice* 34(1):29–43

Frieden J, Stein E, eds. 2001. *The Currency Game: Exchange Rate Politics in Latin America.* Baltimore, MD: Johns Hopkins Univ. Press

Gallagher M, Laver M, Mair P. 1995. *Representative Government in Modern Europe.* New York: McGraw-Hill. 2nd ed.

Garfinkel M, Glazer A. 1994. Does electoral uncertainty cause economic fluctuations? *Am. Econ. Rev.* 84:169–73

Garrett G. 1995. Capital mobility, trade, and the domestic politics of economic policy. *Int. Org.* 49:657–87

Garrett G. 1998. *Partisan Politics in the Global Economy.* Cambridge, UK: Cambridge Univ. Press

Gärtner M. 1999. The election cycle in inflation bias. *Eur. J. Polit. Econ.* 15:705–25

Gärtner M. 2000. Political macroeconomics: a survey of recent developments. *J. Econ. Surv.* 14(5):527–61

Golden DG, Poterba JM. 1980. The price of popularity: the political business cycle reexamined. *Am. J. Polit. Sci.* 24(4):696–714

Gonzalez MA. 1999a. *On elections, democracy, and macroeconomic policy cycles.* Work. Pap., Dept. Econ., Princeton Univ.

Gonzalez MA. 1999b. *Political budget cycles and democracy: a multi-country analysis.* Work. Pap., Dept. Econ., Princeton Univ.

Gonzalez MA. 2000. *On elections, democracy, and macroeconomic policy: evidence from Mexico.* Work. Pap., Dept. Econ., Princeton Univ. http://www.stanford.edu/group/sshi/SpringPapers/gonzalez.pdf

Goodhart LM. 2000. *Political Institutions, Elections, and Policy Choices.* PhD thesis, Harvard Univ., Cambridge, MA

Grier KB. 1987. Presidential elections and

Federal Reserve policy: an empirical test. *So. J. Econ.* 54:475–86

Grier KB. 1989. On the existence of a political monetary cycle. *Am. J. Polit. Sci.* 33:376–89

Grier RM, Grier KB. 2000. Political cycles in nontraditional settings: theory and evidence from the case of Mexico. *J. Law Econ.* 43:239–63

Grilli V, Masciandaro D, Tabellini G. 1991. Political and monetary institutions and public financial policies in the industrial countries. *Econ. Policy* 13:342–92

Grossman G, Helpman E. 2001. *Special-Interest Politics*. Cambridge, MA: MIT Press

Hahm SD. 1996. The political economy of deficit spending: a cross comparison of industrialized democracies, 1955–90. *Environ. Plan. C: Gov. and Policy* 14(2):227–50

Hahm SD, Kamlet M, Mowery D. 1996. The political economy of deficit spending in nine industrialized parliamentary democracies: the role of fiscal institutions. *Comp. Polit. Stud.* 29(1):52–77

Hallerberg M. 2002. Veto players and monetary commitment technologies. *Int. Org.* In press

Hallerberg M, Basinger S. 1998. Internationalization and changes in tax policy in OECD nations: the importance of domestic veto players. *Comp. Polit. Stud.* 31(3):321–53

Hallerberg M, von Hagen J. 1998. Electoral institutions and the budget process. In *Democracy, Decentralisation and Deficits in Latin America*, ed. K Fukasaku, R Hausmann, pp. 65–94. Paris: Org. Econ. Coop. and Dev.

Hallerberg M, Vinhas de Souza L, Clark WR. 2002. Monetary and fiscal cycles in EU accession countries. *Eur. Union Polit.* In press

Harrinvirta M, Mattila M. 2001. The hard business of balancing budgets: a study in public finances in seventeen OECD contries. *Br. J. Polit. Sci.* 31(3):497–522

Havrilesky TM. 1987. A partisanship theory of fiscal and monetary regimes. *J. Money Credit Bank.* 19:308–23

Haynes SE, Stone J. 1988. Does the political business cycle dominate U.S. unemployment and inflation? Some new evidence. See Willett 1988, pp. 276–97

Haynes SE, Stone J. 1989. An integrated test for electoral cycles in the US economy. *Rev. Econ. Stat.* 71(3):426–34

Haynes SE, Stone J. 1990. Political models of the business cycle should be revived. *Econ. Inq.* 28:442–65

Haynes SE, Stone J. 1994. Political parties and the variable duration of business cycles. *So. Econ. J.* 60:869–85

Heckelman JC. 2001. Partisan business cycles under variable election dates. *J. Macroecon.* 23:261–75

Heckelman JC, Berument H. 1998. Political business cycles and endogenous elections. *So. Econ. J.* 64:987–1000

Hewitt C. 1977. The effect of political democracy and social democracy on equality in industrial societies: a cross-national comparison. *Am. Sociol. Rev.* 42(3):450–64

Hibbs D. 1977. Political parties and macroeconomic policy. *Am. Polit. Sci. Rev.* 71(4):1467–87

Hibbs D. 1983. Comment on Beck. *Am. Polit. Sci. Rev.* 77(2):447–51

Hibbs D. 1986. Political parties and macroeconomic policies and outcomes in the United States. *Am. Econ. Rev.* 76(1):66–70

Hibbs D. 1987a. *The American Political Economy: Macroeconomics and Electoral Politics*. Cambridge, MA: Harvard Univ. Press

Hibbs D. 1987b. *The Political Economy of Industrial Democracies*. Cambridge, MA: Harvard Univ. Press

Hibbs D. 1992. Partisan theory after fifteen years. *Eur. J. Polit. Econ.* 8:361–73

Hibbs D. 1994. The partisan model and macroeconomic cycles: more theory and evidence from the United States. *Econ. Polit.* 6:1–24

Hicks AM, Swank DH. 1984a. Governmental redistribution in rich democracies. *Policy Stud. J.* 13(2):265–86

Hicks AM, Swank DH. 1984b. On the political economy of welfare expansion: a comparative analysis of 18 advanced capitalist democracies, 1960–1971. *Comp. Polit. Stud.* 17(1):81–119

Hicks AM, Swank DH. 1992. Politics, institutions, and welfare spending in industrialized democracies, 1960–1992. *Am. Polit. Sci. Rev.* 86:658–74

Huber E, Ragin C, Stephens JD. 1993. Social democracy, Christian democracy, constitutional structure and the welfare state. *Am. J. Sociol.* 99(3):711–49

Imbeau L, Petry F, Lamari M. 2001. Left-right party ideology and government policies. *Eur. J. Polit. Res.* 40:1–29

Ito T. 1990. The timing of elections and political business cycles in Japan. *J. Asian Econ.* 1:135–56

Ito T, Park JH. 1988. Political business cycles in the parliamentary system. *Econ. Lett.* 27:233–38

Iversen T. 1999. *Contested Economic Institutions: The Politics of Macroeconomics and Wage Bargaining in Advanced Democracies.* Cambridge, UK: Cambridge Univ. Press

Jonsson G. 1995. Institutions and macroeconomic outcomes—the empirical evidence. *Swed. Econ. Policy Rev.* 2(1):181–212

Kalecki M. 1943. Political aspects of full employment. *Polit. Q.* 7:322–31

Keech W, Pak K. 1989. Electoral cycles and budgetary growth in veterans' benefits programs. *Am. J. Polit. Sci.* 33:901–11

Keech W. 1995. *Economic Politics: The Costs of Democracy.* Cambridge, UK: Cambridge Univ. Press

Khemani S. 2000. *Political cycles in a developing economy: effect of elections in the Indian states.* Work. Pap. World Bank. http://wbln0018.worldbank.org/Research/workpapers.nsf/5ade973899c860868525673100683 4d5/0bd238deeb3b8f1f852569600052bc35/$FILE/wps2454.pdf

Klein MW. 1996. Timing is all: elections and the duration of United States business cycles. *J. Money Credit Bank.* 28:84–101

Kramer G. 1971. Short-term fluctuations in US voting behavior. *Am. Polit. Sci. Rev.* 65:131–43

Krueger A, Turan I. 1993. The politics and economics of Turkish policy reform in the 1980's. In *Political and Economic Interactions in Economic Policy Reform: Evi-*

dence from Eight Countries, ed. R Bates, A Krueger, pp. 333–86. Oxford, UK: Blackwell

Lachler U. 1978. The political business cycle: a complimentary study. *Rev. Econ. Stud.* 45:131–43

Lachler U. 1982. On political business cycles with endogenous election dates. *J. Public Econ.* 17:111–17

Laver M, Shepsle K. 1996. *Making and Breaking Governments: Cabinets and Legislatures in Parliamentary Democracies.* Cambridge, UK: Cambridge Univ. Press

Leblang D. 2002. The political economy of speculative attacks in the developing world. *Int. Stud. Q.* In press

Leblang D, Bernhard W. 2000a. *Political parties and monetary commitments.* Work. Pap., Univ. Ill. and Univ. Colo. http://sobek.colorado.edu/~leblang/parties.pdf

Leblang D, Bernhard W. 2000b. The politics of speculative attacks in industrial democracies. *Int. Org.* 54:291–324

Lewis-Beck M. 1988. *Economics and Elections: The Major Western Democracies.* Ann Arbor: Univ. Mich. Press

Lindbeck A. 1976. Stabilization policy in open economies with endogenous politicians. *Am. Econ. Rev. Pap. Proc.* 66:1–19

Lohmann S. 1992. Optimal commitment in monetary policy: credibility versus flexibility. *Am. Econ. Rev.* 82:273–86

Lohmann S. 1997. Partisan control of the money supply and decentralized appointment powers. *Eur. J. Polit. Econ.* 13:225–46

Lohmann S. 1998. Rationalizing the political business cycle: a workhorse model. *Econ. Polit.* 10:1–17

Lohmann S. 1999. What price accountability? The Lucas Island Model and the politics of monetary policy. *Am. J. Polit. Sci.* 43:396–430

MacRae CD. 1977. A political model of the business cycle. *J. Polit. Econ.* 85(2):239–63

MacRae CD. 1981. On the political business cycle. In *Contemporary Political Economy,* ed. DA Hibbs, H Fassbender, pp. 169–84. Amsterdam: North-Holland

Madsen H. 1980. Electoral outcomes and macroeconomic policies: the Scandinavian cases. In *Models of Political Economy*, ed. P Whitley, pp. 15–46. London, UK: Sage

Maloney H, Smirlock M. 1981. Business cycles and the political process. *So. Econ. J.* 47(2):377–92

Mani A, Mukand S. 2000. *Democracy and visibility: theory and evidence.* Work. Pap., Dept. Econ., Vanderbilt Univ.

McCallum B. 1978. The political business cycle: an empirical test. *So. Econ. J.* 44:504–15

Mosley P. 1976. Towards a satisficing theory of economic policy. *Econ. J.* 86:59–72

Mosley P. 1978. Images of the floating voter, or the "political business cycle" revisited. *Polit. Stud.* 26:375–94

Moyo D. 1999. *The determinants of public savings in developing countries.* Work. Pap., Dept. Econ., Oxford Univ.

Nordhaus W. 1975. The political business cycle. *Rev. Econ. Stud.* 42(1):169–90

Nordhaus W. 1989. Alternative approaches to the political business cycle. *Brookings Pap. Econ. Act.* 2:1–49

Oatley T. 1999. How constraining is capital mobility? The partisan hypothesis in an open economy. *Am. J. Polit. Sci.* 43(4):1003–27

Olson M. 1965. *The Logic of Collective Action.* Cambridge, MA: Harvard Univ. Press

Olson M. 1982. *The Rise and Decline of Nations.* New Haven, CT: Yale Univ. Press

Olters JP. 2001. *Modeling politics with economic tools: a critical survey of the literature.* Int. Monet. Fund Work. Pap. WP/01/10

Paldam M. 1979. Is there an electoral cycle? A comparative study of national accounts. *Scand. J. Econ.* 81(2):323–42

Paldam M. 1981. An essay on the rationality of economic policy: the test case of the election cycle. *Public Choice* 37(2):287–305

Paldam M. 1989. *Politics matters after all: testing Hibbs' theory of partisan cycles.* Aarhus Univ. Work. Pap. http://ideas.uqam.ca/ideas/data/Papers/aahaarhec1989-8.html

Paldam M. 1997. Political business cycles. In *Perspectives in Public Choice: A Handbook*, ed. DC Mueller, pp. 342–70. Cambridge, UK: Cambridge Univ. Press

Perotti R, Kontopoulos Y. 1998. *Fragmented fiscal policy.* Presented at Nat. Bur. Econ. Res.-Zentrum Europäische Integr.forschüng Conf., Bonn. http://www.columbia.edu/~rp41/webfragm.pdf

Persson T. 1999. The size and scope of government: comparative politics with rational politicians. 1998 Alfred Marshall Lecture. *Eur. Econ. Rev.* 43:699–735

Persson T. 2002. Do political institutions shape economic policy? 2000 Walras-Bowley Lecture. *Econometrica.* In press

Persson T, Roland G, Tabellini G. 2000. Comparative politics and public finance. *J. Polit. Econ.* 108:1121–61

Persson T, Svensson LEO. 1989. Why a stubborn conservative would run a deficit: policy with time-inconsistent preferences. *Q. J. Econ.* May:325–45

Persson T, Tabellini G. 1990. *Macroeconomic Policy, Credibility and Politics.* New York: Harwood Academic

Persson T, Tabellini G, eds. 1994. *Monetary and Fiscal Policy. Volume I: Credibility, Volume II: Politics.* Cambridge, MA: MIT Press

Persson T, Tabellini G. 2000. *Political Economics: Explaining Economic Policy.* Cambridge, MA: MIT Press

Persson T, Tabellini G. 2002. Political economics and public finance. In *Handbook of Public Economics*, ed. A Auerbach, M Feldstein. In press

Pommerehne WW, Hart A, Frey BS. 1994. Tax morale, tax evasion and the choice of political instruments in different political systems. In *Public Finance and Irregular Activities, Supplement of Public Finance*, Proc. Congr. Int. Inst. Public Finance, 49th, pp. 52–69

Pommerehne WW, Schneider F. 1980. Illusions in fiscal politics: a case study. *Swed. J. Polit. Sci.* 5:349–65

Pomper GM. 1971. *Elections in America.* New York: Dodd, Mead

Powell GB. 1982. *Contemporary Democracies: Participation, Stability, and Violence.* Cambridge, MA: Harvard Univ. Press

Powell GB, Whitten GD. 1993. A cross-national analysis of economic voting: taking account of the political context. *Am. J. Polit. Sci.* 37:391–414

Price S. 1998. Comment on "the politics of the political business cycle." *Br. J. Polit. Sci.* 28:201–10

Reid BG. 1998. Endogenous elections, electoral budget cycles and Canadian provincial elections. *Public Choice* 97:35–48

Remmer K. 1993. The political economy of elections in Latin America. *Am. Polit. Sci. Rev.* 87(2):393–407

Rogoff K. 1988. Comment (on Alesina A, macroeconomics and politics). *Nat. Bur. Econ. Res. Macroecon. Annu.* 3:61–63

Rogoff K. 1990. Equilibrium political budget cycles. *Am. Econ. Rev.* 80(1):21–36

Rogoff K, Sibert A. 1988. Elections and macroeconomic policy cycles. *Rev. Econ. Stud.* 55(1):1–16

Rose R. 1980. *Do Parties Make a Difference?* Chatham, NJ: Chatham House

Ross F. 1997. Cutting public expenditures in advanced industrial democracies: the importance of avoiding blame. *Governance Int. J. Policy Admin.* 10(2):175–200

Roubini N, Sachs J. 1989. Government spending and budget deficits in the industrial countries. *Econ. Policy* 8:99–132

Schmidt MG. 1997. When parties matter: a review of the possibilities and limits of partisan influence on public policy. *Eur. J. Polit. Res.* 30:155–83

Schneider F, Frey BS. 1988. Politico-economic models of macroeconomic policy: a review of the empirical evidence. See Willett 1988, pp. 239–75

Schuknecht L. 1996. Political business cycles in developing countries. *Kyklos* 49:155–70

Schuknecht L. 1999. Fiscal policy cycles and the exchange rate regime in developing countries. *Eur. J. Polit. Econ* 15(3): 569–80

Schuknecht L. 2000. Fiscal policy cycles and public expenditure in developing countries. *Public Choice* 102(1–2): 115–30

Schultz KA. 1995. The politics of the political business cycle. *Br. J. Polit. Sci.* 25:79–99

Schumpeter J. 1939. *Business Cycles: A Theoretical, Historical, and Statistical Analysis of the Capitalist Process.* New York: McGraw-Hill

Sheffrin S. 1989. Evaluating rational partisan business cycle theory. *Econ. Polit.* 1:239–59

Shi M, Svensson J. 2001. *Conditional political budget cycles.* Work. Pap., Univ. Wisc. and Inst. Int. Econ. Stud., Stockholm Univ. http://www.iies.su.se/~svenssoj/pbc.pdf

Sieg G. 1997. A model of partisan central banks and opportunistic political business cycles. *Eur. J. Polit. Econ.* 13:503–16

Simmons B. 1996. Rulers of the game: central bank independence during the interwar years. *Int. Org.* 50(3):407–43

Simmons B, Clark WR. 1997. *Capital mobility and partisan economic policy choice: conditional effects of international economic integration on fiscal policy in the OECD.* Presented at Annu. Meet. Am. Polit. Sci. Assoc., Washington, DC, Aug. 28–31

Smith A. 1996. Endogenous election timing in majoritarian parliamentary systems. *Econ. Polit.* 8:85–110

Smith A. 2000. *Election timing in majoritarian parliaments.* Presented at Annu. Meet. Am. Polit. Sci. Assoc.. Washington, DC, Aug. 31–Sep. 3

Stigler G. 1973. General economic conditions and national elections. *Am. Econ. Rev.* 63: 160–67

Suzuki M. 1992. Political business cycles in the public mind. *Am. Polit. Sci. Rev.* 86(4):989–96

Swank DH. 1988. The political economy of government domestic expenditure in the affluent democracies, 1960–1980. *Am. J. Polit. Sci.* 32(4):1120–50

Swank DH. 1992. Politics and the structural dependence of the state in democratic capitalist nations. *Am. Polit. Sci. Rev.* 86(1):38–54

Tabellini G, Alesina A. 1990. Voting on the budget deficit. *Am. Econ. Rev.* 80(1):37–49

Terrones M. 1989. *Macroeconomic policy cycles under alternative structures.* Work. Pap., Dept. Econ., Univ. Wisc.

Thompson W, Zuck G. 1983. American

elections and international electoral-economic cycles: a test of the Tufte hypothesis. *Am. J. Polit. Sci.* 77(2):364–74

Treisman D, Gimpelson V. 2001. Political business cycles and Russian elections, or the manipulations of "Chudar." *Br. J. Polit. Sci.* 31(2):225–46

Tsebelis G. 2002. *Veto Players: How Political Institutions Work*. Princeton, NJ: Princeton Univ. Press

Tufte E. 1975. Determinants of the outcomes of midterm congressional elections. *Am. Polit. Sci. Rev.* 69:812–26

Tufte E. 1978. *Political Control of the Economy*. Princeton, NJ: Princeton Univ. Press

Vaubel R. 1997. The bureaucratic and partisan behavior of independent central banks: German and international evidence. *Eur. J. Polit. Econ.* 13:201–24

Way C. 2000. Central banks, partisan politics, and macroeconomic outcomes. *Comp. Polit. Stud.* 33(2):196–224

Wilensky HL. 1976. *The "New Corporatism": Centralization and the Welfare State*. Beverly Hills, CA: Sage

Wilensky HL. 1981. Leftism, catholicism and democratic corporatism. In *The Development of Welfare States in Europe and America*, ed. P Flora P, AJ Heidenheimer, pp. 345–82. London: Transactions Books

Willett TD, ed. 1988. *Political Business Cycles: The Political Economy of Money, Inflation, and Unemployment*. Durham, NC: Duke Univ. Press

Wright G. 1974. The political economy of New-Deal spending: an econometric analysis. *Rev. Econ. Stat.* 56(1):30–39

Annu. Rev. Polit. Sci. 2002. 5:423–50
DOI: 10.1146/annurev.polisci.5.112801.080943
Copyright © 2002 by Annual Reviews. All rights reserved

TOWARD A NEW POLITICAL METHODOLOGY:
Microfoundations and ART

Christopher H. Achen

*Department of Political Science and Institute for Social Research, University of Michigan,
4252 ISR, Ann Arbor, Michigan 48106-1248; e-mail: achen@umich.edu*

■ **Abstract**   The past two decades have brought revolutionary change to the field
of political methodology. Steady gains in theoretical sophistication have combined
with explosive increases in computing power to produce a profusion of new estimators
for applied political researchers. Attendance at the annual Summer Meeting of the
Methodology Section has multiplied many times, and section membership is among
the largest in APSA. All these are signs of success. Yet there are warning signs, too.
This paper attempts to critically summarize current developments in the young field of
political methodology. It focuses on recent generalizations of dichotomous-dependent-
variable estimators such as logit and probit, arguing that even our best new work needs
a firmer connection to credible models of human behavior and deeper foundations in
reliable empirical generalizations.

INTRODUCTION

Decrying the scientific status of political science has a very long tradition, and not
just from outside the discipline. Burgess (1891) condemned the low intellectual
standards a century ago, and Bentley (1908, p. 162) shortly thereafter proclaimed,
"We have a dead political science." Catlin (1927, p. 142) found no sign of life a
quarter century later: "There is as yet no such thing as a political science in any
admissible sense." The hue and cry has never ceased since.

Almost none of the critics has been entirely wrong. Political science really was
too legalistic in the nineteenth century, too bereft of case studies and statistical
evidence in the 1930s, too ignorant of survey research and statistical methods in
the 1950s, and too resistant to rigorous theory in the1980s.

Even now, much remains to be done on all these fronts. If one puts side by side
an introductory physics book, an introductory economics text, and an introductory
treatment of the political process, it is difficult to be entirely happy with the current
state of the profession. These other fields have serious imperfections and lacunae,
but they also possess a broad-gauge, intellectually powerful, logically integrated,
well-tested framework to convey to freshmen. We do not.

Methodology has customarily been supposed to be part of the solution. Beginning with Charles Merriam's Chicago department in the 1920s and 1930s, and
continuing in each of the succeeding generations, overcoming stasis and creating

1094-2939/02/0615-0423$14.00

the scientific future of the discipline has meant disseminating the newest research techniques. When that has been done, we have always said, then political science will be scientific. We have worked hard, and the dissemination has always been achieved. Indeed, each step made us smarter. But disappointment has always followed. The current era is no exception.

Even at the most quantitative end of the profession, much contemporary empirical work has little long-term scientific value. "Theoretical models" are too often long lists of independent variables from social psychology, sociology, or just casual empiricism, tossed helter-skelter into canned linear regression packages. Among better empiricists, these "garbage-can regressions" have become a little less common, but they have too frequently been replaced by garbage-can maximum-likelihood estimates (MLEs).[1] Beginning graduate students sometimes say, "Well, I don't really understand how these variables relate to each other and the data are bad, but I did use the newest estimator, downloaded from the Internet, and I do report heteroskedasticity-consistent standard errors."

No wonder that a prominent applied statistician, looking recently at one of our more quantitative journals, said (no doubt with a bit of hyperbole), "There is only one item in here I would want to read." He then pointed to an article that was deeply informed about the substance of the problem it addressed but used only cross-tabulations (though it used them intensively and creatively).

Now, fairness requires that a survey of contemporary political methodology acknowledge the field's real achievements. When this author first wrote about the subject nearly 20 years ago (Achen 1983), there were relatively few scholars and accomplishments to report on. Now the field is much too large to cover in an essay, and the statistical sophistication of the discipline has been raised substantially. Although a little flim-flam has emerged to fleece the innocent, so too has much patient and serious development of genuinely new and more powerful statistical tools.

Nevertheless, the present state of the field is troubling. For all our hard work, we have yet to give most of our new statistical procedures legitimate theoretical microfoundations, and we have had difficulty with the real task of quantitative work—the discovery of reliable empirical generalizations. To help the reader see where we stand, the remainder of this essay develops this argument in the context of some recent interesting estimators proposed by prominent political methodologists. Setting aside those statistical proposals that have not stood up to peer criticism, the discussion focuses on some of the best recent work, which demonstrates most clearly what will be needed in the next decades.

The outline of the paper is as follows. First, I review estimators for dichotomous dependent variables, including one of the best-grounded and least-appreciated new estimators of recent years, Nagler's (1994) generalization of logit ("scobit"). This set of estimators is then shown to be easily generalizable beyond scobit to an unmanageably large class. The implication is that creating ever more "generalized" estimators without reference to substantive knowledge, a path we have often

---

[1] I owe the "garbage-can" epithet to Anne Sartori, who makes no claim of originality.

pursued in recent years, leads political methodology astray. Instead, we need reliable empirical knowledge in order to choose among the many possible estimators that might be used in each of our applications.

Next, the paper argues that little dependable empirical knowledge exists in political science because our conventional work habits squander our efforts. Two remedies are suggested. First, we need to exploit formal theory more often to structure our estimators. Second, when no formal theory is available, we need far more serious data analytic procedures to discipline our specifications.

GENERALIZING FAMILIAR ESTIMATORS: FROM LOGIT TO SCOBIT

One group of estimators in very wide use in political science is the probit/logit group. Designed for discrete (often dichotomous) dependent variables, these estimators employ special techniques to keep forecasts meaningful. In the dichotomous case, for example, all logit and probit forecasts are probabilities. They never exceed one or fall below zero, as often happens when linear regression is applied to dichotomous dependent variables. These attractive fits, along with numerical tractability, account for the popularity of probit and logit in applied work. (The log-likelihood functions, though nonlinear in the parameters, are globally concave, so that numerical maximization is easy and reliable.)

In the dichotomous case ("success" or "failure"), both probit and logit generate the probability of a success as the value of a cumulative probability distribution function, that is, as a definite integral of a probability density function. To grasp the underlying intuition in a simple situation, suppose that there is just one independent variable and that it has a positive effect on success. Then the idea is that, if we plotted the probability of success against that variable, the shape of the graph would match some cumulative distribution function (cdf), perhaps a simple one with the stretched S-shape familiar from first courses in statistics. For this purpose, logit uses the standard logistic cdf, whereas probit uses the cdf of the standard normal. In both cases, the effects of the independent variables are nearly linear when probabilities of success are between 20% and 80%, but effects flatten at the extremes to keep probabilities bounded between zero and one.

Thus, to define the logit model, we first recall the density of the logistic distribution: $f_1(z) = e^{-z}/(1 + e^{-z})^2$. Then if P is the probability of success under the logit model, we set

$$P = \int_{-\infty}^{z} f_1(x)\, dx \qquad\qquad 1.$$

$$= F_1(z) = \frac{1}{1 + e^{-z}}, \qquad\qquad 2.$$

where the second line is the cdf of the logistic distribution. If Q is the probability of a failure, we also have

$$Q = 1 - P = \frac{1}{1 + e^z}, \qquad\qquad 3.$$

where the last equality follows from Equation 2.

In statistical applications, the setup is completed with a "link function": The argument z of the cdf is expressed as a (typically linear) function of the explanatory variables. Subscripts are added to denote observation numbers. Thus, in most applications, $z_i = X_i\beta$, where X_i is a (row) vector of explanatory variables for the ith observation, and β is a fixed but unknown coefficient vector.

Under this specification, no matter what values on the real line $X_i\beta$ assumes, forecasts of $P_i = F_1(X_i\beta)$ always stay within the unit interval on which probabilities are defined, since the value of a cdf is itself a probability. This is the attraction of modeling a dichotomous dependent variable using a cdf.

In econometrics textbooks, logit and probit setups are usually generated from a random utility model. The quantity $z_i = X_i\beta + u_i$ is regarded as a utility for attaining or choosing success, where u_i is a stochastic unobserved variable with a known distribution. Successes occur when utility falls above a threshold, conventionally set to zero:

$$p_i = Pr(X_i\beta + u_i > 0) \qquad\qquad 4.$$

$$= Pr(u_i > -X_i\beta), \qquad\qquad 5.$$

where p_i denotes a probability derived from an arbitrary random utility model. Thus, when u_i has some particular distribution with cdf F_u, successes have probability p_i equal to the chance that a draw u_i from its density f_u falls to the right of $-X_i\beta$. This is simply the area under the density to the right of the point $-X_i\beta$, which is one minus the area to the left of the same point:

$$p_i = 1 - F_u(-X_i\beta). \qquad\qquad 6.$$

Now suppose that we model the left-hand-side probability p_i in this equation as a cdf F_p with density f_p, so that

$$F_p(X_i\beta) = 1 - F_u(-X_i\beta). \qquad\qquad 7.$$

Then the density f_p must be the reflection (around zero) of the density of the disturbances f_u. To see this, observe that if f_p and f_u were reflections, then the area to the left of $X_i\beta$ under F_p would equal the area to the right of $-X_i\beta$ on F_u. But this merely restates Equation 7.[2] Hence, in general, a random utility model

---

[2]Alternately, differentiating both sides of Equation 7 with respect to $X_i\beta$ gives $f_p(X_i\beta) = f_u(-X_i\beta)$, which restates the reflexivity in terms of heights of the densities rather than areas under them.

based on a particular density of the disturbances generates a functional form for the probability of success that is the cdf of another density, and the two densities are reflections of each other.

Now if the disturbance density is symmetric around zero, then the density is its own reflection, and therefore F_u and F_p in Equation 7 are the same. Replacing F_p with F_u in Equation 7 and substituting into Equation 6 gives

$$p_i = F_u(X_i\beta) \qquad\qquad 8.$$

for any arbitrary symmetric density such as the logistic or the normal. This is the familiar case seen in textbooks: The probability of observing a success has a cdf shape as a function of the explanatory variables, and that cdf is the same as the cdf of the disturbances in the underlying random utility model.

In particular, when the logistic cdf F_1 with logit success probability P_i is used, then

$$P_i = F_1(X_i\beta) = \frac{1}{1 + e^{-X_i\beta}} \qquad\qquad 9.$$

in parallel with Equation 2; here, again, $z_i = X_i\beta$. Similarly, for the probability of failure, we have

$$Q_i = 1 - F_1(z_i) = \frac{1}{1 + e^{X_i\beta}} \qquad\qquad 10.$$

in parallel with Equation 3. Hence, the random utility approach to motivating the logit model is equivalent to the purely statistical specification in Equations 1 and 2. [The same is true for probit, the sole difference being that the normal (Gaussian) cdf replaces the logistic.] Note, however, the crucial importance of distributional symmetry of the disturbance in moving from Equation 6 to Equation 8, a point to which we shall return.

Taking derivatives in Equation 9 quickly establishes the familiar properties of the logit, for example that in a linear specification, explanatory variables have maximum marginal effect when $P_i = 0.5$, and that marginal effects diminish monotonically and symmetrically around that value, tending to zero as $P_i \to 0$ or $P_i \to 1$.

SCOBIT

In a particular application, a researcher might prefer a cdf different from the logistic or the normal. Perhaps theory or experience indicates that large positive values of the disturbance term in the random utility model are more likely than large negative values, or that the maximum effects of the independent variables occur at a different probability value than 0.5.[3] One way to create such a specification is to note that any real number in the unit interval raised to a positive power remains in the unit interval. In particular, for the logit success and failure probabilities P_i and Q_i, we have that $0 \leq P_i^\alpha, Q_i^\alpha \leq 1$ for any $\alpha > 0$.

After taking note of these considerations, Nagler (1994) uses them to define another estimator, called "scobit" (skewed logit).[4] The idea is to let the new probability of failure be the logit failure probability raised to the power α. Thus, if P_i^* and Q_i^* are the scobit probabilities of success and failure, respectively, we set

$$Q_i^* = Q_i^\alpha = \frac{1}{(1 + e^{X_i \beta})^\alpha} \qquad 11.$$

using Equation 10, and then we adjust the success probability accordingly:

$$P_i^* = 1 - Q_i^\alpha = 1 - \frac{1}{(1 + e^{X_i \beta})^\alpha}, \qquad 12.$$

where we customarily require $\alpha > 0$. Obviously, when $\alpha = 1$, scobit reduces to logit. Thus, scobit is a legitimate generalization of logit; logit nests within it. A routine for estimating the model is now included in the statistical software package STATA.

A useful way to interpret scobit is to use Equation 12 to define a cdf:[5] $F^*(X_i \beta) = P_i^*$. There is no accepted name for this distribution defined by F^*, though it is closely related to the Burr distribution, whose cdf is

$$F_{\text{Burr}}(x) = 1 - (1 + x^c)^{-k} \quad (x \geq 0) \qquad 13.$$

---

[3]There is a technical point here: Because the underlying scale for these threshold models is arbitrary, one can always transform both sides of Equation 7 to get any cdf one likes for the functional form without affecting the fit at all. For example, if one wants the probit cdf Φ to replace some other distribution with cdf F_p on the left-hand side of Equation 7, one would apply the compound function $\Phi[F_p^{-1}(.)]$ to both sides of Equation 7. Thus, in some sense, every threshold model for dichotomous dependent variables is equivalent to a probit setup. But the transforming function nearly always produces elaborately complicated functional forms for the explanatory variables on the right-hand side, with no clear substantive interpretation, and so the point is of no practical importance.

[4]His work is a rediscovery; the estimator was popularized in the statistical literature by Aranda-Ordaz (1981) and is often referred to by his name. The originator is Prentice (1976, p. 766). These earlier authors specify the same likelihood function slightly differently, which obscures their identity with scobit. Prentice, who derives Equation 11 from a more general estimator, multiplies both numerator and denominator on the right-hand side by $(e^{-X_i \beta})^\alpha$. In contrast, Aranda-Ordaz writes $Q_i = 1/(1 + \alpha^{-1} e^{X_i \beta})^\alpha$, which differs from Nagler's Q_i^* by the addition of the constant α^{-1}. But if we let $\alpha^* = \log \alpha^{-1}$, then we can replace α^{-1} with e^{α^*} and simply absorb the constant α^* into the intercept term in $X_i \beta$. This leaves us with the scobit likelihood.

[5]It is easily shown that P_i^* meets the conditions to be a cdf. In particular, it is monotonic in $X_i \beta$.

and 0 otherwise (Burr 1942, p. 217, Equation 20). In fact, it may be shown that the F^* distribution is exponential-Burr. That is, if z has the F^* distribution, then $x = e^z$ is distributed Burr.[6] Because the unlovely name "exponential-Burr" is not used in the literature, I will refer to the distribution most often as the "scobit distribution."[7]

As intuition suggests and Nagler demonstrates, the shape of the underlying density is in general no longer symmetric under scobit, and therefore marginal effects of independent variables in linear specifications are no longer symmetric around $P_i^* = 0.5$. Setting the second derivative of the cdf in Equation 12 to zero gives the (unique) maximum of the density and hence the point of greatest marginal impact:

$$\frac{\partial^2 P_i^*}{\partial z^2} = \frac{1}{(1+e^z)^{\alpha+1}} - \frac{(\alpha+1)e^z}{(1+e^z)^{\alpha+2}} = 0. \qquad 14.$$

Solving gives

$$z = -\log \alpha, \qquad 15.$$

and substitution into Equation 12 gives, for the point of largest marginal impact under scobit, P^*,

$$P^* = 1 - \left[\frac{\alpha}{\alpha+1}\right]^\alpha. \qquad 16.$$

Hence, for example, $P^* \to 0$ as $\alpha \to 0$, and $P^* > 0.5$ if $[\alpha/(\alpha+1)]^\alpha < 0.5$, which occurs when $\alpha > 1$.

Thus, maximal marginal effects under scobit need not occur where the probability of success is 50%, as in logit or probit. Under scobit, maximum impact may occur where the success probability exceeds 50% ($\alpha > 1$) or where it falls below 50% ($\alpha < 1$), an important and potentially useful generalization. As Nagler (1994, p. 253) notes, Equation 16 implies that the point of maximum impact is confined to the interval $(0, 1 - e^{-1})$, or approximately $(0, 0.63)$. When larger points of maximum impact are needed, he essentially proposes switching to the power logit estimator, defined below.

Nagler (1994) applies probit, logit, and scobit to U.S. voter turnout data from the 1984 Current Population Survey from the Census Bureau, showing that scobit gives

---

[6]Morgan (1992, p. 186) sets this derivation of the exponential-Burr distribution as a problem for the student. If one takes derivatives of the F^* and Burr cdfs to get the densities, then standard change-of-variable arithmetic suffices for the demonstration.

[7]Morgan (1992, p. 147) calls the scobit F^* distribution "log-Burr," but this is a verbal slip. As his mathematics demonstrates, scobit is not log-Burr; rather, Burr is log-scobit. (Equivalently, scobit is exponential-Burr.) To see the plausibility of this claim, note that the Burr distribution is non-negative like the log-normal, whereas the scobit distribution, like the normal, covers the entire real line. Thus, the Burr relates to the scobit distribution in the same way that the log-normal relates to the normal, that is, Burr is log-scobit.

a slightly better statistical fit. He also finds that $\alpha \approx 0.4$, implying, from Equation 16, that voters with turnout probabilities of approximately 40% are most affected by the explanatory variables. Of course, probit and logit would have imposed a value of 50% as the point of maximum impact. Thus scobit yields a genuinely different substantive interpretation.

An alternate approach to scobit derives it from a random utility model. Smith (1989, p. 186) and Nagler (1994, pp. 253–54) take this approach, assuming the distribution of the disturbance term to be Burr II.[8] If the Burr II cdf is denoted $F_u^*(z)$, then by definition (Burr 1942, p. 217),

$$F_u^*(z) = \frac{1}{(1 + e^{-z})^\alpha}.$$ 17.

Substituting this F_u^* for F_u in Equation 6 and again using $z_i = X_i\beta$ produces

$$P_i^* = 1 - \frac{1}{(1 + e^{X_i\beta})^\alpha},$$ 18.

and Equations 11 and 12 follow immediately, as desired.

Thus, as with logit, we may arrive at scobit via purely statistical considerations or by the econometric route of specifying a random utility model for individual choice. [In fact, since scobit may be derived in this way from the Burr II distribution, Smith (1989, p. 186) proposed calling the estimator "Burrit."] However, the scobit derivation differs in a crucial way from more familiar estimators. When logit is derived from a random utility model, the symmetric logistic disturbances lead to a logistic cdf functional form for the probabilities. Similarly, for probit, the symmetric normally distributed disturbances imply a normal cdf functional form for the probabilities. For scobit, however, the asymmetric density assumed for the disturbances does not lead to a cdf for the probability of success that has the same distribution. Instead, the assumption of Burr II disturbances leads to a scobit (exponential-Burr) cdf for the functional form.

The Burr II and exponential-Burr distributions are distinct, though closely related, as the disturbance cdf and the cdf for the probability of success must be in any random utility model. They have the relationship shown in Equation 7. As the discussion there implies, the Burr II and exponential-Burr densities must be reflections of each other. Informally speaking, any Burr II density may be converted to the corresponding exponential-Burr density by flipping it so that the left side becomes the right, as the discussion above at Equation 7 implies. In summary, then, under a random utility model, Burr II disturbances generate a cdf for the probability of success P_i^* that corresponds to the scobit (exponential-Burr)

---

[8]Burr (1942) proposed a dozen (unnamed) distributions, of which this is the second. Subsequent authors have usually referred to them by Roman numeral (as in Johnson et al. 1994, pp. 53–54). The "Burr" distribution we have already encountered is Burr XII. Nagler (1994, p. 234, fn. 3) refers to Burr II as "Burr-10," since it appears in Burr's Equation 10.

distribution, and these two distributions have densities that are reflections of each other.

AN ALTERNATE GENERALIZATION
OF LOGIT: POWER LOGIT

In Nagler's scobit, it is the logit probability of *failure* that is subject to exponentiation. The probability of success is then chosen so that the two probabilities add to unity. Of course, one might have proceeded the other way around, raising the logit probability of *success* to the power α and forcing the probability of failure to adjust so that they sum to one. This is the "skewed logistic" of Robertson & Cryer (1974).[9] Because scobit and power logit are both "skewed logistics," however, and because "skewed logistic" is easily confused with "scobit," I have adopted Morgan's (1992, p. 186) alternate name for this estimator, "power logit."

Again using P_i and Q_i to represent the logit probabilities of success and failure, and defining P_i^{**} and Q_i^{**} to be the probabilities of success and failure under power logit, we set

$$P_i^{**} = P_i^{\alpha} = \frac{1}{(1 + e^{-X_i\beta})^{\alpha}} \qquad 19.$$

and

$$Q_i^{**} = 1 - P_i^{\alpha}, \qquad 20.$$

where the first line follows from Equation 9. We again require $\alpha > 0$. Of course, like scobit, this estimator reduces to logit when $\alpha = 1$.

If we interpret P_i^{**} as a cdf, so that $P_i^{**} = F^{**}(X_i\beta)$, then the F^{**} distribution is Burr II. (To see this, compare the definition of Burr II in Equation 17 to the definition of power logit in Equation 19.) That is, the cdf used in the functional form for power logit is the Burr II cdf. Like the scobit density, the Burr II density is asymmetric, so that again, this model allows the independent variables to have a point of maximum influence at probabilities different from 0.5. The largest marginal impact occurs at the point P^{**}, which is

$$P^{**} = \left[\frac{\alpha}{\alpha + 1}\right]^{\alpha}. \qquad 21.$$

Thus, $P^* \to 1$ as $\alpha \to 0$, and $P^* < 0.5$ if $[\alpha/(\alpha + 1)]^{\alpha} < 0.5.$, which occurs when $\alpha > 1$. In contrast to scobit, large values of α reduce the point of maximum impact, whereas small α values increase it. Power logit's point of maximum influence for the independent variables is confined to the interval $(e^{-1}, 1)$, approximately $(0.37, 1)$. This is simply the reflection of the corresponding interval for scobit.

---

[9]Robertson & Cryer set out only the case $\alpha = 2$. Prentice (1976, p. 765) proposed the more general form shown here. It has been studied by Wu (1985) and McLeish & Tosh (1990).

Power logit seems never to have been derived from a random utility model, but it is easy to do so. To make the derivation successful, the density of the disturbances must be the reflection of the density of the power logit (Burr II) cdf P_i^{**}. However, we have already seen that the scobit (exponential-Burr) density is the reflection of the Burr II density. It follows immediately that we need to assume scobit-distributed disturbances here. That is, in a random utility framework, scobit disturbances generate the power logit (Burr II) functional form. A direct proof is straightforward.[10]

In summary, then, the random utility approach to generating scobit and power logit yields the following dual relationship, apparently not previously noticed:

Scobit: Burr II disturbances $\Rightarrow$ exponential-Burr cdf functional form

and

Power logit: exponential-Burr disturbances $\Rightarrow$ Burr II cdf functional form

Put more colloquially, in a random utility framework, scobit disturbances lead to the power logit model, and power logit disturbances imply the scobit model.

Perhaps the clearest way to see the duality relationship between these two estimators is to compare the scobit equation for failure (Equation 11), $Q_i^* = Q_i^\alpha$, and the power logit equation for success (Equation 19), $P_i^{**} = P_i^\alpha$, where again P_i and Q_i are the logit equations for success and failure, respectively.[11] Now from Equations 9 and 10, P_i evaluated at $X_i\beta$ is identical to Q_i evaluated at $-X_i\beta$. Hence, Equations 11 and 19 imply immediately that the probability of obtaining a "failure" under scobit with coefficient vector β is the same as the probability of a "success" under power logit with coefficient vector $-\beta$. Thus, if we give one of these estimators a dataset in which successes and failures have been reversed, the maximum likelihood estimates will not remain the same except for the sign of the coefficients, as they would in logit or probit. Instead, the best fit will switch to a completely different model.

This seemingly minor point has a major consequence for empirical work. With logit and probit, researchers studying turnout, for example, are accustomed to ignoring whether voting should be coded as one and abstention as zero, or vice versa. Reversing the zeroes and ones on the dependent variable has no real statistical consequences. Scobit and power logit do not have that property, however. Reversing the zeroes and ones on the dependent variable for either one of them causes the estimator to switch to the other model. Thus, coding who is a zero and who is a one in a dataset is not a small step with these two estimators: Different choices

---

[10]Use Equation 12 as F_u in Equation 7. This yields a cdf defining F_p on the right-hand side. It has the same form as Equation 19, as desired.

[11]Incidentally, Equations 11 and 19 are not the usual notation for these estimators: I hope that writing them in this fashion makes the relationship and distinction between them clearer than it is in much of the literature.

produce genuinely different fits. In particular, the zero-one reversed fit for scobit yields the coefficients from power logit (with reversed sign), and vice versa.

The good aspect of this model-switching feature of scobit and power logit is that, although we may not have known it, we already have software for power logit. The scobit software in STATA can be used to estimate the power logit model—just reverse the zeroes and ones on the dependent variable, and then at the end, change back the sign of the resulting coefficients. The standard errors, log-likelihoods, and other features of the fit apart from the coefficients will be correct as printed out by STATA.

In summary, both scobit and power logit generalize the logit model. Each offers potential for fitting datasets not well modeled by the symmetric logit and probit estimators. Moreover, for each of them, at least a partial rational choice microfoundation has been successfully laid, since each has been derived rigorously from a particular distribution of the disturbances in a random utility model. Quantitatively skilled graduate students will want both estimators in their toolkits, particularly now that STATA makes appropriate software available.

Political methodologists have long suspected that our familiar estimators were often too restrictive. Dichotomous-dependent-variable models were thought to be a good example. Now we have generated freer models with more parameters and fewer limitations. And we have believed that more generality is always good.

THE PERILS OF GENERALIZING
FAMILIAR ESTIMATORS

Social scientists currently have a wealth of dichotomous-dependent-variable models from which to choose, including many not mentioned here (e.g., Prentice 1976, Stukel 1988, Morgan 1992). Moreover, now that Nagler has shown political scientists the way, other dichotomous-dependent-variable estimators can be generated for our purposes freely and pleasantly.

For example, all the estimators discussed above might be nested inside a single estimator. One way to do this would be to add one new parameter γ and then write the probability of success as a mixture of the scobit and power logit probabilities ("mixit"):

$$P_i^{\mathrm{mix}} = \gamma P_i^* + (1 - \gamma)P_i^{**}, \qquad 22.$$

where $0 \le \gamma \le 1$. Obviously, scobit and power logit are the special cases in which $\gamma = 1$ and $\gamma = 0$, respectively. This new estimator also allows for functional relationships in the data that logit, scobit, and power logit cannot include; it has considerable flexibility. In the contemporary style, this estimator might be proclaimed Generalized Scobit and Power Logit, and preached as GSPL.

Alternatively, rather than constructing a weighted sum of the probabilities of success from the scobit and power logit, we might multiply them instead ("clumpit"):

$$P_i^{\text{clump}} = \frac{(P_i^*)^\gamma (P_i^{**})^{1-\gamma}}{(P_i^*)^\gamma (P_i^{**})^{1-\gamma} + (Q_i^*)^\gamma (Q_i^{**})^{1-\gamma}},$$ 23.

where again $0 \le \gamma \le 1$, and scobit and power logit are the special cases in which $\gamma = 1$ and $\gamma = 0$, respectively. Here, as for all the previous estimators, it is not hard to demonstrate that the standard features of a cumulative distribution function hold for the function defining P_i^{clump}. (In particular, P_i^{clump} is monotonic in its argument.) Like mixit, clumpit has substantial flexibility of fit, and values of all its parameters can be computed by maximum-likelihood estimation, or, if priors are imposed on the parameters, by Bayesian computations.

Still more statistical models for dichotomous dependent variables might be created. All the estimators discussed above start from the logit cdf F_1. They use that cdf to define probabilities of success and failure, and then transform the probabilities in some fashion. Instead, one might start from the normal cdf, define the corresponding probit probabilities, and then transform the probit probabilities in the same ways. Or one might start with the cdf from t-distributions, or the double exponential, or Cauchy, or many others.[12] Combining these possibilities with scobit and power logit, plus the new mixit and clumpit, we have painlessly created in one paragraph more than a dozen brand-new dichotomous-dependent-variable estimators. Extending each of them to polychotomous responses is straightforward, too: One proceeds just as with polychotomous probit. There is no end of opportunities.

By now, though, a concern should have arisen in the reader's mind. For this generality is all too quick. Yes, dozens of estimators are easily created for any situation. Unfortunately, they often fit approximately equally well but give quite different answers. If any of them might plausibly be used on statistical grounds, which one is best for a given problem? Trying them all, besides being unreasonably burdensome, is not even possible; there will always be another ten untried. Purely statistical considerations cannot tell us what to do.

Worse yet, generality is not free. These setups with additional parameters often require surprisingly large datasets to be successful. Consider the best-known generalization of logit, namely scobit. Scobit adds only a single parameter to logit. Yet computational experience with it indicates that samples of 500 are often too small for reliable results when that parameter is added. In Nagler's (1994) own simulations with samples of 500, scobit sampling variances for coefficients were routinely five to ten times larger than those of the corresponding logit, and sometimes 100 or even 1000 times larger. Even in samples of 2000, some coefficients had sampling variances 25 to 100 times larger than logit's. Only in Nagler's study of eligible voters, with nearly 100,000 observations, did the scobit sampling variances

---

[12]It is convenient to use distributions whose support is the entire real line so that out-of-bounds forecasts do not occur, but this allows for log chi-square, log exponential, and many others, as well as those listed above.

settle down to averaging only about twice the size of logit's, a reasonable statistical price to pay for the increased flexibility of fit.

These features of scobit have been investigated by Hanmer, who replicated Nagler's simulations.[13] He finds the source of the problem in occasional wild misestimates of α, the additional scobit parameter, which then cause serious errors in the other coefficients. He also finds that estimates of α are very sensitive to functional form, so that including squared terms in a specification (whether they belong or not) can cause dramatic changes in the estimate of α. Often, the α term seems to capitalize on chance, changing dramatically to try to accommodate one or two data points. In one run, Hanmer found that dropping one observation out of 500 changed the estimated α from 680,000 to 38. Removing one more observation reduced α to 5. The other coefficients sometimes doubled or were cut in half as α changed.

These upheavals took place in data simulated with the same distributions and parameters Nagler used in his own simulations, guaranteed to meet scobit's assumptions, and estimated using the model known to be correct. (The real world would no doubt have been more devious.) Even so, a sample with a truly dramatic error in the estimated α turned up in the first 100 simulated samples Hanmer tried. Serious errors of estimation occurred in about 5% of all 500-observation datasets. Moreover, none of this trouble is unique to scobit. All these findings apply to power logit as well, by the usual trick of reversing the zeroes and ones. And one shudders to imagine empirical and computational experience with mixit and clumpit, which add *two* parameters to logit. In short, if the reader has not already guessed, mixit and clumpit are fakes—mathematically correct but not to be taken seriously. Many a "generalized" estimator glitters emptily.

It is important to understand that nothing in the previous paragraphs indicates that scobit and power logit have no uses, or that the software used to generate their estimates is misleading. To the contrary, the estimators are genuine advances and the software generally works well on what is a difficult numerical estimation.[14] The point is rather that generalizing logit can be very expensive in statistical precision, a point confirmed by theoretical work on scobit (Taylor 1988). Precision is much less an issue when samples have 100,000 cases, as in Nagler's substantive study with Census Bureau data. Then one can let the data speak relatively unaided. But in survey samples of 1000 to 2000, typical of political science work with dichotomous

---

[13]See MJ Hanmer, "An Investigation of Scobit," unpublished manuscript, Department of Political Science, University of Michigan.

[14]Altman & McDonald (2002) find that the scobit maximum-likelihood estimates (MLEs) are numerically hard to compute even in routine cases and that some standard packages, such as GAUSS, occasionally fail to find the true MLEs, even getting the sign wrong on some estimated coefficients. It is possible that the Aranda-Ordaz version of this estimator, which reparameterizes the distribution to lessen the correlation between α and the other coefficients, might help. In any case, this issue (whether the answer printed by the computer program is the correct estimate) is distinct from that discussed by Hanmer (whether the correct estimate is near the truth).

variables, one needs a strong formal-theoretic or detailed data-analytic reason to be using scobit or power logit.

Some readers of this argument have imagined that it applied only to scobit, an estimator not much used in practice. Certainly, they have said, scobit has problems with its standard errors. But that need not stop us from happily creating and using our other substantively atheoretical generalized estimators and MLEs. Hence, the concerns of this paper are easily dismissed.

In fact, however, this defense of conventional wisdom resembles that of the Hapsburgs, who were secure in their belief that the Empire's weaknesses were confined to Serbia. Like Serbia, scobit may expose the issues a little more clearly, but nearly all the new estimators proposed in political methodology in recent years raise the same concerns as does each application of scobit. Since each new estimator imposes a certain structure on the data and often uses up additional degrees of freedom to create statistical generality, why should we believe these assumptions in this problem? Typically, no formal model supports the assumptions, and no close data analysis is presented in their favor. In fact, no matter how devastating those absences, we often write as if we didn't care. For both the creators and the users of our new estimators, simply listing the assumptions seems satisfactory, and we treat the ensuing estimates as findings. Statistical estimators have the logical form *If A, then B*. "Therefore B," we cry.

We have now come to the central issue facing contemporary political methodology. Dozens of estimators might be used in any of our empirical applications. Too often, applied researchers choose the standard ones because they believe methodologists approve of them, whereas methodologists prefer some new, complicated, untested alternative because they know that the standard estimators are often ungrounded in substantive theory, and they hope that the new one might stumble onto something better. Few researchers in either group make a convincing case that their estimator is humming rather than clanking on their dataset. Even the creators of estimators usually do not prove that the supporting assumptions would make rational sense or common sense for the political actors being studied. Nor do they carry out the patient data analysis required to show that their estimator, an arbitrary selection from among dozens that might have been proposed, is more than just computable and plausible, but that its assumptions really match up in detail to the data for which it is intended. If the thing might work on some planet, we think our job is done.

Too many of the new estimators in political methodology are justified solely because they are one conceivable way to take account of some special feature of the data. Perhaps the dependent variable is discrete, or a duration, or a count, or an ecological average, or perhaps partially missing data. Then under some all-too-convenient assumptions, we show that the implied estimates are MLE or Bayes, and we demonstrate that our computers can solve for the parameters. Applied researchers are grateful: "An estimator that takes account of the special features of my data in a way that ordinary regression never did—hooray!" Too often, they rush out to adopt it, not noticing that it may give bizarre answers that standard, simpler, better-tested estimators, perhaps unfamiliar to them, would have avoided.

Once upon a time, our tools were very limited, and econometrics texts taught us, "Decide what sort of data you have, and look up the corresponding estimator." Few questioned the assumptions closely; there were no real alternatives. But those days are long gone. No researcher should suppose now that there is just one statistically reliable technique for a given class of data. There are many, and dozens more are easily created. No one should imagine that some particular newly invented estimator emerging in a prominent political science journal is the only or best way to analyze a dataset. Applied political researchers need to wise up, and political methodologists need to stop ill-using them by promoting particular estimators on abstract grounds of greater generality. The truth is that, for virtually any political dataset in common use, dozens of statistical estimators might be tried, and we simply have not done the work needed to recommend any one of them with scientific honesty.

In short, creating more and more abstract estimators, unrelated to well-grounded empirical generalizations, cannot be the right way to define our job as political methodologists. Statisticians do that for a living, and we will never be as good at their job as they are. Trying to keep up will leave us forever second-rate—at best—and, more importantly, irrelevant to genuine empirical advance in the discipline.

We have a different agenda. One can see it in good statistics texts, wherein the statistician is constantly advised that many techniques are available, and that choosing the right one requires consulting the quantitatively sophisticated researchers in a given field. Inventing new applied estimators is relatively easy, statisticians are told; the trick is to find those that truly fit the data on a particular subject. Ask the specialists, who know the statistical characteristics of the data in detail; then, the texts say, select an estimator on that basis. Right now, though, if statisticians consulted political methodologists concerning the statistical character of our observations, we would have too many second-rate estimators and not enough first-rate answers. What can be done?

MICROFOUNDATIONS

A "microfoundation" for a statistical specification is a formal model of the behavior of the political actors under study. The model might emerge from decision theory, game theory, or some other formalism. Then the statistical setup is derived mathematically from the model, with no further ad hoc adjustments. An independent, normally distributed error term ("white noise") may be added for the inevitable random, nonsystematic deviations from the model.

The simplest example of a dichotomous-dependent-variable estimator that is microfoundation-ready is the probit model. Suppose that some formal model explains the probability of success (say, a country signing a particular treaty) as a function $g(.)$ of certain exogenous variables X_i. Success occurs (the country signs the treaty) according to the threshold model in Equation 4, with many small, random, nonsystematic factors incorporated into an additive disturbance term u_i. (Deriving the existence of additive normal disturbances from the formal model is even better, of course, but not always possible or sensible.) It follows from the formal model, let us suppose, that success occurs when $g(X_i) + u_i > 0$. We may then derive rigorously, as we did in going from Equation 4 to Equation 8,

$$p_i = \Phi[g(X_i)], \qquad 24.$$

where Φ is the cdf of the standard normal distribution.

Equation 24 is the probit model, with some (perhaps complicated) function of the exogenous variables as its explanatory foundation. To use this model is to assert that the model g is the correct representation for the systematic part of the behavior. The Central Limit Theorem justifies the claim that if each of the other, residual factors is nonsystematic and not too intercorrelated, with no subset of those factors dominant over the others, then the disturbance term should be independent and normally distributed. The idea is that a good model fitted to data results in white noise disturbances. That assumption may be disputed, of course, and tested against the data, but it is intellectually coherent and has standard justifications. Thus, probit is not itself a formal model, but it combines easily with one. Much the same can be said for logit, which is essentially indistinguishable from probit in applications. In either case, a formal model plus a justification for white noise disturbances yields a probit or logit setup as a statistical model with microfoundations.

Now let us take up the case of scobit. We have seen that scobit requires disturbances distributed as Burr II. Because there is no reason to believe that the Burr II distribution would occur by chance, it cannot be assumed merely for convenience in a particular application. The same is true for other distributional assumptions used in our estimators, whether Cauchy, t-distributions, truncated normals, or beta distributions. If knowledgeable people are to take the resulting estimators seriously, the distributional assumptions must be defended theoretically and justified with a formal model of the behavior of the political actors. Atheoretical assertions that an estimator follows from *some* arbitrary assumptions, no matter how rigorously, will not persuade. As we have already seen, there are too many possible estimators for any problem. For an estimator to be believed, it requires microfoundations. But when an estimator such as scobit does not use white noise disturbances, how might microfoundations be supplied?

A somewhat artificial case is apparent in the treaty-signing example. Suppose that some formal model implies that a rational governmental decision maker will sign a treaty if any one of the major interest groups in the country supports the treaty. Suppose further that there are α such groups in country i, and that each of them will support the treaty with probability $P_i = F_1(X_i\beta)$, where P_i is the logit probability of support as a function of exogenous factors X_i related to characteristics of the country and the treaty. These probabilities must be identical for each group.

Then the probability P_i^* that the leader will sign the treaty is the probability that at least one of the groups will support it, which is one minus the probability that no group will support it. If $Q_i = 1 - P_i$ is the logit probability of opposition for each group, then the probability of the treating being signed by country i is

$$P_i^* = 1 - Q_i^\alpha, \qquad\qquad 25.$$

which is the scobit model of Equation 12.

Other, similar situations might also generate a scobit specification: "If anyone in the family wants to drive down to vote, we will all go," or "If you can give me one good reason to send a check to Snooky for Senate, I'll send one." When α different conditions are each *sufficient* for success and all have the same logit-based probability of occurring, then the scobit model is mathematically implied. Political actors will behave as if they obeyed a threshold model of choice with Burr II disturbances, but the Burr II assumption will not be arbitrary. Instead, it will be a logical consequence of an underlying formal model with white noise disturbances.[15]

Readers may wish to verify that power logit has much the same potential justification. When α different conditions are each *necessary* for success and all have the same logit-based probability of occurring, then the power logit model is implied. In that case, actors will behave as if they followed a threshold model of choice with exponential-Burr disturbances, but again, the claim that they do so is not arbitrary.[16]

Thus, substantive formal models of a certain kind would give microfoundations to scobit and power logit. They would tell researchers that employing these special estimators is indicated, or even required. As with other estimators, arguing for the use of obscure distributions purely on grounds of computational convenience or aesthetic attractiveness should be avoided. The Burr II and exponential-Burr distributions would be derived from a clean foundational model with routine, conventional logistic errors that required no special pleading for credibility.

The formal model justifying a particular application of scobit or power logit has to be plausible, of course, if the microfoundation strategy is to be successful. The examples of informal models just discussed are all questionable, and they seem to show that model-based justifications for scobit and power logit occur only occasionally. When the posited model justifying an estimator is not persuasive, then a debate will break out. But at least the debate can focus on the signing of treaties, about which political scientists are likely to be knowledgeable, rather than on the occurrence of Burr II disturbances, about which our expertise is negligible. In fact, the latter topic can be ignored. The outcome of the debate on treaty accession will logically determine the choice of estimator. That is what microfoundations are for.

---

[15]For careful thinking about the statistical implications of models with necessary and sufficient conditions, see BF Braumoeller, "Causal Complexity and the Study of Politics," unpublished manuscript, Harvard University.

[16]Microfoundations can be constructed for mixit and clumpit as well, but they are even more specialized than those for scobit and power logit and thus are not to be taken seriously.

Thus, occasionally, models such as scobit, power logit, and other MLEs will be implied by a theoretical model. When they are, they have microfoundations and should be the estimator of choice. More often, though, their usefulness will be found in checking for specification errors. Like many other specification checks and tests, they can help us find model errors. When logit follows from a formal model and power logit does not, but power logit fits better, then we know something is wrong in the formal theory supporting logit or in the implementation of the logit specification. For finding our mistakes, scobit, power logit, and their estimator cousins in other applications are most helpful.

Nagler's (1994) study, for example, shows that our standard specifications for voter turnout are not working in logit and probit. That is an enormously valuable contribution. But in the modern view, the implication is not necessarily that we should abandon logit and switch to one of its generalizations. It is rather that we need to think hard both about the formal theory of turnout and about the specifications we use in logit and probit to study it. (An important step toward a theoretically grounded empirical study of turnout is Sanders 2001.) If we cannot think of any reason why scobit has formal-theory support, however, then jumping to it bears a heavy burden of proof and should be considered with skepticism. Instead, the theoretically defensible goal is either to re-do the theory or, perhaps more commonly, to find and fix the specification errors in the link function. When that has been done in a context where logit has a strong, persuasive formal-theoretic justification, we expect that in the end, logit will usually turn out to have the best fit. Good theory will then be vindicated, and scobit will have played a key auxiliary role in that outcome.

At this point, no doubt, empirical investigators and methodologists accustomed to contemporary political science norms will object. "Look," they will say, "this new Glockenspiel estimator may not have those frou-frou microfoundations you insist on, but it makes theoretical sense by my lights: It takes account of the yodeled nature of my dependent variable, which ordinary regression ignores. Plus it can be derived rigorously from the Cuckoo distribution. Besides, it fits better. The graphs are pretty, at least if not looked at too closely, and the likelihood ratio test rejects the ordinary regression fit at the 0.05 level. Theory-schmeary. Our job is to let the data decide. I'm going to use Glockenspiel. Anything else is choosing a poorer fit." Nearly all of us methodologists have shared these views at some stage of our professional lives.

Nowadays, this is the battle line where the old political methodology and the old political science confront the new. Devotees of the old computing-power-plus-MLE viewpoint are "fitness buffs." If Glockenspiel fits a little better than regression, we have traditionally told ourselves, then it is a better answer than regression or probit. But as we have all learned by our own painful experience, good statistical fitness is not enough. That training regimen too often drives out thinking.

The old style, in which so many of us were trained and which increasing computing power makes even more seductive, is content with purely statistical derivations from substantively unjustified assumptions. The modern style insists on formal theory. The old style dumps its specification problems into a strangely distributed disturbance term and tries to model or correct the resulting mess; the new style insists on starting from a formal model plus white noise errors. The old style thinks that if we try two or three familiar estimators out of 50 possible ones, each with some arbitrary list of linear explanatory variables and fabricated distributional assumptions, and one of them fits better, then it is the right answer. The modern style insists that, just because one atheoretical fit is better than another, that does not make any of them intellectually coherent or satisfying. Instead, a new estimator should be adopted only when formal theory supports it, and not otherwise.

Empirical research closely informed by formal theory has made significant headway in certain fields of political science, notably in studies of U.S. legislators, bureaucrats, interest groups, and the relationships among them—a literature which would require a review article of its own (but see Morton 1999, especially ch. 8). Other examples would include Bartels (1998), who estimates the changing voting power of various American subgroups by exploiting both formal theory about the Electoral College and the extensive datasets provided by the National Election Studies. Bartels has remarked to me that his calculations, like many other formal-theoretic studies of voter turnout, implicitly rely on the scobit α equaling unity, which seems untrue—an example of methodological development influencing theoretical conclusions.

In international relations, Schultz (2001) constructs a model of international bargaining with a free domestic opposition. His explanation for the "democratic peace" (the observation that democracies do not fight each other) implies fresh ways to test for it. Building on related theoretical work by McKelvey & Palfrey (1995), Signorino (1999) shows the striking difference that a formal model makes in the statistical study of international crisis behavior. He pioneers the stage-by-stage statistical modeling of real-world political games. Sartori (2002) exploits a game-theoretic argument to impose a new identifying condition on a selection-bias model of crisis bargaining, and she goes on to provide the most statistically sophisticated analysis of an MLE model yet done by a political scientist. Both the Signorino and the Sartori papers show the power of contemporary formal theory: No methodologist in the old tradition would have thought to propose either of these unfamiliar statistical setups. Both emerge directly from theory, not from econometrics books with their convenient, familiar, substantively unjustified distributional assumptions and functional forms.

TOWARD RELIABLE EMPIRICAL GENERALIZATIONS

Thus far, the discussion has emphasized methodology as the testing of theory. Morton (1999) has admirably reviewed the literature from this perspective. Certainly theory testing is a central task for methodologists. However, methodologists have another role as well, at least equally important. A theory needs things to explain, and finding them is part of our job, too. Much useful theory has emerged bottom-up rather than top-down. One example is the growing literature on Bayes models of public opinion (Zechman 1979, Achen 1992, Bartels 1993, Gerber & Green 1998).

The discovery of thoroughly reliable quantitative generalizations with theoretical bite is often more crucial to the discipline than theory testing. Fecund empirical generalizations certainly exist in political science. The democratic peace may be one such generalization; "party identification predicts the vote very well" seems to be another. Both these propositions have engendered substantial decision- and game-theoretic literatures. Admittedly, both would be more helpful if we knew precisely what "democracy" meant in the first instance and "party identification" in the second, but progress is occurring on both definitions. (On democracy, see Munck & Verkuilen 2002; the revisionist theory of party identification begins with Jackson 1975.)

Neither of these two generalizations about political life came from prior theory. (Yes, Kant had proposed the democratic peace, but almost nobody believed him, and his arguments had been forgotten until empirical researchers surprised everyone with strong evidence.) Both generalizations are important discoveries, and both demonstrate that empirical work often comes before smart theorizing rather than following it, a phenomenon familiar from the natural sciences. Kepler's laws preceded Newton and structured his theorizing; the surprising discovery that black box radiation arrived in discrete units led to quantum mechanics. In short, empirical research has an essential role that involves its own kind of imagination and creativity apart from theory. Empiricists are not simply slack-jawed, dwarfish varlets following the theorist around and washing up the glassware.

We methodologists often find ourselves in Hempel's "context of discovery," with no theories, formal or otherwise, to guide us—a little social psychology, perhaps, but nothing up to the task of making our inferences reliable. Microfoundations remain the gold standard, but often we have to begin with less and search for the empirical regularities that might lead to theory. In that context of high-dimensional problems with too little theoretical structure, how can careless curve-fitting and unreliable findings be avoided?

The usual answer is that, in research problems without microfoundations, we need hard work, insight, and art to see patterns and establish credible empirical regularities. We think of ourselves as following that advice. But our conventional procedures have let us down, and we have had little success. None of the important empirical generalizations in the discipline has emerged from high-powered methodological research. Instead, almost without exception, they were found with graphs and cross-tabulations. Methodological advances, from multiple regression onward, have largely been irrelevant.

To enjoy better times, quantitatively sophisticated empiricists will have to change their way of thinking. Kramer (1986) once wrote that creating a theory is relatively easy; it is learning whether the theory is true that is hard. And he added that political scientists tend to believe the reverse.

Empirical work, the way too many political scientists do it, is indeed relatively easy. Gather the data, run the regression/MLE with the usual linear list of control variables, report the significance tests, and announce that one's pet variable "passed." This dreary hypothesis-testing framework is sometimes seized upon by beginners. Being purely mechanical, it saves a great deal of thinking and anxiety, and cannot help being popular. But obviously, it has to go. Our best empirical generalizations do not derive from that kind of work.

How to stop it? The key point is that no one can know whether regressions and MLEs actually fit the data when there are more than two or three independent variables. These high-dimensional explanatory spaces will wrap themselves around any dataset, typically by distorting what is going on. They find the crudest of correlations, of course: Education increases support for liberal abortion laws, for example. In the behavioral tradition, that counts as a reliable finding. But no one knows why education is associated with that moral position (higher intellect discovering the truth? Mindless adoption of elite tribal norms? Coincidence due to correlation with something else entirely?), and that leaves open the possibility that abortion attitudes do not work the way our simple linear statistical models assume that they do.

Are educated Protestant evangelicals more enthusiastic about relaxed abortion laws than less-educated members of their denominations, for example? In the political science literature, at least, almost no one knows; we have not published the relevant cross-tabulations, and so we know very little about interactions of that kind. Instead, we proceed as we have been trained, looking at the coefficients in large statistical models. Hence, we know only that when linear probit models have mushed their way helplessly through national samples with jumbles of Baptists, Quakers, agnostics, Mormons, Christian Scientists, Jews, Catholics, and Presbyterians—some black, some white, some Asian, and some Hispanic—then education acquires a positive coefficient in predicting liberalism concerning abortion. Whether these different groups of people have unique histories, respond to their own special circumstances, and obey distinctive causal patterns, we do not know because we do not check. In consequence, no real knowledge about the influence of education on abortion attitudes follows from the positive coefficient. Getting rid of this cheap sense of "empirical findings" is probably the central task that quantitative political science faces.

Consider, for example, Nagler's (1994) statistical finding from scobit, discussed above, that the maximum impact of the variables explaining voter turnout occurs when the probability of turnout is approximately 40%. If true, this would be a highly consequential finding, both for political scientists trying to understand why people vote and for political practitioners seeking to target their mobilization efforts. How might it be verified credibly and in detail? Begin with education: Those who have attended college vote more frequently than those who finished only high school. From the cross-tabulations, is the turnout gap between these two groups really largest when the model predicts 40% turnout? Or consider age: Forty-year-olds vote more than thirty-year-olds. Is the gap largest at 40% turnout? How about election-day registration? Is turnout in states with this provision larger than in those without it, and is the gap largest for citizens with a 40% chance of voting?

This is the sort of detailed investigation that truly convinces an alert reader and builds reliable empirical generalizations.

TOWARD RELIABLE ESTIMATORS

Each estimator requires the investigator to be sensitive to its own special features. Consider, for example, the attractive application of heteroskedastic probit to opinion data (Alvarez & Brehm 1995, 1997, 2002). Heteroskedastic probit has the same structure as Equation 8: The probability of a success is given by the cdf of a particular distribution, in this case the normal distribution. Customarily, the normal distribution is derived from a random utility model with normally distributed disturbances, as we have seen.

Unlike ordinary probit, however, in which the disturbances are assumed to be distributed standard normal with fixed variance, heteroskedastic probit allows their variance to depend on exogenous variables. Thus, in the notation of Equation 8,

$$p_i = \Phi_{\sigma_i}(X_i \beta), \qquad\qquad 26.$$

where Φ_{σ_i} is the cdf of a normal distribution with mean zero and variance σ_i.

The specification is then completed by setting the standard deviation of the disturbances, σ_i, equal to a function of exogenous variables Z_i, for example,

$$\log \sigma_i = Z_i \gamma. \qquad\qquad 27.$$

Thus, heteroskedastic probit generalizes ordinary probit in the same way that heteroskedastic regression generalizes ordinary regression, and it is an important model for the same familiar reasons.

The interpretation of the variance part of the model is tricky, however. Anything that generates higher variance will improve the fit. With opinion data, ambivalence is one possibility, if it causes large error variance in responses. Alvarez & Brehm stress this source of higher variance. However, extreme but opposed opinions among respondents, with no ambivalence at all, are another possible source. Careful investigation will be needed to distinguish between these alternatives.

The sorting is made particularly difficult because probit has no natural scale. A heteroskedastic probit model with explanatory variables X_i is completely equivalent to a homoskedastic probit with explanatory variables $X_i/exp(Z_i\gamma)$. (This is the usual "correction for heteroskedasticity" transformation familiar from regression analysis.) In other words, the Z_i variables might enter the equation either because they affect the disturbance variance or because they affect the responses directly.

Nor will it be easy to use the functional form of Equation 27 to separate the two possibilities. The standard deviation σ_i varies only modestly around unity in most applications. Hence, by the usual Taylor series expansion, to a very good approximation,

$$exp(Z_i\gamma) \approx 1 + Z_i\gamma \qquad\qquad 28.$$

where $Z_i\gamma$ is small.

It follows that the multiplicative inverse of $exp(Z_i\gamma)$ is approximately $1 - Z_i\gamma$ plus very small higher-order terms. Assuming that β contains an intercept term β_0, and writing $X_i\beta$ as $\beta_0 + X_{1i}\beta_1$, we find

$$X_i\beta/exp(Z_i\gamma) \approx X_i\beta - \beta_0 Z_i\gamma + \text{small interaction terms in } X_{1i} \text{ and } Z_i. \quad 29.$$

The left-hand side of this equation was constructed because it was the link function in an ordinary probit equation statistically indistinguishable from the heteroskedastic case. But it has turned out to be very nearly, apart from the difficult-to-detect interaction terms, a simple linear specification in X_i and Z_i, the collection of variables that influence the dependent variable directly and those that influence the disturbance variance. (The latter have their sign reversed.)

In short, it will be challenging to distinguish a variable's positive effects on the disturbance variance from its negative effects on the dependent variable (and vice versa). Does education reduce ambivalence, or does it just move opinions in a positive direction? We will be hard-pressed to tell the difference. Trying to estimate both at the same time will make the estimator nearly collinear. Small specifications, carefully formulated with formal theory in mind and relentless data analysis, will be needed to make heteroskedastic probit models yield findings we can rely on with confidence.

Similar remarks might be made about applications of multivariate probit models to vote choice among multiple candidates, with which Alvarez & Nagler (1995, 1998) have done important pioneering work. Such models require careful specification of covariances among error terms if the models are to be identified, and careful testing of the resulting forecasts to check whether the strong assumptions of multivariate normality truly describe the nature of voters' decision making. Much data-analytic experience will be needed before multivariate probit is ready for routine production work.

Making a serious case that an estimator is working well is like validating an empirical generalization—very hard work. Traditionally, we have tried to do both with informal assumptions about the right list of control variables, linearity assumptions, distributional assumptions, and a host of other assumptions, followed by a significance test on a coefficient. But since all the assumptions are somewhat doubtful and largely untested, so are the estimators and the conclusions. The depressing consequence is that at present we have very little useful empirical work with which to guide formal theory. Behavioral work too often ignores formal theory. That might not be so bad if it did its own job well. But it produces few reliable empirical generalizations because its tests are rarely sharp or persuasive. Thus, empirical findings accumulate but do not cumulate.

A RULE OF THREE

Only a more modern approach can halt the proliferation of noncumulative studies. As an instance of the altered perspective I have in mind, I propose the following simple rule, to be applied when no formal theory structures the investigation and we must rely on the art of data analysis:

A Rule of Three (ART):
A statistical specification with more than
three explanatory variables is meaningless.

ART may sound draconian, but in fact, it is no more than sound science. With more than three independent variables, no one can do the careful data analysis to ensure that the model specification is accurate and that the assumptions fit as well as the researcher claims.

Why a rule of three, and not four or two? Rigidity is inappropriate, of course, but the number three is not wholly arbitrary. The guideline is derived from many researchers' experience. Close study of two explanatory factors is usually easy. However, the curse of dimensionality sets in quickly. Collinearity among explanatory factors plagues social science and multiplies the pains of data analysis rapidly as the number of factors rises. Serious data analysis with three explanatory factors is not much like using two, and using four is so hard and so time-intensive that it is almost never done astutely and thoroughly. Sorting out the effects of three variables is a daunting but not impossible task. Hence the rule of thumb: Truly justifying, with careful data analysis, a specification with three explanatory variables is usually appropriately demanding—neither too easy nor too hard—for any single paper.

If one needs several more controls, then there is too much going on in the sample for reliable inference. No one statistical specification can cope with the religious diversity of the American people with respect to abortion attitudes, for example. We have all done estimations like these, underestimating American differences and damaging our inferences by throwing everyone into one specification and using dummy variables for race and denomination. It's easy, but it's useless, and we need to stop.

In any study of political thinking or action, whether abortion attitudes, voter turnout, or international crisis behavior, the various subgroups of actors must be taken seriously and looked at separately and in detail. Cross-tabulation and plotting enforce this mental discipline, and they are the way to start any analysis. But the same logic also implies that when we use our more powerful contemporary statistical tools, we need to subset the sample. Some religious and philosophical communities, for example, have to be set aside in the study of abortion attitudes because we lack adequate data about them. Put bluntly, in most of our empirical analyses, some groups of observations should typically be discarded to create a meaningful sample with a unified causal structure.

Data collection is expensive, and discarding observations will initially seem wasteful. Why confine a probit analysis to African-American abortion attitudes, for instance? The subsample will be much smaller than the full dataset, and it will be harder to speak with confidence about the findings. Instead, why not just throw half a dozen dummy variables and another several linear control variables into the probit analysis to mop up diversity? That would save all the observations. After all, these control variables "matter." Let's put them all in and use all the observations. So goes the conventional wisdom.

Unfortunately, the conventional approach creates devastating inferential consequences. As a brief look at relevant data quickly shows, no one should be studying black Americans' abortion attitudes with a dummy variable for race. A study that gets the unique causal patterns of black Protestants approximately right and throws everyone else out of the sample is better than an analysis that tosses every group into the statistical soup and gets them all wrong. A phony big-sample certitude is no help to anyone.

Similar remarks apply to virtually everything we study. Sometimes patient investigation will show that coefficients vary only a little from one observation to the next, and then our customary procedures will work adequately when applied to the full dataset. But often the causal patterns are dramatically different across the cases. In those instances, subsetting the sample and doing the statistical analysis separately for each distinct causal pattern is critical. Happily, these causally homogeneous samples will need far fewer control variables and make the application of ART easier, because irrelevant subgroups will have been set aside for separate analysis and the corresponding control variables will be unnecessary. Attractive examples of this style of empirical work include Gowa (1999) and Miller (1999).

To do contemporary data analysis, then, we need to consider carefully what explanatory situation we are in. Do the data contain a homogeneous causal path, or several? Because thorough checking is essentially impossible with more than three explanatory variables, ART is crucial to reliable empirical work. Contrary to the received wisdom, it is not the "too small" regressions on modest subsamples with accompanying plots that should be under suspicion. Instead, the big analyses that use all the observations and have a dozen control variables are the ones that should be met with incredulity.

The result of ART, and other rules like it emerging from the new methodology, would be more careful and appropriate choice of samples and much more detailed attention to what the data really say. Political scientists would develop the intimate knowledge of their observations that would constrain our choice of estimators and discipline our formal theories. The easy proliferation of conceivable estimators discussed above would be limited, since assumptions would have to match up to what we knew about our data. Substantively, too, phony generalizations would be caught more often; truly reliable generalizations would have a fighting chance. Political science would have hope, at least, of developing a firm base of empirical knowledge and substantively relevant econometric estimators on which to build.

Some of these substantive generalizations will have been suggested by theory: We will be searching under the streetlamp. But others will have to come from the darkness, unillumined by theory. Searching in darkness requires more self-discipline than we have mustered thus far. ART is meant to help.

SUMMARY AND CONCLUSION

This is the way we political methodologists have thought we should proceed: Pick a problem applied researchers care about. Set up some convenient distributional assumptions, mathematically generalizing what has been done before but not worrying overmuch about the corresponding reality. Then hammer the resulting (perhaps messy) likelihood functions or Bayesian posteriors with relentless computing. A careless substantive example may be included for illustration; there is no need to take it seriously. The enterprise is fun, and it looks fancy and sophisticated.

This approach defines the old political methodology. Helpful as it may have been at one stage of our subfield's development, it is now outdated, for it is profoundly atheoretical. Contrary to what those outside the field often believe, inventing new estimators is not very difficult. With a little work and creativity, dozens can be constructed for any class of estimation problem that interests us so long as substantive theory imposes no constraints. What is horribly difficult is to justify the use of a particular estimator in a given social science dataset—not just hand-wave, but truly justify with theory and evidence, so that a fair-minded but skeptical reader would be convinced. That problem has been almost entirely ignored by the old approach, with the result that political methodology has played little or no role in the key empirical discoveries of the past 30 years in political science.

In a more modern view, radical changes in our work habits are needed. Two avenues for justification of our inferences are open to us, neither of which we have exploited well thus far. The first is to develop microfoundations. This approach ties our estimators to formal theory, letting theory decide which assumptions we should make. In particular, it puts a premium on estimators that can be derived rigorously from a formal model of political actors' behavior, perhaps with the addition of white noise disturbances. Then substantive theoretical foundations are not decorative; they are required. Arbitrary, substantively unjustified distributional assumptions are banned.

The second approach applies when theory is unavailable, perhaps the usual case. Then the requirement is that all the assumptions in the analysis be subjected to ruthless data analysis to assess their validity. No more casual assertions of linearity, no more garbage cans of variables from different literatures, no more endless lists of control variables, no more dubious distributions, no more substantively atheoretical, one-size-fits-all estimators to be applied whenever a certain kind of dependent variable or a certain kind of statistical problem appears. Instead, patient data analysis is required—a clear, detailed demonstration in print that in all the parts of the sample, the same model works in the same way, and that the assumptions hold throughout.

Because doing serious data analysis of this kind is demanding work, I have suggested A Rule of Three (ART). No specification with more than three explanatory variables is at all likely to have been checked adequately. Samples should be chosen and, if necessary, pruned so that three control variables are sufficient. Nothing else should be believed.

Political methodology is a very young field. In its early days, onlookers were delighted by every sign of growth and mastery, no matter how modest. Now adolescence has arrived. Necessary and natural as they were at one time, the old work habits and the old goals suddenly look immature. If further development is to occur, then it is time to insist on different standards of achievement. Formal theory and serious data analysis would remake political methodology, and would give us a far better chance than we now have to contribute to the discipline's search for theoretical understanding of politics.

ACKNOWLEDGMENTS

An earlier version was presented at the Annual Meeting of the American Political Science Association, San Francisco, California, August 29–September 2, 2001. My thanks to many colleagues who attended that panel and made helpful suggestions, including Mike Alvarez, Neal Beck, Henry Brady, Simon Jackman, Gary King, and Jonathan Nagler. Thanks also to Micah Altman, Larry Bartels, David Collier, Jim Granato, John Jackson, Anne Sartori, Phil Schrodt, and John Zaller for recent conversations about the topic of this paper. A fellowship from the Center for the Study of Democratic Politics at Princeton University supported the research, as did the Department of Political Science at the University of Michigan. The paper is dedicated to the memory of my respected Michigan colleague and irreplaceable friend, Harold K. ("Jake") Jacobson, who died unexpectedly while it was being written.

The *Annual Review of Political Science* is online at http://polisci.annualreviews.org

LITERATURE CITED

Achen CH. 1983. Toward theories of data: the state of political methodology. In *Political Science: The State of the Discipline*, ed. A Finifter, pp. 69–93. Washington, DC: Am. Polit. Sci. Assoc.

Achen CH. 1992. Social psychology, demographic variables, and linear regression: breaking the iron triangle in voting research. *Polit. Behav.* 14:195–211

Altman M, McDonald M. 2002. Replication with attention to numerical accuracy. *Polit. Anal.* In press

Alvarez RM, Brehm J. 1995. American ambivalence towards abortion policy. *Am. J. Polit. Sci.* 39:1055–82

Alvarez RM, Brehm J. 1997. Are Americans ambivalent towards racial policies? *Am. J. Polit. Sci.* 41:345–74

Alvarez RM, Brehm J. 2002. *Hard Choices, Easy Answers: Values, Information, and American Public Opinion.* Princeton, NJ: Princeton University Press

Alvarez RM, Nagler J. 1995. Economics, issues and the Perot candidacy. *Am. J. Polit. Sci.* 39:714–44

Alvarez RM, Nagler J. 1998. When politics and models collide: estimating models of multiparty elections. *Am. J. Polit. Sci.* 42:55–96

Aranda-Ordaz FJ. 1981. On two families of transformations to additivity for binary response data. *Biometrika* 68:357–64. Erratum, *Biometrika* 70:303

Bartels LM. 1993. Messages received: the political impact of media exposure. *Am. Polit. Sci. Rev.* 87:267–85

Bartels LM. 1998. Where the ducks are. In

Politicians and Party Politics, ed. JG Geer, pp. 43–79. Baltimore, MD: John Hopkins Univ. Press

Bentley AF. 1908. *The Process of Government: A Study of Social Pressures*. Chicago: Univ. Chicago Press

Burgess JW. 1891. *Political Science and Comparative Constitutional Law*. Boston: Ginn

Burr IW. 1942. Cumulative frequency functions. *Ann. Math. Stat.* 13:215–32

Catlin GEC. 1927. *The Science and Method of Politics*. New York: Knopf

Gerber A, Green DP. 1998. Rational learning and partisan attitudes. *Am. J. Polit. Sci.* 42:794–818

Gowa J. 1999. *Ballots and Bullets*. Princeton, NJ: Princeton Univ. Press

Jackson JE. 1975. Issues, party choices and presidential votes. *Am. J. Polit. Sci.* 19:161–5

Johnson NL, Kotz S, Balakrishnan N. 1994. *Continuous Univariate Distributions*. New York: Wiley

Kramer GH. 1986. Political science as science. In *Political Science: The Science of Politics*, ed. HF Weisberg, pp. 11–23. Washington, DC: Am. Polit. Sci. Assoc.

McKelvey RD, Palfrey TR. 1995. Quantal response equilibria for normal form games. *Games Econ. Behav.* 10:6–38

McLeish DL, Tosh DH. 1990. Sequential designs in bioassay. *Biometrics* 46:103–16

Miller WE. 1999. Temporal order and causal inference. *Polit. Anal.* 8:119–42

Morgan BJT. 1992. *Analysis of Quantal Response Data*. London: Chapman & Hall

Morton RB. *Methods and Models*. Cambridge, UK: Cambridge Univ. Press

Munck GL, Verkuilen J. 2002. Conceptualizing and measuring democracy. *Comp. Polit. Stud.* 35: In press

Nagler J. 1994. Scobit: an alternative estimator to logit and probit. *Am. J. Polit. Sci.* 38:230–55

Prentice RL. 1976. A generalization of the probit and logit methods for dose response curves. *Biometrics* 32:761–68

Robertson T, Cryer JD. 1974. An iterative procedure for estimating the mode. *J. Am. Stat. Assoc.* 69(48):1012–16

Sanders MS. 2001. Uncertainty and turnout. *Polit. Anal.* 9:45–57

Sartori AE. 2002. An estimator for some binary-outcome selection models without exclusion restrictions. *Polit. Anal.* In press

Schultz K. 2001. *Democracy and Coercive Diplomacy*. Cambridge, UK: Cambridge Univ. Press

Signorino CS. 1999. Strategic interaction and the statistical analysis of international conflict. *Am. Polit. Sci. Rev.* 93:279–97

Smith R. 1989. On the use of distributional mis-specification checks in limited dependent variable models. *Econ. J.* 99:178–92 (Suppl: Conf. papers)

Stukel TA. 1988. Generalized logistic models. *J. Am. Stat. Assoc.* 83:426–31

Taylor JMG. 1988. The cost of generalizing logistic regression. *J. Am. Stat. Assoc.* 83:1078–83

Wu CFJ. 1985. Efficient sequential designs with binary data. *J. Am. Stat. Assoc.* 80:974–84

Zechman MJ. 1979. Dynamic models of the voter's decision calculus. *Public Choice* 34:297–315

SUBJECT INDEX

CUMULATIVE INDEXES

CONTRIBUTING AUTHORS, VOLUMES 1–5

CHAPTER TITLES, VOLUMES 1–5

Volume 1 (1998)

Volume 2 (1999)

Volume 4 (2001)